No Longer Separate, Not Yet Equal

No Longer Separate, Not Yet Equal

Race and Class
in Elite College Admission
and Campus Life

*Thomas J. Espenshade
and Alexandria Walton Radford*

IN COLLABORATION WITH CHANG YOUNG CHUNG

PRINCETON UNIVERSITY PRESS
PRINCETON AND OXFORD

Published by Princeton University Press, 41 William Street, Princeton, New Jersey 08540
In the United Kingdom: Princeton University Press, 6 Oxford Street, Woodstock,
Oxfordshire OX20 1TW

Library of Congress Cataloging-in-Publication Data

Espenshade, Thomas J.
No longer separate, not yet equal : race and class in elite college
admission and campus life / Thomas J. Espenshade and Alexandria Walton
Radford ; in collaboration with Chang Young Chung.
p.   cm.
Includes bibliographical references and index.
ISBN 978-0-691-14160-2 (cloth : alk. paper)   1. Minorities—Education
(Higher)—United States.   2. Minority college students—United
States—Social conditions.   3. Private universities and colleges—United
States—Admission.   4. Elite (Social sciences)—United States.
I. Radford, Alexandria Walton,   1980–   II. Chung, Chang Young.   III. Title.
LC3731.E86 2009
371.82—dc22   2009001389

British Library Cataloging-in-Publication Data is available
This book has been composed in sabon

Printed on acid-free paper. ∞

press.princeton.edu

Printed in the United States of America

1   3   5   7   9   10   8   6   4   2

To Our Families

CONTENTS

ILLUSTRATIONS

FIGURES

TABLES

ACKNOWLEDGMENTS

IT IS A PLEASURE to express our appreciation to the many individuals, organizations, and institutions that have contributed to this project. Early research questions were developed in conversations with Stephanie Bell-Rose. William G. Bowen and Harriet Zuckerman helped launch the study and sustained it with their enthusiasm and encouragement. Principal financial support was provided by the Andrew W. Mellon Foundation. Supplemental funding at Princeton University was received from the Office of the Dean of the Faculty, the Education Research Section, the Center for Economic Policy Studies, and a research infrastructure grant to the Office of Population Research from the National Institutes of Health.

We want to thank the colleges and universities that have participated in the National Study of College Experience and their directors of institutional research and registrars for sharing institutional data. We owe a special debt to the more than nine thousand respondents who completed the student survey. These data provide the backbone for our study. Survey data collection was overseen by Edward Freeland, associate director of Princeton University's Survey Research Center, and his capable staff consisting of Marc Weiner (assistant director), James Chu, and Tatiana Shulzycki. Additional data were supplied by The College Board, the Educational Testing Service, Fred Hargadon, Steve LeMenager, Robin Moscato, and Jesse Rothstein.

Princeton University, and especially its Office of Population Research and the Department of Sociology, provided a collegial and supportive working environment. Graduate students who assisted the project include Michelle Fowles, Lauren Hale, Erin Kelly, Ann Morning, and Joan Walling. Undergraduate research assistance was provided by Bryan Bunch, Dan Larach, Zachary Savage, and Suzanne Spence. Methodological and statistical expertise was contributed by Germán Rodríguez, Bonnie Ghosh-Dastidar, Mark Long, Scott Lynch, and Bruce Western. Librarians in the Office of Population Research Library, especially Elana Broch and Joann Donatiello, kept us supplied with a daily stream of pertinent information. We thank Elana Broch and Michiko Nakayama for bibliographic assistance and Wayne Appleton, Jennifer Curatola, and Dawn Koffman for computer support. On the administrative side, the project was smoothly and efficiently coordinated by Melanie Adams, who had overall responsibility for general organizational matters, preparing charts and graphs, and financial oversight. She was ably assisted by Kristen Matlofsky, Judie Miller, Valerie Fitzpatrick, and Colleen Appleton. Jenn Backer skillfully edited the manuscript.

Portions of the final manuscript were read by Melanie Adams, Marvin Bressler, Donnell Butler, Benjamin Colbert, Janet Dickerson, Emily Espenshade, Pamela Espenshade, Edward Freeland, Michael Geruso, Khyati Gokli, Jean Grossman, Laurence Gurman, Fred Hargadon, Angel Harris, Steve LeMenager, Nancy Weiss Malkiel, Peter Paris, Mitchell Stevens, LaTonya Trotter, and Marc Weiner. We are grateful to these individuals for their useful comments and suggestions. Conversations with Thomas Bell, Don Betterton, Robert Crews, Peter Espenshade, Sara Ingraffia, Tom Kane, Elizabeth Knoll, Janet Rapelye, Spencer Reynolds, Frank Richetti, Zachary Radford, and students in the Freshman Seminar on Diversity in Higher Education helped sharpen our thinking on important matters. For their assistance in other ways in enabling us to complete our work, we are grateful to Albert Guerraty, Peter McDonough, T. John Mercuro, Andrew Sokel, Andrew Wechsler, and Robert Wuthnow.

Finally, we wish to express our special gratitude to Chang Young Chung. Chang Chung has been with the project from the beginning. His careful attention and dedication to his craft, his ability to recall the smallest detail, and his unfailing good humor in carrying out all of our statistical programming needs, performing vital database management functions, and interacting with the participating colleges and universities are exceptional and without parallel. We are proud to name him as our collaborator.

No Longer Separate, Not Yet Equal

Chapter One

OVERVIEW

BY THE END OF the 1970s the U.S. civil rights revolution had reached full flower. The Supreme Court in *Brown v. Board of Education* (1954) overturned the "separate but equal" doctrine enshrined in *Plessy v. Ferguson* (1896) and put a constitutional end to forced school segregation based on race. The Civil Rights Act of 1964 etched the *Brown* decision into law and ended legalized racial discrimination in government, employment, and public accommodation. A surge in black voter registration was prompted by the Voting Rights Act of 1965, aided in large measure by federal monitoring efforts built into the law. The Fair Housing Act of 1968 banned racial discrimination in the sale or rental of housing, together with discriminatory practices in lending and insurance. These provisions were supplemented by additional safeguards during the 1970s. Chief among them was the Community Reinvestment Act of 1977, which prohibited "redlining"—the practice of denying mortgages based on the racial composition of the neighborhood. The sweeping changes that *Brown* ushered in took nearly twenty-five years to accomplish, but they effectively put an end to legalized discrimination based on race (Massey, 2007).

Civil and political equality did not guarantee immediate equality in other areas. The effect of the civil rights legislation was to push some discriminatory practices and attitudes underground, making them more subtle, less overt, and harder to detect—what Massey (2007: 110) has described as "discrimination with a smile." In addition, the historical legacy of racial discrimination cannot be eliminated overnight. Some blacks who attended segregated elementary schools prior to the 1954 *Brown* decision are still in the labor force. As a consequence, breaking down legal barriers separating black and white society has not translated either instantaneously or spontaneously into complete equality.

Deep racial divisions in social and economic outcomes remain. Whites and Asians typically exhibit the "best" outcomes, and blacks and Hispanics the poorest. More than 30 percent of white and nearly 50 percent of Asian adults over the age of twenty-five have earned at least a baccalaureate degree, as compared with 18 percent of blacks and just 12 percent of Hispanics. Two-thirds of whites and Asians report they are in excellent or very good health, in contrast to one-half of blacks and Hispanics.

Median household income for whites and Asians is about two-thirds higher than that among black and Hispanic households. Moreover, median household wealth for whites exceeds that for blacks by a factor of ten to one (Wolff, 2007). Poverty and incarceration rates are significantly higher for blacks and Hispanics than for whites and Asians (Western, 2006). Racial patterns of residential segregation suggest that blacks are more spatially isolated from whites than either Asians or Hispanics are, although the degree of segregation of blacks from whites across metropolitan areas has been declining since at least 1980 (Iceland, Weinberg, and Steinmetz, 2002).[1]

QUESTIONS ASKED

Many solutions have been proposed for healing these divisions, but education—and especially higher education—has traditionally been believed by most Americans to be an effective strategy.[2] In this book we address the role of elite higher education in confronting issues of inequality on U.S. college campuses. Specifically, our aim is to draw back the curtain on the selective college experience and take a close look at how race and social class are intimately intertwined with the admission process and with the academic and nonacademic sides of campus life. We ask three central questions. First, to what extent is American elite higher education involved in promoting social mobility? We know, for instance, that the economic return to a college degree is increasing and that the return to a selective college or university education is rising even faster. Therefore, mobility chances in the population are deeply affected by exactly who is profiting from the kind of education selective colleges offer.

[1] Unless otherwise noted, data in this paragraph come from *Racial and Ethnic Diversity: Asians, Blacks, Hispanics, Native Americans, and Whites*, compiled by New Strategist Editors (2006). This source also contains racial comparisons for homeownership rates, median values of owner-occupied housing units, percent of the population lacking health insurance, unemployment rates, percent of the employed population in white-collar jobs, and the living arrangements of children, among other indicators. Each of these tends to substantiate the general finding that the average social and economic status of whites and Asians outranks that of blacks and Hispanics. Other examples can be found in Massey (2007).

[2] In summarizing results from the Brookings Institution's Economic Mobility Project, Sawhill (2008: 6–7) has noted, "There is a widely held belief in America that education is the great leveler, and there is strong evidence that education contributes substantially to earnings and that it can boost the mobility of children from poor and low-income families." For example, 19 percent of adult children with a college degree who were born to parents in the bottom fifth of the income distribution end up in the top fifth of the income distribution. There is a 62 percent chance they will be middle class or higher as adults (Haskins, 2008).

One view is that selective institutions are in the best position to create opportunity for students from traditionally marginalized groups because these schools have wide latitude in choosing whom to recruit, admit, enroll, and graduate. Elite institutions, it is argued, have sufficient numbers of well-qualified applicants as well as the endowments to accomplish the three objectives of greatest concern to admission officers: (1) meeting bottom-line financial targets, (2) enrolling a freshman class capable of doing the academic work, and (3) crafting a first-year class with ample amounts of diversity along racial and other dimensions (Duffy and Goldberg, 1998). Opportunity in higher education has been expanding for racial minorities. In the Ivy League, for instance, black enrollment increased from an estimated 2.3 percent of all students in 1967 (Karen, 1991a) to 5.7 percent by 2006 (National Center for Education Statistics, 2007d). Corresponding proportions of black students at four-year, private institutions rose from 8.2 to 13.4 percent between 1976 and 2005 (National Center for Education Statistics, 2006).

An alternative view is that selective colleges and universities are under great pressure from financial aid officers, trustees, and alumni to enroll the kinds of students who will make minimal demands on their institutions' financial aid budgets and help ensure their alma maters' longevity through continued monetary contributions long after they graduate. In this view, students who are most likely to be admitted, enroll, and graduate are those whose families occupy the more privileged positions in society. By sending their offspring to a selective college or university, parents are hoping to ensure the future success—material and otherwise—of their children. Selective schools are believed by parents to be "reproduction insurance companies" that issue diplomas critical to the future life chances of their children (Stevens, 2007: 255). If this scenario best characterizes the behavior of elite institutions, sociologists would say these colleges are playing a pivotal role in the intergenerational transmission of inequality. Parents who are well-off in their own generation produce children who are as, or even more, successful when they become adults.[3]

The role played by selective institutions in creating opportunity or, alternatively, reinforcing existing inequalities takes on added significance today. Beginning with the Great Depression of the 1930s and continuing to the early 1970s, incomes in the United States were being distributed more equally. But this situation has reversed, and the past three decades have been marked by rising income inequality. The income distribution today is as unequal as it has been since the early decades of the twentieth

---

[3] A forceful exposition of these opposing depictions of selective colleges and universities has been provided by Bowen, Kurzweil, and Tobin (2005). Their concern is whether elite schools are "engines of opportunity" or "bastions of privilege."

century (Piketty and Saez, 2003). The United States is now the most un-equal nation in the developed world (Massey, 2007: 27). If there were no income inequality at all and each family had the same resources, it would matter little whether selective colleges and universities were creating op-portunity. Put differently, if the mechanism that distributes social rewards is such that these rewards are widely dispersed, then somewhat less sig-nificance attaches to the question of mobility chances. But today, when income is highly concentrated at the top of the income distribution, it matters a great deal who in society has the opportunity to receive these rewards. Americans seem quite willing to tolerate a substantial amount of inequality in power, prestige, and other resources provided the chances of securing these rewards are equally distributed across all individuals (Grusky, 2001: 23).

A second set of questions revolves around the use of affirmative action by selective institutions. Most adults, whether or not they have children in college, have heard about affirmative action in higher education. And most of these adults associate affirmative action with admission prefer-ences for members of underrepresented minority groups. But what ex-actly does "affirmative action" mean? What is the rationale, legal or oth-erwise, for race-based preferences? How critical is its use in the creation of racially diverse campuses that are so highly prized by college officials and students alike?[4] How extensively is it practiced? Who are the benefi-ciaries? How much do they benefit? What role do racial preferences play in creating opportunity and upward mobility chances for students to whom the doors of selective colleges and universities might otherwise be shut? Does race-based affirmative action actually harm its intended bene-ficiaries? This could happen if underrepresented minority students are boosted into more competitive academic environments than their aca-demic achievements warrant, and where they are surrounded by excep-tionally talented white and Asian students.

If race-based affirmative action is the primary tool selective institutions rely on to create racial and economic diversity on their campuses, what will happen if the "protective mantle of affirmative action" is with-drawn?[5] What impact would the elimination of affirmative action have on the racial makeup of undergraduate student bodies at selective schools?

[4]Mitchell Stevens (2007: 181) mentions three reasons why selective college admission deans care about racial diversity: (1) race-based preferences constitute a moral imperative; (2) an institution's national prestige depends on the extent of its racial diversity; and (3) re-cruiting non-minority students is easier if a campus can portray itself as racially diverse.

[5]This phrase is adapted from Peter Morrison (1979: 9). Morrison shows that interre-gional migration to the American South and West accentuated regional differentials in pop-ulation growth when overall U.S. population growth slowed in the 1970s and the "protec-tive mantle of natural increase" was withdrawn.

For example, following the passage of Proposition 209 by California voters in 1996, public institutions of higher education were prohibited from considering an applicant's race, ethnicity, or sex in admission. As a consequence, the percentage of underrepresented minority students (African American, Chicano/Latino, and American Indian) in the entering freshman class at UCLA declined from 24.4 in the fall of 1997 to 17.5 in the fall of 1998 (Cardenas, 1998). The number of black students in the first-year class in the fall of 2006 stood at just 100 out of an entering freshman class of about 4,800. This was less than half the number of black students who enrolled in 1997 and the lowest figure in thirty years (Office of Analysis and Information Management, 2007).[6]

Is the UCLA example an isolated instance, or might we expect similar impacts elsewhere if affirmative action were eliminated? Should we believe that other forms of affirmative action that might be more acceptable to a general public—for example, class-based affirmative action—could effectively substitute for racial preferences? Race-based preferences experienced a narrow escape in 2003 when the U.S. Supreme Court approved by the smallest of margins a continuation of race-based affirmative action under tightly drawn conditions (*Grutter v. Bollinger*, 2003) at the University of Michigan Law School. But can we confidently expect that racial affirmative action will be legally permissible forever? Voters in Washington State, Michigan, and Nebraska have prohibited racial affirmative action, other states are considering similar bans, and affirmative action was set aside by gubernatorial action in Florida. There was a possibility that, following the November 2008 elections, more than 30 percent of Americans would live in states where racial preferences in public higher education had been outlawed (Schmidt, 2007d). Conservative appointments to the U.S. Supreme Court since *Grutter* may also suggest that race-based preferences have a limited life expectancy. What are states going to do to maintain racial diversity if they lose the policy tool of affirmative action? What long-term solutions exist to the gradual asphyxiation of racial preferences?

A third issue we address relates to campus life itself. Sometimes lost between a preoccupation with admission practices on the one hand and graduation rates on the other is a concern for students themselves—who

---

[6] In November 2006, voters in Michigan overwhelmingly approved Proposition 2—an amendment to the state constitution whose wording and intent are very similar to those of Proposition 209 in California. The new measure took effect in January 2007 when a portion of the incoming freshman class for the fall of 2007 had already been admitted. Nevertheless, the proportion of minority students (black, Hispanic, and Native American) in the entering freshman class declined from 12.7 percent to 11.4 percent between the fall of 2006 and the fall of 2007. The full effect of Proposition 2 will not be felt until the fall of 2008 (University of Michigan News Service, 2007).

they are, what they learn both inside and outside the classroom, and generally what happens to them while they are in college. We know one thing for certain. Every selective college and university values diversity in all its many forms and has taken deliberate steps to enroll a diverse freshman class. Unlike the broader adult society, diverse racial groups of students are in close contact on campus. Students from different backgrounds sleep in the same dorms; they eat in the same dining halls; they mainly wear the same clothing styles and carry the same backpacks; and they go to class together. College officials have seen to it that racial groups are no longer separate. But does this mean they are equal? There are different ways to anticipate an answer.

There are good reasons to expect that the kinds of student bodies that emerge from highly competitive admission processes at selective institutions are ones in which the outlines of social and economic inequality, so evident in U.S. society, have largely been expunged or at least masked. First, the academic bar for admission is set very high. Only those relatively few students who are judged capable of handling the academic workload are accepted. Second, elite schools tend to want the very best students in all senses of that concept. Students, in other words, are chosen from the upper tail of whatever distribution they belong to (Klitgaard, 1985). Third, all elite institutions have endowments that put them in the top ranks of the college wealth distribution. This institutional munificence is not only a source of generous financial aid. It also subsidizes field trips and other learning initiatives, emergency spending accounts, and other little-noticed interventions that help smooth over latent social class differences. Fourth, students cheer for the same teams, wear the same robes and receive the same diplomas at graduation (Stevens, 2007), and are united in their proud claim to be a "son" or "daughter" of "Ivy U." Students may arrive on campus with some of the rougher edges of inequality still visible. But the socializing experiences they encounter during their college careers are likely to have a homogenizing influence that smoothes out many of the remaining contours of inequality.

On the other hand, a different perspective suggests that, despite the prevalence of these unifying forces, campus life is better characterized as a microcosm of the wider society. If so, the privilege or disadvantage associated with race and social class might not be so easily erased.[7] One

---

[7]For example, as Massey (2007: 52) has observed, "History aside, there are also good social scientific reasons to expect that categorical mechanisms of racial stratification will prove resistant to change. We know, for example, that once learned, cognitive structures do not simply disappear. Racial schemas honed over generations tend to persist in the minds of adults and get passed on to children in conscious and unconscious ways. Likewise, institutions and practices that have evolved over centuries do not just cease to exist when laws change."

area of concern, reinforced by the durability of racial stereotypes, focuses on campus patterns of student interaction across racial and ethnic group boundaries. Admission officers might be doing an excellent job of building a diverse freshman class, only to have smaller and relatively homogeneous subgroups of students break off into their own "silos" once school begins. Moreover, it appears as though the majority of race, ethnic, and gender studies courses are populated disproportionately by members of the groups being studied. If these outcomes are a common occurrence, what do they suggest about the presumed educational and other benefits of attending a diverse campus? The existence at some colleges of "theme dorms" oriented to particular racial or ethnic groups, stories about "all the black kids sitting together in the cafeteria,"[8] and unfortunate racial incidents serve to highlight issues of self-segregation among undergraduate students.[9]

Students from lower-income groups who attend elite institutions may also have a hard time fitting in. Despite the growing generosity of financial aid packages that Harvard, Princeton, Yale, and others among the nation's wealthiest institutions can afford to offer, most needy students are still expected to contribute a modest portion of their support through work-study jobs on campus (Tilghman, 2007). If these positions are highly visible to other students (for example, working at the front desk in the library or helping in the kitchen), they are ostensible reminders of social class distinctions. Other obvious markers include spending large amounts of time in the computer lab because one lacks a personal laptop, declining invitations to eat off campus because free meals are available in the campus dining hall, and not knowing where the Hamptons are (Schweitzer, 2006). Speaking about Yale University, one student who participates in a support group for low-income students called Class Matters said, "I mean I am glad to be part of this club, this very elite, very private club. I just wish someone had given me some clue about what it was beforehand" (Schweitzer, 2006).

If indeed college life reflects the inequality embedded in broader U.S. society, what does it mean? What are its implications, for example, for academic performance in the classroom? Does it suggest that minority students might be having a difficult time holding their own against more

---

[8] "*Why Are All the Black Kids Sitting Together in the Cafeteria?*" is the title of a book about racial identity development by Beverly Daniel Tatum (1997), president of Spelman College.

[9] A series of racially polarizing events, incivility on campus, racial slurs on message boards, and black students being stopped at the campus library and asked to show ID are just some of the examples that prompted one black Trinity College student to say, "There are times when I want to feel good about Trinity, and then. . . . I'm reminded of the underlying disgust that we have here for each other" (Hu, 2006). See also Schmidt (2008).

affluent and perhaps better-prepared white students? What about paying
for college and the burden of college loans and accumulated debt? Who
bears this debt? How does it constrain post-graduation options? What
about satisfaction with college when students look back? How do graduates of selective colleges and universities evaluate their overall undergraduate experience? Are they satisfied with their academic experience?
Do they rate positively their social experiences on campus? We might
expect to see differences by race and by social class in average group levels of satisfaction. If we do, what are the implications? Finally, what do
prospective students and parents who are contemplating sending their
children to elite colleges need to know about these institutions ahead
of time?

RACE, CLASS, AND GENDER

We focus quite intentionally on race and social class, two of the three
meat-and-potatoes dimensions of inequality (along with gender) in the
stratification literature. It is commonly agreed by social scientists that the
concept of race is socially constructed. Whatever physical or genetic differences may exist are largely inconsequential (Brest and Oshige, 1995).
But "race" nevertheless has social meaning.[10] Whenever similarly situated blacks and whites are treated differently in housing and lending
markets—whether in locating suitable housing, being steered toward
particular neighborhoods, or applying for and receiving mortgage loans
(Massey, 2007: 76–84)—then race matters. When blacks without a criminal record are called back for job interviews at lower rates than otherwise
comparable whites who have a conviction for a nonviolent drug offense
(Pager, 2003), then race matters. And when racial profiling is used to
stop, question, and search blacks more often than whites, or when pe-
remptory challenges are used to exclude potential black jurors more frequently than whites (Kennedy, 2001), then race matters.[11]

---

[10] As noted in the introduction to the National Research Council's two-volume study on
racial trends and their consequences in the United States, "The concepts of race and ethnicity are social realities because they are deeply rooted in the consciousness of individuals and
groups, and because they are firmly fixed in our society's institutional life" (Smelser, Wilson,
and Mitchell, 2001: 3). Analyses in this book are conducted using four primary race/ethnic
groupings, including white, black, Hispanic, and Asian. Even though the Hispanic category
is not usually considered a "race," and indeed a separate question about Hispanic ethnicity
is asked on the U.S. decennial census form, we will frequently employ the shorthand term
"race" when we mean a combination of race and ethnicity as these terms are typically
understood.

[11] *Race Matters* is the title of an often frank, yet surprisingly healing, discussion by Cornel
West (2001) of race relations in the United States.

Social class also matters. As David Grusky (2001: 25) has observed, "Class background affects a wide range of individual outcomes," including consumption patterns, values and attitudes, religious affiliation, and voting behavior.[12] Social class influences parenting styles and child-rearing behaviors. Many middle- and upper-middle-class parents are engaged in a process of "concerted cultivation," in contrast to lower- and working-class families whose children are reared using the "accomplishment of natural growth," characterized by a laissez-faire approach (Lareau, 2003). Individuals from upper social classes not only live longer than those from lower social strata, but they are treated differently by doctors, nurses, and hospitals when they become ill (Scott, 2005). Students from poorer and working-class families are more reluctant than their middle-class peers to take risks in the curriculum. The tendency is to avoid courses that sound interesting but in which students fear they might not do well (Alves, 2006). In addition, students from poorer backgrounds are less likely to graduate from high school, enroll in college, and earn a college degree (Kahlenberg, 2004).

We also consider gender, but we do not give it the same attention as race or social class. We have, of course, collected data about and from both men and women. More important, all of our statistical work includes gender as one of the explanatory categories. But we have not emphasized this dimension in our work. To do so would expand the length of our study beyond useful limits. Moreover, gender explains a declining share of variance in both personal and family income, while the explanatory power of class is rising (Massey, 2007: 252–57). Finally, discussions of gender stratification typically focus on discrimination against women, but female students outnumber their male counterparts in two-year and four-year colleges (Chronicle of Higher Education, 2007). In short, we have chosen to emphasize the aspects of inequality in higher education that are arguably the most controversial and receiving the most attention today.

Data for This Study

This study focuses on the selective college experience. We concentrate on schools in this range not because we believe they are representative of all

---

[12] Grusky (2001: 4) defines social classes or strata as discrete groups "whose members are endowed with similar levels or types of assets." Massey describes social strata using the metaphor of layers of sedimentary rock. He notes, "In an analogous manner, societies may be conceptualized as having social strata, different layers that are distinctive in composition and characterized by more or less access to material, symbolic, and emotional resources. Stratification systems order people vertically in a social structure characterized by a distinct top and bottom" (2007: 2).

of American higher education. Clearly, they are not. But we believe that elite higher education is well positioned to assume a leadership role, as recent initiatives in financial aid so amply illustrate. What makes selective institutions worth studying is that they are often in the vanguard of innovative change in higher education.

Our National Study of College Experience (NSCE) is based on an analysis of new data collected from eight academic institutions that are part of the College and Beyond database assembled by the Andrew W. Mellon Foundation. These NSCE schools include public and private research universities in addition to small liberal arts colleges, and they have geographic spread encompassing all parts of the country. The schools in our sample are representative of the most highly rated universities in the United States.[13]

The participating institutions supplied individual student data on all applicants for admission in the fall of 1983, 1993, and 1997. Altogether, there are more than 245,000 records in our administrative database. Administrative data are supplemented by a student survey that was completed by almost 9,100 respondents. Finally, information from existing sources was added to students' records. This includes data from the U.S. Census Bureau, the National Center for Education Statistics, The College Board, the Educational Testing Service, and the U.S. Department of Education. Additional information about the NSCE database is contained in appendix A.[14] Detailed descriptions of how methodological issues are handled can be found in appendix B.

PLAN OF THE BOOK

We take a chronological approach to the process of college application, admission, enrollment, and graduation. Chapter 2 examines characteris-

---

[13] When we compare the characteristics of our eight NSCE institutions against the top 50 universities as rated by *U.S. News & World Report*, we find no statistically meaningful differences between the average characteristics of either group. For example, when the NSCE average is given first, the results are: the 2004 acceptance rate (35% v. 38%); total enrollment in fall 2004 (18,000 v. 18,800); 2004 graduation rate (88% v. 87%); percent of classes with fewer than 20 students (61 v. 57); student/faculty ratio in 2004 (10 v. 11); percent of full-time faculty (93 v. 92); SAT score of entering freshmen (1360 v. 1350); percent of freshmen in the top 10 percent of their high school class (79 v. 79); and average alumni giving rate (32% v. 28%). Data on total enrollment come from the U.S. Department of Education's IPEDS database. The remaining figures are drawn from *U.S. News & World Report* (2005).

[14] Data were originally collected from ten participating NSCE institutions. A decision was subsequently made to refocus the analysis on just eight of these schools. See appendix A for details.

tics of applicants to selective institutions. We consider students' academic qualifications, their demographic and socioeconomic background, and how prominent immigrant and second-generation students are in the applicant pool. We explore strategies students and their parents use to position applicants for admission to the nation's top schools. We ask to what extent these approaches emphasize academic excellence versus extracurricular activities, and how the strategies vary by race and by social class.

Chapter 3 explores the admission process. Here institutional gatekeepers come into the picture. We investigate factors that are most important in determining which candidates are offered a seat in the freshman class. Our analysis provides answers to how strong race-based preferences are and which students benefit the most. Critics of elite college admission policies argue that low-income students receive no extra consideration in admission. We are interested in whether this charge has merit at the most selective institutions. Among all of the strategies students pursue to give themselves an edge in admission, we study what makes a difference and what does not. Finally, we give a preliminary answer to the question of whether, in deciding whom to admit, selective colleges are providing opportunity for underrepresented groups—both in terms of race and class—or are administering an admission process that favors applicants from upper social class categories.

Chapter 4 moves on to consider the characteristics of admitted students who subsequently enroll at selective institutions. We highlight the profiles of matriculants using high school academic performance indicators; demographic, immigrant-, and national-origin background factors; and alternative measures of social class. High school and neighborhood characteristics of enrolled students, and how these vary by race and social class, are featured in the comparisons.

We consider in chapter 5 the extent to which students at selective colleges engage with diversity. We first examine students' participation in ethnic studies courses and ethnically oriented extracurricular activities, and how these tendencies vary by race. From there we focus on patterns of social interaction among students across racial and ethnic categories. Data on the extent of general socializing on campus with members of different racial and ethnic groups, on students' roommates and their ethnic origins, on best-friend networks, and on dating patterns in college permit an examination of social integration or, alternatively, self-segregation. We are especially interested in how the extent of social integration versus racial isolation differs by racial group affiliation.

The topic of academic performance in college is studied in chapter 6. Here we examine graduation rates, choice of college major, and class rank at graduation and how these vary by race and social class. We consider the effects of college selectivity and examine the claim that race-based affirmative action harms its intended beneficiaries by boosting students into exceptionally competitive academic environments. The extent to which academic "underperformance" is prevalent, and whether it persists once other potential explanatory factors are introduced, is also explored.

Elite college tuition has been steadily rising. How students and their families pay for college is studied in chapter 7. We examine tuition levels before and after financial aid is taken into account. We study how net college costs vary by race, by social class, and by type of institution attended (whether private or public and, in the latter case, whether one is an in-state or out-of-state student). Loans figure prominently in whether some students can afford to attend a selective institution. How accumulated loan debt is distributed across different categories of students is assessed. We are especially interested in the financial burden of an elite college education relative to a family's household income and net worth, and how this burden varies by race and social class. These results help us determine how level the financial playing field is among graduates from selective institutions.

Chapter 8 considers a series of broader perspectives on the selective college experience. We take up first the often controversial issue of race-based affirmative action, examining the various justifications for racial preferences and how the U.S. Supreme Court has ruled on these rationales. Next, we explore how much students feel they learned during college from students with different racial or ethnic backgrounds. We examine in particular the connection between learning from difference and having the kinds of experiences in college that put students in close touch with peers from other-race groups. A third topic focuses on students' satisfaction with their college academic and social experiences. We examine how student satisfaction varies by race and by social class. Finally, we continue our exploration of whether selective colleges are engines of opportunity or bastions of privilege. We focus particular attention on how the proportion of enrolled students from upper-middle- and upper-class backgrounds changes across successive entering freshman cohorts. We also examine in one cohort how the proportion of students from high social class backgrounds expands or contracts as one moves from the applicant pool to the set of admitted students, to those who enroll, and finally to those who graduate.

Chapter 9 takes a single issue and studies it from a variety of vantage points. The question is whether there is any realistic alternative to race-based affirmative action that has the capacity to produce the same proportion of underrepresented minority students among the group of admitted students. We examine first the effects of eliminating racial preferences, then of substituting class-based affirmative action for race-based preferences, of combining racial and class-based preferences, of admitting students on the basis of a high class rank in secondary school or SAT scores alone, and of downplaying to varying degrees the importance of an applicant's academic qualifications. Finally, we consider the efficacy of a non-admission strategy. Specifically, we explore the impact on the racial composition of admitted students of closing the racial achievement gap. Our concern is whether closing this gap could preserve shares of under-represented minority students if racial preferences were eliminated.

Chapter 10 examines the implications of our previous findings. In doing so it fleshes out three remaining challenges confronting selective higher education and, more generally, society at large. One of these chal-lenges is the need for an even stronger commitment on the part of selec-tive institutions to provide opportunity to a broad cross-section of under-graduate students. A second challenge focuses on attempts to combat racial balkanization on selective campuses. Colleges and universities must work harder to provide constructive opportunities for students from di-verse backgrounds to come together frequently and productively over the course of their collegiate careers to make the most of campus diversity. Finally, we issue a challenge to all Americans to address the racial achieve-ment gap—a gap that higher education acting alone is incapable of fix-ing. This performance gap affects selective colleges and universities. It also contributes significantly to adult levels of social and economic in-equality; it influences the economy's ability to compete in a global mar-ketplace; and it limits opportunities to open up pathways to leadership for all racial and social class groups.

Chapter Two

PREPARING FOR COLLEGE

INTRODUCTION

"In her desperation, 17-year-old Jessica Roeper found herself wishing that somebody—anybody—in her family had died" (Goldberg, 1997: A1). Why? So she would have something significant to write about in her college application essay. A high school senior stole Bowdoin College's catalogue from the guidance office because of a "fantasy that someone really talented in singing would see the view book and take [her] spot" (Shea and Marcus, 2001: 89). One college applicant told a reporter she had awakened from a nightmare about her college admission prospects, declaring, "Fine. I'm a reject. I'm an outcast" (Goldberg, 1997: B8).[1]

Parents are no less anxious than their children when it comes to college admission. They ask admission officers which elementary schools would best facilitate their children's acceptance to college, as well as how to prepare their second graders for the SAT (Toor, 2000). They encourage their children to play squash for the admission edge it may provide at Ivy League schools (Cruice, 2000; Sharpe, 1999). One father took a year's sabbatical from his job to manage his daughter's college application process (Zernike, 2000). Another called a director of admission to find out if his child's five hundred hours of community service was "enough" (Zernike, 2000). Instead of enrolling their children in wilderness camps to show them how to build campfires, parents send their children to "college admission prep camps" that teach them how to construct the perfect college application essay (Lewin, 2004; Tonn, 2005). For some families, no college admission expense is too great. Parents will pay $9,450 to work one-on-one with a private SAT tutor (Princeton Review, 2008) and hire private consultants costing up to $29,000 to guide their child through the admission process (Shea and Marcus, 2001).

---

[1] These feelings are not all that uncommon. A recent study found that such anxiety during the college admission process is typical of high-achieving high school seniors throughout the country (Hoover, 2007b).

THE CHANGING MARKET FOR HIGHER EDUCATION

How have we arrived at this situation? The majority of American colleges accept 80 percent or more of their applicants (Menand, 2003), and the average acceptance rate nationwide is about 70 percent (Ewers, 2003). Yet college admission angst has probably never been greater, mainly because more students are now competing for relatively few spots at the nation's most prestigious colleges and universities. For example, according to Menand (2003), 1,330 students applied for admission to Yale in 1932, and 72 percent were accepted. In 2008, however, Yale received over seventeen times that number of applications: 22,813. This time, just 8.3 percent of applicants received offers of admission (Finder, 2008b).

The greater number of rejections today is not the result of students being less qualified than their predecessors. On the contrary, elite college applicant pools are more impressive now than in the past, allowing these schools to be even more selective in whom they admit (Soares, 2007: 36). For example, in 2001 Stanford had 5,000 applicants with GPAs of 4.0 or higher and 3,000 applicants with SAT scores of 1500 or better, but only 2,200 available seats in its first-year class (Marcus and Sohn, 2001). Harvard could and did reject 25 percent of applicants with a perfect score on the SAT in 2003 (Menand, 2003), and more than 80 percent of all valedictorians who applied to Harvard in 2001 were passed over (Shea and Marcus, 2001).

Why has the competition at elite colleges increased to such an extent? There are only slightly more students graduating from high school today (3.3 million in 2008; National Center for Education Statistics, 2007b) than there were when the last baby boomers reached college age (3.2 million in 1977; Bronner, 1999). Yet nearly 70 percent of them go directly to college, as compared to roughly 50 percent then (National Center for Education Statistics, 2007c), creating the largest college population America has ever had (National Center for Education Statistics, 2007b). With more and more students heading off to college, one now needs to attend a higher-status institution to gain an advantage in the educational hierarchy (Karen, 2002: 193).[2]

The flight to higher-quality postsecondary institutions described by Paul Attewell (2001) is thus largely the result of families believing that

[2]Similar sentiments have been expressed by Howard Rothman Bowen (1997: 339–42), who contends that in societies with larger college-educated populations, obtaining a greater number of advanced degrees has diminishing returns. The relevant credentials become not the quantity of degrees possessed but instead the caliber of the institutions attended.

college rankings matter. There is a growing conviction that being admitted to one of the nation's top colleges is critical to life satisfaction and professional success (Duffy and Goldberg, 1998; Kirp, 2003). Labor market studies lend some support to this belief. First, attending a more selective institution is associated with a higher probability of graduating (Kane, 1998b; M. Long, 2007b), and graduates from elite colleges are more likely to enter leading graduate and professional schools (Alexander and Eckland, 1977; Bowen and Bok, 1998).[3] Second, there is a positive economic return to a college education, and the increase in this financial payoff has been a prime source of rising income inequality since the 1980s (Ashenfelter and Rouse, 1999; Becker and Murphy, 2007). Students who attend colleges with higher student-average SAT scores, higher tuition, or a variety of other measures of college "quality" tend to have even higher labor market earnings later in life (Behrman, Rosenzweig, and Taubman, 1996; Brewer, Eide, and Ehrenberg, 1999; Daniel, Black, and Smith, 1997; Kane, 1998b; M. Long, 2007b; Loury and Garman, 1995; Zhang, 2005b).[4] Most studies show that attending a college with a 100-point higher average SAT score is associated with a 3 to 7 percent gain in earnings (Dale and Krueger, 2002). These returns to college selectivity have been rising since 1972 (Brewer, Eide, and Ehrenberg, 1999; Hoxby, 2001).

Families' increasing concerns with status, institutional prestige, and educational quality have in turn caused better and more affluent applicants to look beyond their own geographic region for the "right" college to attend (Duffy and Goldberg, 1998). Hoxby (1997) finds that the percentage of students who apply to at least one college outside their home state (or a neighboring state) is rising. This increase is especially pronounced among students with higher test scores. Students are also submitting more applications in general with the hope of gaining admission to at least one

[3] Cookson and Persell (1985) also stress the occupational and financial advantages associated with attending an elite college, including a higher probability of attaining a prestigious position in the business world, becoming a corporate CEO, and sitting on corporate boards. Even after controlling for social origins, high school prestige, and SAT scores, Arnold (2002) finds that Rhodes Scholars achieved greater professional prominence if they attended Harvard, Yale, or Princeton as undergraduates. Brand and Halaby (2006) and Smart (1986) also observe career benefits to elite college attendance. On the other hand, some have argued that the type of four-year college one attends has minimal effects on later educational or occupational attainment (Astin, 1993; Pascarella and Terrenzini, 1991).

[4] Recent work by Dale and Krueger (2002) challenges this emerging consensus. Although they find that students who attend schools with higher tuition do have higher incomes years later, they are skeptical that school selectivity as measured by average SAT scores of entering freshmen is an important determinant of subsequent earnings. They show that "students who attended more selective colleges do not earn more than other students who were accepted and rejected by comparable schools but attended less selective colleges" (1523). Their conclusion rests on the critical assumption, however, that students select which college to attend by choosing randomly from among schools that admit them.

name-brand institution (Finder, 2007). Between 1997 and 2007 the proportion of first-year students at highly selective private universities who submitted between eight and eleven college applications rose from about 21 percent to 29 percent. And the proportion of freshmen who applied to at least a dozen schools more than doubled from 5 percent to 12 percent (Sax et al., 1997; Pryor, Hurtado, Sharkness, and Korn, 2007).[5] Students are not the only ones who have expanded their lists of possible colleges. Premier colleges and universities have grown their lists of possible enrollees as well and have begun recruiting nationally and even internationally for talented students (Duffy and Goldberg, 1998).

These broadened horizons have transformed the market for higher education during the past forty to fifty years from a set of quasi-regional markets into an integrated national market (Hoxby, 2000). Its integration has led to growing stratification among colleges in terms of student ability, tuition, and reputation (Hoxby, 2000), as well as to increased competition at the most prestigious institutions. Currently there is a small number of "winner-take-all" colleges and universities that command a disproportionate share of the most outstanding students (Frank and Cook, 1995). A large proportion of Westinghouse and Presidential Scholars and others with high SAT scores flock to elite colleges (Cook and Frank, 1993). The gap has widened between the average SAT scores of incoming freshmen at top-tier and lower-tier private institutions (Hoxby, 1997). And despite the demographic decline of the 1980s and early 1990s, top schools were able to maintain and improve their reputations for quality. At the same time, second- and third-level institutions fell further behind in terms of selectivity, yield, and the ratio of applications to seats in the first-year class (Duffy and Goldberg, 1998).

ELITE COLLEGE APPLICATION

Each year more than three million graduating high school seniors are faced with choices about whether to apply to college, which schools to apply to, and which one to attend from those at which they have been accepted (National Center for Education Statistics, 2007b).[6] Slightly more than 60 percent of them apply to and enroll in either two- or four-year postsecondary institutions (Hawkins and Clinedinst, 2006). Whether a

[5] Some students apply to more than twenty schools, spurred by an increased use of the common application and a growing number of colleges that waive fees for online applications (Finder, 2006c).

[6] The number of new high school graduates, after having risen from about 2.5 million in 1992, is expected to peak in 2009 and then decline at least through 2014 (National Center for Education Statistics, 2007b).

student reaps the alleged benefits of an elite college education depends on the outcomes of several different stages in the college search process. At each step, individuals and organizations serve as gatekeepers to expand or constrain educational opportunity (McDonough, 1997). In examining seniors' decisions, we are particularly interested in how the roles of various gatekeepers intersect with race and social class to shape who applies to selective colleges and universities.

Hossler, Schmit, and Vesper (1999) identify three stages in the college search process. The first, "predisposition," refers to developing a favorable attitude toward college. Parental support and encouragement are by far the most important determinants of educational aspirations in ninth grade, followed by student achievement and parental education. Teachers and counselors are relatively unimportant at this stage. The "search" stage begins in tenth or eleventh grade as high-ability students with well-educated parents expand their lists of possible college choices. By the end of the junior year, teachers and counselors play a more prominent role in college planning. Seniors who are considering an increasing number of colleges tend to consult more with peers, teachers, counselors, and alumni than with parents. These students are also more likely to have higher grade point averages and to consider more selective and expensive schools. In the "choice" phase, students select the universities to which they will apply and the colleges they will ultimately attend. Sources external to the family, including college admission personnel, become more influential. College costs become a concern to many families, and students and their parents seek out information about financial aid.

Academic achievement in high school is strongly linked to the likelihood of applying to college. Manski and Wise (1983) show that a student's SAT score and high school class rank are positively associated with college application. Given that students do apply, these measures of performance also predict which students apply to the most selective institutions, with better performers more likely to seek admission at top schools. James Davis's (1966) classic frog pond model presumably plays a role in this phase of the application process. Students who are big frogs in small ponds (top students in mediocre high schools) will have higher aspirations as to the type of college they hope to attend than will equally qualified students who are small frogs in big ponds (good but otherwise undistinguished students at elite high schools). In forming a set of schools to which to apply, high-ability applicants are motivated first by an institution's academic reputation and, secondarily, by the social side of college life and by a concern to find a campus where students' academic abilities are similar to their own (Chapman and Jackson, 1987).

Decisions about where, and indeed whether, to apply to college are shaped not just by students' academic achievements but by family socioeconomic status (SES) as well. High SES students are more likely to apply to an elite institution for at least three reasons. First, students' aspirations for academic achievement are closely tied to their parents' level of education. Therefore, students with parents who went to college are more likely to attend college themselves. Second, higher SES students are more likely to score well on the SAT (Chaplin and Hannaway, 1998; J. Rothstein, 2004), and students with high scores are more likely to apply to elite schools (Manski and Wise, 1983). Third, high SES families have the cultural capital and education to know how the selective college admission system operates (McDonough, 1997), as well as the resources to devote to strategies thought to enhance the chances of being accepted.

During each phase of the admission process, high SES families employ a range of tactics "in the struggle to guard against losing ground in the status and economic security game" (McDonough, 1997: 119). In the predisposition phase, high SES parents are more likely than low SES parents to send their children to private schools, move to neighborhoods where the public schools are purportedly better, secure a private tutor to help with homework and basic organizational skills, and encourage their children to take a large number of AP exams and SAT II subject tests. Throughout the search phase, high SES parents are more likely to pay for test preparation courses, take trips to visit colleges the summer before their children's senior year, know how and when to interact with school guidance counselors about the college choice process, and hire an independent counselor to assist in selecting schools and preparing applications. During the choice phase, high SES parents are more likely to encourage early applications (with the knowledge that acceptance rates are higher then than during the regular application period), remind their children of tasks they need to complete and help them make and keep a schedule, assist with personal essays, review an application before it is submitted, pay for applications to multiple colleges, and bear the responsibility of paying for college.[7]

Low SES families, on the other hand, are more passive and reactive toward college and college admission (McDonough, 1997). Many are unfamiliar with relevant college options and rely instead on high school guidance counselors to inform them of possible colleges given their children's academic records. Even if they are aware of the non-school-based admission support services used by affluent parents, many families view them as too costly. Some low SES parents are supportive of their children's aspirations to attend college but are not centrally involved in the

---

[7]For a fuller discussion, see Arenson (2003), Attewell (2001), Avery, Fairbanks, and Zeckhauser (2003), Cookson and Persell (1985), Lombardi (2004), McDonough (1997), and Toor (2001, 2004).

application process. Others limit where their children can apply out of a desire to keep them close to home (a two-hour trip by car is often the outer limit), out of a belief that their offspring should attend only schools where "people are more like us," or because of concerns about cost (Mc-Donough, 1997: 112).[8] Low SES students are also more likely than high SES ones to consider college expenses when defining the set of schools to which they will apply and to assume that college costs will be their own responsibility (McDonough, 1997: 146–47).

Schools, guidance counselors, and teachers also help determine who attends elite colleges by functioning as gatekeepers. Counselors construct an "organizational worldview" that serves to reduce the full range of colleges and universities that students could consider to a manageable subset. This shorter list is informed by the counselor's own experience, as well as by parental and community expectations about appropriate college destinations (McDonough, 1997: 89). At low SES, large public high schools, counselors can be responsible for several thousand students and are often more focused on ensuring that students graduate from high school than on grooming them for college admission (Hawkins and Lautz, 2005; McDonough, 1997). College counselors at private schools, on the other hand, are responsible for fewer seniors, have more resources at their disposal, and have a worldview oriented more toward selective colleges and universities (Cookson and Persell, 1985; Stevens, 2007).

Between these extremes lies a range of organizational responses. Upper-middle-class public high schools use private counselors from the community and parent volunteers to work with college-bound seniors (Mc-Donough, 1997). Paul Attewell (2001) describes a different organizational dynamic in star public high schools. Through differential internal grading systems and access to rigorous science and math courses and AP courses, schools enhance the elite college admission chances of a small number of outstanding students at the expense of other very good candidates. Teachers, too, may intervene on behalf of academically gifted students. This intervention, more common at "low-guidance" high schools, may involve helping students enroll in AP courses (McDonough, 1997: 106) as well as informing students about the admission process and encouraging them to apply to selective institutions (Hossler, Schmit, and Vesper, 1999: 90).

While it may help, this assistance to low SES, high achievers appears to be no match for the even greater number of advantages high SES students

[8] Data from UCLA's annual survey of college freshmen found that the typical baccalaureate freshman cited low tuition and wanting to live near home as factors influencing his decision to attend a particular college, while selective private university students were more likely to be motivated by the school's academic reputation and its rankings in national magazines (Sax et al., 2003).

possess. Data from UCLA's annual survey of college freshmen indicate that high SES students are still overrepresented at selective colleges and universities (Pryor, Hurtado, Sharkness, and Korn, 2007). Compared to all four-year college freshmen, first-year students at very highly selective private universities are more likely to have at least one parent with a graduate degree, to come from families where annual family income exceeds $100,000, and to be unconcerned about financing a college education (Sax et al., 2003). Leonhardt (2004) has observed that "At the most selective private universities across the country, more fathers of freshmen are doctors than are hourly workers, teachers, clergy members, farmers or members of the military—combined." Similar patterns characterize the nation's top public institutions. In 2004, more freshmen at the University of Michigan came from families whose annual income was at least $200,000 than from families that earned less than the national median of $53,000 a year (Leonhardt, 2004).

How do the student bodies at top colleges and universities become so socioeconomically advantaged? Are these the characteristics of elite university applicants, or do elite university student bodies acquire this more affluent form through the sorting that takes place during the acceptance and matriculation processes? In the rest of this chapter, we use applicant data from seven elite universities in the National Study of College Experience (NSCE) to present a more complete picture of the characteristics of applicants to selective colleges. We also examine the strategies applicants employ to try to gain admission and investigate whether use of these tactics differs by students' racial or socioeconomic backgrounds.

THE SELECTIVE COLLEGE APPLICANT
A Brief Profile

During the admission cycle for the class that entered college in the fall of 1997, 67,703 students applied to one or more of seven selective NSCE colleges and universities.[9] Who are these applicants? What is their family background? How academically skilled are they? Table 2.1 provides a brief statistical portrait of NSCE college applicants. More than two-thirds of all applicants are white. Blacks represent 7 percent of this selective applicant pool and Hispanics about 5 percent. Asian Americans comprise one-fifth of all NSCE applicants. This racial distribution of NSCE applicants differs from that of freshmen at four-year colleges nationwide. The American Freshman Survey finds that 79 percent of college

[9] In analyses for this chapter, the individual student or applicant is the unit of analysis. Accordingly, 67,703 is the number of unique individuals in the combined applicant pool to these seven institutions, without regard to how many applications each student submitted or to which NSCE schools. This number is based on a weighted sample of 3,670 respondents.

TABLE 2.1
Descriptive Statistics for the Combined Applicant Pool at Seven NSCE
Colleges and Universities
NSCE Applicant Sample: Fall 1997 Cohort (N = 3,670)

Characteristic	Percent
Race	
White	68.1
Black	6.8
Hispanic	5.2
Asian	20.0
Socioeconomic Status	
Upper	4.9
Upper-Middle	46.8
Middle	37.7
Working	9.3
Lower	1.3
First-Generation College Student	
First Generation	18.1
Not First Generation	81.6
Unknown	0.3
Immigrant Generation[a]	
First	12.0
Second	18.5
Third	17.2
Fourth or Higher	49.9
Unknown	2.4
Sex[b]	
Male	47.1
Female	52.9
High School Academic Achievement	
Top 10% of Class[c]	61.8
GPA A− or Above[d]	81.4
Mean SAT Score[e]	1282.0

Source: National Study of College Experience; Educational Testing Service.

Note: Tabulations based on weighted NSCE college and university applicant sample.

[a]First-generation immigrants include students born outside America's fifty states and Washington, D.C., to at least one foreign-born parent. Second-generation immigrants comprise students born in the United States to at least one foreign-born parent. Third-generation immigrants are born in the United States to U.S.-born parents but have at least one foreign-born grandparent. Individuals counted as fourth-generation immigrants or higher are born in the United States to two U.S.-born parents and four U.S.-born grandparents.

[b]Based on institutional data, NSCE universe (N = 67,703).

[c]Percentage based on NSCE sample applicants reporting class rank in the ETS Student Descriptive Questionnaire (N = 2,808).

[d]Percentage based on NSCE sample applicants reporting high school GPA in the ETS Student Descriptive Questionnaire (N = 3,029).

[e]Mean based on combined institutional and ETS Data (N = 3,538).

freshmen are white, 12 percent are black, and the Asian and Hispanic shares are roughly 5 percent each.[10]

Examined from the standpoint of their socioeconomic backgrounds, applicants to selective NSCE colleges are overwhelmingly middle and upper-middle class. Almost 85 percent of all applicants come from these two socioeconomic categories alone. Fewer than 2 percent consider themselves to be lower class, roughly 9 percent are working class, and just 5 percent report upper-class origins. Nearly 68 percent of applicants have fathers and 61 percent have mothers with at least a college degree. Only about 47 percent of fathers and 42 percent of mothers of college freshmen nationally have attained that level of education (Sax et al., 1997).

First-generation college students are relatively rare at selective colleges and universities, especially when compared to students with a recent immigrant history. Just 18 percent of NSCE applicants do not have a single sibling, parent, or grandparent who has attended a four-year college. Among freshmen nationally the proportion who are the first in their family to attend college is probably larger. Although UCLA's annual survey does not examine siblings' or grandparents' college attendance, it finds that 41 percent of freshmen have fathers who did not attend college, and 44 percent have mothers with no college experience (Sax et al., 1997). While a comparison by immigrant generation cannot be made using UCLA's data, the percentage of elite applicants with immigrant roots is substantial. Roughly 30 percent of all applicants to selective NSCE institutions are immigrants themselves or the children of immigrants.

As Table 2.1 also indicates, 53 percent of NSCE applicants are women. Women also constitute the majority (54 percent) of first-year college students nationwide (Sax et al., 1997: 120). Within both the NSCE applicant sample and the American Freshman Survey, women are more concentrated at public than at private institutions. Women represent 58 percent of the applicant pool at the public NSCE universities, but a little less than half of all applicants are women at the more selective private NSCE colleges. On a national scale, women make up 53 percent of all first-year students at highly selective public universities and 47 percent of all freshmen at highly selective private universities (Sax et al., 1997: 120).

Not surprisingly, applicants to the selective colleges that make up the NSCE are extremely academically accomplished. Nearly two-thirds (62 percent) of all applicants rank in the top 10 percent of their high school class. Eighty-one percent have high school grade point averages (GPAs)

[10]For comparative purposes, we also use UCLA's annual American Freshman Survey, which in 1997 comprised 252,082 college freshmen at 464 universities across the country, to contrast our data on selective college applicants with college freshmen nationwide (Sax et al., 1997: 2).

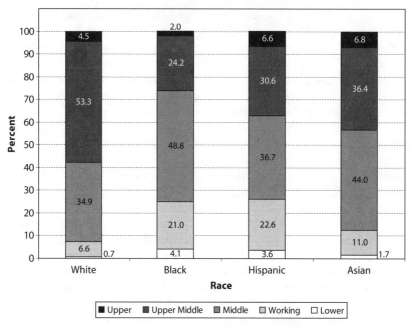

Figure 2.1. Distribution of Socioeconomic Status, by Race; NSCE Applicant Sample: Fall 1997 Cohort (N = 3,670). Note: Differences in socioeconomic status by race are statistically significant at the .001 level. Source: National Study of College Experience.

of A− or above, as compared to just 42 percent of all college freshmen. The average combined math and verbal SAT score of NSCE applicants is 1282—266 points above the national average of 1016 for all college-bound seniors (College Board, 1997).

White applicants are the most affluent student group, followed next by Asians. Blacks and Hispanics are much less likely to come from high SES backgrounds. As shown by Figure 2.1, while 93 percent of white and 87 percent of Asian applicants consider themselves middle class or above, only three-quarters of black and Hispanic applicants fall into this socioeconomic bracket.[11] Applicants differ by race on a related social class measure as well. About 30 percent of black and Hispanic applicants are

[11] Though the majority of white students are upper-middle class, it is important to keep in mind that lower- and working-class applicants are more likely to be white than of any other race. Thirty-seven percent of all lower-class and 48 percent of all working-class applicants are white. Applicants in each SES category are more likely to be white than of any other race because of the much larger number of white students who apply.

TABLE 2.2
Percentage Distribution of Immigrant Generation within Racial Groups
NSCE Applicant Sample: Fall 1997 Cohort (N = 3,670)

Immigrant Generation	White	Black	Hispanic	Asian
First	3.4	8.8	21.4	39.7
Second	6.8	20.6	44.9	50.7
Third	22.8	2.5	19.0	2.6
Fourth or higher	65.3	61.3	13.1	3.5
Unknown	1.7	6.8	1.6	3.5
Total	100.0	100.0	100.0	100.0

Source: National Study of College Experience.
Note: Differences in immigrant generation by race are significant at the .001 level.

the first in their family to go to college. Only about 15 and 22 percent of white and Asian applicants, respectively, make the same claim.[12]

We also can gain a better understanding of the selective college applicant pool by examining the distribution of immigrants in each racial group. Table 2.2 demonstrates that while almost two-thirds of white and black applicants' families have lived in the United States for four or more generations, only 13 percent of Hispanic and less than 4 percent of Asian applicants report the same. About two-thirds of Hispanics and more than 90 percent of Asians are either immigrants themselves or the children of immigrants, as compared to only one-tenth of whites and 30 percent of blacks.

PARENTAL ATTITUDES TOWARD ACADEMICS AND COLLEGE

The way parents approach academics and college influences the way their children prepare for, apply to, and choose colleges (McDonough, 1997). As Table 2.3 indicates, the majority of NSCE applicants come from home environments that promote academics and college attendance. About 57 percent of NSCE respondents agree that a parent or some other adult was involved either "often" or "very often" in helping with homework or making sure they did their homework during their elementary and junior high school years. A slightly larger proportion (61 percent) of applicants come from families in which finishing homework first before participating in other activities (for example, watching TV or playing with friends) was either "often important" or "very important."

[12] Throughout this chapter, the intergroup differences we report in the text, tables, and figures are statistically significant at the .05 level unless otherwise noted.

TABLE 2.3
Academic Orientation of NSCE Applicants' Home Environment
NSCE Applicant Sample: Fall 1997 Cohort

Variable	Percent
Total Sample (N = 3,670)	100.0
Parents or Other Adults Involved in Homework	
Never	8.4
Rarely	14.3
Occasionally	19.9
Often	25.7
Very often	31.4
Unknown	0.3
Families in Which Finishing Homework First Was	
Not at all important	5.8
Not too important	12.9
Somewhat important	19.5
Often important	25.5
Very important	35.3
Unknown	1.1
Mother's College Expectations for Child[a]	
1–5	4.9
6	7.0
7	85.8
Unknown	2.3
Father's College Expectations for Child[a]	
1–5	4.4
6	7.6
7	85.1
Unknown	2.9
Parent(s) Had Opinion about the Type/Quality of College Child Should Attend	
Yes	58.8
No	36.5
Unknown	4.7

Source: National Study of College Experience.
[a]Percent of respondents falling into each category on a seven-point scale (1 = no expectation; 7 = a very strong expectation).

Moreover, most NSCE applicants report that their parents had not only strong expectations that they would attend college but also specific opinions as to the type of university they should attend. Both mothers and fathers earn a mean score of 6.8 on a seven-point scale where 7 reflects their having a "very strong expectation" that their child would attend college. Eighty-six percent of mothers and 85 percent of fathers receive a score of seven from their children. NSCE applicants also feel that their parents had clearly defined college plans for them. Almost three-fifths of applicants agree that their parents had in mind a specific type or quality of college for them to attend.[13]

The only outcome measure presented in Table 2.3 on which applicants differ significantly by race is that which asks whether parents had an opinion as to the quality or type of college the respondent should attend. Seventy-two percent of Asian American applicants responded in the affirmative, as compared to just 45 percent of Hispanic applicants. About 56 percent of both black and white respondents felt their parents envisioned them attending a certain type of institution.

There is a more important differentiation in parental approaches to academics and college when examined by socioeconomic status than by race. This finding supports Annette Lareau's (2003) contention that the styles in which parents raise their children differ more by class than by racial background. Lareau (2003: 1, 66–67) argues that middle-class parents engage in "concerted cultivation," in which they actively work to develop their children's talents in "a concerted fashion." On the other hand, limited financial resources lead lower- and working-class families to adopt a more laissez-faire approach to child rearing (the "accomplishment of natural growth") and "to direct their efforts toward keeping children safe, enforcing discipline, and . . . regulating their behavior in specific areas."

Our data are consistent with this reasoning and show that high SES parents are more involved in cultivating their children's academic lives. As shown in Table 2.4, 60 percent of middle- and upper-middle-class NSCE respondents report that their parents helped with or made sure they completed their homework often or very often, as compared to just 17 percent of lower-class applicants.[14] In addition, nearly two-thirds of

---

[13] Our data show that families who envision a certain type of college are more likely to use the strategies thought to be helpful in gaining admission that we explore later in this chapter. The only strategy such families are not more likely to pursue is hiring a private college consultant, perhaps because they already have colleges selected and do not need a counselor's assistance in this area.

[14] Though upper-class applicants score lower on this measure than expected, when we compare only those applicants with mothers who did not work outside of the home, we find that upper-class parents are "often" or "very often" involved 52 percent of the time, more

TABLE 2.4

Academic Orientation of NSCE Applicants' Home Environment, by Socioeconomic Status
NSCE Applicant Sample: Fall 1997 Cohort (N = 3,670)

Item	Social Class				
	Lower	Working	Middle	Upper-Middle	Upper
Percent of respondents reporting parents or other adults involved in homework often/very often	17.0	43.4	59.8	59.8	47.4
Percent of respondents reporting finishing homework first is often/very important	25.6	45.2	64.9	65.5	63.3
Mean value of mother's college expectation for child[a]	6.0	6.2	6.7	6.9	7.0
Mean value of father's college expectation for child[a]	5.7	6.2	6.7	6.9	7.0
Percent of parents having an opinion as to quality/type of college child should attend	9.6	49.8	51.2	66.6	73.9

Source: National Study of College Experience.
Note: Differences by socioeconomic status are statistically significant at the .05 level.
[a]Based on a seven-point scale in which 1 = no expectation and 7 = a very strong expectation.

applicants in each of the three highest social class categories agree that finishing their homework before engaging in other activities was often important or very important in their homes. Only 26 percent of lower-class applicants and 45 percent of working-class applicants report having families that placed the same emphasis on academics.

A similar pattern emerges on more college-specific questions, with high SES families more engaged in their children's academic future than low SES families. The higher the socioeconomic status of an applicant, the greater her mother's and father's expectation of college.[15] The same holds

than upper-middle-class parents (50 percent) and in the ballpark of middle-class parents (59 percent). This suggests that upper-class families are just as likely to believe that involvement in their children's homework is important but that greater time constraints from high-status employment outside the home may prevent them from participating as much as middle- and upper-middle-class parents. The fact that upper-class parents score highly on involvement measures that do not require as much of a time commitment (belief in the importance of homework first, expectations of college, ideas about the type of college their child should attend) suggests that on the whole they subscribe to the "concerted cultivation" theory of child rearing.

[15]Nationally as well, college expectations for children increase with parental education. In a 2003 Parent and Family Involvement in Education Survey of almost 7,000 students in

true for the type of college envisioned. Nearly three-quarters of upper-class and two-thirds of upper-middle-class parents have specific ideas about the type or quality of college their child should attend. In contrast, less than 10 percent of lower-class and just half of working- and middle-class applicants' parents think their child should study at a particular type of school. One explanation for low SES parents' greater uncertainty may be their lack of personal experience with college. Not having as many college-educated friends or other contacts may make it more difficult for them to know which institutions would accept their children (Konigsberg, 1996; Lareau, 2003). In addition, low SES parents may not perceive an increased value in having their child attend one type or quality of college over another (McDonough, 1997), because 44 percent of lower- and 41 percent of working-class NSCE applicants would be the first in their family to attend any college.

While parents' attitudes toward academics and college shape whether and where students apply, other factors could have a greater bearing on who is actually accepted. We now turn our attention to student behaviors and activities that are believed by many to give applicants an advantage in the competitive college admission process.

INVOLVEMENT IN EXTRACURRICULAR ACTIVITIES

Because of the growing number of highly qualified applicants to America's most selective colleges, extracurricular involvement and leadership potential have become more important to gaining admission (Soares, 2007). But what counts, and how much is necessary? To stand out enough to be admitted on the strength of extracurricular activities, an applicant must excel at the national level in a particular field rather than be well-rounded at the local level (Toor, 2001: 24–25). As Michele Hernández, a former admission officer at Dartmouth, puts it, being the "captain of a team or two, concert mistress of an orchestra, president of the senior class" places an applicant in the middle of the elite college applicant pool. It takes "swimming at the Olympics, playing the violin at Carnegie Hall" to impress selective college admission deans (Hernández, 1997: 116).

---

grades 6 through 12 conducted by the National Center for Education Statistics, 44 percent of parents who had a high school degree or less expected their children to finish college compared to 62 percent of parents with some postsecondary education and 88 percent of parents who had earned at least a bachelor's degree. The findings of the Parent and Family Involvement in Education Survey also suggest that parents of NSCE applicants are more determined to see their children graduate from college than are parents in general. Overall, about 90 percent of the students in the national survey had parents who expected them to continue their education beyond high school, and of these parents, just two-thirds expected their children to earn a bachelor's degree or higher (Lippman et al., 2008).

To receive average if not extraordinary marks in the extracurricular portion of the application, students need to demonstrate a depth of commitment to a few activities rather than perfunctory participation in many activities. Hernández (1997) suggests that students remain active in their extracurricular activities for two years or more in order to demonstrate their dedication. To approximate the way admission officers assess extracurricular participation, we count applicants as involved in an activity only if they are members for at least two years. To further capture applicants' commitment to their extracurricular life, we measure the number of leadership positions and awards they earn.

Types of Extracurricular Activities

The vast majority of NSCE applicants participate in some form of extracurricular activity.[16] Table 2.5 shows the percentage of students participating for at least two years in each of our seven broad extracurricular activity categories. Nearly 80 percent of all applicants participate in some kind of community service, the most common of all extracurricular endeavors.[17] Seventy-one percent engage in an academic activity. Sports, and then performing arts, are the next most common activities with 69 percent and 63 percent involved in each, respectively. Nearly half participate in a group that explores cultural diversity, and over a third hold part-time jobs. Only one-sixth of all respondents are involved in career-oriented activities, the least common among all extracurriculars.

For the most part, different race groups exhibit similar participation rates in these activities. However, as Figure 2.2 shows, involvement in academic and athletic activities does vary significantly by race. Asians are by far the most likely to belong to an academic club, with 84 percent serving as members. Three-quarters of Hispanic, about two-thirds of white, and three-fifths of black applicants are also involved in this type of activity. As for athletics, white applicants are the most likely of all racial groups to join. About three-quarters play a sport for two or more years,

[16] Our data for this section come from the Educational Testing Service (ETS) Student Descriptive Questionnaire (SDQ), which is filled out on a voluntary basis by SAT-takers. Since not all NSCE survey respondents took the SAT and some NSCE SAT-takers decided not to answer the questionnaire, the number of observations is smaller here than in our full applicant sample. Students who did respond to the SDQ reported in which high school years they participated (or expected to participate) in one of twenty-three listed extracurriculars, as well as whether they won an award or held a leadership position in that activity.

[17] Though many applicants and their families believe participating in community service increases chances of acceptance (Sharpe, 1999), Hernández (1997: 113) reports that an in-depth commitment to any activity is weighed the same as in-depth commitment to community service.

TABLE 2.5
Percent of Applicants Participating for Two or More Years
in Each High School Extracurricular Activity Category
NSCE Applicant Sample: Fall 1997 Cohort (N = 3,096)

Activity	Percent
Academic	71.0
Performing Arts	62.9
Athletic	69.3
Community Service	78.4
Cultural Diversity	45.9
Career-Oriented	16.7
Part-time Job	35.8

Source: Educational Testing Service Student Descriptive Questionnaire; National Study of College Experience.

Note: These extracurricular groupings are a condensed version of ETS Student Descriptive Questionnaire items. To be counted as participating in an activity category, students had to belong to at least one organization in that category for at least two years. For example, to be included as having participated in an academic activity, a student would have to be involved in an academic honor society, computer activity, debate or public speaking club, or science/math activity for two or more years. Belonging for one year to the debate team and one year to an academic honor society would not count as participating in an academic activity under our schema. Performing artists include those involved in art, dance, vocal music, instrumental music, theater, journalism, or other literary activity. Athletes comprise members of school spirit clubs (cheerleading, pep squad) as well as intramural, junior varsity, and varsity sports. Community service activities include participating in a community or a religious organization in addition to working in government or political service. Cultural diversity activities consist of ethnic organizations, foreign exchange programs, or foreign language clubs. A co-op work program, junior ROTC, or any other career-oriented activities are considered career-oriented extracurricular endeavors.

as compared to a little less than two-thirds of blacks and Hispanics and slightly more than half of Asians.

There are three extracurriculars in which participation rates differ significantly by socioeconomic status: performing arts, community service, and part-time employment. As shown in Figure 2.3, lower-class applicants are normally among the least likely to participate in these activities, and often by large margins. Notice first that approximately two-thirds of middle- and upper-middle-class applicants and roughly half of working- and upper-class students are involved in the performing arts, as compared to just about a quarter of lower-class applicants. Second, while only two-fifths of lower-class applicants engage in community service,

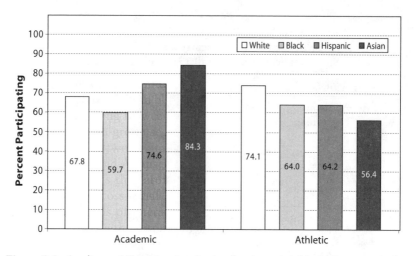

Figure 2.2. Applicants' Participation in Academic and Athletic Extracurricular Activities, by Race; NSCE Applicant Sample: Fall 1997 Cohort (N = 3,096). Note: Racial and ethnic differences are statistically significant at the .001 level. Source: Educational Testing Service Student Descriptive Questionnaire; National Study of College Experience.

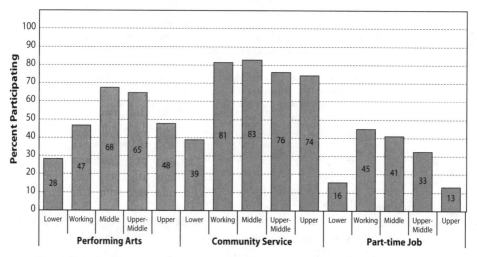

Figure 2.3. Applicants' Participation in Performing Arts and Community Service Extracurricular Activities, and Part-time Jobs, by Socioeconomic Status; NSCE Applicant Sample: Fall 1997 Cohort (N = 3,097). Note: Socioeconomic status differences in participation in performing arts are statistically significant at the .001 level. Differences in participation in community service and part-time jobs are statistically significant at the .05 level. Source: Educational Testing Service Student Descriptive Questionnaire; National Study of College Experience.

about three-fourths or more of all other applicants do. Lastly, 45 percent of working-class, 41 percent of middle-class, and 33 percent of upper-middle-class applicants hold part-time jobs. In contrast, only 16 percent of lower-class applicants work, just slightly more than the percentage of employed upper-class applicants. The pattern by socioeconomic status for part-time job holders may seem anomalous, but as O'Regan and Quigley (1996) explain, lower-income youth tend to have lower rates of employment because of the general economic conditions in the metropolitan communities in which they live and their spatial isolation from non-poor individuals, which curtails their ability to learn of job openings.

Lower-class applicants' less frequent involvement in the activities shown in Figure 2.3 is symptomatic of their lower participation rates in general. Two-fifths of lower-class applicants do not participate in a single extracurricular activity, as compared to less than 3 percent of applicants in other social class categories. While the average lower-class applicant participates in just two extracurricular activities, other applicants are typically involved in close to four.

There are several possible explanations for lower-class applicants' less frequent involvement in extracurriculars. First, Lareau (2003: 3) finds that in contrast to their high SES counterparts, low SES parents do not view their children's participation in organized activities as "an essential aspect of good parenting" and are more likely to consider the cost and time involved as unnecessary burdens. Second, lower-class families often need their children to perform childcare and housework in order to make ends meet (Dodson and Dickert, 2004: 318). This need intensifies when low-income families are headed by a single, particularly working, parent (Dodson and Dickert, 2004). Our data show that these family circumstances do indeed reduce extracurricular participation among lower-class applicants. While lower-class applicants who live with both parents and have a mother who does not work outside of the home are involved in an average of 3.2 activities, lower-class applicants who do not live in two-parent homes and have employed mothers participate in 1.2 activities on average. The fact that three-quarters of lower-class applicants grow up in this latter type of home environment contributes to their having a smaller number of extracurriculars overall.

A third possible explanation for lower-class applicants' less frequent involvement is that their commitment to academic enrichment activities outside school does not leave them enough time to be involved in the more conventional extracurricular activities that the Educational Testing Service (ETS) Student Descriptive Questionnaire (SDQ) captures.[18] Three-fourths

---

[18] Academic enrichment activities typically take place away from school and are not the same as the academic extracurricular activities shown in Table 2.5.

of lower-class NSCE applicants participate in some form of academic enrichment (that is, an additional summer, weekend, college, or distance
learning course outside their high school requirements). Only 52 percent
of other class groups do so. Moreover, while almost 55 percent of lower-
class applicants enroll in after-school workshops or classes, the same is
true of just 21 percent of all other NSCE applicants. Lower-class applicants also devote about nine hours a week tackling their academic enrichment work during the school year, four hours more than other SES groups
spend. The large percentage of lower-class applicants who are deeply involved in academic enrichment seems to reduce their overall number of
extracurriculars. Lower-class applicants who engage in academic enrichment activities have on average just 1.6 extracurriculars to their name,
while those who do not participate in academic enrichment have an average of 3.5 extracurriculars, a number similar to that found for applicants
in other social class categories.

Leadership Positions and Awards

Admission to elite universities depends on more than general participation in extracurricular activities. To stand out among other applicants it
is important to assume leadership roles and win awards as well. Almost
three-fourths of all NSCE applicants who reported their extracurricular
activities in the SDQ held at least one leadership position or earned at
least one award.[19] More than a third had three or more such extracurricular distinctions, and over 10 percent had five or more.

There are racial differences in the number of leadership positions and
awards possessed. Asian students garner the highest average number of
awards or leadership positions (2.3), followed by Hispanics (2.2), whites
(2.0), and then blacks (1.8). As Figure 2.4 shows, while 27 percent of
Asian and Hispanic students have four or more leadership positions or
awards, only 16 percent of whites and 14 percent of blacks hold that
many. Blacks are the most likely to receive no awards; 34 percent have
none. For other racial groups, between 26 and 28 percent of applicants
earn no awards.[20]

---

[19]ETS explains to students who fill out the SDQ that the extracurricular honors they
should note could include, but are not limited to, receiving a varsity letter, being class president, winning a prize in a regional science fair, or participating in the state orchestra.

[20]Black applicants' somewhat lower number of extracurricular distinctions seems to stem
from their slightly lower number of extracurricular activities. While black applicants participate in an average of 4.2 activities, the average is 4.6 for other race groups. The average
number of leadership positions and awards that applicants with 4.2 or fewer activities earn
is 1.5, while those with more than 4.2 activities typically have three honors to their name.
In examining the sample as a whole, the number of leadership positions and awards

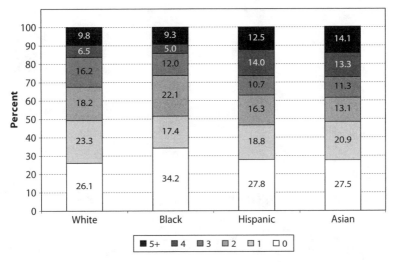

Figure 2.4. Percent of Applicants Achieving Varying Numbers of Awards or Leadership Positions, by Race; NSCE Applicant Sample: Fall 1997 Cohort (N = 3,096). Note: Racial differences in the number of leadership positions or awards applicants earn are statistically significant at the .01 level. Source: Educational Testing Service Student Descriptive Questionnaire; National Study of College Experience.

There are even more striking differences by socioeconomic status. As Figure 2.5 shows, while roughly 20 percent of working-, middle-, upper-middle-, and upper-class applicants have four or more awards or leadership positions, only 6 percent of lower-class applicants have that many. Almost three-fourths of lower-class applicants do not hold a single extracurricular honor, as compared to just over a third of working- and upper-class applicants and a quarter of middle- and upper-middle-class applicants. Lower-class applicants' fewer extracurricular distinctions result largely from their less frequent participation in the SDQ activities from which leadership roles and awards are derived. The average number of awards or leadership positions across social classes follows an inverted

---

applicants win increases monotonically with the number of extracurricular activities in which they participate. This result is likely due to the way in which the SDQ counts awards. An applicant either can have won at least one award in an activity or not won an award in that activity; multiple awards in one activity are not recognized. For example, if a student receives four awards in varsity baseball and five in varsity football he would receive credit for only one award in a varsity sport. Though this way of counting does not precisely capture the way admission officers might view students' awards, for they actually prefer students who are stand-outs in one or two extracurriculars (Hernández, 1997; Sharpe, 1999; Toor, 2001), it still gives a glimpse of which groups are excelling in the extracurricular portion of the application.

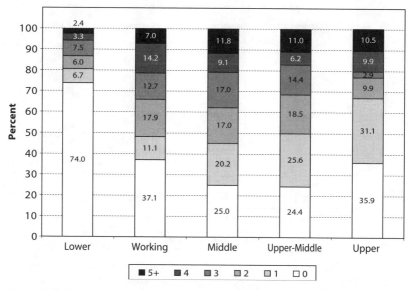

Figure 2.5. Percent of Applicants Achieving Varying Numbers of Awards or Leadership Positions, by Socioeconomic Status; NSCE Applicant Sample: Fall 1997 Cohort (N = 3,096). Note: Social class differences in the number of leadership positions or awards applicants earn are significant at the .01 level. Source: Educational Testing Service Student Descriptive Questionnaire; National Study of College Experience.

U-shaped pattern. It is least for students from the lower-class category (0.7), and then rises to 1.9 for the working-class category and to 2.2 for the middle-class category. Upper-middle-class applicants (2.0) and upper-class students (1.7) exhibit declining average numbers.[21]

High School Academic Achievement

For most applicants to selective colleges and universities, academic performance in high school is more critical to being admitted than is partici-

---

[21] In a logistic regression (not shown) where the dependent variable is coded 1 if an applicant has received 4 or more leadership positions or awards and 0 otherwise, the significantly positive coefficients at the .05 level are for Hispanic and Asian (compared to white) and for female (compared to male). Lower-class applicants receive significantly fewer honors than middle-class applicants. Control variables include immigrant generation, first-generation college student, SAT score, ACT score, high school type, and whether one's high school was identified by veteran Princeton University admission officers as one of the most outstanding high schools in the country.

pation in extracurricular activities. Applicants to our selective NSCE institutions excel in their high school classes. More than a quarter of applicants who reported their high school GPA in the SDQ have an A+ average. More than 60 percent have at least an A average, and more than 80 percent possess an A− or above. While there is little GPA variation by socioeconomic status—about 80 percent of all social class groups have GPAs in the A− to A+ range—GPAs do differ by race. An average of A− or better is earned by almost 89 percent of Asians, 84 percent of Hispanics, and 81 percent of whites, as compared to just 63 percent of black applicants.

Because of grade inflation, admission officers often perceive class rank as a more reliable measure of academic achievement than high school GPA. Not surprisingly, NSCE applicants have achieved strong grades relative to their high school classmates. More than 60 percent of applicants who report class rank are in the top 10 percent of their class, and five out of every six rank in the top 20 percent. But just as with GPA, class rank varies by race. Asians (at 71 percent) are 9 percentage points more likely than whites, 10 percentage points more likely than Hispanics, and 37 percentage points more likely than blacks to be in the top tenth of their class. Three-quarters of applicants from upper-class backgrounds are in the top 10 percent of their high school class. Between 60 and 63 percent of working-, middle-, and upper-middle-class groups are also in the top tenth, but just 27 percent of lower-class applicants rank as highly.[22]

Applicants are also judged by the strength of their high school curriculum and not just by their GPAs or class ranks (Stevens, 2007). Admission officers seek students who "take full advantage" of their secondary school offerings, which means that applicants should enroll (and perform well) in the most challenging courses available. Frequently, the most demanding courses are Advanced Placement (AP) courses, which are high school classes taught at the college level and that culminate in an Advanced Placement examination graded by college faculty and AP teachers. Admission officers look for AP classes on the high school transcript for at least two reasons. First, scores on AP exams provide an indication of how applicants will perform in college, as AP courses and tests more closely approximate the level of work college classes require (College Board, 2006a; Hernández, 1997: 92). Second, selective colleges and universities expect to enroll students who reveal a sincere interest in learning for learning's sake. Admission officers believe that applicants who enroll in AP courses show that drive, because the greater difficulty of AP courses can jeopardize students' GPAs and high school class ranks (Hernández, 1997: 17).

[22] However, differences in class rank by socioeconomic status fail to reach the .05 test for statistical significance. The p-value is .0538.

The number of AP examinations NSCE applicants take varies significantly by race and by social class. ETS records indicate that 72 percent of
NSCE applicants took at least one AP exam. Of these exam-takers, the
average number of tests taken is 3.5. Asians take the most APs with 4.3.
For whites, Hispanics, and blacks the averages are 3.4, 3.2, and 2.7, respectively.[23] The number of AP courses students take generally increases
with applicants' social class. Working-class applicants take an average of
2.9 AP courses, the middle class sits for 3.4, the upper-middle class studies for 3.7, and the upper class enrolls in 4.4. However, lower-class applicants take the highest average number of AP exams of any group: 4.6.[24]

Applicants to selective colleges also perform well on the SAT examination. NSCE applicants have an average SAT score of 1282 compared to a
national average of 1016 (College Board, 1997). As Figure 2.6 shows,
Asians have the highest average score (1334), followed by whites (1284)
and Hispanics (1224). Blacks (1146) score almost 200 points below
Asians. Upper-class applicants earn the highest score of any socioeconomic grouping (1338), followed in descending order by upper-middle-
class (1297) and then middle-class applicants (1268). Lower- and working-
class applicants receive the lowest SAT scores.[25]

To summarize, we find a consistent pattern when examining applicants' academic achievement by race. Asian applicants take the most AP
courses and have the highest GPA, class rank, and SAT score of all racial
groups. Blacks, on the other hand, score the lowest on all four academic
achievement measures. Whites and Hispanics fall in the middle, with a
slightly greater percentage of Hispanics having higher GPAs, but whites
performing slightly better on the other three indicators. Variation in academic achievement by socioeconomic status generally shows a positive

[23] The differences in the mean number of AP courses taken between white and Hispanic
and Hispanic and black applicants are not statistically significant at the .05 level. It is also
worth noting that nationwide there are similar racial gaps in the rate of AP test-taking. Data
from the College Board's *AP Report to the Nation 2006* indicate that the share of African
Americans among AP test-takers in public schools in 2005 was roughly one-half of their
share of graduating seniors. Black students comprised 6.4 percent of the examinee population versus 13.4 percent of seniors. Asian American students have the highest AP participation rates. They made up 10.5 percent of the test-taking population but just 5.2 percent of
public high school seniors. The percentages of whites and Hispanics who take AP examinations are roughly comparable to their percentages among seniors at large. AP exams are
graded on a scale from 1 to 5, and a score of 3 or higher is indicative of some degree of mastery of a subject. The average score on all AP tests taken in U.S. public schools by the class
of 2005 during their high school years was 2.88. Black students had the lowest average AP
test score (1.99) and Asian Americans the highest (3.04) (College Board, 2006a).

[24] However, differences between lower-class and other SES groups are not statistically significant at the .05 level.

[25] However, the difference between lower- and working-class applicants' average SAT
score is not statistically significant at the .05 level.

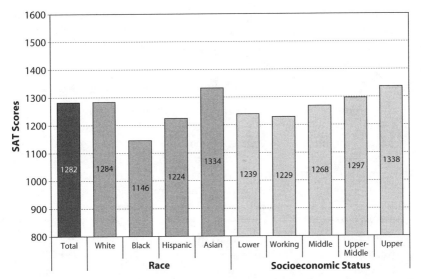

Figure 2.6. Average Combined SAT Scores for NSCE Applicants, by Race and Socioeconomic Status; NSCE Applicant Sample: Fall 1997 Cohort (N = 3,538). Note: Since some applicants only submitted ACT scores, the number of observations is slightly smaller than our full applicant sample. Source: Educational Testing Service; National Study of College Experience.

correlation with social class. Upper-class applicants typically rank highest on standard measures of academic performance in high school.

ADMISSION-ENHANCING STRATEGIES

In this era of increased competition for admission to the nation's top colleges, many students and their families are taking deliberate steps to increase the chances of admission. Strategies that are believed to provide an advantage include the following: choosing to live in a community known for the quality of its public schools; electing to attend a high school other than the public one to which one is assigned (that is, a magnet, parochial, or private school); participating in academic enrichment activities; taking PSAT, SAT, or ACT test preparation courses; hiring a private college consultant; and visiting colleges before applying.[26] This section examines the

---

[26] Applying early is another strategy students use to enhance their chances of college admission (Avery, Fairbanks, and Zeckhauser, 2003). However, we do not have data on which students submitted early applications and cannot draw conclusions about differences in applicants' use of this tactic.

use of these enhancement strategies and whether such use differs by race and socioeconomic status. The next chapter will address whether any of these strategies ultimately helps students gain letters of acceptance.

High School Choice

Although outstanding academic performance in high school is necessary for elite college admission, it is not enough (Espenshade, Hale, and Chung, 2005). Universities need to be confident that students whom they admit are well prepared for their college's academic workload. As a result, the type and caliber of the high school in which "A" grades are earned matter as well. Though applicants who attend strong magnet, parochial, and public schools can often persuade admission officers that they are academically prepared for the rigors of the college classroom, it may be even easier for private school students to make a convincing case.[27]

Moreover, many families and researchers (McDonough, 1997; Persell and Cookson, 1985; Stevens, 2007) believe that private schools provide advantages in college admission beyond just solid academic preparation. For example, McDonough's (1997) investigation of the college application and admission process finds that private schools have more knowledgeable college counselors and place much more emphasis on college admission.[28] In contrast to public schools, college preparatory schools typically employ a counselor devoted solely to college admission (McDonough, 1997). In many cases these counselors have had prior experience working in a college admission office (Cookson and Persell, 1985). Private school counselors' exclusive focus on college counseling and experience in admitting college applicants makes them much more informed about the college admission process than are public high school counselors. For example, Avery, Fairbanks, and Zeckhauser (2003) find that counselors at private schools are more aware of the admission advantage that comes from applying early than are counselors at public schools. College preparatory school students therefore have an informational advantage over students who attend high schools that are less sophisticated about the college admission process.

[27]Private high schools more frequently enjoy a reputation for providing high-quality instruction. Data from the National Center for Education Statistics for the 2001–2 school year indicate that only about 12 percent of all U.S. high schools were non-parochial, private institutions (Broughman and Pugh, 2004: 11; Hoffman, 2003: 2). Yet when two college admissions officers at Princeton University were asked to identify the most outstanding high schools in the country, 32 percent of the institutions on their list fell into this category.

[28]McDonough's (1997) study focused on female students of similar academic standing at a private all-girls school, parochial all-girls school, high SES public school, and low SES public school in California.

In addition, private schools devote much more time to ensuring students' college admission. McDonough (1997: 47, 91) reports that while the private school counselor in her study met with every student for ten to fifteen hours during the college application and admissions process, the high SES public school counselor met with students for a total of about forty-five minutes, and only with those who requested meetings. In addition, students at private high schools profit from the greater amount of time teachers and counselors spend writing better, more detailed letters of recommendation (McDonough, 1997; Sanoff, 1999; Stevens, 2007).[29]

Yet the benefits of attending a private high school may go beyond counselors' better understanding of the process and the greater amount of time school personnel spend on college admission. The most elite private secondary schools also cultivate special relationships with college admission officers, which can then facilitate their students' admission to the most competitive schools (Cookson and Persell, 1985; Hernández, 1997; Mayher, 1998; Toor, 2001). College admission deans take phone calls from private high school counselors and consult with them about applicants (Cookson and Persell, 1985; Toor, 2001: 156–57). They also think twice before rejecting students from private schools, especially the ones that are most well-known.[30] Admission officers want to maintain good relationships with private school counselors so these counselors will continue to encourage students to apply to their institutions, as receiving a large number of applications helps raise a college's selectivity ranking (Stevens, 2007; Toor, 2001).

Despite these potential private school advantages, two-thirds of all applicants to selective NSCE colleges and universities attend regular public high schools. As Figure 2.7 shows, a combined 17 percent attend magnet or parochial schools, and only 14 percent of applicants study at private schools.[31] In addition, just over one-third of all applicants attended their

[29] On the other hand, Michele Hernández (1997: 133) insists that colleges "do not hold an overly general letter against the [often public school] applicant, since it has nothing to do with his academic potential."

[30] Cookson and Persell (1985) recount how two college counselors, one from an elite private school and one from a public high school, sat in on the admissions committee meeting of an Ivy League college to lobby on behalf of their respective students. The public school student was truly outstanding. His SATs were in the 700s and he was top of his class, class president, and a star athlete. The admissions committee rejected this young man and accepted the prep school student who had SATs in the 500s, was in the middle of his class and only an average athlete, and exhibited no strong signs of leadership. The authors conclude that "the admissions officers apparently listen more closely to advisors from select 16 [the most elite private] boarding schools than to public school counselors" (125).

[31] By comparison, less than 4 percent of all high school students nationwide attended non-sectarian private high schools during the 1997–98 school year (Broughman and Colaciello, 1999; Hoffman, 1999). It is worth noting, however, that while private high school students

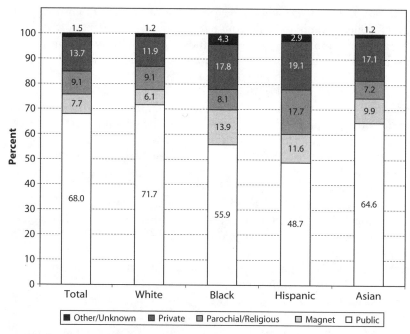

Figure 2.7. Type of High School Attended, by Race; NSCE Applicant Sample: Fall 1997 Cohort (N = 3,670). Note: Racial differences in use of magnet schools are statistically significant at the .05 level. Racial differences in use of public schools are statistically significant at the .01 level. Source: National Study of College Experience.

high school with the expectation that doing so would improve their chances of being accepted to college, essentially using high school choice as a way to enhance their likelihood of college admission.[32]

Race matters when it comes to the types of high schools NSCE applicants attend. Though white applicants are the most socioeconomically

are overrepresented in the NSCE applicant pool, they are not as predominant on elite campuses as they were a generation or two ago. According to Karabel (2005: 127), "By 1930, Princeton—like Yale—was even more insular and dominated by prep school graduates than it had been a decade earlier. . . . [T]he number of public school graduates in the freshman class had dwindled to 94—fewer than the 102 alumni sons entering Princeton that year."

[32] Though some families move to communities specifically for the reputation of their public schools and thus can be considered to exercise school choice, public schools are more frequently the default secondary school. In the NSCE data, only 23 percent of applicants from public high schools claim to have attended their school with the purpose of increasing their odds of college acceptance. In contrast, 43 percent of applicants from magnet schools respond in the affirmative, as do about 70 percent of parochial and private high school students.

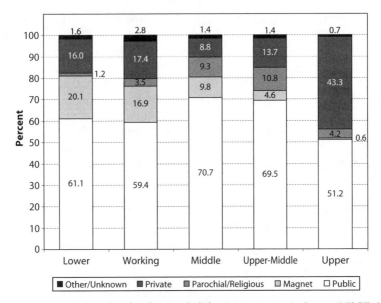

Figure 2.8. Type of High School Attended, by Socioeconomic Status; NSCE Applicant Sample: Fall 1997 Cohort (N = 3,670). Note: Social class differences in use of private schools are statistically significant at the .001 level. Social class differences in use of magnet schools are statistically significant at the .01 level. Source: National Study of College Experience.

advantaged of any of the four racial groups, they are also the most likely to attend tuition-free schools. As indicated by Figure 2.7, more than 70 percent of white applicants attend regular public high schools, as compared to two-thirds of Asians, 56 percent of blacks, and just under one-half of Hispanic NSCE applicants. Meanwhile, less affluent racial groups are more likely to be found at expensive private schools. Between 17 and 19 percent of Hispanics, blacks, and Asians attend private high schools, as compared to 12 percent of whites.[33]

The extent to which students rely on private secondary schools varies by social class, but in a nonlinear way. Figure 2.8 shows that more than

[33] This race difference exists not just in the aggregate. In every SES category except the working class, a greater percentage of black, Hispanic, and Asian applicants attend private schools than do white applicants. The relatively greater concentration of nonwhite students at private schools may mean that, in this highly self-selected sample, parents of nonwhite NSCE applicants simply place a higher value on their children's secondary school education. Yet this result may also be partially the consequence of housing segregation (Massey and Denton, 1993). Compared to white parents of similar economic means, minority parents may find it more difficult to gain residence in high-quality public school districts, leading them to secure other school options for their children.

40 percent of upper-class students graduate from private schools, a higher proportion than in any other class background. At the same time, lower- and working-class applicants are more likely to attend private schools than more affluent middle- and upper-middle-class applicants. It may be the case that there are so many barriers that prevent students from lower- and working-class family backgrounds from applying to elite colleges that those who do apply are more likely to have benefited from the encouragement of a private school. Attending private school may be less necessary for middle- and upper-middle-class students because they can receive the encouragement, information, and preparation they need to apply through their families and/or higher-quality public schools (McDonough, 1997).

Lower-class students are also the most likely of all SES groups to attend their high school in order to enhance their college admission prospects. In this regard, they are more similar to high SES applicants than to middle- and working-class applicants. Fifty-nine percent of lower-class students indicate that they used high school choice as a strategy, followed by about 45 percent of upper-middle- and upper-class students. Less than one-third of working- and middle-class applicants report having attended their high school for the same purpose.

Whether an applicant has attended a public or private secondary school is not all that matters to university admissions officers. Colleges are also concerned with a high school's reputation for academic quality. Students who graduate from schools well-known for their academic rigor— whether private, parochial, public, or magnet—will receive greater recognition for their high GPAs than will students at less demanding institutions. Nevertheless, attending high-caliber schools can also have an adverse effect on chances of admission. In examining more than 45,000 applications to three elite universities, Espenshade, Hale, and Chung (2005) find that, controlling for students' scholastic ability, coming from a school with relatively more highly talented students reduces applicants' chances of being accepted. In other words, the chances of admission are greater for big frogs in small ponds than for equally qualified small frogs in bigger ponds.[34]

[34] Attending a more competitive high school can disadvantage an applicant in several ways. First, reliance on class rank as a measure of high school academic performance can "punish" bright students for having smart peers. Admission officers seldom give students from elite private schools the highest score possible for academic achievement, because being in the top 1 or 2 percent is simply much more difficult at these high schools (Toor, 2001: 94). Second, while letters of recommendation from teachers and counselors at better schools are typically more detailed, they are also less glowing. "Rarely do you see a teacher at one of the top private schools write that a student is 'best of career'" (Toor, 2001: 99). Third, students are sometimes directly compared to the other applicants from their high

In order to ascertain the characteristics of applicants who attend the nation's most academically elite high schools, we asked two seasoned college admission officers at Princeton University to identify for us the "most outstanding secondary schools" throughout the country, without regard to whether these schools are public or private, large or small. The resulting list includes seventy-two elite high schools (the "elite 72"), attended by about 5 percent of all NSCE applicants.[35] There are no significant racial variations in this percentage, but social class makes a difference. Ten percent of upper-class applicants attend an elite high school, followed by about 6 percent of upper-middle-class students. Only about 3 percent of middle-, working-, and lower-class applicants study at one of these most prestigious high schools. Seventy-six percent of applicants from elite secondary schools attend these schools with the idea that doing so will help their chances of college admission.

Academic Enrichment

In addition to relying on high school choice, NSCE applicants also participate in special academic enrichment programs to try to enhance their odds of admission. A little more than half of all NSCE applicants have been involved in a summer, after-school, college, junior college, weekend, or distance learning course or workshop. Thirty percent of all NSCE applicants participate in summer programs, 21 percent in after-school programs, and 17 percent in college or junior college courses. Though there are many worthy academic enrichment programs,[36] admissions officers seem most impressed by students who attend those sponsored by colleges and universities during the summer (K. Cohen, 2002; Hernández, 1997). About one-quarter of all applicants enroll in a college-sponsored program.

Overall, nonwhite students appear more determined than white students to supplement their regular high school curriculum with outside academic enrichment programs. Asian students are the most likely to participate in some form of academic enrichment. Table 2.6 displays the differences that emerge by race for academic enrichment in general and

---

school rather than to the applicant pool as a whole. At least at Brown and at Duke, counselors describe applicants by high school and then make suggestions as to whom the committee should admit from that school (Hernández, 1997: 103; Toor, 2001: 156).

[35] To put this number in perspective, there were 27,341 public and private high schools in this country in the fall of 1997 (Broughman and Colaciello, 1999; Hoffman, 1999). These 72 elite secondary schools represent just 0.3 percent of all existing American high schools.

[36] Such programs include those sponsored by fraternities and sororities or religious groups, as well as more specific programs such as A Better Chance (ABC), Center for Talented Youth (CTY), Jack & Jill, Prep for Prep, Talent Identification Project (TIP), Talent Search, and Upward Bound.

TABLE 2.6
Participation in Supplemental Academic Enrichment Programs,
by Race and Socioeconomic Status
NSCE Applicant Sample: Fall 1997 Cohort

Background	Percent of All Applicants Participating in Any Kind of Academic Enrichment[a]	Percent of All Applicants Participating in College-Sponsored Academic Enrichment[b]
Total Sample (N = 3,670)	52.5	28.2
Race		
White	47.1	25.6
Black	58.8	31.8
Hispanic	55.5	25.6
Asian	68.1	36.7
Socioeconomic Status		
Upper	46.6	33.0
Upper-Middle	57.1	32.8
Middle	47.6	20.8
Working	49.3	33.3
Lower	75.8	26.4

Source: National Study of College Experience.
[a]Racial differences are statistically significant at the .001 level. Social class differences are not significant at the .05 level.
[b]Both racial and social class differences are statistically significant at the .05 level.

for college- or university-sponsored programs. Asians are 21 percentage points more likely than whites to engage in academic enrichment (68 percent) and 11 percentage points more likely to enroll in a college-sponsored program (37 percent). Whites are the least likely to attend general academic enrichment programs (47 percent) or college-sponsored ones (26 percent). Blacks and Hispanics fall in between Asians and whites.

Social class is correlated with the extent to which students participate in academic enrichment. As seen in Table 2.6, lower-class applicants are most likely to be involved in general academic enrichment activities (76 percent), followed by the upper-middle class (57 percent). Almost half of working-, middle-, and upper-class applicants also participate. A different pattern emerges for college-sponsored enrichment. A third of upper-, upper-middle-, and working-class applicants, and a quarter of lower-class applicants enroll in college programs. Just one-fifth of middle-class students do so. Middle-class applicants may attend less frequently because of their family income. It may be too low for them to comfortably afford the rather costly college programs in which upper-middle- and upper-class students participate.[37] Yet, at the same time, it could be too high for them to be eligible for the college programs established specifically for lower- and working-class students.[38]

Test Preparation Services

While participating in academic enrichment may help applicants gain admission, strong test scores remain absolutely critical. Hernández (1997) reports that Ivy League and other selective schools construct an academic index (AI) score for athletes and use the same or comparable formula in judging the academic merits of all applicants. Under the AI, the average math and verbal SAT I score represents one-third of applicants' rating, the average of three SAT II subject test scores counts for another third, and class rank derived from performance in all high school courses makes up the final third (Hernández, 1997: 62). Given that two-thirds of an applicant's academic score can be based on a handful of standardized tests, many students and their families devote significant amounts of time and money to preparing for these exams. About 46 percent of NSCE applicants enrolled in a course designed specifically to improve their SAT, PSAT, or ACT score. Asians (at 54 percent) are the most likely to sign up for a class, followed by blacks (50 percent), whites (44 percent), and Hispanics (40 percent).[39]

Journalists and admission officers tend to focus on the social class dimensions of test preparation. Several articles have been written about how high SES families pay huge amounts of money for test preparation (Gross, 1999; Lewin, 2004; Lombardi, 2003). It is true that courses can be costly—close to $1,000 for thirty-five hours of class instruction with Kaplan or Princeton Review (Chaker, 2005). In light of these costs, admission officers tend to view test preparation as a tool only of the more affluent. It is frequently assumed that poorer and first-generation college students have not had access to test preparation (Hernández, 1997: 110; Lombardi, 2003). This assumption in turn affects the way colleges assess standardized test scores. The same low score is counted against a low SES applicant less heavily than against a high SES one (Hernández, 1997: 110).

[37] In 2002, students living on campus paid $4,792 for one four-week session at Columbia. Brown's seven-week, two-course program cost $6,775, including tuition, room and board, and other fees (Boas, 2002).

[38] Upward Bound and Talent Search, funded by the Department of Education and offered by multiple universities, are two such programs that require participants to be either from lower-income families or potential first-generation college students.

[39] Other researchers have also found Asian and minority students to be more likely than whites to take test preparation courses (Zwick, 2002: 162, 172).

Our data do not support admission officers' suppositions that low SES and first-generation college student applicants are less likely to enroll in some form of test preparation course. First, upper- and upper-middle-class students are not overwhelmingly the most likely to take test preparation courses; the range among all SES groups stretches only twelve percentage points. Upper-middle-class students are the most likely to take such a course, with 52 percent doing so, while working- and middle-class students (at 40 percent) are the least likely to do so. Lower- and upper-class applicants fall in the middle with 45 and 49 percent, respectively, taking a course. Second, in contrast to admission officers' beliefs, first-generation college students are somewhat more likely to take a course than are applicants from families with college experience. More than 55 percent of first-generation college students have participated in test preparation, as compared to just 44 percent of all other applicants.[40]

Applicants who take test preparation courses most commonly receive instruction for a total of five to fourteen hours. Thirty-two percent of all course-taking applicants fall into this category. However, nearly 38 percent of Asian course-takers receive instruction for twenty-five hours or more, as compared to just 22 percent of Hispanic, white, and black course-takers. By socioeconomic status, 85 percent of lower-class applicants who enroll in a course participate for at least twenty-five hours of instruction, as compared to just 22 percent of working- and middle-, 29 percent of upper-middle-, and 45 percent of upper-class applicants.[41]

Almost half of those who enroll in a test preparation course take their class through a private company (for example, Princeton Review or Kaplan). This tendency varies by race, however. As Figure 2.9 shows, only 38 percent of whites who take a test preparation class choose a private company. In contrast, 72 percent of Asians, 56 percent of Hispanics, and 48 percent of blacks enroll through a private firm.[42]

Although participating in some type of test preparation course and the number of hours one spends doing so do not vary substantially with so-

[40]Differences in the use of test preparation courses by socioeconomic status and by first-generation college student status fail to reach statistical significance at the .05 level.

[41]Lower-class applicants may be seeking out more instruction to make up for other areas of the admission process in which they feel disadvantaged. Ninety-four percent of lower-class applicants at public schools obtain instruction for twenty-five hours or more, as compared to only 47 percent of lower-class students at private schools. Eighty-nine percent of lower-class applicants without a private consultant spend that many hours preparing, in contrast to 47 percent of those who have a consultant's help.

[42]These racial differences may be limited to selective college applicants. Using NELS data, Briggs (2004: 223) finds no significant racial differences in students' use of a private test preparation company.

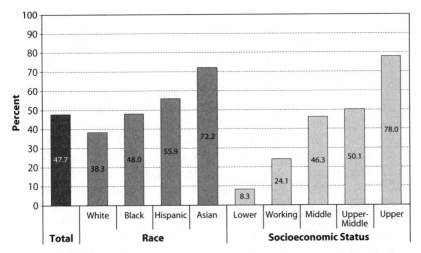

Figure 2.9. Percent of Test Preparation Course-Takers Who Took a Course through a Private Company, by Race and Socioeconomic Status; NSCE Applicant Sample: Fall 1997 Cohort. Note: The data for race and social class are based on 1,581 unweighted cases of students reporting they enrolled in a test preparation course. The proportions in Figure 2.9 reflect weighted tabulations. Differences in the percentage of test preparation course-takers who enrolled in a private course are statistically significant by race at the .001 level and by socioeconomic status at the .01 level. Source: National Study of College Experience.

cioeconomic status, social class is related to the propensity to take a privately sponsored course. Figure 2.9 shows that this tendency rises from 8 percent of all lower-class test preparation takers to 78 percent of those in the upper class. So, while journalists and admission officers underestimate low SES students' access to some form of test preparation, it is true that low SES students are less likely to take private courses. If private classes are more effective at raising students' test scores than are courses sponsored by high schools or other organizations, then low SES students may indeed be at a disadvantage. However, after reviewing six studies that investigated Kaplan's effectiveness and eight studies that explored the efficacy of using Princeton Review, Powers (1993: 29) concluded that "these programs are hardly (if at all) more effective in improving SAT scores than are coaching programs generally."

Use of Professional College Consultants

Another strategy that some applicants and their families use to raise the chances of admission to an elite college or university is to employ professional college consultants or private tutors to assist in the process of selecting colleges and/or completing application forms.[43] Indeed, the college consulting industry has boomed in the wake of inadequate college counseling at many American public high schools (McDonough, 2005),[44] as well as increased competition for admission to elite universities. A 1987 New York State study found that as many as 20 percent of college-bound seniors spoke with a private consultant (McDonough, 1994: 441). According to the Independent Educational Consultants Association (IECA), the percentage of college freshmen who met with private counselors jumped from 1 percent in 1990 to 10 percent in 2000 (Worth, 2000). One longtime counselor predicted that 15 to 20 percent of juniors and seniors attending public high schools in affluent communities hire private college counselors (Worth, 2000).

NSCE data suggest, however, that the percentage of selective college applicants who use a private consultant's services is small and does not vary significantly by race. Our data show that about 12 percent of all NSCE applicants used a private consultant to help choose colleges, and 9 percent employed one to help complete application forms. Five percent of applicants hired a professional consultant to provide both services. About 15 percent of Hispanics, 14 percent of Asians, and 12 percent of blacks and whites use a consultant to help select colleges. Hispanics are also the most likely to hire a professional to help with applications. About 13 percent of Hispanic applicants use a consultant solely for this latter service, as compared to 9 percent of white and Asian applicants and 8 percent of black applicants.

Like the literature on test preparation courses, discussions about the use of private college consultants focus more on its class dimensions, highlighting consultants' high cost and the affluence of those who hire them. Patricia McDonough's (1997) study finds that only high SES parents employ private consultants. McDonough told the *New York Times* that students receiving extra counseling "are mostly white, upper-middle class, with parents who are college educated and have a graduate degree" (Worth, 2000). McDonough (1997: 119) estimates the average family that hires a consultant spends "between $400 and $2,500 to help their children define their postsecondary opportunities and select the college of their choice." Depending on the professional hired, families can pay $520

---

[43] There are estimated to be at least four hundred full-time independent college consultants operating within the United States (Konigsberg, 1996).

[44] The National Association for College Admission Counseling reports that on average 330 students are assigned to one public high school counselor instead of the 100 the American School Counselor Association recommends. Given the many problems public high school students face, counselors spend an average of only ten hours a week counseling students specifically about college (Sanoff, 1999).

to \$29,000 for unlimited hours of service (Konigsberg, 1996; Shea and Marcus, 2001). McDonough (1997: 115) calculates that college consultants charge approximately \$30 to \$125 an hour, while the National Association for College Admission Counseling and the Independent Educational Consultants Association place the hourly rate even higher, somewhere between \$60 and \$200 (Terrell, 1998).

Despite the high cost of private consultants, our data indicate that high SES applicants are not more likely to employ them than are low SES applicants. First, while lower-class applicants are the least likely to hire someone to help select colleges (with just over 4 percent doing so), working-class applicants are the most likely to seek the help of a professional (23 percent). Roughly 11 or 12 percent of middle-, upper-middle-, and upper-class applicants rely on a private consultant for this service. Second, working-class applicants are as likely to hire a consultant for help with completing college applications as are upper-class applicants. Twelve percent of both class groups do so with 9 percent of upper-middle-, 8 percent of middle-, and 4 percent of lower-class applicants following suit. Third, even when we define private consultant use as employing a professional to provide both of these services, the affluent are still not more likely to hire a consultant. It is also worth noting that, in contrast to media depictions, first-generation college students are more likely to employ a consultant for each service individually, as well as both services combined, than are students with family college experience. In sum, at least in elite applicant pools, low SES and first-generation college student applicants are not less likely to hire a private college consultant than are their high SES peers.[45]

There could be at least two reasons why our results differ from those that might be expected. First, the availability of other individuals besides private consultants or tutors to assist applicants during the college admissions process may help explain our consultant results. NSCE data suggest that applicants with family members who guide them through the process are less likely to hire a private consultant. While 20 percent of all applicants with no parental guidance in choosing colleges employ a private consultant, only 4 percent of applicants who have their parents' help use a consultant in addition. Moreover, 16 percent of those who have no assistance from their parents in completing applications seek the expertise of a professional, compared to just 2 percent of those who receive family help. Thus, working-class applicants' greater use of consultants may be the result of their families being less likely to guide them through the process. Just 23 percent of working-class applicants have family help in

---

[45] For all three measures of consultant use, differences by socioeconomic status and by first-generation college student status are not significant at the .05 level.

choosing schools compared to 42 percent of middle-, 50 percent of lower-
and upper-middle-, and 61 percent of upper-class applicants.[46]

Second, our findings and those reported by McDonough and journalists may not be mutually exclusive. Nationally, applicants who employ
consultants may indeed be more privileged. We must remember the applicants NSCE schools attract. Low SES students who apply to these institutions are not average but outstanding. Their excellent performance
may allow them to gain access to resources that a more typical low SES
college applicant could not obtain. For example, the low SES applicants
in our sample may be precisely those for whom some private consultants
engage in pro-bono work (Konigsberg, 1996; Worth, 2000). These high
achievers may also be selected by their high school teachers and administrators to be the primary recipients of the kinds of counseling services
that companies like Kaplan, Princeton Review, and Achieve College Prep
Services now offer to some low SES public high schools (Paul, 2000).
Non-profits, such as Admission Possible, also guide poor students with
high potential through the admissions process (Winerip, 2005).

Visiting Colleges

The final strategy we examine is visiting prospective colleges before applying. Some admission officers view applicants who have already visited
their school as more interested in attending and therefore more likely to
enroll if admitted (Stevens, 2007). By identifying and admitting more
students who are likely to attend, universities can admit fewer students
and thus increase their selectivity, which helps them rise in university
rankings. As a consequence, visiting campus may give an applicant an
edge in the competitive admission process (K. Cohen, 2002; Hernández,
1997; Mayher, 1998).[47] Table 2.7 shows the number of visits NSCE applicants make to prospective colleges before applying. About 15 percent
of students do not visit any colleges before mailing their applications,
about one-third see between three and five schools, and about 23 percent
tour six or more.

White applicants are more likely than nonwhites to make a large number of campus visits. As seen in Figure 2.10, more than a quarter of white
applicants see six or more institutions. Fewer than one-sixth of black,
Hispanic, and Asian students see that many schools. Moreover, whereas

[46] Working-class students are also the least likely to receive family assistance to complete
application forms, though not as dramatically so.

[47] Rachel Toor (2001: 22–23) argues that while showing an interest in a school may be
important at smaller colleges that want to ensure a high yield rate for the smaller number
of students they can accept, prior visits may have no bearing on admission at larger
institutions.

TABLE 2.7
Number of Visits to Prospective Colleges
NSCE Applicant Sample: Fall 1997 Cohort

Number	Percent
Total Sample (N = 3,670)	100.0
0	14.8
1–2	23.2
3–5	33.9
6–9	15.9
10+	7.0
Unknown	5.2

Source: National Study of College Experience.

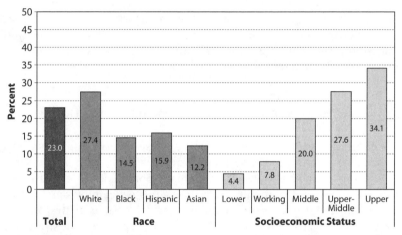

Figure 2.10. Percent of Applicants Visiting Six or More Prospective Colleges before Submitting an Application, by Race and Socioeconomic Status; NSCE Applicant Sample: Fall 1997 Cohort (N = 3,670). Note: Differences in the percentage of applicants making six or more visits are statistically significant by race at the .001 level and by socioeconomic status at the .01 level. Source: National Study of College Experience.

just one-tenth of whites do not visit a single potential college before applying, this behavior is characteristic of about 18 percent of blacks, 22 percent of Hispanics, and 26 percent of Asians. About one-fifth of blacks and Hispanics have at least one college visit paid for in whole or in part by a university, in contrast to less than one-tenth of white or Asian applicants.

The percentage of applicants who visit six or more schools increases with parents' social class background. As shown in Figure 2.10, 4 percent of lower-, 8 percent of working-, 20 percent of middle-, 28 percent of upper-middle-, and 34 percent of upper-class applicants see six or more colleges or universities. While 44 percent of all lower-class applicants have not toured any potential universities, only 19 percent of working-, 16 percent of middle-, 12 percent of upper-middle-, and 13 percent of upper-class applicants have not visited a single prospective college. According to Avery, Fairbanks, and Zeckhauser (2003: 60), low SES students are less likely to visit colleges before being accepted because if they are rejected, the expense of the trip is a loss to a family with already limited means.

The percentage of applicants with visits paid for by a university is strikingly similar for all applicants regardless of their socioeconomic background. Slightly more than 10 percent of applicants are the guest of at least one college, with the exception of upper-class applicants for whom the proportion is just 3 percent. Colleges defray or reimburse expenses for campus visits twice as often for black and Hispanic applicants as they do for lower-class applicants, suggesting that from the standpoint of admission deans, the purpose of offering to pay for these visits is to attract underrepresented minority students rather than students who may be economically disadvantaged.

FACTORS AFFECTING ENHANCEMENT STRATEGIES

We conclude this chapter with a brief analysis of how applicants' race, social class, and other characteristics are related to the use of selected admission-enhancing strategies when many potentially contributing factors are considered simultaneously. To do this we employ the statistical technique of multiple regression analysis, which permits analysts to evaluate the influence of one factor on a particular enhancement strategy on an all-other-things-equal basis. We focus special attention on the effects of applicants' race and social class, the two student traits we have been emphasizing throughout. The outcomes of particular importance include whether students and their families are using school choice to gain an admission advantage, participation in academic enrichment activities, involvement in test preparation programs, and the use of private consultants. Our results are shown in Table 2.8 as a series of multiple regression (in this case, logistic regression) equations.[48]

[48] Frequently throughout this book we will rely on multiple regression to evaluate outcomes. When the dependent variable is of a dichotomous 0 or 1 (that is, "either-or") variety, then logistic regression is an appropriate statistical methodology. A brief word about interpretation might be helpful. The effect of each variable in Table 2.8 is shown as an odds ratio. The "odds" of a particular event happening is the probability of that event divided by one minus the probability of that event. The odds ratio indicates how much higher or lower

We first test use of school choice. Students are assumed to have used school choice as an admission-enhancing strategy if they attended a magnet, parochial, or private high school and did so with the expectation that graduating from such a school would improve their chances of college admission. The results are shown in the first column of Table 2.8. They suggest that nonwhite students are more likely than whites to employ this strategy, but the effect is significantly greater only for Hispanics. All else equal, Hispanic applicants are twice as likely as whites to attend a high school other than the public one to which they are assigned with the belief that it will help their college admission chances. Upper-class applicants are the most likely to use school choice as an admission strategy and middle-class families the least, but none of the variation by social class is statistically important.

By contrast, when we narrow our attention only to those who selected a private secondary school for the college admission advantages it may confer (Cookson and Persell, 1985), we find there is a more substantial association with social class. As shown in the second column of Table 2.8, upper-class applicants are six times as likely as middle-class candidates to attend a private high school with college admission in mind. However, ability to pay does not appear to be the sole determinant of who uses this strategy, because working-class applicants are almost three times as likely as middle-class applicants to attend private school for its anticipated admission benefit. Nonwhite students are once again more likely than whites to pursue this strategy, but the racial variations are not significant.[49]

Black, Asian, and upper-middle-class applicants are relatively more likely to take advantage of academic enrichment opportunities offered outside high school, other things equal. The third column in Table 2.8 displays the odds ratios for participation in some form of supplemental academic enrichment. Blacks and Asians have 93 and 85 percent greater odds, respectively, than do whites of participating in academic enrichment. Upper-middle-class applicants are 65 percent more likely to engage in academic enrichment than are students from middle-class families.[50]

---

the odds are if a variable takes on the value of a particular category instead of the value in the reference category. For example, the first number in the first column in Table 2.8 (1.70) indicates that, everything else constant, the odds of a black applicant attending either a magnet, parochial, or private high school with the expectation that doing so will improve her chances of elite college admission are 1.7 times as high as (or 70 percent *higher than*) the odds for a white applicant.

[49] It is also worth noting that students who attend one of the seventy-two elite secondary schools in the United States are especially likely to hope that their choice of high school will enhance their credentials in the eyes of prospective admission officers.

[50] Immigrant students, especially those with a recent immigrant past (that is, second- and third-generation immigrants), are more likely than applicants with a longer history of U.S. residence to participate in academic enhancement activities.

TABLE 2.8
Odds Ratios from Logistic Regressions for Five Different College Admission Enhancement Strategies
NSCE Applicant Sample: Fall 1997 Cohort

Predictor Variables	Attend a Magnet, Parochial, or Private High School to Improve the Chances of College Admission (1)	Attend a Private High School to Improve the Chances of College Admission (2)	Participate in Any Academic Enrichment Activity (3)	Take an SAT, PSAT, or ACT Test Preparation Course (4)	Hire a Private Consultant to Help Select Colleges and/or Complete Application Forms (5)
Race					
(White)	—	—	—	—	—
Black	1.70	1.61	1.93**	1.25	1.11
Hispanic	2.03**	1.39	1.16	0.60*	1.54
Asian	1.13	1.06	1.85*	1.18	1.43
Socioeconomic Status					
Upper	2.14	5.98***	1.00	1.63	1.25
Upper-Middle	1.42	1.72	1.65*	1.74**	0.93
(Middle)	—	—	—	—	—
Working	1.57	2.91*	1.09	0.92	1.64
Lower	1.27	2.71	2.93	1.07	0.33*
Immigrant Generation					
First	1.16	1.27	1.60	1.77	0.95
Second	1.13	0.82	1.97*	1.92*	0.77
Third	0.92	1.04	2.32**	2.02*	1.57
(Fourth and Higher)	—	—	—	—	—
Unknown	0.53	0.60	3.11*	0.77	0.45

First-Generation College Student					
(No)	—	—	—	—	—
Yes	0.75	0.59	1.22	1.66*	1.17
Unknown	0.12**	0.25	0.38	1.71	1.73
Sex					
(Male)	—	—	—	—	—
Female	1.01	1.31	1.36	1.70**	1.20
High School Type					
(Public)	—	—	—	—	—
Magnet	—	—	1.54	0.55	0.46*
Parochial	—	—	1.25	0.97	1.24
Private	—	—	1.09	1.09	1.02
Unknown	—	—	0.34*	0.24**	0.33
Elite 72 High School					
(No)	—	—	—	—	—
Yes	3.66***	4.28***	1.22	1.67	1.18
SAT Score					
<1000	1.36	1.27	0.94	0.64	2.53
1000–1099	0.82	0.83	0.64	2.05	1.51
1100–1199	1.14	1.55	0.69	0.80	1.65
(1200–1299)	—	—	—	—	—
1300–1399	1.29	2.10	0.68	0.94	1.22
1400–1499	1.14	0.91	0.94	0.84	0.84
1500–1600	0.84	1.41	1.58	0.60	2.19
Unknown	0.63	0.32	0.51	0.48	5.23**

(Continued)

TABLE 2.8 (Continued)

Predictor Variables	Attend a Magnet, Parochial, or Private High School to Improve the Chances of College Admission (1)	Attend a Private High School to Improve the Chances of College Admission (2)	Participate in Any Academic Enrichment Activity (3)	Take an SAT, PSAT, or ACT Test Preparation Course (4)	Hire a Private Consultant to Help Select Colleges and/or Complete Application Forms (5)
ACT Score					
0–15	[a]	[a]	3.41	3.63	[a]
16–19	1.89	0.11	0.45	4.71*	0.53
(20–24)	—	—	—	—	—
25–29	0.92	0.34	0.93	0.50	1.20
30–36	0.75	0.52	1.59	0.61	2.92
Unknown	1.34	1.52	1.01	0.73	2.65
Number of Cases	3658	3658	3670	3670	3658
$F(df_1, df_2)$	2.78(26, 3628)	4.40(26, 3628)	2.32(31, 3635)	2.22(31, 3635)	2.14(30, 3624)
Prob > F	0.0000	0.0000	0.0000	0.0001	0.0003

Source: National Study of College Experience.

Note: Reference categories are in parentheses. The weighted percentage of applicants using strategy (1) is 19.6 percent, strategy (2) is 9.7 percent, strategy (3) is 52.5 percent, strategy (4) is 46.1 percent, and strategy (5) is 17.1 percent.

[a] Some regressions have 3,658 observations because having an ACT score of 0–15 predicted failure perfectly. These 12 observations were dropped from the regression.

*p < .05 **p < .01 ***p < .001

Applicants' social class background seems to matter much more when attention is focused on academic enrichment programs offered by colleges and universities. But it is not just applicants from high SES families who benefit. In results not shown, we performed a logistic regression to examine whether background characteristics affect the odds of participating in the college-sponsored enrichment programs claimed by some to be particularly well regarded by college admission officers (K. Cohen, 2002; Hernández, 1997). Our results suggest that upper-middle-class and upper-class applicants exhibit 80 percent and 373 percent significantly greater odds of being involved, respectively, than do applicants from middle-class families. However, again participation is not dictated solely by ability to pay. Working-class applicants have 241 percent significantly greater odds of enrolling in these programs than do middle-class applicants. This seeming anomaly is partially explained by the existence of such university programs as Talent Search and Upward Bound that are designed to serve socioeconomically disadvantaged students.

Particular applicant categories of race and social class are associated with the use of SAT, PSAT, and ACT test preparation courses. As shown in the fourth column of Table 2.8, Hispanics have 40 percent significantly lower odds than do whites of taking a course. This result is noteworthy because test preparation offers the first example in which white applicants are not the least likely to become involved. Social class also matters. Upper-middle-class applicants have 74 percent greater odds than do middle-class applicants of participating in formal test preparation. It is also worth mentioning that, contrary to admission officers' claims (Hernández, 1997: 110; Lombardi, 2003), first-generation college students exhibit 66 percent greater odds of taking a test preparation course than do applicants from families with college experience.[51]

We also examined the type and amount of test preparation that course-takers receive. Again, in results not shown, black course-takers are 113 percent more likely than whites to take their course through a private firm. Lower- and working-class course-takers are 95 and 70 percent less likely, respectively, to enroll in a private company's course than are middle-class course-takers, but upper-class applicants are 442 percent more likely to do so. In terms of amount of preparation time, upper-class

[51] First-generation college students' high schools appear partially responsible for this result. Twenty-nine percent of all first-generation college students are offered a test preparation course through their high school, as compared to only 16 percent of students whose families have some college experience. Both groups are equally likely to use a private company's services, with about 22 percent doing so. In addition, the regression reveals that second- and third-generation immigrant students are more likely to take test preparation courses than are longer-term U.S. residents. A similar positive association with test preparation is found for female applicants.

applicants who take a course are 3.5 times more likely to have twenty-five hours or more of instruction than are middle-class applicants. Yet lower-class course-takers exhibit even greater odds of preparing for that length of time. They are thirty times as likely as middle-class applicants to do so. To summarize our social class results, upper-middle-class applicants are most likely to take a test preparation course, and there is a strong positive social class gradient to the likelihood of taking such a course through a private company. Yet college applicants from the lower class appear to spend the greatest amount of time in structured test preparation.

Other strategies are less influenced by race and socioeconomic status. Racial variations in using a consultant to help select schools or to complete applications are statistically insignificant. However, lower-class applicants have 67 percent lower odds of hiring a private consultant than do middle-class applicants. Neither race nor social class is related to visiting six or more colleges on an all-other-things-equal basis.

The overall impression one gains from the results reported in Table 2.8 is that, with the few exceptions noted, middle-class white students are less likely than other racial or social class groups to engage in behaviors and activities that are often believed by parents, their children, and even professional counselors to enhance one's chances of entering a selective university. The exceptions have partly to do with the reduced propensity of Hispanic applicants to take test preparation courses and with the greater disinclination on the part of low SES students to hire private counselors to help select colleges or complete application forms. More striking, though just as expected, is the strong positive relation between social class and the tendency to enroll in a test preparation course offered by one of several for-profit companies.

Summary

In this chapter we presented evidence of the growing competition for admission to selective colleges and universities. We explained its increased intensity as a byproduct of more students seeking high-status college degrees in the hope that a credential from a more prestigious institution will improve their economic prospects as the college-educated population expands. To confront the greater anxiety surrounding elite college admission today, students and their parents employ a variety of strategies whose anticipated effect is to increase applicants' chances of being accepted at the school of their choice. These strategies vary and include such measures as choosing a "good" secondary school, supplementing high school coursework with academic enrichment programs, taking standardized test instructional classes, hiring private consultants and tutors, and visiting large numbers of colleges. Many of these strategies have racial and social class correlates. Here we briefly summarize what we have learned about the characteristics of NSCE applicants and their behaviors with respect to preparing for elite college admission.

On average, Asian American applicants appear best poised for college admission based purely on their academic credentials. Not only do Asians have the most distinguished academic records, but they also are most likely to use the enhancement strategies of participating in academic enrichment and taking test preparation courses. Black applicants display the lowest average levels of college preparedness when judged in terms of standard academic achievement measures (high school GPA, class rank, participation in AP courses, and SAT scores). Whites are least likely to attend private school, use high school choice, or engage in academic enrichment activities.

Both high and low SES applicants seem to be better positioned for acceptance than do their fellow applicants from the middle of the socioeconomic distribution. Through targeted college preparatory and enrichment programs, a significant proportion of low SES students who have entered the elite college applicant pool have learned about and gained access to some of the same admission-enhancing strategies that high SES students employ, particularly attending a private high school and using high school choice. Students from the middle classes, on the other hand, often appear trapped. Not only are they least likely to attend a magnet, parochial, or private high school, they are also least likely to take a test preparation course or to have college-sponsored enrichment. One reason may be that families of middle-class applicants lack the cultural capital to be aware of such enhancement strategies. However, it seems more likely that middle-class families feel they have inadequate incomes to take advantage of these opportunities. At the same time, these families are thought to be too financially well-off to be eligible for the free or reduced-cost services and programs available to low SES students. The next chapter examines the factors that affect admission outcomes at selective colleges and universities, including the use of the kinds of enhancement strategies discussed here.

Chapter Three

WHAT COUNTS IN BEING ADMITTED?

INTRODUCTION

Much previous research on access to postsecondary education in the United States is incomplete because it focuses on schools that students attend and overlooks the intervening process of college application and admission (Espenshade, Hale, and Chung, 2005). It is not that gatekeeping functions of colleges and universities are believed to be uninteresting or unimportant but rather that data on who applies and who is accepted are difficult to obtain (Bowen and Levin, 2003; Karen, 1991b). In this chapter we examine factors affecting admission to seven NSCE institutions, all of them academically selective four-year colleges or universities. We will be particularly interested in the roles played by applicants' racial and social class backgrounds. Are admission preferences awarded to particular kinds of applicants? How large are these preferences? How do they compare with the obvious preferences that academically selective institutions have for applicants who have demonstrated a high degree of academic accomplishment, as measured by teacher recommendations, grades, and standardized test scores? We also want to "unpack" racial and ethnic preferences by looking in greater detail at what is behind the labels "black," "Hispanic," and "Asian."

Finally, we return to a central question raised in chapter 2. There we examined a variety of admission enhancement strategies employed by applicants to the nation's top colleges and universities. We also investigated how the use of these strategies varies by an applicant's race and social class. What we did not address is the efficacy of these strategies. Is there evidence that any of these behaviors does, in fact, increase an applicant's chances of being admitted to an elite college or university? We conclude our analysis in chapter 3 with an examination of the association between the use of selective admission enhancement strategies and subsequent admission outcomes.

Answers to these questions will help shed light on the competitive college acceptance process, a process that is often viewed by outsiders as inscrutable and unpredictable (Menand, 2003; Paul, 1995b). In our analysis we concentrate on the top tier of American higher education because it is here that one would expect the importance of various selection criteria to emerge. Most non-selective institutions admit practically everyone who applies (Duffy and Goldberg, 1998; Kane, 1998b).

There are approximately 4,200 degree-granting, postsecondary institutions in the United States, including 2,300 four-year colleges and universities (National Center for Education Statistics, 2004). The choices high school graduates make about whether and where to apply, rather than the college admissions decisions themselves, largely determine how students get sorted among alternative college and non-college destinations (Manski and Wise, 1983).[1] Nevertheless, colleges do exercise gatekeeping functions, and the extent of gatekeeping depends on how selective an institution's admission process is. Two-thirds of freshmen at four-year colleges and universities attend institutions that accept more than 75 percent of applicants. Close to one-quarter attend schools whose acceptance rates fall between 50 and 75 percent. Only at the 146 four-year institutions that Barron's (2000) labels "most" or "highly" competitive are admission rates generally less than 50 percent (Carnevale and Rose, 2004). Acceptance rates at the most elite of these are typically below 20 percent (Fetter, 1995), compared with an average of 71 percent nationwide (Hawkins and Lautz, 2005).[2]

As competition for admission to the top schools has increased, students are submitting more college applications (Astin et al., 2002). Candidates to the most selective institutions apply to more schools than does the average high school graduate. The 1.2 million first-time, full-time students entering four-year colleges and universities as freshmen in 2003 submitted an average of 4.1 applications per student, and nearly 10 percent applied to more than seven colleges or universities (Sax et al., 2003).[3] These students, who represent roughly two-thirds of all high school graduates who applied to and enrolled in postsecondary education (Hawkins

[1]Total estimated fall 2005 enrollment in degree-granting institutions was 16.7 million. Undergraduates accounted for 14.3 million or 86 percent of this total. Full-time students made up 60 percent of all student enrollment; women represented 57 percent; public institutions accounted for a 77 percent share; and students at four-year institutions made up 62 percent of the total (Chronicle of Higher Education, 2004).

[2]Record-low acceptance rates were registered by Ivy League institutions for the Class of 2012, suggesting that "the already crazed competition for admission to the nation's most prestigious universities and colleges became even more intense this year" (Finder, 2008b). Harvard University admitted 7.1 percent of all applicants, Yale admitted 8.3 percent, Columbia 8.7 percent, and Princeton 9.25 percent (Cliatt, 2008; Finder, 2008b).

[3]The universe of schools represented by these 1.2 million entering freshmen include all institutions of higher education admitting first-time freshmen, granting a baccalaureate-level degree or higher, having a listing in the U.S. Department of Education's Integrated Postsecondary Education Data System (IPEDS), and admitting a minimum of twenty-five first-time, full-time freshmen (Sax et al., 2003: 116). In 2003, the national population included 1,539 institutions.

and Lautz, 2005), generated five million college applications.[4] Students attending the most selective public institutions (those where the average combined math and verbal SAT scores of entering freshmen are 1140 or higher) applied to an average of 4.5 schools, and 13 percent of these freshmen submitted more than seven applications. At the most competitive private four-year colleges and universities where average SAT scores for entering students are 1310 or better, freshmen in 2003 submitted an average of 6.3 college applications, and 35 percent of these entering students applied to more than seven schools (Sax et al., 2003). How institutions choose which students to admit from among many worthy applicants says much about the values of the institutions themselves.

APPLICATIONS AND ACCEPTANCE RATES

In chapter 2 we studied the behavior of the 67,703 students who were in the combined applicant pool to seven NSCE institutions in the fall of 1997. A given student was the unit of analysis. As applicants, these 67,703 individuals submitted a total of 79,222 applications to the same NSCE colleges and universities. This chapter views each of these applications as the unit of observation and asks how these applications fared, whether the student submitting the application was admitted or not, and what factors influenced which applicants were admitted to public and private institutions.[5]

From Students to Applications

There were 17 percent more applications submitted than students in the combined NSCE applicant pool in 1997. One possible scenario that is consistent with these figures is that 83 percent of applicants submitted an application to just one NSCE institution, while the remaining 17 percent each applied to two. The actual distribution is shown in the first column of Figure 3.1. Roughly 86 percent of applicants applied to a single NSCE

[4] Aside from increased competition for admission, factors contributing to the upsurge in applications may include the burgeoning popularity of standardized application forms, increasingly aggressive college marketing tactics, and a growing tendency among some colleges and universities to send unsolicited and easy-to-complete application forms to promising students (Farrell, 2006a). Other considerations sometimes mentioned include the growing number of high school graduates, the ease of using on-line application procedures, and expanded financial aid packages (Finder, 2008b).

[5] The 67,703 applicants are represented by 3,670 weighted cases in the NSCE sample data. The 79,222 individual applications are mirrored by 3,829 weighted sample observations. See appendix B for details.

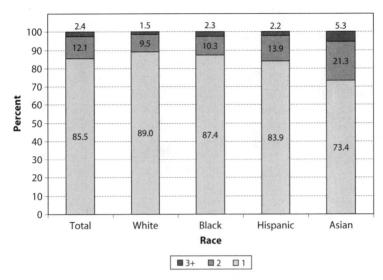

Figure 3.1. Number of Applications per Student in Combined Applicant Pool Submitted to Seven NSCE Institutions, Total and by Race, 1997. Source: National Study of College Experience.

college or university, another 12 percent submitted two applications, and the remaining 2 percent applied to three or more schools. Figure 3.1 also indicates that application patterns differ sharply by race. White students are the most likely to apply to just one school in the NSCE group. Non-white students, especially those from Asian American families, are applying to more on average. When these figures are looked at in another way, white applicants account for 71 percent of all students who submit a single application, in contrast to Asian students, who account for 17 percent. But among students who submit three or more NSCE applications, Asians (at 45 percent) account for the same proportion as whites (44 percent), which suggests that Asians are overrepresented among students who apply to several NSCE institutions.[6]

The average number of applications students submit is positively correlated with social class. About 90 percent of students from lower-class backgrounds apply to just one school, in contrast to just 71 percent of upper-class students. The percentage of students from working-class, middle-class, or upper-middle-class backgrounds who apply to just one school is in the mid-to-high 80s. Part of the SES gradient is no doubt

---

[6] Within the combined NSCE applicant pool, whites make up 68 percent of all students and Asians make up 20 percent (compared to 7 percent for blacks and 5 percent for Hispanics).

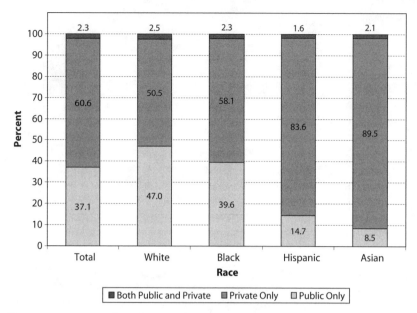

Figure 3.2. Percent of Students in the Combined Applicant Pool to Seven NSCE Institutions Who Applied Only to Public Institutions, Only to Private Institutions, or to Both, Total and by Race, 1997. Source: National Study of College Experience.

created by the cost of applying to college.[7] Even though students from upper-class families make up less than one-twentieth of all students in the combined applicant pool, they account for nearly one-fifth (19 percent) of students who apply to three or more NSCE institutions.

The group of NSCE colleges and universities contains both public and private institutions. Figure 3.2 examines patterns of applications by type of institution. Among all students in the combined applicant pool in 1997, 37 percent apply just to public universities. Another 61 percent apply only to private colleges and universities. Fewer than 3 percent of applicants seek admission at both kinds of schools. Because 15 percent of applicants are applying to more than one NSCE institution but just 2.3 percent are submitting applications to both private and public schools, it becomes clear that multiple applications are confined largely to either the private or the public sector. There is relatively little crossover between types of schools in students' application portfolios.

[7] The College Board Web site reports, "The average college application fee is around $25. (Some colleges charge up to $60, while others don't have an application fee at all.) The fee is usually nonrefundable, even if you're not offered admission. Many colleges offer fee waivers for applicants from low-income families" (College Board, 2006b).

White students are about as likely to apply to public schools as to private ones. By comparison, black applicants exhibit a greater preference for private schools. Hispanic and especially Asian students are substantially more likely to favor private NSCE institutions over public ones. As a consequence, there is a greater minority presence in applicant pools to private NSCE institutions. Nonwhite students represent 43 percent of all students applying solely to private colleges but only 14 percent of those applying only to public institutions.

One might assume that the SES gradient would show a linear relationship such that students from lower-class backgrounds would be most likely to apply to public institutions. But our data do not support this expectation. If anything the association is just the reverse, except for the behavior of upper-class students. The proportion of students applying only to private colleges and universities is highest for the lower class (87 percent). It then declines steadily (71 percent for working-class students and 63 percent for the middle class) before reaching a minimum of 54 percent for upper-middle-class students. The proportion turns up only for students from upper-class backgrounds, 83 percent of whom apply only to private NSCE institutions.

Public and Private Dimensions

The contours of the basic data for chapter 3 are shown in Table 3.1. Here we include the distribution of all 79,222 applications by various categories (for example, by race, social class, gender, and so on) and indicate the proportion of all applicants accepted in each of the categories.[8] Overall, 35 percent of applicants to the seven NSCE institutions were accepted for admission in the fall of 1997. Acceptance rates in this range qualify these NSCE institutions as academically selective. Among other features deserving comment, the overwhelming majority of applicants are either white or Asian. Relatively small proportions (less than 12 percent total) are members of underrepresented minority groups. White and black applicants are admitted at above-average rates. Hispanic applicants face lower admission chances than does the typical NSCE applicant. Acceptance rates are lowest for Asian applicants, just one in five of whom was admitted in 1997 in contrast to roughly one in three applicants overall.

Nearly 85 percent of applicants in the NSCE application pool for 1997 come from middle-class or upper-middle-class families, and only 10 percent have lower- or working-class backgrounds. Rates of admission are

---

[8] To be strictly correct we should refer to the proportion of all applications that are accepted. But we will sometimes use applications and applicants interchangeably with the understanding that applicants are just as unique as applications from the standpoint of a given college or university.

TABLE 3.1
Student Personal and Academic Characteristics, and
Percentage of Applicants Admitted, Fall 1997

Category	Percent of Applicants[a]	Percent Admitted
Total Sample (N = 3,829)	100.0	34.6
Student Personal Characteristics		
Race		
White	66.0	39.2
Black	6.6	41.1
Hispanic	5.3	28.6
Asian	22.1	20.2
Social Class		
Upper	5.2	31.1
Upper-Middle	47.2	38.0
Middle	37.3	33.1
Working	9.1	26.0
Lower	1.2	27.5
Sex		
Male	47.6	31.2
Female	52.4	37.6
Citizenship		
U.S.	93.6	35.4
Non-U.S.	6.4	22.9
Athlete		
Yes	19.7	39.8
No	77.6	33.7
Unknown	2.7	22.0
Legacy		
Yes	22.6	40.3
No	77.0	32.7
Unknown	0.4	74.2
Student Academic Performance		
SAT Score		
< 1000	4.4	28.8
1000–1099	6.3	28.4
1100–1199	13.4	39.9

(*Continued*)

TABLE 3.1 (*Continued*)

Category	Percent of Applicants[a]	Percent Admitted
1200–1299	19.6	32.3
1300–1399	23.2	28.4
1400–1499	17.2	39.9
1500–1600	10.7	41.9
Unknown	5.2	37.0
Sample mean = 1296		
National mean = 1016[b]		
ACT Score		
0–15	0.1	18.5
16–19	0.8	21.1
20–24	7.9	40.1
25–29	13.5	47.4
30–36	11.6	44.9
Unknown	66.2	29.7
Sample mean = 27.4		
National mean = 21.0[c]		
Number of AP Tests Taken		
0	21.1	33.8
1	15.8	35.0
2	11.8	38.0
3	11.1	28.8
4	10.4	39.4
5	8.0	29.9
6	7.4	35.5
7	4.0	32.2
8+	4.6	41.9
Unknown	5.8	33.4
Sample mean = 3.7[d]		
National mean = 2.5[e]		
High School Type		
Public, non-magnet	67.4	34.5
Public, magnet	8.0	33.4
Private	15.2	36.9
Parochial/Religious	8.8	31.0
Unknown	0.7	48.2

(*Continued*)

TABLE 3.1 (*Continued*)

Category	Percent of Applicants[a]	Percent Admitted
Elite 72 High School[f]		
Yes	5.8	35.9
No	94.1	34.5
Unknown	0.1	67.4

Source: National Study of College Experience.

Note: All data are weighted.

[a]Percentages may add up to 100.0 ± 0.1 due to rounding.

[b]The average combined SAT I score for all SAT takers in 1997 (College Board, 2003).

[c]ACT–tested high school graduates in 1997 (American College Testing Program, 1997).

[d]Both the sample and national mean for number of AP tests taken are based on students who took at least one test.

[e]Data are for 1999 (Curry, MacDonald, and Morgan, 1999).

[f]A list of 72 public and private U.S. high schools, considered by two former admission deans at Princeton University to be "top U.S. secondary schools."

generally higher for students from more privileged backgrounds. This pattern becomes more evident when the bottom two classes and the top two classes are grouped together. Students from lower and working classes combined are admitted at a 26 percent rate, compared to a rate of 33 percent for middle-class students and 37 percent for upper-middle-class and upper-class applicants.[9]

Applicants' SAT scores accord fairly well with one's prior expectations. Although the distribution is skewed somewhat to the left, it rises to a single peak for scores between 1300 and 1399 and then declines. The pattern of acceptance rates by SAT score, however, is much more irregular. Roughly 28 percent of students with the lowest SAT scores are admitted. Admission rates then increase to 40 percent for students with scores in the 1100–1199 range, fall back down to 28 percent for scores in the modal range of 1300–1399, and finally increase once again to more than 40 percent when SAT scores surpass 1500. This quite jagged and apparently anomalous pattern has a straightforward interpretation to which we shall return later in this section.

The data in Table 3.1 hide some important differences between applicants to public versus private NSCE institutions. These differences are illustrated in Table 3.2. Slightly more than one-third of the total 79,222 applications were submitted to public colleges and universities. These

[9]A positive correlation between social class and acceptance rates is also found using other measures of socioeconomic status. For example, NSCE students from families who own their own homes have an average acceptance rate of 36 percent. In contrast, applicants whose parents are renters face an acceptance rate of 21 percent.

TABLE 3.2
Differences between Applicants to Public and Private
NSCE Institutions in Acceptance Rates and Standardized
Test Scores, Fall 1997[a]

Category	Applicants to	
	Public Institutions	Private Institutions
Total Sample (N = 3,829)		
Unweighted N	1,033	2,796
Weighted N	27,171	52,051
Overall Acceptance Rate (percent)	55.1	23.8
SAT Score		
Average for all applicants	1205	1341
ACT Score		
Average for all applicants	25.9	29.0
Percent in 30–36 range	17.7	52.1
SAT II (Achievement) Tests		
Percent taking none	50.2	7.4
Average number of tests taken[b]	2.8	3.8
Average test scores(s)	598	649
Percent scoring 650 or above[c]	32.2	56.0
Percent scoring 750 or above[c]	0.7	6.2
Advanced Placement Examinations		
Percent taking none	37.8	14.3
Average number of tests taken[b]	2.6	4.1

Source: National Study of College Experience; Educational Testing Service.

[a]All data are weighted.

[b]Among those taking one or more examinations.

[c]Based on an average SAT II test score for all achievement tests that were taken by a student.

public school applicants were admitted at a 55 percent rate in contrast to an acceptance rate of less than one-quarter (24 percent) for applicants to private institutions. Applicants to private NSCE schools are better prepared academically than their public school counterparts by almost every available indicator. Average SAT scores for private school applicants are 136 points higher than average scores for applicants to public institutions. Applicants to private institutions have higher ACT scores than do public school applicants, are more likely to take SAT II Subject or Achievement Tests as well as Advanced Placement Examinations, and more likely to do better on these supplemental examinations when they do take them.

One might expect that students with higher levels of college preparedness would have a better chance of college admission. While this supposi-
tion is generally correct for applicants to a given institution, the negative
association in Table 3.2 between academic performance and college acceptance rates suggests that we are dealing with institutions that are not
at the same level of academic selectivity. The labels "public" and "private" in Table 3.2 should not be interpreted for the degree of institutional
control they imply as much as for what they suggest about the level of
difficulty in gaining admission. In fact, Barron's twenty-third edition of
Profiles of American Colleges ranks all but one of the private NSCE colleges and universities in their "most competitive" category, whereas the
public institutions fall into the next lower "highly competitive" group
(Barron's, 1998).[10] A second implication of our data follows from the
first. Because of differences in overall levels of academic selectivity as well
as marked fluctuations in the academic caliber of students they admit, the
admission processes of public and private institutions should be examined separately. To combine applications to both kinds of institutions in
a single, composite analysis would lead to results that do not fit the experiences of either kind of institution.

The racial and ethnic composition of applicants to public and private
NSCE institutions for the start of the 1997–98 school year is shown in
Figure 3.3. The first bar in each group of three shows the distribution for
applicants to all seven institutions combined. It is clear that the patterns
for public and private colleges and universities when considered separately are quite distinct, at least for some racial groups. Whites make up
the overwhelming majority (86 percent) of applicants to public NSCE institutions, but they account for barely more than half (56 percent) of the
applications to private schools. At the same time, whereas the Asian share

---

[10] In describing their "most competitive" group of schools, Barron's (1998) reports, "Even
superior students will encounter a great deal of competition for admission to the colleges in
this category. In general, these colleges require high school rank in the top 10% to 20% and
grade average of A to B+. Median freshman test scores at these colleges are generally between 655 and 800 on SAT I and 29 and above on the ACT. In addition, many of these colleges admit only a small percentage of those who apply—usually fewer than one third"
(223). The following descriptors are used for the "highly competitive" institutions: "Colleges in this group look for students with grade averages of B+ to B and accept most of their
students from the top 20% to 35% of the high school class. Median freshman test scores at
these colleges range from 620 to 654 on SAT I and 27 or 28 on the ACT. These schools generally accept between one third and one half of their applicants" (224). The only private
NSCE institution not in Barron's "most competitive" category falls into their "highly competitive" group and is marked with a "+" sign. According to Barron's (1998), "To provide
for finer distinctions within this admissions category, a plus (+) symbol has been placed before some entries. These are colleges with median freshman scores of 645 or more on SAT
I or 28 or more on the ACT (depending on which test the college prefers), and colleges accept fewer than one quarter of their applicants" (224).

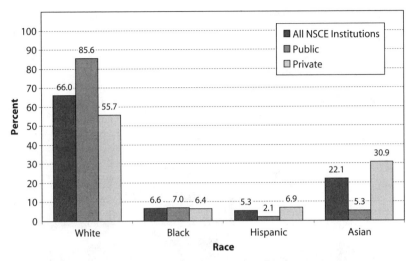

Figure 3.3. Racial Composition of Applicants to Public and Private NSCE Institutions, 1997. Source: National Study of College Experience.

at public institutions (5 percent) is less than the share of black applicants, the Asian share at private institutions (31 percent) is nearly six times greater. At least for the sample of schools we are considering, it is clear that Asian students choosing among academically selective colleges and universities have a strong orientation toward the private sector of higher education. On the other hand, there are relatively few discernible differences in the proportions of black applicants to either type of school. And the overall percentage of Hispanic applicants (5 percent) does reasonably well at characterizing the public and private proportions.

Companion data for applicants disaggregated by social class background are contained in Figure 3.4. It is worth emphasizing first how relatively well-off the applicant pool is from an economic standpoint. More than half of all applicants consider themselves to be upper-middle or upper class. The class backgrounds of applicants to public and private institutions do not differ by as much as their racial and ethnic group affiliations. Nevertheless, private institutions receive disproportionately more applications from students in lower- and working-class families, while students from upper-middle- and upper-class families combined are overrepresented in the public school applicant pool.[11] Differences at the high end of the socioeconomic spectrum are accounted for by what is happening

[11]At the University of Michigan, says Leonhardt (2004), "BMW 3-series sedans are everywhere and students pay up to $800 a month to live off campus, enough to rent an entire house in parts of Michigan."

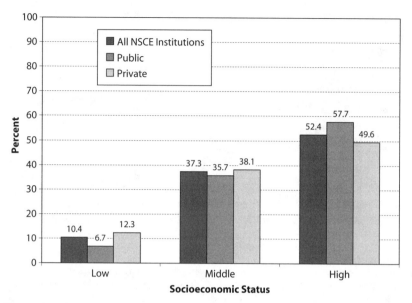

Figure 3.4. Socioeconomic Status Composition of Applicants to Public and Private NSCE Institutions, 1997. Note: Low SES includes lower and working social classes; high SES includes upper-middle and upper social classes. Source: National Study of College Experience.

among upper-middle-class students. These applicants represent 55 percent of the total pool at public institutions in contrast to 43 percent at private schools. Private schools actually attract a larger share of students from the most well-to-do families. Nearly 7 percent of applicants to private colleges and universities are from upper-class families in comparison with just 2 percent of applicants to public institutions. It is apparent that both the most and the least privileged members of society are disproportionately represented in the applicant pools at elite private institutions. On the other hand, applicants to public institutions are comparatively more homogeneous, in terms of both race and socioeconomic status.

The Goals of College Admission

Before considering acceptance rates in more detail or attempting to model admission outcomes at public and private institutions, it is important to set a context for what admission officers at academically selective institutions are trying to do. All college admission officers strive to maintain at least three institutional priorities, often in this order: (1) enrolling sufficient numbers of students to meet bottom-line budget targets, (2) having students of sufficient quality, and (3) ensuring variety and diversity among the student body (Duffy and Goldberg, 1998). Less selective and non-selective institutions usually are preoccupied with the first of these objectives (Kirp, 2003). Only when there is a surplus of quality candidates do institutions have the luxury of employing selection criteria to shape the academic and other compositional aspects of an entering class to best meet institutional objectives.

All of the nation's most academically selective institutions fall into this category.[12] At these colleges and universities, Bowen and Bok (1998: 23–24) identify five institutional objectives that admission officers try to achieve. Most important, admitted students must demonstrate that they have the academic aptitude to do the required work.[13] Beyond that, students are admitted on the basis of their ability to take advantage of an institution's intellectual and other resources and to contribute to the education of their peers; to augment campus diversity, which includes consideration of students' race and ethnicity, geographic origins, religion, socioeconomic status, artistic talent, and athletic ability; to make distinctive long-run contributions to the welfare of society; and to uphold institutional loyalties and traditions. Judgments about these qualities are usually made on the basis of applicants' academic and personal attributes. Secondary school grades, class rank, standardized test scores (SAT I, ACT, SAT II achievement tests), number and variety of honors and AP courses, and difficulty of the secondary school curriculum are important. So, too, are candidates' personal essays, letters of recommendation, extracurricular activities, and (sometimes) campus interviews (Fetter, 1995). These factors are folded into a comprehensive and nuanced, albeit subjective, review of each applicant instead of applying point systems or other mechanical formulas to evaluate students.[14]

[12] Harvard received applications from 27,462 high school seniors for the Class of 2012. More than 2,500 of these candidates scored a perfect 800 on the SAT critical reading test, 3,300 had a perfect score on the SAT math exam, and more than 3,300 were ranked first in their high school class (Finder, 2008b). The applicant pool at Yale totaled 22,813 students (Finder, 2008b) and 21,369 at Princeton (Cliatt, 2008).

[13] Fred Hargadon, former dean of admission at Princeton University, reported in an interview in 1995 that class valedictorians and students with high SAT scores are routinely turned away. Hargadon noted that 1,534 high school valedictorians had applied for admission the prior year and only 495 were offered admission. Similarly, only 24 percent of students who scored between 750 and a perfect 800 on the math SAT were accepted (Paul, 1995a).

[14] Some large public universities, including the University of Michigan and Ohio State University, had relied on a point system for determining admissibility for the large number of applicants they receive each year. These mechanistic procedures were abandoned in favor of a more individualized review following the U.S. Supreme Court decisions in 2003 (Selingo, 2005). At the University of California, Berkeley, following the Regents' 1995 decision banning affirmative action and the 1996 voter-passed Proposition 209 that outlawed race-based preferences in employment and admissions, a new admission process was begun in 1998 that "implemented a more holistic review of applications, where readers gave each

A CONCEPTUAL MODEL

When economists model the college admission decision, an applicant's academic aptitude and other individual attributes are often combined into a measure of "latent quality" or "generalized potential" that is then assumed to be compared with a threshold value unique to each college (Dale and Krueger, 2002; Manski and Wise, 1983). Applicants whose qualifications meet or exceed an institution's minimum threshold are accepted, and others are rejected.[15] We prefer to conceptualize the problem as one in which elite college admission officers attempt to maximize an institutional objective function, subject to constraints. Each applicant i is judged to make a contribution C_i to achieving an institution's multiple objectives.[16] There is also a probability p_i that an applicant will enroll if admitted. Then $C_i \cdot p_i$ is the expected contribution from each applicant who is accepted. The number of seats in the first-year class, S, puts a limit on how many students may be accepted. The expected number of matriculants is the sum of the p_i values for all admitted students, and this sum cannot exceed S. The size of the financial aid budget, F, may also constrain who is accepted. If F_i is the amount of financial aid, whether need-based or merit aid, that is offered to each admitted student, then the sum of $F_i \cdot p_i$ for all accepted applicants must be less than or equal to F. The available amount of financial aid may not constrain the admissions process at every institution. The most elite schools do not offer merit aid, and their admission decisions are made "need-blind" (McPherson and Schapiro, 1998). Admission officers then face the task of choosing which subset of all applicants to admit such that the sum of their expected contributions ($C_i \cdot p_i$) is maximized, subject to constraints on space and (perhaps also) on financial aid.[17]

---

applicant a score for academic achievement and a separate 'comprehensive' score that took account of social and personal obstacles and challenges" (Hout, 2005: 3).

[15]Related formulations are contained in Chan and Eyster (2003) and M. Long (2004b). Epple, Romano, and Sieg (2006) have developed an equilibrium model for higher education that simultaneously predicts student selection into particular institutions, financial aid, educational expenditures, and educational outcomes.

[16]Klitgaard (1985) refers to this contribution as "social value added," or the value to society as measured by later-life contributions that education provides. In his framework, institutions should "select students to *maximize the value added* of the education an institution provides" (60, emphasis in the original).

[17]Anecdotal evidence suggests that this conceptual view of the college admission process, and more generally of the enrollment management process, is correct. William Chace (2006: 12), former president of Wesleyan University and Emory University, recounts, "Admissions officers have to work harder each year to keep up with an increased workload of applications . . . and the schools themselves, looking at the admission rate vs. the yield rate, want to make sure that they have admitted not only those students worthy of admission but exactly those who will actually show up in the fall." Farrell (2006d: A48) describes how

Our model of the elite college admission process has several implications. First, it illustrates why many candidates who could be expected to make a positive contribution to the life of a campus community are denied admission. Their potential contribution may not be deemed high enough, when compared with that of other applicants, or they may be unlikely to enroll if admitted. Second, academic merit is not the only form of merit that admission officers consider. Many different qualities in varying combinations can also help qualify a candidate for admission to a top school (exceptional athletic prowess, a wealthy parent, musical ability, or racial and social class background, to name a few). Third, our model explains the appeal to colleges of binding early decision admission programs. Students who are admitted under early decision are obligated to enroll, so for them $p_i = 1$. At the same time, colleges are reluctant to admit all first-year students through early decision, because there may potentially be even more outstanding students who apply through regular decision.[18] Fourth, children of alumni typically receive a preference in admission decisions. One reason may be that, apart from their personal qualifications and the institutional loyalties they are assumed to possess, they are very likely to enroll if accepted.[19] Fifth, when a financial aid

---

colleges are increasingly relying on statistical models to manage their enrollment numbers. Recalling a conversation with the director of admission at Union College, she writes, "After a human being has read each application and debated its relative merit with the admissions committee, the predictive model's final calculations of such factors as who will accept an offer, or how much an applicant will contribute to tuition revenue, may determine whether the college accepts or rejects a particular student. 'It's like balls running through a pinball machine,' says Mr. Lundquist. 'We put in our picks and run the model to see what the head count looks like, and if it spits out a number that's higher than our financial-aid target, or has too many engineers, or whatever, we have to go back and take some people out and put others in.' In recent years, Mr. Lundquist has had to make some difficult decisions. He has, for instance, told his application readers to pull out names of financially needy students that they had planned to accept. Why? The statistical model had predicted that Union's net tuition revenue would be lower than expected given the students he had chosen to admit."

[18] Despite claims by admission officers that early applicants are generally stronger than regular applicants, Avery, Fairbanks, and Zeckhauser (2003) find that early applicants have somewhat less impressive credentials in terms of SAT scores, class rank, and extracurricular activities than regular applicants at early decision colleges. On the other hand, they do find some support for these claims at early action colleges. These authors also report that "early admits make up slightly more than 20 percent of the entering class at the top universities and colleges that offer Early Decision" (64). Some Ivy League universities, however, filled nearly half of their spaces for September 2003 through early decision admissions (Arenson, 2002). Despite the evident appeal of early admission programs, several elite universities (including Harvard, Princeton, and the University of Virginia) announced in the fall of 2006 they were abandoning this policy to create a more level playing field for low-income students (Farrell, 2006b, 2006c).

[19] Rachel Toor (2001: 211–12), a former admission officer at Duke University, says that yield rates for accepted alumni children and development admits were abnormally high

budget does constrain admission decisions, between two otherwise identical candidates, admission officers have an incentive to admit the one who will cost the institution less. Under these circumstances, admission decisions favor students from more affluent families.[20] Finally, neither C_i nor p_i can be predicted precisely. They are based on admission officers' subjective evaluations, and as such are influenced by randomness and error that can lead to outcomes that are sometimes interpreted by outsiders as capricious or unfair.

MERITOCRACY IN ELITE COLLEGE ADMISSION

Most Americans are firmly committed to notions of meritocracy—the conviction that opportunity and mobility should be based on ability and performance and not on the circumstances of one's birth, including the social position of one's parents. These beliefs carry over to elite college admission. It would be difficult to find many people who would not subscribe to the view that admission to institutions representing the top tier of American higher education should be based on merit. Controversy sets in when one attempts to define merit.

To many students and their parents, merit is viewed as meaning academic merit alone. Standardized test scores, high school grades, and class rank become the arbiters of who should be admitted to elite colleges. But surely this meaning of merit is too narrow. Academic merit is just one component of a more general conception of merit. The merit that a particular candidate for admission may or may not possess must be understood in the context of institutional mission. In this sense, the meaning of merit in admissions can vary through time and across institutions. Female applicants to Ivy League universities had no merit in the days before coeducation, but there was affirmative action for women during and after the transition to coeducation (Karabel, 2005). Similarly, a talented center forward on a Canadian junior ice hockey team might have considerable merit in admissions at Cornell University, especially if Cornell just graduated their starting center forward. But the same individual might have relatively little merit at the University of Pennsylvania, which does not have a men's ice hockey team.

---

because many of these candidates were more mediocre and had fewer acceptances from other, more prestigious, schools.

[20] The substantial admission advantage that is given by some schools to students who will not require financial aid—that is, to "free" students—is summarized by Stevens (2006): "The ability to pay full tuition thus provides a decisive advantage for very good but not stellar academic credentials. . . . 'Free' is actually the high end of a gradient of advantage that directly parallels the amount of need the financial aid office estimates that the candidate will require" (18).

This relative conception of merit in admissions has been expressed most concisely by Jerome Karabel (2005) in *The Chosen*. Since 1900, merit has taken on a succession of different meanings. Early in the twentieth century, merit had a largely academic component and was measured by mastery of, among other things, Latin and Greek. This conception gave way in the 1920s to one of the "all-around man" for whom character, prominent family background, and participation in sports became hallmarks of merit. After the Russians launched their Sputnik satellite in the late 1950s, academic excellence coupled with strong extracurricular participation once again gained ascendancy. During the social upheavals of the 1960s the meaning of merit changed once more, "provoking a seismic cultural shift that elevated the values of 'diversity' and 'inclusion' to a central place in the selection policies of [Harvard, Yale, and Princeton]" (Karabel, 2005: 5). Karabel concludes,

> The history of admissions at the Big Three has thus been, fundamentally, a history of recurrent struggles over the meaning of "merit." Yet beneath the flux has been a consistent pattern: the meaning of merit has shifted in response to changing power relations among groups as well as changes in the broader society. This proposition— that the definition of "merit" is fluid and tends to reflect the values and interests of those who have the power to impose their particular cultural ideals—is the central argument of this book. (5)

Acceptance Rates

Average acceptance rates for applicants to public and private NSCE schools in the fall of 1997 are shown disaggregated by race and social class in Table 3.3. White and black candidates to public institutions are accepted at above-average rates, while admission rates for Hispanics and Asians are substantially below average. At private institutions, white, black, and Hispanic applicants are all admitted at rates higher than that for a typical applicant. More than three out of every ten black candidates are accepted. The admission rate for Asian students is markedly below average—13 percentage points less than that for black candidates.

Admission rates by social class generally exhibit less variation than those by race. No particular pattern by social class is evident among acceptance rates to public institutions. Slightly more than half of all working-class candidates are admitted, and the admission rate rises to nearly two-thirds for upper-class students. When categories are grouped, the acceptance rate for lower- and working-class students combined is 52 percent. It increases somewhat to 57 percent for students from middle-class families, but then falls again to 54 percent for applicants from

TABLE 3.3
Acceptance Rates to Public and Private
NSCE Institutions, by Race and Social Class, Fall 1997

	Percent Admitted	
Item	Public Institutions	Private Institutions
Total	55.1	23.8
Race		
White	56.2	25.7
Black	58.5	31.0
Hispanic	40.8	26.7
Asian	39.9	18.4
Social Class		
Lower	57.8	23.2
Working	51.5	18.3
Middle	57.4	21.2
Upper-Middle	53.7	27.4
Upper	65.0	25.1

Source: National Study of College Experience.

upper-middle-class and upper-class backgrounds. Admission rates to private schools suggest a slightly more positive association with social class. Combining categories shows that 19 percent of students in the bottom two classes are admitted, in contrast to 21 percent of middle-class students, and 27 percent of those from upper-middle- and upper-class families. This positive SES gradient for applicants to private schools is statistically significant at the 5 percent level. In short, whereas admission to public institutions does not appear to favor students from higher social class backgrounds, the admission process at private schools does. Students in the top two social class groups have nearly a 50 percent better chance of being admitted than do students from lower- and working-class families.

Figure 3.5 contrasts acceptance rates by SAT scores for public and private school applicants. The two curves move more or less in parallel fashion and are monotonically increasing throughout the entire SAT range. Controlling for institutional type, higher SAT scores are associated with a higher probability of being admitted. This is the pattern one would expect to find, and it stands in marked contrast to the sawtooth behavior of acceptance rates observed in Table 3.1. The reason for the latter behavior is now clear. The data in Table 3.1 represent an average between acceptance rates at public and private institutions. The SAT scores of public school applicants are concentrated in the 1000–1199 and 1200–1399

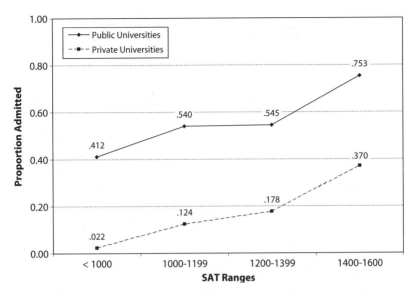

Figure 3.5. Proportion of Students Admitted within SAT Ranges, Applicants to Public and Private NSCE Institutions, 1997. Source: National Study of College Experience.

SAT ranges, which pulls the aggregate average up. But the scores of applicants to private schools are more heavily concentrated in the 1200–1399 and 1400–1600 SAT ranges, which pulls the overall average down closer to the bottom curve in Figure 3.5.[21]

To lay the groundwork for the regression results in the next section, Figures 3.6 and 3.7 show acceptance rates for applicants to private institutions by race and by social class, controlling for candidates' SAT scores. In Figure 3.6 acceptance rates increase monotonically for each race group. In addition, for the same SAT scores, the chances of being admitted are usually highest for black and Hispanic candidates and lowest for Asian applicants. For example, in the highest SAT range (1400–1600), 77 percent of black students are admitted, followed by 48 percent of Hispanics, 40 percent of whites, and 30 percent of Asian candidates. The relatively high proportions of admitted students from the two underrepresented minority groups begin to reflect the influence of affirmative action at elite private institutions. Higher SAT scores are also associated with higher acceptance rates for each social class group as shown in Figure 3.7.

[21] The percentage distribution of SAT scores among public school applicants across the categories less than 1000, 1000–1199, 1200–1399, 1400–1600, and unknown is: 8.7, 32.9, 42.1, 7.7, and 8.5, respectively. The corresponding distribution at private institutions is: 2.1, 12.8, 43.1, 38.5, and 3.4.

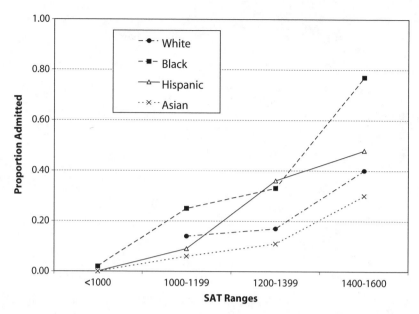

Figure 3.6. Proportion of Students Admitted, by SAT Ranges and by Race, Private NSCE Institutions, 1997. Source: National Study of College Experience.

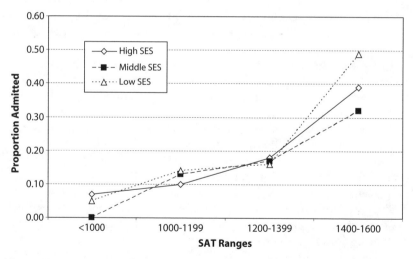

Figure 3.7. Proportion of Students Admitted, by SAT Ranges and by Socioeconomic Status, Private NSCE Institutions, 1997. Note: Low SES includes lower and working social classes; high SES includes upper-middle and upper social classes. Source: National Study of College Experience.

When controlling for SAT scores, however, social class makes little difference to the likelihood of admission until one reaches the highest SAT range. For scores above 1400, admission officers at private NSCE institutions appear to award the highest bonus to lower- and working-class applicants, 49 percent of whom are admitted. Students from upper-middle- and upper-class backgrounds are admitted 39 percent of the time, in comparison to 32 percent for middle-class candidates. Whether these apparent admission preferences by race and class withstand the introduction of additional controls is the subject of the next section.[22]

MODELING ADMISSION DECISIONS

Academically selective colleges and universities, and certainly the most elite ones, are faced every year with many more well-qualified applicants than they can accept. With so many choices, admission officers need criteria for picking and choosing among the most promising candidates. One possibility is to select students at random. But applicants are typically chosen on the basis of their presumed ability to handle the academic workload and to meet other institutional objectives (Karen, 1990; Klitgaard, 1985). At the selective institutions, current conceptions of merit dictate paying attention both to academic potential and to such nonacademic factors as minority status, having a parent or other close relative who graduated from the institution or who is a potential benefactor, participation in athletics and other extracurricular activities, geographic diversity, and contributions to campus life, among others (Freedman, 2003; Zwick, 2002). The criteria that any given institution uses and the relative emphases that are placed on them are generally designed to produce a first-year class that best expresses the values and objectives of the particular institution (Bowen and Bok, 1998). The top colleges and universities in the United States have a sense of shared purpose in this regard.

Empirical studies of the college admission process capture many, but not all, of these selection criteria. Those that are most amenable to statistical analysis are such quantitative measures as standardized test scores, minority status, social class, being a recruited athlete, and legacy status. Students' personal essays, teachers' letters of recommendation, assessments of applicants' contributions to the campus community, and other "soft" variables, while admittedly important in admission decisions, are

[22]Data for public institutions comparable to those in Figures 3.6 and 3.7 have not been shown here because their patterns are somewhat more irregular owing to the smaller number of observations. Even with more observations, it is possible that public universities would not exhibit the same regularities because their admission processes are not as selective as those at the private NSCE schools.

usually excluded, mainly because of the difficulty in obtaining such information. Our plan in this section is to begin with regression results that lay out our principal quantitative findings. Race and social class effects are then interpreted in terms of equivalent numbers of "bonus" points on standardized test measurements and as differences in the probability of being admitted to an NSCE institution. Next we proceed to "unpack" race effects by looking beneath the customary labels of "black," "Hispanic," and "Asian." Lastly, our findings are put in the context of other related research.

Regression Results

The central empirical findings of this chapter are shown in Table 3.4. This table contains six models, three based on applications to public institutions and three to private schools. Models 1 and 4 are additive models for the effects of race and social class, controlling only for an applicant's state of permanent residence and the institution to which an application is sent.[23] These results mirror the descriptive findings in Table 3.3. Hispanic and Asian applicants to public institutions are admitted at significantly lower rates than are whites. At private colleges and universities, blacks have a 29 percent higher chance of admission when compared with white applicants, while the odds of being admitted for Asian candidates are 47 percent (significantly) lower than for whites. There is little association between social class and admission outcomes at public institutions, but the chance of being accepted appears to rise along with an applicant's social class at private institutions.

Contrasts between racial and ethnic groups are brought into sharper relief when controls for applicants' demographic and academic performance characteristics are incorporated (see models 2 and 5). At both types of institutions, there are now positive and larger preferences for black and Hispanic applicants compared with whites, and the Asian disadvantage has increased. At private schools, for instance, the odds of being admitted are more than five times as high for black applicants as they are for whites. The likelihood that an Hispanic student is admitted is double that of a white student. Asian applicants face odds of being admitted that are 67 percent lower than those of white students. Adding these controls has tilted the social class gradient in a somewhat positive direction at public institutions, but the slope has shifted from slightly positive to slightly negative at private institutions. Private colleges and universities appear to

---

[23]Dummy variables for state of residence control for admission preferences tied to geographic diversity. Institution-specific dummy variables account for variation in the overall probability of being accepted.

TABLE 3.4

Odds Ratios from Logistic Regression Estimates of the Effect of Race and Social
Class on Admission Probabilities to Public and Private NSCE Institutions, Fall 1997

Predictor Variables	Public			Private		
	Model 1	Model 2	Model 3	Model 4	Model 5	Model 6
Student Personal Characteristics						
Race						
(White)	—	—	—	—	—	—
Black	1.21	219.85***	804.26***	1.29†	5.26***	4.90***
Hispanic	0.57*	1.64	1.63	0.92	1.99***	2.23*
Asian	0.58*	0.19**	0.37	0.53***	0.33***	0.15***
Social Class						
Lower	3.45	0.93	0.43	0.66	2.02	0.09
Working	1.28	1.02	0.74	0.72	1.42	0.42
(Middle)	—	—	—	—	—	—
Upper-Middle	1.38	1.44	2.42	1.51*	1.32	0.97
Upper	1.87	1.80	0.54	1.06	0.84	0.64
Race-Class Interactions						
Black, Lower			1.42			256.19**
Black, Working			0.79			2.81
Black, Upper-Middle			0.05*			0.93
Black, Upper			—			0.12
Hispanic, Lower			1.42			65.43*
Hispanic, Working			14.97			3.38†

(Continued)

TABLE 3.4 (Continued)

	Public			Private		
Predictor Variables	Model 1	Model 2	Model 3	Model 4	Model 5	Model 6
Hispanic, Upper-Middle			0.28			0.53
Hispanic, Upper			15246.43*			0.40
Asian, Lower			—			610.69***
Asian, Working			7.39			19.62***
Asian, Upper-Middle			0.16			2.54*
Asian, Upper			17.00			2.40
Sex						
(Male)		—	—		—	—
Female		0.80	0.80		1.65**	1.65**
Citizenship						
(U.S.)		—	—		—	—
Non-U.S. Citizen		0.84	0.80		1.83†	1.59
Athlete						
(No)		—	—		—	—
Yes		16.42**	21.83**		2.33***	2.22***
Legacy						
(No)		—	—		—	—
Yes		1.87	1.69		1.23	1.26
Student Academic Characteristics						
SAT Score						
<1000		1.88	1.40		0.02***	0.01***

1000–1099	0.59	0.42	0.17**	0.13**
1100–1199	3.53	2.71	0.53†	0.52†
(1200–1299)	—	—	—	—
1300–1399	0.71	0.48	0.74	0.78
1400–1499	20.12†	18.68	2.85**	3.00**
1500–1600	112.06*	109.11*	4.98***	5.50***
Unknown	0.12	0.11	0.33	0.27
ACT Score				
1–15	0.00**a	0.00***a	—	—
16–19	0.00***a	0.00***a	9.08†	14.74*
20–24	0.09**	0.15*	0.66	0.68
(25–29)	—	—	—	—
30–36	5363.96*	3960.07*	1.85†	1.82
Unknown	0.01***	0.01***	0.78	0.69
Number of AP Tests Taken				
(0)	—	—	—	—
1	0.87	1.29	0.67	0.71
2	9.77**	16.79**	1.01	1.03
3	1.42	2.34	0.67	0.67
4	637.96***	1357.12***	1.07	1.07
5	843.23***	2001.96***	1.43	1.57
6	12089.13***	7380.44***	0.94	0.97
7	0.35	0.28	1.05	0.97
8+	—	—	1.25	1.09
Unknown	6.94	8.71†	0.42	1.75
				0.45

(Continued)

TABLE 3.4 (Continued)

Predictor Variables	Public			Private		
	Model 1	Model 2	Model 3	Model 4	Model 5	Model 6
Number of SAT II (Subject or Achievement) Tests Taken						
1–2		11.54*	12.90*		4.94**	5.56***
(3)		—	—		—	—
4–5		0.90	0.84		1.17	1.24
6–7		991481.7**	439204.6***		1.40	1.27
8+		—	—		2.51	2.49
Average Score on SAT II Tests						
(<650)						
650–749		0.47	0.56		1.69*	1.79*
750+		—	—		4.56**	4.54**
SAT II Information Missing						
(No)						
Yes		0.06*	0.06*		2.32†	2.52*
High School GPA						
A+		1959.71***	2492.85***		3.15*	3.94**
A		18.06***	19.18***		1.84	2.38†
A–		13.21***	15.74***		1.31	1.46
(B+ or lower)						
No response		0.69	0.94		2.13	2.69
High School Class Rank						
Top 10 percent		13.41**	12.48**		7.05***	4.85**
Next 10 percent		11.46**	12.53**		3.64**	2.72*

	(1)	(2)	(3)	(4)	(5)	(6)
(Bottom 80 percent)			—	—	—	—
No response			6.28*	5.12†	1.61	1.08
SDQ Information Missing						
(No)			—	—	—	—
Yes			24.98*	19.79†	8.07***	7.02**
National Merit or Achievement Scholar						
(No)			—	—	—	—
Yes			0.93	1.06	1.50*	1.55*
High School Type						
(Public, non-magnet)			—	—	—	—
Public, magnet			0.15*	0.15*	1.10	1.04
Parochial/Religious			0.18†	0.28	1.17	1.33
Private			2.29	2.69	2.03**	2.27**
Unknown			627.83**	1585.19**	4.08*	3.94*
Elite 72 High School						
(No)			—	—	—	—
Yes			30.72**	34.40**	3.09***	3.25***
Number of Observations	1006	977	977	2767	2765	2765
F	9.09	4.77	4.47	19.41	7.46	6.64
(df1, df2)	(38, 939)	(80, 868)	(90, 914)	(57, 2636)	(102, 2589)	(114, 2608)
Prob > F	0.0000	0.0000	0.0000	0.0000	0.0000	0.0000

Source: National Study of College Experience.

Note: All regressions use weighted observations. Reference categories are shown in parentheses. Geographic area dummy variables (including individual states, Puerto Rico, Washington, D.C., and "other," "foreign," and "unknown" areas) and NSCE institution dummy variables are included in all the above models as control variables, but the estimated coefficients are not reported in the table.

[a] Odds ratio rounds to 0.00.

†p < .10 *p < .05 **p < .01 ***p < .001.

give greater weight to applicants from lower- and working-class families than to students from upper-middle-class or upper-class backgrounds, other things equal. In attempting to evaluate the relative importance of race and social class to admission officers, one would have to conclude (as we did when examining the data in Table 3.3) that admission outcomes are more sensitive to variations in race than to social class affiliation.

Associations between the chances of being admitted to an NSCE college and other demographic and academic performance measures in Table 3.4 generally accord with prior expectations, although there are some notable differences between public and private institutions. Affirmative action exists for female applicants at private schools but not at public ones.[24] Athletes and alumni children are given preference in admission over non-athletes and non-legacies.[25] Higher SAT scores boost admission chances at both private and public institutions. ACT scores also matter to public universities, but less so to private ones where the submission of ACT scores is not as common. Taking a large number of AP or SAT II examinations is associated with a higher admission probability at public schools, but how one performs on those examinations (at least on SAT II

[24]Nationwide, women outnumber men at four-year colleges and universities by about 23 percent (Sax et al., 2004: 126). But at the very top tier of American private research universities, there was an equivalent surplus of men (23 percent) in the combined applicant pools for fall semesters in the 1980s, 1993, and 1997 (Espenshade, Chung, and Walling, 2004). Preferences for female candidates at private schools could be interpreted as an attempt by admission officers to "massage" applicant pools to produce a first-year class with greater gender balance.

[25]Our measures of athlete and legacy status are not as good as we would like. Not all participating institutions were able to report whether an applicant was a recruited athlete or a legacy. Instead, these variables were measured from the NSCE survey data. An applicant was considered to be an athlete if they participated in varsity or other intercollegiate athletics for at least one year in college. A student is assumed to be a legacy if they attended the same undergraduate institution as either their father, their mother, an older sibling, or any other older relative. Being a "legacy" then means that the student is a legacy at the school they ultimately attended, but not necessarily at the NSCE institution(s) to which he or she applied. This fact should result in a weaker measured legacy effect than if legacy status were determined on a school-by-school basis. Stronger legacy effects (equivalent to an odds ratio of 2.858, significant at the .001 level) were obtained by Espenshade, Chung, and Walling (2004). In this examination, based on the experiences of three private research universities, whether a given candidate was an alumni son or daughter was obtained from data supplied by each institution. Finally, the strength of the legacy preference can vary not only across institutions but also within the same college or university. Rachel Toor (2001: 210) describes a practice at Duke of coding alumni children into two categories. The "A" group includes applicants whose parent(s) "had been active and involved with the school since graduation; often this meant that they had a history of consistent giving, but also rewarded were the good soldiers who showed up for reunions and were involved in their local alumni clubs." Applicants in the "B" category "got less of a boost—it simply meant that these people kept their records and whereabouts up-to-date with the alumni office."

Subject Tests) is more consequential at private schools. A student's high school grade point average and class rank are significantly positively correlated with admission chances at both public and private schools, and being a National Merit or National Achievement Scholar is important at private institutions.[26] Finally, the type of high school one attends is related to admission outcomes. Graduating from a public, magnet high school is associated with a lower chance of admission to a public institution, but having a private school diploma helps, especially when applying to a private college or university. An applicant's admission chances at both public and private NSCE schools are significantly improved if he or she graduates from one of the country's seventy-two elite high schools, whether that high school is public or private.[27]

Models 3 and 6 address the question of whether the effects of race are the same for all social class categories or, equivalently, whether the associations between admission outcomes and socioeconomic status are the same for all race groups. To answer this question, we include a set of interaction terms between race and social class in the models for private and public institutions. Some of these interaction terms are individually significant, especially in model 6. Additional tests indicate that the set of interaction terms is jointly significant in both the private and public models.[28] Based on these additional tests, we conclude there is strong evidence that the effect of race depends on social class, and vice versa.

Interpreting the Findings

An easier way to interpret the findings associated with race and social class in Table 3.4 is to convert them into more familiar terms. Many students

---

[26] The National Merit Scholarship Program (begun in 1955) and the National Achievement Scholarship Program (begun in 1964) are two college scholarship programs initiated by the National Merit Scholarship Corporation. Both are based on academic achievement, as judged primarily by a student's score on the PSAT/NMSQT test. The National Merit Scholarship Program is available to all high school students who meet certain eligibility requirements. The National Achievement Scholarship Program was established "to provide recognition for outstanding Black American high school students" (National Merit Scholarship Program, http://www.nationalmerit.org/nasp.php, accessed November 2, 2006).

[27] This is a list of seventy-two secondary schools in the United States that knowledgeable observers would consider to be among the nation's very best. It includes both public and private high schools. The list was compiled by two former Princeton University admission deans who have many years of experience evaluating students from all over the country.

[28] The relevant p-values for testing the null hypothesis of no association are .0034 in model 3 and .0000 in model 6. Stata dropped the interaction terms for Black/Upper class and Asian/Lower class from model 3 because they predicted success or failure perfectly. Three more predictor variables (taking eight or more AP tests, taking eight or more SAT II tests, and attaining an average score of 750 or better on SAT II tests) were dropped by Stata from models 2 and 3 because of collinearity with other explanatory variables.

TABLE 3.5
Race and Social Class Admission Preferences at Public and Private Institutions
Measured in ACT and SAT Points, Fall 1997

	Public Institutions	Private Institutions
Item	*ACT-Point Equivalents (out of 36)*	*SAT-Point Equivalents (out of 1600)*
Race		
(White)	—	—
Black	3.8	310
Hispanic	0.3	130
Asian	−3.4	−140
Social Class		
Lower	−0.1	130
Working	0.0	70
(Middle)	—	—
Upper-Middle	0.3	50
Upper	0.4	−30

Source: National Study of College Experience.

Note: The ACT test is a multiple-choice test that covers four areas: English, mathematics, reading, and science. The ACT is scored in integers, with a maximum of 36 and a minimum of 1. The SAT examination in use in the fall of 1997 had a verbal component (scored from 200 to 800) and a math component (scored from 200 to 800). The estimates in this table control for sex, citizenship, athlete and legacy status, SAT and ACT scores, number of AP tests taken, number of SAT II tests taken, average SAT II test scores, high school GPA and class rank, whether National Merit or National Achievement Scholar, high school type, elite 72 high school, state of residence, and NSCE institution.

who are candidates for admission at state-supported institutions, particularly those in the Midwest, are expected to take and submit scores for the ACT test. The SAT is the more customary standardized test expected of applicants to private institutions. Table 3.5 transforms the strength of admission preferences for members of different racial and socioeconomic groups in models 2 and 5 into their ACT- and SAT-point equivalents, using ACT points at public institutions and SAT point totals at private schools.[29]

[29] To do this, odds ratios in Table 3.4 are first converted back into logistic regression coefficients. Then the coefficients on race and class are interpolated in the ACT scale for public institutions and in the SAT scale at private institutions. The results will be sensitive not only to coefficients on the race and class variables but also to the strength of the ACT and SAT effects (Kane, 2006). These in turn will depend on other measures of academic performance that are included in the model, especially if they are correlated with ACT and SAT scores. Typically, if the correlations are positive, the ACT and SAT effects will be "flatter" or less steep as other indicators of academic merit are introduced. This will have the effect of

The black preference at public schools is equivalent on average to 3.8 ACT points. In other words, a black applicant who receives a score of 27 on the ACT test would have the same chance of admission to a public NSCE institution as a white candidate with an ACT score of 30.8, other things in model 2 the same. There is little effect associated with being Hispanic. The Asian disadvantage is almost as strong as the black advantage. Asian candidates who score 27 on the ACT test could be expected to be as attractive to admission officers at public universities as statistically equivalent white applicants with ACT scores 3.4 points lower, or with an average score of 23.6. Social class effects are rather small. There is a slight admission bonus if a candidate comes from an upper-middle- or upper-class family, but the apparent preference is worth less than one ACT point.

The second column of Table 3.5 indicates the size of admission preferences at private NSCE institutions. Once again, black applicants receive the largest admission bonus—equivalent to 310 SAT points. A black candidate with an SAT score of 1250 could be expected to have the same chance of being admitted as a white student whose SAT score is 1560, all other things equal in model 5. The average admission preference accorded to Hispanic applicants is roughly the same as having an extra 130 SAT points. On the other hand, an Asian candidate with a 1250 SAT score would be just as likely to be admitted at a private NSCE institution as a white student with an SAT score of 1110, other things the same. In general, both the direction and relative magnitudes of admission preferences for different racial and ethnic groups are similar at public and private institutions.[30]

But the same is not true with respect to social class. In contrast to public universities, at private institutions the admission preference is largest

---

magnifying the size of the racial (or social class) preference or disadvantage as measured by their ACT- or SAT-point equivalents. These estimates will also be sensitive to the point in time they are measured. There is some evidence to suggest that the strength of the admission preference for underrepresented minority students has been declining (Espenshade, Chung, and Walling, 2004).

[30] Using the High School and Beyond longitudinal survey of the high school class of 1982, Kane (1998b) showed that racial preference is limited to the top one-fifth of all four-year colleges and universities when ranked by academic selectivity. At these schools, black students have an admission advantage equivalent to two-thirds of a letter grade (for example, A− instead of B) or 400 SAT points. Being Hispanic confers a smaller benefit—slightly more than one-half of a letter grade or 340 SAT points. The coefficient for Asian students is negative, but not statistically significant. With a subset of the private NSCE schools used here and relying on entering cohorts from the 1980s, 1993, and 1997, Espenshade, Chung, and Walling (2004) concluded that the admission bonus for African Americans was equivalent to an extra 230 SAT points (on a 1600-point scale). Hispanic applicants received an admission preference equal to 185 SAT points, and the Asian disadvantage was comparable to a loss of 50 SAT points.

for lower-class applicants and declines more or less monotonically as social class background increases. Lower-class students receive a "plus" factor in admissions compared to middle-class students that is worth approximately 130 SAT points, the same magnitude as the Hispanic preference. At the opposite end of the socioeconomic scale, there is an upper-class disadvantage. These applicants would have to have SAT scores 30 points higher than middle-class students, other things the same, to have the same chance of being admitted.

We do not have all the information we would need to be able to see behind the closed doors of admission offices.[31] Even so, it would be a mistake to interpret the data in Table 3.5 as meaning that elite college admission officers are necessarily giving extra weight to black and Hispanic candidates just because they belong to underrepresented minority groups. This may occur from time to time, especially in situations where two applicants are otherwise equally well qualified. But in our judgment, it is more likely that a proper assessment of these data is that the labels "black" and "Hispanic" are proxies for a constellation of other factors in a candidate's application folder that we do not observe. These unobserved qualities—perhaps having overcome disadvantage and limited opportunity or experiencing challenging family or schooling circumstances—may be positively correlated with the chances of being admitted when a holistic review of an applicant's total materials is conducted.[32] It is these other aspects of race and ethnicity that matter, not race itself. Importantly, if we were able to include these other considerations in our models, we believe the effect of being black or Hispanic per se would be diminished.[33]

A similar reasoning pertains to the so-called Asian disadvantage in admissions. The negative coefficient associated with students from Asian heritage raises the question of whether there are "discriminatory admis-

[31] Rare opportunities to see how admission committees at elite small liberal arts colleges actually function are provided in the ethnographic works of Steinberg (2002) and Stevens (2007).

[32] As noted previously, the NSCE data set does not include all of the information that admission officers presumably evaluate when making admission decisions. Omitted, for example, are letters of recommendation, students' personal statements, lists of extracurricular activities and other talents, and work experience—what we referred to earlier as some of the "softer" variables that matter in determining which students to admit (Fetter, 1995).

[33] A similar view has been expressed by C. Judson King, former systemwide provost and senior vice president for academic affairs at the University of California and current director of the Center for Studies in Higher Education at the University of California, Berkeley. According to King (2005), "It is desirable to include all of the independent measures that are taken into account in the admissions decision to the extent that can possibly be done. . . . If any of the independent measures not taken into account in the analysis are cross-correlated with ethnicity (and everything is cross-correlated with ethnicity to some degree), then what appears to be a racial effect can be a reflection of the omitted variables rather than an actual influence of race."

sions policies against Asian American applicants to elite colleges and universities" (U.S. Commission on Civil Rights, 1992: 104). The two-year review of Harvard's admission policies conducted by the U.S. Department of Education's Office for Civil Rights concluded that "[o]ver the last ten years Asian American applicants have been admitted at a significantly lower rate than white applicants; however . . . this disparity is not the result of discriminatory polices or procedures. . . . We determined that the primary cause of the disparity was the preference given to children of alumni and recruited athletes" (U.S. Commission on Civil Rights, 1992: 120). The Office for Civil Rights also found that Asian applicants were typically stronger than white applicants on most standardized tests and other measures of academic performance (with the exception of the SAT verbal test) and that white applicants were rated higher on such nonacademic indicators as athletics and personal qualifications (U.S. Commission on Civil Rights, 1992: 122n98). It is likely that incorporating in our models an even fuller range of academic performance measures as well as these other nonacademic factors would cast the effect of coming from an Asian background in a different light. With the information at hand, however, we are not able to settle the question of whether Asian applicants experience discrimination in elite college admissions (Espenshade, Chung, and Walling, 2004: 1431n7).[34]

One study that has attempted to evaluate admission decisions by incorporating all of the relevant deterministic factors is a reexamination of a sample of eight thousand applications to the freshman class at the University of California, Berkeley, for the 2004–5 academic year (Hout, 2005). Efforts by the University of California evolved through a series of stages as it sought to comply with the 1995 Board of Regents' decision and the 1996 statewide ballot initiative Proposition 209 disallowing the use of racial preference in university admissions. By 2002 the Berkeley campus had instituted "comprehensive review" that considered both a student's academic potential and the context in which living and learning occurred. Admission decisions for 89 percent of applicants were determined by the average of two independent readers' scores. A thorough statistical analysis of these scores in the context of high school grades and

[34]Karabel (2005) reports that Harvard College deliberately increased the emphasis on subjective and nonacademic factors in the 1920s to check the increasing proportion of Jews on campus. Some observers who believe that Asians are the target of discrimination in admissions have referred to Asians as "the new Jews" (Golden, 2006). In a 1987 *New York Times* article, Berkeley professor Ling-Chi Wang explicitly compared the way Asians are considered in college admissions to the earlier treatment of Jews: "I think all of the elite universities in America suddenly realized they had what used to be called a 'Jewish problem' before World War II, and they began to look for ways of slowing down the admissions of Asians" (Lindsey, 1987).

test scores, family and high school information, extracurricular activities, work experience, obstacles to achievement, and the contents of the personal statement and essay showed that academic considerations—especially high school grades—predominated. Ethnic identity played a statistically significant but substantively small role. To take the most extreme example, Asian American applicants would have to be a bit better than Hispanic students to have the same reader score and therefore the same chance of admission, other things equal. In particular, Asian candidates would have to be in the 79th or 80th percentile of their high school grade distribution to be competitive with Hispanic students in the 75th percentile of their grade distribution.

The remaining 11 percent of decisions were made through a tie-breaking process (because not all students with the same reader score could be admitted through the quotas that existed at the five separate colleges on the Berkeley campus) or through Augmented Review (AR), a "process reserved for applications that seem to be competitive for admission but lack information or present unique circumstances that might make the difference between admission and denial" (Hout, 2005: 6). It was in this small fraction of remaining admission decisions where racial and ethnic identity played more of a role. Black students were significantly more likely to be admitted through the tie-breaking process. Both black and Hispanic students were significantly more likely than students in other groups to be referred for AR review, but once there ethnic differences did not influence who was admitted through AR.[35] Hout (2005: 64) concludes, "My analysis shows that the centerpiece of comprehensive review—the process of assigning read scores—was mainly free of ethnic disparity. . . . [I]t is in AR referral and tie-breaking where ethnic identity plays a role in Berkeley's comprehensive review." It is also Hout's judgment that if all of the factors that go into making up "AR-ness" could somehow be articulated and incorporated into a model, then the measured effects of ethnic identity might largely disappear: "Marking what it is and how that correlates with ethnic identity could explain what appear here as ethnic effects" (6).[36]

---

[35] Black applicants had a 10.8 percent chance of being referred to AR and Hispanic students a 9.5 percent chance, compared to the white proportion of 6.2 percent. The difference between Asian and white applicants was not statistically significant (Hout, 2005: 57).

[36] Prior to 1998, when the passage in 1995 of SP-1 by the California Board of Regents and the passage in 1996 of Proposition 209 by the California voters (both of which banned the use of race, ethnicity, sex, or national origin in the admission process) became effective, race and ethnicity were used along with other factors in the admission selection process. The process, which relied on a somewhat formulaic and mechanistic approach, succeeded in admitting underrepresented minority students in disproportionate numbers. In 1995, for example, underrepresented minority students accounted for 19.5 percent of applicants versus 26.5 percent of admitted students. These percentages reversed sharply in 1998—16.1 percent of applicants compared to 11.2 percent of admitted students (Moore, 2002).

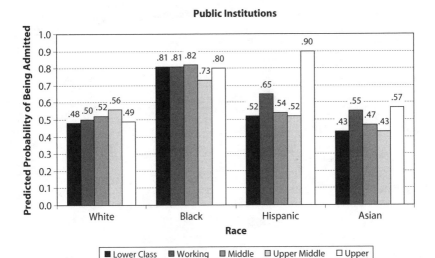

Figure 3.8. Effect of Race and Social Class on the Probability of Being Admitted to Public NSCE Institutions, All Other Things Held Constant, 1997. Note: Based on Model 3 in Table 3.4. Source: National Study of College Experience.

These general caveats also apply to the interpretation of data in Figures 3.8 and 3.9. Here we illustrate, respectively, the implications in Table 3.4 of model 3 for public institutions and model 6 for private institutions. The figures show the predicted probability of college admission for twenty different race-class pairs holding all other characteristics of applicants constant.[37] The black advantage at public universities is apparent in Figure 3.8 as is the fact that predicted probabilities for Asian candidates are generally below those for whites. There is little difference between the average chance that white and Hispanic applicants will be admitted to public institutions. When these expected proportions are weighted by social class within race, the group averages are .54 for whites, .80 for blacks, .57 for Hispanics, and .46 for Asians. Social class also plays a role. For white applicants, social class is related to the expected chance of being admitted in an inverse U-shaped pattern. Upper-middle-class

[37] These calculations are based on the same set of observations used to fit models 3 and 6 in Table 3.4. To derive the estimate for lower-class, white students at public institutions, for example, a predicted probability of admission was calculated from model 3 for each of 977 students using all of each student's observed characteristics, except that race was set equal to "white" and social class was set to "lower." Then a weighted average of these predicted probabilities was formed, using as weights the sample weights of each student. This procedure was repeated for each of the remaining nineteen race-class pairs. The estimates for applicants to private institutions were derived in the same way using model 6.

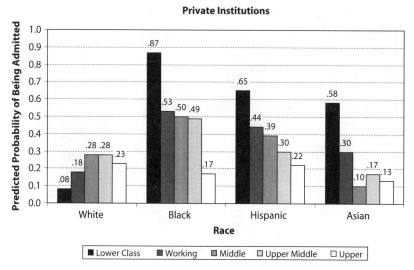

Figure 3.9. Effect of Race and Social Class on the Probability of Being Admitted to Private NSCE Institutions, All Other Things Held Constant, 1997. Note: Based on Model 6 in Table 3.4. Source: National Study of College Experience.

students have the highest expected probability of being accepted. For nonwhite students, a similar inverted U-shaped pattern is evident, except that acceptance rates increase for the upper class. For Hispanic and Asian applicants, in fact, expected admission rates are largest for those from the highest social class backgrounds. With limited budgets for financial aid, public institutions could face incentives to admit a relatively large proportion of students whose families can afford to pay the full educational cost. With these exceptions, however, the social class effects that appear in Figure 3.8 are relatively modest.

The patterns at private institutions shown in Figure 3.9 are markedly different. First, the racial contrasts between whites and nonwhites are more striking than at public institutions. The (weighted) average predicted admission probabilities are .26 for white applicants, .51 for blacks, .37 for Hispanics, and .16 for Asian students. The larger relative differences between predicted admission chances for members of underrepresented minority groups versus whites at private schools compared to public institutions supports Kane's (1998b) conclusion that the extent of affirmative action that is practiced is positively correlated with how academically selective an institution is. Once again, an inverse U-shaped pattern between admission rates and social class is found for whites at private institutions, but the two arms of the "U" are much steeper than at public institutions. White middle- and upper-middle-class applicants to private schools have a substantially greater admission advantage over students from either end of the socioeconomic spectrum than do their counterparts who apply to public universities.

In addition, the SES gradient for nonwhite students at private schools consistently favors candidates from lower- and working-class backgrounds over those from more privileged circumstances. For black and Hispanic students, the expected probability of being accepted falls rapidly and monotonically as social standing rises. In other words, for the private schools in the NSCE data set, there is strong support for the view that admission officers are awarding extra weight to nonwhite students from poor and working-class families—especially to those who are closest to the bottom of the income distribution. Based on the data in Figure 3.8, the same cannot be said about admission practices at public NSCE universities.[38]

The experiences of applicants to the private NSCE schools cast some doubt on the claim advanced by Carnevale and Rose (2004) that the top schools are not providing a class-based preference for low-income students. These authors note that "[w]hile selective colleges purport to provide preferences to low-income students and say they would like to admit more if these students were academically prepared, on average the top 146 colleges do not provide a systematic preference and could in fact admit far greater numbers of low-income students, including minority students, capable of handling the work" (102).

Nor are our results entirely consistent with the findings from a special study conducted by William Bowen and his colleagues of applicants to nineteen academically selective colleges and universities in the fall of 1995 (Bowen, Kurzweil, and Tobin, 2005). These researchers find that, for non-minority applicants with the same SAT scores, there is no perceptible difference in admission chances between applicants from families in the bottom income quartile, applicants who would be the first in their families to attend college, and all other (non-minority) applicants from families at higher levels of socioeconomic status. When controls are added for other student and institutional characteristics, these authors

---

[38] Stevens (2006) has suggested an interpretation for the apparently anomalous treatment of low-income white compared with more privileged white students in private-college admission decisions. Because elite private colleges and universities have access to enough white students in other ways, they intentionally save their scarce financial aid dollars for students who will help them look good on their numbers of minority students. According to Stevens (2006: 30), "Admissions officers often revealed to the researcher their own personal ethical commitments to providing opportunity to members of historically disadvantaged groups, but ultimate evaluative preference for members of disadvantaged groups was reserved for applicants who could be counted in The College's multicultural statistics. This caused some admissions officers no small amount of ethical dismay."

find that "on an other-things-equal basis, *applicants from low-SES back-grounds, whether defined by family income or parental education, get essentially no break in the admissions process; they fare neither better nor worse than other applicants*" (166, emphasis in the original).[39]

This conclusion of no low SES admission preference is corroborated quite well by our findings at public NSCE universities (see Figure 3.8). Within each racial or ethnic group of applicants, the predicted probability of being admitted, on an all-other-things-equal basis, varies relatively little from one social class to another. It is clear that applicants to public universities who come from lower- and working-class family backgrounds do not have an admission advantage compared with other applicants. But we cannot conclude from our findings at private NSCE colleges and universities that there is no SES effect. Figure 3.9 shows that for white applicants to private institutions, there is a low SES admissions disadvantage. White applicants from lower- and working-class families have admissions chances of 8 percent and 18 percent, respectively, in contrast to an expected chance of being admitted that falls in the 20–30 percent range for students from higher SES families. For nonwhite students, on the other hand, there are clear signs of a low SES admissions advantage. Black applicants who come from lower- or working-class families can expect a favorable admissions decision in 87 percent and 53 percent of their cases, respectively. The expected chance of being admitted falls to just 17 percent for upper-class black students. Strikingly similar patterns characterize the admissions chances by social class for Hispanic and Asian applicants to private institutions.[40]

---

[39] Bowen and his colleagues contrast their results with a "friend of the court" brief submitted to the U.S. Supreme Court by Harvard, Brown, the University of Chicago, Dartmouth College, Duke, the University of Pennsylvania, Princeton, and Yale in connection with the two University of Michigan cases. They draw particular attention to factors associated with applicants' socioeconomic status that these eight highly selective private colleges and universities say they "give special attention to" when making admissions decisions—factors including "applicants from economically and/or culturally disadvantaged backgrounds, . . . those who would be the first in their families to attend any college, . . . and those who have overcome various identifiable hardships" (Tribe, 2003: 20). Bowen, Kurzweil, and Tobin (2005: 175) conclude, "What is striking is the juxtaposition of this clear statement of intent with the equally clear empirical finding that, at the schools in our study, there is absolutely no admissions advantage associated with coming from a poor family and only a very small advantage (about 4 percentile points) associated with being a first-generation college-goer; at least that was the case for the '95 entering cohort."

[40] Several factors may help explain why our findings differ from those reported by Bowen and his colleagues. First, we are each dealing with a different set of institutions. The Bowen data include nineteen highly selective institutions—five Ivy League universities, ten liberal arts colleges, and four public flagship institutions. Second, our measures of socioeconomic status are different, although they all depend on students' self-reports. Family income and parental education are the basis for SES categories in the Bowen special study, while we rely

Unpacking Racial Labels

Our analysis of elite college admissions has relied on rather broad racial and ethnic categories. But demographic changes in the U.S. population suggest that the use of such terms as "white," "black," "Hispanic," and "Asian" can disguise a fair amount of heterogeneity beneath the surface. Our concern in this section is to begin to unpack some of this heterogeneity. The main features that will concern us are whether individuals belong to single- or multiple-race groups and their nativity status in terms of immigrant generation.[41]

Nearly 3 percent of children under age eighteen were reported to be multiracial in the 2000 U.S. Census.[42] Although this proportion is small, it has been rising as the proportion of interracial couples increases (Lee and Edmonston, 2005).[43] In addition, both the number of foreign-born individuals in the United States and their proportion of the population have been growing since reaching a low point in 1970. There were 35 million people living in the United States in 2005 who were born elsewhere, making up 12 percent of the total population. The children of immigrants accounted for nearly one in every five U.S. school-age children

---

on students' assessments of their families' social class. As reported in appendix B, however, our subjective measure of socioeconomics status correlates very well with more objective indicators, such as family income and parents' education. Third, Bowen's central conclusion of no admissions advantage for low SES students is derived from an analysis that combines private and public institutions (although most of the colleges and universities in his study are private ones). It is clear from Figures 3.8 and 3.9 that our results are sensitive to whether public or private schools are examined. When Bowen, Kurzweil, and Tobin (2005: 107n26) analyze Ivy League institutions by themselves, they reach conclusions that are much more in line with results we report based on private NSCE institutions and shown in Figure 3.9. Finally, our conclusions depend on logistic regressions (models 3 and 6 in Table 3.4) that incorporate interaction terms between racial identity and social class. When these interaction terms are ignored (see models 2 and 5 in Table 3.4), the additive effects of social class are much weaker. In fact, we would conclude from our models that do not include race-class interaction terms that there is not a statistically significant admissions preference for low SES applicants at either private or public NSCE institutions.

[41] We reserve a more detailed examination of some of these differences, including those associated with national origins, for a discussion of matriculants in chapter 4.

[42] Other sources suggest that the proportion of multiracial children in 2000 was closer to 4 percent, compared with 2.4 percent of Americans of all ages (Jones and Smith, 2001, Table 6, p. 10). Those under age eighteen do not typically fill out census forms; the mother in the household usually does. This difference can influence estimates of the multiracial children population, because parents can be arbitrary in deciding whether to choose one or two categories for their biracial children.

[43] The proportion of interracial marriage has increased from less than 1 percent of all married couples in 1970 to more than 5 percent of couples in 2000. The typical interracial couple involves a white individual and his or her nonwhite spouse (Lee and Edmonston, 2005: 7).

(ages 5 to 17) in 2005. Mexico is the homeland to 30 percent of the foreign-born population, but no other country accounts for more than about 5 percent. The result is a fairly widespread distribution of nationalities among the U.S. foreign-born population (Camarota, 2005).

Our survey data permit us to define four immigrant groups: (1) first-generation—individuals who were born outside the United States; (2) second-generation—native-born persons who have at least one foreign-born parent; (3) third-generation—native-born individuals who have two native-born parents and at least one foreign-born grandparent; and (4) fourth-generation or higher—native-born individuals who have two native-born parents and four native-born grandparents. Nearly one-half (48 percent) of all applications to the seven NSCE institutions are submitted by fourth-or-higher generation immigrant students. These are individuals whose ancestors have had a long history of living in the United States. Almost two-thirds of applications submitted by white and black applicants come from students in the fourth-plus immigrant generation. Not surprisingly, given recent U.S. immigration patterns, two-thirds of Hispanic applications are from candidates in the first or second generation of immigrants. And among Asian applicants, all but about 8 percent of total applications come from immigrants or the children of immigrants.

These patterns differ depending on whether one is examining public or private NSCE institutions. The relevant data are contained in Table 3.6. Two-thirds of applicants to public schools have deep roots in the United States, and only slightly more than 10 percent are first- or second-generation immigrants. By contrast, private schools are more of a magnet for students with a recent immigrant past. Nearly one-half (45 percent) of all applications to private colleges and universities come from first- or second-generation immigrants—four times the proportion at public schools. Fewer than 40 percent are submitted by applicants in the fourth-plus immigrant generation. Two factors account for the differences between public and private schools. First, as shown in Table 3.6, a greater proportion of both white and black applicants to private schools than to public institutions are either immigrants or the children of immigrants. Among black applicants to private schools, for example, just half (51 percent) are in the fourth-plus immigrant group (in contrast to almost 80 percent at public universities). Second, Hispanic and Asian candidates, most of whom come from the first two immigrant groups at both private and public institutions, represent a larger share of all applicants at private schools. These two populations account for almost 38 percent of all applications to private colleges and universities, in contrast to their 7 percent share at public colleges.

It is instructive to examine NSCE applicants by whether they are single-race or multiple-race individuals. By "single race" we refer to students

TABLE 3.6
Immigrant Generation of Applicants to Public and Private
NSCE Institutions, by Race, Fall 1997 (Percentage Distribution)

| | Public | | | | | | Private | | | | |
Immigrant Generation	Total	White	Black	Hispanic	Asian	Total	White	Black	Hispanic	Asian
First	3.0	0.1	5.7	19.8	39.2	16.7	6.8	11.5	19.9	35.0
Second	8.2	4.2	8.4	53.1	54.1	28.1	10.1	28.3	46.6	56.5
Third	19.9	22.6	1.9	15.2	2.7	14.1	21.4	3.1	18.6	2.1
Fourth and Higher	66.6	71.0	79.4	9.7	1.5	38.3	59.4	51.0	13.6	3.3
Unknown	2.3	2.1	4.6	2.2	2.6	2.8	2.4	6.1	1.4	3.1
Total	100.0	100.0	100.0	100.0	100.0	100.0	100.0	100.0	100.0	100.0
N (unweighted)	1,033	308	328	167	230	2,796	766	531	733	766

Source: National Study of College Experience.
Note: Percentage distributions are weighted.

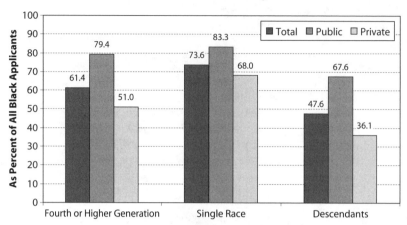

Figure 3.10. Black Applicants to Seven NSCE Institutions Who Are Fourth Immigrant Generation or Higher, Single Race, or Descendants, by Type of Institution, 1997. Source: National Study of College Experience.

who identified themselves as belonging to a single racial or ethnic category in the NSCE survey (the survey permitted individuals to identify with as many races or ethnicities as they considered relevant). For example, among the 52,269 applicants to whom we have assigned the category "white" (based on criteria described in appendix B), 95 percent (or 49,664) marked only the "white" category on the survey. We define these as single-race white applicants, and the remaining 5 percent are considered multiracial. Among all applicants, Hispanics have the smallest single-race proportion (64 percent), partly because many Hispanics, in addition to having an Hispanic ethnic identity, also affiliate with at least one racial group (white, black, or some other race). The single-race proportion for black applicants is nearly three-quarters (74 percent) among applicants to public and private schools combined, and the corresponding Asian proportion approaches nine-tenths (87 percent). For most racial groups, the single-race proportions do not vary much between public and private schools. Blacks are the notable exception. Black applicants to public schools are much more likely to be single race (83 percent) than are private school black applicants (68 percent).

These findings are summarized for black applicants in Figure 3.10. The left-hand panel shows the proportions of black applicants who are in the fourth-or-higher immigrant generation. The middle panel indicates single-race proportions. We show in the right-hand panel the proportion of black "descendants" at public and private institutions. "Descendants" is a phrase used by black undergraduates at Harvard to refer to black students who have descended from the American slave population. It is usually reserved for someone who belongs to the fourth-or-higher immigrant generation and who is not multiracial (Rimer and Arenson, 2004). Our data suggest that black descendants make up roughly half (48 percent) of all black applicants to public and private schools combined. But once again there are sharp differences by type of institution. At public universities black students who are single-race and in the fourth-plus immigrant generation make up two-thirds (68 percent) of all black applicants. By contrast, black applicants to private universities who do not claim any other racial or ethnic identity and whose families have been in the United States for many generations account for only slightly more than one-third (36 percent) of all black candidates.[44]

Aggregate unadjusted acceptance rates for descendant and non-descendant black applicants are shown in Figure 3.11. At both public and private institutions, admission rates are higher for descendants, the group of candidates for whom—in the minds of some people—affirmative action was originally intended. The impact, of course, of these differential outcomes for black students whose families have been in the United States for many generations is to create a pool of admitted students that is more heavily tilted toward descendants than is the pool of applicants.

The regression models in Table 3.4 showed that there are statistically significant racial effects in college admission associated with being black, Hispanic, or Asian. Here we want to ask whether this story is altered if we look behind these broad labels. The results of two additional regression models are shown in Table 3.7. In each regression, the group of black applicants is subdivided into black descendants and black non-descendants. Hispanic and Asian students are disaggregated into three categories that depend on immigrant generation. The additional demographic and academic performance explanatory variables used in models 2 and 5 in Table 3.4 are also included in the models that produce the results shown in Table 3.7.

Estimates for applicants to public institutions in Table 3.7 may be compared with those in model 2 in Table 3.4. The significantly positive influence in Table 3.4 associated with being black has its roots in significantly

[44]Interracial marriage has had an impact on the proportion of single-race applicants in successive immigrant generations. Among Hispanic candidates at private institutions, for example, the percentage of single-race individuals is the following: among the first generation (76 percent), second (68), third (61), and fourth and higher (47). The longer families are in this country and the more interracial intermarriage takes places, the smaller is the remaining fraction of single-race persons. Similar patterns characterize Asian applicants: first generation (93 percent single race), second (90), third (57), and fourth and higher (33).

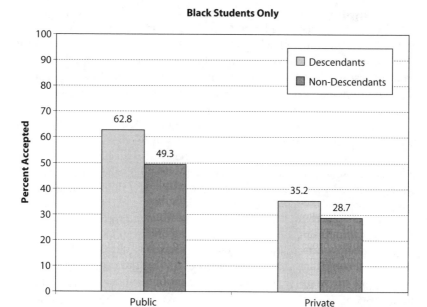

Figure 3.11. Acceptance Rates for Black Applicants to Seven NSCE Institutions, by Type of Institution and Whether Applicants Are Descendants or Non-Descendants, 1997. Source: National Study of College Experience.

positive preferences for both descendant and non-descendant black applicants. Controlling for a broad range of other factors, the preference that admission officers at public institutions extend to black descendants is larger than the one given to black non-descendants whose families have a shorter tenure in the United States. In Table 3.4 there is an insignificantly positive preference for Hispanic applicants to public institutions. None of the generation-specific estimates for Hispanics is significant in Table 3.7. Table 3.4 indicated that Asian applicants faced 81 percent significantly lower odds of being admitted to public universities compared to white students. Unpacking this relative disadvantage suggests that it is associated largely with Asian applicants in the second generation. Asian students who are foreign-born or members of the third-and-higher immigrant generation also face a small admissions disadvantage relative to white applicants, but the difference is not statistically significant. Table 3.7 also incorporates the effects of social class, aggregated here into three categories instead of the five groups used in Table 3.4. Neither the high nor low social class category differs significantly from middle-class applicants in terms of the chances of being admitted. The

TABLE 3.7

Odds Ratios from Logistic Regression Estimates of the
Effect of Race, Immigrant Generation, and
Social Class on Admission Probabilities to Public and Private
NSCE Institutions, Fall 1997

Predictor Variables	Public	Private
Disaggregated Race		
(White)	—	—
Black descendants	333.88***	9.81***
Black non-descendants	106.78***	3.89***
Hispanic first generation	2.35	1.11
Hispanic second generation	0.32	2.79***
Hispanic third and higher generation	12.97	1.68†
Asian first generation	0.11	0.39**
Asian second generation	0.24*	0.27***
Asian third and higher generation	0.15	0.61
Social Class[a]		
Low	1.02	1.44
(Middle)	—	—
High	1.40	1.26
Number of observations	977	2765
F(df1, df2)	4.20(83, 865)	7.46(105, 2586)
Prob > F	0.0000	0.0000

Source: National Study of College Experience.

Note: The models in this table also include as predictor variables the demographic and academic performance variables shown in Table 3.4, along with state-level and institution-specific dummy variables.

[a]"Low" includes lower and working classes; "High" includes upper-middle and upper classes.

†p < .10 *p < .05 **p<.01 ***p <.001

measured positive effect is strongest, however, for applicants from high SES family backgrounds.[45]

The results of a similar analysis for private institutions are shown in the second column of Table 3.7. Once again, the significantly positive preference observed in model 5 of Table 3.4 for black applicants is evident in Table 3.7. The preference is traceable to additional weight given to both black descendants and black non-descendants compared to white students. As in the public example, black applicants to private colleges and universities whose immediate families and ancestors have lived in the United States for a long time receive a stronger weight in admission decisions

---

[45] The two socioeconomic terms combined are jointly insignificant (p-value equals .8318).

than do other black candidates. This difference is statistically significant.[46] These results suggest that the findings in Figure 3.11 of an admission advantage for black descendants hold up at private institutions even after numerous other control variables are introduced into the model.

The admission advantage for Hispanic applicants at private institutions is associated most closely with candidates in the second generation. The odds of being admitted for these students are almost three times as high as they are for comparable white applicants. There are positive preferences, too, for Hispanic applicants in the first and in the third-and-higher immigrant generation, but the effects are not significant. The reduced admission chances that Asian applicants face compared with white students are most closely identified with first- and second-generation Asian immigrants. The negative effect is somewhat larger for Asian applicants in the second generation than for Asian students who are foreign-born. In short, the racial and ethnic influence in Table 3.7 associated with being an Hispanic or Asian applicant at private NSCE institutions is essentially a story about the second generation of immigrants. The difference is that the associations are positive in the case of Hispanic students and negative for Asian applicants. Finally, neither social class influence is statistically significant, and together they are jointly insignificant.[47]

Models for race and class were also estimated including interaction terms between each racial category and social class. Results for applicants to public universities are shown in Figure 3.12 as the predicted probability of being accepted for alternative race-class combinations, holding other things constant. More than 85 percent of applicants to public schools are white. For these students there is a positive correlation between estimated acceptance rates and social class—ranging from 50 percent for white lower- and working-class students to 55 percent (the average for all public school applicants) for upper-middle- and upper-class white candidates.[48]

---

[46] To test this, models in Table 3.7 were rerun using black non-descendants instead of whites as the reference group for racial and ethnic categories. The difference in odds ratios for black descendants and black non-descendants is significant at the 5 percent level for private schools (p-value equals .013) but insignificant for public universities (p-value of .280).

[47] The p-value equals .2795.

[48] In the underlying regression model, three of the eight main effects for race are significant, including positive effects for the two groups of black applicants and first-generation Hispanic students. Interaction terms between first-generation Hispanics and both social class categories are negative, large, and significant. The other significant interaction terms include the negative effect of black descendants with high social class and the two positive terms for second-generation Hispanics with low social class, and first-generation Asians with low social class. Stata dropped from the regression the two interaction terms involving third-and-higher immigrant generation Asians. As a group, the fourteen interaction terms are jointly significant (p-value equals .0009).

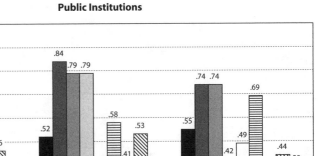

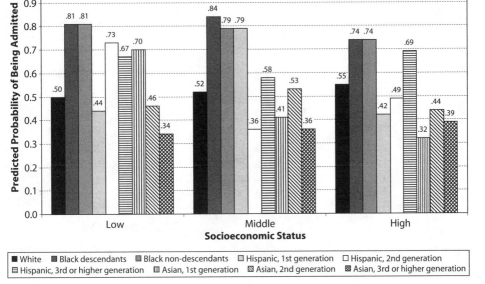

Figure 3.12. Effect of Race, Immigrant Generation, and Social Class on the Probability of Being Admitted to Public NSCE Institutions, All Other Things Held Constant, 1997. Note: Low SES includes lower and working social classes; high SES includes upper-middle and upper social classes. Source: National Study of College Experience.

Estimates involving interaction terms at private institutions are illustrated in Figure 3.13. These results are generally similar to those shown in Figure 3.9. The inverse U-shaped preference pattern by social class is apparent for white students. We observed in Figure 3.9 a negative correlation between social class and acceptance rates for blacks and Hispanics. Here we see that the earlier pattern for blacks is evident only for non-descendants, who comprise roughly two-thirds of all black applicants at private institutions. Black descendants' chances of being admitted remain relatively constant at about 60 percent across all three social classes. The average Hispanic pattern observed previously is found only among second- and third-or-higher generation applicants. It is not apparent among foreign-born Hispanics whose acceptance rate (about 30 percent) is equal to roughly one-half the rate for black descendants at all social classes.[49]

[49] Overall, six of the eight main effects for race are significant (at the 5 percent level)—the main effects for black descendants and black non-descendants are both significantly positive, the coefficients on the three Asian main effects are significantly negative, and the

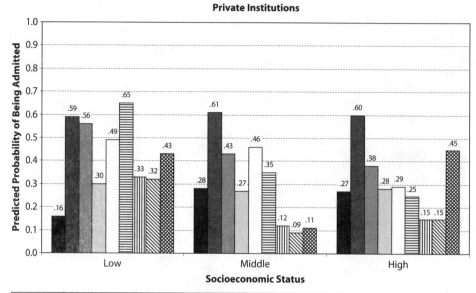

Figure 3.13. Effect of Race, Immigrant Generation, and Social Class on the Probability of Being Admitted to Private NSCE Institutions, All Other Things Held Constant, 1997. Note: Low SES includes lower and working social classes; high SES includes upper-middle and upper social classes. Source: National Study of College Experience.

Related Research

Up to this point we have featured our results on factors affecting the admission process at highly selective institutions. Our conclusions are broadly consistent with an emerging body of related research, which is summarized briefly in this section.

ACADEMIC MERIT

Academic merit is perhaps the essential selection criterion used by elite colleges. As Bowen and Bok (1998: 23) remark, "The most fundamental objective is to be sure that the qualifications of all admitted students are above a high academic threshold." So influential are measures of past

---

second-generation Hispanic effect is significantly positive. Eight of the sixteen interaction terms are significant (at the 10 percent level); the sixteen interaction terms are jointly significant (p-value equals .0000); and the main effect of low social class is negative and significant (p-value of .041), but the main effect of high social class is not significant.

academic performance and future promise that they have become "embedded" in institutional cultures and are now considered normal or natural (Karen, 1990, 1991b).[50] Undergraduate admission offices rely on standardized test scores, high school GPAs, and transcripts, among other things, to make assessments of academic ability (Zwick, 2002).

For admission to Harvard in the fall of 1980, 97 percent of applicants who were rated potential "summa cum laude" graduates were accepted in comparison to fewer than 10 percent of students who were neither "summa" nor "magna" (Karen, 1991b). Rising SAT scores are typically accompanied by monotonic increases in acceptance rates (Bowen and Bok, 1998; Bowen and Levin, 2003; Espenshade, Chung, and Walling, 2004; Espenshade, Hale, and Chung, 2005). High school GPA and SAT scores are important determinants of admission probabilities at all levels of college selectivity. On average, a high school GPA that is based on all Bs instead of all Cs is "worth" about 450 points on the SAT scale; both increase acceptance rates by roughly seven percentage points (Kane, 1998b). Each of these effects is strongest at the most selective colleges (cf. Lillard and Gerner, 1999).[51]

RACE AND ETHNICITY

The recent U.S. Supreme Court rulings in the two University of Michigan affirmative action cases (*Gratz v. Bollinger*, 2003; *Grutter v. Bollinger*, 2003) brought partial, albeit temporary, closure to the issue of whether and how race may be used as one among many factors in "a highly individualized, holistic review" of applicants to postsecondary education. The legal controversy leading up to the Court's decision also revealed

[50] Things have not always been this way. A broad historical account of the changing meanings of merit can be found in Karabel (2005). Karen (1990) points out that the "movement toward meritocracy" did not take root until after World War II, and that "academic ability" was a contested category all along the way, especially by alumni groups whose children stood to be disadvantaged. The Harvard faculty, for example, fought in the late 1950s for admission standards that gave greater weight to scholastic ability. In a related development, admission office philosophies shifted during the 1960s away from recruiting well-rounded individuals to assembling a well-rounded class. Symptomatic of the trend, the mathematics faculty at Princeton pushed for admitting students with high math aptitude, even if applicants were undistinguished in other respects (Bowen and Levin, 2003). To this day, "bright well-rounded kids" are at a competitive disadvantage in the admission process at the most selective institutions in relation to students who appear more "angular" or "well-lopsided" (Toor, 2001: 2, 48; cf. Bowen and Levin, 2003: 60).

[51] Academic ability is also important to graduate and professional schools. LSAT scores and undergraduate GPAs account for about 60 percent of the variation in law school admission decisions for white students (Wightman, 1997). Among applicants to graduate business schools, each college GPA point nearly doubles the odds of admission, and each one-point increase in GMAT-score percentile rank (relative to other applicants to the same school) raises the odds of admission by 3 percent (Dugan et al., 1996).

that racial preferences have a long history in undergraduate and graduate admission programs. Preferences toward underrepresented minority students are not salient if all colleges and universities are grouped together (Kane, 1998b; Lillard and Gerner, 1999; Walster, Cleary, and Clifford, 1971).[52] But at the most selective colleges, black applicants have higher acceptance rates than whites, sometimes by a factor of nearly two to one (Bowen and Bok, 1998; Karen, 1990, 1991b). Admission chances for Hispanics fall in between those for whites and blacks, and those for Asian American students are the lowest.

When controls are added for SAT scores and other variables, the black and Latino advantage relative to whites grows, as does the Asian disadvantage (Bowen and Bok, 1998; Espenshade, Chung, and Walling, 2004). Among schools in the top quintile of selectivity, blacks and Hispanics are between eight and ten percentage points more likely to be admitted than whites (Asian students are six or seven percentage points less likely to be accepted). There is some evidence, however, that the strength of preferences for underrepresented students of color has declined in the past twenty-five years (Espenshade, Chung, and Walling, 2004; Shulman and Bowen, 2001). Race is also considered a "plus" factor in admission to graduate business and law schools (Dugan et al., 1996; Sander, 2004; Wightman, 1997).

SOCIOECONOMIC STATUS

Although the research base is not large, there is evidence that elite private universities extend admission preferences to the least advantaged members of their applicant pools when these preferences are considered on an all-other-things-equal basis. First-generation college students and those from families with annual incomes below $30,000 had higher odds of being accepted to three private research universities in 1997 than did other families. When parental education and family income are combined into one composite SES measure, students in the low SES category have 67 percent significantly higher odds of being admitted than do middle or high SES applicants, a social class bonus that is statistically equivalent to 130 SAT points (Espenshade, Hale, and Chung, 2004).[53]

As noted earlier, based on data from applicants to thirteen institutions in 1995, Bowen, Kurzweil, and Tobin (2005) show that first-generation college students have an admission rate that is 4.1 percentage points significantly higher than that of otherwise similar students. And although

[52] In a June 2003 survey of 451 colleges and universities, only about one-third reported considering race or ethnicity as a factor in admission decisions (National Association for College Admission Counseling, 2003).

[53] This bonus of 130 SAT points is the same amount as the estimated bonus for lower-class students at private NSCE schools shown in Table 3.5.

students from the bottom income quartile are admitted at the same rate as students from the two middle quartiles, the most well-to-do students have a small, but statistically significant, admission disadvantage compared to middle-income students that is equal to 3.1 percentage points. Both this study and the one by Espenshade, Hale, and Chung (2004) suggest that socioeconomic preferences are modest when compared with preferences based on race and ethnicity. Finally, Michael Hout's (2005) analysis of the freshmen admissions program in 2004–5 after Berkeley shifted to comprehensive review showed that the chances of admission were significantly improved for candidates who had participated in a university-sponsored outreach program; who were from low-income families; who had a job that combined academic content, responsibility, or special skills, or who worked because the family needed money; and whose personal statements indicated they had overcome obstacles to achievement.

LEGACIES

Legacy applicants have a parent or other close relative who graduated from the same institution. Legacies are valued because of their presumed greater lifelong institutional loyalties and sometimes because of their gift-giving potential in adulthood (Bowen and Bok, 1998). Legacy candidates are typically accepted at twice the rate of all other applicants (Argetsinger, 2003; Steinberg, 2003), and legacies at Harvard have nearly a three-to-one advantage (Karen, 1990, 1991b). Admission rates for legacies rival and often exceed those for blacks (Bowen and Bok, 1998; Espenshade, Chung, and Walling, 2004). It is sometimes claimed that the overall acceptance rate for legacy applicants is higher because they are more academically qualified (Bowen and Bok, 1998). But the legacy "advantage" persists when such things as SAT scores, minority status, and athletic ability are controlled (Bowen and Bok, 1998; Espenshade, Chung, and Walling, 2004). In Table 3.4 we also found a positive association between being a legacy and admission outcomes. But the effect is not statistically significant, partly because of limitations surrounding how we measure legacy applicants. Data from one selective institution indicate that the legacy advantage for both male and female applicants has fluctuated between 20 and 26 percentage points during the past two decades (Shulman and Bowen, 2001). Espenshade, Chung, and Walling (2004) show that at highly selective private institutions the legacy advantage declined only slightly from 24 percentage points for the 1980s entering cohort to 19 percentage points for the 1997 cohort.

ATHLETES

The role of athletes in university life has been a frequent source of controversy (Report of the Knight Foundation, 2001), and new evidence suggests that a substantial "academic divide" separates recruited athletes from all other students even on elite college campuses (Bowen and Levin, 2003). Athletes, however defined, enjoy a significant and growing admission advantage over other applicants. Athletes at one highly selective university who were "identified by coaches as promising candidates" were admitted at an overall rate of 78 percent and, if their SAT scores were 1150 or higher, the acceptance rate rose to 84 percent (Bowen and Bok, 1998). At other top schools, athletes are admitted at twice the rate of non-athletes (Espenshade, Chung, and Walling, 2004). The advantage if one is a "recruited athlete who appears on a coach's list" is particularly large in the Ivy League—an admission rate in 1999 nearly four times that of other candidates (Bowen and Levin, 2003).

One reason, of course, that athletes appear to have such a strong leg up in the admission competition is that coaches often pre-screen potential recruits and do not encourage them to apply if they have little chance of being admitted (Toor, 2001). Nevertheless, even controlling for SAT scores and other student attributes, athletes are still more likely than non-athletes to be admitted (Espenshade, Chung, and Walling, 2004). In the Ivy League, for example, the adjusted admission rate for recruited male athletes is 66 percent compared to just 15 percent for all other men (Bowen and Levin, 2003). The results in Table 3.4 also show a significant athlete preference. In contrast to the declining minority advantage, data from one school suggest that the athlete edge was twice as large in 1999 as it was in 1976 (Shulman and Bowen, 2001). Other evidence suggests an increasing athlete advantage over time from 25 percentage points in the 1980s to 35 percentage points by 1997 (Espenshade, Chung, and Walling, 2004).[54]

[54]Research has also examined the effects on admission probabilities of applying early, requesting financial aid, and coming from a single-parent family. In the middle SAT ranges (1300–1500), applying early decision or early action to a selective institution can increase admission probabilities by 50 percent compared to applying during the regular cycle. This is equivalent to 100 extra points on the SAT (Avery, Fairbanks, and Zeckhauser, 2003). Requesting financial aid at Harvard had no effect on admission chances, when other factors were controlled (Karen, 1990). Students from disrupted families are at a disadvantage compared to students from intact families in applying to, being accepted at, and eventually attending four-year colleges and universities. The reasons have to do with the lower level of resources in single-parent families (Lillard and Gerner, 1999).

The majority of studies that have examined factors affecting admission outcomes neglect secondary school characteristics—in particular, high schools' academic environments (Bowen and Bok, 1998; Bowen and Levin, 2003; Espenshade, Chung, and Walling, 2004; Shulman and Bowen, 2001; Walster, Cleary, and Clifford, 1971). A few include controls for high school sample stratum (Kane, 1998b) or for school type (public, parochial, or private). Private schools, especially elite boarding schools, have more success than public high schools in placing their students at the most academically selective institutions (Cookson and Persell, 1985; Karen, 1990, 1991b; Persell, Catsambis, and Cookson, 1992). Accounting for

RAISING THE ODDS OF ADMISSION

In this final section we return to a question that was first raised in chapter 2. There we discussed students' involvement in high school extracurricular activities and in a variety of what might be termed college admission enhancement strategies—behaviors that students and/or their parents engage in prior to the point of college application with an eye to increasing the odds of college admission. There is good reason to believe that extracurricular participation helps with college admission, especially if there is evidence that a student is not perfunctorily involved in many activities simply to build a résumé but displays a genuine commitment to and actually excels in a few areas.[55] As noted earlier in this chapter, merit in the eyes of elite college admission deans is more than academic merit, and extracurricular activities offer an additional avenue through which applicants can display the qualities that colleges and universities value.

Research appears to confirm these expectations. Jason Kaufman and Jay Gabler (2004) have investigated the relationship between extracurricular

---

school type fails to capture anything intrinsic about the institution or the quality of the educational experience it offers. At the same time, private schools evaluate applicants on many of the same criteria that elite postsecondary institutions use, and they provide college counseling services and contacts with college admission officers that give private school applicants an edge (Menand, 2003; McDonough, 1997; Yaqub, 2002). Lillard and Gerner (1999) include indicators for the percent of a high school's class going to college and whether the high school is in an urban setting, but these contextual measures are treated as control variables and not featured in the analysis or in their presentation of results. Attewell (2001) not only distinguishes high schools by type—private, exam public, and nonexam public—but also by whether they are "star" high schools. Wightman (1997) includes a measure of undergraduate college selectivity (average SAT or ACT scores of the entering first-year class) and finds it is not a factor in explaining current law school admission practices. Espenshade, Hale, and Chung (2005) test a "frog pond" model of elite college admission proposed by Attewell (2001). They operationalize high school academic context as secondary school–average SAT score and number of AP exams per high school senior. Data on more than 45,000 applications to three elite universities show that high school academic environment has a negative effect on college admission, controlling for individual student scholastic ability. A given applicant's chances of being accepted are reduced if he or she comes from a high school with relatively more highly talented students, that is, if the applicant is a comparatively small frog in a big pond. Direct evidence on high school class rank produces similar findings. School reputation or prestige has a counterbalancing positive effect on college admission. These results suggest that institutional gatekeepers are susceptible to context effects, but the influence of school variables is small relative to individual student characteristics.

[55] One New Jersey college guidance counselor has commented, "Factors other than academic performance and test results—extracurricular activities, artistic talent or some other intangible attribute—come into play more and more when college admissions officials sort through the deluge of applications they receive even from stellar students" (Stern, 2006). Also see Hernández (1997) and Toor (2001).

participation in high school and the probability of attending a four-year college or university. They find that extracurricular "cultural" participation makes some difference. Students who have had hands-on training in the arts have a higher chance of going to college, and having parents who have an interest in the arts boosts candidates' chances of attending an elite college. At the elite college level, being involved with the student newspaper or yearbook benefits boys more than girls, although participation rates in these stereotypically female activities are higher for young women.[56] The authors conclude by saying, "A strong case can be made for continuing efforts to provide extra-curricular opportunities for students that will build their human and cultural capital in ways not ordinarily addressed in the secondary school curriculum" (165). In this section we ask whether there is evidence that doing any of the things customarily believed to influence the odds of college acceptance has the desired effect. Is there anything that parents and their high-achieving children can do to influence outcomes in a period marked by a hectic, at times frenetic, and increasingly competitive rush to be accepted by a name-brand school?

We begin by looking at data in Table 3.8 on the differential participation in extracurricular activities by applicants to public and private NSCE institutions. These data come from the ETS Student Descriptive Questionnaire and are based on students' reports of their extracurricular engagement in high school. Students can indicate on this questionnaire in which of up to twenty-three different extracurricular activities they participated in each of their four years of senior high school. We count students as having participated in a specific activity only if they did so for at least two years. A one-year involvement is ignored because it is likely to be interpreted by admission deans as a half-hearted commitment. All activities are summed to get a count of total extracurricular participation. In addition, the twenty-three activities have been grouped into seven categories, each of which contains relatively similar kinds of activities. Students may also indicate whether they played a leadership role in an organization by, for example, being an officer and whether they won any

---

[56] These findings are interesting on several levels. First, Kaufman and Gabler (2004) find that the effects of exposure to the arts, either directly through hands-on training or indirectly through parents' involvement, are generally the same for young men and young women. Second, the gendered effects of participating in the school newspaper or student yearbook are an example of what Persell, Catsambis, and Cookson (1992) talk about when they discuss the differential rates at which boys and girls convert educational, cultural, and economic assets into attendance at selective colleges and universities. Finally, although one might expect that women's higher participation rates in student newspaper and yearbook would benefit them more than men, selective colleges are often looking for unique individuals (Kaufman and Gabler, 2004).

TABLE 3.8
Participation in Extracurricular Activities and Use of Other Selective Admission
Enhancement Strategies for Applicants to All, Public, and Private
NSCE Institutions, Fall 1997

Item	Percent of Applicants in Each Category		
	Total	Public	Private
Extracurricular Activities/Awards/Leadership Positions[a]			
Large Number of Total Activities	14.6	15.1	14.3
Large Number of Total Awards/Leadership Positions	10.8	8.8	11.8
Large Number of Academic Activities	12.8	8.8	14.9
Large Number of Academic Awards/Leadership Positions	8.0	4.4	9.9**[b]
Large Number of Performing Arts Activities	10.8	9.9	11.2
Large Number of Performing Arts Awards/Leadership Positions	9.5	9.0	9.8
Large Number of Athletic Activities	24.4	27.1	23.0
Large Number of Athletic Awards/Leadership Positions	7.0	7.2	6.8
Large Number of Community Service Activities	6.9	6.9	6.8
Large Number of Community Service Awards/Leadership Positions	8.9	5.4	10.7*
Large Number of Cultural Diversity Activities	9.8	7.7	11.0
Large Number of Cultural Diversity Awards/Leadership Positions	18.4	16.8	19.2
Large Number of Career-Oriented Activities	16.9	17.5	16.6
Large Number of Career-Oriented Awards/Leadership Positions	5.7	3.8	6.7
Held Part-time Job in High School	33.5	52.0	23.8***
Other Admission Enhancement Strategies[c]			
Attend and graduate from magnet, parochial/religious, or private high school to improve chances of college acceptance	20.2	13.8	23.5**
Attend and graduate from private high school to improve chances of college acceptance	10.1	5.1	12.8***
Participate in some kind of academic enrichment program(s) during high school years	54.2	49.0	56.9
Participate in college-sponsored academic enrichment program(s) during high school years	29.2	20.2	33.9**

(*Continued*)

Table 3.8 (*Continued*)

| Item | Percent of Applicants in Each Category | | |
	Total	Public	Private
Take an SAT, PSAT, or ACT test preparation course	46.7	49.2	45.4
Use professional consultant or private tutor to select colleges and/or help complete application forms	18.2	13.2	20.8*
Visit six or more colleges before applying to any schools	23.6	19.3	25.8

Source: Educational Testing Service Student Descriptive Questionnaire; National Study of College Experience.

[a]Data on the number of extracurricular activities, awards, and leadership positions come from the ETS Student Descriptive Questionnaire (SDQ) and are based on information from students who completed the SDQ and whose records could be matched to the NSCE student sample. The SDQ contains information about 23 individual extracurricular activities and whether students participated in each of these in grades 9, 10, 11, and 12. A student had to participate in an activity for two or more years to be counted here. Moreover, SDQ respondents were asked to indicate for each activity whether they have "held a major office or position of leadership" or have "received an award or special recognition for achievement in an activity." These 23 separate activities have been grouped into seven broader categories, using the definitions in Table 2.5, and a total category. Definitions for what constitutes a "large" number of activities or awards/leadership positions are as follows: total activities (9 or 10), total awards (5–10), academic activities (3 or 4), academic awards (2–4), performing arts activities (3–6), performing arts awards (2–4), athletic activities (2 or 3), athletic awards (2 or 3), community service activities (3), community service awards (2 or 3), cultural diversity activities (2 or 3), cultural diversity awards (1–3), career-oriented activities (1 or 2), and career-oriented awards (1 or 2).

[b]The presence of asterisks indicates a statistically significant difference between the percentages for public and private school applicants.

[c]Data on the use of other admission enhancement strategies come from the NSCE survey.

*p < .05 **p < .01 ***p < .001

awards as a result of their participation. We aggregated the numbers of these leadership positions and awards across all activities and, alternatively, grouped them into seven categories.[57] Finally, after examining the distributions for the number of activities students participated in and for

[57]Our measure of extracurricular participation and leadership does not necessarily equate with the information an admission officer would have. For example, while an admission officer would know that a student played varsity football, basketball, and baseball all in the same year, SDQ data only indicate whether or not a student played a varsity sport. So where the admission officer would see three activities, we observe only one. Also, while an admission officer could see that a student was captain and MVP of the varsity football team as a senior and received an award for football at the state level, SDQ data only indicate that the student received an (one) award or leadership position as a varsity athlete. Further, in our analysis a student who received the most improved award on one varsity team would be treated the same as this football superstar. This is important to stress particularly because admission officers like "angular" as opposed to well-rounded students (Toor,

the number of leadership positions or awards they held, we determined for each group of activities and for the total of all activities what constitutes a "large" number of activities and a "large" number of leadership positions or awards by selecting threshold values in such a way that fewer than 20 percent of reporting students fall into the top category.[58]

In the majority of instances in Table 3.8, applicants to private institutions appear to be higher achievers than do students who apply to public schools. They are more likely than their counterparts at public institutions to have a large number of extracurricular participations and frequently to have been a major officer in their club or organization or received special recognition for their participation. For instance, students who apply to private colleges and universities are more likely to have been involved in a large number of academically oriented activities (academic honor society, computer activity, debate and public speaking, or a science or math club) than are students who are aiming toward public schools (15 versus 9 percent). They are also significantly more likely to have won awards or held leadership positions in these activities (10 versus 4 percent). Similarly, applicants to private schools are significantly more likely to have received special recognition for their community service involvement, which includes community and religious activities as well as government or political clubs or activities (11 percent of private school applicants versus 5 percent of applicants to public schools). It is noteworthy that when there are significant differences between private and public school applicants in extracurricular engagements, the differences show up less in the quantity of participation than in the quality of the involvement, if we take as evidence of quality the number of leadership positions earned or awards won. The only activity in which public school applicants have a significant edge over their private school counterparts concerns holding a part-time job during high school. Roughly half of all students applying to public colleges and universities report this kind of involvement, compared to about a quarter of applicants to private schools.

The lower portion of Table 3.8 reports on the use of a variety of admission enhancement strategies that were first discussed in chapter 2.[59] More

---

2001), and the angular applicants are not able to convey their angular status to us through the SDQ data. In fact, our data can make angular students look inactive in extracurriculars because all of their extracurriculars and awards and leadership positions fall into one activity or one category.

[58] There are two exceptions to this coding scheme. First, roughly one-quarter of all reporting students participated in a large number of athletic extracurricular activities. In addition, holding a part-time job during high school—something that a third of students did—does not have a "large" category. Students reported that they held a job or that they did not.

[59] Some of the percentages in this table may differ slightly from those reported in chapter 2. In the previous chapter an individual student in the combined applicant pool was the unit of observation, whereas in this chapter the unit of observation is the application.

than half (54 percent) of all applicants indicated on the NSCE survey that they participated in classes, workshops, or other academic enrichment activities during high school that were designed to supplement their high school coursework. Nearly half (47 percent) said they enrolled in at least one test preparation course (for the SAT, ACT, or PSAT examination). At the other extreme, just one out of every ten applicants attended a private secondary school for the avowed purpose of enhancing their chances of being admitted to a top college or university.

However, as indicated by the last two columns of Table 3.8, there are some important differences between public and private school applicants in the use of these strategies. They are in general adopted much more frequently by applicants to private colleges and universities. These applicants are significantly more likely than applicants to public institutions to elect to attend a secondary school other than their neighborhood public school with the aim of improving their college admission chances, to participate in college-sponsored enrichment activities, and to use a private tutor or professional consultant to help select colleges and/or complete the application form. Only with regard to test preparation activities does the frequency of participation slightly favor applicants to public universities, but the difference is not statistically significant.

In Table 3.9 we examine how extracurricular participation and the adoption of various admission enhancement strategies are related to admission outcomes at private colleges and universities. It should be emphasized at the outset that none of the information in this table is able to establish a cause-and-effect relationship. To be able to say, for example, that having a large number of academic awards or leadership positions leads directly to a higher probability of being admitted to an elite institution would require different kinds of data. We would need an experimental design in which a randomly chosen fraction of our sample was admonished to work hard at academic extracurricular activities and a control group that was not. With the observational (or nonexperimental) data at our disposal, we are at best able to detect relationships—not causal mechanisms—between behaviors and admission outcomes.

The first two columns of Table 3.9 show the percentage of students who are admitted, depending on whether they have intensive extracurricular involvement or adopted particular admission enhancement strategies. The top portion of the table confirms what almost everyone believes— that being able to list a large number of extracurricular activities on one's application (and the awards and leadership positions that can go along with such participation) is associated with a significantly higher probability of elite private college admission. More than one-third of students (35 percent) who claim participation in many extracurricular activities overall are admitted in comparison with one-fifth of students (21 percent)

TABLE 3.9

Participation in Extracurricular Activities, Use of Other Selective Admission Enhancement Strategies, and Acceptance to Private NSCE Institutions, Fall 1997

| | Percent Admitted | | Odds Ratios[b] | |
	Did Have or Use (1)	Did Not Have or Use (2)	Gross Effect (3)	Net Effect (4)
Extracurricular Activities/Awards/Leadership Positions[a]				
Large Number of Total Activities	35.2**[c]	21.0	2.15**	2.49***
Large Number of Total Awards/Leadership Positions	33.9**	21.5	1.17	1.25
Large Number of Academic Activities	31.1*	21.6	1.10	1.18
Large Number of Academic Awards/Leadership Positions	36.9**	21.5	3.16***	3.19***
Large Number of Performing Arts Activities	27.5	22.4	1.61	1.68
Large Number of Performing Arts Awards/Leadership Positions	29.4	22.3	1.13	1.21
Large Number of Athletic Activities	20.2	23.8	0.95	0.97
Large Number of Athletic Awards/Leadership Positions	19.7	23.2	0.92	0.91
Large Number of Community Service Activities	37.1*	22.0	2.13*	2.36**
Large Number of Community Service Awards/Leadership Positions	25.0	22.8	0.73	0.81
Large Number of Cultural Diversity Activities	25.9	22.6	1.01	1.08
Large Number of Cultural Diversity Awards/Leadership Positions	28.7	21.6	0.87	0.92
Large Number of Career-Oriented Activities	22.0	23.2	1.01	1.08
Large Number of Career-Oriented Awards/Leadership Positions	16.2	23.5	0.35*	0.40*

(Continued)

TABLE 3.9 (*Continued*)

| | Percent Admitted | | | Odds Ratios[b] | |
	Did Have or Use (1)	Did Not Have or Use (2)		Gross Effect (3)	Net Effect (4)
Item					
Held Part-time Job in High School	21.6	23.4		1.16	1.11
Other Admission Enhancement Strategies					
Attend and graduate from magnet, parochial/religious, or private high school to improve chances of college acceptance	31.0**	21.3		—	—
Attend and graduate from private high school to improve chances of college acceptance	31.6*	22.4		—	—
Participate in some kind of academic enrichment program(s) during high school years	23.6	23.6		0.86	0.83
Participate in college-sponsored academic enrichment program(s) during high school years	22.7	24.1		0.79	0.77
Take an SAT, PSAT, or ACT test preparation course	19.7**	26.8		0.48***	0.47***
Use professional consultant or private tutor to select colleges and/or help complete application forms	17.7*	25.1		0.87	0.87
Visit six or more colleges before applying to any schools	25.2	23.1		0.80	0.87

Source: Educational Testing Service Student Descriptive Questionnaire; National Study of College Experience.

[a]See Note a in Table 3.8 for definitions and sources.

[b]Odds ratios are estimated from logistic regression equations using the outcome of the admission decision as the dependent variable (coded 1 if admitted, and 0 otherwise). Effects are estimated by incorporating these variables into the full regression model 6 shown in Table 3.4. The reference

group in each case consists of applicants who did not have a large number of activities or awards or who did not use a particular admission enhancement strategy. The "gross" regression effect is obtained by adding extracurricular participation or admission enhancement strategy variables one at a time to the full regression model in Table 3.4. For example, the two total activity variables were considered as one set of variables and entered together; the 13 individual extracurricular activity variables were entered together as one set; and variables for other admission enhancement strategies shown in the lower half of Table 3.9 were entered individually. The "net" regression effects were estimated by incorporating all of the extracurricular and other admission enhancement strategy variables together into one regression. Four alternative net regression effect models were estimated, using different specifications. In each one, the two high school choice strategies were dropped because of high collinearity with the high school type variable already in the regression model. Whether an applicant took a test preparation course, used a private college counselor, or visited a large number of colleges before applying appeared in each of the four specifications. Tabulated odds ratios corresponding to the net effect of total extracurricular activity, having some academic enrichment, taking test preparation, hiring a private counselor, and visiting six or more colleges were taken from the model that included two total extracurricular activity variables and whether a student participated in some academic enrichment program. Effects of the 13 separate extracurricular activity variables were taken from the specification that substituted these variables for the two total activity variables. The effect of having some college-sponsored academic enrichment was estimated from the model that includes two total activity variables and that substitutes college-sponsored academic enrichment for any kind of academic enrichment program(s). Odds ratios are extremely robust across the four alternative specifications.

[c] The presence of asterisks indicates a statistically significant difference between the percentages of applicants who had a large number of activities/awards and those who did not, or between the percentages of applicants who used a particular enhancement strategy and those who did not.

*p < .05 **p < .01 ***p < .001

who have lower levels of engagement. Similar proportions characterize admission outcomes depending on whether students were leaders in their organizations and/or received many recognitions or awards.

But this finding gives no guidance to students about how they should concentrate their extracurricular energies on the assumption that no student can "do it all." Grouping extracurricular activities offers some clues. Significant admission advantages are associated with students who were actively involved in a large number of high school academic activities and who were noted for excelling in these activities by becoming a major officer or earning awards or other honors. The admission edge that is associated with these kinds of academically oriented activities is roughly the same order of magnitude as that for overall extracurricular excellence. Being heavily involved in community service organizations seems to be associated with similar admission rewards. The admission rate for such students approaches 40 percent in comparison with a much lower likelihood of acceptance (22 percent) if students evidence little or no such engagement. For the remaining groupings of extracurricular activities, there is not a significant difference between admission probabilities for students who evidence much participation and those who participate only a little or not at all. In general, however, the small differences in admission outcomes that do exist tend to favor students who have participated a lot. The notable exceptions are for athletics and career-oriented activities (such as a co-op work program, junior ROTC, or other career-oriented activity) where too much involvement might be associated with a smaller chance of college admission. The same could also be said of holding a part-time job during high school.

The lower portion of Table 3.9 examines the relation between acceptance rates and the adoption of particular admission enhancement strategies. Three patterns are evident. First, attending a secondary school other than the neighborhood public school to which one has been assigned is associated with a significantly higher probability of being admitted. The differential is on the order of 10 percentage points, a substantial difference considering that the average acceptance rate at private NSCE institutions is less than 25 percent.[60] Second, there are several strategies that appear not to be associated with acceptance rates. The chances of being admitted are essentially the same whether or not one participates in academic enrichment activities in high school or visits a large number of colleges and universities prior to applying. Third, and perhaps of greatest interest, taking a test preparation course and using a professional consul-

---

[60] Recall from models 5 and 6 in Table 3.4 that graduating from a private (instead of a non-magnet public) high school is associated with significantly higher odds of admission at private NSCE colleges and universities.

tant to help with the college selection and application process are both significantly negatively related to being accepted. One reason this result is surprising, apart from the fact that many prospective students and their parents believe that it does help, is that admission deans are unlikely to know for sure which applicants are adopting these behaviors.[61]

The third and fourth columns of Table 3.9 contain odds ratios associated with extracurricular participation and electing different strategies thought to promote admission chances. Estimates have been developed by incorporating these variables into model 6 in Table 3.4—the full regression model with interaction terms. The column for "gross" effects includes, in addition to the predictor variables in Table 3.4, either the extracurricular activities or the admission-enhancing strategies. Odds ratios that reflect "net" effects include all of the potential predictor variables. It is evident first of all that there are no differences worth mentioning between gross and net effects. Moreover, the following are significantly and positively related to admission outcomes: (1) participating in a large number of extracurricular activities of any kind, (2) emphasizing the quality of participation in academic activities by becoming an important officeholder or receiving other kinds of recognitions for meritorious achievement, and (3) becoming involved with a significant number of community service organizations or projects. These positive associations, the largest of which is for academic excellence outside the classroom, reinforce conclusions based on straightforward tabulations of acceptance rates shown in the first and second columns. In addition, these associations are quantitatively important; the odds of being admitted are more than twice as high for applicants who engage in these activities compared to those who do not.

---

[61] A given student can expect to gain a very small admissions advantage from SAT coaching. First, there is evidence in Table 3.4 that higher SAT and ACT scores are associated with greater chances of admission to public and private NSCE institutions. Second, taking an SAT review course can boost scores, though perhaps not by as much as commercial test preparation services claim. Web sites for the Princeton Review (http://www.princetonreview .com/home.asp, October 18, 2006) and Kaplan Test Prep and Admissions (http://www .kaptest.com/sat, October 18, 2006) guarantee higher test scores or they will refund your initial investment. The Sylvan Learning Center boasts, "After working with Sylvan, three out of four students raise their SAT score 160 points or more" (http://tutoring.sylvanlearning .com/, October 18, 2006). Peterson's online course for the SAT guarantees to raise a student's total SAT score by at least 200 points (out of a maximum total score of 2400) if students complete the full-length version of the course (http://www.petersons.com/, October 18, 2006). Powers and Rock (1999) show that many of these claims are wildly exaggerated. They surveyed a representative sample of 6,700 1995–96 SAT I test-takers and asked respondents about coaching programs in which they had participated. Based on seven alternative models of analysis, Powers and Rock (1999) conclude that coaching (including all special test preparation programs offered to students, excluding those offered by students' high schools) raises the SAT I verbal test score between 6 and 12 points; the estimated improvement on the SAT I math test ranges from 13 to 26 points.

On the other hand, some of the student behaviors are significantly negatively associated with admission chances. Excelling in career-oriented activities is associated with 60 or 65 percent lower odds of admission. These activities include ROTC and co-op work programs. They might also encompass 4-H Clubs, Future Farmers of America, and other activities that suggest that students are somewhat undecided about their academic futures. In addition, our results suggest that taking a test preparation course is associated with at least a 50 percent decline in the odds of being admitted to an elite college, after controlling for the SAT or ACT score that a student receives.[62]

Although the regression results in columns 3 and 4 generally agree with simpler tabulations in the first two columns, there are instances where regression points to a different conclusion. The apparent admission advantage associated with having a large number of leadership positions or awards in extracurricular activities or with participating in a large number of academic activities is not confirmed by the regression results. In addition, whereas the more straightforward tabulations suggest that hiring a private tutor or a professional consultant to help with the college search and application process could be a disadvantage, regression results imply that doing so is not significantly related to the likelihood of being admitted.[63]

---

[62]It is not entirely clear how one should interpret this unexpected outcome, which is found in applications to private and public institutions and in both the regression results and in simpler tabulations. A higher proportion of NSCE applicants (29 percent) than all SAT test-takers in 1995–96 (12 percent) received test preparation from a private company or from some source other than their high school or another high school (Powers and Rock, 1999). At the same time, coached and uncoached NSCE students differ in ways that are common to all SAT takers (see Powers and Rock, 1999). Among NSCE applicants, for example, those who seek coaching are significantly more likely to (1) be Asian students, (2) come from upper-middle- or upper-class family backgrounds, (3) have very well-educated fathers and mothers, and (4) be applying to a private instead of a public NSCE institution. It is possible that the answer has more to do with omitted variable bias. The coefficient in our regression models on taking a test preparation course could be biased (up or down) if there is another variable that is not included in our model that is correlated both with test preparation and with the admission decision. For example, it may be that "weaker" prospects are more likely to feel a need to take a test preparation course. Even though admission deans do not know who has taken test preparation, being a weaker student may reveal itself in other ways (for instance, through teacher recommendations). Briggs (2004) reports that students who are coached on the SAT are more likely than uncoached students to have used a private tutor during high school to help with homework and to have underachieved on the PSAT test relative to their high school GPA in math.

[63]Two potential enhancement strategies, both associated with attending a secondary school other than the public school to which a student has been assigned, have been omitted from the logistic regressions reported in Table 3.9 because they are so highly correlated with high school type, which is already included in the regression models in Table 3.4.

Our findings for public institutions (shown in Table C.3.1) are generally consistent with these results. Students who have earned a large number of awards or recognitions for their extracurricular participation, especially for academically oriented activities, have a significantly higher probability of being admitted than do other students. Against a backdrop of an average admission rate of 55 percent at public universities, the differential advantage is 25 percentage points for excelling at extracurricular activities in general and 36 percentage points for excellence in academic activities. Intensive involvement with either the performing arts or with career-oriented activities appears to be related to a slightly diminished chance of being admitted. Finally, students who have taken test preparation courses are significantly less likely to be accepted than other students. The admission "penalty" associated with this kind of coaching is roughly 25 percentage points at public universities. Regression results have been excluded from Table C.3.1 because the estimates are too unstable.

Summary

In this chapter we have examined factors affecting who is admitted to academically selective colleges and universities. We argued that highly selective institutions have choices about which students to admit. These choices are constrained by the number of seats in the first-year class and (in some cases) by financial aid budgets. But within these constraints, colleges and universities admit that subset of applicants whose anticipated academic and nonacademic contributions to campus life and to society in later years are most likely to advance an institution's mission. The model we developed implies that a candidate's merit, as seen through the eyes of elite college admission officers, consists of more than academic merit. It can encompass a full range of student characteristics that add value to a campus community.

Our analysis is based on data from seven institutions in the National Study of College Experience, representing 79,222 applications for the fall of 1997 entering student cohort. The available information includes students' sex, citizenship, athlete and legacy status, type of high school attended, and a full range of academic performance measures. But the principal focus is on the roles played by a student's race or ethnicity and social class background. Underrepresented minority students have an admission advantage compared to white applicants. Black applicants receive a boost equivalent to 3.8 ACT points at public NSCE institutions and to 310 SAT points (out of 1600) at private institutions, on an all-other-things-equal basis. The Hispanic advantage is less than one ACT point at public schools and equal to 130 SAT points at private institutions.

At public institutions, where the overall acceptance rate is 55 percent for the schools in our sample, acceptance rates are 54 percent for whites, 80 percent for blacks, and 57 percent for Hispanics, when otherwise statistically equivalent applicants are compared. At the private NSCE schools, which have an average acceptance rate of 24 percent, 26 percent of whites, 51 percent of blacks, and 37 percent of Hispanics are admitted, again on an all-other-things-equal basis.

Asian students face an apparent disadvantage in admission compared to whites. At public NSCE institutions, the average acceptance rate is 46 percent for Asians (versus 54 percent for statistically equivalent white students). And at private schools, 16 percent of Asian students are admitted compared to 26 percent of otherwise comparable white students. An unknown proportion of the Asian-white gap in admission chances could be due to factors that admission officers have access to in applicants' folders and that are not in our data set.

Social class background generally receives less weight in admission decisions than an applicant's race or ethnicity. But it does matter, especially at the private schools in our sample. At these institutions, the admission advantage for students from lower-class family backgrounds is equivalent to 130 SAT points. Working-class students receive a boost equal to 70 SAT points. The admission preference accorded to low-income students appears to be reserved largely for nonwhite students. For black, Hispanic, and Asian applicants to private NSCE schools, the likelihood of being admitted is greatest for students from lower-class backgrounds (87 percent for blacks and 65 percent for Hispanics), on an all-other-things-equal basis. This likelihood then falls steeply, typically reaching a minimum for applicants from upper-class families (17 percent for blacks and 22 percent for Hispanics). By contrast, admission chances for whites at private schools are highest for students from middle- and upper-class family backgrounds (28 percent). Lower-class whites are admitted just 8 percent of the time. The acceptance rate for working-class white students rises to 18 percent, but it is still less than the 23 percent rate for upper-class whites. Our findings concerning the substantial low-income preference for nonwhite students at highly selective private institutions come to a different conclusion than recent research conducted by other scholars.

The customary racial and ethnic labels we attach to students can hide a great deal of heterogeneity. We disaggregated black applicants into those we and others have called "descendants" (meaning the descendants of the American slave population—students who belong to the fourth-or-higher generation of immigrants and who identify themselves as black and no other race) and non-descendants. Descendants make up roughly one-half of the overall NSCE applicant pool, but their proportions vary substantially depending on whether public or private institutions are considered. Descendants account for two-thirds of black applicants to public universities, but just one-third (36 percent) of black candidates at private colleges. At both types of NSCE schools, black descendants are accepted at somewhat higher rates than are black non-descendants.

Finally, we explored potential associations between college admission outcomes and extracurricular participation in high school. We examined both the quantity of this participation and its quality, as measured by the number of officer or leadership positions held or awards that were won. After controlling for a broad range of student traits, we found that the quality of academic excellence outside the classroom (for example, assuming leadership roles in an academic honor society, computer activity, debate or public speaking club, or science/math activity) is significantly and positively associated with college admission. So, too, are having a large number of extracurricular activities in general and becoming involved in a wide variety of community service projects. At the same time, being an officer or winning awards for such career-oriented activities as ROTC or co-op work programs has a significantly negative association with admission outcomes at highly selective institutions.

Chapter Four

THE ENTERING FRESHMAN CLASS

INTRODUCTION

We have discussed who applies to selective colleges and who is accepted. Yet it is the students who actually attend elite universities who reap the most long-term career and financial benefits. Who are these matriculants? Sometimes elite college students are depicted by the media as the brightest and most accomplished students the nation has to offer.[1] At other times they are portrayed primarily as individuals born with silver spoons in their mouths (Golden, 2006; Kaufman, 2001; Leonhardt, 2004). Such accounts leave us with contradictory impressions about the students who attend our nation's most selective colleges and universities.

In this chapter we construct a more systematic and comprehensive portrait of elite college matriculants. First, we show how students who are admitted to NSCE institutions differ in their propensity to enroll depending on their race and socioeconomic status. After that, we discuss the academic achievements of NSCE matriculants prior to college. Next, we explore students' racial, multiracial, immigrant, and national origins. Then we examine how matriculants vary on a range of socioeconomic indicators, including parents' education and occupation as well as family income and assets. Finally, we turn our attention to the broader contexts in which elite college students grow up by examining both the racial and socioeconomic composition of matriculants' high schools and neighborhoods.

The data used here differ from those employed in the previous two chapters. First, while chapter 2 examined data about applicants and chapter 3 explored data about applications, this chapter concentrates on students who enrolled at one of our NSCE schools. Second, the previous two chapters relied on data from seven NSCE institutions; this chapter contains data from eight. Third, while the data used in chapters 2 and 3 pertain to students who entered college in 1997, most of the data in this

---

[1] For example, David Brooks (2002: 19) writes with some exaggeration, "The students in the competitive colleges . . . got straight A's in high school and stratospheric board scores. They've usually started a few companies, cured at least three formerly fatal diseases, mastered a half dozen or so languages and marched for breast cancer awareness through Tibet while tutoring the locals on conflict resolution skills and environmental awareness."

chapter encompass a broader set of students—those who entered elite colleges in the 1980s, 1993, and 1997.[2]

YIELD RATES

Yield rates provide the connection between the group of admitted students and those who subsequently matriculate. While being admitted to an elite college no doubt gives students some satisfaction, they cannot have the college experience at that school and the supposed benefits that come along with it unless they enroll (Behrman, Rosenzweig, and Taubman, 1996; Brewer, Eide, and Ehrenberg, 1999; Daniel, Black, and Smith, 1997; Kane, 1998b; Loury and Garman, 1995). Given the advantages of elite college attendance, it is important to understand which students capitalize on their thick acceptance envelopes by matriculating. Overall, about 49 percent of those admitted to one of our NSCE institutions in 1997 chose to enroll. This yield rate (the percentage of those admitted who matriculate) differs depending on the type of institution to which students are accepted. As Table 4.1 indicates, students admitted to a private NSCE college are about nine percentage points more likely to enroll (54 percent) than students admitted to a public NSCE college (45 percent).[3]

Yield rates are correlated with students' racial group affiliation. At private institutions, whites are the most likely to enroll (57 percent), followed by Asians and Hispanics. Black students are the least likely to matriculate, with only 46 percent doing so. Bowen, Kurzweil, and Tobin (2005: 110) and Bowen and Bok (1998: 34) provide a possible explanation for the lower yield among black students. Selective universities' strong interest in admitting the limited number of high-achieving black students

---

[2] Universities were asked to supply data for the earliest year their student information was stored electronically. The precise year during the 1980s that universities began doing so varies by institution. The 1980s cohort is thus used to refer collectively to the following entry cohorts, with the number in parentheses representing the number of schools providing data from that year: 1982 (1), 1983 (3), 1985 (1), 1986 (2), and 1988 (1). See appendix A for more details. As in previous chapters, differences mentioned in the text are statistically significant at the .05 level except where noted.

[3] There are at least three possible explanations for this result. One could be that students who apply to private institutions are more serious about attending if they are admitted because private colleges have more expensive application fees and lengthier applications than public colleges. The difference in yield rates could also reflect the fact that our private colleges are slightly more selective than our public institutions, and students have a tendency to enroll in the most selective college to which they are admitted (Flanagan, 2001; Mayher, 1998). A third possible explanation is that private NSCE institutions admit a larger proportion of their students under early decision programs that require students to matriculate if accepted. Our data do not permit us to investigate this possibility.

TABLE 4.1
Yield Rates at Private and Public NSCE Colleges,
by Race and Socioeconomic Status
NSCE Application Data: Fall 1997 Cohort

	Percentage of Accepted Students Who Enrolled in	
Characteristic	Private NSCE Colleges	Public NSCE Colleges
Total (N = 3,829)	54.1	45.1
Race		
White	56.5	44.8
Black	46.2	48.7
Hispanic	50.2	44.9
Asian	52.1	44.1
Socioeconomic Status		
Upper	67.9	62.7
Upper-Middle	55.5	47.8
Middle	49.3	40.3
Working	53.3	43.8
Lower	55.9	26.2

Source: National Study of College Experience.
Note: Racial and social class differences in yield rates at both types of colleges are statistically significant at the .001 level.

who apply results in blacks having more college acceptances from which to choose, thereby lowering the chances that they will enroll in any one particular institution. Yield rates at public colleges exhibit a different pattern. Even though enrollment rates for black students are roughly the same at private and public NSCE schools, blacks admitted to public institutions have the highest yield rates (49 percent). Hispanics, whites, and Asians are about four or five percentage points less likely to enroll.

For many students going off to selective colleges, the prospect of succeeding academically poses intellectual challenges. But for parents, the financial demands can also be intimidating. So it is not surprising that yield rates vary in systematic ways with family socioeconomic status. At private NSCE institutions, yield rates are related to social class in a U-shaped pattern; they are greatest for upper- and lower-income families and least for the middle class. With a yield rate of 68 percent, upper-class students are by far the most likely to matriculate. Yield rates are also above 50 percent for other social classes—except for the middle class, only 49 percent of whom enroll. Our finding is not unique. Other research also suggests that middle-class students at elite universities have the lowest enrollment rates (Gose, 1998; McPherson and Schapiro, 1991).

Some scholars have suggested that middle-class students are less likely to attend the most selective colleges because they are wooed away by merit-based scholarships from less selective universities that more selective colleges will not match (Bowen, Kurzweil, and Tobin, 2005: 110; Collison, 1993; Gose, 1998; Herring, 2005).[4]

While low and high SES students are offered merit scholarships as well, there are several reasons why middle-class students are believed to have more motivation to accept them. First, middle-class families are often surprised by the amount colleges expect them to pay under need-based aid formulas (Gose, 1998; Herring, 2005). In contrast, low SES students receive a significant amount of need-based aid from almost all of the institutions at which they are accepted, making merit scholarships at less selective schools less enticing (Avery and Hoxby, 2004: 268; Bowen, Kurzweil, and Tobin, 2005: 110). Second, even though both middle and high SES students would save money by attending a less selective school on a merit scholarship, differences in family resources can cause college costs to be a more important factor in middle than high SES students' college choices (Avery and Hoxby, 2004: 268; Gose, 1998; McGinn, 2005).

In contrast to the picture at private schools, yield rates at public institutions are highest for upper social classes and lowest for low-income families. Upper-class applicants who are admitted enroll nearly two-thirds (63 percent) of the time. One reason they are most likely to enroll may be that students from higher social class families are more likely to apply under early decision programs (Avery, Fairbanks, and Zeckhauser, 2003) and are thus bound to attend if admitted. Upper-class students' greater yield rate may also be partially the result of their being more likely to be legacies, because legacy students are thought to be more likely to matriculate (Toor, 2001). Finally, since upper-class students do not have to worry as much about college costs, they may be more able to select schools on the basis of pure preference. College counselors suggest that upper-class students typically prefer to attend the most selective college to which they are admitted (Flanagan, 2001; Mayher, 1998), making them especially likely to gravitate toward NSCE institutions.

Yield rates for lower-income students at public universities typically fall to nearly one-quarter (26 percent). McDonough (1997) offers one possible explanation for lower-class students' less frequent enrollment. She finds that low SES families typically value a college degree from any type of institution and are not as attuned to the possible benefits of attending a more selective college. They may therefore decide that it would

---

[4]Less selective institutions offer merit scholarships to students at the top of their applicant pool in an attempt to improve the academic quality of their student bodies and thus rise in college rankings (Frank, 2005; Hong, 2005; McGinn, 2005).

be better for students to reject a more prestigious public university and attend a nearby public college or local community college. That way, parents reason, students can save money by living at home and perhaps continue the part-time employment they held during high school.[5]

HIGH SCHOOL ACADEMIC ACHIEVEMENT

It should come as no surprise that our NSCE matriculants are exceptionally well prepared for college. Nevertheless, racial gaps do exist. Asian students are typically on top and, on average, blacks are at the bottom. As Table 4.2 indicates, 64 percent of matriculants who report class rank are in the top 10 percent of their high school class, and 60 percent of those reporting high school grade point average (GPA) have averages of A or above.[6] On both measures, Asians are likely to exhibit the most academic success, with Hispanics and then whites not far behind. Blacks, on the other hand, do not possess high class ranks or GPAs nearly as frequently. They are 33 percentage points less likely than Asians to be ranked in the top decile and 30 percentage points less likely to have a GPA of A or above. Yet, despite black students' lower percentages in the top categories, they still perform well in high school, as one would expect of all students who are admitted to selective colleges and universities. More than two-thirds of enrolled black students are in the top fifth of their class or earn a GPA of A− or above.

While high school grades and class rank reveal students' academic achievements within the classroom, SAT scores provide an indication of how students compare nationally. NSCE students receive an average score of 1285 on the SAT.[7] Only 11 percent receive a score lower than

---

[5] Our yield rates by socioeconomic status differ somewhat from those reported by Bowen, Kurzweil, and Tobin (2005: 109). They find that the likelihood of matriculating decreases monotonically with greater family income in their sample of public and private colleges, while we find that yield rates trend in the opposite direction at public colleges and form a more U-shaped pattern at private colleges. This contrast is probably not due to cohort differences, as Bowen, Kurzweil, and Tobin's data are based on students who entered college in 1995 and our yield rate data come from those who started just two years later in 1997. Rather, the difference seems to be due to some combination of the fact that we use a different set of institutions and another measure of socioeconomic status. While Bowen, Kurzweil, and Tobin (2005: 98) divide the family income students report in the voluntary ETS student descriptive questionnaire into quartiles based on America's national income distribution, we use students' appraisals of their socioeconomic status as a whole.

[6] As reported by Finder (2006b), measures of high school class rank are increasingly difficult to obtain from high school officials.

[7] The College Board re-centered SAT scores in 1995. In order to ensure compatibility with scores from our 1997 cohort, we re-centered scores from the 1980s and 1993 cohorts

TABLE 4.2
Percentage Distributions for High School Academic Achievement, by Race
NSCE Matriculant Sample: 1980s, 1993, and 1997 Cohorts

Achievement	Total	White	Black	Hispanic	Asian
High School Class Rank (N = 4,598)					
Top 10%	64.4	64.4	44.1	70.2	76.6
11%–20%	23.0	23.8	28.9	19.9	14.7
Bottom 80%	12.6	11.9	27.1	9.9	8.6
Total	100.0	100.0	100.0	100.0	100.0
% Unknown	29.3	26.9	28.2	24.7	29.3
High School GPA (N = 3,433)					
A+	24.8	24.2	13.9	32.9	32.3
A	34.8	34.6	29.3	32.2	40.2
A−	22.9	23.4	25.1	21.7	18.7
B+ or Below	17.5	17.8	31.8	13.3	8.8
Total	100.0	100.0	100.0	100.0	100.0
% Unknown	22.4	22.2	21.7	20.3	24.6
SAT Score (N = 5,987)					
1500–1600	9.6	8.9	0.9	4.2	21.7
1400–1499	16.4	16.2	5.6	11.8	26.1
1300–1399	22.1	23.1	11.7	25.4	21.0
1200–1299	24.5	25.3	21.0	30.3	18.9
1100–1199	16.1	16.5	22.0	19.0	8.6
1000–1099	8.1	8.0	18.0	7.7	2.7
Less than 1000	3.3	2.0	20.9	1.7	1.1
Total	100.0	100.0	100.0	100.0	100.0
% Unknown	8.9	9.8	8.6	5.2	4.1
Mean SAT Score	1285	1288	1141	1266	1366

Source: National Study of College Experience; ETS Student Descriptive Questionnaire Data.

Note: The percentage distributions displayed in this table are calculated using only known data. Percentages do not always add up to 100 percent because of rounding. Racial differences in high school class rank, high school GPA, and SAT score are statistically significant at the .001 level. All SAT scores reflect the re-centering that occurred in 1995. The variation in the number of observations for each achievement variable is the result of several factors. First, not all students take the SAT, causing a percentage of NSCE students to have unknown SAT scores. Second, while SAT scores were obtained from ETS and from NSCE universities, high school class rank and high school GPA data come from the ETS Student Descriptive Questionnaire (SDQ), which is given to students when they sit for the SAT. Since not all students who take the SAT complete the voluntary SDQ, there are more missing data for high school GPA and class rank. The slightly higher percentage of students with unknown high school class rank is likely due to the fact that many high schools have a policy of not ranking their students (Finder, 2006b). Finally, since the SDQ did not ask most of the students in the 1980s cohort their high school GPA, high school GPA percentages are based only on the 1993 and 1997 cohorts.

1100, more than one-quarter score 1400 or better, and 10 percent earn a score of 1500 or above. To put these figures in perspective, in 2005 the average combined math and verbal SAT score for all college-bound seniors was 1028. Students with a combined math and verbal score of 1400 were in the 96th percentile of all test-takers and those with a 1500 or above were in the 99th percentile (College Board, 2005a).

The racial gradient for SAT scores is similar to those for high school GPA and class rank. Asians are again the most likely to perform well; whites place second, then Hispanics, and finally blacks. The gap between the average SAT scores for Asian and black NSCE students stretches to 225 points. Almost one-half (48 percent) of Asians receive an SAT score of 1400 or better. The next closest competitors are whites, one-quarter of whom have scores this high. Asians' relative performance is even more impressive when we compare the percentage of students earning scores of 1500 or above. Twenty-two percent of Asians receive such high scores, as compared to only 9 percent of whites, 4 percent of Hispanics, and less than 1 percent of blacks. Blacks are not only the least likely to be in the highest SAT categories, they are also the most likely to be in the lowest ones. Twenty-one percent of black students score below 1000, as compared to 2 percent of whites and Hispanics and 1 percent of Asians.[8]

The relation between NSCE college students' socioeconomic status and their high school academic achievement depends on whether we con-

---

using the College Board's SAT I Individual Score Equivalents Table. All SAT scores we report reflect re-centered scores.

[8] An analysis of NSCE data by college type reveals that this gap in SAT scores between blacks and their classmates is smaller at private than at public universities. Black private college students are only six percentage points more likely to earn scores below 1100 (8 percent) than are all other private college students (2 percent). At public colleges, however, black students are 43 percentage points more likely to score below 1100, with 57 percent doing so compared to 14 percent of all other students. The black-white gap in average SAT scores at private colleges is 131 points (1260 versus 1391), while at public universities it is 162 points (1072 versus 1234). Sowell (2004: 146) argues that affirmative action policies are causing the gap in academic preparation between blacks and their classmates to increase as college selectivity decreases. As Gryphon (2005: 11) explains, while Harvard's black freshmen have average SAT scores only 95 points below non-minorities, for Princeton to be as racially diverse it has to employ "preferences large enough to produce a freshman class with a 150-point black-white SAT gap. Because every Ivy League school other than Harvard has attracted and admitted those minority students who would, under race-neutral standards, be well-qualified to attend schools like Wellesley and NYU, these schools must in turn admit minority students whose grades and scores more nearly match those of white and Asian students at schools such as the University of Virginia or the University of Texas." Sowell holds that this "mismatching" of minority students and colleges can have real consequences on campus social relations between blacks and other race groups. He even posits that it can cause white students to leave college with more negative perceptions of blacks than they had when they entered (Sowell, 2004: 148).

sider high school grades or performance on standardized tests. Upper-class students are by far the least likely to have high class ranks or GPAs. As Table 4.3 shows, only 39 percent of upper-class students are in the top tenth of their high school class, as compared to 62 percent of upper-middle-, 70 percent of middle- and working-, and 73 percent of lower-class students. Likewise, upper-class students are about half as likely to have a GPA of A or above and twice as likely to earn a B+ or below as are students from other social classes. Yet a different social class hierarchy emerges when we examine performance on the SAT. On this measure, upper-class students are among the top achievers. They earn the highest average score (1306) and lead (along with upper-middle-class students) in the percentage of students earning scores of 1400 or above. Middle-class students' SAT performance places them in a close third, with lower- and then working-class students farther behind.[9]

There are several possible explanations for upper-class students' weaker in-school performance. One is that upper-class matriculants do not need to have as high a class rank and GPA to be admitted, since they are more likely to be of potential development value and/or children of alumni, statuses that typically provide an admissions advantage (Espenshade, Chung, and Walling, 2004; Toor, 2001).[10] Yet it is problematic to conclude that upper-class students are simply not as bright because their SAT scores demonstrate high academic ability. Instead it seems likely that upper-class students' less impressive classroom performance is due in part to their attending stronger high schools, where higher standards and greater competition from classmates prevent their rank and grades from being as distinguished as they would be at weaker schools. We will discuss the academic quality of matriculants' high schools in greater depth later in this chapter.

RACIAL, IMMIGRANT, AND NATIONAL ORIGINS

The American system of higher education is the envy of the world, and foreign students are being drawn to selective U.S. colleges and universities at record levels (McCormack, 2007). Large numbers of immigrants are also coming to this country (Martin and Zürcher, 2008) and, in increasing numbers, intermarrying with the native-born population, often across racial and ethnic lines (Lee and Edmonston, 2005). Consequently,

[9] Chaplin and Hannaway (1998) and J. Rothstein (2004) have also found that high SES students score better on the SAT than do students from less affluent backgrounds.

[10] Eleven percent of upper-class NSCE students are legacies compared to 3 percent of all other students.

TABLE 4.3
Percentage Distributions for High School Academic Achievement, by Socioeconomic Status
NSCE Matriculant Sample: 1980s, 1993, and 1997 Cohorts

Achievement	Lower	Working	Middle	Upper-Middle	Upper
High School Class Rank (N = 4,598)					
Top 10%	73.4	69.7	69.9	61.5	39.3
11%–20%	15.2	20.2	20.9	24.4	32.8
Bottom 80%	11.4	10.2	9.2	14.1	28.0
Total	100.0	100.0	100.0	100.0	100.0
% Unknown	29.2	33.2	25.0	27.2	30.3
High School GPA (N = 3,433)					
A+	20.5	29.0	28.1	23.3	11.1
A	41.9	35.6	32.5	37.7	20.8
A−	20.3	21.1	23.7	21.8	30.6
B+ or Below	17.3	14.3	15.7	17.3	37.5
Total	100.0	100.0	100.0	100.0	100.0
% Unknown	35.4	29.6	20.2	21.7	26.6
SAT Score (N = 5,987)					
1500–1600	6.2	4.3	9.1	11.2	7.9
1400–1499	10.8	10.5	14.9	18.2	20.4
1300–1399	17.8	16.0	21.7	22.7	29.4
1200–1299	31.8	18.0	23.7	26.4	21.1
1100–1199	14.8	22.6	19.8	12.7	12.5
1000–1099	7.1	16.0	7.3	7.2	8.1
Less than 1000	11.5	12.6	3.5	1.6	0.6
Total	100.0	100.0	100.0	100.0	100.0
% Unknown	12.8	17.4	10.3	6.7	2.5
Mean SAT Score	1230	1198	1278	1305	1306

Source: National Study of College Experience; ETS Student Descriptive Questionnaire Data.

Note: The percentage distributions displayed in this table are calculated using only known data. Percentages do not always add up to 100 percent because of rounding. Social class differences in high school class rank and SAT score are statistically significant at the .001 level. Social class differences in high school GPA are statistically significant at the .01 level. All SAT scores reflect the re-centering that occurred in 1995. The variation in the number of observations for each achievement variable is the result of several factors. First, not all students take the SAT, causing a percentage of NSCE students to have unknown SAT scores. Second, while SAT scores were obtained from ETS and from NSCE universities, high school class rank and high school GPA data come from the ETS Student Descriptive Questionnaire (SDQ), which is given to students when they sit for the SAT. Since not all students who take the SAT complete the voluntary SDQ, there are more missing data for high school GPA and class rank. The slightly higher percentage of students with unknown high school class rank is likely due to the fact that many high schools have a policy of not ranking their students (Finder, 2006b). Finally, since the SDQ did not ask most of the students in the 1980s cohort their high school GPA, high school GPA percentages are based only on the 1993 and 1997 cohorts.

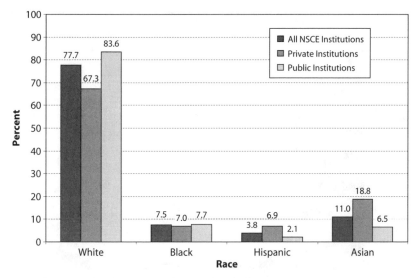

Figure 4.1. Racial Distribution of Matriculants, by College Type; NSCE Matriculant Sample: 1980s, 1993, and 1997 Cohorts Combined (N = 6,350). Note: Differences by college type are statistically significant at the .001 level. Source: National Study of College Experience.

as part of an overall examination of the profile of NSCE students, it is important to consider their racial, multiracial, immigrant, and national origins.

Race

First, we examine students' backgrounds using the four racial categories we have applied throughout this study. Overall, our eight elite colleges are about 78 percent white, 8 percent black, 4 percent Hispanic, and 11 percent Asian. The racial composition of elite institutions varies, however, by college type. As Figure 4.1 reveals, private colleges are more racially diverse than public colleges. Only two-thirds of students at private institutions are white compared to 84 percent of students at public universities. And while private and public colleges have roughly the same percentages of black students, private colleges have three times the proportion of Hispanics and Asians.

The racial composition of universities differs also by cohort. Figure 4.2 illustrates how the racial composition of NSCE institutions has changed over time. While in the 1980s white students made up 85 percent of all elite college students, they now represent slightly less than three-quarters. This decline in the proportion of whites is primarily due to the dramatic

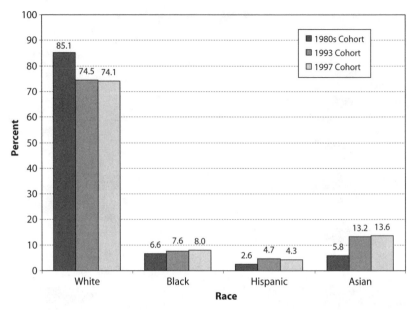

Figure 4.2. Racial Distribution of Matriculants, by Cohort; NSCE Matriculant Sample: 1980s, 1993, and 1997 Cohorts (N = 6,350). Note: Differences by cohort are statistically significant at the .001 level. Source: National Study of College Experience.

increase in Asian students. While the percentage of blacks and Hispanics on elite campuses has each grown by less than two percentage points between the 1980s and the 1990s, Asians' representation has more than doubled from 6 percent in the 1980s to nearly 14 percent in 1997.

Although informative, describing students' backgrounds using only these four racial categories can oversimplify students' racial and ethnic experiences. Some matriculants may have additional racial origins that have also shaped their lives. Others may have grown up exposed to another country's culture as immigrants themselves or as the children of immigrants. In order to develop a more complete picture of elite college students' backgrounds, we next examine students' multiracial, immigrant, and national origins.

Multiracial Origins

Multiracial students' college and other life experiences may differ significantly from those of single-race students. For instance, a study of Hispanic college students found that, in contrast to students who were exclusively Hispanic, Hispanic students with additional racial or ethnic heritages "often were not connected to Hispanic communities, did not speak Spanish, and did not have relatives who were not citizens of the United States" (Morales and Steward, 1996: 8). Multiracial students can also have different college experiences from students who are firmly entrenched in just one racial category (W. Schwartz, 1998). For example, some researchers have noted that multiracial students can feel more isolated. Nishimura (1998) concludes that while some multiracial students are incorporated into single-race social groups and organizations, others are considered suspect by single-race group members. Smith and Moore (2000) report that a need by biracial black students to embrace the non-black part of their identity can cause them to feel more social distance from monoracial black students. Yet other scholars highlight multiracial students' more frequent interactions with different race groups. W. Schwartz (1998) argues that multiracial students' parents, appearance, or cultural upbringing may enable them to travel in multiple racial circles. Indeed, Stephan and Stephan (1991) find that multiracial students have more social interactions with students of monoracial or single heritage backgrounds than single-heritage students have with members of other single-heritage groups.

In order to provide data on multiracial NSCE students we must first define who they are. W. Schwartz (1998) argues that multiracial people can include those who are (1) the biological children of parents of two different races (e.g., black and white) or ethnicities (e.g., Hispanic and non-Hispanic), (2) the descendants of people from different racial or ethnic heritages (e.g., have black, white, and Native American ancestors), or (3) monoracial individuals adopted by parents of a different race (e.g., an Asian child raised by two white parents). To capture these variations we consider students multiracial if they report that (1) their parents belong to different racial categories; (2) they have a parent who is "mixed race" or of two or more races; or (3) they personally are "mixed race," of two or more races, or of a different race from their parents.

Using these criteria we find that almost 8 percent of NSCE students are multiracial. Private universities generally have more multiracial individuals (10 percent) than do public institutions (6 percent). The percentage of multiracial students has grown over time. In the 1980s cohort only 5 percent of all students were multiracial, but this proportion stood at 9 percent in 1993 and 8 percent in 1997. Differences in the percentage of multiracial students by race are even more dramatic. As Figure 4.3 reveals, just 4 percent of students whom we have classified as white report other racial origins. In contrast, 10 percent of Asian students and 20 percent of black students have more than one racial heritage. Hispanics, however, are the most likely to be multiracial. Fully one-half (51 percent) include a category in addition to Hispanic to describe either themselves or a parent.

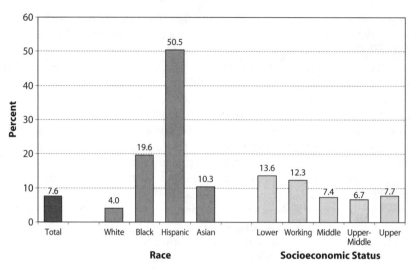

Figure 4.3. Percentage of Multiracial Students, by Race and Socioeconomic Status; NSCE Matriculant Sample: 1980s, 1993, and 1997 Cohorts Combined (N = 6,350). Note: Students are considered multiracial if they report that (1) their parents belong to different racial categories; (2) they have a parent who is "mixed race" or of two or more races; or (3) they personally are "mixed race," of two or more races, or of a different race from their parents. Racial differences are statistically significant at the .001 level. Social class differences are statistically significant at the .01 level. Source: National Study of College Experience.

There are several reasons for this high percentage of multiracial Hispanics. First, Hispanics are more likely to marry outside their own group than are other racial or ethnic populations, producing a larger proportion of mixed-race or mixed-ethnic descendants. While about a quarter of Hispanic couples contain a non-Hispanic spouse, only 16 percent of Asian, 7 percent of black, and 3 percent of white marriages include a spouse of a different racial or ethnic background (Lee and Edmonston, 2005). Second, the U.S. Census Bureau considers Hispanic to be an ethnic category and instructs Hispanics to choose a racial category in addition. For example, in the 2000 decennial census, 48 percent of those who reported Hispanic ethnicity chose a single racial category (white) to describe their race. Eighty percent of Hispanics who listed two races selected white as one of them (Patterson, 2001). Thus, the way in which the census collects data may encourage even Hispanic students with exclusively Hispanic ancestry to select another non-Hispanic category in addition.

Social class differences in the percentage of multiracial students also exist, though they are less pronounced than racial differences. As

Figure 4.3 depicts, low SES students are about twice as likely to be multi-racial as middle-class and high SES students. Part of the SES gradient is explained by the fact that black and Hispanic students, who have the highest multiracial proportions, are disproportionately drawn from lower- and working-class backgrounds.[11]

Immigrant Generation

Immigrant generation is important to consider because families' length of residence in the United States influences students' pre-college and college experiences. Students who come from families who migrated recently are more likely to be familiar with a foreign culture than are students whose families have long resided in the United States. In addition, socioeconomic resources can vary by immigrant generation. Our data indicate that nearly a quarter (23 percent) of NSCE students are first- or second-generation immigrants, about one-sixth are third-generation, and the majority for whom we are able to determine immigrant generation are fourth-generation immigrants or higher (61 percent).[12]

First- and second-generation immigrant students are disproportionately concentrated at private colleges and universities. As indicated by Table 4.4, their share exceeds one-third at private schools, as compared to 15 percent at public institutions. There are two reasons for this difference. First, white and black students at private institutions are more likely than their counterparts at public schools to be immigrants themselves or to have a recent immigrant past. The proportion of first- and second-generation immigrant whites at private colleges (15 percent) is nearly twice that at public universities (8 percent). Likewise, one-third of private university blacks are immigrants or the children of immigrants in contrast to just

---

[11]That said, black and Hispanic students from high SES family backgrounds are more likely to be multiracial than are their low SES counterparts. For example, only 12 percent of lower-class black students are multiracial, as compared to 25 percent of upper-middle-class and 41 percent of upper-class blacks. Similarly, 38 percent of lower-class and 32 percent of working-class Hispanic students identify with a racial or ethnic category in addition to Hispanic, as compared to 57 percent of middle-class, 59 percent of upper-middle-class, and 52 percent of upper-class Hispanics. These patterns mirror trends in black as well as Hispanic intermarriage; both blacks and Hispanics are more likely to intermarry the higher their educational attainment (Lee and Edmonston, 2005).

[12]Immigrant generation is defined so that (1) first-generation immigrants include students born outside America's fifty states and Washington, D.C., to at least one foreign-born parent; (2) second-generation immigrants comprise students born in the United States to at least one foreign-born parent; (3) third-generation immigrants are born in the United States to two U.S.-born parents but have at least one foreign-born grandparent; and (4) fourth-generation immigrants or higher are born in the United States to two U.S.-born parents and have four U.S.-born grandparents.

TABLE 4.4

Percentage Distribution of Immigrant Generation, by Race and College Type
NSCE Matriculant Sample: 1980s, 1993, and 1997 Cohorts Combined

Immigrant Generation	Total	White	Black	Hispanic	Asian
Private Colleges (N = 3,951)					
First	13.9	6.1	14.7	20.8	39.2
Second	20.5	9.3	19.1	46.7	51.8
Third	17.8	22.4	8.4	20.4	3.9
Fourth+	43.7	58.1	51.2	9.9	1.8
Unknown	4.1	4.2	6.7	2.3	3.3
Public Colleges (N = 2,399)					
First	4.6	1.6	1.9	23.5	40.3
Second	10.3	6.7	7.4	40.2	50.6
Third	13.8	15.5	2.5	22.0	3.1
Fourth+	66.4	71.6	80.4	8.8	3.1
Unknown	4.8	4.7	7.7	5.5	3.0

Source: National Study of College Experience.

Note: Racial differences are statistically significant at the .001 level for both private colleges and public colleges. Differences in immigrant generation by college type are also statistically significant at the .001 level.

9 percent of blacks at public universities.[13] Second, there is little difference
between private and public colleges in the proportion either of Hispanic
or of Asian students who are first- or second-generation immigrants. Nevertheless, the proportions for Hispanics (roughly two-thirds) and Asians
(about nine-tenths) exceed those for whites or blacks. In addition, Hispanic and Asian students are about three times relatively more numerous
at private institutions than at public ones (compare Figure 4.1).

[13] While the difference between private and public schools is 25 percentage points in the
NSCE, it is only 6 percentage points in the National Longitudinal Survey of Freshmen
(NLSF), which examines students entering elite colleges in the fall of 1999 (Massey et al.,
2007). The larger gap found in the NSCE may be partially due to its private institutions
being slightly more selective than its public colleges, for Massey et al. (2007) obtain a bigger
gap of 12 percentage points when they compare the percentage of immigrant blacks at the
NLSF's ten most and ten least selective elite colleges. Yet the discrepancy between NSCE
and NLSF results is more likely primarily due to sampling differences. The NLSF comprises
students from twenty-eight institutions but, even more relevantly, it limits participation to
U.S. citizens and a few permanent residents. The earlier waves of data included in the NSCE
cannot explain the variation between NSCE and NLSF results, for the gap between private
and public NSCE schools is even greater (28 points) when we analyze just the 1997 cohort,
which is closest in timing to the data collected in the NLSF. The difference is also not due
to varying operationalizations of "black immigrants." Massey et al. (2007) considered
black students to be immigrants if they have at least one parent who was born outside the
United States. We, too, count black students as first- or second-generation immigrants only
if at least one parent was born abroad.

TABLE 4.5
Percentage Distribution of Immigrant Generation,
by Socioeconomic Status and College Type
NSCE Matriculant Sample: 1980s, 1993, and 1997 Cohorts Combined

Immigrant Generation	Lower	Working	Middle	Upper-Middle	Upper
Private Colleges (N = 3,951)					
First	27.3	22.3	15.1	11.0	14.3
Second	25.9	25.2	18.5	21.3	16.9
Third	13.5	12.8	15.1	21.8	10.0
Fourth+	18.7	35.3	45.5	43.4	55.7
Unknown	14.5	4.5	5.8	2.5	3.2
Public Colleges (N = 2,399)					
First	10.0	7.9	5.0	3.6	4.6
Second	5.3	16.4	9.0	10.4	6.8
Third	5.3	8.7	9.6	17.9	18.7
Fourth+	70.1	61.5	70.0	65.1	61.8
Unknown	9.3	5.5	6.3	3.2	8.1

Source: National Study of College Experience.
Note: Social class differences in immigrant generation are statistically significant at the .001 level for both private colleges and public colleges. Differences in immigrant generation by college type are also statistically significant at the .001 level.

Being a first- or second-generation immigrant at NSCE schools is associated with coming from a lower- or working-class family background. Especially at private colleges and universities, as the socioeconomic status of families increases, the proportion of first- and second-generation immigrant students declines, and the proportion of fourth-and-higher immigrant generation students rises. Moreover, as Table 4.5 indicates, in almost every social class, private colleges have 20 percentage points more first- and second-generation immigrants than do public colleges. Among lower-class students, 53 percent are immigrants or the children of immigrants at private universities, as compared to just 15 percent at public universities—a gap of 38 percentage points. Thus, while selective private colleges are more likely than public institutions to teach immigrant students in general, they are even more likely to educate the most disadvantaged among this group.

National Origins

Because such a comparatively large percentage of students who are enrolled at NSCE institutions have recent immigrant roots, we examine the individual countries from which these students or their parents originate.

White first- and second-generation immigrants are most likely to have roots in Canada or in Western and Eastern Europe. As shown in Table 4.6, however, some white-identified students' families come from India, Egypt, and Iran. Immigrant blacks are primarily from the Caribbean countries of Jamaica, Haiti, and Trinidad and Tobago, or the African countries of Nigeria, Ethiopia, and Kenya.[14] Even Canadian-born black students typically have at least one parent who was born in the Caribbean or Africa.

For first-generation Hispanic students, Mexico is the most common country of origin. However, if we combine the percentages of students who are born in Brazil, Colombia, Argentina, Venezuela, and Peru, first-generation Hispanic students are somewhat more likely to be South American (28 percent) than Mexican (24 percent). The same is not true of second-generation Hispanics, who are roughly between two and three times as likely to have Mexican as South American ancestry. It is also worth noting that although few first-generation Hispanics are of Cuban descent, Cuba is the second most common country of origin for the parents of second-generation Hispanics.

The origins of Asian students also differ by immigrant generation. First-generation Asians are most likely to be born in Taiwan or Korea; sizable proportions also come from India, Hong Kong, Vietnam, China, Canada, and Singapore. Second-generation Asians have predominantly Indian, Chinese, and Korean roots.

Data on the nativity backgrounds of NSCE students also reveal substantial racial differences in the percentage of second-generation students who have two foreign-born parents. Nearly nine-tenths of second-generation Asian students report that both of their parents were born outside the United States, as compared to less than one-third of second-generation whites and just over half of second-generation blacks and Hispanics. These results indicate that second-generation immigrant Asians may be more exposed to foreign norms and cultures than are second-generation immigrants from other racial backgrounds. Such differences may have a bearing on how second-generation immigrant students approach higher education. Data like those in Table 4.6 also help make sense of the proliferation of on-campus organizations that are oriented to students from particular parts of the world.

Multiracial and Immigrant Origins Combined

We conclude this section by combining data on multiracial and immigrant students. We do so for two reasons. First, we want to compare our

---

[14] A notable percentage also report origins in "Other Africa."

TABLE 4.6
Most Common National Origins of First- and Second-Generation
NSCE Matriculants, by Race
NSCE Matriculant Sample: 1980s, 1993, and 1997 Cohorts Combined

Race and Country	First-Generation Immigrants' Birthplace (%)	Second-Generation Immigrants' Father's Birthplace (%)	Second-Generation Immigrants' Mother's Birthplace (%)
White	(N = 152)	(N = 190)	(N = 190)
Canada	16.5	5.9	6.5
USSR	9.2	1.4	0.7
Germany	6.5	4.5	6.6
India	5.5	0.3	0.0
Italy	5.3	8.5	5.1
Egypt	5.0	2.3	1.4
Iran	4.0	3.1	0.6
Poland	3.7	0.4	0.3
United States	0.0	26.9	41.1
Black	(N = 113)	(N = 211)	(N = 211)
Jamaica	19.2	13.1	15.0
Nigeria	15.5	7.7	1.9
Trinidad/Tobago	7.9	5.4	5.7
Canada	7.2	0.4	0.5
Other Africa	6.7	6.3	2.3
Haiti	6.4	7.6	7.5
Ethiopia	4.4	1.1	1.3
Kenya	4.2	0.7	0.0
United States	0.0	23.5	24.9
Hispanic	(N = 219)	(N = 474)	(N = 474)
Mexico	23.7	26.2	32.2
Brazil	7.4	0.6	0.4
Colombia	7.0	4.7	5.7
Argentina	5.8	4.8	3.8
Venezuela	4.3	1.0	0.5
Peru	3.8	1.5	1.8
Spain	3.0	1.6	0.9
Cuba	1.9	11.0	8.8
United States	0.0	24.4	22.5
Asian	(N = 574)	(N = 752)	(N = 752)
Taiwan	18.8	12.0	12.6
Korea	18.1	15.7	16.9
India	11.1	26.1	23.4
Hong Kong	9.7	1.4	3.6
Vietnam	5.5	2.3	2.5

(Continued)

TABLE 4.6 (*Continued*)

Race and Country	First-Generation Immigrants' Birthplace (%)	Second-Generation Immigrants' Father's Birthplace (%)	Second-Generation Immigrants' Mother's Birthplace (%)
China	5.0	20.3	16.9
Canada	5.0	0.0	0.0
Singapore	4.6	0.1	0.2
United States	0.0	6.2	4.8

Source: National Study of College Experience.

Note: The countries listed represent the most common foreign birthplaces of first-generation students by race, with two exceptions. First, we include the United States in order to examine the percentage of second-generation students with one American-born parent. Second, we incorporate Cuba in the Hispanic section because such a large percentage of second-generation Hispanic students have roots there.

findings with other studies of elite college students. Second, our data on applicants, admitted students, and matriculants help explain results that we and others have observed. We find that 26 percent of NSCE students are multiracial *and/or* first- or second-generation immigrants. Asians (at 93 percent) and Hispanics (at 88 percent) are the most likely to fall into this category, and whites (at 13 percent) are the least likely.[15] Nearly one-third (31 percent) of NSCE blacks are first- or second-generation immigrants and/or multiracial.[16] As Figure 4.4 reveals, this percentage has grown in recent years—from 23 percent in the 1980s to 37 percent by 1997—and is larger at private colleges (50 percent) than at public ones (21 percent).

One is not surprised by the high proportions of Asians or Hispanics who are in this group, because the passage of the 1965 amendments to the U.S. Immigration and Nationality Act encouraged widespread immigration from Asia, Mexico, the Caribbean, and Central and South America.[17] Nor should the low percentage of whites be unexpected, because

[15] These figures are not surprising given the high percentage of Asians and Hispanics in the United States who are born abroad. Sixty-four percent of all Asian Americans (U.S. Census Bureau, 2005) and 40 percent of all Hispanic Americans (U.S. Census Bureau, 2004) were born outside the United States.

[16] One might have expected a much lower proportion for blacks, because only about 7 percent of blacks nationally, and 13 percent of black eighteen- and nineteen-year-olds, are first- or second-generation immigrants (Massey et al., 2007).

[17] During the Great Depression in the United States, a time when immigrant flows were at a record low, two-thirds of legal immigrants to this country came from Europe while the remainder originated in the Western Hemisphere. By the 1950s, the European share had fallen to about one-half, the proportion originating in the Americas had grown to nearly 40 percent, and the Asian share (6 percent) was no longer insignificant. The transformations created by the 1965 amendments to the Immigration and Nationality Act were fully manifest by the early 1980s, when the European share of new legal immigrants had declined to

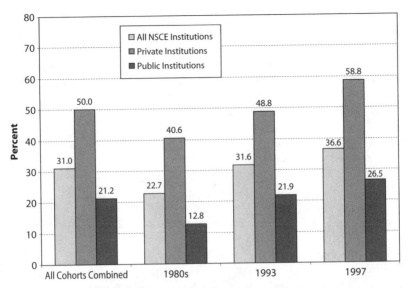

Figure 4.4. Percentage of Multiracial and/or First- or Second-Generation Immigrant Black Students; NSCE Matriculant Sample: 1980s, 1993, and 1997 Cohorts (N = 6,350). Note: Differences by college type are statistically significant at the .001 level. Source: National Study of College Experience.

European immigration to the United States has declined as a share of the legal total, and only modest proportions of white students (less than 5 percent) consider themselves multiracial. On the other hand, the large and rising proportion of black NSCE college students who are multiracial and/or part of the pool of first- or second-generation immigrants signals what in many ways may be the emergence of a new phenomenon, especially at the most academically selective institutions. These black students are on the cutting edge of two confluent trends—a rise in the black intermarriage rate and a growth in the number of black students who are either born outside the United States or have at least one foreign-born parent. Because these students may well be leading a new development in selective higher education, we use the term "vanguards" to refer to black students who are multiracial and/or first- or second-generation immigrant students.[18]

11 percent, the share originating in the Americas remained relatively stable at just less than 40 percent, but the Asian fraction had increased to almost 50 percent of the total legal immigrant flow (Borjas, 1990: 30–39).

[18]The resurgence in black immigration to the United States is described more fully in Kent (2007).

This high percentage of vanguards in the NSCE is not unique. Our results are consistent with what other researchers have observed. Thirty-seven percent of blacks in the 1997 NSCE matriculant cohort are vanguards, compared to 41 percent found in the National Longitudinal Survey of Freshmen's (NLSF) sample of students who entered twenty-eight elite public and private colleges in 1999 (Rimer and Arenson, 2004). Likewise, 59 percent of blacks at private NSCE colleges in 1997 are vanguards, close to the estimate of nearly two-thirds provided by Lani Guinier and Henry Louis Gates Jr. for the proportion of Harvard University's black undergraduate students who are West Indian or African immigrants or their children, or the children of biracial couples (Rimer and Arenson, 2004).

It has been difficult for scholars to explain why such a high proportion of blacks at elite colleges are multiracial and/or first- or second-generation immigrants (Massey et al., 2007). The unique features of NSCE data enable us to provide new insights into this question. Using 1997 cohort data from seven NSCE institutions, we first consider why vanguards represent such a large proportion of black students at elite colleges in general. Then we address why the percentage of vanguards is higher at private colleges than at public ones. Three phases to the college admission process determine the composition of the student body: the application, acceptance, and enrollment stages. In order for vanguard students to represent a higher proportion of enrolled black students than their numbers nationally would suggest, they must either apply, be accepted, or enroll at higher rates than other black students.

One-half (49 percent) of all black applicants to NSCE institutions are vanguards, as shown by Figure 4.5. The percentage of admitted blacks who are vanguards is smaller (just 41 percent), and the percentage among enrolled students is smaller still (40 percent).[19] Thus, the primary reason that vanguard blacks are so highly represented among enrolled black students at NSCE colleges and universities is that they are well represented among all black applicants. Processes operating during the acceptance and matriculation stages of the college admission process serve to decrease the proportion of multiracial and/or first- or second-generation immigrant black students.

NSCE private college campuses have a larger proportion of vanguards among all enrolled black students (59 percent) than do public universities (23 percent)—a gap of 36 percentage points. To understand the reasons

---

[19] Minor discrepancies between Figures 4.4 and 4.5 in the 1997 cohort data are related to the fact that data for Figure 4.4 are derived from eight NSCE institutions whereas seven schools provided the basis for data in Figure 4.5.

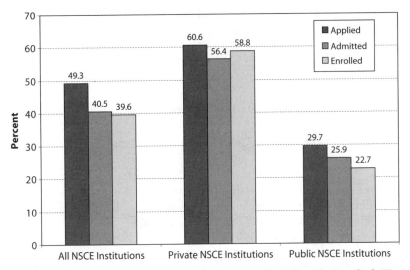

Figure 4.5. Percentage of Vanguard Blacks among All Blacks Who Applied, Were Admitted, and Enrolled in Seven NSCE Institutions, by College Type; NSCE Application Data: Fall 1997 Cohort (N = 3,829). Source: National Study of College Experience.

for this difference, we need to reexamine each stage of the admission process. As shown in the center panel of Figure 4.5, 61 percent of black applicants at private schools are vanguards. This proportion declines to 56 percent at the acceptance stage, suggesting that black vanguards are admitted at slightly lower rates than are nonvanguard blacks. The representation of black vanguards rises to 59 percent at the matriculation stage, which implies that black vanguards who are admitted to private institutions have a somewhat higher tendency to enroll than do other admitted black students.

The story is strikingly different at public universities. Just 30 percent of all black applicants are vanguards, as indicated in the third panel of Figure 4.5. Mirroring the pattern at private schools, black vanguards at public institutions are admitted at lower rates than are other black students, dropping the vanguard proportion to 26 percent at the acceptance stage. But in contrast to behaviors at private institutions, yield rates at public institutions are lower among black vanguards than among nonvanguard blacks, creating a vanguard proportion of 23 percent of all enrolled black students at public universities.

Thus, the principal reason for the greater percentage of vanguards among all black students at private NSCE institutions is that vanguards comprise a much larger share of the black applicant pool at private colleges than at public universities.[20] A secondary factor in explaining the gap is that vanguards have higher yield rates than other blacks at private institutions but lower ones at public schools.

SOCIOECONOMIC CHARACTERISTICS

An analysis of matriculants' socioeconomic backgrounds complements our examination of students' academic achievement and racial and ethnic origins. We illustrate parents' socioeconomic status, education, occupation, income, assets, and housing characteristics. We are particularly interested in how socioeconomic characteristics differ by students' race. To anticipate our results, we find that societal economic divisions by race are also displayed on selective college campuses.

Socioeconomic Status

NSCE matriculants predominantly come from middle-class and upper-middle-class family backgrounds. As Table 4.7 indicates, 84 percent of all students originate in these two socioeconomic categories. Five percent of elite college students report upper-class origins. By contrast, only 10 percent consider themselves working class, and even fewer, just 1 percent, view themselves as lower class. Table 4.7 also shows that the distribution of students by their socioeconomic status is quite similar between private and public universities. Public universities have slightly larger percentages of working- and middle-class students, while private colleges have slightly larger proportions of lower-, upper-middle-, and upper-class students.

Whites and Asians are consistently the most socioeconomically advantaged, while Hispanic and black students are by comparison more disadvantaged. More than one-half of all whites and Asians, but just over one-fifth of blacks, are upper-middle or upper class. By contrast, fewer than 8 percent of white students and less than 12 percent of Asians are lower or working class, as compared to more than one-third of black students and almost 30 percent of Hispanics. While the socioeconomic composition of whites, Asians, and blacks does not differ much by college type, the same is not true for Hispanics. Hispanics who attend public universities are much more likely to be of higher socioeconomic status than are Hispanics

---

[20] This conclusion parallels a related finding in chapter 3. Black descendants comprise a larger share of admitted black students at public than at private NSCE institutions because they account for a substantially larger fraction of black applicants at public than at private schools.

TABLE 4.7
Socioeconomic Status of Enrolled Students, by Race and College Type
NSCE Matriculant Sample: 1980s, 1993, and 1997 Cohorts Combined
(N = 6,350)

Socioeconomic Status	Total	White	Black	Hispanic	Asian
All NSCE Institutions					
Upper	5.0	5.5	1.1	4.3	4.7
Upper-Middle	48.1	51.4	20.5	30.5	49.7
Middle	35.9	35.5	43.4	36.4	33.9
Working	9.9	7.2	30.2	23.4	10.2
Lower	1.1	0.4	4.8	5.3	1.5
Private Colleges					
Upper	6.2	7.4	0.6	5.2	4.6
Upper-Middle	48.8	53.5	22.4	25.4	50.4
Middle	34.0	33.5	42.4	36.3	31.8
Working	9.2	4.7	29.5	27.0	11.0
Lower	1.8	1.0	5.1	6.1	2.1
Public Colleges					
Upper	4.3	4.6	1.3	2.7	4.8
Upper-Middle	47.7	50.4	19.5	40.0	48.5
Middle	37.1	36.4	44.0	36.7	37.4
Working	10.3	8.4	30.5	16.7	8.8
Lower	0.6	0.2	4.6	3.9	0.5

Source: National Study of College Experience.
Note: Racial differences in socioeconomic status for all NSCE institutions, private colleges, and public colleges are statistically significant at the .001 level. Differences by college type in the socioeconomic status of students are significant at the .01 level.

at private colleges. For example, 43 percent of Hispanics at public schools consider themselves upper-middle or upper class compared to 31 percent of Hispanics at private colleges. Likewise, only about one-fifth of public college Hispanics are lower or working class compared to one-third of private college Hispanics. Thus, while at private colleges Hispanics are more likely to share the comparatively lower socioeconomic status background of black students, at public colleges they are more likely to come from higher socioeconomic status backgrounds that begin to approach those of whites and Asians.

Parents' Education and Occupation

Parents of white and Asian students consistently have more education than black and Hispanic students' parents. Table 4.8 indicates that 73 percent of all matriculants have a father with a college degree or better, and

TABLE 4.8

Parents' Education and Occupation, by Race of Student

NSCE Matriculant Sample: 1980s, 1993, and 1997 Cohorts Combined (N = 6,350)

Socioeconomic Status Indicators	Total	White	Black	Hispanic	Asian
Father's Highest Degree					
Less than High School	3.0	2.0	6.3	13.8	4.2
High School	9.8	9.0	20.2	12.2	7.5
Vocational/Associates	11.5	10.9	22.6	15.3	6.3
Bachelor's	27.5	29.6	17.3	18.0	22.6
Master's	20.2	20.4	14.7	18.4	23.1
Professional	16.2	17.3	6.9	11.3	16.1
Doctoral	8.7	8.0	5.2	6.4	17.2
Other or Unknown	3.1	2.8	6.8	4.6	3.0
Mother's Highest Degree					
Less than High School	2.4	1.0	4.7	13.7	6.6
High School	14.8	15.0	17.6	16.5	11.5
Vocational/Associates	18.5	18.0	28.8	22.6	13.1
Bachelor's	32.2	33.3	20.7	21.3	35.7
Master's	23.0	24.3	19.1	17.6	18.2
Professional	3.8	3.2	3.0	2.6	8.4
Doctoral	3.0	2.9	3.4	3.5	3.0
Other or Unknown	2.3	2.3	2.7	2.2	3.5
Father's Occupation					
Executive, administrative, managerial, or professional	68.9	72.5	42.2	53.1	67.0
Technical, sales, or administrative	6.6	6.8	4.5	6.5	7.2
Service (e.g., child care, police and fire, food preparation)	4.6	3.8	8.1	6.3	6.7
Farming, forestry, or fishing	0.9	1.1	0.6	1.4	0.3
Precision production, craft, or repair	5.5	5.3	8.2	7.7	3.7
Machine operator, fabricator, inspector	3.4	2.8	8.7	8.1	2.8
Military	0.9	0.8	2.6	1.1	0.5
Other, Not Applicable, or Unknown[a]	9.2	6.9	25.1	15.8	11.8
Mother's Occupation					
Executive, administrative, managerial, or professional	45.0	46.0	50.5	38.8	36.6
Technical, sales, or administrative	13.3	13.4	12.5	14.0	12.8
Service (e.g., child care, police and fire, food preparation)	9.0	8.5	11.8	11.4	10.1
Farming, forestry, or fishing	0.2	0.2	0.2	0.4	0.1
Precision production, craft, or repair	0.6	0.4	1.6	0.9	1.3
Machine operator, fabricator, inspector	1.6	0.9	5.2	4.3	3.2
Military	0.0	0.0	0.2	0.0	0.0
Other, Not Applicable, or Unknown[a]	30.3	30.6	18.0	30.2	35.9

Source: National Study of College Experience.

Note: Racial differences in father's education, mother's education, father's occupation, and mother's occupation are all statistically significant at the .001 level.

[a]Includes father/mother not working for pay during senior year in high school, didn't have father/mother, don't recall, or missing.

62 percent have a mother who has attained that level of education. While three-quarters or more of white and Asian students' fathers have earned at least a bachelor's degree, only about half of black and Hispanic students' fathers have also done so. Roughly one-quarter of the fathers of blacks and Hispanics have not completed more than a high school degree. White and Asian mothers are about 20 percentage points more likely to have earned at least a college degree than are black and Hispanic mothers.

More than two-thirds (69 percent) of fathers and a little less than half (45 percent) of all mothers of NSCE students are executives, administrators, managers, or professionals (hereafter referred to as executives).[21] White and Asian students' fathers are more likely to be at the top of the occupational hierarchy than are black or Hispanic students' fathers. Seventy-three and 67 percent of white and Asian fathers, respectively, work as executives, compared to 42 percent of black fathers and 53 percent of Hispanic fathers. This comparatively high proportion of fathers of Hispanic students who hold executive or managerial positions is particularly impressive given their relatively more modest academic degree credentials. These race differentials do not apply to mothers of NSCE students. One-half of the mothers of black students work as executives, the largest proportion of any group. White mothers are the next most likely, followed by Hispanic, and then finally Asian mothers. Similarly, black students are the least likely to report that their mothers have no known occupation or are out of the paid labor force.

Family Income and Assets

Income and financial assets are important determinants of a family's socioeconomic status. The first two panels of Table 4.9 display the income and asset distributions of NSCE matriculants based on estimates students gave in the survey. The last two panels exhibit information that NSCE students' families provided in their Free Application for Federal Student Aid (FAFSA). The information families disclose in their FAFSA form has to be verified by tax returns and therefore is likely to be somewhat more accurate than students' estimates.[22] At the same time, however, FAFSA

---

[21] This occupational category includes clergy members, teachers, and people who work in financial services, health diagnosis fields, and the like.

[22] Research suggests, however, that students' self-reports do provide reliable and close approximations of their families' financial situation. A sample of financial aid students at the University of Pennsylvania only overestimated their parents' income by an average of 5 percent (Massey et al., 2003: 25–27). In addition, Bowen, Kurzweil, and Tobin (2005: 98n10) report that an analysis of a nationally representative sample of college students revealed that reports by low-income matriculants of their family's income correspond well with parents' reports. Higher SES students, on the other hand, tend to understate family income.

TABLE 4.9
Percentage Distribution of Household Income and Assets during
Senior Year of High School, by Race

Financial Resources	Total	White	Black	Hispanic	Asian
NSCE Survey Data					
Household Income (N = 5,503)					
$200,000+	15.2	16.3	4.6	8.4	17.2
$150,000–199,999	11.1	11.6	5.0	7.8	12.2
$125,000–149,999	10.6	10.8	7.1	9.2	11.8
$100,000–124,999	10.9	11.9	7.6	4.8	8.2
$75,000–99,999	15.5	16.1	12.2	12.4	14.0
$50,000–74,999	22.2	21.8	29.2	25.0	18.9
$30,000–49,999	9.0	7.7	17.4	14.4	10.8
Less than $30,000	5.6	3.8	16.9	18.0	7.0
Total	100.0	100.0	100.0	100.0	100.0
% Other or Unknown	13.0	12.4	13.6	10.4	17.9
Mean Income (in dollars)	121,360	126,620	78,770	91,260	123,710
Household Assets[a] (N = 3,914)					
$500,000+	24.8	26.1	7.0	15.8	31.2
$300,000–499,999	8.8	9.6	3.9	4.2	8.3
$200,000–299,999	10.5	11.2	6.0	5.9	9.8
$100,000–199,999	12.4	13.2	9.3	7.9	10.7
$50,000–99,999	9.5	9.1	12.7	8.9	10.4
$25,000–49,999	7.2	6.4	10.6	9.2	9.2
$10,000–24,999	10.3	10.2	13.8	9.7	8.4
$2,500–9,999	7.9	6.9	14.3	16.6	6.7
Less than $2,500	8.8	7.2	22.4	21.8	5.4
Total	100.0	100.0	100.0	100.0	100.0
% Other or Unknown	39.9	39.7	41.1	32.5	44.3
Mean Assets (in dollars)	247,450	262,350	101,740	150,810	279,410
FAFSA Data					
Household Income (N = 1,037)					
$125,000+	10.1	11.2	4.9	7.1	9.7
$100,000–124,999	12.5	14.5	5.0	7.4	9.6
$75,000–99,999	18.0	19.8	11.5	13.2	15.3
$50,000–74,999	24.8	25.3	22.7	25.9	23.5
$30,000–49,999	15.7	14.3	24.8	19.3	15.0
Less than $30,000	18.9	15.1	31.2	27.2	26.9
Total	100.0	100.0	100.0	100.0	100.0

(Continued)

TABLE 4.9 (*Continued*)

Financial Resources	Total	White	Black	Hispanic	Asian
% Other or Unknown	59.4	60.9	51.4	47.8	59.6
Mean Income (in dollars)	73,860	80,100	52,700	57,000	62,870
Household Assets[b] (N = 920)					
$200,000+	11.5	10.3	3.3	12.7	22.9
$100,000–199,999	13.2	16.0	4.7	6.2	6.7
$50,000–99,999	9.6	10.0	3.9	8.2	11.8
$25,000–49,999	7.6	8.2	4.3	6.3	7.6
$10,000–24,999	13.1	13.7	6.8	8.3	15.9
$2,500–9,999	18.6	20.0	11.5	14.9	17.4
Less than $2,500	26.3	22.0	65.5	43.5	17.9
Total	100.0	100.0	100.0	100.0	100.0
% Other or Unknown	68.3	69.8	63.2	58.9	66.1
Mean Assets (in dollars)	81,890	78,700	28,250	80,940	133,890

Source: National Study of College Experience; Free Application for Federal Student Aid Data.

Note: Data are based on NSCE matriculants. NSCE survey data include the 1980s, 1993, and 1997 cohorts. FAFSA data are limited to a subset of the 1997 cohort members who applied for financial aid. Racial differences in the percentage distribution in household income and assets are statistically significant at the .001 level in both NSCE and FAFSA samples. NSCE data reflect 1996–97 dollars and FAFSA data reflect 1996 dollars. Percentages do not always sum to 100.0 due to rounding.

[a]Includes savings and investments, but not value of family home, businesses, farms, or retirement plans.

[b]Includes cash, savings, and checking accounts as well as real estate investments other than family home and other investments. Does not include value of family home, businesses, retirement plans, family farms, personal or consumer loans, life insurance, or student financial aid.

data are only available for students from the 1997 cohort who applied for aid. Thus, NSCE data are best used for developing a sense of the income and wealth of all matriculants, while FAFSA data are best employed for exploring the racial differences in income and wealth among those applying for aid.

NSCE survey data indicate that a large proportion of students' families have high incomes and substantial wealth. More than one-third of matriculants come from families whose annual income is $125,000 or more (in 1996–97 dollars). Average family income for all NSCE students is $121,360, compared to an average for all American families in 1997 of $56,900 (U.S. Census Bureau, 2006c). One-quarter of NSCE students' families report total gross assets of at least $500,000, and the mean value of total NSCE household assets is $247,450. By contrast, the average total gross financial assets for all American families in 1995 was $30,960 (Anderson, 1999).

Racial differences in income and wealth are consistent with other indicators of differentials in socioeconomic status. White and Asian students are more likely than their Hispanic and black counterparts to come from families with high incomes. About 40 percent of white and Asian students' families have annual incomes of $125,000 or more. Only one-quarter of Hispanic families and one-sixth of black NSCE families fall into this range. By contrast, one-third of Hispanic and black families report annual incomes below $50,000, as compared to 12 and 18 percent of white and Asian families, respectively. Annual incomes average roughly $125,000 for white and Asian students' families, followed by $91,000 for Hispanic households and $79,000 for black families. Racial differences in average household wealth parallel those in average family income. About one-quarter of white families and more than 30 percent of Asian families have total assets that exceed $500,000, in comparison to just 16 percent of Hispanic households and 7 percent of black families. On the other hand, more than 20 percent of both black and Hispanic families have assets totaling less than $2,500.[23]

NSCE survey data also indicate that there is comparatively greater parity in income across racial groups than in assets or wealth. Table 4.9 shows that while average black family income is 38 percent below the average family income for whites, black family assets on average lag those for white families by 61 percent. Similarly, the average income reported for Hispanic families is 28 percent less than that for white families, but the gap in their respective household assets expands to 43 percent.[24]

NSCE survey data on the proportions of students within each racial category who apply for financial aid and those who receive it are consistent with racial and ethnic patterns in income and wealth. Overall, across the three cohorts of NSCE matriculants, just over one-half (51 percent)

---

[23] These racial differences in assets have important consequences. Oliver and Shapiro (1995) and Conley (1999) have carefully detailed the way in which wealth differences between blacks and whites create a multitude of inequalities in other areas of life, including the completion of higher education (Conley, 1999: 22). They find that these wealth differences exist even between people with similar incomes.

[24] NSCE data also indicate that in almost every income category displayed in Table 4.9 whites and Asians have more in assets than do blacks and Hispanics. For example, Asian and white families earning less than $30,000 a year have $47,110 and $27,990 in assets, respectively, while Hispanics and blacks at that income level have only $15,770 and $12,430 in assets, respectively. Having fewer assets may make one more averse to taking on debt. One report suggests that African American students are more reluctant to borrow for college than are their white counterparts and thus are more likely to work off-campus jobs, even full-time ones, which may lead to lower college completion rates (USA Funds Education Access Report, 2004). Another study found that black students who do take out college loans "express greater perception of burden, even with lower debt-to-income ratios, and less satisfaction that the benefits of borrowing were worth it" than do other students (Baum and O'Malley, 2003).

of all enrolled students applied for financial aid. Instances of requesting financial support are highest for black students (84 percent), followed by Hispanic students (78 percent). Almost three out of every five Asian students (57 percent) requested help in paying for college. Only white students (at 46 percent) were below average in the frequency with which they sought financial assistance for college. The great majority of students who applied for financial aid received it. On average, nearly one-half of students (49 percent) who attended an NSCE institution reported receiving financial assistance. The respective percentages by race are 81 for black, 76 for Hispanic, 49 for Asian, and 44 for white students.[25]

Even among families who perceive that their economic means are inadequate to pay the full costs of tuition, room, and board and who as a result apply for financial aid, our data suggest that selective colleges and universities contain not only academically stellar but also financially advantaged students. As shown in the last two panels of Table 4.9, average family income ($73,860) and average household assets ($81,890) for families requesting financial assistance from NSCE schools far exceed the averages for the typical American family. In addition, the racial hierarchies observed in the NSCE survey data are preserved in the FAFSA data. White and Asian families are disproportionately concentrated in the top income categories, while black and Hispanic families (and some Asian households) are overrepresented among NSCE families with annual income less than $30,000. More than 40 percent of Hispanic households and two-thirds of black families who apply for aid have gross financial assets below $2,500.

Housing

Whether students' parents rent or own their homes is relevant to economic status because owning a home and building equity through ownership is a principal way that many American families accumulate wealth.[26] As shown in Table 4.10, about 90 percent of matriculants' families own their own homes. Rates of ownership are highest for white families (93 percent) and lowest for black families (75 percent).[27] A little less than

[25] Percentages of students who applied for financial aid and who received it are based only on "yes" or "no" responses. Only a small proportion of students (about 3 percent) answered "don't recall" or failed to answer the questions.

[26] For example, based on an analysis of data in 1995 and 1998 from the Survey of Consumer Finances, Straight (2002) has shown that the average older, college-educated, higher-income, black family had $71,000 in net homeowner equity (in 1998 dollars) compared to an average of $77,600 for white families with similar characteristics. Additional information is contained in analyses by Myers and Chung (1996).

[27] These rates, which include data from the 1980s and 1990s, are substantially above U.S. averages, in the aggregate and by race. The average homeownership rate in 1996 for

TABLE 4.10
Housing Tenure, Home Value, and Family Living Arrangements during
Students' Senior Year in High School
NSCE Matriculant Sample: 1980s, 1993, and 1997 Cohorts Combined

Characteristic	Total	White	Black	Hispanic	Asian
Housing Tenure (N = 6,350)					
Owner	90.3	92.6	75.1	83.9	87.1
Renter	7.7	5.7	22.2	14.7	9.6
Do not recall or unknown	2.0	1.7	2.7	1.4	3.3
Home Value[a] (N = 4,337)					
$500,000+	13.8	13.8	4.8	11.7	19.0
$300,000–499,999	16.1	15.7	10.3	14.6	22.8
$200,000–299,999	20.3	21.2	11.7	15.5	20.1
$150,000–199,999	18.1	18.6	16.4	17.9	15.6
$100,000–149,999	18.0	18.5	23.7	16.2	11.3
Less than $100,000	13.8	12.3	33.1	24.1	11.3
Total	100.0	100.0	100.0	100.0	100.0
Do not recall, not applicable, or unknown (%)	24.9	22.5	44.1	28.4	29.5
Respondent Has Own Bedroom (N = 6,350)					
Yes	89.5	91.1	81.1	81.3	87.1
No	9.2	7.8	17.2	18.0	10.9
Unknown	2.3	1.1	1.7	0.7	2.0

Source: National Study of College Experience.
Note: Racial differences in housing tenure, home value, and students having their own bedroom are statistically significant at the .001 level. Home values are adjusted to reflect 1996–97 dollars. Percentages do not always sum to 100.0 due of rounding.
[a]Home value was asked only for students whose parent(s) owned their own home.

one-third of all students estimate their home to be worth more than $300,000, but this proportion ranges from just 15 percent of blacks to nearly 42 percent of Asians. More than 90 percent of white students report that they had their own bedroom while living at home. Ten percentage points fewer black and Hispanic students and four percentage points fewer Asian students are in the same category.

household heads 45–54 years of age was 76 percent (U.S. Census Bureau, 2006b). Home-ownership among American families increased appreciably between 1989 (63 percent) and 1998 (66 percent). The prevalence of homeownership rose for all racial, ethnic, and income groups, and differentials between minority and non-minority families narrowed substantially (Bostic and Surette, 2001). By 2000, homeownership rates were 71 percent for white families and 46 percent for black families, compared to a national average of 66 percent (U.S. Census Bureau, 2006a).

To conclude, in this section we have considered a broad array of indicators that have allowed us to dig deeper into the social and economic backgrounds of NSCE students. We examined social class as perceived by students; parents' education, occupation, income, and assets; the proportion of students who apply for financial aid; and housing characteristics. It is important not to lose sight of the fact that in any group of students, some will be well-off and some not so well-off. One must be careful, in other words, not to assume that all students can be adequately characterized by the general tendencies for the group. Nevertheless, the set of indicators points to one consistent finding. On average, white and Asian students tend to come from more socioeconomically advantaged backgrounds, while black and Hispanic students typically have grown up in less privileged surroundings. Not surprisingly, these conclusions mirror circumstances in the broader U.S. society.

High School Characteristics

We turn next to the environments that matriculants experience prior to college. Matriculants' high school environment is particularly important to consider because it should influence their college readiness and therefore their college academic performance. Academic preparation is crucial to success, yet research shows that school districts with fewer high SES students are less likely to offer college prep and advanced placement (AP) courses (Coleman, 1968; McNeil, 2007). Thus matriculants who attend high schools with more poor students may be less well prepared for college, making their overall transition to university life more difficult.[28]

The composition of matriculants' high schools may also affect students' social lives. College students who grow up attending schools with higher proportions of low SES individuals sometimes report feeling out of place at elite universities where students tend to be from more prosperous backgrounds (Ewers, 2005; Kaufman, 2001). The racial composition of students' high schools may also influence matriculants' ability to socially integrate in college. For example, Massey et al. (2003: 176) find that college students who come from more segregated high schools are significantly more likely to feel social distance from whites. If matriculants feel uncomfortable with the majority of students on campus, it may prevent them not only from excelling academically but also from enjoying the

---

[28] However, tracking students into different levels of classes may mitigate somewhat this socioeconomic influence (Lucas, 1999). LaBrecque (2006) has called for returning the AP examination to its original purpose of enabling students to skip over equivalent college courses. Too often, he argues, AP exams have been used by privileged families as an extra weapon in the competitive admission game.

social aspects of their college experiences (Lewis, 2008; Ostrove and Long, 2007).

The most selective colleges and universities once had the reputation of catering mainly to secondary school students from elite private boarding schools (Cookson and Persell, 1985). This is no longer the case. As Table 4.11 shows, about two-thirds of all NSCE matriculants graduated from public high schools. Only 16 percent come from private schools, about twice the proportion that attend either parochial or magnet schools. Whites are decidedly more likely than nonwhites to attend public schools. Blacks are overrepresented at magnet schools, Hispanics at parochial schools, and Asians at private high schools. Asian students are also the most likely to graduate from one of the country's elite secondary schools, regardless of school type.[29]

White and Asian students are more likely to attend what many would consider the very best secondary schools. We examine the academic quality of matriculants' high schools using as a proxy for quality the average SAT score for all college-bound seniors at a high school who take the SAT test.[30] About 19 percent of all NSCE students come from secondary schools with an average score of 1200 or above, and 13 percent graduate from schools with an average SAT score below 1,000. Roughly 20 percent of both whites and Asians graduate from high schools where the average SAT score is above 1200, in contrast to 12 percent of blacks and 14 percent of Hispanics. By our measure of quality, black and Hispanic students are on average attending weaker high schools than are whites or Asians. The proportion of blacks from schools with scores below 1,000 (37 percent) is more than four times as great as the proportion of Asians (8 percent). Hispanics are twice as likely as whites to attend schools with such low scores.

The socioeconomic status of matriculants' high schools can be approximated by the percentage of high school students who are eligible for free lunch.[31] About 10 percent of students at NSCE college students' high

---

[29] To investigate NSCE students' secondary school environments, we merged our 1997 cohort matriculant sample with data on public schools from the Common Core of Data, on private schools from the Private School Universe Sample, and on both types of high schools from The College Board. These data provide a profile of the type, quality, socioeconomic status, and racial composition of NSCE matriculants' high schools.

[30] Using the high-school-wide average SAT score could be biased by the percentage of high school students who take the SAT test. This indicator may be particularly problematic for high schools in the Midwest since most college-bound students from this region of the country take the ACT, and only a small proportion of high school graduates take the SAT—typically the very best students who want to go to school out of state. For more on this issue, see Espenshade, Hale, and Chung (2005).

[31] This measure captures only students whose family earnings are at 130 percent of the U.S. poverty line or below (U.S. Department of Agriculture, 2005), and it is available only

TABLE 4.11
High School Characteristics, by Race
NSCE Matriculant Sample: Fall 1997 Cohort

High School Characteristics	Total	White	Black	Hispanic	Asian
Type of High School (N = 2,270)					
Public	65.7	68.2	59.8	56.8	58.1
Magnet	7.4	5.9	13.3	10.2	11.4
Parochial/Religious	8.1	8.1	9.6	14.3	4.8
Private	16.4	15.6	14.4	16.4	22.1
Unknown	2.4	2.2	2.9	2.3	3.6
Elite 72 High School (N = 2,270)					
Yes	5.2	5.1	3.9	4.5	6.8
No	91.8	92.7	93.9	90.3	86.6
Unknown	3.0	2.3	2.2	5.2	6.6
Average High School SAT Score[a] (N = 2,270)					
<1000	13.2	11.0	37.0	22.1	8.3
1000–1099	31.3	33.1	27.2	29.1	24.7
1100–1199	33.9	34.3	21.5	28.9	40.3
1200–1299	14.1	15.3	6.9	9.3	13.4
1300–1399	4.2	3.9	4.3	4.6	5.8
1400 or higher	0.2	0.0	0.5	0.3	0.9
Unknown	3.1	2.3	2.6	5.8	6.6
Socioeconomic Composition (N = 1,384)					
Students Eligible for Free School Lunch (%)	9.9	8.5	20.2	18.2	9.4
Racial Composition (N = 1,936)					
White	77.4	82.2	52.5	61.8	69.3
Black	11.8	9.6	36.4	8.8	10.3
Hispanic	4.6	3.2	5.4	21.9	6.7
Asian or Pacific Islander	5.7	4.5	5.2	7.0	13.3
Other	0.5	0.5	0.5	0.5	0.4
Total	100.0	100.0	100.0	100.0	100.0

Source: National Study of College Experience, 1997 cohort; The College Board; the Common Core of Data from 1996 for non–New Jersey Residents; the Common Core of Data from 1995 for New Jersey Residents; and Private School Universe Sample 1998 Data.

Note: Data on high school type, elite 72 high school, and SAT score are based on NSCE survey data. Data on racial composition contain fewer observations because they come from high-school-level data, and some students could not be matched to their high school. Data on free lunch comprise even fewer observations because that information is only asked of public schools.

[a]Average SAT score of graduating high school seniors who took the SAT.

schools qualify for a free lunch. Black and Hispanic matriculants have about twice the proportion of classmates receiving free meals as do white and Asian matriculants.

While white matriculants are the least likely during high school to have an opportunity to interact with students from other racial backgrounds, Asian matriculants are the most likely. This conclusion is based on an examination of racial composition of NSCE students' high schools. These demographic balances (or imbalances, as is sometimes the case) affect opportunities for social interaction in high school. The typical NSCE student attended a high school where 77 percent of the students are white, 12 percent are black, 5 percent are Hispanic, and 6 percent are Asian. The average white attends a high school where more than four in five students are white. In other words, there are just 0.22 nonwhite students for every white student in high schools attended by white NSCE students. By contrast, NSCE minority students are much more exposed than white students to high school peers from other racial backgrounds. Only about one in three students at NSCE blacks' high schools are coethnics, followed by one in five students at Hispanics' schools, and just over one in ten students at high schools attended by NSCE Asian students. Asians are especially likely to attend multiracial schools. Their high schools contain the second highest percentage of whites after whites' own schools, the second highest percentage of black students after blacks' own schools, and the second highest percentage of Hispanics after Hispanics' own schools.[32]

Our data on the racial composition of high schools also reflect moderately high levels of racial segregation, especially for black and Hispanic students. In the absence of any segregation, the racial composition of high schools attended by whites, blacks, Hispanics, and Asians would be the same. However, the proportion of blacks in high schools attended by blacks is 3.1 times as high as it is for the average NSCE student. The corresponding proportion for Hispanic students is 4.8.

NSCE students' perceptions of the racial diversity of their high schools correspond well with the actual high school racial composition data exhibited by the 1997 cohort. As Figure 4.6 illustrates, Asians are the most likely to report attending a very diverse school. Almost one-third claim

---

for students who attended public high schools. Nevertheless, it is a useful gauge of the social class makeup of high school students.

[32] Orfield and Lee's (2006) analysis of primary and secondary public school students nationwide also finds that in 2003–4 whites were the most isolated from other race groups and that Asians were the most likely to attend multiracial schools. Compared to public school students nationwide, white NSCE students are slightly more exposed to Asian and black students, though less exposed to Hispanics. Depending on their race, NSCE minority groups have 22 to 34 percentage points more whites attending their schools than do minority groups in public schools nationally.

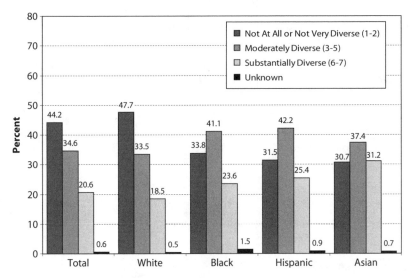

Figure 4.6. Percentage Distribution of Matriculants' Assessments of the Diversity of Their High School, by Race; NSCE Matriculant Sample: 1980s, 1993, and 1997 Cohorts Combined (N = 6,350). Note: NSCE respondents were asked to report how racially or ethnically diverse their high school was using a seven-point scale, with 1 reflecting "not at all diverse" and 7 representing "substantially diverse." Students who gave their school a 6 or 7 were placed in the "substantially diverse" category, those who gave a 3, 4, or 5 were placed in the "moderately diverse" category, and those who gave a 1 or a 2 were placed in the "not at all or not very diverse" category. Racial differences are statistically significant at the .001 level. Source: National Study of College Experience.

that the diversity of their high school was substantial, compared to one-quarter of blacks and Hispanics and less than one-fifth of whites. Almost half of white students rate their school as not at all or not very diverse. The race-specific ratio in Figure 4.6 between the proportion of students reporting their high school is "substantially" diverse and the proportion reporting "not at all" diverse increases monotonically with the proportion of non-coethnics observed in Table 4.11. This suggests that when students think about diversity, they mean the prevalence of other students who are not like them.

Turning to social class, our data suggest that as students' socioeconomic status increases, the likelihood of their graduating from public or magnet schools decreases, and the chance of their becoming alumni from parochial, private, or elite schools rises. However, the results in Table 4.12 indicate that lower-class NSCE matriculants are the exception to this pattern. These students are the least likely of all social class groups to be

TABLE 4.12
High School Characteristics, by Socioeconomic Status
NSCE Matriculant Sample: Fall 1997 Cohort

High School Characteristics	Lower	Working	Middle	Upper-Middle	Upper
Type of High School (N = 2,270)					
Public	45.2	72.3	71.6	62.3	56.4
Magnet	18.7	14.4	7.4	7.0	0.6
Parochial/Religious	3.7	6.5	7.1	8.4	12.4
Private	27.7	4.7	9.2	21.0	29.7
Unknown	4.7	2.1	4.7	1.3	0.9
Elite 72 High School (N = 2,270)					
Yes	15.7	2.0	4.9	4.8	11.7
No	84.3	96.1	92.7	92.5	78.7
Unknown	0.0	1.9	2.4	2.7	9.6
Average High School SAT Score[a] (N = 2,270)					
<1000	41.3	25.4	20.4	7.8	1.0
1000–1099	13.3	36.7	28.5	34.8	15.0
1100–1199	16.7	26.5	33.6	33.8	47.2
1200–1299	23.0	6.8	10.0	16.9	20.6
1300–1399	3.1	2.1	4.8	3.9	6.3
1400 or higher	2.7	0.3	0.3	0.1	0.0
Unknown	0.0	2.1	2.5	2.8	9.9
Socioeconomic Composition (N = 1,384)					
Students Eligible for Free School Lunch (%)	30.6	14.9	11.3	8.1	4.3
Racial Composition (N = 1,936)					
White	42.1	66.3	75.9	80.0	84.2
Black	29.2	19.7	13.8	9.8	4.0
Hispanic	17.9	7.9	4.6	4.1	2.7
Asian or Pacific Islander	10.3	5.2	5.3	5.7	8.7
Other	0.5	0.9	0.4	0.4	0.4
Total	100.0	100.0	100.0	100.0	100.0

Source: National Study of College Experience, 1997 cohort; The College Board; the Common Core of Data from 1996 for non–New Jersey Residents; the Common Core of Data from 1995 for New Jersey Residents; and Private School Universe Sample 1998 Data.

Note: Data on high school type, elite 72 high school, and SAT score are based on NSCE survey data. Data on racial composition contain fewer observations because they come from high-school-level data, and some students could not be matched to their high school. Data on free lunch comprise even fewer observations because that information is only asked of public schools.

[a] Average SAT score of graduating high school seniors who took the SAT.

educated at a public high school and the *most* likely to graduate from an elite high school. Moreover, they are nearly as likely as upper-class students to receive a diploma from a private secondary school.[33]

High school quality also varies by students' social class. Typically, the higher matriculants' socioeconomic status is, the more likely they are to attend schools whose students have high average SAT scores, and the less likely they are to study at schools with low scores. Lower-class students are, once again, the exception to this pattern. Twenty-nine percent of lower-class matriculants received their diplomas from a high school with an average SAT score of 1200 or above, making them more likely than even upper-class students to attend high-scoring schools. Although a substantial proportion of lower-class students attend top secondary schools, an even larger proportion study at the very weakest institutions. Forty-one percent graduated from a school with an average score below 1000, a higher percentage than that of any other social class.[34]

Unlike the results for high school type and quality, the socioeconomic composition of matriculants' high schools is directly correlated with students' own socioeconomic status. Though we only have data from students attending public high schools, we find that the high-school-wide percentage of students who are poor enough to be eligible for a free lunch decreases as matriculants' own socioeconomic status increases. About 31 percent of students at lower-class matriculants' high schools receive a free lunch. For all other socioeconomic groups that percentage is less than half that amount, falling to just 4 percent at upper-class matriculants' schools. Thus, the more prosperous NSCE matriculants are, the

[33] The anomalous situation of low-income students is perhaps traceable to several factors, all of which have to do with an intervention of one kind or another. In some cases, an individual or "sponsor" identifies an exceptionally talented lower-class student and arranges to have her placed in a more rigorous academic environment (Levine and Nidiffer, 1996). This sponsor could be a teacher, relative, minister, or some other influential adult. Some of the more elite private secondary schools also attract low SES or minority students by operating affirmative action programs similar to those at academically selective colleges and universities. Programs such as Prep for Prep and A Better Chance also help channel talented low-income students into college by placing them in high-quality high schools. A number of university summer programs, including Princeton University's Preparatory Program and Harvard University's Crimson Summer Academy, have the goal of identifying academically talented, low-income students in the surrounding community and preparing them for admission to top colleges and universities (Butler, 2006). But these programs do not generally aim to affect the high schools that students attend.

[34] The bimodality in average SAT scores at lower-class students' high schools largely reflects differences in high school type. Seventy-seven percent of the lower-class students at high schools with scores above 1200 attended private schools. Eighty-eight percent of the lower-class students at schools with scores below 1000 studied at regular public or public magnet high schools.

less likely they are to attend high schools with substantial proportions of poor students.

We also find that the more affluent students are, the less likely they are to come from racially diverse high schools. As Table 4.12 indicates, as matriculants' socioeconomic status increases, so does the percentage of white high school classmates. Conversely, the proportion of black and Hispanic students decreases monotonically the greater matriculants' socioeconomic status. The percentage of Asian students at matriculants' high schools follows a nonlinear pattern; lower- and upper-class matriculants' schools have the highest percentages of Asian students.[35]

COMMUNITY CHARACTERISTICS

High schools are not the only contexts that shape matriculants. Neighborhoods and communities in which students grow up should also affect students' academic and social adjustments to college. For example, Massey et al. (2003: 78–86) find that Latino and black undergraduates who are raised in neighborhoods that are more than 70 percent black and/or Hispanic are particularly likely to be exposed to high levels of social disorder and violence, which can impair cognitive functioning. Students who grow up in affluent communities, on the other hand, experience conditions that can facilitate academic success in several ways. First, high SES communities are more able to provide resources to their public schools, which can then be used to better prepare students for the rigor of college classes. Second, Ainsworth (2002) finds that affluent communities' high percentage of college-educated and managerially or professionally employed residents encourages area high school students to develop greater educational degree aspirations, which in turn improve students' academic performance. This neighborhood effect on aspirations may resonate even after students have left their community to attend college, influencing how matriculants approach their college coursework. Third, the socioeconomic composition of matriculants' home communities may shape students' social adjustment to college life as well. Matriculants raised in lower SES communities can find it more difficult to adapt to the social climate of elite colleges than do students more accustomed to living near high SES individuals (Ewers, 2005; Kaufman, 2001).

---

[35] Matriculants' perceptions of their high schools' diversity are congruent with the actual racial composition found in the 1997 cohort's high schools. Low SES students are more likely to report high levels of diversity than are middle-class and high SES students. That said, social class differences in students' self-reports are not statistically significant at the .05 level.

TABLE 4.13
Community Characteristics, by Race
NSCE Matriculant Sample: 1980s, 1993, and 1997 Cohorts Combined

Community Characteristics	Total	White	Black	Hispanic	Asian
Racial and Ethnic Composition (%)					
White	86.1	89.6	57.9	79.5	84.1
Black	9.1	6.7	37.1	7.4	6.1
Hispanic	3.8	2.6	4.7	20.5	5.2
Asian	2.9	2.2	2.3	4.5	7.5
Total	101.9	101.1	102.0	111.9	102.9
Socioeconomic Composition[a]					
Percent with College Degree or More	28.5	28.9	20.3	25.0	32.9
Percent with Professional Degree	11.3	11.5	7.9	9.8	12.7
Percent Employed as Executive, Administrator, Manager, or Professional	34.1	34.4	27.2	31.3	37.8
Median Family Household Income (in dollars)	61,810	62,430	47,860	56,760	69,520

Source: National Study of College Experience; 1980 census; 1990 census.

Note: In an effort to capture the characteristics of communities in which students are raised, data are based on the 1980 census for the 1980s cohort and the 1990 census for the 1993 and 1997 cohorts. The number of observations is slightly smaller than in our full sample because not all NSCE college and university records contained student zip codes that matched census records' five-digit zip-code level summary files. There are 5,277 observations for all variables except for median income, for which the number of observations is 5,279. Racial and ethnic compositions do not sum to 100.0 because those who report Hispanic ethnicity are also instructed to choose a racial category in the U.S. census forms. Dollar figures have been adjusted to reflect 1996–97 constant dollars.

[a]The percents in various educational or occupational categories are based on persons age eighteen or older.

Moderate levels of racial residential segregation characterize the neighborhoods where NSCE students grew up.[36] Table 4.13 illustrates community characteristics according to the race of NSCE students. The average NSCE student lives in an area that is 86 percent white, 9 percent black, 4 percent Hispanic, and 3 percent Asian. Differences by students' race reveal some degree of neighborhood racial segregation, but certainly less than that observed nationwide. For example, the typical black matriculant grew up in a community that is 37 percent black—four times as high as the corresponding proportion for the average NSCE student.

[36] The geographic scope of one's neighborhood is approximated by a student's five-digit zip code. Community characteristics are developed from zip-code files from the 1980 census data for the 1980s cohort and from the 1990 census data for the 1993 and 1997 cohorts.

The contrast is even more striking for Hispanic students, who have more than five times the percentage of Hispanics in their neighborhoods as the average NSCE matriculant. Table 4.13 also indicates that, based on demography alone, white students have limited opportunity to come into contact with nonwhites in their neighborhoods. On the other hand, minority students should have many opportunities to interact with whites in their communities—though not with other nonwhite racial minorities.[37]

These differences in potential exposure to other racial groups are likely to influence campus climate. As Cage (1995) explains, because black college students typically grow up in integrated areas and white college students do not, black students have to teach white students about black culture, while whites have little new to explain to blacks about white culture. In other words, cross-cultural exchanges between black and white students travel in just one direction, from blacks to whites. Since Asians and Hispanics also have had greater exposure to whites than whites have had to them, the cultural exchanges between Asians and whites and Hispanics and whites are likely to be mostly unidirectional as well. In other words, students from nondominant cultures often grow up knowing a good deal about the dominant culture. At the same time, Hispanics, blacks, and Asians have relatively fewer opportunities during their high school years to interact with each other in their neighborhoods, making it more likely that cross-cultural exchanges between them in college will be a two-way street.

Reflecting a societal pattern, white and Asian students have typically grown up in more prosperous communities than have black and Hispanic students. On average, NSCE students live in areas where close to one-third of adults age eighteen or older have a college degree or more, 11 percent hold a graduate degree, and more than one-third work as executives, administrators, managers, or professionals. The median income in communities that produce selective college students is almost $62,000 in 1996–97 dollars. These figures indicate that NSCE students' communities are somewhat more affluent than America as a whole. For instance, the 2000 U.S. census revealed that 24 percent of all Americans age

---

[37] These data reflect the pervasive residential segregation in America that other scholars have underscored. At the same time, all race groups of NSCE students live in communities in which the majority of residents are white. In fact, NSCE blacks', Hispanics', and Asians' neighborhoods contain approximately 25, 43, and 30 percentage points more whites, respectively, than the metropolitan areas inhabited by their racial counterparts nationally (Logan, Stults, and Farley, 2004). NSCE whites also live in communities that are ten percentage points more white (90 versus 80 percent) than suburban and urban whites nationally (Logan, Stults, and Farley, 2004). In short, nonwhite students who attend NSCE schools are not as racially isolated in their neighborhoods as national data would suggest. For more on U.S. patterns of residential segregation, see Massey and Denton (1993).

twenty-five or older had at least a bachelor's degree and the median family household income in 1999 was $50,046 (U.S. Census Bureau, 2000a). Asians generally live in the highest SES communities, followed by whites, Hispanics,[38] and then further behind by blacks. Asian students' communities have 13 percentage points more college-educated residents than do blacks' communities and nearly as large a gap (11 percentage points) in the proportion of residents in executive occupations. The Asian-black difference in median income is even more pronounced. In Asian students' neighborhoods the median family household income reaches almost $70,000, while in black students' neighborhoods that figure is only $48,000.[39]

The relationship between the racial composition of the communities in which NSCE matriculants are raised and students' social class follows the same pattern observed for high schools. Table 4.14 shows that the higher a student's socioeconomic status, the greater the percentage of white neighbors in his or her community and the lower the percentage of black and Hispanic ones. Likewise, the percentage of Asians in the neighborhood falls into a mild U-shaped pattern. The proportion of Asians living in lower- and upper-class students' neighborhoods is slightly higher than the proportion of Asians living in middle SES students' communities.

Not surprisingly, there is a positive correlation between students' family socioeconomic status and the socioeconomic composition of the community in which students are raised. Median income, as well as the

[38]While Hispanics trail whites in the full sample, when we compare just public college students we find that Hispanic students' communities exhibit a higher median family income and higher percentages of residents who are college educated, professionally educated, or employed as executives than do white students' communities. Public college Hispanics are thus similar to whites and Asians not only in their family socioeconomic status but also in their community socioeconomic status.

[39]It is important to remember that the median income in the community does not necessarily match the income of NSCE matriculants' families. About one-third of NSCE Asians and whites and one-quarter of NSCE blacks and Hispanics believe their family's income is greater than that of their neighbors. Hispanics are the most likely to view their family's income as below that of their neighbors (25 percent), followed by Asians and blacks (16 percent) and then whites (14 percent). These data also imply that NSCE students' neighborhoods are segregated by social class. When students are questioned about their social class backgrounds (results shown in Table 4.7), the implicit reference group is families throughout the United States. However, when respondents are asked, "Compared with other families in your neighborhood during your senior year in high school, would you say your household's income was . . . ," the reference group shrinks to one's more immediate surroundings. The fact that racial differences in responses to the relative neighborhood income question are smaller than those to the social class question provides evidence for the existence of neighborhood segregation along social class lines, because families' incomes are much more like those of their neighbors than those of Americans nationally.

TABLE 4.14
Community Characteristics, by Socioeconomic Status
NSCE Matriculant Sample: 1980s, 1993, and 1997 Cohorts Combined

Community Characteristics	Lower	Working	Middle	Upper-Middle	Upper
Racial and Ethnic Composition (%)					
White	63.4	75.4	85.4	88.8	90.3
Black	25.5	18.0	9.9	6.8	4.8
Hispanic	13.3	6.8	3.6	3.2	3.0
Asian	3.6	2.8	2.6	3.1	3.6
Total	105.8	103.0	101.5	101.9	101.7
Socioeconomic Composition[a]					
Percent with College Degree or More	14.6	18.0	24.3	32.8	41.0
Percent with Professional Degree	5.2	6.4	9.3	13.2	17.3
Percent Employed as Executive, Administrator, Manager, or Professional	22.0	25.4	30.7	37.6	44.0
Median Family Household Income (in dollars)	39,180	48,120	55,870	67,150	84,120

Source: National Study of College Experience; 1980 census; 1990 census.

Note: In an effort to capture the characteristics of communities in which students are raised, data are based on the 1980 census for the 1980s cohort and the 1990 census for the 1993 and 1997 cohorts. The number of observations is slightly smaller than in our full sample because not all NSCE college and university records contained student zip codes that matched census records' five-digit zip-code level summary files. There are 5,277 observations for all variables except for median income, for which the number of observations is 5,279. Racial and ethnic compositions do not sum to 100.0 because those who report Hispanic ethnicity are also instructed to choose a racial category in the U.S. census forms. Dollar figures have been adjusted to reflect 1996–97 constant dollars.

[a]The percents in various educational or occupational categories are based on persons age eighteen or older.

percentage of adult community members with a college degree or more, a professional degree, and executive employment, grows with students' increased socioeconomic status.[40] In sum, the socioeconomic characteristics of students' communities share a high degree of similarity with their own families' socioeconomic status; students who are more socioeconomically advantaged themselves come from more socioeconomically advantaged communities.

[40] While the median income of the community rises with students' socioeconomic status, the community's median income does not appear to overtake the income of students' parents. The higher students' socioeconomic status the more likely they are to also perceive their families' income as above that of their neighbors.

Summary

We conclude this chapter by first comparing our findings on the characteristics of students at selective colleges with those observed by Douglas Massey and his colleagues in the National Longitudinal Survey of Freshmen (NLSF)—a sample of white, black, Latino, and Asian students who entered twenty-eight elite colleges in 1999 (Massey et al., 2003).[41] To a close approximation, both the NLSF and NSCE study the same kinds of students—matriculants at academically selective colleges and universities in the United States. The general picture that emerges from a comparison is one of substantial agreement between the NSCE and NLSF in their statistical portraits of students and their families, high schools, and neighborhoods. Differences in outcomes between the two studies seem to be relatively minor and largely explainable in terms of different sampling strategies and/or different measures. For instance, the NLSF includes more institutions, but the NSCE sample contains at least 60 percent more enrolled students. NSCE data encompass a broader time span—three entering student cohorts, the earliest of which capture data from the 1980s. Lastly, the NSCE sample includes all enrolled students—both citizens and non-citizens—whereas the NLSF is limited to U.S. citizens and resident aliens.[42]

Both surveys contain roughly the same proportions of multiracial whites, blacks, and Asians. Differences in the percentage of multiracial Hispanics arise because of the different ways Hispanic ethnicity is measured. The distributions of matriculants by immigrant generation and countries of origin are quite similar between the surveys except for Asian students, 40 percent of whom are first-generation immigrants in the NSCE compared to 32 percent in the NLSF. This small difference is likely due to the inclusion of non-citizens in the NSCE.

Comparing the two studies also reveals that NSCE parents generally come from modestly lower socioeconomic status backgrounds than do NLSF parents. Both fathers and mothers in the NSCE are somewhat less likely than NLSF parents to have completed at least a bachelor's degree, although some of this gap is narrowed when just the 1997 NSCE cohort

---

[41] Bowen and Bok (1998) and Bowen, Kurzweil, and Tobin (2005) examine elite college students, but they do not include information about Hispanic and Asian students' backgrounds. Their findings are therefore not as easily compared to our results as are Massey et al.'s (2003).

[42] The sampling plan for the NLSF sample stipulates the following: "To be eligible for inclusion in the sample, a respondent had to be enrolled at the institution in question as a first-time freshman and be a U.S. citizen or resident alien. Foreign and returning students were excluded from the sample" (Massey et al., 2003: 29).

is considered.[43] The two surveys are comparable, however, in terms of proportions of parents who hold advanced degrees. Black and Hispanic NSCE fathers exhibit lower occupational achievement than their NLSF counterparts. This difference extends to all race groups for NSCE mothers. However, the two surveys have different ways of recording and coding what constitutes a managerial or professional occupation. Rates of homeownership are similar between the NSCE and NLSF, as are the proportions of families whose annual income exceeds $100,000. Only NSCE Asian households stand out for their above-average incomes compared to NLSF Asian families.

School and community differences between the two surveys are also relatively minor. While there is little variation in the proportion of students who attended a public or magnet high school, the notable exception pertains to NSCE Asian students, who are more likely than their NLSF peers to have graduated from a private high school. Also, the proportion of white classmates in NSCE students' high schools, as registered in administrative reports to the U.S. Department of Education, is about ten percentage points higher than comparable proportions self-reported by NLSF students. Some of this difference is doubtless traceable to NLSF students' faulty perceptions. Similarly, the proportion of whites who live in NSCE respondents' neighborhoods is greater than the white proportion in the NLSF. The difference is on the order of 15 to 20 percentage points for nonwhite respondents, but less than five percentage points for whites. Several factors, apart from real differences, may help account for the gap. First, the NSCE proportion is based on census reports, whereas respondents' own estimates underlie the NLSF data. Second, the concept of "neighborhood" in the NLSF is a three-block radius surrounding a respondent's home whereas in the NSCE it is the five-digit zip code. Finally, "white" includes whites and Hispanics in the census data, which may help inflate the percentage of whites in the NSCE analyses. The NLSF keeps these two groups separate.

Though there is extensive symmetry in selective college students' characteristics that are captured in the NSCE and NLSF surveys, substantial differences are apparent when the 1997 entering cohort of NSCE students is compared with all college freshmen in 1997. Based on data from UCLA's American Freshman Survey (Sax et al., 1997), there are three important differences between students who attend America's elite colleges and universities and those who are enrolled at all four-year colleges and

---

[43] Census data reveal, for example, that the percentage of college-educated Americans has increased by more than eight percentage points between the point at which NSCE students first started entering college in the early 1980s and NLSF students entered college in 1999 (U.S. Census Bureau, 2003).

universities. First, Asian students are disproportionately represented (by about nine percentage points) at academically selective institutions compared to all four-year institutions. Second, NSCE students tend on average to be drawn from the upper portions of the socioeconomic status distribution. For example, compared with the fathers of all college freshmen, NSCE fathers are 28 percentage points more likely to have earned at least a bachelor's degree. Almost as large a gap (23 percentage points) exists when mothers are compared. Third, NSCE college students are substantially more "college ready" than their counterparts nationwide. Eighty-five percent of NSCE students earned a high school GPA of A− or better compared with just 42 percent of all four-year college freshmen in 1997. Moreover, in 1997 the average SAT score among NSCE freshmen exceeded the average for all college-bound high school seniors by 257 points out of 1600 (College Board, 1997).

We end by highlighting the four most important findings of this chapter. First, among students who are accepted by NSCE institutions, individuals from upper-class backgrounds are most likely to enroll. Second, Asian students come to NSCE colleges and universities with the strongest academic records and black students with the weakest, as measured by high school grades, class rank, and standardized test scores. Students from low and middle SES families have the best high school records, but high SES students have stronger test scores. Third, a substantial percentage (more than one-third at private schools) of NSCE college students are immigrants or the children of immigrants. The proportion of black NSCE matriculants who are first- or second-generation immigrants and/or multiracial is particularly high at selective colleges and universities (31 percent across all entering cohorts) and is more pronounced at private than at public institutions (50 versus 21 percent, respectively). Fourth, at NSCE institutions as a whole, white and Asian students come from much more affluent families, high schools, and communities than do their Hispanic and black counterparts, thus mirroring patterns in the broader society. The lower socioeconomic position of Hispanic students compared to whites and Asians pertains largely to students at private NSCE institutions. At public universities, Hispanic students enjoy many of the same advantages as their white and Asian peers, while black students remain comparatively more disadvantaged.

Chapter Five

MIXING AND MINGLING ON CAMPUS

INTRODUCTION

The U.S. Supreme Court reaffirmed in *Grutter v. Bollinger* (2003) that there are substantial educational benefits to diversity and declared that student diversity in higher education represents a compelling state interest.[1] There is ample research to illustrate the personal and societal benefits when students interact with classmates from different racial backgrounds. In their comprehensive review of the literature, Chang, Astin, and Kim (2004) report that students who have more cross-racial interaction exhibit greater cognitive development, more positive academic and social self-concepts, higher graduation rates, increased leadership skills, more cultural awareness and understanding, higher levels of civic interest, and greater college satisfaction. Similarly, Levin, Van Laar, and Sidanius (2003) find that sophomores and juniors who have more friendships with students from other backgrounds and fewer friendships with those who share their own background demonstrate less prejudice when they graduate, even after controlling for their prejudice levels as first-year students, pre-university friendships, and other background variables. Van Laar et al. (2005) report that freshmen who are randomly assigned to live with a roommate of a different race exhibit increased interethnic competence and interethnic dating, as well as decreased interethnic unease, symbolic racism, and social dominance orientation.[2]

At the same time, simply attending a diverse college does not guarantee these benefits will materialize. To realize these gains, students must interact with individuals from different backgrounds.[3] Thus, in this chapter,

[1] The Court's simultaneous ruling in *Gratz v. Bollinger* (2003) underscored the fact that while universities can implement policies designed to create a racially diverse student body, these policies must be "narrowly tailored."

[2] See Pidot (2006), however, for a more skeptical view of the social science evidence linking numeric diversity, diversity experiences, and educational benefits of diversity for white and nonwhite students.

[3] As Moody (2001) has pointed out, high schools can be racially heterogeneous and still be substantively segregated if students choose to interact primarily with same-race friends. There is a conceptually analogous situation concerning patterns of racial residential segregation. Cities can be diverse even though neighborhoods within them are racially segregated (Charles, 2003, 2006; Massey and Denton, 1993).

we examine factors that are related to students' engagements in these promising cross-racial interactions. Identifying these influences should help college deans and other administrators create environments in which the educational benefits of a diverse student body are most likely to be maximized.

This chapter examines how students engage with racial and ethnic diversity in numerous areas of college life. Using data on students at all eight NSCE colleges and universities and in all three entering cohorts (1980s, 1993, or 1997), we begin by exploring which students take ethnic studies courses, pursue ethnic extracurricular activities, and choose to live in racially focused housing. Next, we describe how often students interact with faculty and staff from a different racial or ethnic background. Finally, we investigate students' cross-racial social interactions with classmates of a different race in general and with students from specific racial groups. Given the orientation of this chapter, we emphasize how undergraduates' engagement with race and ethnicity varies by respondents' race rather than socioeconomic status.

DIALOGUES ABOUT RACE AND ETHNICITY

There are several ways in which students can become engaged with race and ethnicity during college. One is to enroll in ethnic studies courses. Another is to participate in ethnic activities and organizations. Still a third is to live in a dorm or house that focuses on a specific racial or ethnic heritage. Any of these behaviors is likely to encourage students to grapple with ideas and issues surrounding race and ethnicity. Some of them, such as taking an ethnic studies course about another racial group or participating in an ethnic activity celebrating another racial group, may foster interracial dialogue with faculty, staff, and other students. Yet others, such as participating in an ethnic organization or living in a dorm with students only of a specific heritage, are likely to be particularly conducive to intraracial discussions about race and ethnicity.

Intraracial explorations of race and ethnicity can be just as important as interracial dialogues. For example, Tatum (1997: 72–73) finds that black students in a multiracial high school performed better academically when they started meeting daily as coethnics to discuss issues and problems. Moreover, participating in an organization that is oriented toward a specific race group does not preclude interacting with students of other backgrounds. In fact, there is some evidence that participating in coethnic groupings may facilitate better interracial interactions (Tatum, 1997: 73). Finally, we should note that it may be important for some minority students to immerse themselves in a community of coethnics during college

TABLE 5.1

Focus and Quantity of Ethnic Studies Coursework, by Race
NSCE Matriculant Sample: 1980s, 1993, and 1997 Cohorts
Combined (N = 6,350)

Percent Participating in	Total	White	Black	Hispanic	Asian
African/African American Studies					
Major	0.5	0.2	4.2	0.3	0.3
Minor	1.4	1.0	7.7	0.7	0.4
Course	24.3	20.9	75.6	20.9	15.1
Chicano/Latino Studies					
Major	0.8	0.6	1.1	4.5	0.4
Minor	1.7	1.6	1.5	5.4	1.1
Course	12.1	10.9	19.0	40.7	6.3
Asian/Asian American Studies					
Major	1.0	0.7	0.7	0.2	3.7
Minor	1.0	0.4	1.2	0.7	4.7
Course	17.3	12.8	14.7	13.2	52.2
One or More of the Above					
Major	2.2	1.4	5.5	5.1	4.2
Minor	3.6	2.6	9.5	6.2	5.8
Course	39.6	32.4	79.8	51.2	58.5

Source: National Study of College Experience.
Note: Racial differences for each row item are statistically significant at the .001 level.

in order to further their own racial identity development (Martínez Alemán, 2000; Tatum, 1997) and/or receive the support they need to succeed in a predominantly white university environment (Antonio, 2004: 559–62; Martínez Alemán, 2000).

Ethnic Studies Concentrations and Coursework

First we examine NSCE students' participation in ethnic studies. As the panel at the bottom of Table 5.1 shows, only a small proportion of students major (2 percent) or minor (4 percent) in African American, Latino, or Asian studies, but 40 percent take at least one course in these subject areas.[4] Some racial groups are more likely to sign up for such classes than are others, however. Blacks are most likely to major, minor, or take a

---

[4]While some universities require students to take a course that deals with race or ethnicity before graduating (Levine and Cureton, 1992), none of the schools in our sample has more than 65 percent of students per cohort taking an ethnic studies course. We can therefore reasonably assume that students elected to enroll in these classes.

course in some kind of ethnic studies. Eighty percent enroll in at least one class. Though Hispanics are slightly more likely than Asians to major or minor in ethnic studies, Asians are about seven percentage points more likely than Hispanics to take an ethnic studies course. Whites are the least likely to major, minor, or enroll in an ethnic studies class. More than two-thirds of white students do not participate in a single course.

In terms of the particular types of ethnic studies in which students are involved, African or African American studies appear most popular overall. Table 5.1 shows that almost one-quarter of NSCE matriculants take a course in this area. By comparison, just 12 percent enroll in a Chicano studies course and 17 percent in an Asian studies class. In addition, students are most likely to major, minor, or enroll in ethnic studies courses that mirror their own racial or ethnic backgrounds. Three-fourths of all black students take a class in African or African American studies. Similarly, 41 percent of Hispanic students take at least one course in Chicano or Latino studies, and 52 percent of Asian students enroll in an Asian or Asian American studies course. These percentages are much higher than for non-coethnics taking these classes. Finally, to the extent that African or African American studies courses represent the ethnic studies courses "of choice" on selective college and university campuses, it is partly because they are elected more often by white students over courses in Latino studies (by a margin of ten percentage points) or Asian American studies (by a difference of eight percentage points). In addition, while Asians and Latinos are most likely to take a course about their own ethnic group, they are next most likely to study African Americans.[5]

Ethnic Activities and Organizations

Students are able to explore their own and others' race and ethnicity not only by taking classes but also by participating in ethnic activities and organizations. As Table 5.2 shows, almost 40 percent of all NSCE students engage in one or more ethnic activities. NSCE students are most likely to attend ethnic programs with an African American focus. While 28 percent of NSCE students take part in a Black History month activity at some point during college, smaller fractions participate in Asian month (15 percent) or Chicano month (12 percent) events. The greater involvement in African American programs is again partially due to African Americans' own high levels of participation. Nearly 80 percent of African

[5] Students' greater propensity to take a course on African Americans cannot be attributed only to colleges being more likely to offer a course on this group than on other ethnic groups. Even when we limit the analysis to students who reported that non–African American studies courses were offered at their college, we find that students are still most likely to take an African American studies class.

TABLE 5.2
Participation in Ethnic Extracurricular Activities, by Race
NSCE Matriculant Sample: 1980s, 1993, and 1997 Cohorts Combined (N = 6,350)

Percent Participating in	Total	White	Black	Hispanic	Asian
Ethnic Activity Celebrating					
Black History Month	28.2	24.4	78.5	33.4	19.4
Chicano/Latino History Month	11.9	8.2	29.5	50.2	12.4
Asian American/Pacific Islander Month	14.9	8.6	15.7	20.3	56.8
One or More of the Above	38.2	29.9	79.4	58.1	61.8
Ethnic Organization[a]	20.0	11.7	52.5	37.6	50.5

Source: National Study of College Experience.
Note: Racial differences for each row item are statistically significant at the .001 level.
[a]For the purposes of this analysis students are counted as belonging to an ethnic organization if they cite any of the organizations in which they participated during college to be oriented "toward a specific racial or ethnic group."

American students engage in an activity honoring their own heritage, as compared to 50 percent of Hispanics and 57 percent of Asians. Yet, like participation in African American academic programs, involvement in black activities is also greater because non-black students show greater interest. Not only are whites three times as likely to participate in an African American event as a Chicano or an Asian one, but the most common ethnic activity for Hispanic and Asian students—after one that celebrates their own ancestry—is one that commemorates the heritage of black students.[6]

As Table 5.2 also indicates, 20 percent of all NSCE students belong to an organization that is oriented toward a particular racial or ethnic group. Nevertheless, certain race groups are more likely to put their time and energy toward an ethnic organization than are others. Black and Asian students are the most likely to be members of an ethnic club, although only slightly more than half belong for even as little as one year of college. Next most likely are Hispanic students, close to two out of every five of whom join such an organization. White students are by far the least likely group to belong to an ethnic organization.

Racially Focused Dorms

Lastly, we examine the percentage of students who engage with diversity through their residential environment. Some schools offer matriculants

---

[6]Even analyzing the percent participating out of just respondents who acknowledge that the activity existed at their school indicates that higher percentages of students participate in black activities.

an option of living in an on-campus dorm or house that has a racial or an ethnic theme. Fewer than 2 percent of all NSCE students opt for such a living arrangement, with whites (at 0.5 percent) the least likely to do so. Still, 6 percent of blacks, 5 percent of Hispanics, and 3 percent of Asians choose this residential option for some portion of their college years.[7] Though we do not know the exact ethnic group on which students' race-based housing is focused, we might assume that most students living in such housing reside with classmates who share the same ethnicity.

Students' Interactions with Faculty and Staff

Students engage with race and ethnicity not just in the curriculum but also through the people whom they encounter during college. Some of these individuals are faculty members and staff. Interactions with faculty and administrators of a different race or ethnicity may be particularly important in securing the advantages of diversity. Allport (1979: 276) finds that knowing blacks who occupy a higher occupational social status is particularly effective in lowering racial prejudice about blacks. He predicts that seeing people of other racial backgrounds in high positions should have similar effects.

The vast majority of students at NSCE colleges take most of their courses with white faculty. About 86 percent of white and Hispanic students, 87 percent of Asian, and 90 percent of black students report that at least 50 percent of their professors are white. As a result, most minority students interact with faculty of a different racial background quite often while white students do not. Only 9 percent of white students report that 10 percent or more of their classes are taught by Asian, black, or Hispanic faculty.

Yet even when students are taught by faculty of another background, fruitful cross-racial interactions may be limited depending on the size and structure of the course. The more personal nature of cross-racial interactions with campus adults outside the classroom may actually be more likely to lessen prejudice because these exchanges may be more likely to expose individuals' common interests and humanity (see Allport, 1979: 276). However, despite the benefits of such cross-racial interactions, white students find themselves associating mainly with campus adults who are also white. Only 6 percent claim that their interactions with faculty and staff are never or rarely with whites. Minority students, on the other hand, are far less likely to interact with campus adults of their own

---

[7] This same racial ordering in propensity to live in an ethnically focused dorm holds even when we analyze only students who report that their school offered theme dorms.

TABLE 5.3
Students' Social Relations with Students of
a Different Race or the Same Race
NSCE Matriculant Sample: 1980s, 1993,
and 1997 Cohorts Combined (N = 6,350)

Social Relation	Percent
Socialize Often/Very Often with	
Students of a Different Race	62.8
Students of the Same Race	92.4
Live with at Least One	
Student of a Different Race	51.2
Student of the Same Race	87.8
Have a Close Friendship with a	
Student of a Different Race	50.9
Student of the Same Race	92.5
Date at Least One	
Student of a Different Race	35.8
Student of the Same Race	83.9

Source: National Study of College Experience.
Note: These percentages are based on all students. Students
who do not socialize or who have no roommates, no friends, or
no dates are included in the denominator and considered not to
have experienced the particular type of social relation.

race or ethnicity. Forty-six percent of blacks and Hispanics and two-thirds of Asians meet never or rarely with campus staff and faculty of their background. In sum, minority students are more likely than whites to have cross-racial interactions with faculty and staff both inside and outside the classroom.

STUDENTS' INTERACTIONS WITH OTHER STUDENTS

We now examine students' interactions with each other during college. We are particularly interested in the extent of cross-racial interaction, because defendants in the two University of Michigan cases that went to the U.S. Supreme Court in 2003 argued that creating diversity through the admission process was important in producing a setting in which cross-racial interaction during college could occur. These kinds of interactions, it was alleged, are the ones that lead most profoundly to educational benefits. Table 5.3 highlights the percentage of matriculants who interact with classmates of a different race and of the same race in four different areas of social relations. It shows first that NSCE students are much more likely to have social relations with students of their own race than with those of a different race. Roughly nine-tenths of all students socialize frequently with, room with, and have a close friendship with a classmate from the same race or ethnic group, while five-sixths have dated at least one same-race individual. At the same time, cross-racial interactions are far from rare. General socializing is the most common form of intergroup interaction; nearly two-thirds of all NSCE students socialize often or very often with students of a different race. About half of NSCE matriculants live with a person of a different race at some point during college, and half identify a classmate of a different race among their five closest friends. Dating is the least common, and perhaps most intimate, type of interracial interaction. Just over one-third of all students report dating at least one person from a different racial background while attending their undergraduate institution.

Next we examine the proportion of students from individual race groups who maintain social relations with students from other specific race groups. In this way we can evaluate whether interracial relations between certain groups are more common than interracial relations between other groups. We begin with white students' likelihood of interacting with students from each of the four racial categories.

Whites

White students are much more likely to interact with other whites than with students of color. As Table 5.4 reveals, whites' most common social relation is having a white student as a close friend (97 percent), followed closely by socializing with, rooming with, and then dating another white student (90 percent). In contrast, 57 percent of whites report that they socialize often or very often with students of a different race, 44 percent have a close nonwhite friend, and 42 percent have at least one nonwhite roommate. Less than one-third of whites report dating a nonwhite student.

Whites' interactions with nonwhites are more likely to occur with Asians than with black or Hispanic students. For example, while roughly one-quarter of whites list an Asian student as one of their closest friends or as a roommate, only about 15 percent of whites have this type of relationship with black or Hispanic students. Whites are also more likely to socialize often or very often with Asians than with blacks or Hispanics. The margin of difference is substantial—11 percentage points over blacks and 22 over Hispanics. Whites' margin of interacting with Asian students shrinks, however, when we examine dating. Whites are only slightly more likely to report dating an Asian student than an Hispanic or black classmate.

TABLE 5.4
White Students' Likelihood of Having Social Relations with Students
from Specific Race Groups
NSCE Matriculant Sample: 1980s, 1993, and 1997 Cohorts Combined (N = 2,107)

Students Who Are/ Student Who Is:	Percent Socializing Often/Very Often with	Percent Living with at Least One	Percent Having a Close Friendship with a	Percent Dating at Least One
White	96.3	95.0	97.0	90.0
Of a Different Race	56.5	42.1	43.7	29.5
Black	32.1	16.5	15.8	12.2
Hispanic	21.2	13.6	13.7	12.5
Asian	42.7	26.1	26.3	16.3

Source: National Study of College Experience.

Note: These percentages are based on all white students. In other words, even whites who do not socialize or who have no roommates, no friends, or no dates are included and considered not to have experienced the particular type of social relation.

Blacks

Like their white peers, black students are generally more likely to associate with coethnics than with classmates from other racial or ethnic backgrounds. As Table 5.5 indicates, only with regard to patterns of living arrangements do blacks interact more with non-blacks than they do with other black students. In contrast with whites, however, black students appear to be less insular and more integrated across a broad range of campus experiences. A comparison of Tables 5.4 and 5.5 illustrates that black students are less likely than whites to engage in intraracial social interactions. For example, 87 percent of blacks report socializing often or very often with other black students, whereas 96 percent of whites report socializing this frequently with other white students. Moreover, a larger percentage of black than of white students mentions engaging in interracial interactions. To illustrate, 77 percent of black students say they socialize often or very often with non-black students, but just slightly more than half (57 percent) of whites report socializing frequently with non-whites. These differences imply that the gap between the prevalence of intraracial and interracial interaction is substantially less for blacks than for whites. For instance, a gap of ten percentage points separates the frequency of ingroup versus outgroup socializing for black students (87 versus 77 percent), whereas the corresponding gap for white students is almost 40 percentage points (96 versus 57 percent). Similarly, the difference in terms of ingroup versus outgroup dating behaviors is 34 percentage points for blacks, as compared to 60 percentage points for whites.

TABLE 5.5
Black Students' Likelihood of Having Social Relations with Students
from Specific Race Groups
NSCE Matriculant Sample: 1980s, 1993, and 1997 Cohorts Combined (N = 1,708)

Students Who Are/ Student Who Is:	Percent Socializing Often/Very Often with	Percent Living with at Least One	Percent Having a Close Friendship with a	Percent Dating at Least One
Black	86.5	70.9	87.1	75.9
Of a Different Race	76.6	75.2	62.3	41.8
White	67.5	69.9	52.8	33.9
Hispanic	30.4	11.7	15.7	15.1
Asian	27.5	22.2	22.0	12.0

Source: National Study of College Experience.
Note: These percentages are based on all black students. In other words, even blacks who do not social-ize or who have no roommates, no friends, or no dates are included and considered not to have experi-enced the particular type of social relation.

When black students interact with non-blacks, it is most commonly with white students. More than two-thirds of blacks socialize often or very often with whites or live with a white student.[8] More than half con-sider a white student to be one of their closest friends, and one-third have dated a white student. Blacks are much less likely to engage in the same kinds of social relations with either Hispanic or Asian students—in most cases less than half as likely—at least in part because of the lower repre-sentation of Hispanics and Asians on NSCE campuses. That said, blacks are twice as likely to have an Asian roommate as an Hispanic one and six percentage points more likely to have a close friend who is Asian rather than Hispanic.

Asians

The patterns of social interaction across racial and ethnic lines for Asian students are an extension of the patterns for black students. In particular, Asians are substantially more integrated than either whites or blacks and have social ties to racial outgroups that are as frequent, if not more so, as ingroup ties. As Table 5.6 demonstrates, Asians are actually six percent-age points *less* likely to socialize often or very often with other Asian stu-dents than with students from a different race. Moreover, they are 19 per-centage points less likely to live with another Asian student than with a

[8] By contrast, just one-third and one-sixth of whites, respectively, have the same interac-tions with blacks.

TABLE 5.6
Asian Students' Likelihood of Having Social Relations with Students
from Specific Race Groups
NSCE Matriculant Sample: 1980s, 1993, and 1997 Cohorts Combined (N = 1,475)

Students Who Are/ Student Who Is:	Percent Socializing Often/Very Often with	Percent Living with at Least One	Percent Having a Close Friendship with a	Percent Dating at Least One
Asian	80.6	65.7	79.3	59.1
Of a Different Race	86.6	84.9	79.0	59.0
White	84.6	81.2	75.0	56.6
Black	28.1	17.9	16.7	11.0
Hispanic	22.6	14.4	15.6	9.2

Source: National Study of College Experience.
Note: These percentages are based on all Asian students. In other words, even Asian students who do not socialize or who have no roommates, no friends, or no dates are included and considered not to have experienced the particular type of social relation.

student who is non-Asian. Finally, Asian students are just as likely to form a close friendship with or to date a non-Asian as an Asian classmate.

Asians' interactions with non-Asians transpire overwhelmingly with whites. The percentage of Asians who report social interactions with blacks or Hispanics is no more than one-third of the percentage reporting associations with whites. For instance, while 85 percent of Asians socialize often or very often with whites, only 28 percent spend that much free time with blacks and even fewer (23 percent) do so with Hispanics. Eighty-one percent of Asians live with a white student sometime during college— 63 percentage points more than the percentage who live with a black student and 67 percentage points more than the percentage who live with an Hispanic student. Roughly similar gaps characterize best-friend networks. Lastly, more than half of Asians report dating a white student, but only about one-tenth date a black or an Hispanic undergraduate.

Asian students' greater propensity to interact outside their racial group than is the case for white or black students may be due in part to the variety of cultures, histories, and languages that fall under the Asian umbrella (Espiritu, 1992). While some second-generation Asian Americans find commonality in the experience of being perceived as Asian within America (Espiritu, 1992; Portes and Rumbaut, 2001), others find it just as easy to have social relations with people outside the Asian category as with people inside it who have a different national origin. For example, Radford (2008) shows that first- and second-generation Asian-Indian Americans are more comfortable relating to whites than to East Asians.

TABLE 5.7
Hispanic Students' Likelihood of Having Social Relations with Students
from Specific Race Groups
NSCE Matriculant Sample: 1980s, 1993, and 1997 Cohorts Combined (N = 1,060)

Students Who Are/ Student Who Is:	Percent Socializing Often/Very Often with	Percent Living with at Least One	Percent Having a Close Friendship with a	Percent Dating at Least One
Hispanic	60.9	37.4	50.9	47.2
Of a Different Race	94.3	92.4	93.3	83.7
White	88.0	87.8	85.9	75.3
Black	43.7	21.6	28.3	20.8
Asian	52.1	35.8	40.0	24.8

Source: National Study of College Experience.
Note: These percentages are based on all Hispanic students. In other words, even Hispanic students who do not socialize or who have no roommates, no friends, or no dates are included and considered not to have experienced the particular type of social relation.

Hispanics

If whites are the least well integrated with other students, according to the measures we use here, then Hispanics are the most integrated of the four groups. Based on all of our indicators, Hispanic students are substantially more likely to interact with classmates who do not share their ethnic heritage than with those who do. As Table 5.7 illustrates, more than 90 percent of Hispanics socialize often or very often with, live with, or are close friends with students of a different race. Dating someone of a different race is the least common behavior, as it is for all racial groups. Nevertheless, a very high proportion (84 percent) of Hispanics date interracially. Relations with fellow Hispanics are far less common. Only 61 percent of Hispanics socialize often or very often with other Hispanics, about half have a close friend or date someone who is Hispanic, and only slightly more than one-third have an Hispanic roommate at some point in their college career. To some extent, the patterns for Hispanics are just the opposite of those for whites. If one reverses the first two rows of numbers for Hispanics in Table 5.7, the result would approximate the numbers for whites in the first two rows of Table 5.4.

When Hispanic students interact with non-Hispanics, as they frequently do based on the data we have just presented, their associations occur most commonly with white students. Eighty-eight percent of Hispanics socialize often or very often with whites or live with a white student, 86 percent report that one of their closest friends is white, and three-quarters mention dating a white student. Hispanics are next most likely to associate with Asian students. In fact, Hispanics are more likely than any other group to interact with Asians except for Asians themselves. Likewise, even though Hispanics are least likely to interact with blacks, they are still more likely than any other race group besides blacks themselves to have relations with black peers. For example, 44 percent of Hispanics socialize often or very often with blacks, as compared to just 32 percent of whites and 28 percent of Asians.

Several factors could explain why Hispanic students are more likely to interact with students from other backgrounds than with students of their own ethnicity. First, Hispanics represent only 4 percent of all NSCE students. Thus the relative scarcity of other Hispanic students and the much greater availability of students from other backgrounds may help account for the high percentage of Hispanics who engage in interethnic relations. Second, as discussed in chapter 4, Hispanic students are the most likely to be multiracial. Hispanics are particularly likely to identify as white (Patterson, 2001), and some Hispanics identify as black. Thus some of the interactions discussed here as interracial may not be regarded as such by Hispanic students, because they consider themselves members of these other racial groups as well. Third, Hispanics who attend elite colleges are a heterogeneous group. Within-group differences in socioeconomic status, immigrant generation, and national origin may therefore make it easier for Hispanics to relate to classmates on the basis of factors other than Hispanic roots.

Summary of Cross-Racial Patterns

Our results up to this point suggest that there are differences across the four racial/ethnic groups in how isolated they are from other groups of students or, alternatively, how integrated they are across racial and ethnic lines. Some groups appear to have much more frequent social contact than others with students outside their own racial or ethnic circle. It is useful to have a way of summarizing these differences. One simple approach is to calculate the average difference between the frequency of in-group versus outgroup contact across the four types of social interactions. In Table 5.4, for example, there is a 39.8 percentage point difference in how frequently whites have general social contact with other whites (96.3 percent) compared to nonwhites (56.5 percent). The differences for other forms of social interaction are 52.9 percentage points for living arrangements, 53.3 for friendship networks, and 60.5 for dating patterns. The average of these four numbers is 51.6, which suggests that whites on average are more than 50 percentage points more likely to interact with other white students than with nonwhites. The corresponding figure for black students is just 16.1. For Asians and Hispanics these averages are negative (−6.2 for Asians and −41.8 for Hispanics), meaning that these two groups are typically less likely to interact with ingroup than with outgroup members. Judging from these straightforward indicators, we would have to conclude that the greatest degree of racial separation or social distance on campus is between white and all other nonwhite students. Hispanic students, on the other hand, appear to have more frequent contact with non-Hispanics than with other Hispanics. To some extent, of course, these measures are influenced by the racial and ethnic composition of undergraduate student bodies. White students are in the majority on each of the NSCE campuses. Later in this chapter we will explore how measures of social distance are affected when one takes into account the availability of students from other racial and ethnic backgrounds.

Our results reflecting the behaviors of college students are surprisingly consistent with studies of racial attitudes and perceptions of incoming freshmen at academically selective colleges and universities. Massey et al. (2003: 138–45) constructed measures of social distance by asking entering NLSF freshmen to consider "how close you feel to the people in terms of your ideas and feelings about things." Individual responses ranged from 0 ("very distant") to 10 ("very close"). At one end of the continuum, white students on average feel closest to whites (with a closeness measure of 7.48). At the other extreme, the greatest social distance is exhibited by black students in their attitudes toward Asians (an average closeness measure of 4.35). To compare our results, we return to the data in Tables 5.4 through 5.7. In Table 5.5, for example, the closeness of blacks (the respondent group) to whites (the target group) can be measured by taking an average of the percentages of blacks who have each of the four kinds of social interactions with white students. These percentages range from a high of 69.9 to a low of 33.9, with an average of 56.0 percent.

Several conclusions emerge from a comparison of the NSCE and NLSF data. First, in both surveys the groups that exhibit the greatest social closeness are whites with other whites followed by blacks with other blacks. There is somewhat greater social distance between Asians and other Asians and perceptibly more distance for Hispanics with Hispanics. Second, when cross-race pairs are considered, both surveys indicate that the highest social affinity measures are recorded by Hispanics with whites followed by Asians with whites. Third, in the NLSF data whites feel slightly closer to blacks (5.16) than blacks feel to whites (4.95). This "paradox" (Massey et al., 2003: 140) is not replicated in the NSCE data that examine actual relations with (rather than feelings about) different groups. An average of 56 percent of NSCE blacks have some form of social ties to whites, but just 19 percent of NSCE whites have substantial social interactions with black students. Finally, the greatest social distances in the NSCE data are displayed by whites with respect to Hispanics (15.3) and by Asians with respect to Hispanics (15.5). In the NLSF data, the social distance between these pairs is surpassed only by that of black students with Asians. In the NSCE data just 21 percent of blacks have significant social ties to Asians—a figure that is among the lowest of any of the NSCE social affinity measures. These comparative NLSF and NSCE data suggest that newly enrolled college students' feelings of social distance from different groups may have a lingering impact on patterns of social interaction during their college years.

Socioeconomic Status Differences in Cross-Racial Interactions

Because the extent of students' social interactions with each other plays such a critical role in laying a foundation for the educational benefits of diversity, we comment briefly on how the percentage of students who engage in intraracial and interracial relations varies by socioeconomic status. Our findings indicate that there is a negative correlation between one's social class and the likelihood of interacting with a student of another race or ethnicity for each of the four types of social relations we have been considering—informal socializing, roommate choices, best-friend networks, and dating patterns. In other words, the higher a student's social class background, the less likely he or she is to have substantial social relations with a student from a different racial or ethnic background. Only in the case of dating is the relation not significant at the .05 level. Similarly, there is a positive association between social class and the percentage of students who have social interactions with other students of the same race or ethnicity. Just for closest friends is the relation not statistically significant.[9]

We can now summarize these associations with social class in the same way we did for race and ethnicity. Within each socioeconomic group, students are more likely to interact with students of their same race than with students from another race or ethnic category. But this tendency bears a strong positive relation to social class background. When we take an average across the four types of social interactions, we find that lower-

---

[9] As an illustration, we find that middle-, upper-middle-, and upper-class students are more likely than lower- or working-class undergraduates to have each of the four types of social relations with whites and less likely to have each of these relations with blacks and Hispanics. This pattern is at least partially explained by earlier findings. White students are most likely to interact with other whites, and students from higher SES groups are disproportionately white. Likewise, lower SES students' greater tendency to associate with blacks and Hispanics is partly due to the fact that lower SES students are more likely to be black or Hispanic. Social class differences in the percentage of students interacting with Asians are not significant at the .05 level, suggesting that students from the lower and upper portions of the socioeconomic distribution have similar tendencies to interact with Asian students.

class students are generally just 12 percentage points more likely to interact with a same-race student than with an other-race student. This average percentage increases steadily with higher social class categories—to 27 percentage points for working-class students, to 37 for the middle class, to 43 for the upper-middle class, and finally to 44 percentage points for students from upper-class family backgrounds.

STUDENTS' CROSS-RACIAL INTERACTIONS: HYPOTHESES

As discussed in the introduction to this chapter, cross-racial interactions among students can have a number of positive outcomes. Therefore, to maximize the educational benefits of diversity, it is important to understand the curricular, extracurricular, and other institutional conditions that are associated with the frequency of relations between students from the same or different racial backgrounds. In this section we present several hypotheses about how the ways of engaging race and ethnicity that were described earlier (for example, taking ethnic studies courses, participating in ethnic extracurricular activities and organizations, and living in race-focused dorms) may relate to the chances that students will interact with classmates from their own and from other race groups on our four indicators of social interrelations. We also discuss a few additional hypotheses concerning factors that should be associated with cross-racial social relations. These hypotheses are then tested in the next two sections.

Ethnic Coursework

Because offering a course about a particular racial or ethnic group is especially likely to attract students from that group, we hypothesize that enrolling in an ethnic studies course will be positively related to the likelihood of interacting with students who belong to the race or ethnic group being studied. Moreover, the more coursework about a certain group that students pursue, the more opportunities they should have to form relations with students from that group. In other words, we expect that students who major in, say, Asian American studies will have a greater likelihood of interacting with Asian classmates than students who just take a course in this field.[10]

The effect of studying a particular racial or ethnic group on interactions with other race groups that are not studied is less clear. We hypothesize

---

[10]We are not able to test whether a cause-and-effect relationship exists or which way it might go. In other words, our data do not allow us to determine whether, for example, students enroll in a course on Hispanics because they already interact with Hispanics or, alternatively, whether students' chances of interacting with Hispanics are greater as a result of taking such a course.

that students who pursue black, Chicano, or Asian studies will not be less likely to interact with whites because whites are practically unavoidable on NSCE campuses owing to their large numerical presence. However, students who take courses focused on one minority group may have fewer opportunities to interact with students from other minority groups. This negative relationship between ethnic coursework and interacting with minority students who are not studied should be more pronounced the greater the amount of coursework focused on one particular group. For example, taking a black studies course may not hinder relations with Asians or Hispanics, but majoring in African American studies might.

Ethnic Extracurricular Activities

Being involved in an extracurricular event or organization oriented toward a particular ethnic group should also be positively related to the chances of interacting with students from this group. Specifically, we predict that students who participate in an ethnic event should have a greater probability of interacting with members of the ethnic group being celebrated than would students who do not participate. Similarly, because members of ethnic organizations will most likely share each other's ethnic background, we expect that students who belong to an ethnic organization will exhibit a greater likelihood of interacting with students from their own ethnic group.

The relationship between participating in an extracurricular activity focused on one ethnic group and having social relations with students from other racial groups may depend on the time demands of the particular extracurricular. Because taking part in an ethnic history month event is typically a rather incidental time commitment, we do not believe that such participation will significantly lower students' chances of interacting with groups not being honored by that particular activity. On the other hand, belonging to an ethnic organization is likely to require more of students' time and could limit opportunities to interact with other groups. For example, Sidanius et al. (2004) find that students who belong to segregated fraternities and sororities exhibit increased levels of social distance from students who come from other backgrounds. We therefore expect that members of ethnic organizations will exhibit a lower probability of interacting with students from other backgrounds.

Racially Focused Housing

Although survey participants were not asked to report the race group around which their racial/ethnic heritage theme dorm or focus house is oriented, we might assume that most undergraduates who live in ethnic-focused housing reside with students who share their ethnicity. Because of the amount of time students spend in their residences, we expect racially focused theme dorms and houses to have a similar relationship with social interactions as do ethnic organizations. Namely, students in ethnic-focused housing will have a greater likelihood of intraethnic social relations and a lower likelihood of interethnic ones.

Freshman-Year Roommates and Population Availability

There is evidence that the racial background of one's freshman-year roommate(s) shapes cross-racial interactions. Van Laar et al. (2005) show that being randomly assigned to live with a student of a different race increases interethnic dating and decreases unease with other ethnic groups. Likewise, Boisjoly et al. (2006) find that white students who are randomly assigned a black roommate leave college with more positive attitudes toward diversity and affirmative action. Thus, while our data cannot address whether students choose their first-year roommates or have them assigned, we expect that having a freshman roommate of a different race will increase the odds of interacting across racial boundaries, especially with undergraduates of that roommate's race.

A second variable we examine is the racial composition of the entering class. Gurin (2002) finds that attending a school with a larger percentage of students of color has a positive effect on socializing across racial categories and having close friends from other racial backgrounds. Chang, Astin, and Kim's (2004) results further lead us to expect that the likelihood of students having cross-racial interactions, particularly with minority groups, will be greater on campuses that have higher proportions of minority students.[11]

RESULTS
Interactions with Students of a Different Race

To test these hypotheses, we rely on regression analysis once again because it allows us to examine the influence of particular independent variables from an all-other-things-equal perspective. The outcomes of special interest include whether students (1) socialize frequently with classmates whose racial or ethnic background is different from theirs, (2) live with a student of

---

[11]Rytina and Morgan (1982) developed a conceptual model that merges the axioms of social structural theory with quantitative approaches from social network analysis. They examine contact rates within and between categories of individuals and network densities as a function of the number, including size and proportion, of individuals in different categories.

a different race after freshman year,[12] (3) report that at least one of their five closest friends is of a different race, and (4) date at least one student of a different race. We first examine how a respondent's own race is related to the chances of experiencing each of these social interactions.

Race

Each group of nonwhite students has much greater odds than do whites of interacting with students from other racial backgrounds on all four measures of social interrelations. Hispanics have the greatest relative odds of interacting with students who do not share their ethnic heritage. Table 5.8 shows that compared to whites, Hispanics are 6 times as likely to socialize frequently with, 7 times as likely to live with, 11.5 times as likely to date, and 14 times as likely to be close friends with a student of a different race. Relative to each other, black and Asian students generally have similar odds of interacting with students from different racial backgrounds. Asians, however, are somewhat more likely than blacks to have a close friend from a different racial group and to date someone of a dissimilar race. In sum, Hispanics are most likely to interact with students of a different race, followed by Asians and then by blacks. Whites are by far the least likely to have cross-racial social relations. This conclusion parallels our previous descriptive findings in Tables 5.4–5.7.

Ethnic Coursework

The results regarding ethnic studies coursework provide partial support for our hypotheses. In general, taking at least one course about *one's own* racial group or developing a major or minor area of concentration in the same area is negatively related to interacting with members of other racial groups. At the same time, only the association between majoring in a subject about one's own racial group and having close outgroup friends is significantly negative. Our results also suggest that, on average, engaging with that part of the curriculum that emphasizes issues about *other* racial or ethnic groups is positively associated with the likelihood of cross-racial interactions. The odds of having a close friend of another race and of dating someone from a different racial group are both significantly positively related to taking a course or minoring in a subject, respectively, about people who have a different racial background.

---

[12] While students are often assigned roommates for their freshman year, most students choose their own roommates in subsequent years. Because the goal of this chapter is to explore the social relations that students elect to have with different race groups, we analyze the race of students' roommates after freshman year as an outcome variable and the race of students' roommates during freshman year as a predictor variable.

TABLE 5.8
Students' Social Interactions with Classmates of a Different Race
NSCE Matriculant Sample: 1980s, 1993, and 1997 Cohorts Combined (N = 6,350)
Odds Ratios from Logistic Regressions

Predictor Variables	Socialize Often or Very Often with Students of a Different Race (1)	Live with a Student of a Different Race after Freshman Year (2)	Have a Close Friendship with a Student of a Different Race (3)	Date at Least One Student of a Different Race (4)
Race				
(White)	—	—	—	—
Black	3.17***	2.87***	4.07***	2.84***
Hispanic	5.94***	6.99***	14.05***	11.49***
Asian	3.21***	2.90***	4.53***	3.76***
Ethnic Studies Coursework				
Ethnic Studies Major: Own Race Group	0.74	0.86	0.56*	1.14
Ethnic Studies Minor: Own Race Group	1.01	0.86	0.76	0.91
Ethnic Studies Course: Own Race Group	0.82	0.94	0.80	0.86
Ethnic Studies Major: Other Race Group	0.53	1.01	0.83	0.55
Ethnic Studies Minor: Other Race Group	0.90	1.37	0.68	1.97*
Ethnic Studies Course: Other Race Group	1.11	1.15	1.67***	1.18
Ethnic Extracurriculars				
Ethnic Activity Honoring Own Race Group	0.62**	0.59***	0.46***	0.56***
Ethnic Activity Honoring Other Race Group	2.37***	1.42**	1.42**	2.30***
Ethnic Organization	0.98	0.92	0.69**	0.78*

(Continued)

TABLE 5.8 (Continued)

Predictor Variables	Socialize Often or Very Often with Students of a Different Race (1)	Live with a Student of a Different Race after Freshman Year (2)	Have a Close Friendship with a Student of a Different Race (3)	Date at Least One Student of a Different Race (4)
Residential Environment				
Lived in Race-Focused Housing	0.62	0.58*	0.64	0.61*
Had Freshman Roommate of Different Race	1.85***	2.95***	1.79***	1.39**
Population Availability				
% Nonwhite Students[a]	1.04***	1.03**	1.04***	1.03**
Socioeconomic Status				
Upper	0.59	0.94	0.85	0.96
Upper-Middle	0.79	0.90	1.05	1.16
(Middle)	—	—	—	—
Working	0.93	1.00	1.23	1.15
Lower	0.86	1.41	0.92	0.69
Immigrant Generation				
First	1.07	1.27	1.16	1.23
Second	1.61*	1.71**	1.80**	1.25
Third	1.68**	1.24	1.06	1.02
(Fourth and Higher)	—	—	—	—
Employment				
Had a Job during First Year of College	1.30*	0.97	1.32*	1.14

College Type				
Private Institution	1.92***	1.25	1.33	1.15
(Public Institution)	—	—	—	—
Cohort				
(1980s)				
1993	1.18	0.89	1.29	0.82
1997	1.07	0.77	0.92	0.78
Racial Diversity of High School[b]				
Substantially Diverse	0.97	0.84	1.22	1.14
(Moderately Diverse)	—	—	—	—
Not Very Diverse	0.92	0.85	1.01	1.09
Number of Cases	6,350	6,350	6,350	6,350
$F(df_1, df_2)$	16.59(28, 6203)	23.31(28, 6203)	21.83(28, 6203)	23.45(28, 6203)
Prob > F	0.0000	0.0000	0.0000	0.0000

Source: National Study of College Experience.

Note: The total weighted percentages of students who have these four types of relations are, respectively, (1) 62.8 percent; (2) 40.3 percent; (3) 50.9 percent; (4) 35.8 percent. Reference categories are in parentheses.

[a] Combined percentage of black, Hispanic, and Asian students in entering freshman class at each school.

[b] NSCE respondents were asked to report how racially or ethnically diverse their high school was on a seven-point scale, with one reflecting "not at all diverse" and seven representing "substantially diverse." Students who gave their school a six or seven were placed in the "substantially diverse" category, those who gave a three, four, or five were placed in the "moderately diverse" category, and those who gave a one or a two were placed in the "not very diverse" category.

* $p < .05$ ** $p < .01$ *** $p < .001$

Ethnic Extracurriculars

Estimated relationships between participating in ethnic extracurricular activities and campus patterns of social interactions provide substantially more support for our hypotheses. While students who are involved in own-race functions are less likely to interact in all four social domains with classmates from dissimilar racial or ethnic backgrounds, students who participate in other-race extracurriculars are much more likely than other students to interact across a broad social spectrum with classmates of different backgrounds. In particular, students who participate in their own ethnic group's activity have between 38 and 54 percent lower odds of interacting with students of a different ethnic group, depending on the type of social interaction. Those who engage in another ethnic group's activity, however, have 42 percent greater odds of living with or being close friends with a student of a different race, 130 percent greater odds of dating a student of a different race, and 137 percent greater odds of socializing frequently with students of a different race. In all cases, ethnic activity measures are statistically significant.

Also as predicted, belonging to an ethnic organization is negatively related to the frequency of cross-racial interactions. Students who are members of an ethnic organization have 31 percent significantly lower odds than their non-member classmates of having a close friend of a different race and 22 percent significantly lower odds of dating someone of a different race. At the same time, there is only weak evidence of an association between organizational membership and the frequency of general socializing with classmates of a different race or of having a roommate with some other racial background. Thus, while belonging to an ethnic organization may impede formation of the two more intimate types of social relations, it does not prevent students from interacting with classmates of other racial backgrounds altogether.

Residential Environment

Earlier we hypothesized that students who live in racially focused housing or theme dorms would exhibit a lower probability of interacting with classmates whose race is different from theirs. The results in Table 5.8 support this expectation. The association between residence in a racially oriented theme dorm and patterns of social relations with students from other racial backgrounds is negative for each dimension of social interaction. That said, only the likelihood of living with a classmate of a different race after freshman year or of dating someone from a different racial or ethnic background is significantly lower.

We also expected that having a freshman-year roommate with a different racial background from one's own would promote greater cross-racial socializing on several fronts. This hypothesis is strongly supported by our data. Each of the four types of social interactions is significantly more likely for students who have an other-race first-year roommate than for students who either live by themselves during freshman year or have roommates from the same racial background. As might be anticipated, the greatest increase in the likelihood of socializing associated with having a freshman roommate from another race is for living with someone from a different race after freshman year—nearly a 200 percent increase in the odds. While we cannot say with any certainty that students who live with an other-race classmate during their first year will elect to room with that same individual in subsequent years, this is surely one possibility that must occur with some regularity.

Population Availability

Attending college with students from a broad spectrum of racial and ethnic backgrounds is likely to maximize the opportunity to mix and mingle with other-race classmates. As we noted earlier, one reason that white students appear from our descriptive findings to be the most racially isolated group on campus is the fact that whites typically constitute the great majority of enrolled students. From this vantage point, we examine the association between the availability of nonwhite students and matriculants' odds of having cross-racial social relations. The percentage of nonwhite students is significantly and positively related to the chances of experiencing each type of cross-racial interaction. Specifically, a one percentage point increase in the share of nonwhite students in the entering freshman cohort is associated with a 3 or 4 percent increase in the odds of interacting with students of different racial backgrounds. These results illustrate the importance of having minority students on campus if one wants *all* students to obtain the benefits of cross-racial interactions.

Other Factors

Several other factors are also associated with a greater likelihood of interacting across racial lines. In general, students who are either themselves foreign-born or who are the children or grandchildren of immigrants are more likely to experience each of the four specified types of cross-racial social interrelations than are students in the fourth-or-higher immigrant generation. The strongest and most pervasive associations adhere to second-generation immigrant students. Likewise, holding a job during freshman year is significantly positively related both to the frequency of general patterns of socializing with other-race classmates and to having an other-race close friend. This conclusion parallels work by Chang, Astin, and Kim (2004), who find that having an on-campus job has a positive effect on cross-racial interactions. Finally, students who attend private colleges and universities are generally more likely than students at public universities to interact socially with students from other race groups. The association is significantly positive for socializing often or very often with someone from another race. Bowen and Bok (1998: 236–38) suggest that the residential character and smaller size often typical of selective private institutions are conducive to getting to know and interacting with classmates from a variety of racial and ethnic backgrounds.

Three remaining sets of variables (social class, cohort year, and perceived diversity of high school) are not consistently related to patterns of cross-racial social interaction. The lack of correspondence with social class is somewhat surprising because our previous descriptive findings implied that social distance from other race groups increased the higher the socioeconomic status category to which a student belonged. The results in Table 5.8, which control for the influence of other factors, suggest that these earlier findings are strongly influenced by the correlation between race and social class and by other factors in Table 5.8 with which race and social class are correlated (for example, ethnic coursework and extracurricular activities).

Nor is year of college enrollment significantly related to any dimension of cross-racial interaction. A little detective work shows this result arises because we also control for the proportion of nonwhite students on campus, or "population availability." In other words, cohort year and campus racial diversity are positively correlated. When we redo the analysis by omitting population availability, matriculating in either 1993 or 1997 is significantly positively associated with both the socializing and friendship measures.[13] These results closely match other descriptive findings (not shown) indicating that students' likelihood of interacting with other-race peers has significantly increased since the 1980s on all four of our social relations measures.[14]

---

[13] Including the control for population availability and leaving out any of the other categories of variables in Table 5.8 does not substantially change the cohort results from those already reported. This outcome suggests that increased racial diversity in the student bodies of our selective universities, produced by a combination of factors including race-based affirmative action and perhaps changes in the racial composition of applicants to selective colleges, is the primary reason that strides in cross-racial interaction have occurred over time.

[14] Specifically, students from the two 1990s cohorts combined are eight percentage points more likely to room with and date, 14 percentage points more likely to socialize frequently

Finally, there are no clear patterns of association between the perceived racial diversity of students' high schools and any form of cross-racial social interaction. We include the racial diversity of a student's high school because Gurin (2002) finds that the selection of same-race peer groups among white and African American students at the University of Michigan reflects the segregation of students' pre-college high schools and neighborhoods and is not a reaction to their university experience with diversity. On the other hand, Bowen and Bok (1998: 238) find that "the racial mix of [students'] high school[s] played no role in predicting their college interactions."

RESULTS
Interactions with Students from
Specific Race Groups

In this section we expand the analysis in Table 5.8 by investigating social interactions that NSCE matriculants have with classmates from specific racial or ethnic groups, including whites (Table 5.9), blacks (Table 5.10), Asians (Table 5.11), and Hispanics (Table 5.12). We summarize general findings rather than discussing each table separately.[15]

Race

The relationships between a respondent's race and the chances of interacting with classmates from other specific racial or ethnic groups form four discernible patterns. These patterns are shown in the top panels of Tables 5.9–5.12. First, the odds of *inter*racial contact are lower than the odds of *intra*racial contact for each group of students. All of the 48 associated odds ratios are less than one, and most all of them are highly statistically significant.[16] The behavioral implication is that members of Group B are less likely to interact with members of Group A than members of Group A are to interact with each other. In Table 5.10, for example, white, Hispanic, and Asian students all have lower odds of interacting with blacks than black students do. Although cross-racial social

---

with, and 16 percentage points more likely to be close friends with a person of a different race than are students from the 1980s cohort.

[15] We continue to consider the same four domains of social interaction. The list of explanatory variables used in Tables 5.9–5.12 is essentially the same as, though for nonwhites slightly larger than, the list in Table 5.8.

[16] Just four of the 48 odds ratios are not statistically different from 1.0. Three of these four involve associations between white and Hispanic classmates.

TABLE 5.9

Students' Social Interactions with White Classmates

NSCE Matriculant Sample: 1980s, 1993, and 1997 Cohorts Combined (N = 6,350)

Odds Ratios from Logistic Regressions

Predictor Variables	Socialize Often or Very Often with White Students (1)	Live with a White Student after Freshman Year (2)	Have a Close Friendship with a White Student (3)	Date at Least One White Student (4)
Race				
(White)	—	—	—	—
Black	0.14***	0.16***	0.07***	0.11***
Hispanic	0.34***	0.72	0.31***	0.72
Asian	0.28***	0.37***	0.16***	0.30***
Ethnic Studies Coursework				
Ethnic Studies Major in Nonwhite Group	0.94	0.83	0.79	0.82
Ethnic Studies Minor in Nonwhite Group	0.79	1.06	0.56	0.92
Ethnic Studies Course in Nonwhite Group	1.39	1.24	1.20	1.20
Ethnic Extracurriculars				
Ethnic Activity Honoring Nonwhite Group	1.23	0.89	0.95	0.91
Ethnic Organization, White Student	1.37	1.01	0.79	1.34
Ethnic Organization, Nonwhite Student	0.51***	0.67***	0.50***	0.53***
Residential Environment				
Race-Focused Housing, White Student	0.71	1.28	1.35	0.61
Race-Focused Housing, Nonwhite Student	0.65*	0.85	0.68	0.74
Freshman Roommate Is White	2.71***	4.27***	2.64***	2.42***

Population Availability				
% White Students[a]	0.98	1.00	1.02*	1.00
Socioeconomic Status				
Upper	1.67	0.71	1.77	2.93***
Upper-Middle	1.46	1.01	1.15	1.98***
(Middle)	—	—	—	—
Working	0.98	0.62*	0.84	1.23
Lower	0.90	0.74	0.95	0.53
Immigrant Generation				
First	1.05	0.68	0.97	0.79
Second	1.57*	0.92	1.28	0.96
Third	2.46*	1.06	2.03*	1.21
(Fourth and Higher)	—	—	—	—
Employment				
Had a Job during First Year of College	1.08	0.77*	0.87	1.15
College Type				
Private Institution	0.83	0.68	1.70*	0.77
(Public Institution)	—	—	—	—
Cohort				
(1980s)				
1993	0.72	0.93	1.04	0.64*
1997	0.74	0.83	0.82	0.61*
Racial Diversity of High School[b]				
Substantially Diverse	0.77	0.63**	0.92	0.85
(Moderately Diverse)	—	—	—	—

(Continued)

TABLE 5.9 (Continued)

Predictor Variables	Socialize Often or Very Often with White Students (1)	Live with a White Student after Freshman Year (2)	Have a Close Friendship with a White Student (3)	Date at Least One White Student (4)
Not Very Diverse	1.22	1.16	1.11	1.43
Number of Cases	6,350	6,350	6,350	6,350
$F(df_1, df_2)$	22.01(26, 6205)	24.37(26, 6205)	32.15(26, 6205)	34.63(26, 6205)
Prob > F	0.0000	0.0000	0.0000	0.0000

Source: National Study of College Experience.

Note: The total weighted percentages of students who have these four types of relations are, respectively, (1) 92.5 percent; (2) 84.6 percent; (3) 90.8 percent; (4) 81.6 percent. Reference categories are in parentheses.

[a]Percentage of white students in entering freshman class at each school.

[b]NSCE respondents were asked to report how racially or ethnically diverse their high school was on a seven-point scale, with one reflecting "not at all diverse" and seven representing "substantially diverse." Students who gave their school a six or seven were placed in the "substantially diverse" category, those who gave a three, four, or five were placed in the "moderately diverse" category, and those who gave a one or a two were placed in the "not very diverse" category.

*p < .05 **p < .01 ***p < .001

TABLE 5.10
Students' Social Interactions with Black Classmates
NSCE Matriculant Sample: 1980s, 1993, and 1997 Cohorts Combined (N = 6,350)
Odds Ratios from Logistic Regressions

Predictor Variables	Socialize Often or Very Often with Black Students (1)	Live with a Black Student after Freshman Year (2)	Have a Close Friendship with a Black Student (3)	Date at Least One Black Student (4)
Race				
White	0.27***	0.17***	0.09***	0.11***
(Black)	—	—	—	—
Hispanic	0.30***	0.18***	0.14***	0.19***
Asian	0.18***	0.14***	0.09***	0.11***
Ethnic Studies Coursework				
Major in African/African American Studies	1.65	0.86	2.11	0.63
Minor in African/African American Studies	2.41	1.69	3.70*	3.08*
Course in African/African American Studies	1.23	1.17	1.74**	1.56**
Ethnic Studies Major in Non-Black Group	0.46*	0.66	0.44**	0.63
Ethnic Studies Minor in Non-Black Group	0.57	1.09	0.72	1.23
Ethnic Studies Course in Non-Black Group	1.06	1.19	1.07	1.05
Ethnic Extracurriculars				
Ethnic Activity Honoring Blacks	2.32***	1.59**	1.65**	2.50***
Ethnic Activity Honoring Non-Black Group	1.19	0.99	1.14	1.09
Ethnic Organization, Black Student	2.77***	1.81***	3.29***	1.65***
Ethnic Organization, Non-Black Student	0.93	1.08	0.87	1.01

(Continued)

TABLE 5.10 (Continued)

Predictor Variables	Socialize Often or Very Often with Black Students (1)	Live with a Black Student after Freshman Year (2)	Have a Close Friendship with a Black Student (3)	Date at Least One Black Student (4)
Residential Environment				
Race-Focused Housing, Black Student	0.90	1.17	0.72	0.63
Race-Focused Housing, Non-Black Student	0.52*	0.72	0.98	0.50*
Freshman Roommate Is Black	1.88***	3.08***	2.12***	1.33
Population Availability				
% Black Students[a]	1.09	1.07**	1.07**	0.98
Socioeconomic Status				
Upper	0.79	0.73	0.98	0.79
Upper-Middle	0.82	1.12	0.92	0.87
(Middle)	—	—	—	—
Working	1.29	1.01	1.21	1.01
Lower	0.73	3.27*	1.30	0.73
Immigrant Generation				
First	0.96	1.21	1.19	0.88
Second	0.96	1.35	0.91	0.76
Third	0.86	1.13	1.10	0.76
(Fourth and Higher)	—	—	—	—
Employment				
Had a Job during First Year of College	1.29*	0.84	1.16	1.42

College Type				
Private Institution	1.69***	1.64**	1.59***	1.37*
(Public Institution)	—	—	—	—
Cohort				
(1980s)	—	—	—	—
1993	1.26	0.96	1.26	0.99
1997	1.39*	0.94	1.45*	0.79
Racial Diversity of High School[b]				
Substantially Diverse	1.06	0.88	1.03	1.23
(Moderately Diverse)	—	—	—	—
Not Very Diverse	0.81	0.76	0.88	1.05
Number of Cases	6,350	6,350	6,350	6,350
$F(df_1, df_2)$	29.81(30, 6201)	33.04(30, 6201)	40.40(30, 6201)	42.58(30, 6201)
Prob > F	0.0000	0.0000	0.0000	0.0000

Source: National Study of College Experience.

Note: The total weighted percentages of students who have these four types of relations are, respectively, (1) 36.2 percent; (2) 14.9 percent; (3) 21.7 percent; (4) 17.2 percent. Reference categories are in parentheses.

[a]Percentage of black students in entering freshman class at each school.

[b]NSCE respondents were asked to report how racially or ethnically diverse their high school was on a seven-point scale, with one reflecting "not at all diverse" and seven representing "substantially diverse." Students who gave their school a six or seven were placed in the "substantially diverse" category; those who gave a three, four, or five were placed in the "moderately diverse" category; and those who gave a one or a two were placed in the "not very diverse" category.

*p < .05 **p < .01 ***p < .001

TABLE 5.11

Students' Social Interactions with Asian Classmates

NSCE Matriculant Sample: 1980s, 1993, and 1997 Cohorts Combined (N = 6,350)

Odds Ratios from Logistic Regressions

Predictor Variables	Socialize Often or Very Often with Asian Students (1)	Live with an Asian Student after Freshman Year (2)	Have a Close Friendship with an Asian Student (3)	Date at Least One Asian Student (4)
Race				
White	0.88	0.46***	0.50***	0.39***
Black	0.29***	0.28***	0.32***	0.17***
Hispanic	0.47***	0.41***	0.42***	0.35***
(Asian)	—	—	—	—
Ethnic Studies Coursework				
Major in Asian/Asian American Studies	1.12	0.58	0.63	1.53
Minor in Asian/Asian American Studies	0.66	0.53	0.72	0.99
Course in Asian/Asian American Studies	1.17	1.10	1.57**	1.40*
Ethnic Studies Major in Non-Asian Group	0.60	1.45	0.87	0.40**
Ethnic Studies Minor in Non-Asian Group	0.55*	0.78	0.48**	0.65
Ethnic Studies Course in Non-Asian Group	0.94	1.20	1.03	1.04
Ethnic Extracurriculars				
Ethnic Activity Honoring Asians	3.09***	2.02***	2.51***	1.51**
Ethnic Activity Honoring Non-Asian Group	1.46**	1.01	1.15	1.88***
Ethnic Organization, Asian Student	2.92***	1.49*	2.93***	2.23***
Ethnic Organization, Non-Asian Student	0.94	0.89	0.66*	1.01

Residential Environment				
Race-Focused Housing, Asian Student	0.91	1.29	1.04	0.78
Race-Focused Housing, Non-Asian Student	0.43**	0.93	0.59	0.92
Freshman Roommate Is Asian	2.26***	2.79***	2.18***	1.50**
Population Availability				
% Asian Students[a]	1.07***	1.08***	1.08***	1.05**
Socioeconomic Status				
Upper	0.76	0.91	0.51**	0.70
Upper-Middle	0.93	0.89	0.97	0.95
(Middle)	—	—	—	—
Working	1.10	0.91	1.22	1.37
Lower	0.66	1.04	0.71	0.76
Immigrant Generation				
First	1.10	1.34	1.47*	1.27
Second	1.63**	1.15	1.79**	1.03
Third	1.73**	1.22	1.10	1.03
(Fourth and Higher)	—	—	—	—
Employment				
Had a Job during First Year of College	1.08	0.99	1.16	0.84
College Type				
Private Institution	1.82**	0.85	0.90	1.04
(Public Institution)	—	—	—	—
Cohort				
(1980s)	—	—	—	—
1993	1.30	0.83	1.03	0.95
1997	0.99	0.76	0.78	0.67

(Continued)

TABLE 5.11 (*Continued*)

Predictor Variables	Socialize Often or Very Often with Asian Students (1)	Live with an Asian Student after Freshman Year (2)	Have a Close Friendship with an Asian Student (3)	Date at Least One Asian Student (4)
Racial Diversity of High School[b]				
Substantially Diverse	1.06	0.95	1.22	1.33
(Moderately Diverse)	—	—	—	—
Not Very Diverse	1.06	0.91	0.99	0.97
Number of Cases	6,350	6,350	6,350	6,350
$F(df_1, df_2)$	22.27(30, 6201)	20.36(30, 6201)	24.80(30, 6201)	21.31(30, 6201)
Prob > F	0.0000	0.0000	0.0000	0.0000

Source: National Study of College Experience.

Note: The total weighted percentages of students who have these four types of relations are, respectively, (1) 46.1 percent; (2) 24.1 percent; (3) 32.3 percent; (4) 21.0 percent. Reference categories are in parentheses.

[a]Percentage of Asian students in entering freshman class at each school.

[b]NSCE respondents were asked to report how racially or ethnically diverse their high school was on a seven-point scale, with one reflecting "not at all diverse" and seven representing "substantially diverse." Students who gave their school a six or seven were placed in the "substantially diverse" category, those who gave a three, four, or five were placed in the "moderately diverse" category, and those who gave a one or a two were placed in the "not very diverse" category.

*p < .05 **p < .01 ***p < .001

TABLE 5.12
Students' Social Interactions with Hispanic Classmates
NSCE Matriculant Sample: 1980s, 1993, and 1997 Cohorts Combined (N = 6,350)
Odds Ratios from Logistic Regressions

Predictor Variables	Socialize Often or Very Often with Hispanic Students (1)	Live with an Hispanic Student after Freshman Year (2)	Have a Close Friendship with an Hispanic Student (3)	Date at Least One Hispanic Student (4)
Race				
White	0.71*	0.92	0.55***	0.55**
Black	0.63*	0.47**	0.49**	0.36***
(Hispanic)	—	—	—	—
Asian	0.30***	0.57*	0.41***	0.18***
Ethnic Studies Coursework				
Major in Chicano/Latino Studies	0.85	0.33**	0.37**	0.54
Minor in Chicano/Latino Studies	1.12	1.62	1.19	1.67
Course in Chicano/Latino Studies	1.55**	1.58*	1.82**	1.85**
Ethnic Studies Major in Non-Hispanic Group	0.95	1.73	2.09	0.91
Ethnic Studies Minor in Non-Hispanic Group	0.73	2.04	1.19	1.03
Ethnic Studies Course in Non-Hispanic Group	0.88	0.78	0.80	1.19
Ethnic Extracurriculars				
Ethnic Activity Honoring Hispanics	2.82***	1.96**	1.52*	1.83**
Ethnic Activity Honoring Non-Hispanic Group	1.55**	0.99	1.02	1.42*
Ethnic Organization, Hispanic Student	1.63*	1.30	2.73***	1.42
Ethnic Organization, Non-Hispanic Student	1.07	1.06	0.92	0.90

(Continued)

Table 5.12 (Continued)

Predictor Variables	Socialize Often or Very Often with Hispanic Students (1)	Live with an Hispanic Student after Freshman Year (2)	Have a Close Friendship with an Hispanic Student (3)	Date at Least One Hispanic Student (4)
Residential Environment				
Race-Focused Housing, Hispanic Student	0.92	2.14*	1.17	1.31
Race-Focused Housing, Non-Hispanic Student	1.06	0.60	0.93	0.69
Freshman Roommate Is Hispanic	2.00***	2.41***	3.76***	1.53*
Population Availability				
% Hispanic Students[a]	1.17***	1.18***	1.16***	1.13***
Socioeconomic Status				
Upper	0.47**	0.84	1.01	0.91
Upper-Middle	0.82	0.70*	1.06	0.79
(Middle)	—	—	—	—
Working	0.88	1.29	1.45	1.24
Lower	1.61	1.79	1.14	0.99
Immigrant Generation				
First	1.31	1.21	1.25	1.75**
Second	1.56*	1.41	1.08	1.47
Third	1.34	1.27	1.22	0.91
(Fourth and Higher)	—	—	—	—
Employment				
Had a Job during First Year of College	1.14	1.22	1.45*	0.98

College Type				
Private Institution	1.58**	0.88	1.19	0.99
(Public Institution)	—	—	—	—
Cohort				
(1980s)				
1993	1.29	1.01	1.25	1.02
1997	1.06	0.90	1.16	1.06
Racial Diversity of High School[b]				
Substantially Diverse	0.95	0.85	1.20	0.80
(Moderately Diverse)	—	—	—	—
Not Very Diverse	0.84	0.76	1.17	0.83
Number of Cases	6,350	6,350	6,350	6,350
$F(df_1, df_2)$	19.73(30, 6201)	15.25(30, 6201)	19.22(30, 6201)	18.43(30, 6201)
Prob > F	0.0000	0.0000	0.0000	0.0000

Source: National Study of College Experience.

Note: The total weighted percentages of students who have these four types of relations are, respectively, (1) 23.6 percent; (2) 11.2 percent; (3) 15.5 percent; (4) 13.6 percent. Reference categories are in parentheses.

[a]Percentage of Hispanic students in entering freshman class at each school.

[b]NSCE respondents were asked to report how racially or ethnically diverse their high school was on a seven-point scale, with one reflecting "not at all diverse" and seven representing "substantially diverse." Students who gave their school a six or seven were placed in the "substantially diverse" category, those who gave their school a three, four, or five were placed in the "moderately diverse" category, and those who gave a one or a two were placed in the "not very diverse" category.

*p < .05 **p < .01 ***p < .001

interactions of all four types clearly do occur, the old adage that birds of a feather flock together is well supported by these data.[17]

Second, the social distance between students who do not belong to Group A and their classmates in Group A varies depending on the racial or ethnic affiliation attached to Group A. In particular, we find that the social distance of non-blacks from blacks is the largest and the distance of non-Hispanics from Hispanics is the smallest for students at the eight institutions in our study. Social distance is reflected by the odds ratios associated with race in Tables 5.9–5.12. For example, the odds ratio of 0.14 (see the number in the first row and column of Table 5.9) means the odds that black students socialize often or very often with white students are just 14 percent of the odds that white students socialize this frequently with other whites. When the 12 odds ratios at the top of Table 5.9 are averaged across the three race groups and the four domains of social interaction, the result is 0.31. An interpretation of this result is that, on average, nonwhite students are 31 percent as likely to interact socially with white students as whites are to mix and mingle among themselves. Similar averages computed from Tables 5.10–5.12 show that the social distance of non-blacks from blacks is captured by an average odds ratio of 0.16, of non-Asians from Asians by 0.41, and of non-Hispanics from Hispanics by 0.51. Non-black students are on average just 16 percent as likely as black students to interact with other blacks. On the other hand, non-Hispanic students are typically 51 percent as likely to interact with Hispanic students as other Hispanics are.

Readers should note what these results do *not* mean. They do not necessarily imply that students are more likely to interact with their Asian and Hispanic classmates than they are with whites or blacks. The reason this is so is that an odds ratio is a relative concept that involves both a numerator and a denominator. The numerator in our context captures the likelihood of intergroup interaction, while the denominator reflects the likelihood of within-race interaction. In our data, it is Asians' and Hispanics' lower tendency to interact with coethnics that contributes to making the social distance between them and non-coethnics smaller. To illustrate this point, we recalculated the regression estimates in Tables 5.9–5.12 so that the race group with whom interactions are being studied is the predictor variable of interest and all other race groups combined serve as the reference category. Doing so shows that, on average, Asians

---

[17]This phenomenon is known in the sociological literature as "homophily"—the principle that "contact between similar people occurs at a higher rate than among dissimilar people" (McPherson, Smith-Lovin, and Cook, 2001: 416). Homophily implies that people's social networks are homogeneous with regard to numerous personal characteristics. Race and ethnicity create the strongest divides in personal networks followed by such other characteristics as age, religion, social class, and gender (McPherson, Smith-Lovin, and Cook, 2001).

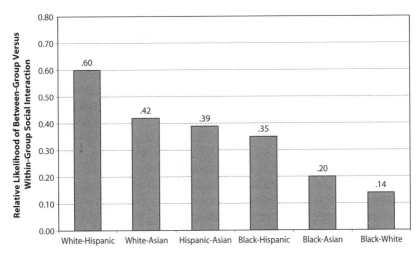

Figure 5.1. Pairwise Racial Patterns of Social Interaction on NSCE College Campuses; NSCE Matriculant Data: 1980s, 1993, and 1997 Cohorts Combined (N = 6,350). Note: To calculate each number in Figure 5.1, we compute the simple arithmetic average of eight odds ratios across four domains of social interaction—four odds ratios for the likelihood that Group A interacts with Group B and four for the likelihood that Group B interacts with Group A. There is no significance to the order in which race groups are listed in the captions below each column bar. Each caption is meant to imply social interaction in both directions. Source: Tables 5.9–5.12.

have just 104 percent greater odds than all other race groups combined of interacting with Asians, and Hispanics have only 83 percent greater odds. By contrast, black students have 621 percent greater odds and white students have 481 percent higher odds of having social relations with coethnics than with non-coethnics.[18]

Third, social interaction is a two-way street. It involves overtures that are initiated by members of Group A and accepted by members of Group B, and vice versa. The relative frequency of these pairwise and reciprocal patterns of social interaction is shown in Figure 5.1. Perhaps most important, the figure indicates that cross-racial interactions involving whites occur frequently, despite the suggestion in Table 5.8 that nonwhites show greater odds of interacting with students of a different race than whites do.

[18] Concluding that the largest social distance is between non-blacks and blacks may appear to contradict our previous finding from Table 5.8 that whites are the least likely to experience cross-racial social interactions. Apart from reasons cited in the text, summary findings based on Tables 5.9–5.12 may differ from those in Table 5.8 for three additional reasons. The average odds ratios we report are unweighted, the regression specifications are slightly different, and, most important, the analyses employ different response variables.

The most frequent form of social interaction between two race/ethnic groups, relative to the amount of contact these groups have with members of their own group, occurs between whites and Hispanics. On average, their odds of having social ties with each other are only 40 percent lower than their odds of interacting with themselves. Whites and Asians, Hispanics and Asians, and blacks and Hispanics occupy the middle of the spectrum, exhibiting between 58 and 65 percent lower odds of between-group than within-group social contact. The greatest relative social distances separating two groups exist for the black-Asian and black-white pairings. Blacks and Asians are typically 80 percent less likely to interact with each other as they are to socialize among their own groups. Even less common is cross-racial, reciprocal interaction involving blacks and whites. Their odds of interacting with each other are 86 percent lower than the odds of within-group social contact.[19]

Fourth, some types of cross-racial relations are easier to form than others. The relevant data are summarized in Table 5.13. To aid interpretation, the first number in this table (0.25) is an average of the three odds ratios in the first three rows of column (1) of Table 5.9. It indicates that nonwhites are about 25 percent as likely as whites are to socialize often or very often with white students. The last row of Table 5.13 reports column averages across all racial groups. This row suggests that the first two types of cross-racial social interactions—general socializing and roommate selections—typically engender the smallest social distances among race groups. In addition, social distances are only slightly greater when close friend networks and dating are involved. In particular, frequent socializing or roommate choices that cross over racial or ethnic boundaries are 60 percent less likely than the same kinds of social interactions that occur within racial groups. Cross-racial friendships or dating partners are 70 percent less likely than similar within-group social ties. All of this is consistent with an observation made earlier in the chapter. The more intimate social relations—in particular, those involving cross-racial close friendships and dating partners—are less common than interactions of a potentially more casual nature.[20]

[19] To illustrate the calculations in this paragraph, the average of the four numbers in the first row of Table 5.9 is 0.12, which means that blacks are only 12 percent as likely to interact with whites as whites are to interact with whites. Likewise, the first row of Table 5.10 suggests that whites are just 16 percent as likely to interact with their black classmates as blacks are to interact with each other. Averaging the two numbers yields 0.14—the number above the column for black-white interaction in Figure 5.1. In other words, blacks and whites are 14 percent as likely (or 86 percent *less* likely) to exhibit cross-racial, reciprocal social interaction as they are to interact with members of their own groups.

[20] Hispanic students occupy a unique role in Table 5.13. Relative to the amount of social interaction that Hispanic students have among themselves, they are the most likely (along

TABLE 5.13

Patterns of Cross-Racial Social Interaction, by Type of Interaction
NSCE Matriculant Sample: 1980s, 1993, and 1997 Cohorts Combined
(N = 6,350)
Odds Ratios from Logistic Regressions

Cross-Racial Interaction with Classmates Who Are	Socialize Often or Very Often with (1)	Live with after Freshman Year (2)	Have a Close Friendship with (3)	Date at Least One (4)
White	0.25	0.42	0.18	0.38
Black	0.25	0.16	0.11	0.14
Asian	0.55	0.38	0.41	0.30
Hispanic	0.55	0.65	0.48	0.36
All Groups	0.40	0.40	0.30	0.30

Source: Tables 5.9–5.12.

Note: Each cell in the first four rows represents an arithmetic average across three re-spondent race groups. Results are not weighted by race. Averages in the final row represent column averages.

Ethnic Coursework

As predicted, taking ethnic studies classes is positively associated with so-cial interaction with the race-ethnic group being studied. This conclusion is particularly true for friendship circles and dating patterns but extends to all four types of social interactions with Hispanic students. Also as ex-pected, developing a minor in African or African American studies shows a larger gain in the likelihood of associating with black students than simply taking an African or African American studies class. The only anomalous results are the significantly negative associations between ma-joring in Chicano or Latino studies and either rooming with an Hispanic student or having a close friendship with someone who is Hispanic.

The results also bear out our hypotheses about relationships between taking courses on one race-ethnic group and interacting with another group. All of the statistically significant relationships in the lower half of the panel involving ethnic studies coursework in Tables 5.10 and 5.11 are negative. Moreover, in every instance these negative relationships are

---

with Asian students) to be named as a participant in frequent between-group socializing, the most likely to have been chosen by non-Hispanics as a roommate after freshman year or as a close friend, and the next most likely (after whites) to be involved in intergroup dating. It is also evident that, for Hispanics, the average odds ratios in the fourth row of Table 5.13 are greater for patterns of social interaction involving general socializing and rooming ar-rangements than they are for friendship networks or dating patterns.

associated with either majoring or minoring in a particular ethnic studies area. Simply taking a class about one race-ethnic group does not seem to lower the likelihood of having social interaction with another race-ethnic group. There does not appear to be any association between the amount of ethnic studies coursework about non-Hispanic students and the chances of interacting with Hispanics. Also, as predicted, taking ethnic studies courses about nonwhites has no significant effect on the likelihood of interacting with white students. Overall, and subject to the caveat about the difficulty of establishing the direction of causation, the results suggest that taking an ethnic studies course may be the most influential facilitator of developing social contacts and interactions with members of the race-ethnic group being examined. These relationships are always positive and are statistically significant in the majority of cases. And in no instance does taking a class about one race-ethnic group significantly reduce the likelihood of having social relations with another group.

Ethnic Extracurriculars

The results for engaging in ethnic extracurricular activities also generally support our hypotheses. Students who participate in an activity celebrating a minority group's heritage have significantly greater odds of engaging in all four types of social interactions with that minority group. Also as predicted, participating in an activity that honors one race-ethnic group does not lower the chances of interacting with members of other race-ethnic groups (including whites). In fact, participating in a non-Hispanic or non-Asian activity is significantly positively associated with the likelihood of socializing frequently with and dating Hispanics and Asians, respectively.

As expected, minority students who belong to an ethnic organization are more likely to interact with classmates from their own race-ethnic group. Asians and blacks who belong to ethnic organizations have significantly greater odds of having all four types of social relations with students who share their ethnicity. Hispanics who are members of ethnic organizations have increased odds of socializing frequently with other Hispanics and of forming a close friendship with an Hispanic student. White students' chances of interacting with other whites are unrelated to membership in an ethnic organization. Perhaps the reason that whites do not fit the pattern of minority students is that the membership of ethnic organizations is likely to be composed primarily of nonwhite students. For white students, therefore, belonging to an ethnic organization is unlikely to reinforce social interactions with coethnics to the same extent that it could if one were a nonwhite student and belonged to an ethnic organization.

Given the presumed time commitment involved in belonging to organizations, we hypothesized that being a member of an ethnically oriented association and belonging to a particular race-ethnic group would reduce the odds of cross-racial social interaction. This expectation is supported only in students' interactions with their white classmates. Nonwhites who belong to ethnic organizations exhibit 33 percent lower odds of rooming with a white student after freshman year and roughly 50 percent lower odds of having any of the three other social relations with whites. With the exception of non-Asian ethnic organization members who display significantly lower odds of having an Asian friend, ethnic organization membership does not significantly affect the likelihood of cross-racial interaction with other minority students.

Residential Environment

Results that connect residence in a racially focused theme dorm to social interactions with members of particular race-ethnic groups are more mixed. Contrary to expectations, whites, blacks, and Asians who participate in race-focused housing do not have significantly greater odds of interacting with coethnics on any of the four types of social relations. There is only one bit of confirmatory evidence. Hispanics who live in race-focused housing exhibit 114 percent higher odds of having an Hispanic roommate after freshman year. There is somewhat greater support for our hypothesis concerning patterns of intergroup relations. With only one exception, living in race-focused housing and not being a member of race-ethnic Group A is negatively related to having social relations with classmates from Group A. The significantly negative associations typically adhere to socializing frequently with members of another group. In sum, our data suggest that living in race-focused housing has little effect on the likelihood of interacting with coethnics, but doing so can lower the chances of interacting with other racial groups.

Also as predicted, students have significantly greater odds of interacting across a broad spectrum of outcomes with classmates from a particular race-ethnic group if they have a freshman-year roommate from that race-ethnic group. For white, black, and Asian students, the largest positive associations are with living with a student of that race after freshman year. For example, students who have a black roommate during their first year in college are more than three times as likely as students without a black freshman roommate to live with someone who is black after freshman year. The smallest positive associations are between freshman roommate's race and dating someone from the same race.[21]

---

[21] In fact, students who have a black roommate during freshman year are just 33 percent more likely than other students to date a black classmate. But this relationship is the only one connected with freshman roommate's race that is not statistically significant. The lack

Population Availability

The data on population availability typically conform to our expectations—universally for Hispanics and Asians and selectively for blacks and whites. Each one percentage point increase in the proportion of Hispanic students on campus is associated with an expected increase in students' odds of socializing frequently with Hispanics of 17 percent, of rooming with an Hispanic student after freshman year of 18 percent, of having a close friend who is Hispanic of 16 percent, and of dating someone who is Hispanic of 13 percent. The percentage of Asian students in the entering cohort is also significantly and positively associated with the chances of having all four types of social relations with Asians, though the size of the associations is typically smaller than for Hispanics. Each additional percentage point in the Asian student share is associated with an increase ranging between 5 and 8 percent in the odds of interacting with Asians. The likelihood of interacting with blacks is not as consistently affected by their proportionate representation on campus. The associations are positive and significant only for roommate choices and close friend networks. Frequent socializing and dating relationships are not affected, suggesting that other factors shape whether students will pursue these latter two activities with their black classmates. Lastly, an increase in the proportion of white students on NSCE campuses is significantly (but only marginally) associated just with the likelihood of having a white student among one's close friends.[22]

---

of significance is not too surprising because romantic relationships are almost always one of the last forms of interaction to occur frequently between race groups, and romantic relationships between whites and blacks have been particularly taboo in American history (Lee and Edmonston, 2005). Even today marriages between whites and blacks are the least common type of intermarriage between America's major racial and ethnic groups (Qian and Lichter, 2007).

[22] Our findings are largely consistent with a study using nationwide data on high school students. Joyner and Kao (2000) report that students' chances of having an interracial friendship rise substantially as the proportion of same-race students in their high school declines. On the other hand, Feld and Carter (1998) show that efforts to integrate schools and to increase interracial contact may backfire if the greater number of minority students is large enough that minority students can satisfy their needs for friendship among members of their own race. In an important nationwide study of high schools characterized by a wide range of racial heterogeneity, Moody (2001) showed that there is a generally positive (although nonlinear) association between the degree of racial heterogeneity and the likelihood of having same-race friends. This conclusion is not inconsistent with a finding by Feld and Carter (1998) that the potential number of cross-race ties increases with racial heterogeneity. As Moody (2001: 703) explains, "As heterogeneity increases in a school, opportunities for making cross-race ties increase, but the observed rate at which cross-race ties are made does not keep up with that opportunity."

Socioeconomic Status

A clear pattern emerges in the relationships between socioeconomic status and the chances of interacting with specific racial groups. In general, there is a positive association between respondents' social class backgrounds and the likelihood of having a range of social ties with white students. On the other hand, the relation between social class and interacting with all groups of nonwhite students is plainly negative. These patterns are evident across all domains of social interaction. They are particularly striking in the case of dating someone who is white and rooming with a black student after freshman year. These results suggest that students may be forming cross-racial social relations on the basis of social class affinities— a kind of assortative socializing along class lines. In other words, higher SES students may be more likely to interact with whites because whites are more likely to share their high socioeconomic status. Conversely, lower SES students may find it easier and more comfortable to interact with blacks and Hispanics because a larger proportion of blacks and Hispanics come from lower socioeconomic status backgrounds as well.

Other Factors

Finally, we assess how other variables relate to interactions with different race groups. First, compared to their classmates who are in the fourth-or-higher immigrant generation, foreign-born students and those with a recent immigrant ancestry are frequently significantly more likely to have social relations with white, Asian, and Hispanic students. The strongest positive associations are with frequent socializing and best-friend networks. Second, students at private NSCE institutions are significantly more likely than their counterparts at public universities to report that they socialize frequently with nonwhite classmates. The pattern of greater interaction with black classmates extends to all four types of social relations. Third, there appear to be relatively few time trends in patterns of social interaction.[23]

CONCLUSION

With all of the attention being given to admitting a racially diverse first-year class, it is natural to assume that today's college students have frequent opportunities to mix and mingle across racial and ethnic lines and

---

[23] On an all-other-things-equal basis, more recent cohorts of NSCE college students are somewhat less likely to date white students and more likely to have frequent social contact with and be close friends with black students.

that they are taking advantage of these opportunities on a regular basis. At the same time, there is sufficient evidence that same-race groups "hang out" together on campus (see Egan, 2007; Lewis, 2008) to raise questions about whether the full potential and promise of diversity are being realized. The analysis in this chapter has shown that, depending on one's perspective, the glass is either half full or half empty. NSCE students do establish social networks that include students of their own race as well as classmates from other racial and ethnic groups. What is difficult to evaluate is whether the extent of cross-racial social interaction that occurs on campus is a lot or a little. In what follows, we offer a brief summary of our principal findings.

Nearly one-third of white students report having taken at least one course in African American, Latino, or Asian American studies. Moreover, 30 percent of whites have participated in an ethnic extracurricular event to celebrate a particular minority group (for example, Black History month). More than one-tenth of white students belong to a campus organization with an orientation toward a specific racial or ethnic group. Even though nonwhite students are more likely than whites to participate in similar kinds of ethnic courses and extracurricular activities, they are surrounded in college by a dominant white culture and engage in this culture in various ways. Nonwhite students attend classes that are populated predominantly by white students. The faculty who teach these courses are overwhelmingly white. Even outside class, most of the adults on campus with whom minority students interact are not members of their own race or ethnic group.

Students from different racial and ethnic backgrounds are also interacting with each other. Data from our eight NSCE institutions indicate that more than 60 percent of students socialize "often or very often" with classmates from a different race. Roughly half have a college roommate from a different race-ethnic background, and a similar proportion of students report having a close friendship with an other-race classmate. Finally, more than one-third of NSCE students report having dated a classmate whose racial or ethnic background is different from their own. In short, the most significant finding from this chapter is that there is frequent social interaction across racial and ethnic lines among enrolled students at the selective schools in our study.[24]

At the same time, it needs to be acknowledged that the amount of social contact *within* racial and ethnic groups is far greater than that

---

[24] This conclusion parallels a finding by Bowen and Bok (1998) from the College and Beyond Study. They report, "So, if there was self-segregation on these campuses—as there surely was in some instances and during 'some part of the day'—the walls between subgroups were highly porous" (231).

between groups. Roughly 90 percent of NSCE students report socializing frequently with, rooming with, and having as one of their five closest friends a classmate from the same racial or ethnic background. About five out of every six students indicate that they dated as least one classmate of their same race or ethnicity. When these patterns are disaggregated by race, it appears that the greatest social distances exist between white and nonwhite students. Partly because white students are the dominant majority on campus, they are about 50 percentage points more likely to interact with other white students than with their nonwhite peers. At the other extreme, Hispanic students are approximately 40 percentage points more likely to have social ties with non-Hispanic classmates than with Hispanic students. Black and Asian students fall in between, with blacks being somewhat closer to whites in terms of their tendencies to interact with classmates like themselves, whereas Asians are more similar to Hispanics.[25]

We offer the following brief conclusions about how respondents' race and other factors are related on an all-other-things-equal basis to the likelihood that members of Group A will interact with members of Group B. First, students in race group A are consistently less likely to establish social ties with classmates in race group B than members of either A or B are to interact socially within their own groups. But when cross-racial interactions do take place, they occur with varying frequency depending on the groups involved. For example, when we control for the relative shares of different racial-ethnic groups on campus, we find that relative to the amount of within-group contact, the greatest social distance occurs between non-black students and their black peers. The black-Asian and black-white gaps are the largest, whereas the smallest relative social distance exists between whites and Hispanics.

Second, some social venues are more conducive to cross-race interactions than others. In particular, intergroup relations are somewhat more

---

[25]Bowen and Bok (1998: 231–33) show that black students in their sample were much more likely to "know well" two or more white students than white students were to be as familiar with blacks. In particular, they report that 88 percent of blacks knew two or more white classmates well, but that only 56 percent of whites knew well two or more black classmates. Our data reflect a similar pattern if we average across the four domains of social interaction (socializing with frequently, rooming with, being close friends with, and dating someone). Among black NSCE students, 56 percent had substantial social ties to whites, whereas only 19 percent of whites were as engaged with blacks. Bowen and Bok also report that blacks and whites were equally likely to know well two or more Asian students (57 and 58 percent, respectively), but that blacks were more likely than whites to know well at least two Hispanic students (54 versus 26 percent, respectively). Our data suggest a different pattern. Whites are somewhat more likely than blacks to interact socially with Asian students (28 and 21 percent, respectively), whereas whites are about as likely as blacks to interact with Hispanics (15 versus 18 percent, respectively).

likely to be found in the context of general socializing or residential rooming arrangements than within the two more intimate forms of social interaction—close friendship networks or dating partners.[26]

Third, our results highlight several campus experiences that can facilitate intergroup interaction. Taking a course about a particular ethnic group, participating in an extracurricular event celebrating an ethnic group's heritage, or joining an organization whose activities are oriented toward an individual minority group are good ways to develop social ties with members of the ethnic group in question, and doing so does not normally appear to interfere with establishing social relations with other nonwhite group members. Moreover, having a first-year roommate from a particular race-ethnic group is associated with a substantially greater likelihood of interacting with members of that group while in college. Not only are there better chances of having a roommate beyond freshman year from that race-ethnic group, but patterns of intergroup social interaction across a broad range of outcomes also seem to be enhanced.

Fourth, we find broad support for a population availability hypothesis. In particular, an increase in the share of students in the entering freshman class who come from a particular race or ethnic group is associated with an increased propensity to develop social ties with members of that group throughout one's college years. This conclusion applies universally to Asian and Hispanic students and selectively to black and (even) white students. It suggests that one effective way that university officials can encourage students to develop social interactions across race and ethnic lines is to ensure critical masses of each group on campus.[27]

Fifth, with the gradual easing of racial tensions in the United States, one might expect to find trends across our three entering student cohorts in the likelihood of intergroup relations. Our descriptive results do show that students who entered college in the 1990s are more likely to have

---

[26] Bowen and Bok (1998: 233) report that the most common settings in which interracial interaction occurred among students who knew well members of other racial groups were "class or study groups" and "same dorm or roommate." This observation is consistent with our findings.

[27] Bowen and Bok (1998: 235) reach a similar conclusion. They find a positive association between the percentage of black students in the 1989 entering freshman cohort and the percentage of white students who knew well two or more black students. A four-percentage-point decline (from 8 to 4 percent) in the proportion of blacks is associated with an eight-percentage-point decline (from 61 to 53 percent) in the proportion of whites who knew well two or more blacks. It is important here to recall Moody's (2001) general conclusion that there is a positive association (at least in high schools and over a broad middle range of values for racial heterogeneity) between the degree of racial heterogeneity at the population level and the odds of nominating a friend of the same race as oneself. His explanation is that race does not become salient until critical masses of minority students are reached. Beyond that point and until higher levels of heterogeneity are attained, more racial heterogeneity leads to a greater chance of having same-race friends.

cross-racial interactions than are students who entered in the 1980s. Regression results, however, indicate that this trend is due not so much to changes in attitudes over time but to changes in the racial composition of the student bodies at selective universities.

Finally, students' social class has a bearing on intergroup relations. As one moves up the social class ladder, the social distance between own-race and other-race individuals increases. Students from higher socioeconomic status backgrounds are more likely to interact with whites and less likely to mix with nonwhites than are middle-class students. On the other hand, lower SES students are less likely to mingle with whites but more likely to interact with black students, as compared to students from middle-class families.

In sum, our data show that students at selective colleges and universities interact frequently with their classmates from other racial and ethnic backgrounds, though not as often as they interact with students who are more like themselves. Moreover, our results suggest that there are policies and programs that universities can implement that may influence the amount of cross-racial interaction on campus.

Chapter Six

ACADEMIC PERFORMANCE

INTRODUCTION

A letter of acceptance to a highly rated college or university is coveted more today than at any other time in the history of American higher education. As proof, one need look no further than to record numbers of applications received by Ivy League and other academically selective institutions or to acceptance rates that, in some instances, have fallen below 10 percent.[1] Half of the respondents in a 2007 nationwide survey of adults supported by the Lumina Foundation for Education believe that a college degree is essential to be successful in the workplace, up dramatically from 31 percent in a similar poll in 2000 (Immerwahr and Johnson, 2007). Parents from upper social classes know instinctively that the top salaries and other professional rewards go to graduates from the "Princetons" and "Harvards" of the academic world. This ingrained belief is surely a reason affirmative action policies have become so controversial. To extend admission preferences at many of this country's top schools to candidates from underrepresented minority groups strikes many as unfair at best and discriminatory at worst. It is for this reason that race-based preferences have been litigated. As we have seen in earlier chapters, the U.S. Supreme Court in 2003 settled matters, at least for the time being, by allowing a consideration of race in admission because of the educational benefits that can flow from a racially diverse student body.

But issues surrounding access and fairness are not the only reason affirmative action has become so controversial. Another important aspect of the debate is the claim that racial preferences are actually harmful to their intended beneficiaries. Critics of race-based affirmative action allege that it boosts underrepresented minority students into more competitive environments than are warranted based on the students' prior academic accomplishments. The consequence is that minority students suffer, not only

---

[1]Princeton University received a record 18,942 applications for the Class of 2011 and admitted 1,838 students for a 9.7 percent acceptance rate. Harvard's acceptance rate for the Class of 2011 was 9.0 percent (also a record), down from 9.3 percent the previous year (Harvard College Admissions Office, 2007; Princeton University, 2007). Applications to selective colleges for the Class of 2012 are setting new records. For example, at Harvard they are up 19 percent over last year to more than 27,000 (Arenson, 2008b).

by graduating at lower rates but also by ranking lower in their graduating classes than they would have if they had attended colleges and universities with students whose academic records were more in line with theirs. Supporters, on the other hand, argue that there are evident advantages to attending and graduating from academically selective institutions. Graduation rates and the chances of attending professional and graduate school are likely to be higher. In addition, graduates of these institutions are thought to have higher lifetime incomes. Moreover, these supporters say, there is no evidence that minority students are mismatched with other students when they attend the most selective institutions. And if class rank suffers, this disadvantage is more than offset by other advantages.

The most comprehensive analysis of empirical data that supports the "fit" or "academic mismatch" hypothesis has been carried out by Richard Sander (2004). Sander examined longitudinal information on the roughly 27,000 students who entered all accredited American law schools in the fall of 1991. The data, which come from the Law School Admission Council, Bar Passage Study, permit one to follow these students through to the completion of law school and then on to whether they took state bar exams and whether they passed in the two- or three-year period following graduation. Sander also studied supplementary data on the employment experiences of these young lawyers. He finds that race-based preferences for black students in law school admission result in higher attrition rates from law school, lower bar passage rates, and subsequent problems in the job market for new lawyers, compared to a race-blind system. In his most damning critique, Sander concludes that racial preferences produce *fewer* black lawyers each year than would be produced under a race-blind system.

A sharply contrasting perspective is offered by Bowen and Bok (1998) in their analysis of College and Beyond (C&B) data on undergraduates. They find no evidence to support the fit (or academic mismatch) hypothesis. Attending a more selective college or university increases graduation rates, is associated with a higher likelihood of earning a professional or doctoral degree, leads on average to greater career success as measured by annual income, and is in most instances correlated with greater involvement (including taking leadership positions) in a broad range of civic activities.

Both Sander and Bowen and Bok recognize that affirmative action programs entail both benefits and costs for underrepresented minority students. And they agree that one of the most important costs is weaker academic performance if minority students struggle when they are placed in more challenging academic environments and are surrounded by other students whose academic records are significantly stronger. But they differ in their evaluation of the relative costs and benefits. For Sander, the modest benefit of school selectivity is more than offset by the negative effect of lower grades (and perhaps less actual learning). For Bowen and Bok, the advantages associated with attending a more selective school trump lower class rank.[2]

The comparatively weaker academic performance of underrepresented minority students at selective schools is to some extent the result of their having more modest academic credentials at the beginning of their college careers. This link between college academic success and college readiness should not be surprising, nor is the finding limited to minority students. Any student whose level of college preparedness, as measured by high school grades and scores on standardized tests, is below the average for all incoming freshmen might be expected to graduate with a class rank below that of many other students. But what study after study has found is that the college academic performance of black students (and to some extent that of their Hispanic peers) is even below what one would predict on the basis of their pre-college academic accomplishments. The reasons for this academic "underperformance" are not well understood, and it is therefore a source of serious concern among college administrators.

This chapter speaks directly to what arguably matters most when students go off to college—how they perform academically. But the chapter also contains valuable data to inform intense debates in higher education. Do the NSCE data support the academic mismatch hypothesis, or do they suggest that minority students derive net benefits from race-based affirmative action policies? What, if any, are the costs to minority students of racial preferences? Do we find evidence of academic underperformance by underrepresented minority students? To answer these questions, we examine college graduation rates, choice of college majors, and overall grades in college. We will be particularly interested in how school selectivity affects these outcomes and in the additional roles played by students' race and social class. Answering these questions requires more data. Therefore, following the collection of the survey data, we returned to the participating NSCE institutions and asked them to supply information about *every* matriculant in each of the three entering cohorts on the following: degree date of undergraduate degree (including an indicator for no degree awarded); field of the awarded degree or current enrolled field of study (using detailed six-digit codes for the classification of

---

[2]Differences in their bottom-line assessments could not be more stark. Sander (2004: 372) concludes, "Affirmative action as currently practiced by the nation's law schools does not, therefore, pass even the easiest test one can set. In systemic, objective terms, it hurts the group it is most designed to help." By contrast, Bowen and Bok (1998: 265) say, "In the eyes of those best positioned to know [black graduates from selective institutions], any putative costs of race-based policies have been overwhelmed by the benefits gained through enhanced access to excellent educational opportunities."

instructional programs); first-year GPA; and cumulative GPA when last observed (e.g., at graduation, withdrawal, or transfer). These data then were merged with information from the NSCE student survey.

Graduation Rates

Graduating from college has a significant and lasting impact on individuals' entire lives. While having some college education is more advantageous than having none, those with a college degree earn even greater rewards. Higher lifetime incomes, greater access to employer-provided health insurance and pension benefits, and better overall health are just a few of the benefits college graduates are more likely to enjoy (Baum and Ma, 2007).

A student's likelihood of graduating, however, depends on where she enrolls. Individuals who matriculate at two-year colleges are very unlikely to earn a four-year degree (Cabrera, La Nasa, and Burkum, 2001). The U.S. Department of Education (2003: 130) reports that only 29 percent of students who begin at community colleges transfer to four-year colleges.[3] Of those who transfer, fewer than 35 percent complete a degree within six years of beginning their higher education. Starting off at a four-year institution is a surer way of eventually earning an undergraduate degree. Even so, just 56 percent of students who begin at four-year colleges complete their degrees in six years (Knapp et al., 2007: 11). There are also differences between public and private universities. Slightly more than half (53 percent) of students at four-year public institutions graduate within six years, in contrast to 62 percent of students at private schools (Knapp et al., 2007: 11). At elite four-year colleges and universities, graduation rates are even higher. Among the academically selective schools in the College and Beyond universe studied by Bowen and Bok (1998), 85 percent of students in the 1989 entering cohort graduated in six years, and an estimated additional 7 percent transferred from their first school and graduated elsewhere within the same period.

Six-year completion rates at the eight NSCE schools studied in the two previous chapters are uniformly high. When averaged across the 1993 and 1997 entering cohorts, they range from a minimum of 84 percent to more than 95 percent.[4] Overall, 89 percent of first-year students earn a

---

[3] Melguizo (2007) points out that black and Hispanic students are overrepresented in California community colleges and that very few successfully transfer to a four-year college.

[4] In this chapter we limit our analysis of graduation rates and class rank distributions to students in the 1993 and 1997 entering cohorts, because these are the two cohorts for which complete information exists. The 1983 entering cohort is missing graduation information for one school out of eight and cumulative GPA data for two schools.

baccalaureate degree in six years.[5] Although it is customary to focus on the proportion of students who graduate within six years of the start of their freshman year, there are some schools—especially those that are largely residential and have sizable endowments—where graduating in four years is the expected norm. The four-year graduation rate at NSCE schools is 74 percent, which suggests that affording students an additional two years in which to complete their undergraduate degrees increases overall graduation rates by 15 percentage points (from 74 to 89 percent).

To study the effects of school selectivity on graduation rates, we grouped these eight colleges and universities into three selectivity categories defined by entering students' math and verbal SAT I scores. An institution qualified for the highest selectivity category if the mean (re-centered) SAT score for freshmen in its 1993 and 1997 cohorts is greater than 1400. Schools in the middle selectivity category have average freshmen SAT scores between 1300 and 1400. An average SAT score below 1300 among entering freshmen places an institution into the lowest selectivity tier.[6] Every selectivity grouping contains at least two schools. Nearly 94 percent of students at the most selective NSCE schools earn diplomas within six years of matriculating as freshmen. This proportion drops modestly to 89 percent among schools in the middle selectivity tier. Among NSCE institutions ranked in the lowest selectivity category, 87 percent of freshmen receive a degree in six years. It is important to remember, however, that an 87 percent graduation rate is still extraordinarily high, not just by national standards but also by comparison with other academically selective schools. For instance, Bowen and Bok (1998) also find that graduation rates increase along with school selectivity. But the six-year completion rate is 81 percent in the lowest of their three tiers.[7] A positive correlation between school selectivity and graduation rates has also been detected by other researchers using different data (Horn, 2006; Kane, 1998a).

[5] These percentages represent first-school graduation rates. Some students—perhaps as many as an extra 7 percent, as estimated by Bowen and Bok (1998)—transferred to other schools and graduated within the same six-year period, bringing the overall completion rate for NSCE students closer to 95 percent.

[6] A student's ACT score was converted to an equivalent SAT score if SAT score was unknown or missing. Just 3 percent of students in the 1993 and 1997 cohorts had neither an ACT nor an SAT score.

[7] Bowen and Bok (1998) use mean unrecentered combined SAT scores among entering freshmen to define their three categories of institutional selectivity. The threshold values they pick are 1150 and 1300, which become roughly 1230 and 1370 on a re-centered basis. These values are not far below the mean re-centered SAT scores of 1300 and 1400 used to define the three NSCE selectivity categories. In the College and Beyond data, graduation rates rise from 81 percent in the least selective category, to 85 percent in the middle category, and to 94 percent among the most competitive schools (Bowen and Bok, 1998: 376).

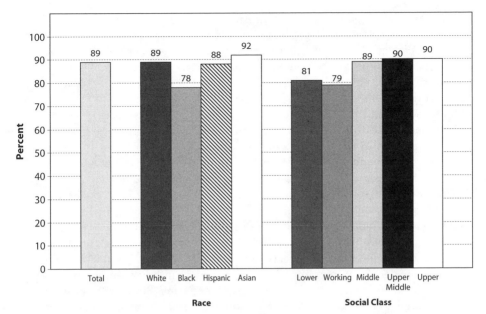

Figure 6.1. Six-Year Graduation Rates at NSCE Institutions, by Race and Social Class; 1993 and 1997 Entering Cohorts Combined (N = 4,390). Note: Racial differences are statistically significant at the .001 level. Social class differences are significant at the .01 level. Source: National Study of College Experience.

More substantial variations are observed when six-year graduation rates are disaggregated by race and ethnicity. The results are shown in Figure 6.1. White and Hispanic students exhibit completion rates close to the average for all students. Black and Asian students define the outer extremes, with just 78 percent of black matriculants earning a degree within six years compared with 92 percent of their Asian peers.[8] This racial ordering is preserved when a four-year time frame is used. Completion rates are highest for Asians (80 percent), followed by whites (75 percent), Hispanics (71 percent), and blacks (57 percent). However, the Asian-black graduation gap stretches from 14 to 23 percentage points when four-year graduation rates are substituted for six-year ones. Put differently, black students display the largest "catch-up" when graduation outcomes are observed after six years. Using this expanded window of opportunity means an additional 21 percent of black freshmen earn their degrees. The gains are less for other groups, including Asians who exhibit the smallest

[8] A similar racial pattern in graduation rates is evident nationally among all four-year institutions (Knapp et al., 2007) and at other elite colleges and universities (Bowen and Bok, 1998; Ehrmann, 2007; Horn, 2006).

increase (at 12 percentage points). Anecdotal impressions formed by observing Princeton undergraduates suggest that many students who get into academic difficulty and are asked to take a semester off come back to campus with a greater sense of purpose and receive better grades thereafter, even though their ultimate graduation date may have been delayed as a result.[9]

NSCE students from more modest economic circumstances generally are less successful than their better-off peers in completing their bachelor's degrees in six years. Figure 6.1 shows graduation rates by social class. Approximately eight out of ten students from lower- or working-class families manage to graduate in six years, compared to roughly nine out of ten from higher social class backgrounds. This class divide expands when we consider four-year graduation rates. Just 53 percent of lower-class students and 64 percent of those from working-class families graduate in four years. Among students from more affluent families, four-year graduation rates range between 71 and 78 percent. A similar socioeconomic gradient in graduation rates is evident in other samples of students at elite colleges and universities (Bowen and Bok, 1998; Bowen, Kurzweil, and Tobin, 2005) and in more representative national samples of college students (Ficklen and Stone, 2002; Hebel, 2007). A recent report from the Pell Institute (Engle and O'Brien, 2007) finds that only 12 percent of students from the bottom quartile of family income will earn a bachelor's degree by age twenty-four compared to 73 percent of students from families in the top income quartile. Part of this gap is caused by differences in rates of college enrollment. But even among those who do enroll, students from lower-income backgrounds are less likely to persist to degree completion.

Simple tabulations can tell us only so much about the issues raised at the beginning of this chapter. To investigate how college selectivity, race, and social class affect graduation rates and other academic outcomes, it is necessary to isolate the effects of these factors holding constant other variables that might also play a role. Regression analysis permits us to examine these effects on an all-other-things-equal basis. We begin the analysis in the remainder of this section by returning to conclusions about graduation rates derived from the College and Beyond database and ask how well our results agree with those reported earlier by Bowen and Bok (1998). Following that, we consider an expanded model that incorpo-

---

[9] One of this book's authors (Espenshade) served as the departmental representative for sociology at Princeton from 1998 to 2001 and had an opportunity to observe first-hand the comings and goings of sociology majors. The departmental representative in each department is responsible for monitoring the academic progress of all undergraduate concentrators.

rates a number of additional explanatory variables suggested by Bowen and Bok but not included in their analyses.

The Bowen and Bok Model

The most thorough examination of the academic mismatch hypothesis in the context of highly selective undergraduate colleges and universities has been conducted by Bowen and Bok (1998). They find that, controlling for other factors that are likely to influence graduation rates, there is a strong positive and statistically significant association between school selectivity and the likelihood of graduating in six years. Students who attend a school in the most selective category have the greatest probability of graduating, followed by students who enroll at an institution in the middle range of selectivity. Matriculating at a college or university in the lowest selectivity tier is associated with the lowest graduation probabilities. It is these results that Bowen and Bok (1998: 88) point to when arguing that the C&B data provide a strong refutation of the mismatch hypothesis.[10]

The first step in our analysis is an attempt to replicate Bowen and Bok's findings using NSCE data. Our results are in surprisingly good agreement with theirs. The first column of Table 6.1 shows the odds ratios from a logistic regression in which the dependent variable is whether a student who enrolled at one of the eight NSCE institutions in either 1993 or 1997 graduated within six years of matriculation. The predictor variables have been chosen deliberately to match as closely as possible the predictor variables selected by Bowen and Bok (1998: 381).[11] Note first that school selectivity is positively and significantly associated with graduation outcomes. Students who attend the most selective NSCE institutions are twice as likely to graduate in six years as are students at the least selective schools. NSCE students who enroll at a school in the second most selective tier are 18 percent more likely than students in the bottom tier to graduate in the same six-year time frame. Our results are completely consistent with those found in the C&B data, and we would have to conclude that there

[10]Nationally representative data are consistent with this general conclusion based on selective institutions. Melguizo (2008) asks whether the higher graduation rates of students at selective institutions are due to characteristics of the institutions or whether they result from enrolling more academically qualified students. Using data from the National Education Longitudinal Study high school senior class of 1992, Melguizo finds that school selectivity matters. There is a strong positive relation between school selectivity and the likelihood of completing a bachelor's degree. The result holds for both black and Hispanic students.

[11]The only important difference is that our model also includes a variable for cohort year.

TABLE 6.1
Odds Ratio Results from Logistic Regressions Examining
Six-Year Graduation Rates
NSCE Matriculant Data: 1993 and 1997 Cohorts (N = 4,390)

Predictor Variables	Bowen and Bok Model[a] (1)	NSCE Model[b] (2)
Race		
(White)	—	—
Black	0.47***	0.57**
Hispanic	0.83	0.53**
Asian	1.26	0.68
Social Class		
Upper-Middle and Upper Class	1.08	0.69
(Middle Class)	—	—
Lower and Working Class	0.55*	0.78
College Selectivity		
Most Selective Tier	1.99**	1.68
Second Most Selective Tier	1.18	1.29
(All Other Colleges)	—	—
Immigrant Generation		
First	—	3.09***
Second	—	1.87**
Third	—	1.11
(Fourth and Higher)	—	—
Unknown	—	1.14
Employment during First Year of College		
(None)	—	—
Less than ten hours per week	—	1.11
Ten or more hours per week	—	0.63*
Unknown	—	0.81
Satisfaction with College Social Experience[c]		
(Very Satisfied)	—	—
Not Very Satisfied	—	0.33***
Unknown	—	0.34*
Parents Owned Home during Senior Year of High School		
Yes	—	2.03**
(Other and Unknown)	—	—

(*Continued*)

TABLE 6.1 (*Continued*)

Predictor Variables	Bowen and Bok Model[a] (1)	NSCE Model[b] (2)
Parents Helped with Homework during Primary School		
Yes	—	1.61*
(Other and Unknown)	—	—
High School GPA		
A+	—	2.67*
A	—	1.93
A−	—	1.17
(B+ or lower)	—	—
Unknown	—	0.83
Elite 72 High School Graduate		
Yes	—	4.67***
(Other and Unknown)	—	—
Number of Observations	4,390	4,390
F	8.77	5.39
(df1, df2)	(20, 4291)	(63, 4248)
Prob > F	0.0000	0.0000

Source: National Study of College Experience.

Note: Both models use weighted observations. Reference categories are shown in parentheses.

[a]This model reestimates with NSCE data the model that Bowen and Bok (1998: 381) used to explore six-year graduation rates at College and Beyond institutions. This model controls for gender, cohort, SAT I score, high school class rank, and attending a women's college, although the coefficients are not reported.

[b]Like the Bowen and Bok model, this model controls for gender, cohort, SAT I score, high school class rank, and attending a women's college. In addition, this model controls for first-generation college student status, legacy status, recruited athlete status, whether received financial aid, number of Advanced Placement (AP) exams taken, number of SAT II exams taken, average SAT II score, National Merit or National Achievement Scholar status, and high school type.

[c]Students considered "very satisfied" rate their overall college social experience a 6 or 7 on a seven-point scale, in which 1 represents "least satisfied" and 7 represents being "most satisfied." Students considered "not very satisfied" gave their experience a score between 1 and 5.

*p < .05 **p < .01 ***p < .001

is no support in our data for the mismatch hypothesis when we examine that hypothesis using the framework of the Bowen and Bok model.[12]

Table 6.1 also provides the first indication in the NSCE data of academic underperformance by underrepresented black and Hispanic students. Black students who are statistically equivalent to whites in terms of college attended, SAT scores, high school class rank, and other control variables nevertheless have 53 percent significantly lower odds than whites of graduating within six years. Hispanic students are 17 percent less likely than comparable white students to graduate in the same time period. Asian students have slightly higher graduation chances than whites on an all-other-things-equal basis. Social class behaves in the expected way. Students from lower- and working-class family backgrounds are 45 percent significantly less likely than otherwise equivalent middle-class students to graduate within six years. Those from the most prosperous families are the most likely to graduate in this period.[13]

An Expanded Model

When we consider an expanded model, however, with a larger number of plausible covariates, results bearing on the mismatch hypothesis are not quite as definitive. The second column of Table 6.1 presents the odds ratios from our preferred model for studying six-year graduation rates. This expanded model includes all of the predictor variables from the first column plus others. A student's immigrant generation status might be important, especially because of the presence of large numbers of first- and second-generation immigrants. High school academic performance as registered by high school GPA is likely to be related to college graduation chances for obvious reasons. Our expanded model also includes several explanatory variables noted by Bowen and Bok (1998: 68–82 passim) for their potential importance but not incorporated in their model. These encompass employment during the first year of college (as an additional dimension of family socioeconomic status and also as a constraint on time available for studying), satisfaction with one's college social ex-

---

[12] The main differences between Bowen and Bok's regression results and ours are, first, that both school selectivity effects are significant (at the 5 percent level) in Bowen and Bok's analysis while attending only a most selective school is significant in ours. Second, in Bowen and Bok's regression, the odds of graduating in six years are three times as large for students at a school in the top selectivity tier rather than the bottom selectivity tier. In our analysis, the corresponding odds are just twice as large.

[13] The direction and relative magnitudes of our race and SES effects are the same as those Bowen and Bok (1998: 381) observe in their analysis of C&B data, but all of their race and SES coefficients are significant at the 5 percent level. In model 1 of Table 6.1, only the black and low SES effects are significant.

perience, whether parents owned their own home (as an added measure of accumulated wealth), whether parents helped with homework (an indicator of parental child-rearing behaviors), and whether the student attended one of seventy-two elite secondary schools (as an indicator of college preparedness). This model also contains several new control variables, including legacy and recruited athlete status, first-generation college student, whether the student received financial aid, and a set of more complete pre-college academic performance measures.

The first point to observe about the results in the second column is that while there is still a positive association between school selectivity and graduation rates, the evidence opposing the mismatch hypothesis is not as convincing as it was in our replication of the Bowen and Bok model. Students who enroll at one of the most selective NSCE schools can expect to have two-thirds higher odds of graduating in six years than do students at the least selective NSCE institutions. Students who matriculate at colleges in the middle tier have somewhat lower odds of graduating in six years than do students at the most elite schools. But they nevertheless have nearly a 30 percent greater chance of graduating in the same period as compared to students in the lowest tier. But it is important to emphasize two aspects of these new results. The graduation advantage that top-tier schools have over bottom-tier ones is smaller (as measured by odds ratios) compared to the model in the first column. Moreover, neither of the odds ratios for school selectivity in the expanded model is statistically significant at the 5 percent level.[14] Nevertheless, the totality of the evidence, while perhaps not quite as compelling as it was in the previous model, suggests that the advantages of school selectivity outweigh the costs and that, on balance, greater school selectivity is still associated with a somewhat higher chance of graduating, for both minority and non-minority students alike.[15] Under no reasonable

[14] The regression coefficient for the most selective tier of schools has a p-value of .074, meaning that the coefficient would be considered significant at the 10 percent level. We also estimated model 2 in Table 6.1 for each race group separately. In no instance does either of the top two tiers of institutional selectivity have a statistically significant effect. Attending a top-tier NSCE institution instead of a bottom-tier one has a positive association with graduation rates for all groups except Hispanics. On the other hand, attending a school in the middle tier has a somewhat negative effect for all groups except white students.

[15] This conclusion is supported in work by Small and Winship (2007), who use C&B data to examine school-to-school variation in black graduation rates. Some scholars have argued that these differences are due to institutional factors and not to variation in student bodies. Small and Winship find evidence for an "institutional hypothesis." Of eight institutional factors considered, however, only school selectivity (mean SAT score for the entering freshman class) is statistically significant. Greater school selectivity improves graduation rates, more so for blacks than for whites.

interpretation can our results be viewed as supporting the academic mismatch hypothesis.[16]

Our expanded model contains stronger evidence for academic underperformance by black and Hispanic students. Both groups of students now have about a 45 percent significantly lower likelihood of graduating in six years, controlling for numerous other factors including a broad range of academic merit variables. On the other hand, social class is no longer significantly related to graduation outcomes, perhaps because some of the newly included predictor variables capture other more nuanced aspects of socioeconomic status.

Finally, the additional variables whose coefficients are reported in Table 6.1 typically have the expected effects.[17] Immigrant generation is strongly and monotonically associated with timely graduation. One might expect that language difficulties and other issues of immigrant adjustment associated with recency of arrival would create barriers to successful completion of academic work. But the effects seem to operate the other way around, perhaps reflecting stereotypical immigrant values of hard work and wanting to please parents.[18] Graduating within six years from an NSCE school is positively associated with home ownership (perhaps because home equity can be tapped to pay college bills), parental help with homework in primary school (perhaps reflecting the value that parents attach to doing well in school), high school GPA, and attending an elite high school. On the other hand, holding down a job during the

---

[16]Richard Sander's (2004) more systemic analysis of law school students' performance takes into account the complete range of accredited U.S. law schools from the most prestigious to the least. He discovered that at the most elite law schools, the advantages of law school selectivity were large enough to offset the costs, so that the net impact was zero. Sander (2004: 441) concludes, "At the most elite schools (the schools attended by the one-eighth of black students with index scores above 700), the advantages of low institutional attrition entirely offset lower grades." It is possible that we are seeing some of the same features operating in our results. In other words, had we been able to examine the undergraduate experience across a broader range of colleges and universities—and not just at the most selective ones—our conclusions about whether there is evidence favoring the mismatch hypothesis might have been somewhat different.

[17]With the exception of cohort year, the remaining variables mentioned in note b to Table 6.1 are generally statistically insignificant. Other things equal, students in the 1997 entering cohort had 57 percent greater odds of graduating within six years than students who started college in 1993.

[18]Although the outcome measure is not entirely comparable, U.S. census data have shown that first- and second-generation European, Caribbean, African, and Hispanic immigrants between the ages of twenty and twenty-four are more likely to possess four-year college degrees than are their counterparts from third-or-higher generation backgrounds (Rong and Brown, 2001: 550; Rong and Grant, 1992).

first year in college[19] and being dissatisfied with the social aspects of college life appear to be stumbling blocks to graduating with the majority of one's peers.[20]

Differences between models 1 and 2 in Table 6.1 in the measured effects of race and college selectivity (and their associated levels of statistical significance) can be accounted for almost entirely by the inclusion in model 2 of just three additional blocks of variables—immigrant generation, social satisfaction with college, and an expanded array of pre-college academic performance indicators.[21] Black students are on average the least satisfied with the social aspects of their undergraduate college experience, and we know from model 2 that being dissatisfied with college predicts college attrition. Therefore, part of the negative effect in model 1 associated with being black is picking up a greater degree of college dissatisfaction.[22] As we noted in chapter 4, large proportions of Hispanic and Asian students on NSCE campuses are first- or second-generation immigrants. Model 2 suggests that being foreign-born or having at least one parent who is born outside the United States is associated with a much higher probability of graduating in six years. This feature alone is sufficient to account for the more negative Hispanic coefficient in model 2 than in model 1. Asian students have the additional advantage of extremely impressive academic credentials, not all of which are captured in model 1, and which tend to be positively correlated with graduation outcomes. Both immigrant generation and the extra academic performance measures in model 2 help account for the lower odds ratio for Asians in

[19] See Ishitani (2006: 864) and Singell and Stater (2006: 381) for reviews of the contradictory conclusions other studies have reached regarding the effect of different types of work-study employment on graduation.

[20] Our results on the effects of being satisfied with college life are consistent with those of Bowen and Bok (1998: 194), who conclude, "Predictably, students who finished at the C&B schools they entered originally were more positive in their evaluations than students who left prior to graduation. Two-thirds of the matriculants who graduated from their first school were 'very satisfied' [with their undergraduate education], as contrasted with 40 percent of those who transferred and graduated from other schools and 32 percent of those who dropped out and did not graduate from any school." Tinto (1993) and M. Fischer (2007) also find that lack of successful social integration into campus life is a cause of undergraduate attrition.

[21] These additional academic indicators include the number of AP and SAT II exams a student takes, the average score on SAT II exams, high school GPA, and whether a student is a National Merit or National Achievement Scholar.

[22] This finding is consistent with other studies that have suggested that an inhospitable social environment (Cross, 1998; M. Fischer, 2007), lack of a sense of social belonging on campus (Bowen and Bok, 1998: 82–84; Clark and Crawford, 1992; M. Fischer, 2007), or just the college experience itself (Vars and Bowen, 1998: 472) negatively affects black students' graduation rates and grades.

model 2. Finally, the extra academic performance variables in model 2 are largely responsible for the weaker effects of college selectivity—at least the top tier of selectivity—in model 2. This result suggests that the reason students at the most selective NSCE schools have the highest odds of graduating (as shown in model 1) is due not so much to the intrinsic characteristics of the institutions they attend, although these surely must matter to some extent, but instead to their students' superior academic credentials that are not fully captured in model 1.[23]

Of greater interest, however, to the debate over the merits of the academic mismatch hypothesis is the question of why our conclusions based on model 2 in Table 6.1 differ from those reported by Bowen and Bok (1998). The estimated effects of college selectivity warrant special attention. We conclude that students who matriculate at one of the schools in the top tier of selectivity are roughly 1.7 times as likely to graduate as students who enroll at a bottom-tier institution. But this effect is not statistically significant (at the 5 percent level). Bowen and Bok find that students enrolled in the top tier institutions are significantly more likely than students in the lowest tier to graduate in six years. Moreover, the expected margin of their advantage is on the order of three to one.

There could be several reasons for these disparate findings. To some extent, the fact that the set of institutions we study—although all of them are academically selective—and the entering cohorts involved are different may help explain these discrepancies. More important, we believe, our regression estimates are based on roughly 4,400 cases, whereas Bowen and Bok have at their disposal more than 32,000 observations. If we had a larger sample on the same NSCE schools, then each of our coefficients would be estimated more precisely and levels of statistical significance would be higher. Finally, the inclusion of additional covariates may largely account for the observed differences. In other words, it is possible that the effect of institutional selectivity would be less important in the Bowen and Bok (1998: 381) model if they had expanded their model to include the predictors in our model 2, especially those that capture more completely the pre-college academic accomplishments of matriculants. One might even venture the tentative conclusion that this reason is the most important one. We say this because we were able to replicate reasonably closely the Bowen and Bok findings in model 1 using a smaller number of observations, a different set of schools, and two more recent cohorts.

---

[23]Regarding differences in the effects of socioeconomic status, coming from a lower- or working-class family background has less of a negative effect in model 2 than in model 1, because model 2 incorporates additional variables often related to parents' social class (for example, employment during first year of college and parents' homeownership status).

College Major

The choice of a major field of study in college probably ranks just behind the decision to earn a college degree in terms of its impact on students' futures and, in particular, their future earnings (Daymont and Andrisani, 1984; Roksa, 2005; G. Thomas, 1985). For example, college majors that rely heavily on mathematics are positively correlated with higher future incomes (Fogg, 2004; Hecker, 1996). One's college major has an especially strong influence on earnings in the early stages of professional careers. About 95 percent of the gender gap in earnings among recent college graduates can be explained by differences in college major (McDonald and Thornton, 2007). Choice of major is also associated with the decision to pursue a graduate degree, which in turn influences careers and lifetime income (Simpson, 2001).

What majors do our NSCE students choose? How do their selections compare with those made by students at other kinds of colleges and universities? Our discussion is based on students in the 1997 entering cohort, because this is the only cohort for which all eight NSCE institutions supplied data on college major. We concentrate on the 89 percent of cohort members who graduated within six years and for whom college major is reported. Among broadly identifiable fields of concentration, NSCE students are most likely to major in the social sciences (24 percent), followed by humanities (18 percent), natural sciences (14 percent), and engineering (11 percent).[24] Figure 6.2 shows that the miscellaneous "other" major category captures the largest share of NSCE students (33 percent). This category includes such majors as education, business, architecture, agriculture, health, and communications—undergraduate majors that are more common at public than at private colleges and universities.

Data from the American Freshman Survey—a national survey of first-year college students conducted by UCLA as part of the Cooperative Institutional Research Program—allow us to put NSCE students' choices about a college major into a broader context. A comparison based on

---

[24] Our grouping of individual majors into broader categories is very similar to the scheme used by Bowen and Bok (1998: 354). Humanities includes American studies, art, art history, classics, English literature, foreign languages and literature, history, letters, music, theater, philosophy, and religion. Social science includes anthropology, area studies, economics, government, political science, psychology, and sociology. Natural science includes astronomy, atmospheric sciences, biological sciences, chemistry, geological sciences, mathematics, physics, and statistics. Engineering includes all branches of engineering, along with computer and information sciences. Other is a miscellaneous category that includes agriculture, architecture, environmental design, business, management, communications, education, and health sciences, among other things.

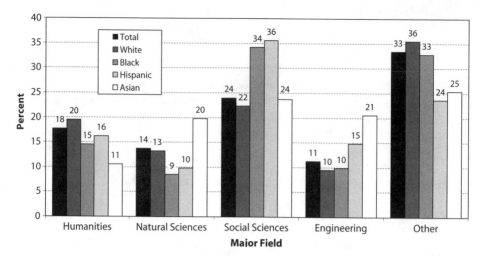

Figure 6.2. Distribution of College Majors at NSCE Institutions, by Race; 1997 Entering Cohort (N = 1,993). Note: Differences by race in natural sciences, social sciences, and other majors are statistically significant at the .01 level. Differences by race in humanities and engineering majors are significant at the .001 level. Results are based on students who graduated within six years with a known major. Percentages may not sum to 100 because of rounding. Source: National Study of College Experience.

majors actually chosen by NSCE students and "probable" majors selected by incoming freshmen in 1997 at the nation's most selective private colleges shows that the agreement is reasonably good. In no case is there more than a six percentage point difference in the proportion of NSCE students who select one of the major fields shown in Figure 6.2 as compared to freshmen at selective private colleges across the country (Sax et al., 1997: 102–3). Larger discrepancies materialize, however, when NSCE students are juxtaposed with all first-year college students. A major in the humanities, natural sciences, or social sciences is selected by 56 percent of NSCE students in contrast to just 31 percent of freshmen at all four-year institutions who expect to make the same decision (Sax et al., 1997: 22–23).

The major fields of study elected by NSCE students are sharply differentiated by race. Details are shown in Figure 6.2. Black and Hispanic students are overrepresented in the social sciences but are conspicuous by their relative absence from the natural sciences. Asian students are substantially overrepresented in both the natural sciences and engineering but choose to major only infrequently in the humanities. On the other hand, white NSCE students are somewhat more likely than nonwhites to major in the humanities and marginally less likely to select one of the social sciences. In their analysis of elite students in the 1989 entering cohort at C&B schools, Bowen and Bok (1998: 71) found that black students were more likely than whites to major in the social sciences, less likely to major in the humanities, and equally as likely as whites to pick engineering or natural sciences as a major. We find a similar pattern in the NSCE data. The only exception seems to be in the natural sciences, where blacks are four percentage points less likely than whites to be found.[25]

Social class differences in the choice of college major are not as pronounced as racial differences among NSCE students. The one important exception is the field of engineering. As we move up the social class ladder, students' inclination to major in engineering drops off sharply. More than two-fifths (42 percent) of lower-class students and 20 percent of students from working-class backgrounds major in engineering, as compared to 12 percent of those from the middle class, 10 percent from the upper-middle class, and just 6 percent of upper-class students. Upper-class students are much more likely to major in one of the social science or "other" fields in Figure 6.2; more than four out of five upper-class NSCE graduates (81 percent) landed in one of these two areas of concentration.[26]

CLASS RANK AT GRADUATION

The day parents bring their children to campus for the start of freshman year is a time of great excitement and anticipation at most colleges and

[25] Other studies that use more representative samples of college students report that white freshmen are more likely to express a desire to major in a career-oriented field such as education or business, and that Hispanics disproportionately indicate a preference for engineering (Leppel, Williams, and Waldauer, 2001). Asian students are commonly found majoring in the natural sciences and engineering, even outside the NSCE or C&B college setting (Escueta and O'Brien, 1991; Goyette and Mullen, 2006).

[26] Bowen, Kurzweil, and Tobin (2005) also find that lower-income students are somewhat more likely to major in engineering. Risk tolerance may explain some of these social class differences. Saks and Shore (2005) present evidence that a career in business is financially riskier than a career in engineering. They then show that wealthier students are significantly more likely to major in business than are lower SES groups. They posit that upper-class students may be more likely to pursue business because they have a higher risk tolerance because of their family's greater resources. Risk tolerance may also explain upper-class NSCE students' preference for social science majors. Since many private elite liberal arts institutions do not offer business as a major, students may seek majors that appear more aligned with areas of business. Economics may seem like good preparation for a career in finance, and psychology and sociology may be viewed as helpful for careers in marketing or advertising. The fact that Cole and Barber (2003) find that students who major in the social sciences are more likely to be interested in business careers than in other careers lends further support to this idea.

universities. Perhaps more than anything else, parents want their children to be happy in college and to graduate. But how students subsequently perform in their classes and the grades they receive are surely of concern to parents and students alike, to college faculty and graduate school admission officers, and perhaps even to future employers. Performing well and making the "dean's list" can be not only a source of pride to students but a confidence booster as well. On the other hand, students who struggle just to keep their heads above water may find that the academic side of college life is stressful and not totally satisfying. In this section we examine how students perform in their college coursework and ultimately where they rank in their graduating class. We focus on students who graduated within six years in the 1993 and 1997 entering cohorts at our eight institutions and ask how race and social class are associated with their academic class standing. Of special relevance to issues raised at the beginning of this chapter is whether affirmative action has the cost identified by others of lowering the class rank of students who attend the most academically selective institutions. We also want to know whether the NSCE data contain evidence of academic underperformance by underrepresented minority students. To begin the analysis, we focus on class rank distributions by students' race and social class. Following that, we investigate the determinants of class rank at graduation on an all-other-things-equal basis.

Before proceeding, it is worth mentioning some important points about the construction of our dependent variable—where students' cumulative GPAs at graduation place them in their graduating classes relative to their peers. We rely on percentile class rank at graduation, a variable that can range between zero and 100. A student who graduates in the 80th percentile, for example, has performed better than 79 percent of other students in the graduating class, but 20 percent of his or her classmates have done even better overall. We use data on cumulative GPA provided by institutional registrars because of well-known validity problems associated with students' self-reported grades and test scores (Kuncel, Credé, and Thomas, 2005; Zimmerman, Caldwell, and Bernat, 2002).[27] In addition, we convert cumulative GPAs into percentile class ranks to adjust for potential differences in grading standards across NSCE campuses and for the possibility of grade inflation over time (Sabot and Wakeman-Linn,

[27]Following a thorough review, Kuncel, Credé, and Thomas (2005: 63) conclude that "self-reported grades should be used with caution." Students more commonly overreport than underreport their GPAs, sometimes by a factor of two to one or even more. In general, students with low actual GPAs and, to a lesser extent, cognitive ability tend to report their grades less reliably. On the other hand, self-reported grades can be a reasonably good reflection of actual grades for students with high ability and good grades (Kuncel, Credé, and Thomas, 2005).

1991). Finally, our procedures position each NSCE survey respondent in the percentile class rank distribution of *all* students in that respondent's graduating class.[28] Our percentile class rank data are institution and cohort specific but are then pooled for analysis purposes.

The class rank distribution among all NSCE sample respondents who graduated within six years of matriculating matches very closely the entire percentile class rank distribution among all NSCE college and university graduates. Roughly equal percentages of respondents come from each class rank quintile, and the median class rank at graduation among survey participants is the 52nd percentile. This suggests that our NSCE sample as a whole is not biased toward students whose grades are exceptionally good or poor, and that we can have confidence in generalizing from the sample population to all NSCE students.[29]

Class rank distributions are, however, sharply differentiated by race. White students tend to graduate with above-average grades, whereas underrepresented minority students are disproportionately concentrated toward the bottom of their graduating class. The details are shown in Figure 6.3. Roughly one-quarter of white graduates rank in the top 20 percent of their class, and less than one-sixth fall into the lowest quintile. The picture for black students is distressingly different. Fully one-half of all black graduates end up ranked in the lowest 20 percent of the class. Just 5 percent of black students graduate in the highest 20 percent. The class-rank profile for Hispanic students is a little closer to all students, but they still find themselves overrepresented among students with below-average grades. One-third of graduating Hispanic students fall into the lowest quintile, as compared to only 10 percent who graduate in the top quintile. Asian students come closest to matching the class rank distribution of all NSCE students combined. About 20 percent of graduating Asian students fall into each class rank quintile. We have focused here on just the highest and lowest quintiles, but the same general patterns by race are evident if we ignore the extreme quintiles and concentrate on the distribution between the 20th and 80th percentiles.

---

[28] An alternative would have been to gauge percentile class rank relative only to other NSCE sample respondents who graduated from the same school in the same cohort. This approach has obvious problems, especially if students who responded to the survey are drawn disproportionately from either the upper or lower portion of the class rank distribution for all students.

[29] Class rank quintiles are defined in terms of all graduating seniors, not just those who are survey respondents. Each quintile captures 20 percent of the graduating class. The lowest quintile refers to the bottom 20 percent of students in terms of class rank, the second lowest quintile to students whose class ranks are between the 20th and the 40th percentile, and so on. The median is a number that divides a distribution into two halves of equal size.

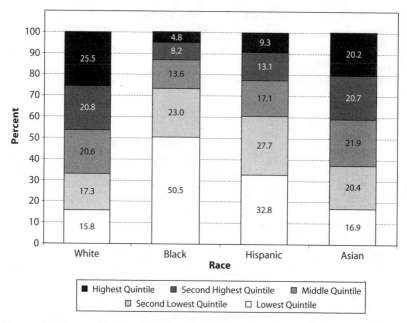

Figure 6.3. Percentile Class Rank at Graduation for Those Graduating from NSCE Institutions within Six Years, by Race; 1993 and 1997 Entering Cohorts Combined (N = 3,788). Note: Racial differences in class rank are significant at the .0001 level. Source: National Study of College Experience.

A simpler way to describe the essential story in Figure 6.3 is to focus on the median percentile ranking for each race group. By this measure, too, whites perform best while blacks and Hispanics typically lag behind. The median class rank at graduation for white students is the 57th percentile, which means that one-half of whites are ranked higher than the 57th percentile and one-half are ranked lower. The median ranking for blacks is the 20th percentile. For Hispanic students the median is somewhat higher (32nd percentile), while Asians, for whom the median class rank is the 52nd percentile, are fairly typical of all NSCE students. There is a difference of 37 percentage points between the median class ranks of whites and blacks. A gap of this magnitude has another interpretation. The typical black student is outperformed by 84 percent of white students. Alternatively, 86 percent of black students do less well in their college coursework than does the typical white student. Gaps exist, too, between Hispanic and white students, although they are not as pronounced as black-white differences. The overall Hispanic-white difference in median class rank is 25 percentage points. The typical Hispanic student

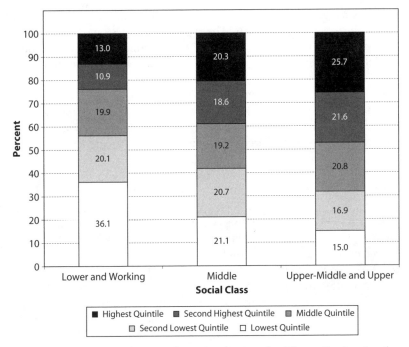

Figure 6.4. Percentile Class Rank at Graduation for Those Graduating from NSCE Institutions within Six Years, by Social Class; 1993 and 1997 Entering Cohorts Combined (N = 3,788). Note: Social class differences are significant at the .001 level. Source: National Study of College Experience.

ranks below 75 percent of white students. Seen another way, 75 percent of Hispanics rank below the median white student.[30]

When graduating seniors are disaggregated by social class rather than by race, students from affluent family backgrounds exhibit better grades and higher class ranks than do students of more modest means. The data in Figure 6.4 group lower- and working-class students together, and combine students from upper-middle and upper social classes. Just 13 percent of students in the lowest socioeconomic status group rank in the top one-fifth of their graduating class, as compared to 20 percent of middle-class students and more than one-quarter of students in the highest social class category. An opposite pattern is observed when we focus on the lowest class ranks. More than one-third (36 percent) of students from lower- and working-class families rank in the bottom quintile. This proportion falls steadily to 21 percent of middle-class students and to only 15 percent of

[30] These comparisons are based on interpolations in more detailed race-specific class rank distributions.

graduates in the highest social class groups. Median class ranks for each group follow a similar pattern. The typical student from the lowest SES group graduates in the 33rd percentile. The median middle-class student has a class rank in the 48th percentile, while the typical upper-middle- or upper-class student graduates in the 58th percentile.[31]

Of course, the determinants of where a student is ultimately ranked in his or her graduating class extend well beyond race and social class. Students' pre-college academic records have a lot to do with subsequent outcomes. How competitive a college or university is, as judged by the academic qualifications of its students, can also be expected to affect the comparative standing of any given student. The best way to assess the importance of any factor or set of variables for students' percentile class rank at graduation is to examine these determinants on an all-other-things-equal basis. This is what we do next. We will be particularly interested in whether affirmative action policies have the anticipated cost of lowering the final class rank at graduation for students who are the principal beneficiaries of race-based policies. In other words, does school selectivity have a negative effect on one's class rank, holding other things constant? Research has also found evidence of academic underperformance by underrepresented minority students. When we control for a large set of high school academic performance measures, is it still the case that black and Hispanic students perform less well in their college coursework than do white and Asian students? To answer these questions, we use regression analysis applied to the 3,788 observations in Figures 6.3 and 6.4—students who graduated in six years and for whom class rank data exist.

---

[31] Grouping social classes the way we have in Figure 6.4 suggests steady improvement in college academic performance as one looks across socioeconomic groups from the lowest to the highest. This pattern is generally true, but there is an unanticipated reversal among upper-class students. The most privileged students have an overall class rank distribution that is more in line with middle-class students and that occasionally falls between middle-class and working-class graduates. Median percentile class ranks for each SES group show this pattern clearly: 18 for lower-class students, followed by 34 for the working class, 48 for the middle class, 59 for the upper-middle class, and then a decline to 48 among upper-class students. Data from a separate Princeton study provide some insight. As part of the Campus Life in America Student Survey (CLASS) project, freshmen and juniors who were enrolled at six universities in the fall of 2004 were asked to identify their three most important priorities for their time in college. We isolated the responses of students who attended the four institutions most like the selective schools in the NSCE sample—Princeton, Emory, UCLA, and the University of Miami. "To learn as much as possible inside the classroom" was mentioned by 15 percent of lower-class students as one of their three most important college priorities, followed (in steady progression) by 18 percent of working-class respondents, 23 percent of the middle class, and 27 percent of upper-middle-class students, before dropping back to 25 percent for upper-class respondents. This social class gradient in the pattern of responses bears a close correspondence to median percentile class ranks reported above for each of the five social class categories.

Our first important finding from the NSCE data is that students who enter college with a given set of academic qualifications can be expected to perform less well in their coursework and grades relative to other students if they attend a more selective college or university than one that is not as selective. The evidence is contained in model 1 of Table 6.2. Here we see that students who attend an NSCE school in the most selective tier can expect to graduate with a class rank that is 18 percentile points lower than they could have anticipated if they had attended one of the least selective institutions. Moreover, students who graduate from an institution in the second tier of selectivity are likely to suffer a class rank penalty of 15 percentile points, as compared to students who graduate from a school in the lowest selectivity tier. To the extent that affirmative action lifts underrepresented minority students into higher-tier institutions than they might have attended without racial preferences, one of the costs of these preferential policies—perhaps the principal cost—is a lower ultimate class rank. It must be emphasized, however, that the expected negative effect of school prestige and selectivity on class rank applies to *all* students and not just to students who are targets of affirmative action.[32] Moreover, the effect should not be all that surprising. It is another illustration of the "little frog in a big pond" phenomenon studied more than forty years ago by the sociologist James Davis (1966).[33]

Our second important conclusion is that even when we control for students' academic qualifications when they enroll in college—and we have a long list of such controls—we find evidence of academic underperformance on the part of all nonwhite NSCE students. The most severe effects are recorded by black students. But both Hispanic and, perhaps somewhat surprisingly, Asian students also receive grades that are generally below those one would expect on the basis of high school grades, high school class rank, and standardized test scores. The results in Table 6.2 suggest that black students can expect to graduate with a class rank that is more than 17 percentile points lower than otherwise equivalent white students who attend the same institution. The fact that numerous other researchers have documented the same phenomenon using different data (Bowen and Bok, 1998: 78; Massey and Mooney, 2007) does not make it any less painful to acknowledge. The good news is that what was originally a 37 percentage point black-white difference in median class ranks (57 for whites compared to 20 for blacks) has now been reduced to just

[32] In results not shown, we find the same negative effect of school selectivity when model 1 in Table 6.2 is fit to each race group separately.

[33] Bowen and Bok (1998: 73–74) report a similar class rank penalty in their C&B data: "Competing against fellow students with very strong academic credentials naturally affects one's class rank, even though this disadvantage may well be counterbalanced by other benefits."

TABLE 6.2
OLS Regression Results for Percentile Class Rank at Graduation[a]
NSCE Matriculant Data: 1993 and 1997 Cohorts (N = 3,788)

Predictor Variables	(1)	(2)
Race		
(White)	—	—
Black	−17.3***	−8.1***
Hispanic	−14.9***	−4.9***
Asian	−9.9***	−2.8*
Social Class		
Upper-Middle and Upper Class	3.4	1.8
(Middle Class)	—	—
Lower and Working Class	−3.1	1.3
College Selectivity		
Most Selective Tier	−18.4***	−4.9**
Second Most Selective Tier	−15.4***	−3.6*
(All Other Colleges)	—	
Athlete		
(No)	—	—
Yes	−4.6*	−0.1
Legacy		
(No)	—	—
Yes	−1.7	−2.3
Sex		
(Male)	—	—
Female	10.0***	6.3***
Immigrant Generation		
First	6.7**	−0.7
Second	3.2	−0.9
Third	3.2	0.5
(Fourth and Higher)	—	—
Unknown	0.3	−1.1
Satisfaction with College Social Experience[b]		
(Very Satisfied)	—	—
Not Very Satisfied	3.6*	1.2
Unknown	2.9	2.7
College Major		
(Humanities)	—	—
Natural Science	−6.9**	−7.1***
Social Science	−3.1	0.3
Engineering	−9.6**	−7.0***
Other	−1.5	−1.8
Undeclared or Unknown Major	−1.8	−2.5
Missing Major, Institutional Level[c]	−2.4	−1.8

(*Continued*)

TABLE 6.2 (*Continued*)

Predictor Variables	(1)	(2)
SAT Score		
<1000	−22.0***	−8.2**
1000–1099	−15.3***	−7.2**
1100–1199	−7.3**	−1.8
(1200–1299)	—	—
1300–1399	3.3	1.5
1400–1600	8.7**	3.1
Unknown	−1.9	−2.2
Average Score on SAT II Tests		
(<650)	—	—
650–749	5.5**	0.9
750 and above	19.8***	8.9***
Unknown	−2.1	0.1
High School GPA		
A+	16.3***	6.3**
A	9.9**	3.8
A−	2.8	1.9
(B+ or lower)	—	—
Unknown	−3.2	−3.3
First Year Percentile Class Rank		
Highest Quintile	—	60.3***
Second Highest Quintile	—	44.0***
Middle Quintile	—	27.5***
Second Lowest Quintile	—	11.9***
(Lowest Quintile)	—	—
Missing 1st Year Class Rank, Individual Level	—	40.7***
Missing 1st Year Class Rank, Institutional Level[c]	—	32.5***
Constant	40.3***	12.8***
Number of Observations	3,788	3,788
R-Squared	0.314	0.687

Source: National Study of College Experience.

Note: Both models use weighted observations and control for first-generation college student status, whether received financial aid, parents' home ownership during senior year of high school, homework help from parents during primary school, hours spent in employment during first year of college, number of Advanced Placement (AP) exams taken, number of SAT II exams taken, high school class rank, National Merit or National Achievement Scholar status, high school type, elite high school attendance, cohort, and attending a women's college. Reference categories are shown in parentheses.

[a]For those who graduate within six years.

[b]Students considered "very satisfied" rate their overall college social experience a 6 or 7 on a seven-point scale, in which 1 represents "least satisfied" and 7 represents being "most satisfied." Students considered "not very satisfied" gave their experience a score between 1 and 5.

[c]Institution(s) did not provide this information for any of its students in this cohort.

*p < .05 **p < .01 ***p < .001

17 percentile points when black and white students with statistically equivalent profiles are compared. In other words, observed differences between blacks and whites in terms of college readiness and other measurable characteristics account for 20 points, or slightly more than one-half, of the initial 37 percentile points separating the class rank of the typical white and black student. Compared to comparable white students at the same institution, Hispanics can expect to graduate with a class rank that is 15 percentile points lower. Even Asian students, long believed by some to be academic superstars, end up graduating with a class rank that is on average 10 percentage points below the class rank of similar whites.[34]

Our third conclusion based on results in Table 6.2 is that other factors also influence college academic performance. Students who have the strongest academic skills, as measured by high school grades and scores on the SAT I and SAT II exams, can expect to rank appreciably higher in their graduating class, other things equal. These effects are generally large and statistically significant.[35] Women tend to outperform men by an average of ten percentile class rank points.[36] Choice of college major can also affect class rank. Majoring in one of the natural sciences or engineering is associated with a seven to ten percentage point decline in expected class rank. Athletes pay a small class rank penalty, but children with alumni connections do not. We also find evidence that first-generation immigrants and students who are not particularly satisfied with the social side of their college experience also possess a slight class rank advantage at graduation.[37] On the other hand, contrary to the pattern observed in

[34] The reason this result is surprising is that academic underperformance is usually talked about in the context of black and Hispanic students. It is not clear what contributes to underperformance by Asian students. Some of the standard explanations advanced for blacks do not seem to apply to Asians.

[35] Geiser and Santelices (2007) tracked 80,000 students admitted to the University of California system and concluded that high school GPA is a better predictor than standardized test scores not only of freshman-year grades in college but also of four-year college outcomes including cumulative college grades and the likelihood of graduating.

[36] Other studies have also found that women earn higher grades than men (Sax, 2007; Young, 2004).

[37] This latter result, while a bit counterintuitive, is not unique to NSCE data. Princeton's CLASS project asked juniors to report their cumulative college GPA and to rate their satisfaction with the social aspects of their college experience using the same scale as in the NSCE survey. Like NSCE matriculants, students at UCLA, the University of Miami, Emory, and Princeton who were more socially dissatisfied earned higher GPAs than their classmates who were highly satisfied. Authors' tabulations from other NSCE data provide a possible explanation for this result. NSCE students who express the lowest levels of social satisfaction also report spending relatively few hours per week in extracurricular activities. Moreover, students who spend less time in extracurricular activities tend to have high grades, perhaps because they have more time to study and make use of that time to their academic

Figure 6.4, social class is not related to class rank when other factors are held constant, perhaps because some of these other factors include additional indicators of socioeconomic status.[38]

All students who are admitted to elite colleges and universities are presumed to have the ability to handle the academic workload. But this does not mean that all of them face the same kinds of transitions from high school to college. Students who attend the nation's most elite private boarding schools may notice little difference between the academic demands of secondary school and those they confront in college. But for others whose high school academic preparation might have been less rigorous, or for students who are the first in their family to go to college, the transition to postsecondary school might be more difficult. Students who are less well prepared could face greater academic challenges, at least initially, and it could take them a semester or even longer to develop the kinds of study skills that permit them to feel more confident that the academic playing field has been leveled.

The data we have collected on percentile class rank at the end of freshman year permit an analysis of factors that influence how well students perform on tests, term papers, oral presentations, and other things that determine grades during the first transition year in college. Our regression analysis uses the same explanatory variables as model 1 in Table 6.2, but the data are limited to 2,224 students in the 1997 entering cohort for whom we have first-year percentile class rank.[39] In results not shown, school selectivity effects are noticeable within nine months. Attending a

---

advantage. Unfortunately, the NSCE survey contains no direct information on hours per week spent studying. Some additional supporting evidence about how time allocation may affect grades comes from employment hours per week. In the regression in model 1 in Table 6.2, in results not shown, graduates who had a job during their first year in college that took more than ten hours per week could expect to have a final class rank 1.5 percentile points lower than students who had no job during their freshman year, but the effect is not statistically significant.

[38] Our results in model 1 are broadly consistent with those reported by Bowen and Bok (1998: 383). The note at the bottom of Table 6.2 includes a list of other control variables used in model estimation. In general, the effects of these variables when included in model 1 are not statistically significant.

[39] Percentile class rank at the end of freshman year is calculated in the same way as percentile class rank at graduation, except that it is not limited to students who graduate within six years. All students with a first-year GPA are included in the analysis regardless of their graduation outcomes. Forty-six students in the 1997 cohort (out of 2,270) were omitted because they were missing GPA information. We exclude the 1993 cohort because two institutions were unable to supply the requisite first-year GPA data for any of their students. The only differences between our regression model for first-year percentile class rank and model 1 in Table 6.2 are that the former excludes a variable for cohort year (because only 1997 cohort data are being used), and the variables for college major are dropped (because most students do not declare a major until after their freshman year).

school in the most selective NSCE tier is associated with a reduction of 22 percentile points in class standing as compared to enrolling at a school in the lowest selectivity category. Matriculating at one of the colleges in the second most selective tier can be expected to lower one's class rank by 15 percentile points compared to students in the lowest tier. Academic underperformance is also widespread by the end of freshman year. Black students rank 13 percentile points behind equivalent white students. Hispanic students are at the same disadvantage, while a gap of ten points opens up between Asian and white students. Standard indicators of academic preparation—high school GPA and scores on SAT I and SAT II exams—play the same role in determining percentile class rank at the end of the first year as they do at graduation. The same is true for being a first-generation immigrant. Likewise, students' social class has an inconsequential effect on first-year class rank, just as it does on class rank at graduation. And graduating from a secondary school that is either private or elite (whether public or private) is not associated with percentile class rank after one year of college (or at graduation), suggesting that whatever initial advantage these schools might have conferred in terms of college readiness is temporary and has vanished by the end of freshman year.

Other factors appear to operate differently in the first year than they do over a student's entire college career. For instance, being a first-generation college student lowers first-year class rank by five points; working a job for ten or more hours per week reduces first-year class standing by six points; and attending a women's college is associated with a higher first-year class rank of seven points, all other things equal. None of these variables is significant in the percentile class rank at graduation equation. On the other hand, whether one is female, an athlete, or dissatisfied with the social aspects of college life makes little difference to first-year class standing, although all of these factors matter at graduation.

We suspected that how a student performs in her first year of college might be a strong predictor of her ultimate class rank at graduation, and indeed this is the case. Model 2 in Table 6.2 reestimates model 1 by including one additional predictor variable—a student's percentile class rank (measured in quintiles) at the end of freshman year. Note first that the inclusion of just this one extra variable results in a substantial boost in the R-squared value. In model 1 we are successful in explaining 31 percent of the overall variation in the dependent variable. But in model 2 the proportion of variance explained jumps to 69 percent. This is a very high percentage by almost any standard, certainly in regressions using cross-sectional data. Second, the effects of first-year percentile class rank are strong and in the expected direction. The higher a student ranks at the end of freshman year, the higher she is predicted to rank at graduation. A student in the highest quintile at the end of her freshman year can expect at graduation to rank fully 60 percentile points higher than an otherwise equivalent student who is in the bottom 20 percent of the freshman class. Ranking in the second highest quintile after just one year in college is predicted to result in a class standing 44 percentile points higher than a comparable student whose grades put her into the lowest quintile after freshman year. We are not suggesting there is some kind of iron law whereby a student's first-year class standing is fully determinative of where in the class she graduates. But clearly, the academic firepower a student displays during freshman year builds momentum that typically carries her a long way to graduation.

The remaining coefficients in model 2 have an interesting interpretation, especially when considered in light of model 1. Take as an example the effect of being female. Model 1 suggests that women have a ten-point class rank advantage at graduation over otherwise comparable men. Model 2 tells us that holding other variables in this model constant—including percentile class rank after freshman year—women have a graduation class rank advantage over men of 6.3 percentile points. So between two otherwise identical students—one male and one female—who have the *same* class rank at the end of their first year, the woman will subsequently outperform the man by an additional 6.3 percentile class rank points by the time they graduate. Put more generally, coefficients in model 2 indicate approximately how much of the ultimate difference in class rank attributable to a given variable can be expected to develop after a student's freshman year is over. Coefficients in model 1 show the total difference in class rank measured over a student's entire college career. Therefore, subtracting coefficients in model 2 from those in model 1 gives a rough estimate of how much of the ultimate class rank differential arises during a student's first year in school. Accordingly, during freshman year, women (who eventually graduate within six years) do somewhat better in their coursework and grades than equivalent men (who also graduate in six years). Their superior performance gives them a percentile class rank advantage over men of approximately 3.7 percentage points. After freshman year, women continue to perform better than men, and their class rank advantage grows by an additional 6.3 percentile points. By the time graduation comes, women have garnered a cumulative class rank advantage over men equivalent to ten percentile points.

Notice that the coefficients in model 2 are generally smaller in absolute value (or closer to zero) than those in model 1. This suggests not only that some of the gap attributable to a particular explanatory variable develops during freshman year but also that the gap continues to build in later years. Black students, for example, lag behind comparable whites by about nine percentage points after one year, but the gap grows by an additional eight percentage points by graduation time, resulting in a total deficit of more than 17 points relative to comparable whites. For Hispanic and Asian students, the majority of the overall class rank gap at graduation develops during freshman year, although the academic distance from whites continues to expand in subsequent years.[40]

The overall impact on class rank at graduation appears to be concentrated in the first year for several other variables as well. College selectivity is a case in point. Freshman-year class rank is lowered by approximately 14 percentage points if one attends a college in the most selective tier and by roughly 12 percentage points if a student enrolls in a second-tier NSCE institution, as compared to attending a school in the lowest selectivity category. Students can expect an additional class rank penalty between the beginning of sophomore year and the end of senior year of only about five points at the most selective schools and less than four points at those in the middle tier. The effect of being a recruited athlete or a first-generation immigrant is even more concentrated in the first year. The disadvantage associated with being an athlete develops entirely during freshman year and apparently does not increase thereafter. The same is true for the advantage that adheres to being a first-generation immigrant; the total effect is almost identical to the effect during the first year.[41]

Coefficients on college major are an exception to the overall pattern. Here there is little difference between models 1 and 2. This tells us there is only a small first-year effect on class rank at graduation stemming from college major choice. Virtually all of the effect is concentrated in what

[40] Academic credentials exert their expected influence throughout a student's college career.

[41] There could be at least two alternative explanations for the attenuation in coefficient values between models 1 and 2 in Table 6.2. First, by including first-year percentile class rank in model 2, we add another control variable for students' ability to do college-level work. Coefficients in model 2 therefore may be smaller in absolute value than those in model 1 not because the effects on student academic performance of individual predictor variables contract in later years, but rather because first-year class rank is capturing effects of other determinants of cumulative class rank omitted from model 1 but which are nevertheless correlated with variables that are included in model 1. Second, another reason performance gaps may be smaller after freshman year is that upper-level undergraduates are starting to sort themselves into courses and majors in which they earn better grades. Freshmen, on the other hand, take a more standardized set of courses because they have graduation requirements they must fulfill. This less flexible curriculum during freshman year may expose differences in students' overall ability. Scholars present evidence of students sorting themselves into easier and more difficult college majors depending on their early college performance. Sabot and Wakeman-Linn (1991) report that undergraduates' likelihood of taking a second course in a given subject decreases the lower the grade they earn in their first course in that field. In another study, students who switched from engineering to another major had GPAs 0.5 points lower on a four-point scale than those who stayed (Ohland et al., 2004). Other research suggests that when students do not perform well in their initial science classes, they tend to forego their interest in science and switch into the social sciences or humanities where grades are generally higher (Elliott et al., 1996).

happens after freshman year. Majoring in one of the natural sciences comes with a price—a lower class rank at graduation equal to seven percentile points. But none of this price arises during freshman year. This makes intuitive sense because most students do not declare a major until the start of junior year. Many students experiment during freshman year and even into their sophomore year by taking courses in a wide variety of subjects and only then begin to focus on a major. Students who plan on being engineering majors, however, fall into a different category. Prospective engineering majors are expected by some schools to declare their intent when they apply, or at the beginning of freshman year, and then to start right away taking an often lengthy sequence of demanding engineering courses. This practice explains why engineering majors experience a loss of almost three percentile points even in the first year, although most of their nearly ten-point reduction in class standing at graduation occurs after freshman year.

CONCLUSIONS

In this chapter we have found that underrepresented minority students at selective colleges and universities graduate at lower rates than do their white and Asian classmates. Moreover, among students who do graduate, blacks and Hispanics end up with grade point averages in the lower ranks of their class. To some extent these findings should not be especially surprising, because black and Hispanic students are more likely to come from socioeconomic backgrounds and to attend the kinds of elementary and secondary schools that leave them relatively less well prepared for the academic rigors of selective colleges. But, as our regression analyses have shown, even when black and Hispanic students are compared against otherwise equivalent white and Asian students, underrepresented minorities still do not perform as well as their white or Asian peers. Although racial gaps are reduced, both graduation rates and class ranks are lower for blacks and Hispanics even after controlling for a broad array of pre-college academic performance measures and other background characteristics.[42]

Researchers often use the term academic "underperformance" to refer to the phenomenon in which minority students do not perform as well as expected given their high school academic records. Experiences prior to college (including school, home, peer, and neighborhood environments)

---

[42] On an all-other-things-equal basis, Asian students have significantly lower class ranks than do whites, but there is no statistically significant difference in graduation rates between Asians and whites.

as well as those encountered during college (e.g., discrimination, reduced teacher expectations, feelings of not belonging, and stereotype threat)[43] have been advanced as possible reasons why black and Hispanic students do not do as well as predicted.[44] Even though theories abound, no one has yet conclusively identified the causes of academic underperformance.[45]

Given this underperformance, some have raised doubts about the effects of affirmative action, arguing that racial preferences do underrepresented minority students more harm than good. What affirmative action does, all sides would agree, is make it possible for minority students who are the beneficiaries of race-based preferences to attend more selective institutions than they would otherwise. There is evidence in our data that doing so gives these students a greater likelihood of graduating than if they attended a less selective college or university. We find, for instance, that the odds of graduating are twice as large if a student enrolls at one of the most selective NSCE schools as compared to entering a school in the lowest selectivity tier. The claim is only somewhat less strong when we control for a larger set of potential explanatory factors. There is no support in our data for the proposition advanced by the academic mismatch hypothesis that minority students are likely to fail in higher numbers if they attend a more selective college or university.

At the same time, however, we find that going to a more selective institution puts many black and Hispanic students in head-to-head competition with a larger number of academically talented white and Asian students, with the result that minority students typically rank lower in their graduating class than if they were not so overmatched. Our class rank penalty, estimated on an all-other-things-equal basis, is equivalent to 18 percentile points if one graduates from a school in the most selective NSCE tier as compared with a school in the lowest tier, and 15 percentile

---

[43] Stereotype threat refers to the social-psychological phenomenon of test anxiety (and subsequent low test performance) that is triggered when a member of an underrepresented minority group is afraid that his test performance will confirm negative racial stereotypes about the mental abilities of a racial group of which he is a member (Steele, 1997; Steele and Aronson, 1998).

[44] For comprehensive reviews of factors hypothesized to influence academic underperformance, see Bowen and Bok (1998: 78–88), Cole and Barber (2003: 128–38), and Massey et al. (2003: 1–19).

[45] Racial gaps in collegiate academic performance have been called "one of academe's touchiest subjects" (Schmidt, 2007c). Colleges and universities, for example, generally refuse to report grades broken out by race. However, the tide may be slowly turning. At least, college officials are starting to discuss the problem more openly. Begun in 2001, the Consortium on High Achievement and Success—a group of more than thirty private liberal arts colleges and small universities—is addressing these issues. Initial efforts have focused on best practices of what is working on different campuses, but as yet few proven strategies have been identified (Schmidt, 2007c).

points if a student graduates from a second-tier institution as compared to one in the bottom tier. This penalty pertains to all students who receive an admission boost on the basis of nonacademic criteria, but it affects especially black and Hispanic students for whom admission bonuses are the largest.[46]

For many underrepresented minority students, then, affirmative action entails an inherent trade-off—a degree from a more prestigious institution, which is clearly advantageous for later-life outcomes, achieved at the price of a lower class rank at graduation, which may have its own associated disadvantages. How should one evaluate this trade-off? What is the likely net effect of these opposing tendencies? Our judgment—based on the available evidence and on commonsense considerations—is that, in most instances, the positive effects of school selectivity override the negative consequences of lower class rank. The selectivity of a student's undergraduate college is positively associated with graduation rates,[47] and graduating from a more selective college facilitates earning a graduate or professional degree,[48] greater career advancement,[49] and higher future income.[50] In addition, the grades students receive in their college coursework and where they ultimately rank in their graduating class are not the sum total of the value of a college education, and their influence on later-life accomplishments may fade with the passage of time (Bowen and Bok, 1998: 89).

There are several other reasons for expecting that the influence of college selectivity might predominate over class rank. First, both employers and professional and graduate school admission deans seek applicants with particular qualifications. Many gatekeepers appear to believe that elite colleges have proportionately more candidates of the type they seek

[46] The size of admission bonuses for black and Hispanic applicants to NSCE schools is discussed in detail in chapter 3. For an analysis of admission preferences for underrepresented minority students, athletes, and legacies at three private NSCE universities, see Espenshade, Chung, and Walling (2004).

[47] Alon and Tienda (2005), Bowen and Bok (1998), Kane (1998a), Light and Strayer (2000), M. Long (2007b), Small and Winship (2007).

[48] Alexander and Eckland (1977), Bernstein (2003), Bowen and Bok (1998), Brand and Halaby (2006), Eide, Brewer, and Ehrenberg (1998), Zhang (2005a).

[49] Arnold (2002), Brand and Halaby (2006), Cookson and Persell (1985), Smart (1986).

[50] Behrman, Rosenzweig, and Taubman (1996), Brewer, Eide, and Ehrenberg (1999), Daniel, Black, and Smith (1997), Kane (1998a), Loury and Garman (1995), Zhang (2005b). M. Long (2007b) finds that college selectivity positively affects subsequent household income but that there are weaker effects on hourly wages. Most of the studies cited in this and the previous three footnotes control for pre-college credentials. Those that are able to control, in addition, for undergraduate grades also find that students in general as well as minority students are more likely to attend graduate school (Bowen and Bok, 1998; Zhang, 2005a) and earn higher incomes (Bowen and Bok, 1998) if their undergraduate degree comes from a more selective college.

and thus concentrate their recruitment efforts or give special consideration to applicants at such schools at the expense of less selective institutions (Bernstein, 2003; Hansen, 2006). It may be because elite colleges are believed to do a better job preparing their graduates with the kinds of job skills they will need later on (Becker, 1975). Alternatively, prospective employers and graduate schools may rely on selective schools either as a signaling device or credentialing service that reduces search time and costs for those wanting to recruit talented college graduates (Collins, 1979).

Second, both employers (Hansen, 2006) and graduate schools (Bernstein, 2003; Weiss, 1997) seem to recognize the greater difficulty of earning high grades at more selective schools and give more latitude in evaluating class rank. For example, Hansen (2006: 60) reports that "some organizations take the top 30 percent of students from Ivy League schools but insist on the top five percent for other schools."[51] The class ranks of underrepresented minority graduates of elite colleges may be especially downplayed as part of affirmative action programs.[52]

Finally, it may be difficult for outstanding students at less selective institutions to gain recognition for how high they rank in their class as compared to equally talented individuals at more selective schools. One reason is that academic performance is typically calibrated and reported in terms of cumulative GPA and not class rank (Ahmadi, Raiszadeh, and Helms, 1997; Cole et al., 2007).[53] In addition, grade inflation and grade compression at the more selective schools conspire to make almost every student look like a very strong student.[54] Even though small differences in GPA can mean substantial changes in class rank, these latter

[51] Although a study of elite undergraduate admissions has found that students of equal ability have less of a chance of being admitted if they attend a more selective rather than less selective high school (suggesting that class rank does matter), the same study has also found that "admission officers place less weight on class rank if applicants come from schools where there is a high concentration of talented students and where differences among the top students are small and difficult to discern" (Espenshade, Hale, and Chung, 2005: 285). These issues have not been investigated in graduate school admissions.

[52] For example, Bowen and Bok (1998: 113) find that blacks in the middle third of their class are seven percentage points more likely than whites in the top third to complete studies at an elite professional school. Even blacks in the lowest third of their class are nine percentage points more likely than whites in the middle third of their class to receive an elite graduate degree (Bowen and Bok, 1998: 113).

[53] See also Bernstein (2003), McKinney et al. (2003), Weiss (1997), Wertheimer (2002).

[54] The extent of grade inflation and compression appears to be positively correlated with institutional selectivity. As Cole and Barber (2003: 201) report, "It is certainly not true today that the distribution of grades in various types of school is the same. In the schools in our sample only a small minority of students at the elite schools receive GPAs of B− or less. . . . At the state universities about 40 percent receive GPAs or B− or less and at the HBCUs 59 percent receive GPAs of B− or less."

differences are overshadowed when GPA is the chief currency of academic performance.[55]

Although the evidence suggests that there are career advantages across a wide variety of outcomes if a student attends a more selective rather than a less selective college, there may be instances in which a lower class rank matters more than higher school selectivity. In a classic article, James Davis (1966) studied the career decisions of college-age men. Davis hypothesized that a student's decision to pursue a "high-performance" career is based in large part on the "student's judgment of his own academic ability," which he evaluates by comparing his performance with that of his college classmates rather than with university students as a whole. As a result, "GPA standing on the local campus" is more likely than college selectivity to shape students' self-evaluations of academic ability and therefore career decisions. If attending a more selective college causes students with a given scholastic aptitude to have less confidence in their abilities and thus forego intellectually challenging career fields, these students may indeed improve their future prospects by attending a less selective university. Davis (1966: 31) thus advised parents sending their sons off to college, "It is better to be a big frog in a small pond than a small frog in a big pond."

A major study of career aspirations of highly talented minority students offers some support for this "frog-pond" hypothesis. Cole and Barber (2003) ask what factors influence underrepresented students to choose academia as a career and what policy options are available to increase the racial and ethnic diversity of college faculties. After analyzing data on more than 7,600 graduating seniors in the spring of 1996 from thirty-four schools—highly selective, small liberal arts colleges; Ivy League universities; somewhat less selective, large public flagship universities; and historically black colleges and universities—the authors conclude that the small numbers of minority faculty are due to supply constraints. In other words, black and, to a lesser extent, Hispanic students are failing to pursue graduate Ph.D. programs in sufficient numbers. According to Cole and Barber, the reason is that affirmative action policies have the consequence that able minority students at selective schools are competing with even better-prepared white and Asian students, making it harder for minorities to excel. Performing relatively less well in turn

---

[55] For example, a 2002 Princeton graduate with a B average may seem like a solid candidate, comparable even to someone with an A average at a less selective college, but this GPA masks the fact that this Princetonian would actually rank 923rd out of 1,079 students, or below the 15th percentile of his class (Malkiel, 2003). Moreover, when grade compression is such that 65 percent of all Princeton graduates have an average of B+ or higher (Malkiel, 2003) and half of all Harvard undergraduates have A or A− averages (Belluck, 2002), a class rank penalty of 18 points is practically impossible to detect in GPA.

lowers the academic self-confidence of these minority students and leads to lower career aspirations, just as Davis (1966) would predict. The result is that minority students are less likely to choose college professor as a career. In fact, Cole and Barber (2003: 208) conclude that African American students would be twice as likely to pursue academic careers if they attended nonelite schools rather than elite ones.[56]

One could argue that college teaching is an exceptional case. Evidence favoring this conjecture is provided by Bowen and Bok (1998: 95–106). They find in the C&B data that 24 percent of black students in the 1976 entering cohort aspired to a Ph.D., in contrast to 18 percent of whites. Yet, in the final analysis, doctoral degrees were earned by 4 percent of black students as compared to 7 percent of white students.[57] At the same time, these authors find little evidence to suggest that, as a result of attending a more selective university, high-achieving black undergraduates are shying away from careers that require professional degrees. Black graduates from C&B schools are as likely to earn business degrees and more likely to earn law and medical degrees than are their white classmates, despite the fact that whites typically have higher class ranks. Bowen and Bok suggest that any greater slippage for black than for white students between original graduate or professional school aspirations and ultimate degree attainment can be explained by blacks having not only higher aspirations upon entering college but also less information about career opportunities.

To conclude, then, although attending a more selective college negatively affects students' relative GPAs when students' ability is held constant, the literature suggests that the benefits in terms of educational attainment, occupational status, and earnings outweigh this downside risk. Although more research is needed on the career decisions and life outcomes of black and, particularly, Hispanic students at a wider range of undergraduate institutions, the advantages of a degree from a more selective college appear to hold for all students, including minority students. On the whole, the evidence does not support assertions made by mismatch proponents. Instead, affirmative action, which enables more underrepresented minority students to gain access to selective colleges than would a race-blind admission policy, appears to help more than harm minority students' futures.

---

[56] Elliott et al. (1996) reach a similar conclusion with respect to underrepresented minority students who choose scientific career fields.

[57] Smaller black-white gaps in both initial aspirations for a doctorate and enrollment in Ph.D. programs are apparent among members of the 1989 entering cohort, leading Bowen and Bok (1998: 95–100) to speculate that things may be changing.

Chapter Seven

SHOULDERING THE FINANCIAL BURDEN

INTRODUCTION

The high cost of college tuition tops Americans' list as the most important issue facing higher education (Smallwood, 2006). According to the College Board (2007a: 14), average student expenses at four-year colleges for the 2007–8 academic year range from $17,300 for in-state public college students to $27,800 for out-of-state public university matriculants and to $35,400 for private college undergraduates.[1] Even after we subtract the average amounts students receive in grants and education tax benefits, 2007–8 college costs (including tuition, fees, room, and board) are still $10,000 at four-year public colleges and universities and $23,000 at four-year private institutions (College Board, 2007a: 17). At a 5 percent annual rate of increase, one year of college is projected by 2023–24 to cost an average of $40,250 at public institutions and $82,750 at private ones (Oregon College Savings Plan, 2006).[2]

College costs were not always this high. As Figure 7.1 indicates, in 1977–78 the average inflation-adjusted published price for one year of tuition, room, board, and fees was approximately $6,900 at four-year public universities and $14,400 at their private college counterparts (College Board, 2007a: 11). By 2007–8 these figures had nearly doubled at public institutions, climbing to $13,600, and increased by almost 125 percent at private ones, reaching more than $32,300 (College Board, 2007a: 11).[3]

[1] These figures include tuition and fees, books and supplies, room and board, transportation, and other expenses (College Board, 2007a: 14).

[2] The projected four-year total at an Ivy League college rises from $194,874 for students beginning college in 2004–5 to $634,173 at the start of the 2024–25 school year. Average college costs are based on tuition and fees, room and board, books and supplies, transportation, and other expenses for the 2004–5 school year. Projected future costs are calculated using a "proprietary college inflation factor developed by College Money" (Oregon College Savings Plan, 2005).

[3] There is some debate as to why college costs have risen so rapidly. The National Commission on the Cost of Higher Education reported that they could not identify a "single, tidy explanation for the tuition spiral" but included technology, facilities, student and parent expectations about amenities, regulations, administrators, faculty salaries, and financial aid as possible causes (Gladieux, 2004: 36). Some scholars argue that decreases in state budget allocations are also crucial to understanding the increasing tuition prices observed at public colleges (Ehrenberg and Rizzo, 2004; Kane, 1999: 9; McPherson and Schapiro,

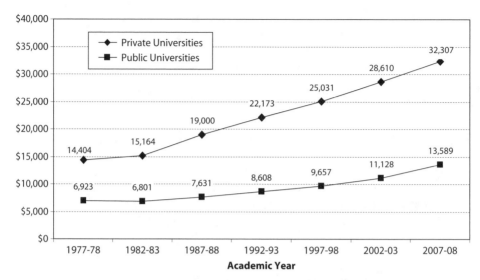

Figure 7.1. Average Tuition, Room, Board, and Fees Charged by Four-Year Public and Private Universities for One Year of College, 1977–2008. Note: Results represent the average price four-year public and private universities advertise as full-time students' one-year costs, weighted by full-time undergraduate enrollment. All dollar values reflect constant 2007 dollars. Source: Trends in College Pricing, College Board (2007a: 11).

1998: 25). Others have observed that tuition goes up even when state lawmakers increase college funding (Smith, 2007b). Referring to other factors highlighted by the commission, Ehrenberg and Rizzo (2004) concur that technology, student services, and financial aid have raised prices, but they add that pressure for institutions to be the best in every aspect together with increasing costs in conducting scientific research have contributed as well. Ehrenberg (2002) suggests that the system of shared governance among faculty, trustees, and administrators, in addition to the roles played by the federal government and alumni, have also conspired to keep rising costs unchecked. Kane (1999: 9), on the other hand, differs with the commission's and Ehrenberg and Rizzo's (2004) contention that financial aid is driving up costs, but he does agree that rising faculty salaries have escalated prices at public colleges. Baumol and Blinder (2006: 522–23) explain that rising faculty salaries tend to cause college costs to grow faster than the rate of inflation, due to a principle known as the "cost disease of personal services." They note that real wages tend to rise at the same rate as labor productivity. In other words, as employees become more productive, their wages increase. Yet positions that require direct, interpersonal interaction, such as teaching, cannot become more productive. In fact, the quality of education professors provide is thought to decrease with increased productivity because increased productivity (that is, more students per faculty member) would require professors to spend less personal time with each student. To prevent professors from switching to careers where wages are rising due to growing productivity, schools increase professors' wages by similar rates. However, since professors' raises are not offset by gains in their productivity, their services become ever more expensive compared to goods and services that have seen improvements in efficiency, leading college tuition to increase faster than the rate of inflation.

The rising cost of an undergraduate education has attracted the attention of federal lawmakers and public officials. Senator Charles Grassley, the top Republican on the Senate Finance Committee, has urged wealthy colleges to spend a higher percentage of their endowments to stabilize or reduce tuition costs (Blumenstyk, 2008). The current version of the House Higher Education Act proposes that the U.S. Department of Education publicly identify universities that increase tuition and fees by more than their sector's average and require these colleges to form committees to develop "cost-reduction opportunities" (Field, 2008). Concerns over affordability have also led the secretary of education's Commission on the Future of Higher Education (2006) in its final draft report to encourage colleges and universities to find innovative ways at the institutional level to control costs, improve productivity, and expand the supply of higher education. A major motivation behind such proposals is to prevent students from low SES families from being priced out of the market for higher education.

Indeed, lower SES Americans are not attending college, especially the more expensive colleges, at the same rate as higher SES Americans. High-achieving, low-income students are about 20 percentage points less likely to attend college than are high-achieving, high-income students (Kahlenberg, 2006). When low-income students go to college, they have increasingly enrolled at less expensive community, two-year private, and for-profit colleges (K. Fischer, 2006b; Gladieux, 2004: 21; McPherson and Schapiro, 1998: 44–47). Those low SES students who attend four-year universities typically enroll at schools with smaller endowments and less selective admissions. In 2004–5, for instance, one-third of all students at four-year colleges had enough financial need to qualify for and receive federal Pell grants. By contrast, only 20 percent of all students at the thirty-one best-endowed public flagship universities and just 14 percent of all students at the fifty-nine wealthiest private colleges were similarly eligible (K. Fischer, 2006b). Only 10 percent of the undergraduates at the nation's most selective colleges were Pell grant recipients in 2001–2 (Heller, 2004: 158).[4]

While low SES students are underrepresented at the more elite and expensive four-year colleges and universities, researchers still debate whether this result is due to college costs.[5] Data from the National Center for

[4] While Pell grant eligibility depends on several factors (U.S. Department of Education, 2006: 5), researchers often use Pell grants to identify low-income students. One study found that 90 percent of Pell grant recipients at four-year colleges in 1999–2000 came from families with annual incomes less than $41,000 and 75 percent came from families with annual incomes less than $32,000 (Heller, 2004: 157).

[5] See Kahlenberg (2006) for a summary of the argument that cost is the driving force and Forster (2006) for a synopsis of the position that insufficient academic preparation is the primary factor.

Education Statistics indicate that, while total prices at four-year public and private colleges rose between 1992–93 and 1999–2000, low-income students' net price did not increase when grant aid is considered (Horn, Wei, and Berker, 2002). Yet even if net price has not grown for the most financially vulnerable, affording college may still be difficult. One study finds that 63 percent of four-year public university students nationwide do not have enough funds between their expected family contribution and financial aid package (including scholarships, grants, work-study jobs, and tax credits) to meet their college costs. Middle-income families face an average annual shortfall of about $5,000, which increases to $6,600 for low-income families (Southern Regional Educational Board, 2006).

Debt can loom large if families receive insufficient financial aid. Nationally, both the percentage of students who assume loans and the amounts they borrow have increased dramatically in recent years. In 1993 less than half of all four-year college students took out loans, but by 2004 two-thirds of such students did (Project on Student Debt, 2006).[6] Graduates with debt owed about 58 percent more in 2004 than they did in 1993, even controlling for inflation (Project on Student Debt, 2006). In 2004, the typical four-year public college graduate with debt faced $15,500 in loans, and his private college counterpart confronted $19,400 (College Board, 2005b: 12).[7]

Such debt has important consequences for students and the choices they face after college graduation. According to the State Public Interest Research Group's Higher Education Project, 23 percent of four-year public college students graduate with too much debt to repay their loans by working as teachers, and 37 percent owe too much to serve as social workers. Private college students are even less likely to be able to start

---

[6] Between 1995–96 and 2003–4, the proportion of all undergraduates who received either a subsidized or an unsubsidized federal Stafford loan rose from one-quarter to one-third (Wei and Berkner, 2008).

[7] Today the average indebted graduate from a private college owes $24,200 (Egan, 2008). Each year since 2001, the proportion of undergraduate funding in the form of grant aid has declined (College Board, 2005b: 5). Usher (2006) finds that up-front grants and scholarships are more effective than loans in encouraging low-income students to attend and complete college. Singell, Waddell, and Curs (2006) examine whether the introduction of merit-based aid programs harms the college access of needy students. Prior research has found that the enrollment effects of merit aid are large and significant, whereas the enrollment effects of need-based aid are modest and insignificant. These authors use panel data on Pell grant recipients to study the effects on low-income students of the introduction of Georgia's Helping Outstanding Pupils Educationally (HOPE) program, a program designed to retain the best of Georgia's high school graduates at in-state institutions. They find that HOPE scholarships have had the largest impact on the enrollment of low-income students at Georgia's two-year and less selective four-year institutions. Nevertheless, Pell students have not been crowded out of Georgia's more selective institutions.

careers in these fields. Thirty-eight percent cannot afford to teach, and 55 percent cannot repay loans on a social worker's salary (Swarthout, 2006).[8] These statistics are of particular concern in light of a White House report that predicts that U.S. school districts will need to hire an additional 2.2 million teachers over the next decade (The White House, 2006). Debt may also prevent college graduates from pursuing careers that require advanced degrees. University graduates from the class of 1993 who had at least $5,000 of debt were significantly less likely than debt-free students to enroll in graduate or professional school within the year (Millet, 2003).[9] Another study finds that 42 percent of college graduates who do not pursue graduate school blame student loan debt (Baum and O'Malley, 2003).[10]

The remainder of this chapter examines these issues as they pertain to students at selective colleges. How much does it cost to attend an NSCE institution? How do students pay for college, and what proportion of expenses do different sources cover? Once grant aid is figured in, what are students' net costs? What percentage of students borrows to pay for college? How much money do students owe upon graduation if they take out loans? What percentage of family members assumes debt to help finance their children's education, and how much do they typically need to repay? Lastly, how large of a financial burden does a selective college education place on students and their families? Throughout this chapter we

[8] Harvard Law School began a new program in the fall of 2008 that waives third-year tuition for law students who intend to spend five years working for nonprofit organizations or the government. Reporting on these changes, Jonathan Glater (2008b) writes, "For years, prosecutors, public defenders and lawyers in traditionally low-paying areas of the law have argued that financial pressures were pushing graduates toward corporate law and away from the kind of careers that they would pursue in the absence of tens of thousands of dollars in student loans."

[9] On the other hand, Schapiro, O'Malley, and Litten (1991) find that high debt does not significantly affect whether graduates of elite Consortium on Financing Higher Education (COFHE) institutions enroll in graduate programs in the arts and sciences immediately following college graduation.

[10] The implications of debt can also be appreciated by examining the effects that eliminating it has had on some groups of students. In 2001 Princeton University removed all loans from students' financial aid packages and replaced them with grants (Quiñones, 2005). A survey of the first group of financial aid students to have spent all four years of college under this new no-loan policy found that lack of undergraduate debt had an impact on two-thirds of the students' post-college plans (Quiñones, 2005). Graduates specifically asserted that not having to repay loans made it possible for them not only to attend graduate school but also to pursue lower-paying jobs in education and nonprofit organizations (Quiñones, 2005). Rothstein and Rouse (2007) also report that graduates from one selective institution shifted toward lower-salary jobs in public service once loans were replaced with grants. Gates Millennium Scholars who leave college with no debt have also been observed to choose careers more rooted in their personal interests and less based on economic concerns (Gertner, 2006).

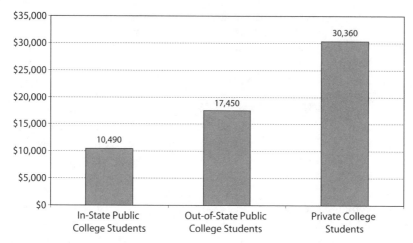

Figure 7.2. Students' Estimated Average Total Cost (Tuition, Fees, Room, Board, and Books) of First Year of College, by Type of Student; NSCE Matriculant Sample: 1980s, 1993, and 1997 Cohorts Combined (N = 6,327). Note: All dollar values reflect constant 1996–97 dollars. The number of observations is slightly smaller than the full matriculant sample because of missing data. There are 1,071 in-state public, 1,316 out-of-state public, and 3,940 private college student observations. Source: National Study of College Experience.

focus on how social class and the type of institution a student attends affect these economic aspects of students' college educations. The majority of the data come from the NSCE matriculant sample, which comprises students who enrolled in one of eight selective colleges in the 1980s, 1993, and 1997.

PAYING FOR HIGHER EDUCATION

Total College Costs

The cost of a selective college education varies substantially. As Figure 7.2 indicates, NSCE private college students estimate that their tuition, fees, room, board, and books cost about $30,400 (ignoring financial aid) for their first year of college alone.[11] Public college matriculants face much lower costs, although average prices are different for in-state and out-of-state residents. Out-of-state students attending the same schools as their

[11] All dollar values reflect constant 1996–97 dollars unless otherwise noted. Differences reported in the text are statistically significant at the .05 level unless explicitly stated otherwise.

in-state classmates need approximately $17,500 to cover one year of expenses, $7,000 more than the $10,500 required of their in-state peers.[12]

College Choice

Do these sticker prices influence where students go to college?[13] Prior studies have suggested that high SES parents are willing to pay more for college because they believe that attending a selective private college is critical to their children's future success (Chinni, 2006; Duffy and Goldberg, 1998; Easterbrook, 2004; Flanagan, 2001; Glater, 2006; Mayher, 1998; McDonough, 1997).[14] Others claim that middle-class and high SES parents encourage their children to attend more expensive, selective private colleges rather than public universities in an effort to convey social status (P. Cohen, 2006). Another perspective suggests that top students make the decision to attend more expensive private and out-of-state colleges on their own and are not pressured to do so by their parents (Lipman Hearne, 2006).[15] At the same time, lower- and working-class parents, and even some middle-class families, face incentives to send their children to public in-state institutions as a way of reducing college costs.

For some social class groups, anticipated college costs may influence the type of school students attend. Data in Figure 7.3 show that upper-class students are overrepresented at the more expensive private colleges. Students from middle-class families are disproportionately represented at in-state public institutions, suggesting that they may enroll in colleges with the lowest costs as a way of reducing their expenses.[16] Though the

---

[12] Because costs vary not just by college type (public college vs. private college) but also by students' residency status at public colleges (in-state vs. out-of-state), this chapter analyzes how students pay for college using three student-type categories (in-state students, public colleges; out-of-state students, public colleges; and students at private colleges).

[13] The role of financial aid in decisions about where to go to college is explored in detail in Hoxby (2004).

[14] As noted in chapter 2, researchers who have investigated post-college outcomes find that graduating from an elite college provides career and financial benefits (Arnold, 2002; Behrman, Rosenzweig, and Taubman, 1996; Brand and Halaby, 2006; Brewer, Eide, and Ehrenberg, 1999; Cookson and Persell, 1985; Daniel, Black, and Smith, 1997; Kane, 1998b; Loury and Garman, 1995; Smart, 1986; Zhang, 2005b). Opposing viewpoints, however, suggest that the advantages of an elite college education are overstated and that bright students will succeed wherever they attend (Astin, 1993; Dale and Krueger, 2002; Pascarella and Terrenzini, 1991).

[15] As compared to students with SAT scores below 1300, students with scores of 1300 or higher downplay their parents' influence in their college choice and are more likely to enroll in a university outside their state and/or in a private college (Lipman Hearne, 2006: 22–25).

[16] Yield rates discussed in chapter 4 also support this idea. Middle-class NSCE students are the least likely of all social class groups to accept the offers of admission extended by elite private universities.

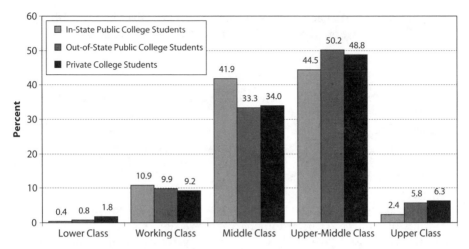

Figure 7.3. Percentage of Students from Each Social Class in Each Student Type Category; NSCE Matriculant Sample: 1980s, 1993, and 1997 Cohorts Combined (N = 6,350). Note: Differences in the percentage of working- as well as upper-middle-class students by student type are not statistically significant at the .05 level. Differences in the percentage of upper-class students by student type are statistically significant at the .05 level. Finally, differences in the percentage of lower- as well as middle-class students by student type are statistically significant at the .01 level. Source: National Study of College Experience.

pattern for working-class students is what one might expect, the differences across student types are not significant. Lower-class students appear to be overrepresented at private colleges and universities, contrary to expectations.[17] In sum, while choosing a less expensive college can assist students in financing their education, it appears that most lower- and working-class families do not use this approach.[18] Instead, students who

[17] While lower-class NSCE students' college choices appear not to be motivated by posted sticker price, lower-class students nationally seem to be more cost conscious. Bridget Long (2004) finds that low-income high school graduates from 1992 are less likely to choose to attend a more expensive college than are students from higher socioeconomic backgrounds.

[18] However, some argue that even high SES individuals are starting to make use of college choice as a cost-cutting strategy. Michael McPherson and Morton Schapiro (1998: 44–47) find that the percentage of high-income students who enrolled in four-year private colleges declined between 1980 and 1994 while the percentage enrolling at four-year public colleges increased. Others also report that more and more high SES students are attending public colleges (Quinn, 2006; Tooley and Howell, 1995). Upper-class NSCE matriculants, however, have not become significantly more represented among in-state or out-of-state public university matriculants over time. Instead, the opposite has occurred; their proportion among private university undergraduates increased to 9 percent in the 1997 cohort from 5 percent in the 1980s cohort and 4 percent in the 1993 cohort. On the other hand, upper-middle-class NSCE matriculants have become more prevalent among in-state public college

attend selective colleges meet the costs of their education by (1) securing grants or scholarships; (2) taking out loans; (3) working; and/or (4) receiving financial assistance from family members.[19] Next we explore how student type and social class affect NSCE undergraduates' use of these four different funding methods. Then we examine the proportion of college expenses paid for by each of these sources depending on student type and socioeconomic status.

Grants and Loans

Students access grants and loans primarily through their financial aid packages.[20] As Figure 7.4 shows, about half of all NSCE matriculants are financial aid recipients,[21] and most students who apply for aid receive

---

students. While in the 1980s and 1993 cohorts upper-middle-class students made up 39 percent of all in-state public college students, in the 1997 cohort they made up 55 percent. Nevertheless, this growth does not coincide with a significant decline in the percentage of upper-middle-class students among out-of-state public or private college matriculants. Among out-of-state public college students, the percentages of enrolled students who are upper-middle-class are 48 in the 1980s, 53 in 1993, and 49 in 1997. The corresponding figures for private colleges and universities are 47 in the 1980s, 49 in 1993, and 51 in 1997. The differences across time at public institutions for out-of-state students and for students at private institutions are not statistically significant at the .05 level. Thus although upper-middle-class students are representing a larger share of in-state public college students, this is not the result of upper-middle-class students moving away from elite private and out-of-state public colleges.

[19] It should be noted, however, that students do not always select the most economically prudent scholarship and aid packages. Avery and Hoxby (2004) found that students sometimes select grants simply because they have names attached, that students are excessively attracted by loans and work-study, even when such offers are worth less than grants, and that students more strongly consider grants' shares of college costs than the grants' total amounts.

[20] While less common, students can and do obtain scholarships from foundations, organizations, and businesses outside their university. Both parents and students can also secure private loans to help meet educational expenses, although such loans typically charge higher interest than those offered in aid packages (Burd, 2006). While taking out private loans to pay for college was once uncommon, its use has grown significantly in recent years as government loan limits have not adjusted to keep pace with increasing college costs (Baum and O'Malley, 2003; College Board, 2005b; Glater, 2006). Students are also increasingly paying for college tuition on credit cards; 24 percent of students charge their tuition on credit cards, and the resulting credit card debt is a significant cause of dropping out of college (McGlynn, 2006).

[21] Nationally, 62 percent of college students received aid in 1996–97 (Boggess and Ryan, 2002: 17). Elite college students are less likely to be on aid because they tend to be from more socioeconomically advantaged family backgrounds. For example, in Table 4.9 we showed that less than 15 percent of all NSCE students have family incomes of less than $50,000. In sharp contrast, 57 percent of all college students have family incomes in this range (Boggess and Ryan, 2002: 5).

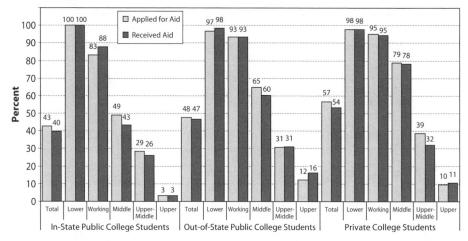

Figure 7.4. Percentage of Students Applying for and Receiving Financial Aid during First Year of College, by Type of Student and Socioeconomic Status; NSCE Matriculant Sample: 1980s, 1993, and 1997 Cohorts Combined (N = 6,350). Note: Social class differences in the percentage of students applying for as well as receiving aid within each student category are statistically significant at the .001 level. Differences by type of student in the percentage applying for and receiving aid are also statistically significant at the .001 and .01 levels, respectively. The fact that the percentage of matriculants receiving aid is sometimes larger than the percentage applying can be attributed to the fact that some schools award merit scholarships to students regardless of whether they applied for financial aid. Source: National Study of College Experience.

it.[22] The figure also indicates that the higher students' socioeconomic status is, the less likely they are to use aid as a way to fund their college degree.[23] Overall, about 98 percent of lower-class NSCE students collect financial aid, as compared to 12 percent of upper-class students. Though

---

[22] The Free Application for Federal Student Aid (FAFSA) form, which students typically complete when they apply for financial aid, is even longer than most tax forms, with its 128 questions, and can be confusing (Farrell, 2007b; Selingo, 2006). We therefore investigated whether matriculants who applied for aid received assistance from certain sources in completing the forms. Compared to other social classes, lower-class students are less likely to receive help from their guidance counselors, and working-class students are less likely to receive assistance from their parents. Presumably to make up for the lack of help from these sources, lower- and working-class undergraduates are slightly more likely to consult with teachers, private consultants, peers, and other adults than are undergraduates from other social class groups. By student type, in-state public college students are also slightly more likely to receive assistance from both guidance counselors and teachers, while enrollees at private colleges are more likely to have their parents' help. The help of private college financial planners in filling out financial aid forms is on the rise, and families that earn between $50,000 and $150,000 are most likely to use this new service (Farrell, 2007b).

[23] This finding holds true nationally as well (Boggess and Ryan, 2002: 14).

social class appears to be the primary factor affecting who seeks out grants and loans, college costs also matter. In-state public college undergraduates are least likely to request and receive aid, followed next by out-of-state public college undergraduates, and then their private college counterparts.[24] This trend is particularly true of working-, middle-, and upper-middle-class matriculants. For example, among the middle class, less than half of in-state public college students apply for financial aid in contrast to almost two-thirds of their out-of-state public college counterparts and more than three-quarters of their private college peers.

Student Employment

Another way students fund their undergraduate educations is by working during college.[25] Figure 7.5 illustrates NSCE matriculants' use of freshman-year employment. We note first that the percentage of undergraduates with jobs differs by student type. About one-third of public college freshmen are employed, as compared to almost one-half of private college freshmen.[26] Second, students' likelihood of working varies by socioeconomic status. In general, matriculants from lower-, working-, and middle-class backgrounds are more likely to be employed than are upper-middle- and upper-class matriculants. Third, this social class gradient grows more pronounced the greater the college costs that students confront. For example, lower- and upper-class in-state public college students are about equally likely to work. In contrast, the differential between lower- and upper-class students is 33 percentage points for out-of-state public college students and 72 percentage points for students at private universities.[27]

[24] This result also occurs nationally. A smaller percentage of public college students receives aid than do private college students (Boggess and Ryan, 2002: 14–15; Knapp et al., 2007: 3; Wasik, 2006).

[25] We should note, however, that this strategy can backfire. If students earn more from their jobs than government-imposed caps allow, their financial aid can be reduced or even eliminated (Burd, 2003, 2006).

[26] Nationally, students are even more likely to work. Seventy-two percent of all full-time undergraduates were employed full- or part-time in 1996–97 (Boggess and Ryan, 2002: 5–6). NSCE private college students are more likely to be employed than are their counterparts at public colleges, perhaps because they are more likely to receive financial aid. Financial aid packages require students to make some contribution toward their college costs and usually encourage students to meet at least part of these obligations by accepting work-study positions.

[27] Figure 7.5 also suggests that lower-class out-of-state public and private college students are more likely to be employed than lower-class in-state public college students. The reason may be that the former groups not only face greater college costs but also come from families with lower incomes and fewer assets than lower-class in-state college students. Average family income for lower-class in-state students at public institutions is $24,700, as compared to $21,000 for lower-class out-of-state students at public institutions and $22,700 for lower-class students at private colleges and universities. Differences in average family

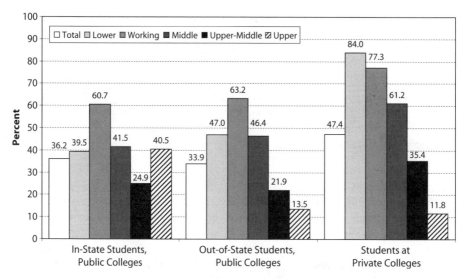

Figure 7.5. Percentage of Students Who Held a Job during Their Freshman Year of College, by Type of Student and Socioeconomic Status; NSCE Matriculant Sample: 1980s, 1993, and 1997 Cohorts Combined (N = 6,350). Note: Social class differences in the percentage of students working during their freshman year are statistically significant at the .001 level within each student type category. Differences by type of student are also statistically significant at the .001 level. Source: National Study of College Experience.

Social class and type of school attended are also associated with the number of hours students work at a job. Figure 7.6 shows the median number of hours NSCE students worked per week during their freshman year if they held a job.[28] High SES matriculants consistently worked fewer

assets follow the same pattern across the three types of students—$12,600, $6,600, and $10,200, respectively. At the same time, upper-class out-of-state public and private university matriculants are less likely to be employed than their in-state public college counterparts, perhaps because their families have greater financial resources than do the families of upper-class in-state public college students. Across the three student types (in-state at public institutions, out-of-state at public institutions, and students at private institutions), average family income is $234,000, $266,000, and $267,000, respectively. Corresponding mean asset values are $428,000, $486,000, and $592,000.

[28] Scholars debate the effects of hours of employment on academic performance. Although Horn and Berktold (1998) argue that employment adversely affects the academic performance of students who work more than fifteen hours a week, Nonis and Hudson (2006) observe no relationship between time spent working and a student's GPA. Strauss and Volkwein (2002) find that working more hours is, in fact, positively correlated with GPA. As discussed in chapter 6, NSCE matriculants who worked ten or more hours per week during their freshman year have significantly lower odds of graduating in six years, but not significantly lower class ranks, compared to students who did not have a job. Working fewer than ten hours a week has no significant effect on either academic performance measure.

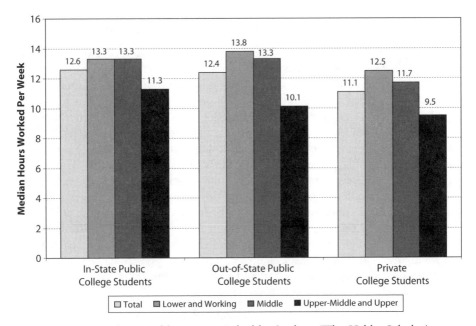

Figure 7.6. Median Weekly Hours Worked by Students Who Held a Job during Their Freshman Year of College, by Type of Student and Socioeconomic Status; NSCE Matriculant Sample: 1980s, 1993, and 1997 Cohorts Combined (N = 2,970). Note: Median hours worked per week are based only on students who were employed during their freshman year and who reported the number of hours they worked. As a result there are 394 in-state public, 528 out-of-state public, and 2,048 private college student observations. Differences by student type in the distribution of hours worked are statistically significant at the .001 level. Social class differences are also statistically significant at the .001 level among both out-of-state public college students and private college students. Social class differences among in-state public college students are statistically significant at the .05 level. Source: National Study of College Experience.

hours than their middle-class and low SES counterparts.[29] Given their families' greater resources, high SES students may not work as many hours because they are less dependent on their job earnings to meet expenses. Employed students at public colleges work between one and two hours more each week than do employed students at private colleges.[30]

[29] Median hours per week are calculated using only respondents who were employed during their freshman year and who reported the number of hours they worked. To ensure that the median hours presented in each category are based on a sufficient number of students, we have condensed our five social classes into three socioeconomic groupings. The pattern displayed is similar to that observed using five social classes.

[30] This result may occur because public and private universities suggest that undergraduates work for different lengths of time. For example, the financial aid offices at elite public

Financial Assistance from Family Members

Family members can also help pay for students' undergraduate educations. In fact, federal financial aid programs expect all parents except those with very low incomes to contribute some amount toward their dependent children's education.[31] About 84 percent of NSCE students report that their relatives gave them some amount of money to help finance their first year of college.[32] While this percentage does not differ significantly by student type, it does by social class. Only about one-third of lower-class students (32 percent) and two-thirds of working-class matriculants (66 percent) receive funds from their family compared to 83, 90, and 87 percent of middle-, upper-middle-, and upper-class students, respectively. These findings are consistent with those reported by McDonough (1997: 146–47), who shows that money is not a factor in choosing colleges for many of the high SES students she studied; these students assumed that their parents would take care of college costs. Low SES students, however, assumed that college expenses would be their responsibility.

Proportion of College Costs Covered by Different Sources

What is the relative importance of these various college funding mechanisms? Overall, matriculants' families are the primary source of support, providing 58 percent of total college costs.[33] Grants pay for about one-fifth, loans to students and parents meet a little more than one-tenth, and students' employment, savings, and other sources finance the final one-tenth of the bill. As Figure 7.7 illustrates, however, there are differences by student type and by social class. Family and student contributions cover a slightly larger proportion of public college students' costs, while grants and loans meet a somewhat larger percentage of private college students' expenses. By social class, the percentage of costs financed by

---

colleges such as the University of California, Berkeley (2006) and the University of Virginia (2005: 3) indicate that students can be employed in work-study jobs for up to twenty hours a week. In contrast, Harvard College (2006: 7) reports that working eight hours a week is appropriate for students heavily involved in extracurriculars and that working twelve hours completely fulfills students' expected contributions. At Princeton University, financial aid students are required to work 7.5 hours per week if they are freshmen and 8.5 hours if they are sophomores, juniors, or seniors (Tilghman, 2007).

[31] The amount of money parents are asked to provide depends on individual family circumstances, but it is based primarily on family income and assets. Kane (1999: 25) illustrates how these two variables determine a family's expected contribution.

[32] Nationally, only about two-thirds of dependent college students' parents did so in 1986–87 and 1992–93 (Stringer et al., 1998: 17).

[33] This percentage is quite similar to figures for the country as a whole. Nationally, parents cover about 55 percent of their children's college costs (Stringer et al., 1998: 3).

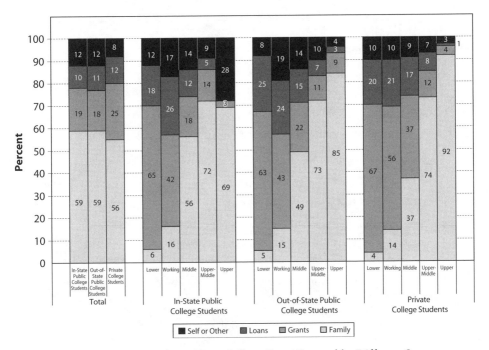

Figure 7.7. Percentage of First-Year College Costs Covered by Different Sources, by Type of Student and Socioeconomic Status; NSCE Matriculant Sample: 1980s, 1993, and 1997 Cohorts Combined (N = 5,909). Note: Percentages may not always sum to 100 because of rounding. Due to missing data, there are 992 in-state public, 1,229 out-of-state public, and 3,688 private college student observations. The "family" category includes only the amount families pay immediately to universities. Any amount families pay for using loans falls under the loans category. The "grants" category includes not just federal, state, and college awards in financial aid packages but also scholarships students obtain from other sources. Likewise, the "loans" category is composed of federal loans to parents and students in financial aid packages as well as private loans that students and parents take out independently. Finally, the "self or other" category comprises funds not only from students' employment during the academic year but also from summer work, savings, and other miscellaneous sources. Proportions are based on 1996–97 constant dollars. Source: National Study of College Experience.

relatives increases the higher matriculants' socioeconomic status,[34] while the percentage paid for with grants decreases. The figure also illustrates that compared to other social class groups, working- and middle-class undergraduates generally fund a higher percentage of college costs using their own or other sources. Lower- and working-class students cover a

[34] The same is true nationally (Stringer et al., 1998: 4).

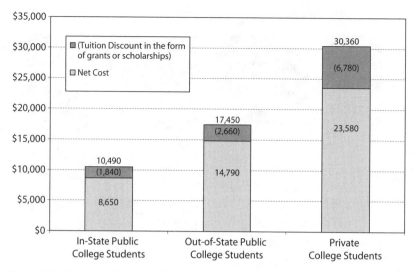

Figure 7.8. Students' Estimated Total Cost, Tuition Discount (Grants and Scholarships), and Net Cost (Total Cost Minus Tuition Discount) of First Year of College, by Type of Student; NSCE Matriculant Sample: 1980s, 1993, and 1997 Cohorts Combined (N = 6,327). Note: All dollar values reflect constant 1996–97 dollars. The number of observations is slightly smaller than our full matriculant sample because of missing data. There are 1,071 in-state public, 1,316 out-of-state public, and 3,940 private college student observations. Source: National Study of College Experience.

higher proportion through loans, a fact that has a direct bearing on debt accumulation.[35]

Net Cost of Attending Selective Colleges

As noted above, grants cover 20 percent of the typical NSCE student's first-year college costs. Because grants never have to be repaid, they essentially represent a discount off of the advertised total college cost, leaving many undergraduates with lower net costs than the sticker price would suggest.[36] Figure 7.8 illustrates NSCE matriculants' average first-year total cost, tuition discount, and net cost by student type. It shows that discounts range between 15 percent for out-of-state students at pub-

---

[35] Later in this chapter, we more fully investigate the role of both student and parent debt in financing elite university educations.

[36] We use net cost to represent total cost minus grant and scholarship aid only. Some researchers also subtract tax breaks (College Board, 2007a) or even loans (Horn, Wei, and Berker, 2002) in determining students' net costs.

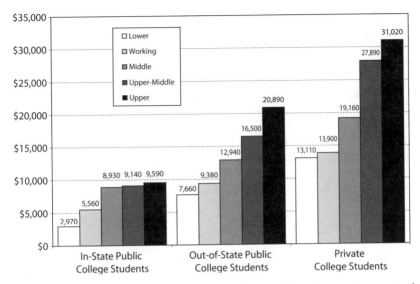

Figure 7.9. Students' Estimated Net Cost (Total Cost Minus Tuition Discount) of First Year of College, by Type of Student and Socioeconomic Status; NSCE Matriculant Sample: 1980s, 1993, and 1997 Cohorts Combined (N = 6,327). Note: All dollar values reflect constant 1996–97 dollars. The number of observations is slightly smaller than our full matriculant sample because of missing data. There are 1,071 in-state public, 1,316 out-of-state public, and 3,940 private college student observations. Source: National Study of College Experience.

lic universities and 22 percent for students at private institutions. The dollar amount saved is positively related to the original total college costs. For example, the average in-state public college student's first year bill is reduced by $1,840 once grants and scholarships are included, while the average private college student's costs shrink by $6,780.[37] Yet even these grant discounts do not fully equalize students' costs at selective colleges. Private university students still face first-year net costs that are $9,000 greater than net costs for out-of-state public college students and $15,000 more than those for in-state public college students.

These differences in net cost by student type occur not just in the aggregate but within every socioeconomic category. As Figure 7.9 illustrates, regardless of students' social class, the least expensive undergraduate option is an in-state public college, followed by an out-of-state public college. On average, it is most costly to attend a selective private college

---

[37] The same results are found nationally, with private college students receiving more grant money than public college students (College Board, 2007a: 16–17; Kane, 1999; Wasik, 2006).

or university, even considering grant aid.[38] The figure also shows that within each student category, a lower socioeconomic status is associated with smaller net costs. For example, while upper-class students at private colleges pay approximately the full price with their annual bill of $31,020, their lower-class peers face much reduced statements of only $13,110. In the end, social class determines net costs as much or more than student type. For instance, upper-middle- and upper-class out-of-state public college matriculants contribute more money for their education (after the tuition discount) than do lower- or working-class matriculants at private colleges. Likewise, middle-, upper-middle-, and upper-class in-state public college students are charged a higher net dollar amount than are lower-class out-of-state public college students.

ACCUMULATED COLLEGE DEBT

Student Debt

Even the net costs incurred in attending a selective college are often too much for students to shoulder immediately. Thus, in order to meet college payments, 40 percent of NSCE students take out a loan. Figure 7.10 depicts how the percentage of NSCE matriculants facing educational debt upon graduation differs by student type and by social class. Public

---

[38] This result may not be as true today. Since the last NSCE cohort enrolled in college, several selective private universities have increased the amount of financial aid they give in the form of grants to lower- and middle-income students. For example, starting in 2001 Princeton eliminated all loans from the financial aid packages students receive and replaced them with grants (Quiñones, 2005). Stanford and Yale no longer require families making less than $45,000 a year to contribute any money toward their child's education, while Harvard and the University of Pennsylvania make the same offer to families earning less than $60,000 and $50,000 a year, respectively (Hill and Winston, 2006a; Tomsho, 2006; Wasley, 2006; Winter, 2005). Yale and Harvard have both raised the income ceiling on eligibility for financial aid to close to $200,000. MIT now matches the amount students receive in Pell grants with institutional grants, providing individual students with as much as $4,050 in additional grant aid each year (Lipka, 2006). Public universities have increased their grant aid to low-income students as well. The University of North Carolina at Chapel Hill enables students from families at or below 200 percent of the federal poverty line to graduate debt free if they spend ten to twelve hours a week in a work-study position (Brown and Clark, 2006; University of North Carolina at Chapel Hill, 2006). The University of Virginia gives grants instead of loans to matriculants with family incomes at or below 200 percent of the poverty line (Turner, 2006; University of Virginia, 2006). Grant aid to low SES students has also increased at the University of Minnesota, the University of Maryland at College Park, Michigan State University, Miami University in Ohio, and at public universities in Indiana and Oklahoma (Brainard, 2006; Brandon, 2006). Given these changes, low-income students and their families probably should no longer assume that a particular type of college will always be the least expensive. Those trying to find the cheapest elite college option will have to compare the financial aid programs offered by specific universities.

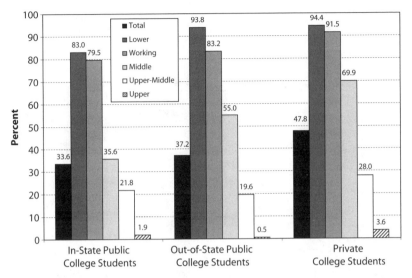

Figure 7.10. Percentage of NSCE Students with Personal Educational Debt at the Time of Graduation, by Type of Student and Socioeconomic Status; NSCE Matriculant Sample: 1980s, 1993, and 1997 Cohorts Combined (N = 6,350). Note: Social class differences in each student type category are statistically significant at the .001 level. Differences by type of student are also statistically significant at the .001 level. There are 1,077 in-state public, 1,322 out-of-state public, and 3,951 private college student observations. Source: National Study of College Experience.

college matriculants are less likely to owe money from their undergraduate education than are private college matriculants. Slightly more than one-third of in-state and out-of-state public university students have loans, as compared to almost half of all private university graduates. Moreover, the likelihood that a student has debt is negatively related to his or her socioeconomic status. For example, at least 80 percent of lower- and working-class undergraduates have loans, as compared to fewer than 5 percent of upper-class undergraduates.

The amount of money students assume in debt is also important.[39] The typical NSCE student with loans owes $15,910 at the time of graduation. In Figure 7.11 we show the median amounts that indebted students borrow by student type and social class. The results indicate that the size of their loans increases along with matriculants' college costs. In-state students who have debt from attending public universities owe about

[39] While there are limits on how much students can borrow through federal programs (U.S. Department of Education, 2006), students can always take on additional debt through private loans, credit cards, and arrangements with family members (Burd, 2006; Glater, 2006; J. King, 2005; Nellie Mae, 2005).

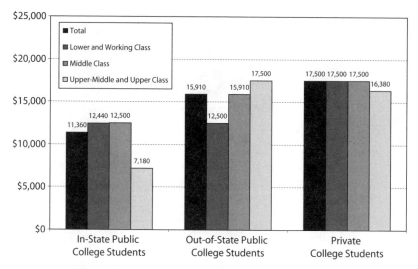

Figure 7.11. Median Amounts Owed by Students Who Have Personal Educational Debt at the Time of Graduation, by Type of Student and Socioeconomic Status; NSCE Matriculant Sample: 1980s, 1993, and 1997 Cohorts (N = 3,427). Note: All dollar values reflect constant 1996–97 dollars. There are 544 in-state public, 679 out-of-state public, and 2,204 private college student observations. Source: National Study of College Experience.

$11,400; their out-of-state peers tackle loans of about $15,900; and their private college counterparts need to repay $17,500. Differences in the amount of money graduates owe by student type are much smaller than one might expect given the much larger differences in their annual net costs. For example, although the typical indebted private college student has annual net costs that are $9,910 greater than the typical indebted in-state public college student, the amount the indebted private college student owes for his or her entire undergraduate education is only $6,140 greater. Likewise, while NSCE private college students with debt have annual net costs that are $6,120 greater than their out-of-state public university counterparts with debt, these private college alumni owe just $1,590 more from all of their undergraduate years. These results reveal that higher net costs do not necessarily translate into equally larger student loans. Private college matriculants are meeting their much larger net costs through means other than just greater personal borrowing.

The amount of money that NSCE graduates owe according to social class forms two distinct patterns depending on student type.[40] Among

[40]In Figure 7.11 we present three condensed socioeconomic status categories rather than our usual five. The results depicted are very similar to those observed using five social class groups.

in-state public and private college matriculants, low SES and middle-class students owe approximately the same amounts while their high SES classmates owe less. Out-of-state public college graduates follow a different pattern. For them, debt increases along with students' socioeconomic background. While low SES out-of-state students take out loans of about the same size as their in-state counterparts, middle-class and, especially, high SES out-of-state students face much larger debts than do their in-state equivalents.[41]

Parental Debt from Students' Undergraduate Education

Parents and other family members sometimes also assume debt to help finance NSCE students' college educations. About 11 percent of all respondents report that a relative has borrowed for them. As Figure 7.12 indicates, this percentage differs by student type and social class. Families of students at private colleges are more likely to take on debt than are in-state or out-of-state public college students' families. In addition, the likelihood of parents having some debt when their children graduate from college bears an inverse U-shaped relation to social class. In every student category, middle-class parents are the most likely to borrow. These results suggest that middle-class families find it more difficult than other socioeconomic groups to meet their expected contributions using existing financial resources.

The typical parent (or other family member) who assumes debt for their NSCE student's undergraduate education owes $15,910. As Figure 7.13 demonstrates, there tends to be a positive correlation between loan debt and parents' social class, with the overall pattern being most pronounced at private colleges and universities. In other words, within each student category, middle and high SES families tend to owe more than their low SES counterparts. Turning to student type, the greater students' total college costs are, the greater their families' median debt. Parents or

---

[41] Lower-class in-state and out-of-state public college students may face similar levels of debt because their financial circumstances qualify them for similar need-based grants. Middle-class and high SES out-of-state public college matriculants, on the other hand, may take out more in loans than their in-state counterparts because they are ineligible for some of the merit-based grants available to in-state students. For example, in an effort to keep bright students in the area, Arkansas, Florida, Georgia, Louisiana, New Mexico, South Carolina, West Virginia, and Massachusetts allow their high school graduates who meet and maintain certain academic standards to attend in-state public colleges for free (Cauchon, 2004; Fischer, 2006a; Glater, 2006). States and colleges are increasingly shifting the grant aid they provide from need-based to more merit-based criteria (Cauchon, 2004; College Board, 2005b; Fischer, 2006a; Gladieux, 2004: 34). In 1994, the country awarded $1.2 billion in merit scholarships. In 2004 that figure reached $7.3 billion (Finder, 2006a).

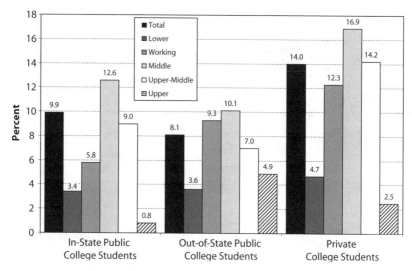

Figure 7.12. Percentage of NSCE Students Whose Parents or Other Family Members Have Incurred Debt as a Result of Student's Undergraduate Education, by Type of Student and Socioeconomic Status; NSCE Matriculant Sample: 1980s, 1993, and 1997 Cohorts Combined (N = 6,350). Note: Differences by type of student and social class are statistically significant at the .01 level. Differences by social class among private college students are statistically significant at the .001 level. However, differences by social class among in-state public college students as well as among out-of-state public college students are not statistically significant at the .05 level. Source: National Study of College Experience.

other relatives of in-state public college matriculants typically owe about $8,000; parents and family members of out-of-state public college students must repay $17,500; and those of private university matriculants confront a debt of approximately $22,700. For middle-class parents, loan debt doubles from almost $9,000 to nearly $18,000 if their children go to private or out-of-state public universities instead of in-state public institutions. Low SES parents' debt is around $11,000 greater if their children opt for a private rather than a public undergraduate education.

The variation in the amount families owe by student type is more pronounced than the variation in the amount students themselves owe (see Figure 7.11). For example, the typical private university graduate with debt owes $6,140 more than the typical in-state public university alumnus with debt. In contrast, the typical private college student's family owes $14,780 more than the family of a typical indebted in-state public college student. These results suggest that when students and their families are

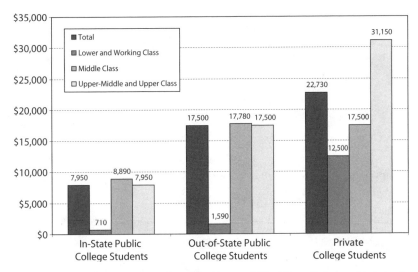

Figure 7.13. Median Amounts Owed by Parents Who Have Debt as a Result of a Student's Undergraduate Education, by Type of Student and Socioeconomic Status; NSCE Matriculant Sample: 1980s, 1993, and 1997 Cohorts (N = 860). Note: All dollar values reflect constant 1996–97 dollars. There are 103 in-state public, 144 out-of-state public, and 613 private college student observations. Source: National Study of College Experience.

unable to meet costs immediately, the balance is more apt to be transferred in the form of larger loans to parents than to students.[42]

Multiple Factors Considered

It is important to examine on an all-other-things-equal basis the factors associated with whether children and/or their parents face accumulated debt from students' undergraduate educations. Our results are shown in two logistic regressions in Table 7.1. We begin by examining an NSCE student's chances of taking out a loan to help finance college. The results in the first column indicate that student type continues to affect whether undergraduates borrow. Not surprisingly, given their lower net costs, in-state public college students have 65 percent lower odds of borrowing than do private university students. Relative to students at private institutions, out-of-state public college students have 49 percent lower odds of

---

[42] This outcome may occur because the federal government's Plus Loan program allows parents to borrow as much as the total cost of their children's education minus any financial aid received, while students face the same federal caps on Stafford and Perkins loans regardless of their college costs (U.S. Department of Education, 2006).

TABLE 7.1

Odds Ratio Results for the Likelihood That Students or Their Families Have Loans to Repay at the End of NSCE Students' Undergraduate Education NSCE Matriculant Sample: 1980s, 1993, and 1997 Cohorts Combined

Predictor Variables	Student Acquires Debt	Parent or Other Relative of Student Acquires Debt
Type of Student		
In-State Students, Public Colleges	0.35***	0.53**
Out-of-State Students, Public Colleges	0.51***	0.52**
(Students at Private Colleges)	—	—
Socioeconomic Status		
Upper Class	0.01***	0.20*
Upper-Middle Class	0.26***	0.75
(Middle Class)	—	—
Working Class	3.49***	0.55*
Lower Class	5.41***	0.20***
Race		
(White)	—	—
Black	2.19***	1.63**
Hispanic	1.99***	1.57**
Asian	0.88	1.37
Cohort		
(1980s Cohort)	—	—
1993 Cohort	1.37*	1.42
1997 Cohort	1.38*	1.37
Immigrant Generation[a]		
First	1.07	0.71
Second	1.06	0.64*
Third	0.71*	0.91
(Fourth and Higher)	—	—
First-Generation College Student[b]		
Yes	1.48*	1.62*
(No)	—	—
Unknown	0.23	5.95
Gender		
(Male)	—	—
Female	1.17	0.90

(Continued)

TABLE 7.1 (*Continued*)

Predictor Variables	Student Acquires Debt	Parent or Other Relative of Student Acquires Debt
Number of Household Members[c]		
(Four or Fewer)	—	—
Five or More	1.63***	1.06
Unknown	1.01	0.05
Two Parents in Same Household[d]		
(Yes)	—	—
No	1.60**	0.80
Unknown	0.62	1.02
SAT Score[e]		
<1000	1.17	0.82
1000–1099	1.03	1.52
1100–1199	0.91	1.13
(1200–1299)	—	—
1300–1399	0.81	1.17
1400–1499	0.94	0.99
1500–1600	0.91	0.83
Unknown	1.71	0.38**
Number of Cases	6,350	6,350
F (df$_1$, df$_2$)	23.24 (28, 6,203)	4.5 (28, 6,203)
Prob > F	0.0000	0.0000

Source: National Study of College Experience.

Note: Reference categories are in parentheses.

[a]First-generation immigrants include students born outside America's fifty states and Washington, D.C., to at least one foreign-born parent. Second-generation immigrants comprise students born in the United States to at least one foreign-born parent. Third-generation immigrants are born in the United States to U.S.-born parents but have at least one foreign-born grandparent. Individuals counted as fourth-generation immigrants or higher are born in the United States to two U.S.-born parents and four U.S.-born grandparents.

[b]First-generation college students are students who reported they were the first in their immediate family (including grandparents, parents, and siblings) to go to a four-year college.

[c]Number of household members comprises all individuals who were members of the household during the respondent's senior year of high school, including those away at college.

[d]Students living with both of their parents in the same household during their senior year of high school are placed in the "Yes" category. Students in any other type of known parental arrangement are placed in the "No" category.

[e]SAT scores are based on institutional data and ETS score reports. All SAT scores reflect the re-centering that occurred in 1995. Students who lacked SAT scores but possessed ACT scores had an SAT score simulated for them using an ACT-SAT conversion chart.

*$p < .05$ **$p < .01$ ***$p < .001$

acquiring educational debt. Social class is inversely related to the likelihood that an individual student will accumulate college debt. Upper- and upper-middle-class students' odds of having debt are 99 and 74 percent lower, respectively, than those for middle-class students. Meanwhile, working- and lower-class graduates have 249 and 441 percent greater odds of loan obligations, respectively, than do their middle-class counterparts. These regression results are completely consistent with the patterns observed in Figure 7.10. Race is associated with the chances that students will have loan obligations. Within the same social class, both black and Hispanic students are roughly twice as likely as whites to take on debt.[43] In addition, the odds of having to repay loans are higher among more recent graduates,[44] first-generation college students, students from large families, and graduates who did not live with two parents in the same household during their senior year of high school.[45]

Turning to the second column of Table 7.1, which reveals the likelihood that a parent or other family member assumes debt to help an NSCE student with educational expenses, we find that student type is again an important factor. Parents of students who graduate from public institutions are about half as likely as private school graduates' families to have taken on debt. The odds that families will borrow to help finance their children's undergraduate education are greatest for middle-class parents and then decline toward both ends of the socioeconomic spectrum. Working-class families are 45 percent significantly less likely than middle-class families to borrow on their children's behalf. Both lower- and upper-class families are only one-fifth as likely as middle-class families to borrow to finance a child's undergraduate education. Thus the descriptive results from Figure 7.12, which showed that middle-class families are most likely to take on debt, hold up even when additional

[43] This result may occur partly because social class does not completely capture differences in resources between underrepresented minority students and whites (Conley, 1999). NSCE black and Hispanic matriculants have lower incomes, and particularly lower assets, than do whites of their same social class.

[44] Students' odds of borrowing may have grown in part because the reauthorization of the Higher Education Act in 1992 increased student access to subsidized loans and enabled even those students without perceived need to secure unsubsidized federal loans (J. King, 2005).

[45] Although the association is not statistically significant, the regression results also suggest that matriculants with high SAT scores generally have lower odds of debt than do matriculants with low scores. This pattern may be explained by the fact that high-scoring NSCE students (as well as high-scoring students nationally) are more likely to come from families with high incomes than are students with lower scores (Chaplin and Hannaway, 1998; Rothstein, 2004). Another explanation may be that high-scoring students are more likely to qualify for merit scholarships than are lower-scoring students, thereby reducing their need to borrow.

control variables are introduced. Black and Hispanic families are more likely than white families to resort to borrowing to finance their children's education. The same can be said about the parents of first-generation college students.

The Financial Burden of Attending an Elite College

We gain a better appreciation of the financial burden that college costs impose on students and their families by relating costs and accumulated debt to the ability of families to pay. To measure college affordability or, conversely, relative economic hardship, we have constructed ratios that reflect both the net cost for the first year of college and the total debt from a student's undergraduate career (student plus parental debt) as a proportion, first, of annual family income and then of assets. The results are shown in Table 7.2 and tell two stories. First, financial burden is positively correlated with overall college costs. For example, first-year net costs represent 11 percent of in-state public college students' family income and 17 percent of family income for out-of-state public college students. For students at private colleges, the proportion rises to 28 percent. Second, as SES increases, financial burden generally decreases. Net costs for lower-class students at private universities represent approximately 92 percent of their families' yearly income. In contrast, upper-class private college students' net costs comprise only 13 percent of annual family income. Similar patterns can be observed in the remaining three panels in Table 7.2.

Do student type and social class continue to have a relation to financial burden once we control for other relevant variables? To answer this question we fit four ordinary least squares (OLS) regressions using the financial burden ratios in Table 7.2 as dependent variables. Each OLS regression includes the control variables from Table 7.1. The two debt ratio regressions also control for whether students have some portion of their college loans forgiven in exchange for undertaking certain careers or participating in special programs.[46] The results are shown in Table 7.3.

---

[46] There are many ways in which students can have their educational debt erased. For example, some teachers can be absolved of up to 100 percent of their Stafford loans. Teachers, nurses, medical technicians, law enforcement officers, Vista Corps workers, Peace Corps members, and U.S. Armed Forces personnel can have as much as all of their Perkins loans forgiven (U.S. Department of Education, 2006). AmeriCorps graduates also receive an education award that they can apply toward either their undergraduate student loans or future studies or training (AmeriCorps, 2006). As of 2001–2, forty-three states had also adopted one or more workforce contingent loan forgiveness programs as well (Kirshstein et al., 2004).

TABLE 7.2

Mean Values of Ratios for Net Cost of First Year of College and Total Undergraduate Debt
as a Proportion of Family Income and of Assets

NSCE Matriculant Sample: 1980s, 1993, and 1997 Cohorts Combined

Net Cost and Total Debt Ratios	Total	Lower	Working	Middle	Upper-Middle	Upper
Net Cost of First Year of College Divided by Family Income (N = 5,687)						
In-State Students, Public Colleges (N = 952)	0.11	0.19	0.14	0.12	0.08	0.06
Out-of-State Students, Public Colleges (N = 1,195)	0.17	0.51	0.28	0.18	0.13	0.09
Students at Private Colleges (N = 3,540)	0.28	0.92	0.41	0.33	0.21	0.13
Net Cost of First Year of College Divided by Family Assets (N = 4,563)						
In-State Students, Public Colleges (N = 729)	1.08	1.39	1.72	1.20	0.82	0.21
Out-of-State Students, Public Colleges (N = 916)	1.44	2.83	2.75	2.13	0.72	0.05
Students at Private Colleges (N = 2,918)	2.22	6.84	4.17	3.56	0.76	0.11
Total Debt from College Divided by Family Income (N = 5,035)						
In-State Students, Public Colleges (N = 861)	0.10	0.71	0.35	0.10	0.05	0.01
Out-of-State Students, Public Colleges (N = 1,042)	0.16	1.17	0.39	0.22	0.06	0.01
Students at Private Colleges (N = 3,132)	0.31	1.57	0.74	0.45	0.11	0.01
Total Debt from College Divided by Family Assets (N = 4,101)						
In-State Students, Public Colleges (N = 669)	1.89	8.42	6.91	1.51	0.86	0.04
Out-of-State Students, Public Colleges (N = 808)	2.89	6.77	3.95	4.73	1.60	0.00
Students at Private Colleges (N = 2,624)	3.25	12.24	7.84	5.36	0.53	0.01

Source: National Study of College Experience; 1993 and 1997 FAFSA Data.
Note: Net cost is defined as total cost minus grant and scholarship aid. Total debt includes both the student's and the family's educational debt. Total assets comprise savings and investments but do not include value of family home, businesses, retirement plans, or farms. If students from the 1993 and 1997 cohorts did not report family income or assets in the NSCE survey, we used the income and asset information they provided in their FAFSA form, if available. We adjusted all dollar values to reflect 1996–97 constant dollars before calculating any ratios. The number of observations varies because of missing data.

TABLE 7.3
Regression Results for Net Cost of First Year of College and Total
Undergraduate Debt as a Proportion of Family Income and of Assets
NSCE Matriculant Data: 1980s, 1993, and 1997 Cohorts Combined

Predictor Variables	Net Cost of First Year of College/ Family Income	Net Cost of First Year of College/ Family Assets	Total Debt from College/ Family Income	Total Debt from College/ Family Assets
Type of Student				
In-State Students, Public Colleges	−1.18***	−1.13***	−0.50***	−0.51**
Out-of-State Students, Public Colleges	−0.52***	−0.50***	−0.32***	−0.24
(Private College Students)	—	—	—	—
Socioeconomic Status				
Upper Class	−0.58***	−1.70***	−0.58***	−1.21***
Upper-Middle Class	−0.25***	−1.07***	−0.31**	−0.83***
(Middle Class)	—	—	—	—
Working Class	−0.15	0.31	0.15	1.91***
Lower Class	0.49**	1.21***	1.03***	7.71***
Race				
(White)	—	—	—	—
Black	−0.64***	−0.23	0.10	0.37**
Hispanic	−0.42***	−0.04	0.01	1.94
Asian	−0.02	−0.26	0.07	−0.76
Cohort				
(1980s Cohort)	—	—	—	—
1993 Cohort	0.17*	0.45**	0.11	0.22
1997 Cohort	0.29***	0.67***	0.03	0.20
Immigrant Generation[a]				
First	0.17*	0.13	0.07	0.04
Second	0.09	−0.04	0.00	−0.15
Third	0.06	−0.16	0.05	0.00
(Fourth and Higher)	—	—	—	—
First-Generation College Student[b]				
Yes	0.10	0.10	0.22*	0.23
(No)	—	—	—	—
Unknown	0.42*	1.60	0.99**	−0.69
Gender				
(Male)	—	—	—	—
Female	0.10	0.42***	−0.01	0.10
Number of Household Members[c]				
(Four or Fewer)	—	—	—	—
Five or More	−0.14*	0.12	−0.01	0.07
Unknown	0.15	0.94*	−0.73	−0.10
Two Parents in Same Household[d]				
(Yes)	—	—	—	—
No	0.12	0.06	0.01	0.10
Unknown	−0.03	−0.66	0.46	−0.38

(Continued)

TABLE 7.3 (*Continued*)

Predictor Variables	Net Cost of First Year of College/ Family Income	Net Cost of First Year of College/ Family Assets	Total Debt from College/ Family Income	Total Debt from College/ Family Assets
SAT Score[e]				
Less than 1000	−0.08	−0.26	−0.06	0.25
1000–1099	0.28**	0.17	0.18	0.25
1100–1199	0.09	−0.02	−0.08	−0.02
(1200–1299)	—	—	—	—
1300–1399	−0.03	0.16	−0.06	0.03
1400–1499	−0.19	−0.19	−0.14	0.10
1500–1600	−0.22	−0.04	−0.16	−0.01
Unknown	−0.09	0.15	−0.10	0.06
Some Portion of College Loans Forgiven[f]				
Yes	—	—	0.23	0.73*
(No, but have loans)	—	—	—	—
No loans to forgive	—	—	−4.77***	−5.24***
Unknown	—	—	−0.18	−0.43
Constant	−1.68***	−1.63***	−1.23***	−0.59**
Number of Observations	5,687	4,563	5,035	4,101
R-Squared	0.1503	0.1605	0.8020	0.7254

Source: National Study of College Experience; 1993 and 1997 FAFSA Data.

Note: Net cost is defined as total cost (tuition, fees, room, board, and books) less financial aid in the form of grants and/or scholarships. Total debt includes both the student's and the family's educational debt. If students from the 1993 and 1997 cohorts did not report family income or assets in the NSCE survey, we used the income or asset information they provided in their FAFSA form, if available. We adjusted all dollar values to reflect 1996–97 constant dollars before creating the ratio variables. To address skewness in the dependent variables and the fact that some students reported having no debt upon college graduation, we added .001 to each dependent variable and took the log of it before performing each regression. Results were robust across alternative formulations of the dependent variable, including tobit estimates. Reference categories are in parentheses. Coefficient estimates are derived from ordinary least squares regression.

[a]First-generation immigrants include students born outside America's fifty states and Washington, D.C., to at least one foreign-born parent. Second-generation immigrants comprise students born in the United States to at least one foreign-born parent. Third-generation immigrants are born in the United States to U.S.-born parents but have at least one foreign-born grandparent. Individuals counted as fourth-generation immigrants or higher are born in the United States to two U.S.-born parents and four U.S.-born grandparents.

[b]First-generation college students are students who reported they were the first in their immediate family (including grandparents, parents, and siblings) to go to a four-year college.

[c]Number of household members comprises all individuals who were members of the household during the respondent's senior year of high school, including those away at college.

[d]Students living with both of their parents in the same household during their senior year of high school are placed in the "Yes" category. Students in any other type of known parental arrangement are placed in the "No" category.

[e]SAT scores are based on institutional data and ETS score reports. All SAT scores reflect the re-centering that occurred in 1995. Students who lacked SAT scores but possessed ACT scores had an SAT score simulated for them using an ACT-SAT conversion chart.

[f]The variables in this category are derived from students' responses to whether any portion of their undergraduate loans was forgiven. When these variables are omitted from the regressions examining debt, the results are qualitatively the same although some of the coefficients are larger in absolute value. The regressions examining net cost do not include variables from this category since having loans forgiven after graduation should not affect first-year net cost.

*p < .05 **p < .01 ***p < .001

Net Cost Ratios

Findings pertaining to net cost ratios are completely consistent with patterns observed in Table 7.2. Associations between each relative net cost measure and type of student on the one hand and student's social class on the other are contained in the first two columns of Table 7.3. Other things being equal, the financial burden relative to family income of attending an NSCE institution is smallest for in-state students at public universities. It is somewhat larger for out-of-state students at public universities and greatest for students who enroll at private colleges. Likewise, there is a smooth gradient across social classes in relative net cost burdens. Net cost relative to family income is highest for lower-class students—a burden nearly 50 percent greater than for middle-class students. As students come from successively higher SES backgrounds, their relative net cost of attending college declines. Relative costs faced by students from the upper-middle class are 25 percent below those for middle-class students. If one comes from the highest social class category, the relative burden shrinks to 58 percent below that for students from the middle class.

Conclusions are unchanged when net cost is considered relative to family assets. The only difference is that the relative burden of paying for college is now even more sensitive to changes in socioeconomic status. These results suggest that even though high SES students and their families are faced with higher net costs for college than are low SES families (see Figure 7.9), high SES families experience less economic hardship when paying for college because their greater financial resources enable them to afford these higher costs more easily.

Other student characteristics also shape net cost ratios. Underrepresented minority students face significantly lower cost-to-income ratios than do comparable whites. The relative burden is 64 percent smaller for blacks and 42 percent less for Hispanics.[47] Moreover, there is striking evidence that the affordability of a college education has been declining. Net cost relative to income is 17 percent higher for the 1993 entering cohort than for students who went to college in the 1980s. For students who enrolled as freshmen in 1997, the net cost of the first year in college relative to family income is 29 percent larger than during the 1980s. Parents' and students' ability to afford a college education appears to be declining even faster if financial burden is judged relative to family assets. Students who entered in 1997 faced first-year costs relative to

---

[47] To determine if minority students of all social classes have smaller financial burdens than their white counterparts we ran the two net cost OLS regressions again, this time with race and social class interaction terms. The results indicate that while lower-class minority students enjoy smaller net cost ratios than do whites, high SES minorities generally do not.

assets that are 67 percent higher than those experienced by their 1980s counterparts.

Total Debt Ratios

Relative debt burden is related to student type and to students' social class backgrounds in the same way as relative net cost. The results are shown in the last two columns of Table 7.3, which examine the combined total amount of student and family college debt in relation to ability to pay. Relative debt burden is greatest for students who are enrolled at private colleges and universities and least for students at in-state public institutions. Moreover, debt in relation either to family income or to family assets is largest for students from lower-class backgrounds and smallest for students from families that are the most advantaged. The debt burden placed on low SES students and their families is especially heavy when measured as total debt divided by assets. The total debt/asset ratio for working-class students represents an increase of nearly 200 percent over that for middle-class students. Students from lower-class backgrounds face debt/asset ratios that are roughly 770 percent larger than those confronted by middle-class families. These findings support earlier conclusions based on Table 7.2.[48] However, unlike the case for relative net cost, there is a slight suggestion that black and Hispanic students face higher total debt ratios than comparable white students.[49] Blacks, for example, have average debt/asset ratios that are 37 percent greater than those for whites.[50] In addition, there is only weak evidence that total debt ratios are increasing over time or that college is becoming increasingly unaffordable.[51]

[48] Regressions that include interaction terms between student type and social class indicate that the benefits of attending public institutions as an in-state student are even greater for low and high SES students than the average effects in Table 7.3 suggest.

[49] While black and Hispanic students may generally have greater relative debt burdens than whites, by including race–social class interaction terms in models for total debt ratios, we find that low SES minority students have relative debt burdens that are smaller than those of low SES whites.

[50] Blacks' total debt/asset ratio may be larger than whites' because NSCE blacks have substantially fewer assets than do NSCE whites from the same social class. Differences in total debt and family income between whites and blacks of the same socioeconomic status are not nearly as large. Oliver and Shapiro (1995) and Conley (1999) have also documented that the assets disparity between blacks and whites is much larger than the disparity between these two groups in income.

[51] Although other research suggests that the percentage of Americans with educational loans and the amount of debt people owe have increased dramatically (Project on Student Debt, 2006; Washburn, 2004), these conclusions are not reflected in NSCE data. First, neither the percentage of students with debt nor the percentage of parents with debt has changed significantly between our three cohorts. Second, controlling for inflation, the

Our survey asked students whether any portion of their undergraduate loans was forgiven, perhaps in exchange for services or conditional on post-graduate study. Having loans reduced in this way could also affect students' and families' college indebtedness. The results in Table 7.3 are at once unsurprising and surprising. Students who have no loans to forgive understandably exhibit the lowest debt ratios. But the finding that having some portion of loans absolved is associated with higher debt burdens is counterintuitive. Debt/asset ratios are 73 percent higher for students with debt absolution. The answer lies in the fact that students who have loans forgiven still face several thousand dollars more in total debt than do other indebted students.[52] Further, the differential impact of having loans forgiven on debt/income versus debt/asset ratios is partially explained by the fact that students with loans forgiven have an average of $63,430 less in family assets than do other students with debt. The difference in family income between students with loans absolved and other students with loans is not nearly as great as the difference in assets.

To summarize, on an all-other-things-equal basis, the economic burden that students and their families shoulder to obtain a selective college education depends on whether a student attends a public or private institution, whether he or she is an in-state or out-of-state student, and the family's social class. In-state public college students have the smallest relative burden, followed by out-of-state public college matriculants. Private college students' hardship is on average the greatest. Low SES undergraduates' relative financial burden is larger than that of high SES undergraduates. Other factors that we examined are not as consistently related to the affordability of an elite college education.

SUMMARY

In this chapter we have discussed the total cost and the discounted net cost (total cost minus any grant and scholarship aid) of a selective college education, the ways in which students pay for their undergraduate degrees, and the debt and overall financial burden that result from attending an NSCE college or university. We find first that studying at an academically selective four-year college can be expensive but that the price of an elite education varies substantially depending on where students

---

average total amount indebted NSCE students and their families owe is only slightly greater in the 1997 cohort than in the 1980s cohort ($22,240 versus $21,120, a difference of $1,120).

[52] In addition, most state loan forgiveness programs only relieve students between $2,000 and $5,000 of debt per year of service (Kirshstein et al., 2004: 3).

attend. Students can save thousands of dollars by enrolling in highly se-lective public, rather than highly selective private, universities. They can reduce their costs even more if they attend a public college within their home state. Yet despite these potential cost savings, our data in-dicate that only middle-class students are significantly more likely to en-roll at in-state public colleges than at the other more expensive NSCE institutions.

Second, not all students pay the advertised tuition. Nearly half receive some kind of financial aid. The more limited students' economic resources are, the larger the grants they receive from colleges. The resulting net costs that students face can be several thousand dollars a year less than the prices that colleges publish, with private universities tending to give a larger dollar tuition discount. Even with this reduction, however, private institutions remain NSCE students' most expensive option. Students in every social class face lower net costs at in-state and out-of-state public universities.

Third, students at NSCE institutions use a variety of methods to meet their undergraduate expenses. Those from higher social classes rely pri-marily on family members to fund their degrees, while those of lesser means are more likely to depend principally on grants and scholarships. Given universities' high costs, undergraduates of all socioeconomic back-grounds can meet only a small portion of their expenses on their own by working during college or contributing prior savings. NSCE college ma-triculants who cannot otherwise cover all of their college costs assume debt. Lower SES matriculants and their families use loans to cover a larger fraction of their financial obligations than do families with greater economic resources.

Fourth, the likelihood of borrowing varies by student type and by so-cial class. As the net costs facing students go up so does the probability that they, as well as their relatives, will assume debt. The chances of stu-dents taking out a loan are inversely related to their socioeconomic sta-tus, while the likelihood of students' parents taking out a loan is greatest among middle-class families.

Finally, attending a selective college or university does not represent the same financial sacrifice for all students or their families. The costs for in-state and out-of-state public college matriculants weigh less heavily on their families' economic resources than do the expenses associated with a private institution. Even though low SES students face smaller net college costs than high SES students do, the costs and total debt that low SES matriculants incur from their undergraduate educations represent larger fractions of their families' income and assets than is the case for more af-fluent students. In other words, the grant aid that low SES students receive does not completely make up for their families' lesser means. Relative to their ability to pay, affording an elite education is still most financially burdensome for lower-income families.

The greater financial burden that confronts lower SES students and their families has several potential adverse consequences. It may discourage many lower SES students from applying to academically selective colleges and universities or from enrolling if they are accepted. The high economic cost relative to ability to pay may lead to higher rates of attrition for lower- and working-class students. And the accumulated debt for students who persist through graduation may constrain post-graduate opportunities in ways that higher SES students can ignore.

Chapter Eight

BROADER PERSPECTIVES ON THE SELECTIVE COLLEGE EXPERIENCE

INTRODUCTION

In previous chapters we looked carefully at how race and social class influence who applies and who is admitted to academically selective colleges and universities and how these same factors shape subsequent experiences on campus. In the final three chapters, beginning with this one, we adopt a broader perspective on contemporary issues facing higher education. In this chapter we address four questions. First, which students are the actual beneficiaries of affirmative action in the college admission process? Are these students the same as the intended beneficiaries? Second, selective institutions in higher education rest their defense of race-conscious admission practices on the educational benefits that are expected to flow from diversity. What evidence is there in our data about how much students learn from classmates who belong to racial groups different from their own? Third, how satisfied do students say they are with their undergraduate education? Are there important differences by race or by social class in overall levels of satisfaction? Finally, U.S. society is stratified in so many different ways, and there is evidence, at least as far as income is concerned, that the degree of inequality has increased since the early 1970s (Johnston, 2007). Education has traditionally been viewed as the key to upward mobility. What role do the NSCE institutions play in this process? Do they provide avenues for large numbers of capable, low-income students to advance in society beyond the circumstances of their birth? Or, in sociological language, are they actively engaged in the intergenerational reproduction of inequality? Put somewhat differently, in the words of William Bowen and his colleagues (Bowen, Kurzweil, and Tobin, 2005), do elite colleges and universities function as "engines of opportunity" or as "bastions of privilege"?

AFFIRMATIVE ACTION FOR WHOM?

The story of who gets admitted to academically selective institutions is a story about preferences. As we saw in chapter 3, preferences are extended to students who have high scores on standardized tests, who are recruited athletes or alumni children, who do well academically in high school as reflected by their high school GPA and class rank, and who graduate from secondary schools with outstanding reputations. Significant consideration is also given to members of underrepresented minority groups. At both public and private NSCE schools, the largest race-sensitive preference is associated with black "descendants"—black students in the fourth-or-higher immigrant generation who are not multiracial and who can be considered, to a good first approximation, to be descendants of the American slave population. Next in line are other black candidates—typically those who are first- or second-generation immigrants and/or who are multiracial. Hispanic students also receive an admission bonus. At public universities, this bonus is largest for Hispanics in the third-or-higher immigrant generation, whereas second-generation applicants receive the largest Hispanic preference at the private colleges. Asian students, as we have seen, experience a disadvantage in admission at both public and private institutions when measured on an all-other-things-equal basis. The largest negative impact appears to be concentrated among Asian applicants who are second-generation immigrants.

Racial preferences like these often arouse strong passions. They also point to a controversy within a controversy. One very vocal group is opposed to any kind of race-conscious admission preference. Others are strong advocates. But even among supporters of affirmative action, there are differences of opinion. Many feel that there are important educational benefits from diversity and that all forms of difference, not just racial or ethnic, contribute to a richer intellectual environment on campus. Others who have grown up within a strong civil rights tradition counter that the original intent of affirmative action has been diluted; too many different groups, not all of whom have faced institutionalized discrimination, are now covered by affirmative action.

Opposition to Affirmative Action

All too frequently, debates about affirmative action fail to include a definition of terms. Christopher Edley Jr. (1996), dean of the Boalt Hall Law School at the University of California, Berkeley, has defined affirmative action as "any effort taken to expand opportunity for women or racial, ethnic and national origin minorities by using membership in those groups that have been subject to discrimination as a consideration [in decision making or allocation of resources]" (16–17). A broader definition, which does not include the qualifier that recipient groups have been subject to prior or current discrimination, has been offered by Brest and Oshige (1995: 856): "An affirmative action program seeks to remedy the significant underrepresentation of members of certain racial, ethnic, or other groups through measures that take group membership or identity into account. Such measures range from actively searching for and recruiting members of particular groups to counting group identity as a 'plus' in the admissions or hiring process."

Opposition to affirmative action is often based on the claim that it is illegal because it constitutes reverse discrimination. Jennifer Gratz and Patrick Hamacher, both of whom are white, applied for admission to the University of Michigan's undergraduate program in the mid-1990s. They were both Michigan residents, and although they met the university's standards for admission, they were ultimately rejected. The university used a point system for deciding the vast majority of admission outcomes. Underrepresented minority candidates (including African Americans, Hispanics, and Native Americans) were automatically awarded 20 points of the 100 points necessary to guarantee admission. Gratz and Hamacher subsequently filed suit against the university and its president at the time, Lee Bollinger, claiming that the university's use of racial preferences violated the Equal Protection clause of the Fourteenth Amendment to the Constitution, Title VI of the Civil Rights Act of 1964, and 42 U.S.C. § 1981 (*Gratz v. Bollinger*, 2003).

At about the same time, Barbara Grutter—also a white resident of Michigan—applied for admission to the University of Michigan law school. In contrast to the procedures used by the university's undergraduate admission office, the law school had a more flexible admission policy by which all of a candidate's credentials were evaluated individually and "holistically." Notice was taken of a candidate's racial and ethnic background, along with many other academic and nonacademic factors. Even though Grutter had achieved a 3.8 undergraduate GPA and a LSAT score of 161, she was denied admission. She, too, filed suit against the university and its president, alleging that the Law School gave too much consideration to minority candidates' race. The result, she argued, was that applicants from certain minority backgrounds had a much better chance of being admitted than other students with equivalent academic credentials but who belonged to disfavored racial categories. Her suit was based on the same legal challenges as those of Gratz and Hamacher (*Grutter v. Bollinger*, 2003).

In both of these cases, petitioners' arguments are based on a fairly literal reading of the law. The Thirteenth Amendment, ratified in 1865, abolished slavery once and for all throughout the United States. The Fourteenth Amendment, passed by Congress in 1866 and ratified by the necessary three-fourths of all states in 1868, granted citizenship to recently freed slaves and protected their civil liberties. The key passage is in section 1: "nor shall any State . . . deny to any person within its jurisdiction the equal protection of the laws." The Reconstruction Era proved short-lived, however, and many of the liberties guaranteed by the Fourteenth and Fifteenth Amendments eroded during the next one hundred years. Not until the 1950s and 1960s did equal treatment under the law become reinvigorated (Foner, 2004).[1] Title VI of the 1964 Civil Rights Act provides that, "No person in the United States shall, on the ground of race, color, or national origin, be excluded from participation in, be denied the benefits of, or be subjected to discrimination under any program or activity receiving Federal financial assistance." The qualifier "receiving Federal financial assistance" covers all major colleges and universities (both public and private) that receive federal research dollars, Pell grant assistance, or some other source of federal money. Finally, Title 42 (chapter 21, subchapter I, section 1981) of the U.S. Code contains the following language concerning equal rights: "All persons within the jurisdiction of the United States shall have the same right in every State and Territory . . . to the full and equal benefit of all laws . . . as is enjoyed by white citizens." We turn next to the question of whether any of these apparent prohibitions against discrimination on the basis of racial classifications has any exceptions.[2]

[1] According to Foner (2004), "By the turn of the century, the Fourteenth and Fifteenth Amendments had become dead letters throughout the South. A new racial system had been put in place, resting on the disenfranchisement of black voters, segregation in every area of life, unequal education and job opportunities, and the threat of violent retribution against those who challenged the new order."

[2] In addition to legal arguments, a number of practical considerations have been raised in opposition to affirmative action. First, it is argued that affirmative action in higher education has the effect of boosting minority students into academic environments that are more competitive than is warranted based on their academic achievements. In these environments, underrepresented minority students find it difficult to compete against more talented white and Asian students with the consequence that their academic self-esteem, grades, and class rank suffer by comparison (Sowell, 1972, 1993; Thernstrom and Thernstrom, 1997). Sander (2004) has made this argument in the context of law schools, bar passage rates, and jobs with major law firms. A similar argument has been used to explain the relatively small numbers of black and Hispanic faculty in colleges and universities (Cole and Barber, 2003). Sander's research has been criticized on numerous grounds (for examples, see Ho, 2005; Wilkins, 2005). Bowen and Bok (1998: 59–70) reject this "fit" or "mismatch" hypothesis, pointing out that graduation rates for black students are higher the more selective the college or university they attend. On the other hand, Bowen and Bok (1998: 72–78) find that, controlling for a student's own SAT score and high school grades, class rank is lower when that student attends a more competitive college. The authors conclude, "Competing against fellow students with very strong academic credentials naturally affects one's class rank, even though this disadvantage may well be counterbalanced by other benefits" (73–74). In another test using graduation rates for black and Hispanic students who attended college in the 1980s and early 1990s, the "mismatch" hypothesis has been rejected by Alon and Tienda (2005). Thernstrom and Thernstrom (1999: 1605–8) contend that looking at graduation rates is only half of the picture. How students perform relative to each other for those

Nonremedial Justifications

When it appears that race has been used to deny equal treatment to different groups of individuals, courts have deemed classification on the basis of race a "suspect classification" that is subject to "strict scrutiny." There are two parts to the strict scrutiny test, and both must be met for the racial classification to be considered within the bounds of the law. The first concerns intended goals or aims. The particular activity or program in question must serve a "compelling governmental interest." The second part pertains to the means by which the ends are achieved. The means must be "narrowly tailored" to achieve the stated purpose.

In evaluating both the undergraduate and law school admission practices at the University of Michigan, the Supreme Court in 2003 agreed with Justice Lewis Powell in *Regents of the University of California v. Bakke* (1978). In that case, in an opinion that was interpreted to be the opinion of the Court, Powell believed that racial quotas used by the medical school at the University of California, Davis, to guarantee minority students a minimum number of seats in the first-year class were unconstitutional. At the same time, he argued that race could be used in a flexible manner as one of many factors considered in admission. His underlying contention was that diversity served an educational purpose: "The atmosphere of 'speculation, experiment and creation'—so essential to the quality of higher education—is widely believed to be promoted by a diverse student body" (*Regents of the University of California v. Bakke*, 1978: 312). Moreover, the educational benefits that flow from diversity serve a compelling state interest. The Supreme Court in both *Gratz* and

---

who graduate is also worthy of greater study. See also footnote 8 in chapter 4. Second, opponents have argued that perpetuating affirmative action covers over a more serious problem—lower levels of minority academic achievement—and postpones the day when serious action is taken to remedy it. In arguing against extending affirmative action to all campuses in the University of Wisconsin system, a former member of the Board of Regents said, "[Affirmative action] is cheap and easy, and it makes it look like people are doing something as opposed to spending real money" (Schmidt, 2007b). A similar sentiment has been attributed to Ward Connerly, the moving force behind state ballot initiatives to outlaw affirmative action: "Mr. Connerly is unbothered: If black and Hispanic students are rare at selective universities, the solution is better academic preparation, not special treatment in admissions. 'Every individual should have the same opportunity to compete,' he said. 'I don't worry about the outcomes'" (Lewin, 2007a). Third, in his dissent from the majority opinion in *Grutter*, Justice Clarence Thomas (2003) argued that affirmative action stigmatizes blacks and other beneficiaries of racial preferences (26) and lowers a necessary incentive for hard work and academic preparation because underperforming students believe that affirmative action will give them the necessary edge (30). Finally, Glenn Loury (1997), an economist at Brown University, has argued that affirmative action rewards marginal blacks and harms marginal whites, thereby raising the average credentials of whites and lowering it for blacks. This in turn erodes the perception of black competence.

Grutter agreed with Powell that "student body diversity is a compelling state interest that can justify the use of race in university admissions" (*Grutter v. Bollinger*, 2003: 13).[3]

But as to whether the means used to achieve student body diversity are narrowly tailored, the Court reached different conclusions in *Gratz* and *Grutter*. By a 6–3 majority, the Court in *Gratz v. Bollinger* (2003) decided that the undergraduate admission policy of automatically awarding a certain number of points to minority candidates violated the Equal Protection clause of the Fourteenth Amendment as well as the 1964 Civil Rights Act and Title 42 of the U.S. Code. The Court believed that the policy was too mechanistic and formulaic and therefore not narrowly tailored to achieve the compelling interest of a diverse student body. On the other hand, the law school's more flexible system of considering a candidate's race or ethnicity as one factor among many in a "holistic" evaluation of credentials was judged (by a slim 5–4 majority) to be narrowly tailored and therefore lawful (*Grutter v. Bollinger*, 2003). Consequently, the "diversity rationale" on which colleges and universities have relied since *Bakke* as justification for race-sensitive admission policies (Palmer, 2001) was upheld by the Court in those instances where admission practices are sufficiently nuanced.[4]

Drawing on the numerous amicus briefs submitted to the Court by corporate leaders and military officers, among others, Justice O'Connor introduced another, more pragmatic, rationale for a diverse student body— that it better prepares students for an increasingly diverse workforce and society. O'Connor wrote, "In order to cultivate a set of leaders with legitimacy in the eyes of the citizenry, it is necessary that the *path to leadership* be visibly open to talented and qualified individuals of every race and ethnicity" (*Grutter v. Bollinger*, 2003: 20, emphasis added). Scott Page's (2007) recent work parallels this conclusion. In experiment after experiment, Page found that diverse groups of problem solvers—people with diverse cognitive toolkits—outperformed groups selected on the basis of the

[3]In his dissent, Justice Clarence Thomas argued that the "educational benefits of diversity" do not rise to the customary standard of a compelling state interest. Previously, compelling state interest, or "pressing public necessity" as it is sometimes called, was reserved for cases involving national defense as in the internment of Japanese Americans during World War II (Thomas, 2003: 3). In a related case, the Fifth Circuit ruled in 1996 in *Hopwood v. Texas* (1996) that institutions of higher education do not have a compelling state interest in enrolling a racially diverse student body.

[4]At the same time, some ambivalence about the diversity rationale seemed to characterize the Court. This is reflected not only in the narrowness of the 5–4 majority but also by the suggestion on the part of Justice O'Connor that even this rationale might contain a sunset provision. At the conclusion of the majority's opinion in *Grutter*, O'Connor noted, "We expect that 25 years from now, the use of racial preferences will no longer be necessary to further the interest approved today" (*Grutter v. Bollinger*, 2003: 31).

highest individual ability. He concluded that "diversity trumped ability" (xx). It was corporate leaders who pointed out to him the powerful advantages of identity diversity in the workplace. Two changes have moved corporations in this direction. First, the business world is becoming more global, involving interactions with many different kinds of people from all over the world. Moreover, the nature of work in corporate settings has become more team focused where people need to be able to work with others whose backgrounds are different from their own (xxi).[5]

Remedial Justifications

Even among supporters of affirmative action there is a debate about how far the benefits of racial preferences should extend. Are some people more deserving of the benefits than others? Edley (1996: 173) expresses it succinctly: "The problems of justification and tailoring lead naturally to the question of which groups should be included in affirmative action."

The remedial justification for affirmative action centers on remedying the present effects of past discrimination (Palmer, 2001). This differs from the nonremedial interest, discussed in the previous section, which focuses on promoting the educational benefits of diversity (Palmer, 2001). The Supreme Court has not endorsed a university's taking remedial affirmative action as a way of combating "general societal discrimination." On the other hand, a university may act to remedy the present effects of its *own* past discrimination if there is sufficient evidence for its behavior (Palmer, 2001: 85).[6] Despite the prohibition on affirmative action to remedy general societal discrimination, some legal scholars believe that the remedial justification should be given more weight than the nonremedial

---

[5] A final pragmatic reason to consider race-sensitive admissions has been pointed out by Attewell and Lavin (2007). They show that increasing access to education among disadvantaged students reduces educational gaps in the next generation. Their study is based on interviews with women who entered the City University of New York in the early 1970s under CUNY's open admissions policy. The children of these women were more likely to succeed in school and earn college degrees. In addition, the women were more likely to raise their children in stable two-parent families, to earn higher incomes, to expect their children to go to college, and to be involved in their children's schoolwork. Other pro–affirmative action rationales can be found in Cohen and Sterba (2003), Katznelson (2005), and Wise (2005). A useful history of the challenges to affirmative action at the University of Michigan is contained in Stohr (2004). A wide-ranging review of whether affirmative action improves or impedes efficiency and performance in education, the labor market, and contracting is provided by Holzer and Neumark (2000). Holzer and Neumark (2006) examine the evidence on the costs and benefits of affirmative action from the standpoint of the beneficiaries and society at large.

[6] At other times, the Supreme Court has required universities to take remedial affirmative action to dismantle a de jure segregated system of higher education as in the case of Mississippi (*United States v. Fordice*, 1992).

interest (Edley, 1996: 140).[7] Brest and Oshige (1995) take the argument one step further. They acknowledge the nonremedial interest in affirmative action, and they advance two justifications for remedial action. First, there is the corrective justice argument that "seeks to compensate individuals for wrongful injuries" including wrongful discrimination against members of a group (865, 898). There is also the distributive justice rationale, which argues that disadvantaged groups in society should be prevented from falling below some socioeconomic threshold, whether or not discrimination is the source of their disadvantage (867). These authors conclude, "Notwithstanding the Court's narrow view, we consider affirmative action as a means to social justice as well as for its educational benefits. . . . [A] discussion of a subject of such broad importance ought not be limited to the particular rationales favored at any one time by a particular alliance of justices" (858).

A second axis of the debate turns on who within the remedial justification is entitled to the benefits of race-based preferences. Even though he did not use the phrase "affirmative action," President Lyndon Johnson in his commencement address at Howard University in 1965 laid the groundwork for measures that go beyond ensuring nondiscrimination. Moving beyond freedom to opportunity and ultimately to achievement was the goal. But it was also clear, because of the special character of "Negro poverty," that African Americans were the intended beneficiaries of such measures.

> But freedom is not enough. You do not wipe away the scars of centuries by saying: Now you are free to go where you want, and do as you desire, and choose the leaders you please. You do not take a person who, for years, has been hobbled by chains and liberate him, bring him up to the starting line of a race and then say, "you are free to compete with all the others," and still justly believe that you have been completely fair.
>
> Thus it is not enough just to open the gates of opportunity. All our citizens must have the ability to walk through those gates. This is the next and the more profound stage of the battle for civil rights. We seek not just freedom but opportunity. We seek not just legal equity but human ability, not just equality as a right and a theory but equality as a fact and equality as a result. (Johnson, 1965)

---

[7]Edley's (1996: 52) reasoning is that, "It would be a classic lawyer's error to focus exclusively, or even primarily, on the law—as it is or as it should be. The struggle to define civic norms and values is far broader than that." In a similar vein, he argues, "We would do well, therefore, to put the matter of courts, laws, and litigation to one side. We should focus instead on deciding what we believe to be right, for any given institution and set of circumstances" (159).

An emphasis on past discrimination gives African Americans a special claim to the benefits of remedial affirmative action and sets them apart from other groups (including immigrants) who could demonstrate disadvantage but not necessarily equivalent discrimination (Graham, 2002: 141–42). As Edley (1996) comments, "Social science confirms there is still discrimination against all [racial minorities], but slavery has made for important differences and for an important element shared by almost all African Americans" (xix). Later he concludes, "[T]he voluntarily disadvantaged have a lesser claim on our solicitude if the remedy in question is the morally costly one of race-conscious decision making. All wrongs are not equally compelling" (176). A similar sentiment has been expressed by Brest and Oshige (1995: 899): "African Americans are the paradigmatic group for affirmative action, an extraordinary remedy which was designed to ameliorate the legacy of a history of slavery and pervasive discrimination against them based on their race—a legacy that persists today."[8]

Graham (2001, 2002) has pointed out that in the span of a relatively few years following the mid-1960s, what had been efforts to end discrimination because of race quickly became transformed into affirmative action. Discrimination as the defining eligibility criterion blended into disadvantage. And the number of beneficiary groups expanded to incorporate not just other racial minorities and immigrants but also women, the disabled, and other claimant groups.[9] Not everyone was happy when it appeared that affirmative action programs were losing focus (Graham, 2002: 131–33). Writing in the *Washington Post*, Charles Krauthammer (2001) exclaimed,

> Affirmative action was invented to help blacks as redress for the centuries of state-sponsored slavery and discrimination. But as other groups—women, Hispanics, Native Americans; the list is ever expanding—claimed a piece of the grievance pie, affirmative action molted into "diversity." Diversity is simply the attempt to achieve rainbow representation for its own sake, without any pretense of

[8] Brest and Oshige (1995) also question whether affirmative action should extend to immigrants unless it can be demonstrated that "a group has suffered from discrimination, and its present disadvantaged status is substantially attributable to that discrimination" (874).

[9] According to Graham (2002: 9), "Beginning in 1969 with the Nixon administration, the nondiscrimination provisions were transformed into affirmative action programs benefiting an expanding array of protected class groups. African Americans, the chief beneficiaries of both the intended reforms of 1964–65 and the minority preference programs of the 1970s, were joined as claimants by mobilizing constituencies representing feminists, Hispanics, the disabled, American Indians, and to a lesser extent the aged, Asians, and gays and lesbians. Paralleling this was an effective mobilization by environmentalists and advocates of consumer rights and worker safety. This was America's postwar 'rights revolution.'"

redress or justice. . . . When affirmative action was about justice, it at least had moral force.

A Question of Values

So where does this leave us? We are surrounded by a swirling set of competing claims (Edley, 1996: 40). There are legal principles and laws intended to constrain behavior. There are moral and ethical claims of social justice. Mounting evidence of the educational benefits of campus diversity deserve attention. And so do practical considerations centering on opening up pathways to leadership. In the end, how much weight to accord each of these claims is a question of vision and of one's values (Edley, 1996). Justice O'Connor's majority opinion in *Grutter* attempted to strike a balance among competing claims. Race-sensitive preferences in admissions were upheld for the time being, but with the added expectation they would no longer be needed by 2028. It may not take that long before the Supreme Court has an occasion to revisit these issues.[10]

LEARNING FROM DIFFERENCE

One of the strongest claims made in the literature on diversity in higher education is that there are educational benefits to diversity. Students learn more, their horizons are expanded, and they are forced to think in original and less automatic ways when they live and come into contact with other students whose backgrounds and perspectives differ from their own (Gurin, 2002; Witt, Chang, and Hakuta, 2003). One of the most eloquent statements of this argument has been offered by William G. Bowen,

---

[10] In June 2006 the U.S. Supreme Court agreed to rule on what measures, including considering the race of individual students, local school districts may use to achieve racial integration in public schools (Greenhouse, 2006; Liu, 2007). The cases involve school-choice plans in Seattle, Washington (*Parents Involved in Community Schools v. Seattle School District*, No. 05–908), and Louisville, Kentucky (*Meredith v. Jefferson County Board of Education*, No. 05–915). In commenting on the differences between these cases and the University of Michigan cases, Greenhouse (2006) observed, "The new cases do not ask the court to revisit [*Grutter v. Bollinger*], and the justices are unlikely to do so. But the implications are far-reaching nonetheless. The eventual decision, roughly a year from now, could not only set the court's path in this area but could also shape the climate in which government policies with respect to race will be debated." By a narrow 5–4 decision, the Court ruled in June 2007 that public school systems cannot attempt to achieve racial balance in individual schools by taking account of a student's race, thereby invalidating programs in Seattle and metropolitan Louisville (Greenhouse, 2007).

former president of Princeton University and the Andrew Mellon Foundation. Writing in 1977 as president of Princeton, Bowen contended,

> In a residential college setting, in particular, a great deal of learning occurs informally. It occurs through interactions among students of both sexes; of different races, religions, and backgrounds; who come from cities and rural areas, from various states and countries; who have a wide variety of interests, talents, and perspectives; and who are able, directly or indirectly, to learn from their differences and to stimulate one another to reexamine even their most deeply held assumptions about themselves and their world. As a wise graduate of ours observed in commenting on this aspect of the educational process, "People do not learn very much when they are surrounded only by the likes of themselves."
>
> In the nature of things it is hard to know how, and when, and even if, this informal "learning through diversity" actually occurs. It does not occur for everyone. For many, however, the unplanned, casual encounters with roommates, fellow sufferers in an organic chemistry class, student workers in the library, teammates on a basketball squad, or other participants in class affairs or student government can be subtle and yet powerful sources of improved understanding and personal growth. (1987, 427–28)

Some of the evidence supporting these claims has been cited in earlier chapters.[11] Much of the analysis has been conducted by Patricia Gurin, a social psychologist at the University of Michigan, and her colleagues. Based on their research covering national samples of undergraduates as well as students at the University of Michigan, Gurin (2002) concludes, "It is clear . . . that interaction with peers from diverse racial backgrounds, both in the classroom and informally, is positively associated with a host of what I call 'learning outcomes' . . . [including] engagement in active thinking processes, growth in intellectual engagement and motivation, and growth in intellectual and academic skills." As we noted earlier, this body of scholarly work was relied on by Justice Sandra Day O'Connor when she wrote for the majority in *Grutter v. Bollinger* (2003).

There is a question in the NSCE survey that relates to learning from difference. Early on in the questionnaire, before students had time to form much of an impression about the survey's content or purpose, respondents were asked, "On a scale from 1 to 7 (1 = nothing at all and 7 = a substantial amount), how much have you learned from students of different racial and ethnic backgrounds who attended the same college or

---

[11] See also Orfield (2001), Gurin et al. (2002), and W. Bowen (2007) for affirming views. A contrary position has been taken by Rothman, Lipset, and Nevitte (2003) and Pidot (2006).

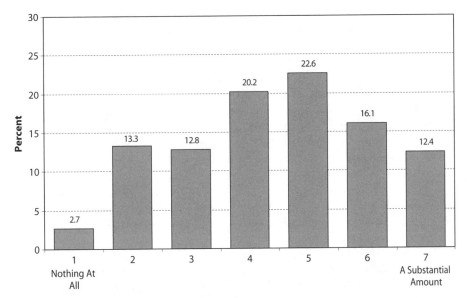

Figure 8.1. How Much Students Learned from Other Students of Different Racial and Ethnic Backgrounds. Note: NSCE Matriculant Sample, Eight Institutions (N = 6,271). Source: National Study of College Experience.

university as yourself?" The range of responses is shown in Figure 8.1 for the nearly 6,300 individuals who answered this question. Fewer than one-third (28 percent) of respondents believe they learned a lot from other students with different racial backgrounds (response categories 6 and 7). An equivalent proportion (29 percent) thought they had learned little or nothing at all (response categories 1, 2, and 3). Close to one-half of all students (43 percent) responded in the middle range of categories (4 and 5), suggesting they felt they had learned something, but neither a lot nor a little, from different kinds of students.[12]

It is difficult to judge from the data presented in Figure 8.1 whether the educational benefits of diversity are large, small, or somewhere in between for students at the NSCE colleges and universities in our study. As we will see later in this chapter when we discuss students' satisfaction with their academic and social experiences in college, responses to these questions are clustered much closer to the positive end of the scale. By contrast, the distribution in Figure 8.1 has more of a bell shape to it—high in the middle and lower at either end.[13]

[12] The mean across all students is between response categories 4 and 5 (an average of 4.45).

[13] Some context is provided by results of a survey conducted in the spring of 2006 among students at the University of California. More than 40 percent of students surveyed

What we can say is that there are statistically significant differences by race, social class, cohort, and type of institution attended in how much students perceive they learned from other students from different racial and ethnic backgrounds. White students, for example, feel they learned the least. Just 26 percent thought they had learned a lot from nonwhite students, while nearly 32 percent responded in one of the three lowest categories. Black students are somewhat more optimistic than whites; 36 percent believe they learned a lot from non-blacks in contrast to 23 percent who say they learned little or nothing. Asian students are similar to blacks—38 percent answered in one of the two highest categories in comparison to 16 percent who fell into one of the three lowest rankings. Hispanic students are far and away the most sanguine about their diversity experiences. Forty-five percent of Hispanics say they learned a lot from their non-Hispanic classmates, while just one in every seven (14 percent) feels they learned little or nothing.[14]

The social class gradient in learning from difference tends to favor students from lower and working classes. For example, 37 percent of lower- and working-class students combined feel they learned a lot from students with different racial backgrounds. This proportion falls monotonically across higher social classes to 29 percent among middle-class students, 26 percent for the upper-middle class, and 23 percent among students from the upper class.[15] Recent cohorts of college students feel they learned more from their other-race peers than do older cohorts. For instance, 31 percent of students who enrolled in NSCE colleges or universities in 1993 or 1997 indicated they learned a lot from other kinds of students in

---

reported that "their understanding of others was often improved through personal interactions with other students who differed from them" (Chatman, 2008: 1).

[14] The attitudes of white students may be partially conditioned by their feelings about affirmative action. Whites may tie a question about "how much you learned from people of other backgrounds" to their feelings on affirmative action in a way that black and Hispanic students might not. In other words, white students, because they feel they are apt to lose the most from affirmative action, may have a higher threshold that needs to be reached to feel that they have learned enough from people of other races for affirmative action to have been "worth it." National polling data lend some support to this speculation. In a February 2003 nationwide Time/CNN survey, taken about the time when the last respondents were completing the NSCE student survey, only 33 percent of white adults said they approve and 55 percent disapproved of "affirmative action admissions programs at colleges and law schools that give racial preferences to minority students" (Roper Center, 2003). On the other hand, 65 percent of black respondents and 60 percent of Hispanic respondents approved of such programs. In the same survey in a question asked only to white adults, 30 percent of respondents said they were either "very" or "somewhat" concerned that "because of affirmative action, you will be passed over for a job or admission to a college."

[15] At the other end of the distribution, just 22 percent of lower- and working-class students together say they learned little or nothing from difference, in contrast to 29 percent of middle-, 30 percent of upper-middle-, and 32 percent of upper-class respondents.

contrast to just 23 percent of students who matriculated in the 1980s. Finally, attending a private college seems to be more conducive to learning from difference than enrolling at a public university. Among students at private NSCE institutions, 37 percent indicated they learned a lot from their other-race classmates, while only one-quarter (24 percent) of students at public institutions feel the same way.[16]

Exploring the Mechanisms

In chapter 5 we explored patterns of cross-racial social interaction among students on NSCE college campuses. We were particularly interested in four kinds of social outcomes—how often students engaged in general socializing with other-race classmates, whether they had an other-race roommate sometime after freshman year, whether one of their five closest friends in college was someone of a different race, and whether they ever dated a college classmate whose racial or ethnic background is different from their own. What we learned there, both from simple descriptive tabulations and from regression analysis, is that white students are more distanced from their nonwhite college classmates than is the case for any other racial group. In other words, white students have a greater tendency than blacks, Asians, or Hispanics to interact exclusively with members of their own racial group. The earlier data suggested that whites are on average 52 percentage points more likely to interact with other white students than with nonwhite students, when the average is taken across all four domains of social interaction. This measure of social isolation falls to 16 percentage points for black students. The patterns are reversed for Asian and Hispanic students. Asians are six percentage points more likely to interact with *non*-Asian students than with other Asians. Hispanics are the most likely to interact with other-race peers. On average, Hispanics are 42 percentage points more likely to interact with *non*-Hispanics than with other Hispanic students.

There is good reason to believe that the amount of social interaction students have with other-race peers is a key factor leading to learning from difference. The sharing and exchanging of ideas and perspectives that are thought to be conducive to learning and the associated challenges to customary modes of thinking cannot happen unless there is sufficient mixing and mingling among students from different backgrounds (Light, 2001). Our data provide strong evidence to support these beliefs. Figure 8.2 examines the relationship between patterns of social interaction and the extent of learning from difference. Arrayed along the horizontal axis are the four types of cross-racial interactions that were

[16]Differences by sex are not statistically significant in a two-way tabulation.

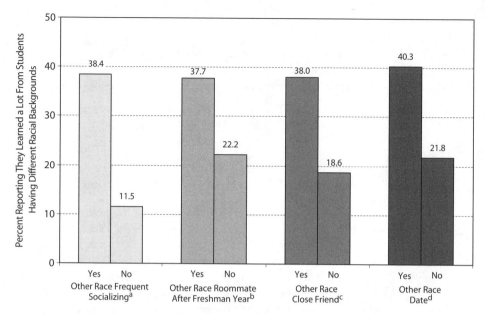

Figure 8.2. Patterns of Social Interaction on Campus and Whether Students Learned a Lot from Diversity. Note: NSCE Matriculant Sample, Eight Institutions (N = 6,271). Learned "a lot" means students responded in one of the two highest categories (a "6" or a "7") in Figure 8.1. The variables for patterns of social interaction are the dependent variables in Table 5.8. All differences between pairs of yes-no responses are significant at the .0001 level. [a] = Socialize often or very often with students of a different race; [b] = Live with a student of a different race after freshman year; [c] = Have a close friendship with a student of a different race; [d] = Date at least one student of a different race. Source: National Study of College Experience.

studied in chapter 5. In each case, students are divided into two groups—those who reported they experienced this type of interaction while in college and those who said they did not. The vertical axis shows the percentage of students in each category who said they acquired a significant amount of learning from their other-race classmates. These are the students who responded with either a "6" or a "7" to the learning-from-difference question shown in Figure 8.1.

The overall patterns are very clear. Students who experienced any of the four types of cross-racial social interaction are much more likely to report a substantial amount of learning from difference than are students who did not engage very much with their other-race classmates. For example, the first bar in Figure 8.2 shows that 38 percent of students who socialized often or very often with peers of a different race reported they learned a lot from these cross-race engagements. By contrast, as shown in the second bar, only 12 percent of students who did not socialize this frequently reported a substantial amount of learning from difference. Strikingly similar differences in learning outcomes between students who engaged with their other-race peers and those who did not are evident for the three remaining types of social interaction. In general, it appears that students with significant amounts of cross-racial interaction while in college are roughly twice as likely to report a substantial amount of learning from their other-race classmates as those who interacted less often with students from other race or ethnic groups. For each of the four types of social interaction, the differences in learning outcomes are highly statistically significant.

It is now apparent why white students feel they learned the least from their other-race peers while in college and why Hispanic students feel they derived the greatest educational benefits from diversity. White students experienced the most racial isolation on NSCE college campuses. Typically, they were more likely to interact with other white students than with nonwhite classmates across the four types of social interaction we have examined. White students' comparatively low levels of interracial social interaction deprive them of the kinds of productive social engagements that promote learning from difference. Hispanic students, on the other hand, are the most likely of any of the four racial-ethnic student groups to exhibit cross-racial versus intra-ethnic social interaction. Given the link between cross-racial engagement and positive reports of learning from difference, it is not surprising that Hispanic respondents are the most likely to believe they learned a lot from classmates with different racial and ethnic backgrounds.[17]

The take-away lesson is evident. When students seize opportunities to interact frequently with their peers from other racial and ethnic backgrounds and when this interaction occurs on more than a casual or superficial level, positive learning experiences can result.[18] Our findings lend support therefore to claims that there are educational benefits to diversity. They provide additional evidence for the conclusion that there is "a wide range of educational benefits when students interact and learn from each other across race and ethnicity" (Bowen, 2007: 21–22). The sobering

[17] Part of the reason why whites are more racially isolated is that only one in five students they pass as they walk through campus is from a different racial or ethnic background. Hispanics, blacks, and Asians have a much greater likelihood of mingling with students who do not share their race because their percentages on campus are much smaller. As shown in Figure 4.1 the racial composition of NSCE matriculants is 78 percent white, 8 percent black, 4 percent Hispanic, and 11 percent Asian.

[18] Allport (1979) has shown that contact with other racial or ethnic groups that is too superficial can reinforce negative stereotypes and not have positive learning outcomes.

and discouraging fact, however, is that not all students open themselves to these opportunities. Among NSCE students 37 percent indicate they never socialized, or did so only rarely or occasionally, with other-race classmates while in college. Half (49 percent) experienced only same-race roommates during college—a proportion that rises to 60 percent when restricted to the period after freshman year when students are typically allowed to choose their own roommate(s). One-half of students (49 percent) also report that none of their five best friends in college was someone from a racial or ethnic background different from their own. Finally, nearly two-thirds of students (64 percent) report never dating someone from a different racial background during college. These numbers leave room for improvement. There is reason to believe that if college and university administrators implemented policies and programs that yielded more cross-race social interaction—especially by white students with their nonwhite classmates—the perceived educational benefits from diversity would increase.

Interactions That Matter Most

Figure 8.2 shows that all four types of cross-racial social engagement can lead to positive learning outcomes. Before leaving this discussion we want to ask whether some types of interracial social encounters are more productive than others. In a regression (not shown) we examined the association between whether a student believed that he or she had learned a lot from diversity and whether the same student experienced any of the types of interracial social interaction shown in Figure 8.2. The regression controlled only for the NSCE institution the student attended. Coefficients on each of the four social interaction variables are positive, confirming the picture in Figure 8.2. However, in only two instances—frequent socializing and interracial dating—are the coefficients statistically significant at the 5 percent level or better.[19] The coefficient on frequent socializing is the largest of the four. Students who report that they socialized often or very often with other-race classmates are more than three times as likely to report a substantial amount of learning from other-race peers.[20]

In a second regression (not shown) we added controls for all of the variables in Table 5.8 as well as for sex, SAT score, high school type, and whether the high school is one of the nation's most elite secondary schools. Several conclusions stand out. First, the effects of the particular types of

[19] These two coefficients are significant at the .000 level. The coefficient on other-race close friend has a p-value of .063.

[20] Odds ratios associated with each type of interracial social interaction are 3.05 (other-race frequent socializing), 1.15 (other-race roommate after freshman year), 1.28 (other-race close friend), and 1.60 (other-race date).

interracial social interaction are largely unchanged from the simpler regression. The coefficients associated with each of the four variables are all positive and have essentially the same magnitudes; only the coefficients on frequent socializing and interracial dating are statistically significant; and frequent socializing with other-race classmates has the largest influence on learning from difference (an odds ratio of 2.9 in contrast to 1.5 for cross-racial dating). Second, students who attend an elite secondary school are only half as likely as other students to report they learned a significant amount from other-race classmates. On the other hand, having a job during freshman year is associated with a 30 percent higher likelihood of reporting significant learning from difference.[21] Third, the effects of race and social class are jointly insignificant. In other words, when members of different race and social class groups have equivalent amounts of cross-racial social interaction on campus, they have roughly the same chance of reporting a significant amount of learning from difference. However, it is precisely because these groups exhibit varying amounts of social distance from each other that they disagree about how much they believe they learned during college from classmates with racial and ethnic origins that differ from their own.[22]

SATISFACTION WITH COLLEGE

College administrators should be, and indeed they are, concerned with how satisfied students are with their undergraduate education. College satisfaction has been linked to lower attrition rates, greater persistence through college, and higher graduation rates (Bowen and Bok,

---

[21] This result is consistent with one reported by Chang, Astin, and Kim (2004), who find that holding an on-campus job has a positive effect on cross-racial interactions.

[22] In addition to the variables mentioned above, two ethnic studies coursework variables—taking a course about members of one's own race and developing an ethnic studies major about another racial group—are positively and significantly (at the 5 percent level) related to learning from difference. These associations suggest a straightforward approach to enhancing the educational benefits of diversity that many institutions are already pursuing as part of creating a more diverse curriculum. With respect to ethnic extracurricular activities, participating in an ethnic activity that honors another race group and belonging to an ethnic organization are both significantly positively related to learning from difference. Neither residential life variable—living in race-focused housing and having a freshman roommate whose race is different from one's own—is significantly related to learning outcomes. At the same time, we cited literature in chapter 5 showing that having a randomly assigned first-year roommate from a racial background different from one's own leads to more interethnic dating, decreased unease with other ethnic groups, and (for white students with a black roommate) more favorable attitudes toward diversity and affirmative action (Boisjoly et al., 2006; Van Laar et al., 2005).

1998: 194; Brown, 2000; Donohue and Wong, 1997).[23] It is also reasonable to suppose that students who are the most satisfied with their college experience will be the ones who are most engaged in alumni activities, most likely to contribute financially to their alma maters, and most willing to recommend their school to prospective students.

Numerous studies have examined the sources of college satisfaction. College satisfaction has been correlated with the variety of campus diversity initiatives (Humphreys, 1998) and opportunities to interact with a broad array of students (Bowen and Bok, 1998: 240). Students who exhibit a high degree of involvement in campus activities (University of Maryland, 1986) and in academic and nonacademic work (Astin, 1999), who give positive reports of their learning and development during college (Pike, 1993), who are highly satisfied with the quality of academic instruction and their social involvement (Einarson and Matier, 2005), and who participate in athletics (Pascarella and Smart, 1991) also tend to be the most satisfied with their undergraduate education. Finally, students who report receiving adequate amounts of financial aid (Taylor and Olswang, 1997), who receive social support and make use of campus resources (Brown, 2000), who have high levels of academic motivation (Donohue and Wong, 1997), and who are the most satisfied with their jobs after college (Pike, 1994) are the ones who report being very satisfied with their college years.

In the NSCE survey, we measured students' satisfaction with two aspects of their undergraduate education—their academic experiences and their social experiences. The degree of satisfaction was measured in both cases on a seven-point scale ranging from 1 (least satisfied) to 7 (most satisfied).

Academic Experience

Respondents were asked how they would evaluate their overall college academic experience. In some cases this retrospective evaluation occurred within a few years of having left college. But for the oldest members of the NSCE study—those who enrolled in college in the early 1980s—this look back may have occurred some fifteen years after graduation. Responses for the more than 6,200 NSCE matriculants who answered this question are shown in Figure 8.3. Overall, former students appear to be highly satisfied with the academic aspects of their undergraduate

[23] Achievement motivation and, for African American students, sources of social support have also been identified as factors related to persistence and college graduation (Brown, 2000; Donohue and Wong, 1997). See also Berger (2001–2) for a review of organizational studies and recommendations for improving the effectiveness of retention efforts on campus.

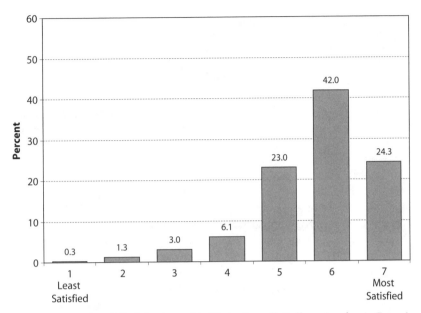

Figure 8.3. Students' Satisfaction with Their Overall College Academic Experience. Note: NSCE Matriculant Sample, Eight Institutions (N = 6,249). Source: National Study of College Experience.

education. Two-thirds of all respondents (more than 66 percent) gave a rating of "6" or "7" to their academic experiences. Even when students evaluated their academic experiences less favorably, the most common response was a "5" rating. Very few students—just one in ten—indicated either ambivalence (a rating of "4") or some degree of dissatisfaction with the overall academic aspects of their undergraduate education. Given the academically elite nature of the institutions in our study and the substantial status and prestige value associated with attending them, it is reassuring to see that most students had highly favorable evaluations of the formal education they received.

As might be expected, however, particular groups of students vary in how enthusiastic they are about their academic experiences during college. Hispanic students are in general the most positive. More than 70 percent report that they are highly satisfied with their overall academic experience.[24] At the other extreme, 55 percent of black students report being highly satisfied. White and Asian students fall in between; 67 percent of white students and 65 percent of Asians give their college academic

---

[24] We consider students who rated their academic or social experiences in college with a "6" or "7" to have been highly satisfied with those experiences.

experiences a highly favorable rating of "6" or "7." Differences by race and ethnicity are statistically significant (at the 5 percent level). Overriding these differences, however, the most important point to take away is that solid majorities of each racial-ethnic group, including African American students, are strongly satisfied with the education they received.

There is a positive and statistically significant relation between social class and satisfaction with academic experiences. Approximately 61 percent of lower- and working-class students combined are highly satisfied with their college academic life. This proportion increases to 63 percent for middle-class students and rises again to 70 percent when upper-middle- and upper-class students are combined. Once again, clear majorities in each social class report being very satisfied with the academic side of college life. On average, students who attended private NSCE institutions report being slightly more satisfied with their academic experiences than do students at public universities, although the differences are small and not statistically significant. Roughly 68 percent of matriculants at private schools and 65 percent of matriculants at public institutions report being highly satisfied with their academics. Students in the middle of our three entering cohorts—those who enrolled in 1993 as opposed to either the 1980s or in 1997—are the most positive about their academic experiences. More than 71 percent of respondents in this entering cohort are highly satisfied with their academic experiences, in contrast to 65 percent of students from the 1980s cohort and 63 percent of respondents in the 1997 cohort. Finally, women in our study are significantly more positive about the academic aspects of their undergraduate education than are men. Nearly 69 percent of women, in comparison to 63 percent of men, are highly satisfied with their academic experiences.

In a regression (not shown), we examined the association between being highly satisfied with one's college academic experience and a variety of explanatory variables.[25] Doing so allows us to control for the potential influence of other factors and to examine the association between overall academic satisfaction and other variables on an all-other-things-equal basis. Many of the descriptive findings reported above are confirmed by the regression analysis. Blacks are 34 percent significantly less likely than whites to be highly satisfied with their overall academic experiences. On the other hand, both upper-middle-class and upper-class stu-

---

[25] Explanatory variables included (dummy) variables for NSCE institution, race, social class, individual student SAT score, average SAT score of the entering college first-year class, cohort, sex, whether first-generation college student, immigrant generation, high school type, whether high school belongs to a group of seventy-two elite U.S. high schools, perceived racial diversity of one's high school, whether student had a job during the first year of college, the percentage of nonwhite students in the entering freshman class, and overall satisfaction with one's college social experience.

dents are significantly more likely than middle-class students to be highly satisfied—33 percent more likely in the former instance and 90 percent more likely in the latter. Women are significantly more likely than men to be satisfied with their academic experiences, while students who matriculated at any of the public institutions in our study are consistently significantly less satisfied on average than are their counterparts at each of the private colleges and universities. One's entering cohort is not significantly related to academic satisfaction, although our descriptive findings showed otherwise. Perhaps not surprisingly, students who are highly satisfied with their overall college social experiences are significantly more likely to report academic satisfaction as well.

Finally, there is a suggestive pattern to the coefficients on individual students' SAT scores and the average SAT score for entering freshmen. Even though these coefficients are not statistically significant, there is a generally positive association between satisfaction with academic aspects of college life and one's own SAT score. Better students, in other words, seem happier with the quality of their academic experiences. At the same time, the negative coefficient on average SAT score for all entering students[26] implies that, controlling for an individual student's academic credentials, students are less satisfied with their overall college academic experience when they attend college with relatively more talented peers—perhaps because their relative class rank suffers. This finding is reminiscent of "frog pond" effects found in other contexts (cf. Espenshade, Hale, and Chung, 2005). For example, in a classic essay, James Davis (1966) found that controlling for individual student academic merit, college-age men were less likely to opt for a high-performance career field the more competitive their college academic environment was. Davis cautioned parents who were sending their sons off to college, "It is better to be a big frog in a small pond than a small frog in a big pond" (31).

Social Experience

NSCE survey respondents were asked a companion question about how satisfied they are with their overall social experience in college. The distribution of responses is shown in Figure 8.4. As was the case with appraisals of college academic experience, students' assessments of their social life in college are heavily concentrated at the most favorable end of the spectrum. Nearly three out of every five (58 percent) respondents give an overall rating of "6" or "7" to social life, indicating they are highly satisfied with their social experience in college. At the same time, this

---

[26] A p-value of .055 suggests that the coefficient is nearly statistically significant at the 5 percent level.

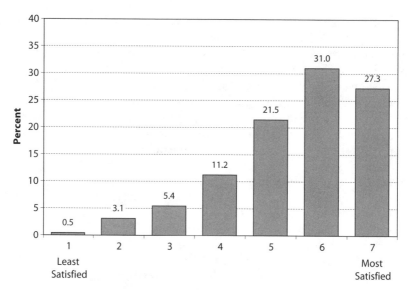

Figure 8.4. Students' Satisfaction with Their Overall College Social Experience. Note: NSCE Matriculant Sample, Eight Institutions (N = 6,207). Source: National Study of College Experience.

solid majority is somewhat less enthusiastic about the social aspects of college life than they are with their academic experiences. Just 10 percent of respondents give their academic experience a rating of "4" or less. By contrast, 20 percent of NSCE respondents give a similar range of scores to their social experience. It is perhaps not too surprising that students at elite academic institutions are more highly satisfied with their overall academic experience than they are with the social side of campus life, especially given the high level of academic talent among the student body and the faculty.

Despite respondents' highly supportive attitudes overall toward social life on campus, some groups of students express higher degrees of satisfaction than others. There are statistically significant differences by race and by social class. Black students express the least amount of satisfaction with their social experience, just as they did with their overall academic experience, and whites display the most satisfaction. Fewer than half (44 percent) of black students are highly satisfied with their overall social experience, in comparison to 60 percent of whites. Clear majorities of Hispanics (57 percent) and Asians (56 percent) are highly satisfied with their social experience. A positive relationship exists between social class and general social satisfaction. As a group, 46 percent of lower- and working-class students are highly satisfied with their social experience in college. This proportion rises to 57 percent for middle-class students and to 62 percent when upper-middle- and upper-class students are combined.[27] It is important to note that in each of these cases, and in every other instance in which the aggregate of all respondents was divided into subgroups, students are more positive about the academic aspects of their undergraduate education than about the social aspects. In other words, the proportion of respondents giving their academic experience a rating of "6" or "7" is consistently greater than the proportion who rated their social experience just as highly.

In a reversal from the pattern for academic experience, a significantly larger fraction of students at public NSCE institutions (61 percent) is highly satisfied with their college social experience than is the case for students at private NSCE colleges and universities (54 percent). Part of the explanation might be the reputation that some public institutions—even academically selective ones—have for being "party" schools. This reversal means that the gap between academic and social satisfaction is particularly large at private schools. At these colleges and universities, there is a difference of 14 percentage points in the proportion of students who are highly satisfied with their academic versus their social experience. At the public institutions, this gap is reduced to just four or five percentage points. Students from the 1993 entering cohort are more satisfied with their social experience than are students in either the earlier or later first-year classes, but the differences are not significant. And in another reversal, men appear to be more highly satisfied than women with their college social experience (60 percent compared to 57 percent), but the difference is not statistically significant.

In a regression (not shown) in which the likelihood of being highly satisfied with one's college social experience is the outcome variable, relatively

[27] To put these findings in perspective, our tabulations from the 2000 General Social Survey—a nationwide survey of more than 2,800 adults—indicate there is a positive correlation between life satisfaction and socioeconomic status. When respondents were asked, "Taken all together, how would you say things are these days?" 28 percent of those with less than a high school degree said they were "very happy," a figure that rises monotonically with more education to 45 percent among those with a graduate degree. When respondents are grouped by a socioeconomic index that reflects occupational prestige, 27 percent of those in the bottom one-sixth of the range said they were "very happy" compared with 42 percent of those in the top one-sixth. An alternative approach that does not rely on global evaluations of one's life but on real-time assessments of one's feelings shows that people with above-average income are barely happier than others in moment-to-moment experience (Kahneman et al., 2006). In a wide-ranging literature review of the relation between income and subjective well-being (SWB), Diener and Biswas-Diener (2002) conclude that more money may increase SWB if it means avoiding poverty or living in a developed country. But over the longer term, more money may have little relation to increasing SWB if most of it is gained by well-off individuals whose material desires rise along with their incomes, a phenomenon commonly referred to as being on a "hedonic treadmill" (Kahneman et al., 2004).

few coefficients are statistically significant at the 5 percent level.[28] Black students are 38 percent significantly less likely than whites to be highly satisfied with their campus social experience. Working-class students are 36 percent significantly less likely than middle-class students to be highly satisfied with their campus social life. In addition, students who held a job during their first year of college are significantly less satisfied with their social life than are students who were not working. Perhaps this difference reflects the possibility that students who are working, including those on financial aid and holding campus jobs, have less time (and money) to participate in social activities on and off campus. As anticipated, students who are satisfied with their academic experience also tend to be highly satisfied with their social life.

It is worth asking why, despite generally high levels of enthusiasm for both their academic and social experiences, NSCE students from less privileged family backgrounds—principally black and lower-income students—are less satisfied with the totality of their college experience than are white students from wealthier circumstances. Perhaps it has something to do with the level of comfort students feel with their college surroundings. Many academically elite institutions radiate affluence. Many were started, or at least substantially sustained, by wealthy white men. As of mid-2006, the eight institutions in our study had a combined endowment approaching $50 billion, or an average of $6.25 billion per institution. In 2006 only six universities in the country had a larger total endowment (Van der Werf, 2007). The unavoidable daily contact with tangible signs of institutional prosperity and the mixing and mingling that goes on between lower- and upper-income classmates can be intimidating to students from less privileged backgrounds (Kaufman, 2001).

The following story told to one of us by our faculty colleague, Miguel Centeno, illustrates the way feelings of disenfranchisement can manifest themselves. The Princeton University Preparatory Program (PUPP) was started in 2001 under the influence and direction of Professor Centeno. PUPP is designed to identify academically talented, low-income students in area high schools near Princeton, New Jersey, and prepare them for admission to academically selective colleges and universities throughout the country. In the summers before their tenth- and eleventh-grade years, students take enriched high school courses at Princeton University and participate in a variety of field trips. The summer prior to senior year includes more coursework plus internships with local businesses and nonprofit organizations. Throughout the program, close contact is main-

---

[28] This regression equation contains the same set of explanatory variables as the regression for academic satisfaction, except that satisfaction with academic life is substituted for satisfaction with social life in the social life equation.

tained with students' high schools, and participants' academic progress is monitored. During the senior year, help and encouragement are offered to PUPP students to guide them through the college application and admission process. At the close of the three-year program there is a "graduation" exercise at Princeton to commemorate successful completion. At the conclusion of one of these exercises, a parent of a PUPP student asked Centeno, "Is it all right now if we sit on the grass?" It is difficult to imagine that students from PUPP families will derive the same satisfaction from their college experience or feel as entitled to all the opportunities college has to offer as a student whose Princeton heritage extends back four or five generations.

Related Studies

Bowen and Bok (1998) use one survey item to gauge satisfaction with undergraduate education. Satisfaction is measured on a five-point scale ranging from very satisfied to very dissatisfied. More than 60 percent of students in the 1976 College and Beyond (C&B) entering cohort and nearly two-thirds of all respondents in the 1989 entering cohort report being "very satisfied" with the undergraduate education they received. Blacks are just four or five percentage points less likely than whites to say they are very satisfied. The black-white difference disappears completely in a regression analysis that is limited to students who graduated from the C&B institution in which they first enrolled. Mooney (2005) has analyzed college satisfaction among juniors in the National Longitudinal Survey of Freshmen, a sample of students who entered C&B institutions in the fall of 1999. To measure satisfaction, Mooney combines answers to three questions in which students were asked to rate on a five-point scale their satisfaction with their intellectual development, their social life, and their overall college experience. In a regression analysis based on more than 2,600 respondents, she finds that blacks have significantly lower evaluations of their overall college experience than do whites—by nearly 0.7 points on a 15-point scale. Asians, too, report that their college satisfaction is less than that of whites—by 0.4 points out of a total of 15 points.[29]

Patterns in the NSCE data are corroborated by responses in 2006 from more than 14,000 seniors at twenty-nine academically selective private colleges and universities. When asked to rate their overall satisfaction with their undergraduate education, 40 percent of these seniors reported they were "very satisfied." Another 49 percent said they were "generally satisfied," and just 5 percent stated they were dissatisfied

---

[29]Both of these race effects are statistically significant at the .01 level.

(Broh, 2007).[30] Blacks and whites define the limits of the racial spectrum with 29 percent of blacks and 43 percent of whites indicating they were very satisfied with their college education. There is a positive association between students' family income and level of satisfaction. Among students with total annual family income less than $75,000, 37 percent said they were very satisfied with their education. This percentage rises to 39 percent for students whose family income is between $75,000 and $150,000, and increases again to 43 percent when annual family income is greater than $150,000.

The 2006 senior survey also asked students to evaluate the quality of their social life on campus, using a four-point scale that ranges across "very dissatisfied," "generally dissatisfied," "generally satisfied," and "very satisfied." Seniors are typically less satisfied with their college social experience than with their undergraduate education overall. Just 30 percent of respondents said they were "very satisfied" with their campus social life. Once again, this percentage is least for black students (21 percent) and greatest for whites (33 percent). In addition, the proportion of students saying they were very satisfied with their social life increases with family income, from 25 percent when income is below $75,000, to 30 percent if income is between $75,000 and $150,000, and to 34 percent if annual family income is greater than $150,000. Data from the 2006 college senior survey reinforce the conclusion drawn from the NSCE student survey that black and lower-income students express lower average levels of satisfaction than do other students when asked to evaluate the years they spent as undergraduates.

A nationwide survey of college seniors that uses a college satisfaction question much like the one employed by Bowen and Bok (1998) has been conducted by the Higher Education Research Institute at UCLA. Approximately 38,000 seniors at more than 125 four-year colleges and universities were asked in 2000 to rate their satisfaction with their "overall

[30] This figure of 40 percent is quite a bit lower than the roughly 60 percent of respondents in the C&B study who said they were "very satisfied" with their undergraduate education (Bowen and Bok, 1998). Several reasons may account for this gap—apart from true differences in overall satisfaction—including a slightly different universe of colleges and universities, different cohorts involved in the analysis, and whether the survey was conducted among current students or among those who were looking back on their undergraduate years with the perspective that experience brings. Perhaps most important, although the two surveys use the same five response categories, the alternatives are not presented in the same order. In the 2006 senior survey, the first-listed choice is "very dissatisfied" and one has to move through four more choices before coming to "very satisfied." In the C&B study, respondents are presented with "very satisfied" as the first alternative. These different orderings may induce C&B respondents to choose "very satisfied" more frequently than do students in the senior survey even if participants in the two surveys are equally well satisfied with their undergraduate education.

college experience" using a four-point scale. Data from the *2000 CIRP College Student Survey* show that 29 percent of seniors were "very satisfied" with their undergraduate experience. Another 54 percent indicated they were "satisfied," and the remaining 17 percent were either "neutral" or "dissatisfied" (Pryor, 2007). This broader and nationally representative cross-section of college seniors is generally less highly satisfied with their undergraduate education than are students who attended the academically selective C&B institutions.

All juniors at six universities (Princeton, Emory, University of Miami, Michigan State, UCLA, and Portland State University) were asked through a Web-based survey in the fall of 2004 to evaluate how satisfied they were in their first two years in college with their overall academic and social experiences. These questions formed part of the Campus Life in America Student Survey (CLASS) project—a study conducted by Princeton University and designed to measure the extent of undergraduates' engagement with diversity experiences and their satisfaction with these experiences. An advantage of comparing our NSCE findings with those from the CLASS project is that identical question wording is used in both surveys to evaluate satisfaction with different aspects of campus life.

In the CLASS data, just over half (52 percent) of respondents said they were highly satisfied with their academic experiences, and an almost identical proportion (53 percent) indicated a high degree of satisfaction with their social experiences. This reported level of satisfaction is less than that exhibited by NSCE respondents. Moreover, CLASS respondents are equally well satisfied with the academic and social dimensions of their undergraduate education, whereas NSCE respondents are more enthusiastic about the academic aspects of college. Differences in satisfaction by race and ethnicity are relatively small in the CLASS data. On the other hand, there are quite large variations by social class. For example, fewer than one-third (31 percent) of lower-class students report being highly satisfied with their social experiences. This proportion rises steadily across successively higher social classes, reaching 63 percent for upper-class students—a span of 32 percentage points. The gap between the proportion of lower- and upper-class students who report a high degree of satisfaction with their academic experiences is half as large—a range of 17 percentage points.

RECYCLING OPPORTUNITY

America is believed to be a land of opportunity—a place where anyone can grow up to be successful regardless of his or her social origins. Scholars debate how true this was in the past (Viadero, 2006b). But it does not seem like an accurate characterization of U.S. society today. The intergenerational reproduction of social inequality is particularly acute in the upper and lower tails of the distribution of income and wealth. In her examination of the intergenerational transmission of wealth inequality, Lisa Keister (2005) finds that 45 percent of those born into families in the lowest quintile of wealth accumulation end up in the lowest quintile as adults. At the other end of the spectrum, 55 percent of individuals born into the top 20 percent of wealthiest families end up in the top 20 percent in their own generation. Correlations are less strong for individuals in the middle quintiles, but they still hover around 35 percent.

Even though the United States has one of the highest percentages among all industrial countries of young people going to college, it also has a relatively low level of equality in terms of overall educational opportunity (Beller and Hout, 2006). Partly as a consequence, the United States occupies a median position in international comparisons of occupation mobility. It ranks even lower when intergenerational income mobility is stressed, falling behind Canada, Finland, Great Britain, Sweden, Norway, and possibly Germany (Beller and Hout, 2006).

The system of elite private secondary and postsecondary education in the United States has been implicated in this process (Bowen, Kurzweil, and Tobin, 2005; Cookson and Persell, 1985; Dickert-Conlin and Rubenstein, 2006).[31] Critics charge that current institutional arrangements distribute advantage to sons and daughters who are already privileged by their parents' status (Golden, 2006; Sacks, 2007b). All too infrequently, it is claimed, do selective institutions provide opportunities for upward social mobility. For example, data from the Higher Education Research Institute at UCLA show that 40 percent of freshmen at the nation's forty-two most selective public universities in 2003 came from families whose annual income exceeded $100,000—up from 32 percent in 1999—at a time when fewer than 20 percent of families overall were making that much (Leonhardt, 2004). UCLA data also show that among the 250 most selective colleges and universities in 2000, 55 percent of entering freshmen came from families in the top quarter of the income distribution compared to only 12 percent who came from the bottom quarter. Just fifteen years earlier, the upper quartile of the income distribution accounted for 46 percent of entering freshmen in contrast to 13 percent of students from the bottom quartile. The squeeze is evidently being felt most by families in the middle two quartiles, whose share of entering freshmen fell from 41 percent in 1985 to 33 percent in 2000 (Leonhardt, 2004). A forty-year review of CIRP data by the Higher Education Research

---

[31] For the most recent research and what can be done about these issues, see Haveman and Smeeding (2006), and McPherson and Schapiro (2006a).

Institute at UCLA shows just how durable these trends have become. In 1971 the median parental income of all college freshmen at four-year institutions was 46 percent higher than the national average. By 2006, parental income of first-year college students exceeded the national average by 60 percent (L. Smith, 2007a).

An analysis by the Chronicle of Higher Education of federal Pell grant data for the academic year 2004–5 reveals that nearly one-third of undergraduates at all four-year colleges and universities were Pell grant recipients, compared to only 14 percent of undergraduates at the nation's wealthiest 59 private colleges and 20 percent of students at the 31 best-endowed public universities (K. Fischer, 2006b). These figures show in another way how institutions of higher education, and the students who attend them, are segregated by income level. Haveman and Smeeding (2006) provide data on how college choice is structured by family income. The children of families making more than $90,000 in 1999–2000 are overrepresented at private, four-year institutions, whereas those whose family income is less than $30,000 are disproportionately concentrated at public, two-year colleges. Selingo and Brainard (2006) argue that the gap between the haves and the have-nots in higher education—among students as well as institutions—is growing. Tendencies to award merit scholarships principally to students from higher-income families have contributed to growing inequality in higher education (Farrell, 2007a). So, too, have rapidly rising tuition costs, determined efforts by successful families to ensure the future success of their children, and a growing emphasis by schools themselves on the financial bottom line (Leonhardt, 2004; Sacks, 2007a).

How are our NSCE institutions doing in this regard? Are they participating, perhaps unwittingly, in the recycling of opportunity from one generation to the next?[32] Or are they creating opportunities for socioeconomically disadvantaged students to enjoy the same intellectual and economic rewards that their more privileged peers receive by attending and graduating from some of the nation's most outstanding colleges and universities? It might be argued that if more than a small dent is going to be made in the current process, it must begin with elite institutions. These are the schools that are in the best position financially to admit more low-income students. And they are also in the enviable position of being able to select from a large pool of qualified applicants and thus to shape an entering class that best meets institutional objectives (Duffy and Goldberg,

---

[32] This phrase is motivated by Robert Shireman's (2002) plea to enroll a more economically diverse freshman class. He points to "a disturbing social stratification in our nation's colleges and universities—both public and private," and urges institutions in a position to do so to encourage upward mobility rather than "recycle prestige."

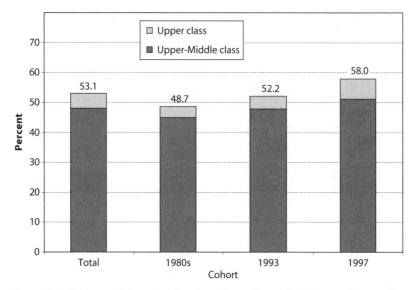

Figure 8.5. Percent of Enrolled Students from Upper-Middle- or Upper-Class Backgrounds, by Cohort. Note: Eight NSCE Institutions (N = 6,350). Source: National Study of College Experience.

1998). There are some hopeful signs. We provided evidence in chapter 3 that private NSCE institutions extend a significant admission bonus to low-income nonwhite students on an all-other-things-equal basis. But is this enough?

Rising Affluence

Figure 8.5 shows the percentage of entering NSCE students who come from upper-middle-class or upper-class families. More than half (53 percent) of freshmen overall are from what we might call privileged backgrounds. What is more important is the trend across the three cohorts. In a relatively short period of time—between the early to mid-1980s and 1997—the proportion of entering NSCE freshmen from upper-middle- or upper-class backgrounds increased from 49 to 58 percent. A growth of six percentage points (from 52 to 58 percent) in the span of just four years between 1993 and 1997 is quite striking.

These aggregate changes have been accompanied by increases in percentages of both upper-middle- and upper-class students. The fraction of upper-middle-class students rose from 45 percent in the 1980s to 48 percent in 1993 and to 51 percent by 1997. The corresponding share of upper-class freshmen increased from almost 4 percent in the 1980s to

7 percent by 1997. This progressive upscaling of entering freshmen cohorts has come at the expense of the middle class, whose share of first-year students dropped from more than 39 percent in the 1980s to 33 percent by 1997. There was also a small decline in the proportion of students from lower- and working-class backgrounds combined—from 12 percent in the earliest cohorts to 9 percent by 1997. This evidence shows clearly that our academically selective NSCE institutions are not immune from trends characterizing many of the nation's top schools. Whether intentionally or not, students at NSCE institutions are being drawn from ever more affluent family circumstances.

These trends characterize both private and public NSCE institutions. If anything, they are more pronounced at public universities—a seeming contradiction to the mandate state-supported institutions have to serve the needs of a broad cross-section of their states' populations. Among private colleges, the proportion of entering freshmen in the top two social classes rose from 52 percent in the 1980s to 59 percent by 1997. Among the public institutions, the corresponding percentages increased from 47 percent in the earliest cohorts to 57 percent in 1997. Within each cohort, the proportion of more privileged students is higher at the private than at the public institutions. But the private-public gap narrowed to just two percentage points by 1997 from roughly five or six percentage points in the 1980s.

The middle class is being squeezed at both the private and public NSCE institutions. Its share of entering first-year students at private colleges declined from 37 to 31 percent between the 1980s and 1997. The corresponding percentage over the same period at public universities fell from 40 to 34 percent. The combined share of lower- and working-class students among entering freshmen at public universities also fell from 13 to 9 percent. At private schools, the combined lower- and working-class proportion showed no trend—rising from 10 to 13 percent and then falling back again to 10 percent in the three successive cohorts.

What is perhaps even more surprising is the fact that rising levels of affluence characterize each of the four racial-ethnic groups. Among white NSCE matriculants, the combined proportion of upper-middle- and upper-class students increased from 51 percent in the 1980s to 63 percent by 1997. Among black students, the growth over the same period is from 17 percent to 28 percent, a relative increase that far outstrips that for white students. The growth in relative numbers of well-to-do blacks is offset by a decline from 40 percent to 29 percent in the combined proportion of lower- and working-class black students. For Hispanic students, 33 percent came from more privileged circumstances in the 1980s in contrast to 38 percent in 1997. And, finally, for Asian students, 53 percent were from the top two social class categories in the 1980s in contrast to

57 percent by the late 1990s. The growing social class stratification that characterizes NSCE students is not confined, as some might suspect, to white and Asian students. Underrepresented minority students are caught up in this trend as well.

Processes Generating Stratification

By the time college freshmen arrive on campus, they have already survived a number of hurdles. They have graduated from high school, applied to college, been admitted to at least one postsecondary institution, and made a decision about where to enroll. Colleges and universities do exert gatekeeping functions. But many of the other decisions that ultimately determine the makeup of the entering first-year class are made by students with the help of their parents, other influential adults, and peers. Some insight into the processes generating the data in Figure 8.5 is captured in Figure 8.6. This figure is based on survey data for students who applied to the seven NSCE institutions that were able to provide information on all applicants and all matriculants for the fall of 1997. It shows the evolving social class composition of NSCE students as they first select themselves into the applicant pool, then as colleges and universities screen these applicants and decide which ones to admit, and finally as students make decisions about whether to enroll in an NSCE institution.

The first bar in Figure 8.6 shows that more than half (52 percent) of the students in the combined applicant pool to seven NSCE institutions in 1997 come from families in the top two social class categories. This is an extraordinarily high proportion. About 5 percent report they are from upper-class backgrounds, and the remaining 47 percent indicate they come from upper-middle-class families. Colleges and universities have some influence in shaping the composition of their applicant pools through a variety of outreach activities, especially to nontraditional feeder schools. But for the most part, a process of self-selection determines who makes their way into the applicant pools at the nation's most selective schools and, for that matter, to postsecondary institutions in general.

The social class backgrounds of students who applied to NSCE institutions are substantially different from those of all applicants to college for the fall of 1997. Data on all entering college students are available from the annual American Freshman Survey conducted by the Higher Education Research Institute at UCLA. These data pertain to all first-time, full-time freshmen at nearly 2,700 postsecondary institutions, including four-year colleges and universities as well as two-year colleges. To a first approximation, matriculants at these institutions represent the pool of high school graduates applying to college. There are striking differences in family income between applicants to NSCE institutions and all college

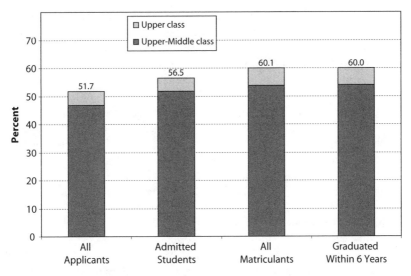

Figure 8.6. Social Class Profile of NSCE Students from Application to College Graduation, 1997 Cohort. Note: Seven NSCE Institutions (N = 3,670). Source: National Study of College Experience.

applicants. Slightly more than one-quarter (28 percent) of NSCE applicants had parents whose annual family income fell below $50,000, in contrast to nearly one-half (47 percent) of all college applicants in 1997. At the other end of the income scale, 18 percent of NSCE applicants reported family incomes of $150,000 or higher in comparison to just 7 percent of college applicants overall (Sax et al., 1997).

Equally sharp differences are apparent in parents' levels of educational attainment. Approximately 12 percent of the fathers of NSCE applicants had no more than a high school education. By contrast, 37 percent of the fathers of all college applicants had a high school diploma or less. On the other hand, one-half (49 percent) of NSCE fathers had earned at least one degree beyond the bachelor's degree (a master's degree, professional school degree, or doctorate), whereas just one-sixth (17 percent) of the fathers of college applicants overall held a graduate degree. Similar differences characterize mothers' level of education. Among mothers of NSCE applicants, 31 percent had a graduate degree in contrast to just 12 percent of all mothers of college applicants (Sax et al., 1997). The fundamental lesson to be drawn from these comparisons is that the most important reason NSCE freshmen come from such privileged social class backgrounds is that students from relatively affluent families are disproportionately represented in the applicant pools at NSCE institutions. For a whole set of reasons, including the perceived cost of attending elite colleges and universities as well as a desire to go to college not too far from home, students from middle- and lower-class backgrounds are less likely to apply to elite schools in the first place (McDonough, 1997).

The second point to observe in Figure 8.6 is that actions by selective college admission deans produce a social class profile for admitted students that is more affluent than that for all applicants. As indicated by the second bar in Figure 8.6, almost 57 percent of all students admitted to the same seven NSCE institutions for the fall of 1997 come from upper-middle- or upper-class families. The only way this can happen is if acceptance rates are positively correlated with an applicant's social class background. This is the case for all seven NSCE schools in the aggregate. At the seven public and private NSCE schools together, acceptance rates in the fall of 1997 were 26 percent for lower- and working-class applicants combined, 33 percent for those in the middle class, and 37 percent for applicants from upper-middle- and upper-class families.

But when the data are disaggregated by private and public institutions, only the private institutions admit a higher percentage of students in higher social class categories. Acceptance rates for the fall of 1997 at public NSCE universities are 52 percent for lower- and working-class applicants combined, 57 percent for middle-class students, and 54 percent when upper-middle- and upper-class applicants are grouped together. At the private colleges and universities, on the other hand, there is a statistically significant positive association between social class and acceptance rates. Just 19 percent of lower-/working-class applicants were accepted, compared with 21 percent of middle-class students, and 27 percent of those from upper-middle-/upper-class backgrounds. We discovered in chapter 3 that private NSCE institutions give an admission preference to lower- and working-class nonwhite students on an all-other-things-equal basis. Although this low SES preference weakens the tendency for selective private colleges to accept a higher proportion of applicants from higher social class categories, it evidently is not strong enough to overcome it.

The final piece of the puzzle in an explanation for the generally high social class backgrounds of NSCE matriculants is contained in the third bar in Figure 8.6. Three-fifths (60 percent) of entering NSCE freshmen come from upper-middle- or upper-class families—a higher proportion than the fraction of more privileged students in either the pool of applicants or admitted students. Once acceptance letters are sent out from NSCE colleges and universities, students in the higher social class categories are more likely to accept those offers and enroll in the first-year class. The rising proportion of NSCE students from upper-middle- or upper-class backgrounds as one moves from application to admission to enrollment is offset by declines in the proportion of students from other social class categories. The proportion of middle-class students, for example, falls from 38 percent of all applicants to 36 percent of admitted students to 32 percent of matriculants. Students from lower- and working-class families combined account for 11 percent of applicants but just 8 percent of admitted and enrolled students.

In short, at each stage in the deliberations—beginning with the decision by students to apply to an NSCE college or university and continuing with actions taken by institutional gatekeepers and finally to enrollment choices by students and their families—the process winnows down the pool of applicants. Those who survive are not just fewer in number. They are also drawn from families that rank progressively higher on the socioeconomic ladder.[33] Students who apply to NSCE institutions are more privileged on average than applicants to all colleges and universities in the country. But NSCE matriculants come from even more affluent backgrounds. In the growing stratification that ensues, selective institutions of higher education are not simply passive observers. The private colleges and universities, at least, are active participants in a process that confers, concentrates, and finally consolidates advantage among the social groups that are already the most well-to-do in American society.[34]

[33] To avoid the possibility that a small amount of double counting in the pool of admitted students might be affecting our results (that is, in a few instances, the same student might have applied to and been accepted by more than one NSCE institution), we double-checked our conclusions against data from the three largest private schools. On a school-by-school basis, we examined the social class profile of applicants, admitted students, and enrolled students. When these results are averaged across the three schools, we find that 49 percent of applicants, 58 percent of admitted students, and 62 percent of entering first-year students come from upper-middle- or upper-class family backgrounds. This pattern is entirely consistent with the data in Figure 8.6.

[34] The only other study of which we are aware that tracks the socioeconomic profile of students along the path from college application to acceptance to matriculation is the one by William Bowen and his colleagues (Bowen, Kurzweil, and Tobin, 2005). They analyze data for the 1995 entering cohort collected from nineteen academically selective colleges and universities—five Ivy League universities, ten academically selective liberal arts colleges, and four flagship state universities. Their measures of socioeconomic status include the proportion of students from low-income families (defined as families in the bottom quartile of the income distribution) and the proportion of students who are the first in their families to attend college (families where neither parent has more than a high school education). They find, as we do, that low SES students are underrepresented at these elite institutions. However, their data indicate that the proportion of socioeconomically disadvantaged students changes relatively little across the pool of applicants, admitted students, and matriculants. They conclude, *"This consistent pattern suggests that socioeconomic status does not affect progression through these stages"* (100, emphasis in the original). By contrast, the NSCE data described earlier in this section show that the shares of middle and low SES students both decline as one moves along the path from application to enrollment. We would conclude from our data that the SES profiles of students are substantially altered as they progress from applicants to matriculants.

The final bar in Figure 8.6 shows the social class composition of students who graduate from their NSCE institutions within six years of matriculating. Sixty percent come from upper-middle- or upper-class backgrounds. This proportion is the same as the one among entering first-year students. Nearly 6 percent of all graduates claim an upper-class family background, while the remaining 54 percent report coming from upper-middle-class circumstances. The progressive upgrading of students' socioeconomic characteristics exhibited by the transition from college application through admission to enrollment is clearly arrested once students begin their college careers. NSCE college graduates are no more privileged on average than their peers with whom they began their college careers. This means that there are no substantial differences between the six-year graduation rates for upper-middle- and upper-class students compared to their lower SES classmates. This is what our data show.[35] Overall, 91 percent of NSCE freshmen at these seven institutions in the fall of 1997 graduated within six years. The corresponding percentages for individual social class categories are 87 percent for lower-class students, 90 percent for the working class, 91 percent for the middle class and upper-middle class, and 85 percent for upper-class students.[36]

Table 8.1 separates the transitions shown in Figure 8.6 into their public-private and racial-ethnic components. Public and private institutions start out at different places in terms of the social class mix of their applicants, but they end up at the same place by the time students graduate. Among public institutions, 57 percent of applicants are either upper-middle or upper class compared to 49 percent of applicants to private colleges and universities. In other words, applicant pools at the private NSCE institutions are characterized by somewhat greater socioeconomic diversity. But 60 percent of both public and private graduating classes contain students from more privileged backgrounds. Convergence in these two pathways arises from actions by admission officers at private colleges and universities whose practices favor applicants from upper-income families. There is essentially no difference between public and private schools in the social class profiles of admitted students. More so

---

[35] As a reminder to readers, the data in Figure 6.1 pointed to a slightly different conclusion. There we showed that overall six-year graduation rates are 89 percent. Rates are approximately 80 percent for lower- and working-class students, as compared to roughly 90 percent for students from middle-class or higher backgrounds. The reason for these differences is that Figure 6.1 is based on data from eight NSCE schools and for the combined 1993 and 1997 entering cohorts.

[36] The story is essentially the same if one uses a four-year instead of a six-year graduation window. Sixty percent of four-year NSCE graduates come from upper-middle-class or upper-class backgrounds. Four-year graduation rates, which are 81 percent overall, include 71 percent for the lower class, 81 percent for the working class, 82 percent for the middle class, 81 percent for the upper-middle class, and 76 percent for upper-class students.

TABLE 8.1
Combined Percentage of Upper-Middle and Upper-Class Students in Successive
Stages of the Application-to-Graduation Process, 1997 Cohort

Category	All Applicants	All Accepted Students	All Matriculants	Graduated within Six Years
All Students	51.7	56.5	60.1	60.0
Public	56.9	56.6	60.9	60.4
Private	49.1	56.3	59.4	59.6
White	57.8	61.1	65.4	64.9
Black	26.0	25.0	27.6	27.7
Hispanic	37.1	38.2	38.3	39.4
Asian	43.2	55.2	56.1	56.2

Source: National Study of College Experience.
Note: Based on seven NSCE institutions.

at private than at public institutions, there is a progressive shedding of students from lower SES backgrounds as one moves from the initial application stage through to college graduation.

When one considers the transitions made by different racial and ethnic groups, the big story is what happens between application and matriculation. There is little further change in social class profiles between enrollment and graduation. The socioeconomic composition of both white and Asian students, which is already tilted toward the upper end of the distribution in the NSCE applicant pool, is further skewed by decisions surrounding admission and matriculation. Among whites, the proportion of more privileged students increases from 58 percent of applicants to 65 percent of enrolled students. The corresponding rise among Asians is from 43 percent to 56 percent, with the largest jump (12 percentage points) determined by who is admitted. The picture is substantially different for underrepresented minority students. Their more modest socioeconomic circumstances compared to whites and Asians are apparent in the applicant pool, and the successive stages of the application-to-matriculation process do little to alter these profiles. Roughly three-quarters of black students and almost two-thirds of Hispanic students in the applicant pool report that they come from lower-, working-, or middle-class backgrounds. The same is true of black and Hispanic matriculants.

These data point to a wide and growing gap between the socioeconomic characteristics of white and Asian students on the one hand and black and Hispanic students on the other. Initial differences in their social class backgrounds are reinforced and magnified as students move from application to admission to enrollment. In short, the socioeconomic stratification along racial and ethnic lines that we find on NSCE college campuses is even greater than what is observed among those who aspire to attend these institutions. This growing divergence in socioeconomic fortunes between white and Asian students versus underrepresented minorities means that blacks and Hispanics are bearing the weight of socioeconomic diversity. It may also serve to reinforce the confluence of race and class stereotypes at the nation's most selective colleges and universities. Finally, these data suggest that more than a few underrepresented minority students may face a double burden on their campuses if they feel they are emblematic of both racial and economic diversity.

Postscript

In response to charges that elite colleges and universities have become "bastions of privilege" rather than "engines of opportunity" (Bowen, Kurzweil, and Tobin, 2005; Kahlenberg, 2004) and that they are losing market share of lower-income students to two-year and for-profit colleges (K. Fischer, 2006b), the nation's top public and private academic institutions have begun more aggressive campaigns to recruit economically disadvantaged students through expanded financial aid programs and outreach activities to identify and attract financially needy students.[37] Many of these efforts have been concentrated at private colleges and universities with substantial endowments (Columbia, Harvard, MIT, Princeton, Smith, Stanford, the University of Pennsylvania, Williams, and Yale, among others).[38] But public flagship universities, including the University of Virginia through its AccessUVa initiative (Tebbs and Turner, 2006; Turner, 2006) and the University of North Carolina through the Carolina Covenant (Brown and Clark, 2006; K. Fischer, 2006b), have also renewed their commitment to lower-income students. Although these programs have had an important symbolic effect, in the judgment of some observers, they have had modest impacts and "done little so far to alter the composition of the student bodies of the nation's elite institutions" (K. Fischer, 2006b).

[37] Expanded outreach activities and financial aid initiatives help lower-income students only at the application and matriculation stages of the college enrollment process. If the admission stage is also contributing to growth in the number of affluent students, as our data suggest it is, then other remedies might also be in order. This topic will be explored further in chapter 9 through simulations of alternative admission policies.

[38] Davidson College announced in March 2007 that it was eliminating loans from its financial aid packages. Starting in August 2007 students with demonstrated financial need will have that need met entirely through grants and student employment. The new initiative is expected to cost $3.5 million annually. Davidson officials believe that they are the first national liberal arts college to eliminate loan debt (Lipka, 2007).

Summary

In this chapter we have considered several broader issues facing elite higher education. First, controversy continues to surround affirmative action in college admission despite the U.S. Supreme Court's 2003 decision in the two University of Michigan cases. Forces opposed to racial preferences have not been silent. Those who believe in the educational benefits of many different kinds of diversity support admission preferences not just for underrepresented minority and low-income students but also for other kinds of applicants who will help create a more heterogeneous campus. Then there are those who feel that the original intent of affirmative action has been diluted by targeting too broad an audience and that the strongest (and perhaps only) preference should be reserved for African Americans who have suffered the most from institutionalized discrimination. How much weight one gives to each of these alternative arguments depends on one's values. The Supreme Court's attempt in *Grutter* to reconcile competing claims might be interpreted as a balancing act in which each party has won at least a partial, but perhaps only provisional, victory.

Second, our survey data provide mixed results when respondents are asked how much they believe they learned in college from classmates whose racial or ethnic background is different from their own. Just as large a proportion (29 percent) feels they learned little or nothing at all as believes they learned a substantial amount (28 percent). There is strong evidence that students are most likely to feel they have learned a lot from diversity when they have taken advantage of opportunities to interact with other-race classmates in a variety of social domains—general socializing, roommate selections, friendship networks, and dating patterns. The sobering realization, however, is that not all students readily grasp these opportunities. White students in particular tend to be the most racially isolated on campus, and in turn they feel they have learned the least from diversity. Hispanic students are at the other end of the spectrum, with respect both to patterns of interracial social interaction and to assessments of how much they learned from difference.

Third, students who attend the nation's most selective colleges and universities are typically more satisfied with their undergraduate education than are students at all four-year institutions. Solid majorities of NSCE students are highly satisfied with both academic and social aspects of their college experience. There are, nevertheless, important differences by race and social class in overall levels of satisfaction. White and Hispanic students display the most positive attitudes about their undergraduate education, while black students are the least enthusiastic. The more pessimistic assessments of black students as compared to whites remain when differences are examined on an all-other-things-equal basis. High SES students are significantly more positive than low SES students about both their academic and social experiences.

Finally, there is a growing tendency for students at all four-year colleges and universities to be drawn from the upper end of the family income distribution. And students who attend the most selective of these institutions are an increasingly privileged subgroup of all college students. A rising share of students at NSCE institutions comes from upper-middle- and upper-class family backgrounds. NSCE applicants exhibit a markedly higher family income profile than do all applicants to U.S. colleges and universities. But the subsequent processes of admission and decisions about where to enroll create an even more well-to-do cast to students who subsequently arrive on campus. Especially at private NSCE institutions, the chances of being admitted are positively correlated with social class background. It would not be an exaggeration to conclude that elite higher education plays an important role in the intergenerational production and maintenance of social inequality in the United States.

Chapter Nine

DO WE STILL NEED AFFIRMATIVE ACTION?

INTRODUCTION

We devoted an entire chapter in this book to understanding how the elite college admission process works. Part of our reason for doing so was to remove some of the mystery and air of apparent secrecy that surrounds these practices (Paul, 1995b; Steinberg, 2002). In this chapter we revisit the subject of college admission, but now we have a different purpose. Here we are interested not so much in what admission practices are but rather in what they could or even should be. Part of the rationale for re-visiting admissions is that this is the ground of greatest contestation. In many instances, disagreement is ignited by a system of admission prefer-ences whereby one candidate is given an edge over another on grounds other than academic performance. Scholars debate the role played by preferences for alumni children (Karabel, 2004; Massey and Mooney, 2007), recruited athletes (Shulman and Bowen, 2001; Bowen and Levin, 2003), and students from upper social classes (Golden, 2006). But the most heated controversy has been reserved for admission preferences for members of underrepresented minority groups. Even though the Supreme Court's ruling in 2003 appeared to resolve these issues, at least for the time being, forces opposed to race-conscious admission practices have not been quiet.

In addition, elite college admission deans and their staffs exercise enor-mous power and influence over the lives of aspiring college matriculants. Even though the stages that lead from college application to admission, to enrollment, and finally to graduation are influenced much more by in-dividual decisions and behaviors of thousands upon thousands of young people and their parents, institutional actors play a larger role than any comparable number of students and parents. Likewise, it is far easier for a small number of highly selective colleges and universities to alter their admission practices than to expect myriad individual families to lead a reform movement.

Some opponents of affirmative action have sought to accomplish through public referenda what they have been unable to achieve in the courts. The use of affirmative action in public education, employment, and contracting was banned by voters in California in 1996 (Proposition 209) and in Washington in 1998 (Initiative 200). More recently, voters in Michigan in November 2006 overwhelmingly approved Proposal 2, known as the Michigan Civil Rights Initiative. Proposal 2 amends Michigan's state constitution by prohibiting state agencies and institutions, including public universities, from operating programs that grant preferences based on race, color, ethnicity, national origin, or gender (Schmidt, 2006b). These new policies took effect in December 2006, midway through the admission season, thereby creating two distinctly different admission systems for students entering Michigan State University, Wayne State University, and the University of Michigan in the fall of 2007 (June and Schmidt, 2007). Supporters of these ballot initiatives have targeted nine other states (Arizona, Colorado, Missouri, Nebraska, Nevada, Oregon, South Dakota, Utah, and Wyoming) for a kind of "Super Tuesday" referendum in November 2008 (Schmidt, 2007a).[1]

These recent developments and the prospect of further constrictions raise the question of where do we go from here in terms of outreach, recruitment, and admission policies. They have driven public institutions into a search for alternatives—alternatives that are at once race-neutral and that preserve racial and ethnic diversity on their campuses.[2] The Law School at Wayne State University, for example, has adopted a new policy that lets admission officers give extra consideration to students who have grown up on an Indian reservation or in Detroit, whose population is largely black, or have overcome disadvantage. Other schools are focusing on the educational pipeline, including targeting mostly minority high schools, using more minority recruiters, and establishing summer preparatory programs for talented students from disadvantaged high schools. Ohio State University has begun a magnet school that concentrates on math and science to prepare potential applicants. It is also establishing stronger ties to poorer students as early as the elementary grades to begin the planning process for college (Lewin, 2007a).

The controversial nature of race-sensitive admission practices at elite colleges and universities prompts two questions. What are the conse-

---

[1]Nebraska was the only state to approve the ballot initiative in November 2008. It was narrowly defeated in Colorado. Supporters failed to obtain enough valid petition signatures in Arizona, Missouri, and Oklahoma. Ward Connerly's group, the American Civil Rights Coalition, had earlier opted to suspend its efforts in the remaining states (Wiedeman, 2008a, 2008b).

[2]The vice-provost at the University of Missouri was quoted as saying, "Just this morning, we had a conversation along the line of how we would continue to ensure diversity at our campus if we could not consider race." And Mary Sue Coleman, president of the University of Michigan and a champion of affirmative action, said, "Of course, you want to look at family income, and being the first in the family to attend college and those kinds of factors, of course we do that, but it doesn't get us to a racially diverse student body" (Lewin, 2007a).

quences of alternative admission policies for the racial and social class backgrounds of admitted students and for their academic qualifications? In addition, are there policies that do not take race into account that can nevertheless maintain the same racial/ethnic composition of admitted students that exists under race-based admission practices?[3] A useful way to address these questions is through the use of microsimulation. Microsimulation is a modeling strategy that allows users to answer a number of "what-if" questions. In this chapter we explore the impacts of a number of different (and hypothetical) admission policies on the race-ethnic, social class, and academic performance characteristics of the admitted student population at seven NSCE institutions.

Initially, we consider the implications of removing the positive admission preferences for black and Hispanic candidates, holding everything else constant. This qualifier is important, because in practice both students and institutions are likely to react to a change in incentives signaled by the elimination of affirmation action. Minority students may have a lower tendency to apply to an institution that no longer appears as committed to attracting a diverse student body. Incentives for white and Asian candidates may also be rearranged. Yield rates could be affected if admitted minority students are more likely to want to attend a college where there is a larger critical mass of students of color. At the institutional level, universities that are required not to consider race in admissions, but that are nevertheless committed to educating students from all backgrounds, may change the admission weights attached to various applicant characteristics in an effort to preserve minority enrollments. In our simulation exercises we ignore these second-order effects and concentrate on the initial impact of a change in admission policies on characteristics of admitted students, holding the composition of the applicant pool constant. The outcomes of these first-round impacts offer a good guide as to how students and universities are likely to react.[4]

---

[3] One could easily imagine that a change in admission strategies might be evaluated along a number of dimensions, including a college's bottom-line financial situation, long-run prospects for raising money from alumni, an institution's ranking in *U.S. News & World Report*, or the performance of its athletic teams. But the impact on the number of underrepresented minority students is often privileged in these debates. As Carnevale and Rose (2004: 154) observe, "[A]ffirmative action defines the policy debate over admissions to selective colleges. All other proposals for expanding access and choice are measured by their implications for affirmative action. As a result, any discussion of selective college admission gets hopelessly entangled in a thicket of race, partisan politics, and idealism. Opposition to affirmative action has become a bottleneck for exploring the role of socioeconomic status, or other nonracial categories of disadvantage, in admissions."

[4] Potential effects on students' application behaviors have been noted by Bowen and Bok (1998), Conrad (1999), and Klitgaard (1985); on yield rates by Bowen and Bok (1998), Conrad (1999), and Dugan et al. (1996); and on institutional response mechanisms by

Our findings are based on regressions for public and private institutions that incorporate interaction effects between race and social class (see Table 3.4). These are our preferred models for understanding the roles played by a variety of student characteristics and qualifications in the elite college admission process. In the results that follow, the effects of alternative admission policies are captured by adjusting the weights attached to different admission criteria. Doing so effectively means we are examining potential changes in how applicants are evaluated for admission, not changes in the applicant pool itself. Later in this chapter we will explore the impact of a different profile to the student applicant pool by assuming that society has succeeded in closing the academic achievement gap between underrepresented minority students on the one hand and white applicants on the other. The microsimulation results discussed here are the most comprehensive of any we know, not only in terms of the scope of alternative admission policies that are considered but also with respect to the range and level of disaggregation employed for students' characteristics.[5]

Fryer, Loury, and Yuret (2007) and Guerrero (2002). There is some evidence that these are more than just theoretical possibilities. Mark Long (2004a) finds that after the elimination of affirmative action, black and Hispanic students in California and Texas are predicted to send fewer SAT-score reports to top-tier in-state public institutions, while white and Asian American students are predicted to send more. On the other hand, Card and Krueger (2004) find no change in the tendency of highly qualified underrepresented minority students to send their SAT scores to the most selective public colleges and universities in either Texas or California. Other features of the application process were also unaffected by the elimination of affirmative action, including the number of schools to which scores were sent and the lower bound on the quality of such schools. In the state of Washington in the fall of 1999, the year after the passage of public referendum I-200 that prohibited government "from discriminating or granting preferential treatment based on race, sex, color, ethnicity or national origin in public employment, education, and contracting," the number of minority freshmen and the transition rate from high school to college fell from the fall of 1998 by more than 25 percent for black students and by roughly 40 percent for Hispanics. These impacts were felt almost entirely at the University of Washington, the flagship public institution. While some of the change can be attributable to a change in admission policies, most of the decline was due to fewer applications from minority students (Brown and Hirschman, 2006). Institutional response mechanisms have been registered in California. Following the University of California Regents' decision in 1995 ending affirmative action, the faculty at the University of California, Berkeley, law school voted to downgrade the importance attached to LSAT scores and other indicators of academic preparedness from "greatest" to "substantial" weight (Guerrero, 2002: 91–92).

[5] The microsimulation results are derived from models 3 and 6 in Table 3.4 for public and private institutions, respectively. The methodology follows one used by Mark Long (2004b). Each observation used to estimate the regression model in Table 3.4 is passed through the model and a probability of college admission is estimated. The predicted probability is multiplied by that observation's sampling weight to derive the expected number of admitted students with that set of characteristics. The total number of admitted students under each

ELIMINATING AFFIRMATIVE ACTION

Table 9.1 shows the expected effects of eliminating affirmative action at private NSCE colleges and universities.[6] The first two panels reflect observed baseline data under race-based policies in effect in 1997. Private institutions received 51,836 applications for the 1997 entering cohort. Of these, 12,233 were accepted, resulting in an average acceptance rate of 23.6 percent.[7] The third panel indicates the expected outcome if admission strategies are altered to remove the positive preferences for black and Hispanic candidates. Everything else is kept the same, including the lower acceptance rate for Asian applicants compared to whites. A comparison of characteristics of the admitted student population under current policy (the second panel) with characteristics assuming no affirmative action (the third panel) suggests both the direction and magnitude of the effect of a policy that no longer gives extra weight in admission to members of underrepresented minority groups.[8]

---

simulation is controlled to the observed number accepted under current policy in 1997. Separate control totals for private and public institutions are matched by adjusting the constant term in the underlying logistic regression equation in cases where the predicted number of admitted students is too high or too low. The average SAT score for the admitted class is based on observed SAT scores and an ACT score-to-SAT score conversion table if only an ACT score is known. Guy Orcutt (1957; Orcutt et al., 1961), an economist at the University of Wisconsin, pioneered the use of microsimulation as a policy analysis tool.

[6] Text tables provide summary tabulations, with an emphasis on private colleges and universities. More detailed information for private and public NSCE institutions is contained in Tables C.9.1–C.9.11. The effects of implementing the same admission policies are generally milder at public institutions than at private ones, except for the adoption of top 10 percent plans. This result parallels the conclusion in Bowen and Bok (1998: 41) that the impact of eliminating affirmative action on the racial profile of enrolled students is greatest at the nation's most academically selective institutions and falls as institutional selectivity declines. This result may be related to the fact that the most selective institutions have the largest number of applicants relative to the number of seats in the first-year class. They therefore have the greatest room to maneuver in terms of giving preferential treatment to various subgroups of the applicant pool to shape an entering class that best meets institutional objectives.

[7] These numbers differ slightly from those shown in Table 3.2 because the simulation tables are based only on the sample observations used to estimate models 3 and 6 in Table 3.4. Model 3 is estimated from 977 cases, 56 fewer than the total of 1,033 cases in the application sample for public institutions. Model 6 is based on 2,765 observations, 31 fewer than the total sample of 2,796 at private colleges and universities.

[8] It is customary among some economists to compare simulated effects of alternative scenarios with the *simulated* baseline or current policy instead of the actual observed outcomes. But in our case the simulated number of accepted students is identical to the actual number under current policy. Moreover, for all variables that are used as predictor variables in the regression prediction equations in Table 3.4, the simulated distributions match the

TABLE 9.1
Effect of Eliminating Affirmative Action at Private Institutions:
Simulation Results, Fall 1997

			Difference from Observed Baseline Admitted If	
	Observed Baseline Applications	Observed Baseline Admitted	No Affirmative Action[a]	Race-Neutral Admission[b]
Item				
Total	51,836	12,233	0	0
Race (%)				
White	55.7	59.9	4.6	−6.5
Black	6.3	8.3	−4.7	−5.5
Hispanic	7.0	7.9	−2.1	−3.2
Asian	31.0	23.9	2.2	15.1
Social Class (%)				
Lower	1.6	1.6	−0.8	−1.2
Working	10.7	8.3	−2.0	−4.3
Middle	38.0	33.4	−0.4	5.8
Upper-Middle	43.0	49.6	2.5	−0.5
Upper	6.8	7.2	0.7	0.1
Race and Social Class (%)				
Minority, bottom 2 classes	3.5	4.5	−3.3	−3.6
Non-minority, bottom 2 classes	8.8	5.4	0.4	−1.9
Minority, top 3 classes	9.8	11.7	−3.5	−5.1
Non-minority, top 3 classes	78.0	78.4	6.4	10.5
Mean SAT Score	1,340	1,405	5	10

Source. Table C.9.1.

[a]This simulation eliminates preferences for black and Hispanic applicants but keeps the Asian disadvantage.

[b]This simulation removes all consideration of race or ethnicity.

observed data exactly. This includes the distribution of admitted students by race, social class, race combined with social class, high school GPA, and high school class rank, all of which appear in detailed tables in appendix C. The agreement is very good, but not exact, for distributions involving simulated SAT score, which is constructed from a combination of observed SAT and ACT scores. For example, the average observed SAT score among admitted students in Table 9.1 is 1405. The corresponding mean SAT score among admitted students in the simulated baseline results is 1402. For all of these reasons, in our analysis in this chapter we compare the simulated impacts of alternative admission strategies with actual outcomes observed under current policy.

If preferences for minority students were eliminated, acceptance rates for black and Hispanic students—especially for black applicants—would be dramatically reduced. The acceptance rate for blacks could be expected to fall from 31 percent under current policy to 13 percent, reducing the number of black students admitted by more than half. Acceptance rates for Hispanic applicants would also fall, from 27 to 20 percent. Underrepresented minority students currently account for more than 16 percent of admitted students, but this overall share would decline to less than 10 percent with the loss of affirmative action. Blacks would see their share decline the most—from 8 to 4 percent. Hispanics would experience a loss from 8 to 6 percent. White and Asian students gain in almost equal proportions from seats not filled by minority applicants. It is expected outcomes like these that concern proponents of affirmative action. How can academically elite institutions of higher education serve as vehicles for social mobility—to open up "pathways to leadership" in Justice Sandra Day O'Connor's words—if the number of underrepresented minority students at these selective colleges and universities were to become so very small?[9]

Judging from students' social class backgrounds, current admission policies have the effect of creating a more privileged group of students when compared with all applicants. For example, the proportion of students claiming an upper-middle- or upper-class background increases from roughly 50 percent among applicants to nearly 57 percent among admitted students. But with the elimination of affirmative action, the extent of socioeconomic diversity would decline still further. Now 60 percent of admitted students ($= 49.6 + 2.5 + 7.2 + .7$) could be expected to come from at least an upper-middle-class family. Despite these changes, academic qualifications of admitted students would be only slightly affected. For example, average SAT scores—an admittedly simplistic measure of academic merit—could be expected to increase from 1405 under current policy to 1410 without affirmative action.

More striking changes can be expected if admission officers followed a race-neutral policy in which no regard is given to any candidate's race. In this scenario, shown in the last panel of Table 9.1, not only are positive preferences for minority candidates removed but the so-called Asian penalty is removed as well. In this simulation, all regression weights for nonwhite candidates are set equal to those for whites. Alternatively, one could assume that all candidates are white (and keep all of their other

---

[9] Whenever simulation results are presented in this chapter, either in the text or in tables, the terms "minority students" and "underrepresented minority students" are used interchangeably to refer to black and Hispanic students. "Non-minority" is used to mean white and Asian students.

characteristics) and obtain the same result. With these assumptions, acceptance rates for minority students would decline even more—to less than 11 percent for blacks and to 16 percent for Hispanics. Minority shares among admitted students would fall to under 8 percent, less than half their overall proportion under current practice. White applicants would also suffer. Their acceptance rate would drop to 23 percent—less than the average acceptance rate of 24 percent and lower than the white rate under racial affirmative action (25 percent). Asian students would be affected the most. Nearly three out of every ten Asian applicants would be accepted under a race-neutral policy, compared to fewer than two out of every ten in 1997. Asian candidates could be expected to comprise nearly 40 percent of all accepted students, compared to less than 25 percent under current policies.

A race-neutral policy would have hardly any effect on the proportions of students in the top two social classes. But greater compression into the middle class is likely. Correspondingly, the number of admitted students from lower- and working-class backgrounds would decline by more than half. The greater degree of demographic and socioeconomic homogeneity created by a color-blind policy is also suggested by the fact that nearly 90 percent of admitted students could be expected to be non-minority (either white or Asian) and come from one of the three highest social classes. Academic profiles of admitted students would continue to inch upward under a race-neutral policy, with average SAT scores reaching 1415.

These results are broadly consistent with other research. Using nationally representative data, Mark Long (2004b) finds that the share of blacks, Hispanics, and Native Americans among all accepted students at the nation's most elite colleges (those in the top decile) would decline from 11 to 8 percent if admission preferences for these underrepresented minority students were eliminated. At the five College and Beyond (C&B) schools for which they have detailed admissions data, Bowen and Bok (1998) conclude that imposing "race-neutrality" in admissions, that is, assuming that acceptance rates for blacks are the same as those for whites within each SAT range, would reduce the overall black acceptance rate in 1989 from 42 to 13 percent. At the most selective of the C&B schools, imposing the same race-neutral assumptions could be expected to decrease the share of black students among all enrolled students from 8 to 2 percent (Bowen and Bok, 1998). Removing all consideration of race at three top-tier private universities is likely to reduce the share of admitted black and Hispanic students from 17 to 7 percent and to increase the acceptance rate for Asian applicants from 18 to 23 percent (Espenshade and Chung, 2005). Similar consequences for underrepresented minority students could be felt in graduate management education programs

(Dugan et al., 1996) and in American law schools (Sander, 2004; Wightman, 1997).

Conclusions drawn from these hypothetical simulations have been corroborated by several real-world "natural experiments." In at least four states where the use of race-conscious admissions in public higher education has been eliminated by judicial decree, executive or Board of Regents' decisions, or public referenda, one can observe a decline in minority enrollments. Decisions by the University of California Regents in 1995 and California's voters in 1996 to eliminate the use of race in public education had their initial impacts on graduate programs in 1997 and on undergraduate admissions in 1998. The number of underrepresented minority students who were admitted to the University of California, Berkeley, law school declined by 66 percent between 1996 and 1997, from 162 to 55. The number of accepted black applicants fell from 75 to 14, none of whom chose to enroll. The admission of Hispanic candidates declined by 50 percent. Altogether the minority share in the first-year class was reduced from 26 percent in 1994 to 5 percent in 1997 (Guerrero, 2002).

Similar impacts were felt among undergraduate programs. At Berkeley, underrepresented minority students comprised 10 percent of all admitted students in 1998 compared to 23 percent in the previous year. The largest impacts were felt by black students, whose admitted numbers fell by 66 percent (Guerrero, 2002). Acceptance rates for black and Hispanic candidates also declined substantially at UCLA but were offset by small increases for Asian Americans (Committee on Undergraduate Admissions and Relations with Schools, 1999).[10] The general picture is not very different in Washington (Brown and Hirschman, 2006), Texas (Tienda and Niu, 2006), or Florida (Horn and Flores, 2003).[11] The single overarching conclusion from our simulations and these many empirical studies

---

[10] A decade after Proposition 209 was passed, black students made up just 2 percent of the first-year class at UCLA in the fall of 2006 and only 3 percent in the University of California system (Lewin, 2007a).

[11] An analysis of freshmen enrollment patterns at five public flagship institutions in California, Texas, and Florida between 1990 and 2005 shows that black, Hispanic, and white enrollment shares declined following the elimination of racial preferences. Asian shares increased, especially in California (Colburn, Young, and Yellen, 2008). But because these states were also undergoing rapid demographic changes during the same period, it is not clear how much of changing enrollment patterns should be attributed to the loss of race-based affirmative action. Our simulations, shown in Table C.9.7, indicate that both whites and Asians increase their shares among all admitted students at NSCE public institutions when race-neutral admission practices are introduced. But the percentage gains are larger for Asian applicants.

has been appropriately summarized by Kane (1998b: 432): "The proportion of minority students at these [selective] colleges would be extremely low if admissions committees ignored the race or ethnicity of
applicants."[12]

More Weight for Low-Income Students

Anthony Carnevale and Stephen Rose (2004) make a case for including
class-based or economic affirmative action in addition to race-based affirmative action. Today's low-income students are underrepresented not
only in higher education generally but also at the nation's most selective
institutions. At the 146 most competitive four-year colleges and universities, 74 percent of students come from the top quarter of the socioeconomic distribution (based on family income and parental education and
occupation), and 10 percent come from the bottom half of the distribution. Only 3 percent of enrolled students at these academically selective
institutions come from the bottom quarter of the socioeconomic distribution (Carnevale and Rose, 2004). Because it is commonly agreed that
there are social and economic benefits to attending college—benefits that
are accentuated by graduating from an elite institution—students who
have fewer economic advantages to begin with because of their family
circumstances have disproportionately less access to opportunity in their
own generation.

Despite institutional claims that low-income students are already being
given extra consideration in admission (recall the evidence from chapter 3)
and that colleges would like to admit more students from poor and
working-class backgrounds if only their academic backgrounds were
stronger, Carnevale and Rose (2004: 102) argue that "on average the top
146 colleges do not provide a systemic preference [to poor and working-

---

[12] A companion analysis for California has been conducted by Conrad and Sharpe (1996),
who argue that a change in admission policy is likely to change the composition of the applicant pool and to have an adverse effect on yield rates (see also Lomibao, Barreto, and
Pachon, 2004). Florida governor Jeb Bush preemptively implemented an executive order
("One Florida") in 1999 that eliminated the use of race or sex in state employment, government contracting, and higher education. Concurrently, he inaugurated the Talented 20 policy that guaranteed automatic admission to Florida's system of public universities to public
high school graduates who finished in the top 20 percent of their class and completed a required set of academic coursework. This new policy took effect with undergraduate admissions for fall 2000. Roughly one-third of students admitted to the Florida State University
system were Talented 20 students in 2000 and 2001. But systemwide the racial and ethnic
distribution of enrolled students changed relatively little between 1999 and 2000 (Horn
and Flores, 2003).

class students] and could in fact admit far greater numbers of low-income students, including minority students, capable of handling the work." They estimate that there are perhaps as many as 300,000 such students with the ability to complete a bachelor's degree who do not attend a four-year college. These students—the "low-hanging fruit"—should be the first priority in a policy to increase socioeconomic diversity in four-year institutions (136).

Bowen, Kurzweil, and Tobin (2005: 161) are also concerned with ways that elite colleges and universities could "do more, at the institutional level, to address the disadvantages associated with low socioeconomic status." Their proposed solution, like that of Carnevale and Rose, is to increase preferences for students from lower social classes while maintaining current admission practices regarding underrepresented minority groups. They cite four reasons to give more admission weight to low-income candidates: (1) because this group of students is substantially underrepresented at selective institutions, increasing their numbers would expand the educational benefits of diversity; (2) it would open up additional pathways to mobility and opportunity in the same way that race-conscious affirmative action does; (3) students who have worked hard to overcome disadvantage and present themselves as credible candidates for admission deserve extra consideration; and (4) poor and working-class students do not underperform academically in the same way that other groups of students do. Implementing both class- and race-based preferences would therefore help tilt the balance at academically selective colleges and universities away from institutions that are "bastions of privilege" toward ones that are "engines of mobility and opportunity" (Bowen, Kurzweil, and Tobin, 2005).

Table 9.2 contains our simulations of the impact of three alternative admission policies at private colleges and universities designed to give more weight to low-income applicants. It is assumed in each simulation that race-based affirmative action remains in effect. In the first simulation (shown in the second panel) the emphasis placed on candidates from lower-class backgrounds is magnified by equating it to the weight currently accorded black applicants. More weight is also given to working-class applicants by equating their preference with that of Hispanic candidates. By assigning the greatest social class consideration to members of the bottom two groups, this admission strategy produces substantially more socioeconomic diversity. The share of admitted students from lower- and working-class families more than doubles, from 10 percent under current policy to 21 percent. Giving low-income applicants more weight also increases racial diversity. The proportion of admitted students who are nonwhite rises from 40 to 43 percent, with the principal gains accruing to black and Hispanic students.

TABLE 9.2
Effect of Giving More Weight to Low-Income Students at Private Institutions:
Simulation Results, Fall 1997

		Difference from Observed Baseline Admitted If		
Item	Observed Baseline Admitted	Substitute Black and Hispanic Weights for Lower and Working Classes	Substitute Legacy Weight for Lower Class[a]	Substitute Legacy Weight for Lower and Working Classes[a]
Total	12,233	0	0	0
Race (%)				
White	59.9	−2.4	−0.4	−2.7
Black	8.3	1.0	0.2	1.2
Hispanic	7.9	0.9	0.1	1.1
Asian	23.9	0.4	0.1	0.4
Social Class (%)				
Lower	1.6	3.6	3.2	2.9
Working	8.3	7.2	−0.3	8.7
Middle	33.4	−4.1	−1.1	−4.4
Upper-Middle	49.6	−5.8	−1.6	−6.3
Upper	7.2	−1.0	−0.3	−1.1
Race and Social Class (%)				
Minority, bottom 2 classes	4.5	3.3	0.6	3.7
Non-minority, bottom 2 classes	5.4	7.5	2.3	7.9
Minority, top 3 classes	11.7	−1.3	−0.3	−1.4
Non-minority, top 3 classes	78.4	−9.5	−2.5	−10.2
Mean SAT Score	1,405	−17	−7	−19

Source: Table C.9.2.
[a]The legacy weight, equivalent to an odds ratio of 2.858, is based on an estimate for the 1997 cohort in the work by Espenshade, Chung, and Walling (2004, Table 7, p. 1442).

Economic affirmative action has a large impact on poorer non-minority applicants. Minority students in the bottom two social classes increase their share of admitted students from roughly 5 to 8 percent. However, a larger increase is registered by lower- and working-class white and Asian applicants, whose share of the total grows from 5 to 13 percent. This increase is substantial enough that it is no longer as likely to appear to the casual observer that minority students make up the lion's share of the low-income population on campus.[13] The growth in the number of admitted students from modest economic circumstances is also large enough to reverse the positive association between social class and acceptance rates. Under a broad policy of class-based affirmative action that gives as much weight to students from lower- and working-class families as is now being given to underrepresented minority students, acceptance rates are greatest for students in the lowest socioeconomic categories.[14] Offsetting these gains, the share of white and Asian students in the top three social classes falls by roughly ten percentage points. In addition, giving this much extra admission weight to lower-income candidates can be expected to depress academic credentials among the admitted student population. The average SAT score falls nearly 20 points from 1405 under current policy to 1388. In addition, smaller proportions of admitted students have high school grades that place them in the A+ range or in the top 10 percent of their high school class.

A milder form of class-based preferences, but still stronger than the version that exists under current policy, would be to assign the equivalent of a "legacy" preference to low-income students and to restrict it to applicants from lower-class families. We experiment here with a "legacy thumb on the scale" because it corresponds to the type of economic affirmative action considered by Bowen, Kurzweil, and Tobin (2005: 178). The strength of the legacy preference is equivalent to an odds ratio of 2.858, taken from a 1997 estimate for three private research universities by Espenshade, Chung, and Walling (2004). It suggests that alumni children have odds of admission that are nearly three times as high as those for non-legacy applicants. A legacy preference of this magnitude is stronger than the main effect for Hispanic students in model 6 of Table 3.4 but weaker than the main effect of being black.

The third panel of Table 9.2 traces the expected outcomes of substituting a legacy-equivalent weight for the weight now being given to lower-class applicants, keeping other things the same. There are gains in socioeconomic diversity compared to current policy—lower- and working-class

[13] Even under current policy, white and Asian students account for the majority of admitted students in the bottom two social classes. But with this version of economic affirmative action, their share rises from slightly more than one-half (55 percent) to nearly two-thirds (62 percent).

[14] In the baseline case reflecting current policy, admission rates are 18.9 percent for low SES students (combining lower- and working-class students), 20.7 percent for middle SES students, and 26.9 percent for high SES students (combining upper-middle and upper classes). Under the scenario in the second panel of Table 9.2, acceptance rates are 39.7 percent for low SES students, 18.2 percent for middle SES students, and 23.7 percent for high SES students.

students raise their combined share of admitted students from 10 to 13 percent—but they are not as pronounced as those registered in the prior simulation. Moreover, they are achieved by an increase solely in the proportion of admitted students who come from lower-class families, from less than 2 up to 5 percent. Working-class students, along with applicants in all other social class categories, see their shares of admitted students fall. Finally, this policy results in only modest changes in the racial composition of the admitted student population and in their academic credentials.

A policy that gives this legacy-size preference to students from both lower- and working-class family backgrounds could be expected to have even stronger effects on socioeconomic diversity because there are so many more working-class than lower-class students in the applicant pool. But how much stronger? The answer is contained in the last panel of Table 9.2 where a legacy preference has been substituted for preferences currently given to lower- and working-class applicants. The degree of socioeconomic heterogeneity produced is roughly equivalent to, or perhaps slightly greater than, the amount created by substituting black and Hispanic preferences for lower- and working-class students. Now admitted students in the bottom two social classes make up 22 percent of the total. The effects on racial composition are also somewhat accentuated as the proportion of admitted minority students grows to 19 percent. The largest percentage point changes compared to current policy affect white and Asian students at both the bottom and the top ends of the socioeconomic distribution. There are only small differences in average SAT scores or in high school grades between the simulations in the second and fourth panels.

Overall, these simulations indicate that extending stronger class-based preferences to students who come from less privileged economic backgrounds is likely to result in more socioeconomic diversity (depending on the magnitude of these additional preferences), in slightly more racial diversity, and in a marginally weaker academic profile for the group of admitted students. Clearly, there are trade-offs involved in expanding economic affirmative action, just as there are winners and losers whenever elite college admission officers exercise discretion in making decisions. How far private colleges and universities will want to move in this direction, and indeed how far they can afford to move, will depend on the perceived costs and benefits of the contemplated changes.[15]

---

[15] Middle-class students have the lowest acceptance rates in the simulations shown in the third and fourth panels of Table 9.2. In the third panel, acceptance rates are 24.6 percent for low SES students, 20.1 percent for middle SES students, and 26.1 percent for high SES students. In the fourth panel, the corresponding acceptance rates are 41.3, 18.0, and 23.5 percent.

The only other comparable simulations of the effects of economic affirmative action combined with racial preferences are those prepared by William Bowen and his colleagues (Bowen, Kurzweil, and Tobin, 2005).[16] Their simulations examine what would happen "if students with family incomes in the bottom quartile were given the same admissions advantage, within each SAT range, now enjoyed by legacies" (178). The conclusions reached by our respective approaches are surprisingly similar, especially given the differences in the set of schools and the underlying methodology. The principal differences center on average admission probabilities (ours are lower because all of our schools are highly selective private institutions), the impact on racial diversity (we find that giving greater weight to lower-income students increases the proportion of underrepresented minority students in the admitted pool), and acceptance rates and shares among the admitted student population for lower SES minority students (we find these increase when greater low-income weight is used in admissions, in contrast to Bowen et al., who detect little change).

Three kinds of costs attributable to class-based preferences are cited by Bowen, Kurzweil, and Tobin (2005). Admitted students may have somewhat lower test scores and grades; a larger proportion of low-income students in the overall student body will put added pressure on financial aid budgets; and students from more modest economic backgrounds are likely to contribute less to their alma maters after graduation. These authors estimate that financial aid budgets would need to expand by about 12 percent (just under $2 million per year at private liberal arts colleges and between $5 and $6 million at private universities) to accommodate the additional low-income students that would be enrolled using an approach that puts a legacy thumb on the scale.[17]

Bowen and his colleagues conclude from their simulations that the average SAT score for the entering class "remains essentially unchanged" by admitting more low SES students. By comparison, our results suggest a decline of 17 SAT points if lower- and working-class candidates are given the same weight as black and Hispanic applicants. But that is not all. In our simulations the share of students with grades in the top

[16]Carnevale and Rose (2004: 138–50) also present what they describe as simulations designed to explore alternative admissions strategies. But their analysis, based on data from the National Education Longitudinal Study of 1988 and the High School and Beyond Study, is more about alternative ways the national applicant pool might be conditioned to meet desirable goals. They do not examine the effect of alternative admission policies per se. Once pools of applicants who are qualified for admission to selective four-year colleges and universities are created, "colleges will have to face the challenge of deciding which candidates to accept" (148).

[17]Davidson College is expected to spend an additional $3.5 million per year to replace all loans with scholarships and student employment in its financial aid packages (Lipka, 2007).

10 percent of their high school class is expected to decline from 81 percent of all admittees under current policy to 77 percent. These two changes by themselves could be expected to lower an institution's overall score in the *U.S. News & World Report* (2005) rankings of national universities by 0.56 points.[18] When a lower annual giving rate is factored in, the total decline could be as much as 0.77 points.[19] Some of these changes are likely to have a cascading effect. Freshman retention and six-year graduation rates may decline if the college preparedness of entering students is reduced. Having to devote a larger fraction of an institution's overall budget to financial aid could degrade faculty salaries, increase average class size, and lower the proportion of full-time faculty, all of which in combination would reduce a school's ranking. Further declines are likely if peers lower their assessments of an institution's quality or if an institution's drop in the rankings produces a less competitive pool of applicants in the future.[20]

It is difficult to estimate the combined effect of these various factors, all of which are variables in the *U.S. News* rankings. Conservatively, however, we might imagine that a university's overall score might fall by 2 points—say, from 95 to 93 or from 66 to 64. Hypothetical changes such as these could drop the University of Pennsylvania (now ranked fourth overall with a score of 95) into a tie for seventh with Cal Tech and MIT (with a score of 93). Alternatively, Brandeis, which is tied for thirty-fourth position, could fall into a tie for fortieth place with Boston College if its score went from 66 to 64.

It is likely that many colleges and universities, when contemplating how far they can go in accepting more low SES students, are limited by

[18] This estimate is based on our internal analysis of published *U.S. News & World Report* (2005) data. We regressed an institution's overall score on the factors used to compile the rankings. Scores range from 42 to a maximum of 100 for the 114 nationally ranked universities.

[19] Bowen, Kurzweil, and Tobin (2005: 181–82) cite the following alumni giving rates by family income quartiles when students were undergraduates: 38 percent for the bottom income quartile, then 50, 59, and 62 percent as one moves up the income quartiles to the top quartile. We used these giving rates along with Bowen et al.'s estimate of how large the fraction of all bottom income quartile students would be among enrolled students under current policy and under the legacy thumb (the proportion rises from 10.6 to 16.7 percent) to conclude that the overall alumni giving rate could be expected to fall by 1.1 percentage points under their version of class-based affirmative action.

[20] Monks and Ehrenberg (1999) show that the cascade effect can operate in both an upward and a downward direction. In their analysis of thirty-one selective private colleges and universities, an improvement in an institution's relative standing in one year was followed in the next year by more applications (which increased an institution's selectivity), a higher yield rate, a higher average SAT score for members of the entering class, and fewer demands on the financial aid budget. If an institution fell in the rankings, then all of these things would happen in reverse.

the additional cost of grants and scholarships for needy students. But for universities with large endowments and whose overall economic health is robust, the loss of institutional prestige could be a more important deterrent to admitting more low-income students than the higher price tag required for financial aid. If *U.S. News & World Report* could be persuaded to include as a factor in its rankings the proportion of lower-income students in the first-year class, as the Washington Monthly College Guide (2006) does by incorporating the percentage of students who receive Pell grants, selective colleges and universities might be more willing to increase the share of such students on its campuses.[21]

Substituting Class for Race

Social and political conservatives who have been skeptical of the merits of race-conscious affirmative action have argued that in the areas of education, employment, and public contracting, preferences should be granted on the basis of socioeconomic disadvantage and not race or gender. Doing so would benefit all low-income families, but especially minority families who are disproportionately poor and working class. The most eloquent statement of the case for substituting social class preferences for race-based ones has been made by Richard Kahlenberg (1996: 209).

> Class-based affirmative action is a highly radical idea, but radical in the most American way. Americans hold doggedly to notions of family and liberty, but they also believe in a sort of rough equality of opportunity that gives the underdog a real chance in life. Racial preferences do a poor job of advancing that goal. Indeed, they have divided the very people who would naturally champion policies to bring

---

[21] This is not a new idea. The argument has been made before, but apparently without much success, by Ehrenberg (2003: 15): "Nowhere in the rankings methodology . . . is there any mention of the income distribution of an institution's students' families, the education levels of the institution's students' parents, nor the fraction of its students for whom English is a second language. Institutions that recruit students from underrepresented and disadvantaged populations—students who tend to have lower scores on entrance exams—and that do a wonderful job educating these students through to graduation should be more highly valued than the *USNWR* methodology currently permits." Changes in the ranking factors and in the weights assigned to them have been made from time to time, frequently in response to pressure from institutions that stood to gain from a change in the formula (National Opinion Research Center, 2000). For example, the yield rate was dropped in 2004 and faculty salaries have been adjusted for regional cost of living differentials (Ehrenberg, 2003). A general critique of the *U.S. News & World Report* ranking methodology has been provided by Clarke (2002). A more radical proposal that is being advanced by Lloyd Thacker, director of the Education Conservancy, calls on college and university presidents not to participate in *U.S. News & World Report* and other institutional rankings (Fain, 2007).

about greater fairness. A system of preferences for the disadvantaged offers a far bolder and more appropriate way of promoting Jefferson's vision of a natural aristocracy—a state in which children, born into all walks of life, can flourish in a way we have never truly allowed.

Moreover, Kahlenberg argues, class-based preferences will create not only more racial diversity than race-neutral policies but also more socioeconomic diversity than race-based affirmative action ever has. To the extent that people learn when exposed to others with different perspectives and backgrounds, differences based on socioeconomic position can be just as beneficial as racial and ethnic diversity. Indeed, in Kahlenberg's opinion, from an educational standpoint, "the new enrichment of class diversity will more than offset any decline in racial diversity" (165).

Just how far can class-based preferences go in restoring the racial diversity that would be lost by eliminating affirmative action? Is it correct to argue that class-based affirmative action can substitute for race-based affirmative action and achieve the same outcome? Answers to these important questions at private institutions are contained in Table 9.3. Once again the profile of students admitted under current policy is shown in the first panel, while the second panel indicates the likely effects of lifting racial affirmative action (that is, preferences for black and Hispanic applicants) and replacing it with a system of expanded social class preferences. Stronger low SES preferences are achieved by substituting the sizes of black and Hispanic preferences for those normally accorded to applicants from lower- and working-class families, respectively. It is immediately apparent that such a substitution would produce a decline in the minority share of admitted students by more than one-third, from 16 to 10 percent. Without any doubt, class based preferences cannot achieve the same ends as racial affirmative action. Even though, as we have seen in Table 9.2, adding economic affirmative action on top of racial affirmative action raises slightly the underrepresented minority share of admitted students, preferences for black and Hispanic applicants are such an important boost to minority applicants that removing them drastically undercuts minority students in the aggregate pool of accepted students. One does not have to worry that elite college admission officers will be able "to use class as a Trojan Horse for race" (Kahlenberg, 1996: 166).

It is to be expected that low-income students will increase their representation with economic affirmative action, as they do from 10 percent of admitted students (for lower- and working-class students combined) to 17 percent. Moreover, one can confidently predict that substituting class for race will greatly benefit low SES white and Asian students while having the most detrimental effects on upper SES black and Hispanic applicants.

TABLE 9.3
Effect of Substituting Other Policies for Affirmative Action at Private Institutions:
Simulation Results, Fall 1997

		Difference from Observed Baseline Admitted If		
Item	Observed Baseline Admitted	No Affirmative Action, More Low-Income Weight[a]	No Affirmative Action, More Low-Income Weight, Less Emphasis on Academic Performance[b]	No Affirmative Action, More Low-Income Weight, No Weight to Academic Performance[c]
Total	12,233	0	0	0
Race (%)				
White	59.9	3.0	2.4	2.2
Black	8.3	−4.3	−2.5	−0.7
Hispanic	7.9	−1.7	−1.0	−0.6
Asian	23.9	2.9	1.1	−0.9
Social Class (%)				
Lower	1.6	2.5	3.0	3.4
Working	8.3	4.5	6.7	8.4
Middle	33.4	−4.0	−5.2	−5.1
Upper-Middle	49.6	−2.9	−4.7	−7.4
Upper	7.2	−0.2	0.2	0.7
Race and Social Class (%)				
Minority, bottom 2 classes	4.5	−1.5	−0.4	0.2
Non-minority, bottom 2 classes	5.4	8.5	10.1	11.5
Minority, top 3 classes	11.7	−4.4	−3.2	−1.6
Non-minority, top 3 classes	78.4	−2.6	−6.5	−10.2
Mean SAT Score	1,405	−5	−34	−76

Source: Table C.9.3.

[a]This simulation eliminates affirmative action for black and Hispanic applicants, but substitutes black and Hispanic weights for lower and working classes, respectively.

[b]This simulation eliminates affirmative action for black and Hispanic applicants, but substitutes black and Hispanic weights for lower and working classes, respectively. The weight given to SAT and ACT scores, high school GPA, and high school class rank is reduced by one-half.

[c]This simulation eliminates affirmative action for black and Hispanic applicants, but substitutes black and Hispanic weights for lower and working classes, respectively. Zero weight is attached to SAT and ACT scores, high school GPA, and class rank.

Our simulation confirms this expectation. Acceptance rates for non-minority applicants in the bottom two social classes increase from 15 to 38 percent, while those for black and Hispanic applicants in the top three socioeconomic groups fall from 28 to 18 percent. This parallels Tom Kane's (1998b: 448) conclusion that "class is a very poor substitute for race for selective colleges seeking racial diversity. The problem is simply one of demographics." We see this in our data, too. Although black and Hispanic students are overrepresented (compared to whites and Asians) among all applicants from lower- and working-class families, they still constitute a modest fraction (29 percent) of all such applicants. Thus, any proposal to increase preferences for students from socioeconomically disadvantaged backgrounds will affect a large number of white and Asian students as well. Finally, it is worth noting that there is no substantial change in the academic profile of admitted students when the status quo is replaced by adding class and removing race-based preferences.

Other research agrees with our conclusions (Conrad and Sharpe, 1996; Cancian, 1998; Kane, 1998b; Carnevale and Rose, 2004; Bowen, Kurzweil, and Tobin, 2005). The consensus has been summarized by Carnevale and Rose (2004: 153): "Hence, income-based policies are not an effective substitute for conscious racial and ethnic enrollment targets."[22] The most reliable and complementary set of simulations to ours have been carried out by Bowen, Kurzweil, and Tobin (2005). Their results are completely consistent with those reported here. If current admission policies are altered to substitute class-based preferences for affirmative action for members of underrepresented minority groups, the acceptance rate for whites and Asians in the bottom income quartile could be expected to increase from 30 to 49 percent. Offsetting this change, admission probabilities for minority students in the upper three income quartiles would fall from 51 to 26 percent.[23]

Fryer, Loury, and Yuret (2007) have developed a model that predicts that if universities are prevented from practicing race-based affirmative action but nevertheless want to maintain representational goals (that is, a desired degree of racial diversity), they will combine a color-blind approach with one that "flattens" the function linking the admission outcome to a candidate's academic qualifications. Institutions will end up placing less weight on academic factors and more weight on social background characteristics. In the long run, the authors say, a policy of this kind undercuts incentives for students to work hard in high school and

[22] For one possible dissenting view, see Basten et al. (1997).

[23] The only small discrepancy affects the proportion of white and Asian students in the upper SES categories. In our simulations the share of this group among all admitted students falls slightly from 78 to 76 percent. In Bowen et al.'s companion projections, the share of non-minorities in the top three income quartiles grows somewhat from 79 to 81 percent.

lowers the average quality of the applicant pool. Tom Kane (1998b), too, has observed, "Unless elite colleges dramatically reduce their reliance on high school grades and standardized test scores, class-based preferences cannot do much to cushion the impact of the elimination of race-based preferences" (433). Behavioral changes at the institutional level following the termination of race-based preferences in public higher education suggest that these conclusions are more than economists' theoretical predictions. In California, for example, "The law schools are responding to Board of Regents' mandate by decreasing the weight given to UGPA and LSAT scores and by increasing the weight on other factors" (Conrad and Sharpe, 1996: 42).

How far can a relaxed emphasis on candidates' academic qualifications go toward restoring the racial diversity lost by eliminating affirmative action? How realistic is it to expect that paying less attention to high school grades and standardized test scores could soften the impact, as Tom Kane has suggested? The second panel in Table 9.3 has already examined the effect of substituting class-based for race-based affirmative action. In the third panel we retain these assumptions and, in addition, assume that college admission officers place less weight on standard indicators of applicants' academic merit. More specifically, it is assumed that just half the normal emphasis is given to a student's high school GPA, high school class rank, and SAT and/or ACT score.[24] If the desired degree of racial diversity is assumed to be represented by that achieved under current policy, then an approach that downgrades the weight given to academic performance moves institutions in the preferred direction, compared to results in the second panel, but it does not move them far enough. Underrepresented minority students' share increases from 10 to 13 percent of all admitted students and their acceptance rate rises from 18 to 22 percent when less attention to academic performance is combined with both class-based and color-blind affirmative action.

The social class distribution is also affected. There is now somewhat more socioeconomic diversity as lower- and working-class admittees make up a 20 percent share compared to a 17 percent share if academic performance is evaluated using current policy standards. More racial and socioeconomic diversity is offset by declining proportions for whites and Asians in the top three social classes. More important, less emphasis on

---

[24]What halving the importance of academic indicators means in practice is illustrated by the odds ratio of 3.94 associated with a high school GPA of A+ in model 6 of Table 3.4. Having a high school GPA in this range means that a candidate's odds of being admitted are 294 percent greater, other things equal, than a student whose GPA is B+ or lower. Flattening by one-half the function that relates admission outcomes to high school GPA means that A+ students would now have 147 percent higher odds of admission compared to B+ students. This implies an odds ratio of 2.47, which is substituted for 3.94 in the simulations.

prior academic performance will lower the academic qualifications of the admitted class. The average SAT score for all admitted students falls to 1371—34 points below the average under current practice. And the proportion of admitted students with high school grades in the A+ range or who graduated in the top of their class is noticeably lower compared to the status quo.

We simulate a more extreme version of this policy in the last panel of Table 9.3. Here the admission office is assumed to assign zero weight to high school grades, class standing, and SAT or ACT performance. This simulation is not particularly realistic. It is difficult to imagine any admission dean at an elite private institution who would advocate such a position. But the simulation is valuable nonetheless because it indicates how hard it is to devise an acceptable alternative to race-based affirmative action that preserves today's critical mass of underrepresented minority students. The degree of racial and economic diversity would increase still further if academic qualifications were ignored altogether. Underrepresented minority students would see their share among admitted students increase to 15 percent, their acceptance rate would rise to 26 percent (equal to that for white applicants), and the proportion of lower- and working-class students would grow to 22 percent—slightly more than the highest proportion of lower-income students we have seen in any simulation thus far. Even though the minority student share approaches the share under current policy, it still falls somewhat short (15 versus 16 percent).

But whatever gains have been achieved on the racial diversity front by relaxing academic standards have come at a steep price in terms of academic credentials of the entering class. The average SAT score for admitted students is expected to drop to 1329—76 points below the average under current policy. Other measures of academic performance also suffer. The proportion of admitted students with high school grades in the A+ range is cut in half, from 42 percent under the status quo to 22 percent if grades are ignored. And the fraction of students who graduate in the top 10 percent of their class is also substantially reduced, from more than 80 percent under current policy to just slightly more than 50 percent if grades no longer matter to admission deans.[25]

Projecting our simulation results beyond the fourth panel suggests that some combination of high school grades and standardized test scores would have to be given *negative* weight in order to restore the racial and ethnic balance accomplished by current policy. This sobering assessment is corroborated by simulations based on C&B data and prepared by

---

[25] Announcing a policy that disregards academic credentials would be likely to encourage even weaker students to apply, thereby lowering still further the academic merit of the admitted first-year class.

Fryer, Loury, and Yuret (2007: 25–26), who suggest that an optimal color-blind admission policy would end up giving "less weight to test scores, more weight to high school grades, and more weight to social background factors" compared to current race-based affirmative action. The majority of the seven schools they study would have to give negative weight to SAT math scores to achieve representational objectives for black and Hispanic students.

In this section we have shown that class-based affirmative action is not a satisfactory substitute for race-based affirmative action. Even a vigorous policy of increasing admission weights given to lower- and working-class students to equate them with weights that current policy assigns to underrepresented minorities falls substantially short of maintaining today's percentages of admitted black and Hispanic students. Economic affirmative action has some effect in raising the proportion of minority students in the admitted pool, but its primary impact is (as its name suggests) to increase the proportion of socioeconomically disadvantaged students on campus. If applicants' prior academic accomplishments were overlooked to a sufficient extent, or possibly even given reverse weight here and there, it might be possible to maintain the racial and ethnic balances achieved by a more conventional race-based affirmative action policy. But to do this would require paying a very high price in terms of the academic qualifications and college readiness of students who enter today's elite private colleges and universities. Trustees, alumni, and faculty are not likely to sit by quietly if such a plan were even contemplated, much less proposed or implemented.

X-PERCENT PLANS

In 1996 the Fifth Circuit Court of Appeals ruled in *Hopwood v. Texas* that the University of Texas Law School did not have a compelling state interest in creating a racially diverse student body. With race-based affirmative action declared invalid, minority undergraduate freshman enrollments at both the University of Texas at Austin and at Texas A&M University tumbled. Black enrollment at the Austin campus, for example, fell from 5 percent of the freshman class in 1995 to less than 3 percent in 1997. There were equally sharp drops for Hispanic students (Tienda and Niu, 2006). Also in 1997 the Texas legislature passed a provision guaranteeing admission at the in-state public institution of their choice to any Texas high school senior who graduated in the top 10 percent of his or her class (Horn and Flores, 2003). The bill was touted as a race-neutral alternative that could have the same effect on minority representation on campus as the more traditional form of race-based affirmative action.

But in fact, H.B. 588 depended on neighborhood and school racial segregation and concentrated disadvantage to have any chance of being effective (Tienda and Niu, 2006).

How useful are X-percent plans? Can they restore ethnic balances lost by banning race-conscious affirmative action? An analysis of percentage plans in Texas, Florida, and California has concluded that they are not effective in maintaining racial diversity on public campuses, partly because many of the students who are admitted under these plans would have been accepted anyway (Horn and Flores, 2003). An analysis of nationally representative data by Mark Long (2004b) comes to a similar conclusion. Removing affirmative action and replacing it with a plan that automatically accepts the top 10 percent of high school graduates results in a net loss in the share of admitted students who are members of underrepresented minority groups. The extent of the "rebound" or "bounce back" in minority shares arising from percent plans depends on whether institutions are public or private and on the degree of institutional selectivity, but it is uniformly less than 50 percent and typically one-quarter or less.[26]

Our analysis of these issues at public NSCE institutions is shown in Table 9.4. We emphasize potential implications of implementing percentage plans at public schools because bans on race-based affirmative action have targeted public flagship universities and because percentage plans have been adopted at these institutions as race-neutral substitutes. The first panel of Table 9.4 shows the profile of admitted students under racial affirmative action at public institutions. Black and Hispanic students together account for more than 9 percent of all admitted candidates, and five out of every six underrepresented minority students who are accepted are black. Under a policy of no race-conscious affirmative action (shown in the third panel of Table C.9.7), the minority share of admitted students declines to less than 6 percent. But the loss of affirmative action affects only black students. The number of admitted black applicants falls by 46 percent from 1,110 to 600, while the number of admitted Hispanic students remains essentially unchanged.

Adopting a 10 percent plan at public NSCE institutions makes an inconsequential difference in restoring racial and ethnic balances. Two

---

[26] If race-conscious affirmative action is eliminated just at public colleges and universities, the underrepresented minority share among all admitted students at all colleges and universities is simulated to decline from 16.1 to 15.8 percent. The share rises only to 15.9 percent with a top 10 percent plan at public institutions, a rebound of about a quarter. At the top-quality decile of all colleges and universities, an affirmative action ban lowers the combined black and Hispanic share of admitted students from 10.6 to 7.8 percent. If a 10 percent plan also affected all colleges and universities, the minority share could be expected to rebound to 8.8 percent, just about a third of the way back to its initial level (M. Long, 2004b).

TABLE 9.4
Effect of Top 10 Percent Plans at Public Institutions:
Simulation Results, Fall 1997

Item	Observed Baseline Admitted to Public	Difference from Observed Baseline Admitted If	
		No Affirmative Action, Admit Top 10% First[a]	No Affirmative Action, Admit In-State Top 10% First[b]
Total	14,185	0	0
Race (%)			
White	87.3	3.3	3.3
Black	7.8	−3.4	−3.4
Hispanic	1.5	0.1	0
Asian	3.4	0	0.1
Social Class (%)			
Lower	0.5	−0.1	−0.2
Working	6.1	1.6	−0.4
Middle	38.1	−3.0	0.6
Upper-Middle	52.5	2.1	0.1
Upper	2.8	−0.6	0
Race and Social Class (%)			
Minority, bottom 2 classes	2.6	−1.2	−1.1
Non-minority, bottom 2 classes	4.0	2.7	0.5
Minority, top 3 classes	6.7	−2.1	−2.3
Non-minority, top 3 classes	86.7	0.6	2.9
Mean SAT Score	1,206	27	5

Source: Table C.9.4.

[a]This simulation admits all applicants to public NSCE institutions who rank in the top 10 percent of their high school class. After eliminating race-based affirmative action for black and Hispanic applicants, the usual criteria were applied to the remaining 32.3 percent of admitted students.

[b]This simulation admits all in-state applicants to public NSCE institutions who rank in the top 10 percent of their high school class. After eliminating race-based affirmative action for black and Hispanic applicants, the usual criteria were applied to the remaining 65.2 percent of admitted students.

alternative percentage plans are considered in Table 9.4. Shown in the second panel are the simulation results of accepting all applicants who rank in the top 10 percent of their high school class, regardless of applicants' state of permanent residence.[27] Approximately two-thirds (68 percent) of all admitted students come in under this percentage plan, while

[27]We also disregard whether applicants attend public or private high schools. This is similar to H.B. 588 in Texas, as long as the high school is accredited (Horn and Flores, 2003: 16).

the remaining one-third are admitted by procedures that reflect current policy except that race-based affirmative action for black and Hispanic applicants has been eliminated. The results in the third panel assume that automatic admission to public institutions is granted only to in-state students who rank in the top 10 percent of their class. Roughly 35 percent of admitted students are accepted under this percentage plan. The remaining 65 percent of admittees are evaluated using criteria in current policy except that, once again, race-conscious affirmation action is assumed to be no longer in effect.[28] The minority student share is about 6 percent under both of these two top-ten plans, compared with slightly less than 6 percent if affirmative action is eliminated with no percentage plan to replace it. Percentage plans at public NSCE institutions do little to increase the minority presence on campus if affirmative action is eliminated. When compared with race-based policies, they result in a sharp drop in the number of black students. A top 10 percent plan extended to applicants from all states raises, of course, the proportion of admitted students in the top decile of their high school class. Other aspects of the admitted student profile are only marginally affected. The distributions of admittees by social class and high school GPA are much the same under either percentage plan as they are with race-sensitive policies.[29]

Admission by SAT Scores

We made the case in chapter 3 that admission deans at elite colleges are looking for the most meritorious students to admit from among the many candidates in their applicant pools and that merit in the eyes of these

---

[28] Following the adoption of the top 10 percent plan in Texas, approximately 20 percent of all students from Texas who were admitted systemwide were percent-plan eligible. In 2001 at the University of Texas, Austin, and Texas A&M campuses, nearly half of the admitted class from Texas ranked in the top 10 percent of his or her high school class (Horn and Flores, 2003).

[29] If private NSCE institutions admit only students who rank in the top 10 percent of their high school class, the underrepresented minority share of accepted students is 6 percent, less than half the proportion under current policy (16 percent). In Table 9.1 we observed that eliminating affirmative action at private colleges would lower the minority share to 9 percent. Therefore, introducing a 10 percent plan produces no rebound whatsoever in the minority student share lost by ending affirmative action. Asian applicants receive the biggest boost from percentage plans. Their acceptance rate increases from 18 percent under current policy to 25 percent if a 10 percent plan is adopted, and their share of admitted students rises from 24 to 33 percent. Moving to a 10 percent plan also concentrates socioeconomic backgrounds of admitted students around the middle class and results in a small increase (14 points) in the average SAT score of members of the admitted group. For more details, see Table C.9.4.

admission officers constitutes more than academic merit. Bowen and Bok (1998: 31) have also argued that it is not realistic to assume that applicants will be admitted just "by the numbers."[30] Nevertheless, at least in the minds of some parents, overall merit is equated almost exclusively with academic merit narrowly conceived. There are traditions that encourage this way of thinking. At City University of New York, for example, admission to the Honors College is not influenced by athletic ability, being an alumni child, being a member of an underrepresented minority group, or having wealthy parents. Instead, entrance depends on high school grades, SAT I/ACT scores, an essay, and recommendations (City University of New York, 2006). Many of the students who are admitted come from relatively poor and/or immigrant family backgrounds. In 2005 the average standardized test score for members of the entering class was in the 93rd percentile nationwide ("Rebuilding the American Dream Machine," 2006). Moreover, a highly competitive entrance examination governs admission to some of the best-known public high schools in the United States, including Stuyvesant and Bronx Science in New York City, Boston Latin in Boston, and Lowell High School in San Francisco (Attewell, 2001).[31]

The simulations in Table 9.5 address what might happen if academic merit, and indeed only a candidate's SAT score, were all that mattered for admission to private colleges and universities. We first ranked applicants by their SAT scores and then selected candidates with the highest scores until the admitted class was completely full. In the end all candidates with scores of 1460 or higher (and some students with scores of 1450) were admitted. Accepting students by this admittedly narrow criterion even of academic merit produces a college campus from which nearly all black students have disappeared. The fraction of underrepresented

[30] These authors argue, "Given the multiplicity of considerations that affect undergraduate admissions decisions, it is hard to imagine that anyone would favor a directive to admit simply 'by the numbers' and offer places only to those students with the highest test scores and high school grades" (Bowen and Bok, 1998: 31).

[31] Competitive entrance examinations have a long history. They were used by the Chinese Imperial Civil Service as early as 200 B.C. It is generally agreed that university entrance exams were in use in England and Germany by the mid-1800s, although there are claims that the Sorbonne required a passing score on an admissions test as early as the thirteenth century and that the practice originated in Spain in the late sixteenth century. In the United States during the late 1800s it was common for each university to have its own entrance requirements, including courses that students had to have taken in high school. To add some consistency to this situation a group of a dozen northeastern universities in 1900 established the College Entrance Examination Board. This board developed a common entrance examination that a large number of colleges and universities agreed to accept. Initially dependent on essays, this test later evolved into a series of multiple-choice questions. Known then as the Scholastic Aptitude Test (and today just as the SAT test), it was first given in 1926 to eight thousand students (Zwick, 2002).

TABLE 9.5
Effect of Admitting Students by SAT Scores Alone at Private Institutions:
Simulation Results, Fall 1997

Item	Observed Baseline Admitted	Difference from Observed Baseline Admitted If Admission by SAT Scores Only[a]
Total	12,233	0
Race (%)		
White	59.9	−1.6
Black	8.3	−7.4
Hispanic	7.9	−5.4
Asian	23.9	14.4
Social Class (%)		
Lower	1.6	−1.4
Working	8.3	−6.1
Middle	33.4	5.1
Upper-Middle	49.6	1.1
Upper	7.2	1.1
Race and Social Class (%)		
Minority, bottom 2 classes	4.5	−4.1
Non-minority, bottom 2 classes	5.4	−3.3
Minority, top 3 classes	11.7	−8.7
Non-minority, top 3 classes	78.4	16.2
Mean SAT Score	1,405	107

Source: Table C.9.5.
[a]This simulation admits all students with SAT scores of about 1450 and higher.

minority students among all accepted students declines from 16 percent with affirmative action to just over 3 percent under the new regime. Acceptance rates fall dramatically for both black and Hispanic students, but the largest declines are registered by black students, for whom the probability of being admitted drops from 31 to 3 percent. The number of black students who are accepted falls by nearly 90 percent, from 1,016 to 110. Even the number of admitted Hispanic students declines by more than two-thirds.[32] Asian students would gain from the openings created by

[32] A real-world counterpart to these simulation results comes from enrollment trends for black students at the three most prestigious campuses of the City University of New York. CUNY adopted more stringent admission criteria in 2000 and 2001. Applicants for admission to CUNY's baccalaureate programs had to achieve a certain score on the SAT

minority students whose admission is no longer viable under the new SAT-only policy. The Asian share among admitted students increases from 24 to 38 percent, and the number of Asian students who are accepted grows by more than 60 percent. Asian applicants, who have the lowest acceptance rate (18 percent) under current policy, would be admitted at the highest rate (30 percent) under the revised practice of admitting students by a single criterion.[33]

An SAT-only admission policy could also be expected to affect students' socioeconomic profiles. Comparing the first and second panels in Table 9.5 suggests that the social class distribution of admitted students would have a smaller variance and be concentrated around middle- and upper-middle-class students. Because SAT scores tend to be positively correlated with students' social class backgrounds and because we are selecting only students with the highest scores, it is not surprising that the proportion of lower- and working-class students among the admitted pool drops sharply, from 10 percent under current policy to less than 3 percent. Nor is it surprising that the average SAT score for members of the admitted group jumps by more than 100 points—from 1405 to 1512—when only those with the highest scores are admitted. Selecting on SAT score also produces an admitted cohort with stronger high school grades, not only with respect to class rank but also with GPAs in the A+ and A range.[34]

---

examination, the New York State Regents' exam, or CUNY's own entrance examination. Between 1999 and 2005, black enrollment declined from 40 to 30 percent of all undergraduate students at City University, from 20 to 15 percent at Hunter College, and from 24 to 14 percent at Baruch College (Arenson, 2006).

[33]Partly to generate more applications from underrepresented minority students and to create greater racial diversity on their campuses, a growing number of selective colleges and universities is moving away from the simulation described here and no longer requiring the submission of SAT or ACT scores. Smith College and Wake Forest University are the latest additions to this list (Lewin, 2008). Admission officials at Wake Forest plan to make the strength of the high school curriculum selected, high school grades, writing ability, extracurricular activities, and an applicant's character as reflected in letters of recommendation the primary criteria for admission. Part of the rationale for the new policy is the mounting evidence that high school grades are better predictors of college success than are standardized test scores. New studies by The College Board show that no individual component of the new SAT test—not critical reading, math, or writing—predicts first-year college GPA as well as high school GPA (Kobrin et al., 2008). Even the combined score (out of 2400) on the new SAT test does not do as well as high school GPA in predicting first-year college GPA. For women and minorities, however, the combined SAT score does somewhat better than high school GPA (Mattern et al., 2008).

[34]These results are generally consistent with other similar studies. Espenshade and Chung (2005) report simulations that admit students at three private research universities solely on the basis of SAT score. Mean SAT scores among admitted students rise from 1405 to 1512, exactly the same as in Table 9.5. The share of admitted students who are white goes from

Eliminating the Racial Achievement Gap

Up to this point we have examined a broad spectrum of alternative admission policies, including ones that remove preferences for underrepresented minority students, add weight for poor and working-class applicants, replace race-based preferences with class-based ones, deemphasize to varying degrees the importance of traditional indicators of academic performance in high school, substitute percentage plans when race-based affirmative action is eliminated, and admit students on the basis of SAT scores alone. While the impact of these policies on the profile of admitted students varies, each has at least some effect on the distribution by race, social class, SAT score, high school class rank, or high school GPA. But the most important conclusion to draw from these simulations is that *there is no alternative admission policy with the capacity to preserve minority student shares observed under racial affirmative action.*[35] If these institutions wish to maintain a critical mass of minority students on their campuses, there is not any feasible and compelling policy on the horizon—at least not one within easy reach—that can accomplish this objective other than a system of race-conscious admission preferences that operate in the context of a holistic and individualized review of all the factors in a candidate's application folder.[36]

51.4 to 47.7 percent (if we exclude students who failed to report their race, most of whom are white); for blacks the share falls from 9.0 to 0.9 percent; for Hispanics, from 7.9 to 2.2; for athletes, from 10.2 to 1.9; and for legacies, from 6.5 to 3.2. Asians students are the only group whose share increases when SAT scores predominate in selection—from 23.7 percent under current policy to 38.7 percent. Had Harvard's Class of 1975 been chosen on the basis of SAT verbal scores alone, the proportion of admitted students who were legacies would have fallen from 13.6 to 6.1 percent, of athletes from 23.6 to 4.5, and of black students from 7.1 to 1.1. The proportion of students on financial aid would have remained essentially unchanged at 55 percent (Klitgaard, 1985: 29).

[35] As early as 1999, a group of ETS researchers had been working on a race-neutral formula to identify "strivers"—students who had overcome significant forms of disadvantage. It was thought that giving more admission weight to strivers could produce black and Hispanic enrollments at least as large as those achieved by racial affirmative action, especially if the striver formula took family wealth and savings for college into account. This research became mired in controversy and is no longer supported by ETS (Schmidt, 2006a).

[36] This conclusion reinforces earlier assessments that are based on considering a more limited set of alternatives. For example, Carnevale and Rose (2004: 150) conclude, "But ultimately there is no better way to guarantee a certain level of racial diversity than by employing race per se." Mark Long (2004b: 1033) says, "Given the persistent gaps in test scores and other measures of academic preparedness between under-represented minorities and white and Asian American students, affirmative action appears to be the only effective tool in maintaining minority enrollment in top-tier colleges." This conclusion applies with equal force to public flagship universities in California, Texas, Washington, and Florida

There is one more simulation worth exploring. As noted in chapter 2, NSCE applicants, who by any standard are among the most talented anywhere, are characterized by a racial academic achievement gap. Average SAT scores, for example, vary systematically by racial or ethnic group affiliation. As shown in Figure 2.6, white students who applied to one of the NSCE institutions in the fall of 1997 had an average SAT score of 1284, in contrast to 1146 for blacks, 1224 for Hispanics, and 1334 for Asians. Admission preferences for black and Hispanic applicants compensate to some extent for these performance differentials (Ferguson, 2001). What would happen if racial achievement gaps could be eliminated? Would affirmative action programs still be needed to preserve black and Hispanic shares of admitted students?

A simulation in which test-score gaps have been closed has not been selected arbitrarily. Thoughtful scholars are increasingly pointing to this path as the way out of the tangle of controversy created by affirmative action programs. In the aftermath of Michigan's new ban on affirmative action, Mabel Freeman, assistant vice president at Ohio State University, was quoted as saying, "When we saw what was coming down the road, we started looking to other models, but no other model results in as much diversity. . . . The only long-term solution is to do better in the pipeline and make sure all kids get the best education possible, K–12" (Lewin, 2007a). Glenn Loury (1997) has argued that rather than relying on preferential affirmative action (which he labels "patronizing"), emphasis should be put instead on "developmental" affirmative action to enhance performance.

> Such a targeted effort at performance enhancement among black employees or students is definitely not color-blind behavior. . . . What distinguishes it from preferential hiring or admissions, though, is that it takes seriously the fact of differential performance and seeks to reverse it directly, rather than trying to hide from that fact by setting a different threshold of expectation for the performance of blacks. (41)[37]

(M. Long, 2007a). Kane (1998b: 451) stresses the trade-off between race blindness in admissions and racial diversity on campus. Trying to circumvent this trade-off by relying less on academic performance measures and more on social background factors to preserve a given level of racial diversity entails large efficiency losses in the short run and undermines incentives to hard work in the longer run (Fryer, Loury, and Yuret, 2007). Reports of the effects of race-neutral admission alternatives in medical school have reached similar conclusions (Steinecke et al., 2007).

[37] Thernstrom and Thernstrom (1999: 1631) leave little doubt about where they stand. They conclude their review of Bowen and Bok's (1998) *The Shape of the River* by saying, "As long as the average black high school senior reads at the eighth-grade level, efforts to engineer parity in the legal and medical professions are doomed to failure. For a generation,

Even Sandra Day O'Connor's "expectation," expressed on behalf of the majority in *Grutter v. Bollinger* (2003: 31), that in another twenty-five years we will no longer need to rely on race-sensitive admission practices to achieve the educational benefits of diversity suggests we may be in a transition period now to something beyond affirmative action.

Our final set of simulations assumes that the black-white and Hispanic-white academic achievement gap has been closed. Methodological details about how this is done are explained in appendix B. In brief, we can say that black and Hispanic test scores and other measures of academic performance (including the number of SAT II and AP tests taken; SAT I, SAT II, and ACT Composite scores; high school GPA and class rank; and whether a student is a National Merit or National Achievement Scholar) are replaced with scores of "similarly situated" white applicants where controls are introduced for social class and other student characteristics. These imputations have the effect of raising academic performance profiles for black and Hispanic students while leaving unaffected those for whites and Asians.[38] Eliminating the test-score gap raises average SAT scores among all applicants at private colleges by ten points (from 1340 to 1350). The average SAT score increases by 25 points (from 1189 to 1214) among applicants to public universities when racial achievement gaps are closed.[39]

Table 9.6 shows the results of these new simulations for private colleges and universities. These represent to our knowledge the first-ever attempt to show how the profile of admitted students might be affected if a way could be found to narrow and then close gaps in test scores and other indicators of academic performance between black and Hispanic applicants on the one hand and white students on the other. The first panel in Table 9.6 includes a statistical portrait of admitted students under current conditions—that is, under a policy of positive admission preferences for black and Hispanic candidates coupled with existing differences in academic performance between underrepresented minority students versus whites and Asians. This panel is brought over from Table 9.1 as a point

---

now, preferences in higher education have been a pernicious palliative that has deflected our attention from the real problem."

[38] Some observers argue that it is a mistake to focus on white achievement as the standard. Because Asian Americans often perform better than whites, the achievement gap should be viewed in the context of Asian students' performance versus that of whites, blacks, and Latinos (Maxwell, 2007).

[39] We need to emphasize that eliminating racial academic achievement gaps does not mean that average scores on measures of academic performance will be equal among blacks, Hispanics, and whites. Rather, the propensity score matching technique that is used equalizes measures of academic performance between blacks (or Hispanics) and whites for similarly situated whites, that is, after controlling for social class and other student characteristics.

TABLE 9.6

Effect of Eliminating the Racial Achievement Gap and Affirmative Action at Private Institutions: Simulation Results, Fall 1997

Item	Observed Baseline Admitted	Applications with No Achievement Gap	Difference from Observed Baseline Admitted If	
			Admitted with No Achievement Gap, but Keeping Affirmative Action[a]	Admitted with No Achievement Gap, No Affirmative Action[b]
Total	12,233	51,836	0	0
Race (%)				
White	59.9	55.7	−5.1	0.3
Black	8.3	6.3	5.3	−0.3
Hispanic	7.9	7.0	2.2	−0.2
Asian	23.9	31.0	−2.4	0.1
Social Class (%)				
Lower	1.6	1.6	0.5	−0.6
Working	8.3	10.7	1.2	−1.4
Middle	33.4	38.0	1.8	1.3
Upper-Middle	49.6	43.0	−3.0	0.4
Upper	7.2	6.8	−0.6	0.2
Race and Social Class (%)				
Minority, bottom 2 classes	4.5	3.5	2.2	−2.0
Non-minority, bottom 2 classes	5.4	8.8	−0.5	0
Minority, top 3 classes	11.7	9.8	5.3	1.6
Non-minority, top 3 classes	78.4	78.0	−7.0	0.4
Mean SAT Score	1,405	1,350	8	13

Source: Table C.9.6.

[a] This simulation shows the profile of admitted students assuming the black–white and Hispanic–white achievement gap has been closed. It is further assumed that current admission practices remain in effect, including the positive preferences for black and Hispanic applicants and the Asian disadvantage.

[b] This simulation shows the profile of admitted students assuming the black–white and Hispanic–white achievement gap has been closed. It is further assumed that affirmative action for black and Hispanic applicants has been eliminated, though the Asian disadvantage remains.

of reference. Next in Table 9.6 we show the composition of the applicant pool to private NSCE institutions assuming no academic achievement gap. The profile is identical to the one included in Table 9.1 for all race and social class characteristics of applicants. But on measures of academic performance, applicants in Table 9.6 (with raised scores for blacks and Hispanics) present a stronger profile.

The third panel in Table 9.6 addresses the question of what would happen if the academically "reconditioned" applicant pool were treated by admission officers in the same way as are today's applicants. We can anticipate the general direction of the change; black and Hispanic applicants would look more attractive. With both affirmative action and their stronger academic credentials in place, minority students would be even more likely to be accepted relative to white and Asian candidates. We should expect their representation among admitted students to increase relative to current conditions. Table 9.6 shows that this is indeed the result. The share of admitted students who are black or Hispanic increases by almost one-half compared with current outcomes (from slightly more than 16 percent to nearly 24 percent). Offsetting these gains, shares of white and Asian admitted students fall—from 60 to 55 percent for whites and from 24 to 22 percent for Asian students. The social class distribution of admitted students is also affected by these changes. As expected, with more underrepresented minority students in the admitted pool, lower- and working-class students make up a somewhat larger fraction of all admitted students (12 percent) than they do with current conditions (10 percent).

The final panel of Table 9.6 addresses what might be accomplished at private colleges and universities if affirmative action preferences for blacks and Hispanics were lifted at the same time as their academic credentials were upgraded in the manner assumed here. This is the kind of situation envisioned by Loury (1997: 41) when he argues for "a concerted effort to enhance performance, while maintaining common standards of evaluation." A comparison of the first and last panels shows that the proportion of underrepresented minority students among all accepted applicants would hardly be affected. In either case, approximately 16 percent of admitted students would be black or Hispanic. Nor would admitted shares for white or Asian applicants change very much. On the other hand, there is an indication that the socioeconomic profile of admitted students would be slightly higher with no achievement gap and no affirmative action. The proportion of lower- and working-class students falls from 10 percent under current conditions to 8 percent in the simulation.

Table 9.7 lays out the implications of the same set of assumptions for public NSCE universities. Once again as a point of reference, we show in

TABLE 9-7
Effect of Eliminating the Racial Achievement Gap and Affirmative Action at Public Institutions: Simulation Results, Fall 1997

Item	Observed Baseline Admitted	Applications with No Achievement Gap	Difference from Observed Baseline Admitted If	
			Admitted with No Achievement Gap, but Keeping Affirmative Action[a]	Admitted with No Achievement Gap, No Affirmative Action[b]
Total	14,185	25,826	0	0
Race (%)				
White	87.3	85.9	-4.3	-1.7
Black	7.8	7.4	3.5	0.9
Hispanic	1.5	2.1	1.1	1.0
Asian	3.4	4.7	-0.3	-0.1
Social Class (%)				
Lower	0.5	0.5	0.3	0.1
Working	6.1	6.5	-0.1	-0.5
Middle	38.1	36.6	0.4	0
Upper-Middle	52.5	54.1	-0.6	0.4
Upper	2.8	2.4	0.1	0
Race and Social Class (%)				
Minority, bottom 2 classes	2.6	2.4	0.5	-0.2
Non-minority, bottom 2 classes	4.0	4.6	-0.3	-0.1
Minority, top 3 classes	6.7	7.1	4.1	2.0
Non-minority, top 3 classes	86.7	85.9	-4.3	-1.7
Mean SAT Score	1,206	1,214	36	31

Source: Table C.9.11.

[a]This simulation shows the profile of admitted students assuming the black–white and Hispanic–white achievement gap has been closed. It is further assumed that current admission practices remain in effect, including the positive preferences for black and Hispanic applicants and the Asian disadvantage.

[b]This simulation shows the profile of admitted students assuming the black–white and Hispanic–white achievement gap has been closed. It is further assumed that affirmative action for black and Hispanic applicants has been eliminated, though the Asian disadvantage remains.

TABLE 9.8
A Comparison of the Profiles of Admitted Students under Two Conditions:
Current Policy (Affirmative Action with an Achievement Gap) versus
No Affirmative Action and No Academic Achievement Gap, Private and
Public Institutions Combined, Fall 1997

Item	Current Policy	No Affirmative Action, No Achievement Gap
Total Admitted	26,418	26,418
Race (%)		
White	74.6	73.8
Black	8.0	8.4
Hispanic	4.5	4.9
Asian	12.9	12.9
Social Class (%)[a]		
Low	8.1	7.0
Middle	35.9	36.6
High	56.0	56.4
Mean SAT Score	1299	1321

Source: Tables C.9.6 and C.9.11.

[a]"Low" includes lower and working classes; "High" includes upper-middle and upper classes.

the first panel the profile of admitted students under race-based policy.
The second panel includes a portrait of all applicants to public institutions after the academic credentials of minority students have been raised.
The proportion of blacks and Hispanics among all admitted students can be expected to increase from 9 percent under current race-based policy to 14 percent (third panel) when enhanced academic performance measures are combined with affirmative action for underrepresented minority students. But when these positive admission preferences are removed, the share of black and Hispanic students falls back to 11 percent (fourth panel), a figure that is only slightly larger than the share realized under today's conditions at NSCE public universities. Socioeconomic profiles of admitted students vary inconsequentially between current policy and either of the two simulations.

A summary of our findings is contained in Table 9.8 where we combine the simulation results from private and public NSCE institutions and consider the aggregate effects among all the schools in our study population. The first column shows the actual racial and socioeconomic profile of admitted students in the fall of 1997. The second column indicates how the profile could be expected to change if affirmative action bonuses for black and Hispanic applicants were dropped, and simultaneously the academic performance of black and Hispanic students was improved to levels achieved by white applicants who are in similar circumstances. The remarkable and totally unexpected conclusion one draws from the comparison is that *there is essentially no difference whatsoever in the shares of black and Hispanic students admitted under the two conditions.* Whether we consider current practice or a situation where black and Hispanic applicants have been put on an equal academic footing with their white counterparts after affirmative action has been lifted, approximately 13 percent of all admitted students are members of underrepresented minority groups. If anything, minority student shares might be slightly larger in the simulation.

These results are very encouraging. Their message is that, in the long run, the way to create a diverse racial and ethnic mix of students on elite college and university campuses is through a process in which all students compete for admission on a level academic playing field. In such a situation, affirmative action would no longer be needed to guarantee a critical mass of minority students. While positive preferences for athletes, legacies, or members of other subgroups of applicants might still be utilized to achieve other institutional objectives, admission bonuses for underrepresented minority students would no longer be necessary to achieve the balance of different racial and ethnic groups observed today.[40]

It is also instructive to see how little change there is in the proportions of white and Asian students among accepted candidates. Roughly 74 percent of the ranks are filled by white students under either condition, and there is no change at all expected in the proportion of Asian students (13 percent) out of those who have been admitted. The comparison also suggests that admitted students in the simulation will be drawn from somewhat higher social class backgrounds than those of actual admittees, although the differences are not at all large. If it is believed that the simulated proportions of admitted lower- and working-class students are too low, even by today's standards, giving slightly more consideration in the admission process to low-income students could be expected to restore a more socioeconomically desirable shape to the first-year class.[41]

[40] Encouraging a varied mix of well-qualified students to apply is also a crucial step in the process. This suggests that admission deans need to emphasize outreach and recruitment as an ongoing and important part of their day-to-day responsibilities.

[41] We also experimented to see what impact a completely race-neutral admission policy would have when applied to an applicant pool with no racial academic achievement gap. The proportion of students admitted to private institutions who are Asian increases to 37 percent. The white student share declines to less than 50 percent, while black and Hispanic students each make up roughly 7 percent of admitted students. At public institutions, the same assumptions imply the following shares among admitted students: white (85 percent), black (9 percent), Hispanic (between 2 and 3 percent), and Asian (4 percent).

There is reason to believe that our estimates of the simulated proportions of admitted black and Hispanic students in Table 9.8 could be too low. One can easily imagine that having stronger academic qualifications would encourage more black and Hispanic students not only to complete high school but also to aspire to attend some of the most elite colleges and universities in the United States. These heightened aspirations are likely to be reflected in larger proportions of underrepresented minority students in applicant pools at both selective private and public institutions. There is every reason to expect that these larger proportions of highly qualified black and Hispanic applicants would be matched by larger proportions of such students among all candidates who are accepted and then among those who enroll in the first-year class. By focusing on the consequences of improved academic performance among a *fixed* group of students in NSCE applicant pools, we may have overlooked some of the potentially important second-round effects that could increase minority representation even more at the nation's top colleges.

Summary

This chapter has used microsimulation analysis to investigate likely impacts on the composition of admitted students of alternative admission policies at academically selective universities in the United States. One of our major concerns is with the representation of black and Hispanic students in the overall pool of admitted students. Under current admission policies, which consider membership in a racial or an ethnic minority group to be a plus factor in admission, black and Hispanic students account for slightly more than 16 percent of all students who were admitted to private NSCE colleges in the fall of 1997 and somewhat more than 9 percent of all admitted students at public universities. We looked at how these proportions could be expected to change under a variety of alternative scenarios, including (1) eliminating race-based affirmative action programs, (2) moving to a completely race-neutral admission policy, (3) adding extra weight for applicants from lower- and working-class family backgrounds on top of affirmative action preferences, (4) substituting economic or class-based affirmative action for race-based affirmative action, (5) reducing the emphasis given to a candidate's academic credentials, (6) giving priority to applicants who rank in the top 10 percent of their high school class, and (7) admitting students solely on the basis of their SAT scores.

In this exhaustive examination of a wide variety of potential admission policies, we have looked for but have not found any feasible policy alternative to the current practice of race-sensitive admission that has the capacity to generate the same minority student representation on campus.

The closest we have come among private institutions is a 15 percent minority student share among all admitted students, achieved by lifting affirmative action, adding more weight for low-income students, and paying no attention whatsoever to students' academic qualifications. This policy stands no chance of being implemented at any academically selective institution. On the public side, a maximum minority student share of 7 percent is registered, again by substituting more low-income weight for affirmative action and disregarding academic credentials.

As a last set of simulations, we considered the implications of improving test scores and other academic performance measures of black and Hispanic applicants relative to their white counterparts. In particular, we examined the effects of closing the racial academic achievement gap. The remarkable insight from this analysis is that improving the academic performance of underrepresented minority students constitutes the only viable, long-run strategy for preserving meaningful minority representation on elite college campuses if race-based affirmative action is eliminated. No amount of tinkering with admission practices can match the power or attractiveness of this solution. We are led, then, to an answer to the question: Where do we go from here? The U.S. Supreme Court in 2003 handed race-conscious affirmative action a reprieve. However, with the Court newly reconstituted and with expanding (and so far largely successful) efforts to ban affirmative action through state ballot initiatives, affirmative action's remaining life expectancy is uncertain. In the meantime, we need to make closing the racial achievement gap a high societal priority and to move aggressively and with the greatest determination to make it happen.

Chapter Ten

WHERE DO WE GO FROM HERE?

IN THIS CONCLUDING chapter we pull back from the detailed analyses in earlier chapters and ask: What does it all mean? What are the lessons to be learned? And where do we go from here? Preceding chapters have stressed themes of inequality and how they manifest themselves by race and social class at academically selective colleges and universities. We have examined strategies used in preparing for admission to selective colleges, the strength and varieties of admission preferences conferred, and social class differences by race and ethnicity. We have also studied how graduates from selective schools evaluate their undergraduate experience in terms of satisfaction with the social and academic sides of college life, how much was learned by associating with different kinds of students, and how social class mediates the cost of college.

Rather than repeat these chapter summaries, we prefer instead to use this final chapter to draw out the implications of the most significant aspects of inequality that our research has uncovered. There are three issues in particular we wish to highlight. One is the unique role that elite higher education plays in perpetuating intergenerational inequality in America. A second is a tendency on the part of some undergraduate students after they arrive on campus to withdraw into relatively homogeneous racial subgroups and spend their college years without much cross-racial social interaction. These patterns of behavior have significant implications for the educational benefits of diversity. Finally, racial and ethnic differences in academic achievement—differences that emerge well before students apply to college—persist over the course of students' college careers and affect many things that selective universities do, from recruitment and admission to the conferring of degrees. Each of these issues poses important challenges, both for leaders of higher education and for society as a whole. Our discussion will include recommendations for how these challenges can be met. Throughout, readers are referred to previous chapters for more information by relevant chapter numbers placed in bold brackets (for example, [6]).

REPRODUCING INEQUALITY

Intergenerational transmission of inequality is a hallmark of most human societies. Individuals who occupy the top rungs on the socioeconomic ladder produce children who tend to be advantaged when they reach adulthood. Conversely, parents of lesser means have offspring who, as adults, tend to be disproportionately concentrated at the bottom of the social and economic distribution. These outcomes are not preordained or inevitable, of course, but there are strong correlations pointing in this direction. We should be surprised if it were otherwise, because the rich and powerful in society are the ones who make society's rules.

It is easy to see how income and wealth inequality are reproduced. Laws governing the accumulation and disposition of property and other assets make it possible for the well-to-do to distribute wealth to their children in tax-advantaged ways. But what happens when it comes to such achieved statuses as educational attainment or occupational status? In these instances, where individual accomplishment is prized, who one's parents are may be less relevant. We know that the economic return to a college education has continued to increase (Mishel, Bernstein, and Allegretto, 2007). Further, given that one has a college degree, the economic payoff to attending an elite college or university is also rising [2]. Therefore, which students pass through the gates of the nation's most distinguished academic institutions matters a great deal to patterns of social and economic inequality. If access is improving for children in lower- and working-class families, then elite higher education might be opening pathways to upward mobility for many less advantaged, but nevertheless highly talented, students. But if elite higher education is serving mainly the offspring of those who are already privileged in society, then these institutions might justifiably be held accountable for aiding and abetting a process that recycles opportunity and reinforces existing patterns of inequality from one generation to the next.

Economic advantage among parents begets educational advantage for their children. We noted earlier [2] that high school students with better grades and test scores are the ones most likely to apply to college. And students with the strongest academic credentials tend to apply to the most selective colleges and universities. We also pointed out that parents' socioeconomic status, including family income and education, is highly correlated with children's academic aspirations and performance. When we also factor in the economic reality that the return to a college degree is rising and the return to an elite degree is rising even faster, we are witness to the anatomy of intergenerational inequality. Parents who do very well in their own generation have children who in turn do very well when they become adults.[1]

Forces that produce American-style inequality are gathering strength. A widening gap separates the incomes of families with college students

---

[1] A fuller account of this "reproduction thesis" is contained in Stevens (2007: 10–13).

compared to all families. At the same time, the family incomes of students at selective colleges and universities are drifting away from the family incomes of all college students. Between 1997 and 2006, the difference between the median family income of students at the nation's most selective four-year nonsectarian colleges and the median family income of all four-year college students rose by 22 percent [8]. Over time at NSCE institutions, students are being drawn from higher and higher rungs on the social class ladder [8]. Students at both public and private NSCE schools, as well as all four racial-ethnic groups, reflect these new realities. This socioeconomic version of continental drift has clear implications for the social reproduction of inequality across generations. Increasingly, more opportunity is being transmitted via elite college destinations to those who are already privileged by their parents' position in society.[2]

At least two factors influence trends in who receives the economic prizes elite higher education confers. First, because of rapidly rising costs of higher education, families who send their children to college—and especially to a selective college—are coming from points farther out in the upper tail of the family income distribution (Leonhardt, 2004). Second, the income distribution itself is being stretched, so that the same point in the upper tail of the distribution corresponds to a higher annual income. New work by Piketty and Saez (2003) shows that the share of gross personal income claimed by the top 1 percent of tax filing units rose from 8.2 percent in 1980 to 17.4 percent in 2005—a concentration of income at the top of the distribution not seen since 1936.[3]

Disadvantages faced by lower-income students are compounded by financial aid policies. State support for public higher education has dwindled, leaving a larger share to be paid by families (McPherson and Schapiro, 2006b). At the same time, the purchasing power of federal Pell grants for low-income students has declined (Gerald and Haycock, 2006). Merit aid deployed to attract desirable candidates who might otherwise enroll elsewhere is rising faster in total dollars than need-based aid for low-income students (Long and Riley, 2007). Inadequate financial aid lowers

---

[2] One consequence is that intergenerational income mobility has declined and is now no greater than that in Europe (Levy and Temin, 2007). The United States also ranks behind northern Europe but ahead of other European countries in intergenerational educational mobility (Pfeffer, 2007).

[3] The original essay by Piketty and Saez (2003) carried the data on income inequality through 1998. The latest data to 2005 can be found on Saez's Web site, http://www.econ .berkeley.edu/~saez/ (accessed March 2007). An increase in the economic return to a college degree is mentioned prominently as a reason for the rise in income inequality (Becker and Murphy, 2007). But policy and institutional factors have also been implicated, including the declining bargaining power of unions, a falling real value for the minimum wage, lower marginal tax rates for the highest earners (Levy and Temin, 2007), and a growing emphasis on pay-for-performance practices (Lemieux, MacLeod, and Parent, 2007).

enrollment rates for poorer and working-class students who have been admitted to selective colleges (Avery and Hoxby, 2004; Linsenmeier, Rosen, and Rouse, 2006) and contributes to higher attrition among students who have enrolled (Ishitani and DesJardins, 2002; Stinebrickner and Stinebrickner, 2007).

The Role of Higher Education

Elite higher education also contributes to the problem of reproducing inequality. When we examine the socioeconomic profiles of students who apply to, are accepted by, enroll at, and finally graduate from NSCE colleges and universities, we find there is a growing representation at each successive stage of students from upper-middle- and upper-class family backgrounds [6, 8]. In crafting a class, elite institutions take what are already exceptionally privileged applicant pools and put them through a sieve that preserves even more advantage. These features characterize both private and public NSCE schools, but they come into sharper contrast at private colleges and universities.[4] Beyond that, despite relatively generous financial aid packages that NSCE schools are able to offer, the financial burden of a college education—whether measured by first-year net costs or total debt in relation to family income or net worth—weighs most heavily on lower- and working-class students and least so, or not at all, on upper-middle- and upper-class students [7]. Accumulated college debt constrains post-graduation options for students, encouraging many to seek higher-paying jobs instead of less remunerative public service positions (Rothstein and Rouse, 2007).

Before suggesting that selective colleges and universities are perhaps not doing enough to reverse the decline in socioeconomic diversity on their campuses, it is important to acknowledge some of the useful steps they are taking. In the absence of these measures, the growing homogenization around students from upper-middle- and upper-class backgrounds would be even greater. First, racial affirmative action is expanding opportunity for black and Hispanic students who, on average, come from lower socioeconomic backgrounds than do white or Asian students. Eliminating affirmative action at the group of private colleges in our study is expected to reduce the proportion of admitted students from lower- and working-class families from 10 to 7 percent, and increase the share of upper-middle- and upper-class students from 57 to 60 percent. The expected changes at public universities are in the same direction [9].

---

[4]Soares (2007), for example, is critical of Yale University and other similarly elite schools for the overwhelming importance of family wealth in admission decisions.

Second, private NSCE institutions already practice class-based affirmative action [3]. The average admission bonus is worth 130 SAT points for lower-class applicants, as compared to middle-class students. For working-class applicants, the plus factor is worth 70 SAT points. At the other end, upper-class applicants pay a modest price in admission equivalent to 30 SAT points. The low SES benefit at private colleges is reserved largely for nonwhite applicants for whom the probability of being admitted, on an all-other-things-equal basis, is greatest for lower-class students and then declines as social class rises. For white students, admission chances vary with social class in an inverted U-shaped pattern. They are smallest for low and high SES applicants and largest for white students from middle- and upper-middle-class backgrounds. Although these efforts to attract more low-income students are laudable, they are not strong enough to overcome upper-class privilege in admission. At private NSCE colleges and universities there is still a positive correlation between students' social class position and the chances of being admitted—ranging from 19 percent for lower- and working-class students combined, to 21 percent for the middle class, and to 27 percent when upper-middle- and upper-class applicants are grouped together.

Third, selective colleges and universities are responding to calls to increase financial aid and expand eligibility.[5] Some schools (including Princeton, Davidson, Amherst, the University of Pennsylvania, and Swarthmore) have eliminated loans for all students with demonstrated financial need (Hoover, 2007a). Harvard announced that families with annual incomes of up to $180,000 would be eligible for financial aid, to assist middle-class and upper-middle-class students and keep Harvard financially competitive with major state universities (Rimer and Finder, 2007). Yale followed suit by raising the upper limit on family income to $200,000 (Arenson, 2008a). Other institutions have announced partial no-loan programs or voided tuition for students whose family income is below a certain level.[6]

---

[5]Recent accounts have called unflattering attention to the rising share of students from upper-income backgrounds in elite higher education (Golden, 2006; Sacks, 2007a, 2007b; Soares, 2007). At the same time, there has been a groundswell of scholarly appeals to enroll more low-income students (Bowen, Kurzweil, and Tobin, 2005; Kahlenberg, 2004; McPherson and Schapiro, 2006a).

[6]Brown, Duke, Stanford, Columbia, Washington University, and Williams, among others, have increased financial aid and expanded eligibility (Bloomberg News, 2008; Finder, 2008a; Glater, 2008a; Rimer and Finder, 2007). Columbia University received a $400 million gift from an alumnus, the amount to be used entirely for financial aid (Lewin, 2007b). Such gifts may not be as visible as a new building with a donor's name, but they may in the end have greater value added.

So What (More) Is to Be Done?

As noted above, there are numerous factors that contribute to the rise in income inequality in America. It is unrealistic to expect that there is much higher education can do by itself to reverse them. At the same time, we would like to believe that the nation's most selective colleges and universities—and certainly the best endowed among them—could do more to increase mobility chances even if income inequality is increasing. What this means in practical terms is that selective institutions should aspire to *socioeconomic neutrality*. In other words, they should aim to preserve the socioeconomic composition of students in their applicant pools in the social class profiles of students whom they admit, enroll, and graduate. If the proportion of high SES students did not increase (as it does now) across the various stages leading from application to admission and finally to graduation, then elite higher education would be doing its fair share—and perhaps more—to open up and protect pathways to upward mobility for academically talented members of society's less advantaged groups. It goes without saying that the good these institutions could do would be undermined if low-income students had large loans to repay following graduation.[7]

Socioeconomic neutrality is a high standard and bound to meet numerous objections. The first is that there are not enough talented, lower-income students in the country to go around. Or, perhaps more likely, the numbers exist but these students are not thinking about applying to top-tier colleges and universities. So the challenge to selective institutions begins with recruitment and the need to identify and attract more low-income students of high ability into their applicant pools. One is reminded here of the way recruited athletes make their way onto coaches' lists for admission. Academic deans could learn a lesson or two from their athletic departments. The available evidence suggests the task is not impossible. Hill and Winston (2006b) show there are sufficient numbers of high-ability (SAT scores of 1420 or higher), low-income (in the bottom two quintiles of the family income distribution) students nationwide to permit the twenty-eight academically selective private colleges known as the "COFHE schools" to increase their numbers of highly talented, lower-income students to mirror national proportions.[8] Carnevale and

---

[7] It is also clear that a policy that creates more campus socioeconomic diversity has the potential to add significantly to the overall educational benefits of diversity.

[8] The Consortium on Financing Higher Education (COFHE) is an organization of private colleges and universities, formed in 1971 for the purpose of examining how selective institutions can provide exceptional educational opportunities for talented students and meet best practices in fiscal management.

Rose (2004) have estimated there are perhaps as many as three hundred thousand low-income students with the potential to achieve high SAT scores but who are not attending a four-year college. They refer to these students as "the low-hanging fruit in any policy strategy to increase socioeconomic diversity in four-year colleges, including selective colleges" (136). The point made by these studies is that supply constraints are not keeping colleges and universities from expanding their numbers of economically disadvantaged students. Rather, the focus should be on encouraging more of the most promising students of modest means to apply to a four-year college in the first place.

Admission policies represent the second step in maintaining socioeconomic neutrality. Here the objection one often encounters is that more low-income students cannot be admitted without sacrificing academic standards. Our research has shown that in the applicant pools at selective private NSCE institutions there are already sufficient numbers of highly qualified, lower-income students to admit more of such students, thereby preserving social class neutrality in admissions without compromising the average academic credentials of students who are accepted.[9] Simulations for private schools support this conclusion [9].[10]

There are four scenarios that produce a proportion of upper-middle- and upper-class students in the accepted pool that is no higher than the proportion in the applicant pool. Two of these simulations involve giving more weight in admission to lower- and working-class applicants while keeping race-based affirmative action intact.[11] Neither alternative results in an appreciable drop in the average SAT score for the admitted class (a decline to 1388 in one case and to 1386 in another, compared with 1405 under current practice). A third simulation involves admitting candidates to private institutions based solely on their high school class ranks and GPAs, together with information on SAT scores.[12] Here the average SAT score of admitted students increases to 1419. Only when racial affirmative action is eliminated and replaced by more low SES weight in admission, and no attention is paid to ACT or SAT scores or to high school class ranks and GPAs, is there a noticeable decline in academic standards

---

[9] The issue surrounding admission is largely moot at public NSCE institutions, because aggregate acceptance rates are uncorrelated with candidates' social class backgrounds [8].

[10] Bowen, Kurzweil, and Tobin (2005: 180) also report that admitting more low SES students leaves academic standards as measured by average SAT scores of the entering class "essentially unchanged."

[11] In the first instance, lower- and working-class applicants are shown the same preference as black and Hispanic candidates, respectively. In the second scenario, legacy preferences are assigned to lower- and working-class applicants.

[12] In this scenario admission officers are assumed to ignore other factors that are usually considered, including race, social class, gender, athlete and legacy status, and the like.

(to an average SAT score of 1329 for the admitted class—a decline of between 5 and 6 percent).

Another step elite institutions can take to "do more" to increase equality of opportunity is to ensure that lower-income students who do enroll have the possibility of graduating at the same rate as all other students. Failure to graduate represents a loss of individual student talent as well as institutional resources. Even though some of our earlier data suggested no significant social class differentials in graduation for enrolled students, these data were based on seven NSCE schools in 1997 [8]. A fuller accounting of graduation rates for matriculants at all eight NSCE colleges and universities for the combined 1993 and 1997 entering cohorts suggests low SES students are at a disadvantage. Roughly 80 percent of lower- and working-class students graduate in six years, as compared with 90 percent of students from higher social class families [6]. Part of the reason for higher attrition among lower-income students is inadequate financial aid and mounting loan obligations (Baum and Saunders, 1998; Engle and O'Brien, 2007).

The good news in all of this, however, is that we already have solid evidence from the experience of our NSCE institutions that social class neutrality is possible—at least for members of underrepresented minority groups [8]. For black and Hispanic students in the 1997 cohort, the proportions from upper-middle- and upper-class family backgrounds increase by no more than two percentage points when one compares the applicant pool with those who graduate within six years of matriculation. By contrast, proportions in the top two social classes increase by seven percentage points for white students and by 13 percentage points for Asians.

Socioeconomic neutrality requires paying attention to other conditions surrounding college completion besides graduation rates. The playing field for lower-income students cannot be level if the loans they are required to accept in order to finance their educations leave them with substantially higher debt burdens than those faced by other students. At the present time, though, this is the reality at most academically selective institutions. But financial aid is expensive, and it has to compete for dollars against other institutional priorities. Being able to come up with the requisite amount of financial aid to attract and retain students is often the critical stumbling block to creating more socioeconomic diversity. A report from the Advisory Committee on Student Financial Assistance (2006), a committee that provides advice to the secretary of the U.S. Department of Education on financial aid policy, has concluded that during the 1990s between 1.0 and 1.6 million bachelor's degrees were lost among college-ready students from low- and moderate-income families because of tuition price barriers. The committee estimates that another 1.4 to 2.4 million bachelor's degrees will be foregone during the current decade.

So another potential objection to our proposal that selective institutions could promote social mobility by remaining socioeconomically neutral is that the proposal is simply unrealistic. It would cost too much money to implement. Michael McPherson, president of the Spencer Foundation, and Morton Schapiro, president of Williams College—two academic leaders who have written widely on financial aid matters—say flatly,

> Only a relative handful of private colleges and universities can afford to admit the freshman class without regard to family financial capacity and at the same time meet the financial needs of all those admitted students who choose to enroll. . . . Indeed, the reality is that even many nationally ranked and highly selective private universities and colleges would stagger under the burden if they succeeded in enrolling many more low-income students. (McPherson and Schapiro, 2006b: 7)

There is no easy rebuttal to this argument. The first requirement in assembling an entering freshman class is to meet bottom-line financial targets (Duffy and Goldberg, 1998), and no matter how one looks at it, these efforts cost money. Davidson College officials estimate that their no-loan program will cost $3.5 million per year (Lipka, 2007). Amherst College expects to spend an extra $1.6 million in just the first year to replace loans with grants (Hoover, 2007a). When Princeton announced its full no-loan policy in 2001, university officials estimated that the new program and other enhancements to financial aid would cost $5 million (Marks, 2001). Harvard's new proposal will require increasing spending on financial aid by $22 million each year beginning with the 2008–9 academic year (Rimer and Finder, 2007). Yale's new financial aid policy will raise spending on undergraduate aid by $24 million (Arenson, 2008a). Higher spending from endowments and increased alumni contributions are expected to pay for the new initiatives. One reason these programs are affordable is that highly selective institutions enroll relatively few low-income students, at least in relation to less competitive colleges and universities (McPherson and Schapiro, 2006b).

A final objection to our proposal is that, even if highly selective colleges and universities manage to enroll more disadvantaged students and stabilize the social class profiles of students as they progress from application to graduation, the overall effect on higher education more broadly will be very small. Part of the argument is that there will merely be substitutions between tier-one and tier-two institutions, with the first-tier institutions taking some of the low-income students who would otherwise have gone to a second-tier school with little net impact (McPherson and Schapiro, 2006b). Another part is that elite colleges and universities—the ones that are in the best position to take in more students from less privileged backgrounds—enroll only about 2 percent of the nation's freshman class, so that their efforts, even if effective, are not likely to amount to very much (McPherson and Schapiro, 2006b). The obvious counterargument is that these same highly selective schools are the leaders in American higher education (W. Bowen, 2006). What they say, and more especially what they do, can help set "the tone at the top." Their presidents have a bully pulpit from which to help mold public opinion and shape public policy. This latter point is particularly important, because higher education is going to need the partnership of state and federal governments if sufficient financial aid dollars are going to be pried loose to make a significant difference.

INEQUALITY IN SOCIAL INTERACTIONS

Our research has shown that there is a moderate amount of mixing and mingling across racial and ethnic lines among NSCE undergraduates [5]. Roughly two-thirds of respondents said they socialized frequently with students from other races; one-half had a roommate from a different race; another one-half indicated that at least one of their five closest friends in college was from a different racial or ethnic group; and one-third of students said they dated someone in college from another racial group. From this perspective, the glass looks half full. But looked at in another way, the glass is half empty. One-third of students socialized much less frequently or not at all with members of other racial groups; one-half lived only with students from their own racial group or never had a roommate; and one-half indicated that all of their closest friends in college shared their race or ethnicity.

We also showed that cross-racial social interactions matter a great deal in terms of learning from difference [8]. Even though substantial fractions of NSCE students were ambivalent about how much they learned from students whose racial and ethnic backgrounds differed from their own, and despite the fact that just as many respondents felt they learned only a little as those who said they learned a lot, interacting across racial and ethnic lines is linked to educational benefits. Students who participated in interracial associations in any of four different settings—including frequent general socializing, roommate choices after freshman year, best-friend networks, or dating—were roughly twice as likely to indicate they learned "a lot" from difference as students who did not have these kinds of beneficial interactions.

The lesson for college and university administrators seems clear. Maximizing the educational benefits of diversity requires creating opportunities for students to come together in meaningful ways across racial and ethnic categories. The challenge to colleges and universities is to "move beyond Michigan" and make the most of diversity. By this we mean that it is not enough for selective institutions to admit a racially diverse class, relying in part on principles of race-based affirmative action guaranteed in *Grutter v. Bollinger*. Diversity work does not end at the admission office. Once students matriculate, the challenge to administrators is to identify students who are unlikely to have, or perhaps even want, much in the way of cross-racial interaction—and we have observed that their numbers are not small—and develop the kinds of policies and programs that are likely to foster productive interracial contact.

This challenge is made more formidable by the fact that there are inequalities in social interactions. The strength of affinities that exist within and between racial and ethnic groups depends on the groups being considered. Social distance is not independent of race or ethnicity. Our research has shown that white students are the most racially isolated group on campus.[13] Whites are more likely than any other racial or ethnic group to interact exclusively with other coethnics and least likely to interact with non-coethnics. Among nonwhite students, blacks are the most racially insular. Hispanics are the least self-segregated group, interacting with non-Hispanics more frequently than they do with other Hispanic students. Given these patterns, it is not surprising that 46 percent of Hispanic students believe they learned a lot from other students with different racial or ethnic backgrounds in contrast to just 26 percent of white students [8].

An examination of the prevalence of social interaction among alternative pairs of racial or ethnic groups reveals the existence of a racial gradient. Interaction is most common when one of the groups is white, and it is least likely to take place when one of the groups is black. In particular, information derived from descriptive tables [5] shows that the greatest social distance separates blacks and other nonwhite groups. The smallest social distance tends to occur between whites and either Asians or Hispanics. When we control for factors that might influence the frequency of interracial contact, including the relative availability of different groups on campus [5], we still find that the likelihood of cross-race interaction is greatest when the groups involved are whites and Asians or whites and Hispanics. Blacks register the lowest levels of contact in their associations with whites, Asians, or Hispanics. Interactions between Asians and Hispanics occur with intermediate frequency.

The realization that the level of contact among members of two different racial-ethnic groups on NSCE campuses depends very much on which

---

[13] Other research using different data has come to the same conclusion (Chang, Astin, and Kim, 2004; Smith et al., 1997).

two groups these are suggests in another way that interracial contact is not yet on an equal footing for all groups concerned. It also raises the bar for colleges and universities. While more cross-race contact of a productive type would be welcome no matter which groups are participating, the particular challenges facing university officials seem first to encourage more white students to become involved with their nonwhite counterparts. In addition, however, the largest social cleavages appear to separate underrepresented minorities from white and Asian students. This suggests that whites and Asians should be encouraged to take advantage of opportunities to become better acquainted with their black and Hispanic peers, and vice versa.

Difficulty of the Challenge

Meeting this challenge is complicated by the fact that general attitudes among incoming college freshmen are moving in counterproductive ways. Data from the annual freshmen survey conducted by UCLA's Higher Education Research Institute suggest four important nationwide trends (Sax et al., 2004: 10–11): (1) a declining proportion of first-year students indicates that promoting racial understanding is an important personal goal; (2) a rising percentage believes that racial discrimination is no longer a problem in America; (3) smaller proportions say they frequently socialized with someone of a different race/ethnicity while in high school; and (4) declining fractions of freshmen report the chances are "very good" they will socialize with someone from a different racial group while in college. When responses are disaggregated by racial category, whites consistently display the least "integrationist" attitudes and behaviors. Most of these trends have been evident since 1990 (Pryor, Hurtado, Saenz, Santos, and Korn, 2007).

In addition, encouraging more social connections across racial and ethnic lines means confronting the fact that students' attitudes and behaviors on American college campuses are rooted in racial attitudes in American society more generally (Levin, 2003: 97). Children absorb these attitudes while they are growing up and bring them to college, just as surely as they come with bicycles, iPods, and backpacks. Beverly Daniel Tatum (2007), a longtime student of racial identity development and now president of Spelman College, puts it this way:

> Our choice of friends is shaped in part, if not wholly, by our sense of self-definition, particularly in adolescence and adulthood. But self-definition does not emerge in a vacuum. It is shaped by a lifetime of social interactions, molded by messages received about who we are in the world, how others perceive us, and with whom we

should seek connection. In a society where racial group membership is still a meaningful social characteristic, the development of racial identity is relevant to how our social connections are formed and maintained. (86)

She goes on to say,

Even when parents have positive racial attitudes, children can absorb the prejudices of their peers and the wider cultural media. The specific content of those prejudices, and their targets, will vary depending on where students have grown up and what their life experience has been. But we can be sure that all members of our campus population have come to college with stereotypes and prejudices about some other segment of our student body. (109–10)

Despite signs of progress in racial attitudes—for example, there is growing support among whites for ideals of racial equality and integration—there is also evidence of persistent negative racial stereotypes and growing alienation among many blacks (Bobo, 2001). Camille Charles (2006) has conducted a thorough study of racial attitudes and preferences for racial neighborhood composition in Los Angeles. Two of her findings are particularly noteworthy. First, substantial proportions (more than 50 percent) of whites and, especially, Asians hold negative stereotypes about blacks and Latinos. Only a small fraction (less than 5 percent) of Asians harbors negative views about whites. Second, respondents to her survey were asked to describe the racial composition of their "ideal neighborhood." The racial group that is most preferred is one's *own* group. This is the case for each group of survey participants, but it is truest for whites and least so for native-born Asians. Further, whites are the most desired outgroup, while blacks are least preferred. Charles (2006: 125) concludes that racial attitudes and patterns of preferences for neighborhood racial composition both "follow a now-predictable racial hierarchy: whites are always the most preferred outgroup and blacks the least preferred; Asians and Latinos, in that order, are located in between these two extremes."

There is a wide arc of evidence linking racial attitudes and preferences in the adult population to student behaviors in the campus "neighborhood." For one thing, racial attitudes among adults in Los Angeles are quite similar to those held by adults nationwide (Charles, 2006: 115). Second, the degree of correspondence between the percentage of one racial group holding negative stereotypes about another group in Charles's Los Angeles data and the proportion of one campus group having substantial social contact with another group in the NSCE data is remarkable. High proportions holding negative stereotypes (e.g., whites about blacks or Latinos) are highly correlated with low levels of social interaction on campus.[14] Third, as noted in an earlier chapter [5], students' racial attitudes—measured at the beginning of their freshman year by the degree of social distance separating one racial group from another—are strongly associated with subsequent patterns of cross-racial behavioral interactions in the NSCE data. Finally, racial differences in students' socioeconomic status—differences we have documented in many ways with respect to parents' education, occupation, income, homeownership, and wealth [4] or having college loans to repay [7]—no doubt help solidify racial prejudices on campus, just as racial attitudes and socioeconomic inequality are mutually reinforcing in the broader society (Bobo, 2001; Charles, 2006).

So What's to Be Done?

An accumulating body of evidence suggests there are educational benefits to diversity. Social interaction in college with diverse peers has positive learning and democracy outcomes (Gurin et al., 2002). Cross-race connections in the form of having meals or studying together, dating, or interacting in the classroom contribute to intellectual ability, social skills, and civic interest (Chang, Astin, and Kim, 2004). Beyond individual students and the institutions they attend, diverse college campuses also contribute to private enterprise and the economy as well as society at large (Milem, 2003). But as Light (2001) and numerous others have pointed out, realizing these benefits requires not only a structurally diverse campus environment but also sufficient social interaction across racial and ethnic group lines.

There are reasons to be hopeful that greater amounts of cross-racial interaction can be encouraged despite the obstacles we have mentioned. It is possible for colleges and universities to push back against the forces of negative racial stereotypes and attitudes that are generated by, among other things, entrenched patterns of racial residential segregation. One reason is that college is a time when young people are open to new ideas and experimentation. Minds that have been formed around one way of looking at the world can be trained to consider, if not always adopt, new perspectives. In addition, researchers who have begun to study "peer effects" in college have shown that students do learn from and influence each other (Winston and Zimmerman, 2004). Finally, we know from available evidence that there are strategies university officials can adopt to increase the amount of interracial contact among undergraduates.

[14] A similar point is made by Charles (2006: 129): "A growing body of research points to the direct effects of negative racial stereotypes on preferences for integration. As expected, the more negatively a particular racial group is perceived, the less desirable members of that group are as potential neighbors, and this is especially true for whites' perceptions."

What are some of these strategies? We showed earlier that the likelihood of students interacting with peers whose racial backgrounds differ from their own is positively associated with taking a course about another racial or ethnic group, participating in an ethnic activity celebrating some other racial group (e.g., a Black History month event), having a freshman-year roommate from another race, holding a job during the first year of college, or attending a campus with a substantial presence of nonwhite students [5]. The good news in all of this is that students' characteristics (apart from their race) do not seem to impact cross-racial interactions very much. But what students and institutions *do* matters a great deal.

We also showed that some kinds of social connections matter more than others in influencing students' assessments of how much they learn from students from other racial or ethnic backgrounds [8]. General socializing with members of other racial groups—provided it is of the "often" or "very often" kind—and interracial dating have more powerful effects on learning from difference than having either cross-race roommates after freshman year or interracial friendship networks. Of these two, general socializing is the single most influential kind of interracial contact in producing educational benefits of diversity. This conclusion suggests an avenue college administrators may want to pursue. The more public and less intimate types of social contact are easier to form and are more prevalent than interracial friendship networks or dating [5]. Moreover, encouraging more frequent general contact across racial lines is likely to receive broader public support than efforts to promote interracial dating. As Larry Bobo (2001) has noted in his study of American racial attitudes, "In general, the more public and impersonal the arena, the greater the evidence of movement toward endorsing ideals of integration and equality" (271).

Colleges will of course want to experiment with their own curricular and co-curricular initiatives. But one that is worth considering is suggested by our own empirical evidence that having a job during one's freshman year is positively associated with the likelihood of campus cross-racial contact and with learning from difference. We cannot tell from our data what kinds of jobs these are, but it is reasonable to speculate that work-study students are coming into contact with members of other racial and ethnic groups in fulfilling their financial aid obligations. Why not extend these benefits to all students? Why not have a mandatory "community service" activity? Students could work in small, multiracial groups on a variety of projects within the campus community or off campus. Such programs would not only encourage the kinds of cross-racial, equal-status contact in pursuit of a common objective that Allport (1979) showed produces positive results in reducing prejudice. If these group projects replaced work-study requirements for students who receive financial assistance, they would also have a secondary benefit of helping erase social class distinctions. At present, it is all too easy for students from more affluent circumstances to recognize students who are on financial aid by the kinds of campus jobs they hold.

Additional strategies that hold promise for increasing productive cross-racial contact among undergraduates have been suggested by other researchers. Some of these strategies feature residential life initiatives. Light (2001) focuses on the importance of embedding diversity in first-year residential living arrangements. Antonio (2004) finds that freshman-year roommates provide a basis for male students' friendships throughout college. A final observation relevant to residential life comes from the Campus Life in America Student Survey (the CLASS project) at Princeton University's Office of Population Research. The purpose of the CLASS project is to see whether it is possible to derive from the experiences of a set of higher education institutions a set of "best practices" for maximizing the educational benefits of diversity. The CLASS project has collected student survey and institutional data from six colleges and universities (Princeton, Emory, University of Miami, Michigan State, UCLA, and Portland State). Freshmen were interviewed in the fall of 2004 and again in 2006 and asked about the extent of their diversity experiences and how satisfied they are with these experiences. Roughly one hundred institutional representatives were interviewed to collect qualitative data about a range of university policies, programs, and practices with respect to diversity. The CLASS project is relating what institutions do to a range of student-level outcomes to find out what works and what does not.

One set of analyses conducted so far finds that the race of one's first-year roommate matters for diversity outcomes. Stephanie Grace (2007) focuses on the result of a natural experiment. Most of the schools in the CLASS project use random assignment of freshman-year roommates. She shows that students who have roommates whose race or ethnicity is different from their own rate more positively the quality of their interracial interactions and are significantly more open to diversity experiences by their junior year than are students with same-race first-year roommates. Friendship patterns throughout college are also affected by one's freshman-year roommate. Having a freshman roommate from another race or ethnicity is associated with having a best friend in junior year whose race is different. Moreover, the best friend's race is more likely to match the roommate's race. Finally, Grace shows that the proportion of one's closest friends in junior year who are from other races is positively affected by having a first-year roommate from another race or ethnicity. In addition, the racial composition of the friendship network is more likely to reflect the first-year roommate's race. In short, residential housing arrangements freshman year can have a number of positive diversity consequences.

Finally, campus leaders can also insist on a policy of inclusion, provide incentives for co-sponsorship of events by two or more student groups, and set a tone that fosters a positive campus climate. Gurin et al. (2002) have found that informal interactional diversity is frequently more effective than classroom diversity in producing positive educational benefits. Tatum (2007) provides numerous examples of curricular and co-curricular initiatives, including multicultural course requirements. Chang, Astin, and Kim (2004) find that the percentage of students of color on campus, the proportion of students who work part-time on campus, and (at the student level) living on campus are all positively related to higher levels of cross-racial interaction.[15]

We do not yet have a sufficient appreciation for the full arsenal of diversity initiatives that can be deployed to increase interracial contact among undergraduates and maximize the educational benefits of diversity. Certainly, more cross-institutional studies are needed (Smith et al., 1997). More commitment and experimentation at the institutional level will also be required to move the focus of diversity beyond the doors of the admission office and onto the college campus. This will be hard work, and the path will not always be smooth. But we do know some things already. Proximity by itself is not enough (Edley, 1996). One cannot expect to throw together a racially mixed group of undergraduates and expect good things to happen automatically (Hu, 2006). Colleges and universities cannot afford to "leave serendipity to chance" (Kuh, 2001: 294). Efforts must be *intentional* (Kuh, 2001; Simmons, 2007), and they must provide *structured opportunities* for intergroup interaction (Smith et al., 1997; Tatum, 2007). If we know anything at all, it is this: "There is more to [building community] than sitting around a campfire holding hands and singing 'Kumbaya'" (Edley, 1996: 265).

INEQUALITY IN ACADEMIC ACHIEVEMENT

The two issues we have discussed so far in this chapter present challenges mainly to deans and other administrators at selective colleges and universities. Ensuring social class neutrality in the process that admits, enrolls, and ultimately graduates exceptionally talented students in ways that do not favor upper socioeconomic status groups is an issue for selective colleges and those who lead them. Adopting policies and programs that take

---

[15] Other examples of successful diversity initiatives include mentoring programs and ethnic residential theme houses. But these are related more to increased student satisfaction, retention, and academic success than to interracial contact (Smith et al., 1997).

full advantage of the educational benefits of diversity and that will encourage routine and frequent social interaction among students from all racial, ethnic, and social class backgrounds is again a challenge for student leaders and administrators overseeing campus life. The final challenge, however, is far greater—too large, in fact, for selective colleges and universities to tackle by themselves. As suggested by the title of an article by Christopher Jencks and Meredith Phillips (1998a)—"America's Next Achievement Test"—this is an issue facing society as a whole. It is the challenge posed by the racial gap in academic achievement.

This racial gap is reflected in academic records of applicants to selective colleges. White and Asian students typically have the strongest grades and test scores, whereas the scholastic credentials of black and Hispanic candidates rank lower. For example, among applicants to NSCE schools in the fall of 1997, Asian students had an average SAT score of 1334, as compared to an average of 1146 for black students—a gap of nearly 190 points [2]. Whites rank 50 SAT points behind Asians, and Hispanic applicants are 60 points behind whites (but still almost 80 points ahead of blacks). Eighty-nine percent of Asian applicants had a high school GPA of A− or better, in contrast to 63 percent of blacks. And 71 percent of Asian candidates ranked in the top 10 percent of their high school graduation class, as compared to 34 percent of black applicants.

Gaps in pre-collegiate academic performance persist among students who enroll at NSCE schools [4]. There is a difference of 225 points between the average SAT scores of Asian and black matriculants. Seventy-seven percent of Asian students graduated in the top 10 percent of their high school class, in contrast to 44 percent of black students. College academic performance shows the same stark differences [6]. At our eight NSCE institutions, 92 percent of Asian students graduate within six years, as compared to 78 percent of black students. Among those who graduate, the typical black student ranks in the 20th percentile in contrast to the typical white student, who graduates in the 57th percentile.

One might be tempted to conclude from these data that there is something perverse about the composition of elite college applicant pools. It may seem that only the brightest Asian students are seeking admission to top schools, whereas among black and Hispanic students it is the more average who are the ones eager to attend. But the hard truth is that America's most selective colleges and universities attract the very best Asian, white, black, and Hispanic applicants. It's just that these students, when arrayed by race, are not located at the same place along the spectrum of academic accomplishment.[16] To put the matter somewhat differently,

---

[16] In the 2000 cohort of SAT test-takers, blacks were 14.3 percent of all black and white participants, but they were substantially underrepresented in the upper tail of the overall

applicants to elite colleges and universities are drawn almost uniformly from the upper tails of their respective race-ethnic academic distributions. The unmistakable fact, however, is that these distributions are not perfectly aligned. White and Asian students on the whole outperform black and Hispanic students on the whole on the kinds of academic performance measures that matter most to selective colleges and universities.

The story at elite institutions is just the tip of the iceberg. What is happening there offers a window on a wider world that illustrates the magnitude of a much deeper and more pervasive societal problem. A large body of evidence has demonstrated that the racial test score gap is real, it emerges early in children's lives, and it widens as children age and move through school.[17] The best information we have suggests that genetic differences do not account for racial gaps (Dickens, 2005; Nisbett, 2007). No racial gaps in mental functioning were detected among a nationally representative sample of ten thousand children born in 2001 and tested at ages eight to twelve months (Fryer and Levitt, 2006a). However, social class differences in the inventory of children's vocabulary words emerge at about eighteen months (Farkas, 2004). By age three, the SES vocabulary gap is bigger and it continues to grow as children age, largely because of the amount of verbal interaction parents have with their children (Farkas, 2004; Hart and Risley, 2003). By the time children enter kindergarten, racial differences in both cognitive and nonacademic skills and knowledge are "moderate to large" (Le et al., 2006; Phillips and Chin, 2004). Black children lag about one year behind whites in vocabulary skills (Farkas, 2004), and blacks are significantly behind whites in both reading and math—a gap that widens by the end of first grade (Fryer and Levitt, 2004).

Differences observed at kindergarten entry are accentuated as children move through school. Gaps widen by third grade (Fryer and Levitt, 2006b) and are wider still by fifth grade (Le et al., 2006).[18] By twelfth grade black students have fallen roughly four years behind whites.[19] For

---

distribution. Blacks were less than 1 percent of blacks and whites who had perfect scores of 1600, and they accounted for just 1.4 percent of blacks and whites who had scores of 1400 or above—a threshold that includes roughly 65 percent of students admitted to the most selective schools (Krueger, Rothstein, and Turner, 2006).

[17] Some have suggested that the test score gap is merely a reflection of racially biased standardized tests, not real differences in academic achievement between races (Berlak, 2001). But most academics have concluded that, due to modern testing techniques, test bias accounts for only a small proportion of the gap (Kober, 2001).

[18] Fryer and Levitt (2006b) add that the largest racial gaps at the end of third grade are in the skills most crucial to future academic and labor market success. Inferior schools for blacks no longer seems to be the explanation.

[19] Very little progress has been made on this front in the past forty years. The Coleman Report (Coleman et al., 1966), required by Congress as part of the 1964 Civil Rights Act,

instance, data from the National Assessment of Educational Progress (NAEP; "The Nation's Report Card") show that average reading scores for blacks at age seventeen are the same as those for whites at age thirteen, and the lag in average mathematics scores is almost as great (Perie, Moran, and Lutkus, 2005).[20] Majorities of black and Hispanic students who took the NAEP test in twelfth grade were ranked below "Basic" in five out of eight subjects tested (National Center for Education Statistics, 2007a). Blacks fared worst while Hispanic students did only marginally better. By contrast, white and Asian students who performed below Basic were not a majority in any subject area. At least one-third of white students scored at the "Proficient" or "Advanced" level in three out of eight subjects. Comparable proportions of Asian students were rated at the same level on four out of eight tests. In no subject area tested did the proportion of black or Hispanic students attaining proficiency or advanced status surpass 20 percent.[21]

Racial differences in SAT scores and other measures of educational success show similar gaps. Among high school graduates in 2007 who participated in the SAT program, the average score on the combined critical reading and mathematics tests was 1092 for Asian students—230 points higher than the average score (862) for black participants (College Board, 2007b). Whites had the best scores on the critical reading and writing components; Asians tested best in mathematics. The mean scores for black students on all three tests were roughly at the 25th percentile of all test-takers. Rates of being left behind a grade, lower-track placement in high school, being suspended or expelled, and graduating high school are differentiated by race in the same way (Hauser, 2004; KewalRamani et al., 2007; Kozol, 1991; Lucas and Paret, 2005; Mishel and Roy, 2006; Swanson, 2004). Finally, college enrollment and degree completion are generally highest for whites and Asians and lowest for blacks and Hispanics (Kane, 2004).

---

also concluded that black children start out school behind white children and never catch up. At that time, black school children in sixth grade lagged 1.9 years behind their white counterparts. By twelfth grade the average gap widened to nearly four years, the same as it is today (Viadero, 2006a).

[20] Racial gaps in NAEP reading and math scores narrowed between the early 1970s and the late 1980s but since then have remained constant or even reversed (Harris, 2006; Kane, 2004). Ferguson (2001) attributes at least part of the slowdown to popular culture, especially the rise in hip-hop (for which 1988 was a watershed year), for adversely affecting the amount of leisure reading done by black and Hispanic youth.

[21] NAEP achievement levels are defined as follows: Basic denotes "partial mastery of prerequisite knowledge and skills that are fundamental for proficient work at a given grade"; Proficient represents "solid academic performance. Students reaching this level have demonstrated competency over challenging subject matter"; and Advanced represents "superior performance" (National Center for Education Statistics, 2007a).

How important a problem is the racial gap in academic achievement? The statistics we have presented surely paint a dismal picture, but are the underlying issues they reflect all that significant? A report from the College Board (1999: 1) calls eliminating the racial test score gap "the most important educational challenge for the United States." It is that, but it is more than that. Abigail Thernstrom and Stephan Thernstrom (2003: 247) in their book *No Excuses* refer to the racial gap in skills and knowledge as "the most important civil rights issue of our time." It is that, too. Successfully attacking the racial academic achievement gap represents the next stage in the struggle for social justice and equal opportunity. But it is even more than that. The racial gap in grades, test scores, and other measures of the skills, abilities, and knowledge that children acquire is arguably the most pressing domestic issue facing the United States at the beginning of the twenty-first century. To understand why, we need to appreciate the consequences of the persistent racial gap in academic accomplishment.

For one thing, the racial academic performance gap lies at the heart of many adult forms of social and economic inequality. Racial gaps in cognitive skills and knowledge that develop over the life course, beginning soon after a child's birth and continuing through to the completion of high school, are not just random, disconnected events. Rather, they represent outcomes linked together in a chain of cumulative causation. What happens at one age influences what happens later on. Small differences that emerge early in children's lives can become magnified in a pattern of cumulative advantage or disadvantage. What starts off as a racial gap in school readiness quickly becomes an academic achievement gap, which is followed by a graduation gap, a labor-market skills gap, a wage gap, and eventually a poverty gap. It is for this reason that Jencks and Phillips (1998b: 3–4) have concluded that "reducing the black-white test score gap would probably do more to promote [racial equality in America] than any other strategy that commands broad political support."

There is abundant evidence that gaps in skills and knowledge at one age are predictive of achievement at later ages. A child's linguistic accomplishment by age three is highly correlated with language skills in the third grade (Hart and Risley, 2003). Academic and nonacademic school readiness skills at kindergarten entry are closely linked with math and reading scores in the fifth grade (Le et al., 2006). Differences in school readiness skills—especially early math, reading, and attention skills—are strongly associated with later school reading and math achievement (Duncan et al., 2007). One-half of the black-white achievement gap in twelfth grade is explained by performance differences between students at kindergarten entry (Phillips, Crouse, and Ralph, 1998). A student's grades and test scores in the eighth grade predict the likelihood of college completion for adults in their mid-twenties (Phillips and Chin, 2004). Scores on tests of core academic skills in junior and senior high school are highly predictive of who later holds a bachelor's degree (Sum et al., 2007). Finally, black-white test score gaps measured in the eighth grade account for all of the racial wage gap among women in their late twenties and much of the gap for young men (Neal and Johnson, 1996).[22]

Patterns of cumulative advantage and disadvantage continue into adulthood and manifest themselves in a broad spectrum of socioeconomic inequalities. For example, racial gaps in academic accomplishment have been linked to racial differences in educational attainment and earnings that in turn are related to racial inequality in crime, health, and family structure (Jencks and Phillips, 1998a). Children who are behind at kindergarten entry do less well in school and are likely to become teenage parents, to engage in criminal activity, and to be unemployed as adults (Ludwig and Sawhill, 2007; McLanahan and Sandefur, 1994). Scores on tests administered to teens in junior and senior high school are highly correlated with ultimate educational attainment, which in turn is strongly linked to later-life employment opportunities, earnings, time spent in poverty or near poverty, and individuals' net impacts on government revenues and expenditures (Sum et al., 2007). Other aspects of social and economic inequality among adults—including differences in Internet use (DiMaggio et al., 2004), incarceration rates (Western, 2006), and wealth and homeownership (R. Rothstein, 2004)—have been associated with early life differences in cognitive skills and knowledge. There is every reason to believe that these differences in adult outcomes would be reduced if a way could be found to narrow racial performance gaps among children and adolescents.

A second reason racial gaps in academic success matter is that they affect workforce quality and the competitiveness of the U.S. economy. Domestic forces are combining to produce a "perfect storm" for poorly educated Americans (Kirsch et al., 2007). These forces include (1) substantial disparities by race and ethnicity in the distribution of job-related skills, (2) economic restructuring, which implies that nearly half of all new jobs generated between 2004 and 2014 will require a college degree, and (3) demographic trends, especially the rising Hispanic share of the population. To illustrate this last point, between 1972 and 2006, the combined

---

[22]Measured differences even at birth can also have long-lasting effects. McCormick, Gortmaker, and Sobol (1990) show that low birth-weight babies, and especially very low birth-weight infants, are at significantly greater risk of being placed in special education classes and/or repeating a grade compared to normal weight infants. And Paneth (1995) finds that low birth-weight outcomes are more prevalent among black mothers than among white mothers. Low birth-weight babies (less than 2,500 grams) accounted for 13.6 percent of all black babies in 1991, as compared to 5.8 percent of white babies.

Hispanic and non-Hispanic black share of the U.S. school-age population 5–17 years old rose from nearly 20 percent to 35 percent (U.S. Census Bureau, 1974, 2007), and it is projected to increase further to more than 43 percent by 2050 (U.S. Census Bureau, 2000b).[23] The U.S. economy is not so large, nor is the size of the population with few labor-market skills so small, that we can afford to be complacent in the face of this mounting problem.

Global forces are also putting pressure on American families with inadequate education. The end of the cold war and the integration of China, India, and the former Soviet-bloc republics into the international market-oriented, capitalist production system greatly increased the number of "hard-working" and "low-paid" workers around the world (Polaski, 2007), effectively doubling the number of workers in the global economy from roughly 1.5 billion in 2000 to 3 billion (Freeman, 2007) and creating a global oversupply of labor (Polaski, 2007). A global labor market has been accompanied by a more aggressive search by business owners for attractive wage-skill combinations wherever in the world they can be found (International Monetary Fund, 2007). This major shift in where "capital finds labor" has left unskilled U.S. workers falling behind. Prior to about 1990, workers in the United States faced little competition from low-wage workers in India, China, or the Soviet Union (Freeman, 2007). Now the situation is much different. The doubling of the global workforce "has presented the U.S. labor system with its greatest challenge since the Great Depression" (Freeman, 2007: 129). U.S. workers who are most affected are those whose skills most resemble the skills of the majority of workers in the newly expanded global labor pool. Typically, these are individuals with the fewest labor market credentials.[24] Labor economists believe that "[t]he challenge for American workers is to obtain work skills that differ sufficiently from those being

[23] Nearly all of this increase is due to trends in the Hispanic population. The Hispanic share alone increases from 6 percent in 1972 to a projected 30 percent by 2050. Projections of the U.S. population by Jeffrey Passel and D'Vera Cohn (2008) at the Pew Hispanic Center suggest a growth from 296 million in 2005 to 438 million by 2050, 82 percent of which is attributable to immigrants arriving during the period and their U.S.-born children.

[24] "Offshoring"—the movement of jobs out of the country—presents a new but related set of problems. Whether jobs are at risk can no longer be easily captured by the old divide of "low-end" and "high-end" work (Blinder, 2006). Jobs that are most susceptible to offshoring are "impersonal services . . . that can be delivered electronically from afar with little or no degradation of quality" (Blinder, 2007). For example, taxi cab drivers, janitors, and most physicians are unlikely to see their jobs go abroad. But radiologists, accountants, typists, and computer programmers are more at risk. These processes have been aided by low-cost communication and computer technology (Levy and Murnane, 2006). A framework for understanding the labor market impacts of offshoring is contained in Grossman and Rossi-Hansberg (2006).

produced in huge numbers overseas to keep U.S. wages high" (Freeman, 2007: 138).[25]

Yet, at the very time we need a better-educated population to compete with other rapidly modernizing countries and to avoid a decline in living standards (New Commission on the Skills of the American Workforce, 2007), growth in the quality of the U.S. workforce has slowed or stagnated (Carneiro and Heckman, 2003).[26] The outcome has been relatively flat wages for many individuals, especially those with a high school education or less. The typical U.S. worker has experienced downward pressure on wages and benefits for the past thirty years. Adjusted for inflation, average weekly earnings of non-supervisory employees in 2007 were 5 percent below their 1964 levels (Polaski, 2007). Earnings for men in their thirties have remained relatively flat for the past four decades, and much of the increase in family incomes is accounted for by more women working (Isaacs, 2007). A recent poll of working families found that nearly half of respondents believe their children will be "worse off" than they are when it comes time for them to enter the labor market and raise their own families (Herbert, 2007). Unless new steps are taken, it does not appear that the situation will change any time soon. Researchers at the Educational Testing Service project that by 2030 average levels of literacy and numeracy among the working-age population will have declined by 5 percent (Kirsch et al., 2007). The takeaway message is unmistakable. America needs a *more* educated, not a less educated, labor force.

Therefore, the challenge—and it is an urgent challenge facing all Americans—is to identify the factors responsible for the racial academic achievement gap and take the necessary corrective steps to close this gap as soon as possible. Time alone is an unreliable ally. Given the slow rate of convergence in black-white test outcomes over the past thirty years, it

---

[25] Carneiro and Heckman (2003: 86) seem to agree. They write, "The problem is clear. The supply of skilled [U.S.] workers is not keeping pace with demand. How to increase the supply of skilled workers in an economically efficient way is not so clear." Reflecting on the impacts of freer international trade, Paul Krugman (2007) observes, "Still, there's little doubt that the pressure of globalization on American wages has increased. . . . The highly educated workers who clearly benefit from growing trade with third-world economies are a minority, greatly outnumbered by those who probably lose." A global labor market also creates added competition for highly skilled U.S. workers. One indication is America's declining competitiveness in science and technology. American exports of high-technology products exceeded imports by $54 billion in 1990. But by 2001 the United States had become a $50 billion net importer of high-tech manufactured goods (Committee on Prospering in the Global Economy of the 21st Century, 2007: 14). The biennial report on science and engineering of the National Science Board (2008), the parent body of the National Science Foundation, calls attention to lagging high school skills in science and math, and to persistent racial gaps in knowledge and test scores.

[26] Carneiro and Heckman (2003: 86) claim that "America has an underclass of unskilled and illiterate persons with no counterpart in northern Europe."

is likely to take another century at least to eliminate the black-white gap in average SAT scores (Krueger, Rothstein, and Turner, 2006) or to reach black-white parity in average reading and math scores among the highest 5 or 10 percent of all students—the part of the distribution from which selective colleges and universities draw most of their students (Hedges and Nowell, 1999).[27] The No Child Left Behind Act of 2001 aims to eliminate the racial gap in academic achievement by the end of the 2013–14 school year by stressing accountability standards and sanctions for school districts failing to meet them. But no serious observer believes the act will succeed in its current form. Critics complain that there are insufficient funds to accomplish the stated objectives (Armor, 2008), and early assessments show little or no improvement in the racial gap in NAEP reading and math scores (Lee, 2006).

There is general agreement about the set of broad factors responsible for the racial academic achievement gap, but no consensus on their relative importance or on the most effective ways or places at which to intervene. Part of the gap is due to racial differences in social class backgrounds (Baum and Ma, 2007; College Board, 1999). These account for somewhere between one-third and two-thirds of the overall racial gap (Hedges and Nowell, 1999; Phillips et al., 1998). But there are still important black-white gaps within income groups (Krueger, Rothstein, and Turner, 2006).[28] Other factors whose importance has been documented include home environments, schools, and neighborhood conditions.[29] But no one knows for sure how all these factors interact to produce such widespread racial gaps in skills and knowledge. In the absence of a convincing paradigm that commands broad respect, proposing policy remedies is like

[27] To the extent that black-white gaps are narrowing, it seems to be because the lowest-performing black students are doing better relative to low-performing whites. Black-white gaps in the upper tails are more stable (Hedges and Nowell, 1999). Within cohorts, however, black-white gaps grow faster for initially high achievers. Reardon (2008) finds that reading and math scores diverge more between kindergarten and fifth grade for students who entered kindergarten with high reading and math test scores than for students with low scores.

[28] Yeung and Conley (2008) have suggested that part of the remaining gap may be due to black-white differences in wealth that exist for families with similar incomes. These authors find that liquid assets, particularly in the form of stocks or mutual funds, are positively related to school-age children's test scores.

[29] A more detailed listing would have to include student characteristics and attitudes (Kalil, Pattillo, and Payne, 2004), family structure (McLanahan and Sandefur, 1994) and parental child-rearing practices (Brooks-Gunn and Markman, 2005; Cheadle, 2008), neighborhoods and peer groups (Davis, Jenkins, and Hunt, 2002; Duncan and Magnuson, 2005; Suskind, 1998), schools and teachers (Greenwald, Hedges, and Laine, 1996; Krueger and Whitmore, 2001; Lee, 2007; Page, Murnane, and Willett, 2008; Phillips and Chin, 2004), health, nutrition, and the physical environment (Currie, 2005; Kozol, 1991; Lang, 2007; Rothstein, 2004), and racial prejudice and discrimination (College Board, 1999).

throwing darts in the dark. We are never quite sure where the target is or whether we have aimed in the right direction once a program has been launched.[30]

So What's to Be Done?

The racial gap in academic performance plays a much more central role in problems that loom large today than almost anyone realizes. It contributes significantly to most adult forms of social and economic inequality, and it figures prominently in the ability of the U.S. workforce and economy to compete successfully in world markets. Many public policies are directed to combating the symptoms of this underlying problem, but this approach is both expensive and inefficient. What is needed is a declaration of war on the root causes. We propose a Manhattan Project for the behavioral and social sciences—a project with the same scale, urgency, and sense of importance as the original Manhattan Project.[31] We call this project the American Competitiveness and Leadership Project. Its aims are twofold: (1) to identify the causes and cumulative consequences of racial gaps in academic achievement and (2) to develop concrete measures that can be taken by parents, schools, neighborhoods, and the public sector all working together to close these gaps on a nationwide scale. We should not be satisfied with demonstrated success in small-scale, localized projects.

The American Competitiveness and Leadership Project (ACLP) will entail close and continuous monitoring of the lives of a large sample of children followed from birth to roughly age eighteen, or onto the first

---

[30]Christopher Jencks and Meredith Phillips (1998a) have concluded, "The number of people who think they know how to eliminate racial differences in test performance has shrunk steadily since the mid-1960s" (47). "While we are convinced that reducing the black-white test score gap is both necessary and possible, we do not have a detailed blueprint for achieving this goal—and neither does anyone else" (53). Even though this assessment is ten years old, most observers would agree the conclusion is still valid (Armor, 2008: 323–24; Wray, 2006: 2). A more sanguine position has been adopted by Rouse, Brooks-Gunn, and McLanahan (2005: 13): "We know how to help a child begin school ready to learn. We know how to begin to close racial and ethnic gaps in school readiness. We simply must decide to do so."

[31]The original Manhattan Project developed the atomic bombs dropped on Hiroshima and Nagasaki, Japan, in August 1945. It was formally known as the Manhattan Engineer District, and was organized and controlled by the U.S. Army Corps of Engineers. It lasted from 1942 to 1946, occupied three main sites (Oak Ridge, Tennessee; Los Alamos, New Mexico; and Hanford, Washington) as well as hundreds of smaller ones, and employed as many as 125,000 people at one time (Hales, 1997). Manhattan Project costs, including capital and operations costs from 1942 to 1945, eventually totaled almost $2 billion—$28.5 billion in constant 2007 dollars (Schwartz, 1998; U.S. Bureau of Labor Statistics, 2008).

step of their postsecondary plans. Like the Manhattan Project, the ACLP will of necessity involve interdisciplinary teams of researchers at multiple sites of universities and research institutes around the country. And like the Manhattan Project, the ACLP will be an important element of our national self-defense viewed broadly. But unlike the Manhattan Project, research for the ACLP will be conducted in the open, and it will be for peaceful rather than destructive purposes. The ACLP is an extraordinarily ambitious project, likely on a scale previously unimagined in social or behavioral science research. It will have to monitor a large birth cohort—perhaps as many as fifty thousand children—partly to allow for natural attrition in the sample over time but also to locate important causal mechanisms that would otherwise be hidden by smaller samples. Data generated by this project will doubtless consume the time of hundreds of graduate students, faculty, and research scientists at our leading research and teaching institutions.[32]

We will not have to wait twenty years for useful findings to emerge, because racial gaps develop in the first few years of life. What we learn from the ACLP can be applied almost immediately, beginning to make a difference in the lives of children not that much younger than children in the ACLP study cohort. But even if it takes somewhat longer to identify practical steps that can be adopted, the sooner we begin the sooner progress can be measured. After all, it has been more than forty years since the Coleman Report issued its findings on factors contributing to the black-white gap in school performance (Coleman et al., 1966). Too little progress has been made in the intervening period.

All Americans stand to benefit from the American Competitiveness and Leadership Project, especially individuals whose life chances will be made brighter as a result. But there are several groups that have a particular stake in its success: academically selective institutions in higher education, corporate America, U.S. taxpayers, and the philanthropic sector.

HIGHER EDUCATION

Closing the racial gap in academic achievement would benefit selective colleges and universities by reducing their dependence on affirmative action to create a racially balanced undergraduate student body. As we showed in our simulations of the effects of alternative admission practices, if admission deans are obligated to forego race-sensitive admission strategies while racial achievement gaps remain at today's levels, the pro-

---

[32] There should be room in the ACLP for doing randomized experiments. If following the day-to-day experiences of a large number of children suggests patterns that might be causally linked, we should be able to develop programs, evaluate them, and learn how to replicate them on a larger scale.

portions of black and Hispanic students on elite college campuses will fall dramatically [9]. On the other hand, if black-white and Hispanic-white achievement gaps are eliminated, race-based affirmative action policies would no longer be necessary to preserve current shares of underrepresented minority students among admitted students.

The need to close racial academic achievement gaps takes on greater urgency because restrictions on the use of racial affirmative action are tightening. Residents in four states (California in 1996, Washington in 1998, Michigan in 2006, and Nebraska in 2008) have passed referenda that prohibit the use of affirmative action in public education. The measure was on the ballot in Colorado in November 2008, and petition drives were under way in three other states (Arizona, Missouri, and Oklahoma) to gather enough valid signatures to put the measure before voters. If one also includes Florida, whose governor curtailed racial preferences in state government in 1999, then more than 31 percent of the nation's population live in states that have banned affirmative action in public education or are trying to do so (Schmidt, 2007d). Beyond that, Justice Sandra Day O'Connor seemed to establish a sunset provision for race-conscious admission policies when, writing for the majority in *Grutter v. Bollinger*, she declared, "We expect that 25 years from now, the use of racial preferences will no longer be necessary to further the interest approved today" (*Grutter v. Bollinger*, 2003: 31). The conservative tilt to the U.S. Supreme Court in the meantime has created added pessimism that race-based affirmative action will last that long. Even if it does, the reprieve will be short-lived. Students who turn age eighteen and are preparing to go off to college in the year 2028 will be born in 2010, leaving little time to address academic achievement gaps.

Finally, achieving racial parity in academic achievement would facilitate other goals of selective institutions—creating more racial diversity among faculty and greater socioeconomic diversity among undergraduates. Earlier we reported evidence that some underrepresented minority students at top schools may be reluctant to choose college teaching as an occupation if their comparatively low standing in their graduating classes causes them to doubt their intellectual capabilities [6]. With no racial gaps in test scores, there would be less reason for black and Hispanic students to form negative academic self-concepts. Second, to promote greater economic diversity in their student bodies, a number of elite institutions are aiming to make college more affordable by eliminating loan requirements and providing extra grant aid to lower- and middle-income families. But closing racial gaps in academic success would probably do more for socioeconomic diversity by expanding the number of highly qualified, low-income students in selective college applicant pools than all the new scholarship dollars put together.

CORPORATE AMERICA

Closing the racial gap in academic achievement has beneficial consequences for the competitiveness and productivity of the American economy. A better-educated workforce is a more productive workforce. Estimates from the Alliance for Excellent Education (2007) suggest that higher incomes would add more than $300 billion to the nation's economy if students who dropped out of the high school class of 2006 had graduated instead. Beyond that, racial achievement gaps impede diversity in the workplace, not only in entry-level positions but up and down the corporate ladder. Diversity improves corporate competitiveness in a variety of ways. In problem solving, diverse groups typically outperform an individual of extraordinary ability or even homogeneous groups of the best and brightest (Page, 2007). In addition, workers who possess "diversity capital" are not only better at functioning within a team-oriented organizational framework but more equipped to relate to a diverse clientele from varying cultures and nationalities in a rapidly globalizing world.[33] Finally, as younger workers increasingly value diversity in their personal lives and work settings, employers are finding that workforce diversity is a valuable aid in recruiting new employees.[34] For all of these reasons, corporate leaders are often the ones making the connection between racial/ethnic workplace diversity and diverse perspectives, and top management has become a pro-diversity champion (Page, 2007).

Developing corporate leaders for a more diverse world also depends on sufficient workplace diversity. All too often, however, one finds a shrinking pipeline as one looks at upper levels of management. For instance, while 15 percent of college graduates are black or Hispanic, they represent just 8 percent of MBA students at the top twenty-five business schools, only 3 percent of senior management positions, and 1.6 percent of Fortune 1000 chief executives (Stodghill, 2007). Closing the racial academic achievement gap would help expand this pipeline, not just in the

---

[33] This argument played a prominent role in the U.S. Supreme Court's thinking in the University of Michigan cases. "Major American businesses," Justice O'Connor wrote, "have made clear that the skills needed in today's increasingly global marketplace can only be developed through exposure to widely diverse people, cultures, ideas, and viewpoints" (*Grutter v. Bollinger*, 2003: 18).

[34] A group of Stanford University law students has begun handing out "diversity report cards" to major law firms. Law students are being encouraged to select future employers partly on their diversity profiles. The Stanford students plan to send their rankings to the general counsels at the Fortune 500 companies and encourage them to use the rankings in choosing law firms to work with (Liptak, 2007). In addition, colleges are responding to prospective students' desires to attend schools with racial diversity. Lewis (2008) has observed that sixteen of the top twenty universities as ranked by *U.S. News & World Report* have Web sites with easily accessible statements or statistics "promoting diversity."

corporate world but in all sectors of society.[35] In the words again of Justice O'Connor, "In order to cultivate a set of leaders with legitimacy in the eyes of the citizenry, it is necessary that the path to leadership be visibly open to talented and qualified individuals of every race and ethnicity" (*Grutter v. Bollinger*, 2003: 20).[36]

U.S. TAXPAYERS

For U.S. taxpayers the benefit of closing the racial gap in academic achievement is a lower total tax bill for the same level of public services. Individuals with improved education and greater labor market success have higher earnings and pay more in taxes to federal, state, and local governments. At the same time, they make fewer claims on public sector services. Examples include lower government expenditures for law enforcement, public health care, income-based public assistance (including food stamps and housing), and special education placements in elementary and secondary school (Alliance for Excellent Education, 2007; Holzer et al., 2007; Levin et al., 2007; Ludwig and Sawhill, 2007). More education is also associated with a lower likelihood of becoming a teenage parent or using drugs and a greater chance of having better-educated and healthier children (Alliance for Excellent Education, 2007; Ludwig and Sawhill, 2007).

Dollar estimates suggest that fiscal impacts of parity in racial test scores are overwhelmingly positive. Holzer et al. (2007) show that children's experience with poverty in their parental home is associated with lower earnings and productivity, higher crime rates, and poorer health as adults.

[35] Higher education provides another example where the pipeline to leadership is racially constricted. Roughly one-half of all college and university presidents are age sixty-one or older and poised to retire soon. Progress in diversifying these top ranks has been slow. Women lead 23 percent of the nation's colleges and universities, and persons of color lead just 14 percent, including minority-serving institutions. A report from the American Council on Education finds that the prospects for greater gender diversity are much greater than those for racial diversity among college presidents. Women currently make up 38 percent of chief academic officers—second-in-command positions from which college and university presidents are usually drawn. Persons of color make up 16 percent of all senior administrators and less than 10 percent of chief academic officers (King and Gomez, 2008).

[36] The link between racial performance gaps and a shortage of nonwhite leaders in responsible positions in many different sectors of society has been made forcefully in a study by The College Board (1999) titled *Reaching the Top*. The report asks where leaders for a diverse society will come from. Their answer is, "Until many more underrepresented minority students from disadvantaged, middle class, and upper-middle class circumstances are very successful educationally, it will be virtually impossible to integrate our society's institutions completely, especially at leadership levels. Without such progress, the United States also will continue to be unable to draw on the full range of talents in our population during an era when the value of an educated citizenry has never been greater" (2).

They calculate that costs to the U.S. economy stemming from childhood poverty are about $500 billion per year, or nearly 4 percent of gross domestic product. Levin et al. (2007) highlight the public benefits of converting high school dropouts into high school graduates. They estimate that lifetime benefits (in 2004 dollars) are $209,000 for each new graduate. To achieve these benefits would cost a median amount (over five targeted educational interventions) of $82,000 per student. Their figures imply a net public economic benefit of $127,000 per student or, equivalently, a benefit-cost ratio of more than 2.5. If this intervention could be scaled up and reduce by half the 700,000 high school dropouts each year, Levin et al. (2007) calculate the annual net benefits to the public would total roughly $45 billion.

PHILANTHROPIC SECTOR

The American Competitiveness and Leadership Project will give foundations concerned with child welfare and, especially, the education of children and adolescents a much clearer idea of where to target their resources effectively. More broadly, eliminating the racial gap in academic accomplishment promotes a stronger society and a healthier democracy. Individuals with more education and higher earnings are more likely to volunteer in civic activities and have more tolerant attitudes (Alliance for Excellent Education, 2007; Baum and Ma, 2007). Higher socioeconomic status is also positively associated for all racial-ethnic groups with higher rates of political participation, including contacting elected officials, contributing money, and voting (Leighley and Vedlitz, 1999; Verba, Schlozman, and Brady, 2004).

Final Words

When the Swedish economist Gunnar Myrdal was invited in the late 1930s by the Carnegie Corporation of New York to conduct a comprehensive study of the "Negro in the United States," he concluded rather grimly that "the Negro problem in America represents a moral lag in the development of the nation and a study of it must record nearly everything which is bad and wrong in America" (Myrdal, 1944: xix). Despite American "imperfections" and "shortcomings," however, Myrdal voiced great optimism for the future: "*not since Reconstruction has there been more reason to anticipate fundamental changes in American race relations, changes which will involve a development toward the American ideals*" (xix, emphasis in the original). To some people reading these words written two-thirds of a century ago, Myrdal must seem overly optimistic or even a bit naïve. Surely we have made great progress as a nation, but we are not there yet. The races are no longer separate, but they are not yet equal—not on selective college campuses or more generally in American society. Time alone may eventually accomplish this objective, but time is not on our side. Success is more urgently needed. The American Competitiveness and Leadership Project has the potential to do more for race relations and racial equality in this country than any other initiative currently under consideration.

Appendix A

THE NSCE DATABASE

To answer the research questions in chapter 1, it was necessary to collect new data to describe the processes of applying to and attending academically selective colleges and universities. The backbone of the National Study of College Experience (NSCE) database is an institutional data file constructed with the cooperation of ten institutions that were part of the College and Beyond (C&B) database assembled by researchers at the Andrew W. Mellon Foundation (Bowen and Bok, 1998).[1] These ten colleges and universities have geographic spread, and they represent public universities, private research universities, small liberal arts colleges, and historically black colleges and universities.[2] No institution refused our invitation to participate in the National Study of College Experience.

Each NSCE school was asked to supply individual student information on all applicants for undergraduate admission in the fall of 1983, 1993, and 1997.[3] We requested information on whether each applicant was accepted, whether the applicant enrolled if accepted, a variety of student identifiers, demographic characteristics including place of residence at time of application, high school attended, high school academic performance, other student information including whether applicants were

[1] The complete institutional data file for the College and Beyond database includes data from the following thirty-four institutions (historically black colleges and universities are denoted by an asterisk). Public universities: Miami University (Ohio), University of Michigan (Ann Arbor), University of North Carolina (Chapel Hill), and Pennsylvania State University. Private universities: Columbia University, Duke University, Emory University, Georgetown University, Howard University*, Northwestern University, University of Notre Dame, University of Pennsylvania, Princeton University, Rice University, Stanford University, Tufts University, Tulane University, Vanderbilt University, Washington University, Xavier University*, and Yale University. Private liberal arts colleges: Barnard College, Bryn Mawr College, Denison University, Hamilton College, Kenyon College, Morehouse College*, Oberlin College, Smith College, Spelman College*, Swarthmore College, Wellesley College, Wesleyan University, and Williams College.

[2] In exchange for their participation in the National Study of College Experience, we agreed to protect the identity of each school and to safeguard the confidentiality of all student information.

[3] NSCE institutions were asked to provide data for the fall 1983 entering cohort or the earliest date at which they began electronic record keeping. One institution provided data for 1982, five for 1983, one for 1985, two for 1986, and one for 1988. The median entering cohort is 1983.

TABLE A.1

Number of Applications to Ten NSCE Institutions, by Institution Type,
Entering Cohort, and Application Status

| | Application Status | | | |
	Applied, Not Accepted	Accepted, Not Enrolled	Accepted, Enrolled[a]	Total
Public Universities				
1983	11,230	5,227	10,754	27,211
1993	10,050	7,312	11,569	28,931
1997	12,188	8,232	12,285	32,705
Private Colleges and Universities				
1983	34,108	5,694	7,418	47,220
1993	36,412	8,158	8,087	52,657
1997	41,195	7,410	8,156	56,761
Total	145,183	42,033	58,269	245,485

Source: National Study of College Experience.

[a]One institution supplied data only on all matriculants. The remaining nine provided individual-level information on all applicants in all three cohorts.

recruited athletes or alumni children, family and household socioeconomic data, financial aid packages, and academic performance in college.

Data on the size and composition of the NSCE institutional database are shown in Table A.1. Altogether there are 245,485 student records, excluding transfers and graduate students. Roughly 36 percent of all records come from public universities, and applications to private colleges and universities account for the remaining 64 percent. Approximately 30 percent of all records come from the 1983 cohort, another 33 percent come from 1993, and the 1997 cohort is responsible for 36 percent of all cases. One school that was asked to participate in the study toward the end of institutional data collection was able to supply data only for all matriculants, not all applicants. When data from this one institution are removed from Table A.1, acceptance rates at public universities range between 51 and 58 percent across the three cohorts. Corresponding acceptance rates for private colleges and universities fluctuate between about 27 and 31 percent. For the total sample of nine institutions, the overall acceptance rate is 37 percent. There is less variation in yield rates according to type of institution. The fraction of admitted students at public institutions who enrolled varies between 45 and 55 percent across the three cohorts. Yield rates fluctuate between 50 and 57 percent at private schools. For the total sample, the overall yield rate for all cohorts combined is 51 percent.

A second component of the core NSCE database is a survey data file. A sixteen-page questionnaire was mailed to a stratified random sample of 18,164 unique individuals in the institutional database. The sample focused mainly on enrolled students in each of the three entering cohorts, but sample members were also drawn from students who applied for admission in 1997 and were rejected as well as from applicants who were accepted in 1997 by a given NSCE institution but who chose not to enroll. The survey instrument includes items related to satisfaction with college, patterns of social interaction on campus, course selections and participation in extracurricular activities, college expenses including financial aid and educational debt, pre-college experiences with a particular emphasis on pre-college preparation for admission to academically selective colleges and universities, help with the application process, and family demographic and socioeconomic background characteristics. The NSCE student survey gathered data from 9,085 respondents. A complete copy of the NSCE survey instrument is included at the end of this appendix (see Exhibit A.1).

These two core components of the NSCE database were supplemented with existing data from other sources. Information on the characteristics of public and private high schools was obtained through the National Center for Education Statistics (NCES) from its Common Core of Data (CCD) and the Private School Universe Survey (PSS), and from The College Board through its High School Survey. These data can be matched to individual student records using the high school's College Entrance Examination Board (CEEB) identification number on the college application. To approximate the characteristics of neighborhoods where applicants grew up, we appended to student records data from the 1980 and 1990 U.S. Census of Population and Housing using the five-digit zip-code level files. The Educational Testing Service (ETS) supplied data on student standardized test scores and on student responses to the Student Descriptive Questionnaire (SDQ), a voluntary questionnaire that students are asked to complete when they register for the SAT exam. Aggregate high school data on average SAT scores of college-bound seniors and on the number of AP exams taken by students in each high school were obtained from The College Board. Finally, the U.S. Department of Education provided data from the Free Application for Federal Student Aid (FAFSA) for a sample of 1997 cohort members.

Although two historically black colleges and universities (HBCUs) are represented among the ten schools in the NSCE institutional universe, data from these two HBCUs do not figure prominently in our analysis. One reason is that the primary focus of this study is on the race and class dimensions of college admission and campus life, but most HBCUs have little racial or ethnic diversity among their student populations. Beyond this, most studies of diversity in higher education use as their study populations schools where the majority of students are white. Finally, the institutional data received from the two HBCUs were less complete in some respects than data from the other eight NSCE institutions. Our main results therefore are derived from institutional and survey data at eight majority white colleges and universities.

EXHIBIT A.1: NATIONAL STUDY OF COLLEGE EXPERIENCE QUESTIONNAIRE

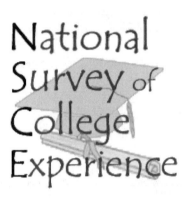

National Survey of College Experience

An Important National Study of Applicants to Selective U.S. Colleges and Universities and Their Subsequent Educational Experiences

A. Have you ever been enrolled for at least one semester in an undergraduate college or university in the United States?

       (CIRCLE ONE)

YES .... 1 ⟶ (GO TO NEXT PAGE)

NO .... 2 ⟶ (SKIP TO QUESTION 34 , PAGE 9)

Please return your completed questionnaire to:

Princeton Survey Research Center
Princeton University
169 Nassau St
Princeton, NJ 08542-7007

If you have questions, please call Dr. Edward Freeland at 1-800-305-0950

SECTION A: SOCIAL NETWORKS AND ACTIVITIES ON CAMPUS

In which undergraduate institution did you enroll as a first-year student?

Name of Institution: _____ City and State:_____

If you attended more than one institution for your undergraduate studies, answer the questions with respect to the institution that you attended for the longest period of time. If you attended two schools for the same length of time, base your answers on your experiences at the school you last attended.

1. On a scale from 01 to 07 (01 = least satisfied and 07 = most satisfied), how would you evaluate your overall college...

	(Circle one on each line)						
	Least satisfied ◀					▶ *Most satisfied*	
a. **academic** experience?	01	02	03	04	05	06	07
b. **social** experience?	01	02	03	04	05	06	07

2. On a scale from 01 to 07 (01 = not at all and 07 = a substantial amount), how racially and ethnically diverse was your **high school**?

(Circle one)						
Not at all ◀			▶	A substantial amount		
01	02	03	04	05	06	07

3. Compared with your high school, how racially/ethnically diverse was your **college**? Was your college . . . ?

(Circle one)

Less diverse 1
About the same 2
More diverse 3
Don't recall 7

4. Overall, how would you compare the amount of interaction you personally had with members of other racial/ ethnic groups in college as compared to high school?

(Circle one)

Less in college 1
About the same 2
More in college 3
Don't recall 7

5. On a scale from 01 to 07 (01 = nothing at all and 07 = a substantial amount), how much have you learned from students of different racial and ethnic backgrounds who attended the same college or university as yourself?

(Circle one)						
Nothing at all ◀			▶	A substantial amount		
01	02	03	04	05	06	07

6. During your undergraduate years, how often did you interact outside of class with adults (e.g. administrative staff or teachers) in the college community?

(Circle one)

Never .... 1 Skip to Q. 10
Rarely .... 2 ⎤
Occasionally .... 3 ⎬ Go to Q. 7
Often .... 4 ⎪
Very often .... 5 ⎪
Don't recall .... 7 ⎦

7. Were these interactions primarily with...?

(Circle one)

Administrative staff (e.g., deans, department staff, coaches) 1
Teachers (e.g., professor, lecturer) 2
Both 3
Don't recall 7

8. In general, how would you describe the nature of these interactions?

(Circle all that apply)

Tutoring 01
Academic counseling or advising 02
Career or job counseling 03
Financial counseling or advising 04
Athletic coaching 05
Employer 06
Mentoring 07
Friendship 08
Programming projects or events 09
Other – *Specify:* _____ 95
Don't recall 97

9. How often were these adults with whom you interacted **outside of class** of your...

(Circle one on each line)

	Never	Rarely	Occasion-ally	Often	Very often	Don't recall
Same gender?	1	2	3	4	5	7
Same race/ ethnicity?	1	2	3	4	5	7

10. Where did you live each year as an undergraduate?

(Circle all that apply on each line)

	On-campus dorm or apartment	Off campus		Don't recall
		With parents or other relatives	Other apartment or house	
Freshman year	1	2	3	7
Sophomore year	1	2	3	7
Junior year	1	2	3	7
Senior year	1	2	3	7

11. Did you ever live in an on-campus theme dorm/ focus house (e.g., language dorm, fraternity house, ethnic house)?

(Circle one)

Yes 1
No, but school did offer one or more of these .... 2 ⎤
No, school did not offer .... 3 ⎬ Skip to Q.13
Don't recall .... 7 ⎦

12. What was the theme or focus?

(Circle one or more codes in each column)

	Freshman Year	Sophomore Year	Junior Year	Senior Year
Academic (e.g., honors, humanities)	01	01	01	01
Athletic	02	02	02	02
Language	03	03	03	03
Fraternity or sorority	04	04	04	04
Racial / ethnic heritage ...	05	05	05	05
Other – *Specify:*	95	95	95	95
Other – *Specify:*	95	95	95	95
Didn't live in theme dorm focus house this year	96	96	96	96

13. During your undergraduate years, how often did you **socialize** on campus with students of the following racial/ethnic groups?

(Circle one on each line)

	Never	Rarely	Occasionally	Often	Very Often	Don't recall
American Indian/Native American or Alaska Native	1	2	3	4	5	7
Asian or Asian American	1	2	3	4	5	7
Black or African American	1	2	3	4	5	7
Hispanic or Latino	1	2	3	4	5	7
Native Hawaiian or Other Pacific Islander	1	2	3	4	5	7
White	1	2	3	4	5	7

14. Of the people you **dated** at your undergraduate institution, how many were . . . . . ?

(Circle one on each line)

	0	1	2	3	4	5 or more
American Indian/Native American or Alaska Native	0	1	2	3	4	5
Asian or Asian American	0	1	2	3	4	5
Black or African American	0	1	2	3	4	5
Hispanic or Latino	0	1	2	3	4	5
Native Hawaiian or Other Pacific Islander	0	1	2	3	4	5
White	0	1	2	3	4	5

15. List the first names of **five** of your closest friends at your undergraduate institution. Then indicate the race/ethnicity and gender of each person.

(Circle all that apply on each line)

First name	American Indian/ Native American or Alaska Native	Asian or Asian American	Black or African American	Hispanic or Latino	Native Hawaiian or Other Pacific Islander	White	Other Race or Ethnic Group	Gender	
								M	F
1.	01	02	03	04	05	06	07	1	2
2.	01	02	03	04	05	06	07	1	2
3.	01	02	03	04	05	06	07	1	2
4.	01	02	03	04	05	06	07	1	2
5.	01	02	03	04	05	06	07	1	2

16. Think back to your roommate(s) during each year of college. First indicate the total number of roommates you had each year. Then indicate the race/ethnicity of these roommates.

(Circle all that apply on each line)

	Number of Roommates Each Year	American Indian/Native American or Alaska Native	Asian or Asian American	Black or African American	Hispanic or Latino	Native Hawaiian or Other Pacific Islander	White	Other Race or Ethnic Group
Freshman year.........	_____	01	02	03	04	05	06	07
Sophomore year	_____	01	02	03	04	05	06	07
Junior year	_____	01	02	03	04	05	06	07
Senior year..............	_____	01	02	03	04	05	06	07

17. As an undergraduate, did you participate in the following activities or courses?

(Circle one on each line)

Activity/Course:	Yes, did participate	No, did not participate		Don't recall
		School did offer	School did not offer	
American Indian/Native American Month activities	1	2	3	7
Asian American/Pacific Islander Month activities	1	2	3	7
Black History Month activities	1	2	3	7
Chicano/Latino History Month activities	1	2	3	7
Women's History Month activities	1	2	3	7
Other multicultural activity	1	2	3	7
American Indian/Native American course	1	2	3	7
Asian/Asian American Studies course	1	2	3	7
African/ African American Studies course	1	2	3	7
Chicano/ Latino Studies course	1	2	3	7
Jewish Studies course	1	2	3	7
Gender/ Feminist/ Women's Studies course	1	2	3	7
Other Ethnic Studies course – *Specify:* _____	1	2	3	7
Other Ethnic Studies course – *Specify:* _____	1	2	3	7

18. In the courses that you took as an undergraduate, roughly what percent of your teachers were...?

(Circle one on each line)

	None	1-9%	10-24%	25-49%	50% or more	Don't recall
Female	0	1	2	3	4	7
American Indian/Native American or Alaska Native ..	0	1	2	3	4	7
Asian or Asian American	0	1	2	3	4	7
Black or African American	0	1	2	3	4	7
Hispanic or Latino	0	1	2	3	4	7
White	0	1	2	3	4	7

19. What were your undergraduate major/minor areas of concentration?

(Circle all that apply in each column)

Area of concentration	Major	Minor
Asian/Asian American Studies	01	01
African/African American Studies	02	02
Chicano/Latino Studies	03	03
Jewish Studies	04	04
Other Ethnic Studies	05	05
Gender/Feminist/Women's Studies	06	06
Other (Chemistry, Sociology, etc.)	07	07
None/Did not have	96	96

20. Did you participate in any of the following extracurricular activities or clubs as an undergraduate?

Please indicate your participation for each year, whether you were ever a leader, officer or captain, and whether the activity had a particular gender or racial/ethnic orientation.

College Activity or Club	(Circle all that apply on each line)					Were you ever a Leader, Officer or Captain?	Was this club or activity oriented towards a particular…	
	Freshman	Sophomore	Junior	Senior			Gender group?	Racial / ethnic group?
Varsity intercollegiate athletics	01	01	01	01	➡	❏ Yes ❏ No	❏ Yes ❏ No	❏ Yes ❏ No
Other intercollegiate athletics	02	02	02	02	➡	❏ Yes ❏ No	❏ Yes ❏ No	❏ Yes ❏ No
Intramural athletics	03	03	03	03	➡	❏ Yes ❏ No	❏ Yes ❏ No	❏ Yes ❏ No
Performing arts (e.g. music, theater) ...	04	04	04	04	➡	❏ Yes ❏ No	❏ Yes ❏ No	❏ Yes ❏ No
College newspaper, radio, yearbook ...	05	05	05	05	➡	❏ Yes ❏ No	❏ Yes ❏ No	❏ Yes ❏ No
Student government (e.g. class officer, student senate)	06	06	06	06	➡	❏ Yes ❏ No	❏ Yes ❏ No	❏ Yes ❏ No
Student political group	07	07	07	07	➡	❏ Yes ❏ No	❏ Yes ❏ No	❏ Yes ❏ No
Volunteer services (e.g. tutoring, community outreach)	08	08	08	08	➡	❏ Yes ❏ No	❏ Yes ❏ No	❏ Yes ❏ No
Fraternity or sorority	09	09	09	09	➡	❏ Yes ❏ No	❏ Yes ❏ No	❏ Yes ❏ No
Pre-professional or academic club (e.g Pre-Law Society)	10	10	10	10	➡	❏ Yes ❏ No	❏ Yes ❏ No	❏ Yes ❏ No
Religious club or community	11	11	11	11	➡	❏ Yes ❏ No	❏ Yes ❏ No	❏ Yes ❏ No
Cultural organization (e.g. South Asian Students Association)	12	12	12	12	➡	❏ Yes ❏ No	❏ Yes ❏ No	❏ Yes ❏ No
Other – Specify:_____	95	95	95	95	➡	❏ Yes ❏ No	❏ Yes ❏ No	❏ Yes ❏ No
Other – Specify:_____	95	95	95	95	➡	❏ Yes ❏ No	❏ Yes ❏ No	❏ Yes ❏ No
Did not participate in any extra-curricular activities or clubs this year	96	96	96	96				

*If you did not participate in **any** of the activities listed in Question 20, please **skip** to Question 22.*

21. On average, how many hours per week did you spend on all these activities combined?

(Circle one)

Less than 5 hours 1
5-9 hours 2
10-14 hours 3
15 hours or more 4
Don't recall 7

SECTION B: COLLEGE EXPENSES

22. *For the following questions, think back to your first year in college.*

Did you **receive** financial aid during your first year of college?

(Circle one)

Yes 1
No 2
Don't recall 7

23. What was the total cost (tuition, fees, room, board, and books) of your first year in college? (This is the cost before financial aid was applied.)

(Circle one)

Less than $1,000	01
$1,000-2,499	02
$2,500-4,999	03
$5,000-9,999	04
$10,000-14,999	05
$15,000-19,999	06
$20,000-30,000	07
More than $30,000	08
Don't recall	97

24. How much of your **first year's** educational expenses (tuition, fees, room, board, and books) **reported in Q. 23** did you cover with money from each of the sources listed below?

(Circle one on each line)

	None	Less than $1,000	$1,000-2,499	$2,500-4,999	$5,000-9,999	$10,000-14,999	$15,000-19,999	$20,000 or more	Don't Recall
Contribution from parents or other family member	00	01	02	03	04	05	06	07	97
Own funds (e.g. savings, summer work, academic year work)	00	01	02	03	04	05	06	07	97
Federal/state grant or scholarship	00	01	02	03	04	05	06	07	97
Grant or scholarship from college or university	00	01	02	03	04	05	06	07	97
Grant/ scholarship from another source outside of college or university	00	01	02	03	04	05	06	07	97
Federal student loan (e.g. Stafford, Perkins)	00	01	02	03	04	05	06	07	97
Federal loan to parents (e.g. PLUS)	00	01	02	03	04	05	06	07	97
Loan from a private institution to you	00	01	02	03	04	05	06	07	97
Loan from a private institution to your parents	00	01	02	03	04	05	06	07	97
Other sources	00	01	02	03	04	05	06	07	97

25. Did you have a job during your first year of college?

(Circle one)

Yes	1
No	2 } Skip to Q. 27
Don't recall	7

26. On average, how many hours a week did you spend at your job(s) during your first year of college?

(Circle one)

Less than 5 hours	1
5-9 hours	2
10-14 hours	3
15-19 hours	4
20-24 hours	5
25 or more hours	6
Don't recall	7

EDUCATIONAL DEBT

27. *For the following questions, think about the amount of educational debt at the time you left/finished college. If you are currently in school, you are asked to predict what your debt will be when you graduate.*

When you left/finished college, about how much money did **you** (not your parents) owe in loans related to your undergraduate education?

(Circle one)

None	00 Skip to Q. 30
$1-999	01
$1,000-2,499	02
$2,500-4,999	03
$5,000-7,499	04
$7,500-9,999	05
$10,000-14,999	06
$15,000-19,999	07 } Go to Q. 28
$20,000-29,999	08
$30,000-39,999	09
$40,000-49,999	10
$50,000-75,000	11
More than $75,000	12
Don't recall	97

28. At that time, did you consider the amount of your educational debt to be...?

(Circle one)

A little	1
An average amount	2
A lot	3
Don't recall	7

29. Was any portion of the loans for your undergraduate education forgiven in exchange for services or conditional on post-graduate study?

(Circle one)

Yes	1
No	2
Don't recall	7

30. When you left / finished college, about how much money did **your parents** (or other family members) owe in loans related to your undergraduate education?

(Circle one)

None	00
$1-999	01
$1,000-2,499	02
$2,500-4,999	03
$5,000-7,499	04
$7,500-9,999	05
$10,000-14,999	06
$15,000-19,999	07
$20,000-29,999	08
$30,000-39,999	09
$40,000-49,999	10
$50,000-75,000	11
More than $75,000	12
Don't recall	97

32. Did you attend the same undergraduate college as ...

(Circle one on each line)

	Yes	No
Your father?	1	2
Your mother?	1	2
An older sibling?	1	2
Any other older relative?	1	2

33. Do you have an undergraduate degree?

(Circle one)

Yes	1 Skip to Q. 34
No	2

33a. What is the highest year of undergraduate education you have **completed**?

(Circle one)

Freshman	1
Sophomore	2
Junior	3

SECTION C: PRE-COLLEGE EXPERIENCES

34. *For questions 34 and 35, think back to your* **elementary and junior high school** *years.*

    How often was a parent or another adult involved in helping with or making sure you did your homework?

    (Circle one)

    Never 1
    Rarely 2
    Occasionally 3
    Often 4
    Very often 5
    Don't recall 7

35. In your family, how important was it to finish your homework first before you could participate in other activities (e.g. play with friends, watch TV, etc.)?

    (Circle one)

    Not at all important 1
    Not too important 2
    Somewhat important 3
    Often important 4
    Very important 5
    Don't recall 7

36. On a scale from 01 to 07 (01 = no expectation, 07 = very strong expectation), how strong was each parent's expectation that you would go to college?

    (Circle one on each line)

	No expectatio	←→			Very strong expectation		No Parent
Mother	01	02	03	04	05	06 07	00
Father	01	02	03	04	05	06 07	00

37. Did either of your parents have in mind a particular type or quality of college that you should attend?

    (Circle one)

    Yes 1
    No 2
    Don't recall 7

38. At the time you applied to college, had any of your immediate family members (e.g., brothers, sisters, parents, grandparents) already attended a 4-year college or university?

    (Circle one)

    Yes 1
    No .... 2 } Skip to Q. 40
    Don't recall 7

39. Which immediate family member(s) had already attended a 4-year college or university?

    (Circle all that apply)

    Brother(s) or sister(s) 01
    Parent(s) 02
    Grandparent(s) 03
    Other – *Specify:* _____ 95
    Don't recall 97

40. Were you a National Merit Scholar or National Achievement Scholar?

    (Circle one)

    Yes 1
    No 2
    Don't recall 7

41. Did you **apply for** financial aid for your first year of college?

    (Circle one)

    Yes 1
    No 2
    Don't recall 7

ACADEMIC ENRICHMENT

42. Please think about your high school years, including both the academic school years and the summers. Did you participate in classes, workshops, or other **academic enrichment** activities in addition to your high school coursework that were designed to supplement your school work?

    (Circle one)

    Yes 1
    No .... 2 } Skip to Q. 47
    Don't recall 7

43. What were these activities?

    (Circle all that apply)

    Summer course 01
    After-school workshop/ course 02
    Weekend course 03
    Course at a college or junior college 04
    Distance learning/ Correspondence course 05
    Other – *Specify:* _____ 95
    Don't recall 97

44. Whose idea was it for you to participate?

(Circle all that apply)

Parent or other relative 01

Guidance counselor or advisor 02

Teacher 03

Self 04

Other – *Specify:*_____ 95

45. How many hours **per week** did you usually devote to these activities? Your best estimate is fine.

 a. during the academic year? _____ hours per week

 b. during the summer?.......... _____ hours per week

46. Were these programs sponsored by:

(Circle all that apply)

A college or university 01

A high school (your own or another school) 02

A private company (e.g. Huntington Learning, Sylvan Learning, etc.).................... 03

Other group or organization:

 A Better Chance(ABC) 04

 Center for Talented Youth (CTY) 05

 Fraternity or sorority 06

 Jack & Jill 07

 Prep for Prep 08

 Religious group or organization 09

 Talent Identification Project (TIP) 10

 Talent Search 11

 Upward Bound 12

 Other – *Specify:*_____ 95

 Don't recall 97

PREPARATION FOR COLLEGE

47. Have you ever enrolled in an SAT, PSAT, or ACT test preparation course?

(Circle one)

Yes 1

No .... 2 ⎫ Skip to Q. 50

Don't recall .... 7 ⎭

48. Was the course sponsored by. . . ?

(Circle all that apply)

Your high school 01

A private company (e.g. Princeton Review, Kaplan, etc.) 02

Another group or organization *Specify:*_____ 95

Don't recall 97

49. How much total time did you spend taking one or more of these courses?

(Circle one)

Less than 5 hours 1

5-14 hours 2

15-24 hours 3

25-49 hours 4

50 or more hours 5

Don't recall 7

50. Have you ever used a private tutor to help prepare for the SAT, PSAT, or ACT test?

(Circle one)

Yes 1

No .... 2 ⎫ Skip to

Don't recall .... 7 ⎭ Q. 52

51. How much total time did you spend being tutored privately for one or more of these tests?

(Circle one)

Less than 5 hours 1

5-14 hours 2

15-24 hours 3

25-49 hours 4

50 or more hours 5

Don't recall 7

52. Which of the following best describes the high school from which you graduated?

(Circle one)

Public (regular/non-Magnet) 01

Public (Magnet) 02

Parochial/Religious 03

Private 04

Other – *Specify:*_____ 95

53. Did you attend this school with the expectation that it would improve your chance of being accepted to college?

(Circle one)

Yes 1

No 2

Don't recall 7

54. After you graduated from high school, did you do a post-graduate year at any other public or private secondary school before applying to college?

(Circle one)

Yes 1

No 2   Skip to Q. 56

55. Did you do this with the expectation that it would improve your chances of getting into the college of your choice?

(Circle one)

Yes 1

No 2

Don't recall 7

56. **Before you applied to any schools**, how many colleges or universities did you visit to see if you might like to go there?

(Circle one)

None .... 1 Skip to Q. 58

1 or 2 2

3-5 3

6-9 4

10 or more 5

Don't recall 7

57. Were any of these trips paid for (at least in part) by the college or university?

(Circle one)

Yes 1

No 2

Don't recall 7

58. Who were the influential individuals who helped you . . . .?

(On each line, circle all that apply.)

	No one	Your parents or other family members	A guidance counselor or advisor from your high school	A teacher at your high school	A professional consultant or private tutor	Peer	Other adults (e.g. employer, friend)	Don't recall	Didn't apply for aid
a. Select colleges?	00	01	02	03	04	05	06	97	
b. Complete the application forms (excluding recommendations)?	00	01	02	03	04	05	06	97	
c. Prepare applications for **financial aid?**	00	01	02	03	04	05	06	97	96

SECTION D: FAMILY BACKGROUND

59. Please indicate where the following members of your biological family were born:

(Circle one on each line)

	In the US	In Puerto Rico	Somewhere outside the US	If outside of the US, specify country code (enter 3-digit code from list on back cover):	Don't know
a. Your mother	1	2	3 ⟶	___ ___ ___	7
b. Your mother's mother	1	2	3 ⟶	___ ___ ___	7
c. Your mother's father	1	2	3 ⟶	___ ___ ___	7
d. Your father	1	2	3 ⟶	___ ___ ___	7
e. Your father's mother	1	2	3 ⟶	___ ___ ___	7
f. Your father's father	1	2	3 ⟶	___ ___ ___	7

60. Where were you born?

(Circle one)

The United States .... 1 } Skip to
Puerto Rico .... 2 } Q. 63

Somewhere outside the United
States 3

61. In which country were you born? (*Enter 3-digit code from the list of countries on the back cover.*)

3-digit country code: ____ ____ ____

62. What was your citizenship status at the time you applied to college?

(Circle one)

US citizen by birth (including born abroad of American parent(s)) 01

Naturalized US citizen 02

Permanent resident alien (non-citizen) 03

Temporary resident (non-citizen) 04

Other – *Specify:*_____ 95

63. Are you male or female?

(Circle one)

Male 1

Female 2

64. What race/ ethnicity do you consider yourself to be?

(Circle one or more)

American Indian/Native American or Alaska Native 01

Asian or Asian American 02

Black or African American 03

Hispanic or Latino 04

Native Hawaiian or Other Pacific Islander 05

White 06

Other – *Specify:*_____ 95

65. What is your **mother**'s race/ ethnicity?

(Circle one or more)

American Indian/Native American or Alaska Native 01

Asian or Asian American 02

Black or African American 03

Hispanic or Latino 04

Native Hawaiian or Other Pacific Islander 05

White 06

Other – *Specify:*_____ 95

Don't know 97

66. What is your **father**'s race/ ethnicity?

(Circle one or more)

American Indian/Native American or Alaska Native 01

Asian or Asian American 02

Black or African American 03

Hispanic or Latino 04

Native Hawaiian or Other Pacific Islander ... 05

White 06

Other – *Specify:*_____ ... 95

Don't know 97

67. *Now please think about your senior year in high school as you answer these next questions.*

At the beginning of your **senior year** in high school, with whom did you live?

(Circle one)

Two parents, same household 01

Two parents, separate households 02

Your mother only 03

Your father only 04

Other – *Specify:*_____ 95

68. At the beginning of your senior year in high school, how many people were members of your household? *(Include yourself and other individuals away at college.)*

(Circle one)

One 01

Two 02

Three 03

Four 04

Five 05

Six 06

Seven 07

Eight or more 08

Don't recall 97

69. Was your father (or father figure, if you lived with another adult man) working for pay at any time during your senior year in high school?

(Circle one)

Yes .... 1- Go to Q. 70

No .... 2 }
Didn't have father .... 3 } Skip to Q. 72
Don't recall .... 7 }

70. What kind of work was your father (or father figure) doing, that is, what was his primary occupation at that time?

(Circle one)

Executive, administrative, managerial, or professional occupation (e.g. financial services, clergy, health diagnosis, teacher) 01

Technical, sales, or administrative support occupation, including clerical 02

Service occupation (e.g., child care provider, police and fire, food preparation) 03

Farming, forestry, or fishing 04

Precision production, craft, or repair occupation (e.g. mechanic, heating and air conditioning, construction, cabinet maker) 05

Machine operator, fabricator, inspector (e.g., textile sewing machine, taxi cab driver, welder) 06

Military 07

Don't recall 97

71. Was this position. . . ?

(Circle one)

With a private company or organization (including non-profit) 1

In the public sector (e.g., any type of government position – municipal, state, or federal) 2

Self-employment 3

Don't recall 7

72. What is the highest level of schooling your father (or father figure) has completed?

(Circle one)

Less than high school graduate 01

High school graduate 02

Vocational training or some college, but no degree 03

Associate degree 04

Bachelor's degree (e.g. BA, AB, BS) 05

Master's degree (e.g. MA, MS, MEng, MEd, MSW, MBA) 06

Professional school degree (e.g. MD, DDS, DVM, LLB, JD) 07

Doctorate degree (e.g. PhD, EdD) 08

Other – *Specify:*_____ 95

Don't recall 97

73. Was your mother (or mother figure, if you lived with another adult woman) working for pay at any time during your senior year in high school?

(Circle one)

Yes 1

No 2

Didn't have mother .... 3 } Skip to Q. 76

Don't recall 7

74. What kind of work was your mother (or mother figure) doing, that is, what was her primary occupation at that time?

(Circle one)

Executive, administrative, managerial, or professional occupation (e.g. financial services, clergy, health diagnosis, teacher) 01

Technical, sales, or administrative support occupation, including clerical 02

Service occupation (e.g., child care provider, police and fire, food preparation) 03

Farming, forestry, or fishing 04

Precision production, craft, or repair occupation (e.g. mechanic, heating and air conditioning, construction, cabinet maker) 05

Machine operator, fabricator, inspector (e.g., textile sewing machine, taxi cab driver, welder) .. 06

Military 07

Don't recall 97

75. Was this position. . . ?

(Circle one)

With a private company or organization (including non-profit) 1

In the public sector (e.g., any type of government position – municipal, state, or federal) 2

Self-employment 3

Don't recall 7

76. What is the highest level of schooling your mother (or mother figure) has completed?

(Circle one)

Less than high school graduate 01

High school graduate 02

Vocational training or some college, but no degree 03

Associate degree 04

Bachelor's degree (e.g. BA, AB, BS) 05

Master's degree (e.g. MA, MS, MEng, MEd, MSW, MBA) 06

Professional school degree (e.g. MD, DDS, DVM, LLB, JD) 07

Doctorate degree (e.g. PhD., EdD) 08

Other – *Specify:*_____ 95

Don't recall 97

77. During your senior year in high school, what is your best estimate of your household's total annual income? *(Consider annual income from all sources before taxes.)*

(Circle one)

Less than $10,000 01

$10,000-19,999 02

$20,000-29,999 03

$30,000-39,999 04

$40,000-49,999 05

$50,000-74,999 06

$75,000-99,999 07

$100,000-124,999 08

$125,000-149,999 09

$150,000-199,999 10

$200,000-250,000 11

More than $250,000 12

Don't recall 97

78. Compared with other families in your neighborhood during your senior year in high school, would you say your household's income was...?

(Circle one)

Far below average 1

Below average 2

Average 3

Above average 4

Far above average 5

Don't recall 7

79. Which one of the following categories best describes your family's **social class** during your senior year in high school?

(Circle one)

Lower class 1

Working class 2

Middle class 3

Upper-middle class 4

Upper class 5

Don't recall 7

80. During your senior year in high school, did your family own or rent the home in which you lived?

(Circle one)

Own 1

Rent .... 2 ⎫ Skip to

Don't recall .... 7 ⎭ Q. 84

81. Was your home....?

(Circle one)

Under mortgage 1

Paid for in full (i.e. no mortgage) .... 2 ⎫ Skip to

Don't recall .... 7 ⎭ Q. 83

82. What is your best estimate of the amount of mortgage debt that remained to be paid on your home (during your senior year in high school)?

(Circle one)

Less than $25,000 01

$25,000-49,999 02

$50,000-74,999 03

$75,000-99,999 04

$100,000-124,999 05

$125,000-149,999 06

$150,000-199,999 07

$200,000-249,999 08

$250,000-299,999 00

$300,000-399,999 10

$400,000-500,000 11

More than $500,000 12

Don't recall 97

83. What was the estimated market value of your family home during your senior year in high school? In other words, how much do you think it would have sold for if it had been put up for sale then?

(Circle one)

Less than $50,000	01
$50,000-74,999	02
$75,000-99,999	03
$100,000-124,999	04
$125,000-149,999	05
$150,000-199,999	06
$200,000-249,999	07
$250,000-299,999	08
$300,000-399,999	09
$400,000-499,999	10
$500,000-1,000,000	11
More than $1,000,000	12
Don't recall	97

84. During your senior year in high school, did you have your own bedroom?

(Circle one)

Yes	1
No, shared a bedroom with someone else	2

85. What is your best estimate of your household's **total assets other than your family home** during your senior year in high school? Count savings and investments as part of assets, but do not count the value of businesses, farms or retirement plans.

(Circle one)

Less than $2,500	01
$2,500-9,999	02
$10,000-24,999	03
$25,000-49,999	04
$50,000-99,999	05
$100,000-199,999	06
$200,000-299,999	07
$300,000-399,999	08
$400,000-500,000	09
More than $500,000	10
Don't recall	97

86. Please enter your full date of birth below:

_____ / _____ / 19____
    Month   Day   Year

87. If you have any comments, please write them in the space below:

Thank you for completing this questionnaire. Please mail it back
in the postage paid envelope addressed to:

Princeton Survey Research Center
Princeton University
169 Nassau St
Princeton, NJ 08542-7007

Country	Code	Country	Code	Country	Code
Afghanistan	200	India	210	Ukraine	195
American Samoa	060	Indonesia	211	Uruguay	387
Argentina	375	Iran	212	Venezuela	388
Armenia	185	Iraq	213	Vietnam	242
Australia	501	Ireland/Eire	119	Yugoslavia	147
Austria	102	Israel	214		
Azores	130	Italy	120		
Bahamas	333	Jamaica	343	**IF DON'T KNOW SPECIFIC**	
Bangladesh	202	Japan	215	**COUNTRY, PLEASE USE ONE**	
Barbados	334	Jordan	216	**OF THE CODES BELOW:**	
Belgium	103	Kenya	427		
Belize	310	Korea/South Korea	217/218	Asia	245
Bermuda	300	Laos	221	North America	304
Bolivia	376	Latvia	183	Central America	318
Brazil	377	Lebanon	222	South America	389
Burma	205	Lithuania	184	Caribbean	353
Cambodia	206	Malaysia	224	Europe	148
Canada	301	Mexico	315	Middle East	252
Chile	378	Morocco	436	North Africa	468
China	207	Netherlands	126	Other Africa	462
Colombia	379	New Zealand	514	Pacific Islands	527
Costa Rica	311	Nicaragua	316		
Cuba	337	Nigeria	440	Elsewhere (includes country not	
Czech Republic	155	North Ireland	142	known)	555
Czechoslovakia	105	Norway	127		
Denmark	106	Pakistan	229		
Dominican Republic	339	Palestine	253		
Dominica	338	Panama	317		
Ecuador	380	Peru	385		
Egypt	415	Philippines	231		
El Salvador	312	Poland	128		
England	139	Portugal	129		
Ethiopia	417	Romania	132		
Figi	507	Russia	192		
Finland	108	Saudi Arabia	233		
France	109	Scotland	140		
Germany	110	Singapore	234		
Ghana	421	Slovakia/ Slovak Republic	156		
Great Britain	138	South Africa	449		
Greece	116	Spain	134		
Grenada	340	Sweden	136		
Guam	066	Switzerland	137		
Guatemala	313	Syria	237		
Guyana	383	Taiwan	238		
Haiti	342	Thailand	239		
Holland	126	Trinidad & Tobago	351		
Honduras	314	Turkey	240		
Hong Kong	209	U.S. Virgin Islands	078		
Hungary	117	USSR	180		

Appendix B

NOTES ON METHODOLOGY

Appendix B describes how several methodological issues have been handled. We begin with issues that pertain generally to all chapters. At the end, we discuss closing the racial academic achievement gap, a topic that is relevant to the simulations in chapter 9.

NSCE SURVEY DATA

Drawing the Sample

A major new data collection effort centered on the NSCE survey. With the institutional records as the sampling frame, it was decided to concentrate most of the sample on matriculants at the ten NSCE institutions in the 1983, 1993, and 1997 entering cohorts. The target number of responses from matriculants in each cohort was 2,400, distributed across racial and ethnic groups as follows: 800 white, 900 black, 400 Asian, and 300 Hispanic students. In addition, it was desirable to have a sample of all applicants in the 1997 cohort to facilitate an examination of factors associated with the process of college application and admission. The sample of matriculants was supplemented therefore with a target number of 1,000 respondents from the 1997 cohort who applied to an NSCE institution and were rejected and another 1,000 individuals who were accepted but chose not to enroll. In both of these cases, efforts were made to produce equal numbers of white, black, Asian, and Hispanic respondents. Altogether, the NSCE survey was designed to yield 9,200 completed interviews with 2,900 white, 3,200 black, 1,700 Asian, and 1,400 Hispanic students.

The initial portion of survey data collection was subcontracted to RoperASW in Princeton, New Jersey. Roper estimated that the proportion of sample members locatable would range between 56 and 81 percent (depending on race/ethnicity, cohort, and enrollment status) with an overall average of 66 percent. Furthermore, it was assumed that an average of 75 percent of sample members who were contacted would respond to the questionnaire. Expected sample response rates varied between 61 and 86 percent, again depending on race, cohort, and enrollment category.[1]

---

[1] Projected respondent location rates and sample response rates, conditional on sample members being located, were highest for whites and the same but lower for all nonwhites,

These estimates implied that roughly one-half of all individuals who were drawn into the sample would eventually complete a questionnaire. Working backward, this meant that a sample of roughly 18,400 would be needed to yield 9,200 respondents.

Because of the decision to focus the sample on matriculants in the 1983 and 1993 cohorts and on all applicants in 1997, the effective size of the sampling frame was reduced from 245,485 total application records in the institutional data file to 127,294 records. Prior to sampling, these data were arrayed into twenty-five rows—five cohort/enrollment status categories for each of five race/ethnic groups (white, black, Asian, Hispanic, and other/unknown)—and ten columns corresponding to each NSCE institution. Within each row of the table, target numbers of sample members were derived from assumed sample location rates, sample response rates conditional on being located, and target numbers of respondents.[2] Finally, target numbers of sample members for each row of the table were distributed across institutions to yield, as nearly as possible, equal numbers of sample members at each college and university.[3] Then for each cell or sample stratum in this table, sample members were selected by random sampling without replacement. A total sample of 18,491 student records was chosen. After removing individuals who appeared more than once, we were left with a final sample of 18,164 unique persons.

Collecting the Data[4]

ROPERASW

In the summer of 2000, Roper received a file containing 18,164 sample records, including the sample member's full name, social security number, date of birth, and address at the time of application to college. Efforts were made to locate current addresses and telephone numbers for

---

highest for the 1997 cohort and progressively lower for earlier cohorts, and highest for accepted and enrolled students, lower for accepted but not enrolled, and lowest for students who were not accepted.

[2] We assumed that most of those for whom race was either "other" or "unknown" in the institutional data were in fact white. Subsequent analysis of responses to NSCE survey questions on race bore out this assumption.

[3] This procedure typically meant that sampling fractions varied by institution because the ten NSCE institutions exhibited considerable variation in the sizes of their student bodies. At some of the smaller institutions, this procedure sometimes resulted in sampling rates of 100 percent for some categories of nonwhite students. Ten sampling strata were empty because one participating institution was able to supply data just for matriculants.

[4] This section draws on survey methodology reports prepared by Linda Lepping at RoperASW (RoperASW, 2002) and by Edward P. Freeland and Marc D. Weiner at Princeton University's Survey Research Center (Freeland and Weiner, 2003). A more detailed description than the one provided in the text of how the NSCE survey data were collected is available from the authors.

all sample members. The study then consisted of two steps: a mail survey and a telephone follow-up with individuals who failed to respond to the mailing efforts. A total of 3,036 completed interviews were obtained through the mail-out, mail-back questionnaires.[5] An additional 747 telephone interviews were completed, for a total of 3,783 interviews for all modes of data collection.

Questionnaires completed by mail were entered using computer-assisted data entry (CADE). Data entered via CADE were 10 percent verified with a random sample of all mail completes. The verification was accomplished by entering the responses twice and comparing the two entries for accuracy. The failure rate achieved in the 10 percent verification was low enough not to warrant a 100 percent verification effort.

PRINCETON UNIVERSITY SURVEY RESEARCH CENTER

The Princeton University Survey Research Center (SRC) resumed data collection in September 2001 with a goal of reaching the original target of 9,200 completed interviews. Under the direction of the SRC, the second phase of the project consisted of a redesign of the survey materials and procedures, the addition of a project Web site and the option to complete the survey online, and an extensive telephone locating effort to determine the most current correct mailing addresses for all original sample members who had either not yet completed a questionnaire or refused participation. The SRC worked the same sample as RoperASW, and no question wording changes were made to the survey instrument.

Data collection began in April 2002, with the mailing by SRC of the first set of questionnaires. At this time, the sample file had a total of 14,381 records, 8,300 of which had already been attempted by Roper, and the remaining 6,081 as entirely new cases. Excluded from this sample were the 3,783 sample members from whom Roper had already obtained completed interviews. The SRC obtained 5,302 additional completed questionnaires. Most of these (4,661) were completed by paper/mail, and the remaining 641 were completed online. When added to Roper's 3,783 completed responses, the total number of completed NSCE responses is 9,085—a figure within 1.25 percent of the original target number.

---

[5] In an effort to understand why the response to the mailings was lower than anticipated, RoperASW randomly selected one hundred non-responders who had been sent all the mailings and for whom a telephone number was available. RoperASW research staff called each of these individuals seeking to verify that they had in fact received the mailings. As a result of this experiment, it was discovered that a significant number of the 1997 mailings had been sent to parents' addresses and that many parents had not forwarded the packages to their children's college addresses. When asked, many parents affirmed that their children usually picked up any mail that came in during the school year when they returned home for break.

TABLE B.1
Final Status Codes

Final Status	Count	Known to Be Eligible	Known to Be Ineligible
Complete—SRC	5,302	Yes	
Complete—Roper	3,783	Yes	
Refused (presurvey)	705	Yes	
Refused (during survey)	223	Yes	
Not Usable	202		Yes
Not Reachable	23		Yes
Deceased	58		Yes
Not Locatable (presurvey)	374		Yes
Not Locatable (during survey)	1,431		Yes
Failed Verification: Ineligible	16		Yes
Failed Verification: Eligibility unknown	12	Eligibility unknown	
Unknown/No Response	6,035	Eligibility unknown	
Total	18,164		

Source: National Study of College Experience.
Note: The data reflect final disposition assignments from both the Survey Research Center at Princeton University and RoperASW. For a detailed discussion of the reconciliation of the codes assigned by Roper to the codes assigned by the SRC, see "Supplemental Notes on Reconciling Final Status Codes as Between the Survey Research Center and Roper" in Freeland and Weiner (2003).

All completed questionnaires received were subjected to a test to verify that the person completing the questionnaire was in fact the intended respondent. This was done by comparing data from the administrative records (e.g., date of birth, sex, race, etc.) with the responses in the questionnaire. As a result of this comparison, 28 completed questionnaires were identified as having been completed by someone who was probably not the intended respondent. These questionnaires are not counted as completed cases for calculation of the response rate, nor are they included in the analysis files. A summary of the final status codes assigned to each case is shown in Table B.1.

Response Rate Analysis

To define responses that qualify as "completed interviews," we first identified a subset of thirteen *priority* questions from the NSCE survey instrument. These consisted of question numbers 15, 16, 27, 28, 38, 39, 58a, 58b, 58c, 59, 60, 61, and 64. A respondent had to answer at least one priority question for his or her interview to be considered "complete." All 9,085 interviews passed this basic test. Sample response rates are calculated as the total number of completed interviews divided by the number of sample members "at risk" of responding to the questionnaire. More specifically, we follow convention among public opinion research professionals and define sample response rates as "the number of complete interviews with reporting units divided by the number of eligible reporting units in the sample" (American Association for Public Opinion Research [AAPOR], 2004: 3, 28). Eligible reporting units consist of those specifically named persons who had an opportunity to answer the questionnaire and chose either to respond or not to respond. Other individuals were not eligible for a variety of reasons, including the fact that no contact was made with them at any point in the survey. Finally, there is a group of sample members whose eligibility status is unknown.

It is customary to report response rates in studies using sample survey data, but researchers do not always make clear their methodology for calculating response rates and frequently they are not consistent in their use of terminology.[6] AAPOR (2004) provides formulas for six different response rates, ranging from those yielding the lowest to the highest response rates. We have selected an intermediate formula, the Response Rate 3 (RR3) method, defined by AAPOR (2004: 28–29) as

$$RR3 = \frac{I}{(I + P) + (R + NC + O) + e\,(UH + UO)}$$

where
  I = complete interview
  P = partial interview
  R = refusal and break-off
  NC = non-contact
  O = other ineligible
  UH = unknown if household/occupied housing unit
  UO = other unknown, and
  e = estimated proportion of cases of unknown eligibility that are eligible.

[6] As noted by the American Association for Public Opinion Research (AAPOR) (2004: 28), "Numerous outcome rates are commonly cited in survey reports and in the research literature. The same names are used to describe fundamentally different rates and different names are sometimes applied to the same rates. As a result, survey researchers are rarely doing things in a comparable manner and frequently are not even speaking the same technical language. As Groves and Lyberg (1988) have noted, 'There are so many ways of calculating response rates that comparisons across surveys are fraught with misinterpretations.' Among the more common terms utilized are response, cooperation, refusal, and contact." AAPOR advises that it is insufficient and unacceptable to report that "the response rate is X" (American Association for Public Opinion Research, 2004: 32). It is also necessary to report on exactly which response rate method is being used (e.g., "Response Rate 2 was X").

TABLE B.2
Disposition Categories for Calculating Overall Response Rate

| Completed Interview | Eligibility Status | | | Total |
	Eligible	Ineligible	Unknown	
Yes	9,085	0	0	9,085
No	928	2,104	6,047	9,079
Total	10,013	2,104	6,047	18,164

Source: National Study of College Experience.

In the NSCE the number of complete interviews (I) is 9,085, and there are no partial completes (P). An additional 928 individuals are eligible but refused to participate (R). The ineligibles (NC and O) include 2,104 persons who were not reachable, deceased, or not locatable prior to or during the survey. Finally, there are 6,047 individuals remaining in the total sample whose eligibility status is unknown (UO).[7] All 18,164 sample cases are organized according to their disposition status and shown in Table B.2.

Several methods exist for estimating the eligibility rate e (AAPOR, 2000: 36n25). In his review of seven alternative methods for estimating e in random-digit-dialing telephone surveys, Tom Smith (2003: 8–9) argues there is no "gold standard" for estimating eligibility rates and "no general eligibility rate that can be applied to all or even most surveys." What is important is to be clear on the method applied. We base our estimate of e on the "proportional allocation or CASRO method," which assumes that "the ratio of eligible to not eligible cases among the known cases applies to the unknown cases" (T. Smith, 2003: 1–2). In Table B.2 there are 6,047 cases where the sample member did not complete a questionnaire and where the eligibility status is unknown. Among known eligibility cases that did not complete an interview, 30.6 percent ($= 928/(928 + 2,104)$) were eligible. Using this estimated value for e, the overall response rate in Table B.2 calculated using the RR3 method is $9,085/(9,085 + 928 + e \cdot 6,047)$ or $9,085/11,863.8 = 76.6$ percent.

An overview of response rates in the NSCE survey calculated by race, cohort, and enrollment status is contained in Table B.3. The overall estimated NSCE survey response rate based on 9,085 completed interviews

[7] The category UH is used only in random-digit-dialing telephone surveys. Persons with unknown eligibility status include twenty-eight individuals who failed verification in the sense that although they returned a completed questionnaire, it could not be verified that they were the intended respondents. These questionnaires are not counted as completed cases when calculating response rates nor are they used in the analysis files. See Table B.1 for details.

TABLE B.3
Response Rates and Number of Completed Responses, by Race, Cohort,
and Enrollment Status

		Race					
Cohort	Enrollment Status	White	Black	Hispanic	Asian	Other & Unknown	Total
1983	Enrolled	70.3[a] (532)[b]	70.5 (880)	77.7 (231)	71.2 (438)	63.2 (242)	70.2 (2,323)
1993	Enrolled	74.0 (531)	74.9 (797)	79.3 (414)	73.0 (432)	82.4 (192)	75.6 (2,366)
1997	Applied/Not Accepted	76.2 (129)	87.6 (215)	79.4 (255)	79.0 (227)	81.2 (115)	81.2 (941)
	Admitted/Not Enrolled	85.0 (156)	85.4 (221)	86.9 (263)	78.8 (254)	93.0 (97)	85.2 (991)
	Enrolled	76.2 (545)	80.8 (825)	76.7 (384)	74.7 (480)	75.0 (230)	77.5 (2,464)
Total		74.7 (1,893)	76.8 (2,938)	79.5 (1,547)	75.4 (1,831)	77.0 (876)	76.6 (9,085)

Source: National Study of College Experience.

[a]Response rates (%) calculated using Response Rate 3 method in American Association for Public Opinion Research (2004).

[b]Number of completed responses in parentheses.

is 76.6 percent. Apart from two outliers (63.2 and 93.0 percent), more than two-thirds of individual stratum response rates lie between 70 and 80 percent, and the remaining ones fall between 80 and 90 percent. Response rates vary with cohort in the expected way; they are highest overall for the 1997 enrolled students (77.5 percent), then somewhat lower in the 1993 cohort (75.6 percent), and finally lowest in 1983 (70.2 percent). On the other hand, contrary to expectations, response rates are not greatest among enrolled students in 1997. Students in the 1997 cohort who were admitted but did not enroll as well as those who were not admitted have higher response rates (85.2 and 81.2 percent, respectively). Nor do response rates vary by race and ethnicity in the expected way. Overall response rates are highest for Hispanic students (79.5 percent) and lowest for whites (74.7).

Table B.4 contains additional and illustrative response rate measures from the NSCE survey, each derived using the RR3 method. Response rates are progressively lower the older the cohorts of entering students. Overall, response rates are marginally higher at private institutions than

TABLE B.4
Response Rates and Number of Completed Responses, by Entering Cohort,
Institutional Type, Race, and Sex

| | Entering Cohort | | | |
Item	1983	1993	1997	Total
Type of Institution				
Public	72.5[a]	71.8	79.6	75.6
	(700)[b]	(784)	(1,390)	(2,874)
Private	69.1	77.6	80.8	77.0
	(1,623)	(1,582)	(3,006)	(6,211)
Race				
White	70.3	74.0	77.8	74.7
	(532)	(531)	(830)	(1,893)
Black	70.5	74.9	82.6	76.8
	(880)	(797)	(1,261)	(2,938)
Hispanic	77.7	79.3	80.1	79.5
	(231)	(414)	(902)	(1,547)
Asian	71.2	73.0	78.1	75.4
	(438)	(432)	(961)	(1,831)
Other/Unknown	63.2	82.4	82.6	77.0
	(242)	(192)	(442)	(876)
Sex[c]				
Male	66.6	68.9	74.9	70.9
	(1,020)	(924)	(1,601)	(3,545)
Female	72.3	80.3	84.0	80.5
	(1,299)	(1,442)	(2,793)	(5,534)
Total	70.2	75.6	80.5	76.6
	(2,323)	(2,366)	(4,396)	(9,085)

Source: National Study of College Experience.
[a]Response rates (%) calculated using Response Rate 3 method in American Association
for Public Opinion Research (2004).
[b]Number of completed responses in parentheses.
[c]The final sample of 18,164 individuals was missing a value for sex in the institutional
data in 46 cases and in the completed responses in 6 cases.

at public ones. Women display response rates that are roughly ten percentage points higher than those for men.

Response rates reported in Tables B.3 and B.4 are conservative and
may understate the true response rates. In staff discussions we assigned
nearly 1,000 sample members to unknown eligibility when a good case

could be made that they should be considered ineligible and not at risk of completing the survey. In addition, Princeton's Survey Research Center contacted very few current students at their college addresses. The questionnaire was sent instead to their home address. It is unknown whether parents set the survey aside for their children until vacation, forwarded it to them at their campus address, or discarded the materials. If a questionnaire was delivered by the U.S. Postal Service, we treated it as received by the student and considered the student eligible to participate in the survey, but we really do not know whether the student had a choice about whether to complete the questionnaire. Surely in some proportion of these cases, sample members should have been put into the "unknown eligibility, no returned questionnaire" category. Finally, in a review of methods for calculating eligibility rates, Tom Smith (2003) refers to the RR3 method (also known as the "proportional allocation" or "CASRO method") as conservative and not leading to inflated estimates of response rates.

ANALYSIS SAMPLES AND WEIGHTING

Because the sample for the NSCE survey was drawn with varying sampling fractions and because response rates vary by sample stratum, it is necessary to weight the survey data to reflect institutional population totals. As a preliminary step, it is necessary to expand the number of completed responses to account for duplicates. The 18,491 student records were sampled from a universe of 127,294 records. Some persons were represented in the sample more than once. Before attempting to contact any sample members, we removed 327 duplicate records from the sample to avoid sending multiple survey instruments to the same person, leaving 18,164 unique individuals. Completed responses were received from 9,085 members of this group. Prior to constructing weights and before attempting any analyses, 185 duplicate records for individuals who completed the survey were restored or cloned, and survey responses were attached to each of these multiple sample occurrences.[8] As a consequence, survey data available for analysis consist of 9,270 completed responses, obtained from 9,085 separate individuals.

---

[8]Responses were duplicated or cloned to account only for the multiplicity of times the same student appeared in the sample, not in the universe. For example, a student may have applied to three NSCE institutions and therefore appears three times in the universe for the 1997 cohort. But if just two of these cases were drawn into the sample and if this individual responded to the survey, then only one additional set of duplicate responses needed to be created, not two.

The weights depend on the kinds of analyses we expect to perform. Most of our analyses will be based on one of three study populations.

1. All *persons* in the combined applicant pools. In this case a unique person or student is the unit of analysis. For example, we might be interested in examining pre-college preparation strategies among all applicants in our data. These studies call for a person weight.

2. All *applications*, where the application is the unit of analysis. We could be interested, for example, in studying decisions made by admission officers across multiple institutions. Because some students applied to more than one NSCE institution, their application to each of those schools, and not the student, is the unit of analysis for this type of investigation. Here we need an application weight.

3. Lastly, all *matriculants* to NSCE institutions. The unit of analysis is the matriculant, each of whom is unique because a person can enroll at only one institution. If, for example, we want to examine the socioeconomic characteristics of these individuals or their patterns of social interaction on college campuses, then we need a matriculant weight.

P-Sample

Although all eight non-HBCUs in our institutional data set supplied data on matriculants, one was prevented by time constraints from providing data on all applicants. This institution was omitted from analyses pertaining to the behaviors of students in the combined applicant pools as well as from studies of factors determining admission to academically selective colleges and universities. Thus, the P-sample or "person" sample corresponds to the set of unique individuals who applied for admission to one or more of *seven* NSCE institutions in the fall of 1997. There was a total of 79,222 applications submitted to these seven schools, but some students applied to more than one NSCE institution. As a result, these applications correspond to 67,703 unique individuals or applicants in the P-universe. These 67,703 individual applicants are represented by 3,670 unique individuals in the P-sample.

Weights for P-sample members are based on application *pathways*.[9] A unique application pathway consists of the set of one or more of the seven P-sample institutions to which someone in the institutional data of 67,703 unique applicants has applied, supplemented by information on the outcome of each application process (that is, rejected, accepted but did not enroll, accepted and subsequently enrolled). A total of 958

[9] We are grateful to Germán Rodríguez for suggesting this approach.

distinct pathways are represented by the institutional data. Some of these pathways, however, are not represented by any individuals in the P-sample, so it was necessary to combine similar pathways at the institutional level to ensure that each resulting pathway contained at least one P-sample member. After collapsing, there were 496 separate pathways in the population.[10] Then the P-weight for each unique population/universe pathway is calculated as the number of persons in the population in application pathway i with race j ($j = 1$ (white), 2 (black), 3 (Hispanic), 4 (Asian) and 5 (other/unknown)) divided by the number of persons from the numerator in pathway i and race j who also appear as sample respondents. The P-weights are designed to permit analyses that reproduce the population of all unique individuals in the combined applicant pools to these seven institutions. The P-sample is the primary analysis sample used in chapter 2. The unweighted racial and ethnic distribution of P-sample membership includes 1,070 white students, 811 blacks, 829 Hispanics, and 960 Asians for a total of 3,670. When weighted using P-weights, the percentage distribution becomes: whites (68.1), blacks (6.8), Hispanics (5.2), and Asians (20.0).

A-Sample

The A-sample or "application" sample uses the individual application as the unit of analysis. In the population there are 79,222 applications for admission in the fall of 1997 to the same seven institutions used for the P-sample. These universe applications are represented by 3,829 applications in the A-sample. The A-sample is relied on for analyses in chapter 3 of the admission process at academically selective institutions, and the associated weights are designed to reproduce the total number of applications in the population. Both the A-sample and associated A-universe contain multiple applications from the same individual, but these duplicates are intentional. A-weights are calculated specific to 105 individual sampling strata (= 1 cohort (fall of 1997) × 3 enrollment statuses (rejected; accepted but did not enroll; accepted and later enrolled) × 5 races (white, black, Hispanic, Asian, other/unknown) × 7 institutions). The A-weight for 1997 for each sample respondent in cell i (= college), j (= race), k (= enrollment category) is the number of people in category ijk from the institutional or population data divided by the number of respondents in the NSCE survey in category ijk. Cells involving the three

[10] Before the application pathways were combined, the distribution of these outcomes by race/ethnicity is as follows: white (334), black (158), Hispanic (134), Asian (256), other and unknown races (76). After some aggregation, the race/ethnic distribution of the remaining 496 pathways is: white (112), black (102), Hispanic (93), Asian (150), and other and unknown races (39).

enrollment statuses must be combined to determine the total number of applications from members of race/ethnicity *j* to institution *i*.

M-Sample

Much of the analysis in chapters 4 through 8 deals with various aspects of campus life and relies on data about matriculants at *eight* NSCE institutions, one more institution than is reflected in the P-sample or in the A-sample.[11] The M-sample or "matriculant" sample also differs from the P- and A-samples in that it incorporates a time dimension. Enrolled students at each of the eight institutions in the fall of 1983, 1993, and 1997 are incorporated into the analysis. Moreover, the M-sample is a somewhat "thicker" sample in comparison to the other two. There are 54,471 unique persons or matriculants in the population compared with 6,350 separate individuals in the M-sample. M-weights are designed to reproduce the universe of enrolled students at each institution in each cohort year. They are calculated specific to 120 population cells (3 cohorts (1983, 1993, and 1997) × 5 races (white, black, Hispanic, Asian, other/unknown) × 8 institutions). The M-weight for matriculant sample respondents in category *i* (= college), *j* (= race), *k* (= cohort) is the number of matriculants in category *ijk* from the institutional or population data divided by the number of sample respondents in the NSCE survey in category *ijk*.

For each of the analysis samples (P, A, and M), sample weights are calculated using five race and ethnicity categories including the category "other and unknown." However, as discussed below in the section titled "Race and Ethnicity," sample respondents in the "other and unknown" group were subsequently reallocated to one of four primary race groups for analysis purposes. When this reallocation was performed, sample respondents retained the weights they were assigned as members of the "other/unknown" race group.

RACE AND ETHNICITY

An increase in interracial marriage in the United States has contributed to growth in the size of the multiracial population. Marriages involving individuals from different racial backgrounds increased as a percentage of all marriages between 1990 and 2000 (Farley, 2002). Levels of outmarriage are particularly high among American Indian and Hispanic men and women as well as for Asian women, and are above average for Asian

---

[11] The risks of some slight inconsistencies in results across chapters stemming from different numbers of schools taking part (seven in some cases and eight in others) seem to us slight in comparison to the advantages of being able to include additional data from the one institution that was able to supply information only about its enrolled students.

and black men. In recognition of these demographic changes, the U.S. Census Bureau in 2000 altered the way it collects data on race and ethnicity. Three significant changes were made on the decennial census long form. Questions about Spanish/Hispanic/Latino origin were placed ahead of questions concerning race. The varieties of printed racial categories from which respondents could select were modified. Most important, respondents could identify with more than one racial group.[12] In the 2000 census, 6.4 million Americans or 2.6 percent of the total population reported two or more races (Farley, 2002). The multiracial population made up 4 percent of all persons under age eighteen (Qian, 2004a). The most common combinations among the multiple-race population in 2000 are white and some other race (32 percent), white and American Indian (16 percent), white and Asian (13 percent), and white and black (12 percent) (Farley, 2002). These data suggest that when members of minority racial groups marry outside their own group, they typically marry someone who is white.

While the new census race questions permit a more textured and accurate demographic and social description of the U.S. population, they nevertheless pose challenges to researchers and policymakers who frequently seek parsimony in their analyses (Goldstein and Morning, 2002). Most studies would obscure the main story if they attempted to deal with all of the varieties of respondents' multiple-race backgrounds. As a consequence, researchers commonly attempt to associate members of their study populations with a single race as a satisfactory first approximation (Cole and Barber, 2003; Massey et al., 2003). We have taken this approach here even though NSCE survey respondents were encouraged to mark as many racial/ethnic categories as applied to them.

The racial and ethnic composition of the 9,085 NSCE survey respondents as reported by the ten participating NSCE institutions is shown in row 1 of Table B.5. Because there was oversampling of nonwhite students, the resulting unweighted distribution is not representative of the underlying population. Nevertheless, 20.8 percent of sample members were listed as white on their college application, 32.3 percent as black, 17.0 percent as Hispanic, 20.2 percent as Asian, and 9.6 percent fell into the "other" or "unknown" race category.[13] A preliminary step in the

[12] On the 1990 decennial census long form, respondents to the race question were instructed to "Fill ONE circle for the race that the person considers himself/herself to be." In 2000 the instructions were modified as follows: "Mark one or more races to indicate what this person considers himself/herself to be" (Farley, 2002).

[13] The total institutional file of all students applying to ten NSCE institutions across three entering cohorts includes 245,485 applicant records. The race/ethnic breakdown of these individuals is: white (59.1 percent), black (10.8 percent), Hispanic (4.0 percent), Asian (14.9 percent), other race(s) (3.1 percent), and unknown race (8.1 percent).

Institutional and Analysis Race/Ethnicity Categories among Completed Interviews
Compared to Target Sample

Item	Race/Ethnicity						
	White	Black	Hispanic	Asian	Other	Unknown	Total
1. Reported by NSCE institutions	1,893	2,938	1,547	1,831	378	498	9,085
2a. Analysis categories after reallocating 876 Other and Unknown cases[a]	2,552	2,994	1,565	1,974			9,085
2b. Percent distribution	28.1	33.0	17.2	21.7			100.0
3a. Number of cases reallocated	+659	+56	+18	+143	−378	−498	0
3b. Number allocated as percent of row 1	34.8	1.9	1.2	7.8			0
4a. Target sample	2,900	3,200	1,400	1,700			9,200
4b. Percent distribution	31.5	34.8	15.2	18.5			100.0

Source: National Study of College Experience.

[a]For details on the methods for reallocating 876 "other" and "unknown" race cases to single-race categories, see Table B.7.

research involved reassigning each of the 876 sample members whose racial affiliation was listed either as unknown or as belonging to a group or some combination of groups other than white, black, Hispanic, or Asian to one of these four principal categories. Details on how this reallocation was performed are provided at the end of this section.[14] To summarize these procedures, we first accepted the racial designations provided by NSCE institutions for the students who were identified as white, black, Hispanic, or Asian (WBHA). For most of the remaining students, we relied on responses to the NSCE survey race questions if respondents marked only one race and it fell into WBHA. For the relatively small number of additional cases, a principal race group was assigned based on a combination of factors including parents' race or the responses of multiple-race individuals in other surveys when asked about their "primary" racial identification or when asked to choose just a single race.

The distribution of all NSCE sample respondents according to their analytic single-race categories is shown in rows 2a and 2b of Table B.5. This is the "race" variable we use for substantive analyses in later chapters. White and black respondents constitute the two largest groups, followed

[14]The number of Native Americans or Alaska Natives was too small to warrant a separate analytic category.

by Asians and Hispanics. Three-fourths of the 876 individuals whose institutional race was either other or unknown were reclassified as white (row 3a), followed next by Asian. Very few sample respondents were reassigned to the black or Hispanic groups. These reclassifications increased the number of white respondents based solely on institutional race designations by almost 35 percent (row 3b). Much smaller impacts were felt in each of the nonwhite categories.[15] Rows 4a and 4b of Table B.5 illustrate the race designations of the original target sample. We aimed to achieve 9,200 completed questionnaires. As noted previously, our achieved sample came within 1.25 percent of this total. Further, a comparison of the percentage distributions in rows 2b and 4b shows that the race-ethnic distributions of the achieved and expected target samples are quite close.

The NSCE survey question on respondent's race asked individuals, "What race/ethnicity do you consider yourself to be?" and then instructed them to select as many categories as applied from among the following: American Indian/Native American or Alaska Native; Asian or Asian American; Black or African American; Hispanic or Latino; Native Hawaiian or Other Pacific Islander; White; and Other (specify). Table B.6 shows respondents' reported race on the NSCE survey and their designated race for analysis purposes. There is a substantial amount of consistency between the two variables. Overall 7,610 or 83.8 percent of all sample members cited the same race in the NSCE survey as their analytic race determination. This fraction, however, varies by race group. It is highest for whites (91.3 percent), lowest for Hispanics (63.0 percent), and at intermediate levels for blacks and Asians (roughly 86 percent).[16]

It is evident that each analytic race group contains a significant amount of multiple-race diversity. Although most individuals who were designated white for analysis purposes also claimed to be white in the survey, nearly

---

[15] Our findings are consistent with those from other recent research. Based on national data from the U.S. Department of Education's Integrated Postsecondary Education Data System, or IPEDS, Daryl Smith and his colleagues report that there has been a dramatic rise in the number and percentage of students who are designated by their home institutions as "race/ethnicity unknown," either because students failed to report race/ethnicity on their college application forms, or selected more than one race/ethnicity category, or chose "other" (Smith et al., 2005). Nationwide the percentage rose from 3.2 percent of enrolled students in 1991 to 5.9 percent of those enrolled in 2001. Using data from three selective, private liberal arts colleges in California, these authors conclude that "overall, a sizeable portion of students in the unknown category are white, in addition to multiracial students who may have selected white as one of their categories" (Smith et al., 2005: 1).

[16] Internal consistency can be viewed from another perspective. "White" is the primary analytic category for 92.5 percent of individuals who selected only "white" in the NSCE survey. These percentages exceed 99 percent for respondents who claimed the single race/ethnicity of "Black," "Hispanic," or "Asian" in the NSCE survey.

TABLE B.6
Racial and Ethnic Diversity within the Four Primary Race Categories

Race/Ethnicity as Reported in NSCE Survey[a]	Primary Analytic Categories									
	White		Black		Hispanic		Asian		Total	
	Number	Percent	Number	Percent	Number	Percent	Number	Percent	Number	Percent
White[b]	2,329	91.3	23	0.8	132	8.4	35	1.8	2,519	27.7
Black	2	0.1	2,586	86.4	3	0.2	3	0.2	2,594	28.6
Hispanic[c]	2	0.1	6	0.2	986	63.0	0	—	994	10.9
Asian[c]	3	0.1	5	0.2	6	0.4	1,709	86.6	1,723	19.0
White/Black[d]	0	—	102	3.4	0	—	1	0.1	103	1.1
White/Hispanic	4	0.2	2	0.1	241	15.4	1	0.1	248	2.7
White/Asian[e]	17	0.7	0	—	1	0.1	58	2.9	76	0.8
Black/Hispanic	0	—	38	1.3	9	0.6	0	—	47	0.5
Black/Asian[f]	0	—	22	0.7	0	—	0	—	22	0.2
Hispanic/Asian[g]	0	—	0	—	27	1.7	5	0.3	32	0.4
Native American[h]	68	2.7	2	0.1	2	0.1	7	0.4	79	0.9
Black/Native American	0	—	36	1.2	0	—	0	—	36	0.4
Other/Unknown[i]	68	2.7	85	2.8	86	5.5	81	4.1	320	3.5
Miscellaneous[j]	16	0.6	44	1.5	47	3.0	19	1.0	126	1.4
Missing	43	1.7	43	1.4	25	1.6	55	2.8	166	1.8
Total	2,552	100.0	2,994	100.0	1,565	100.0	1,974	100.0	9,085	100.0

Source: National Study of College Experience.

[a]Survey respondents were asked to circle all categories that applied to them. Categories include I (American Indian/Native American or Alaska Native), A (Asian or Asian American), B (Black or African American), H (Hispanic or Latino), P (Native Hawaiian or Other Pacific Islander), W (White), and O (Unspecified Mixed Race or Other Race/Ethnicity).

[b]Includes W (2,485) and WI (34, all coded W for analysis purposes).

[c]Includes A (1,676), AP (11), and P (36).

[d]Includes WBI (25).

[e]Includes WA (64), WP (5), and WAP (7).

[f]Includes BA (19), BP (2), and BAP (1).

[g]Includes HA (19), HP (11), and HAP (2).

[h]Includes American Indian/Native American or Alaska Native.

[i]Includes Unspecified Mixed Race or Other Race/Ethnicity.

[j]Includes numerous small categories, the largest of which are WO (18), BO (17), and HO (11).

3 percent claimed to be solely Native American or Alaska Native. Among blacks, the most prominent non-black combination is black-white, accounting for 3.4 percent of all black sample members. Nearly 40 sample members who were designated black identified with a black-Hispanic combination. There is greater diversity among the Hispanic analysis race category. Fewer than two-thirds of these individuals claimed only an Hispanic affiliation in the survey. More than 130 or 8.4 percent of all Hispanics reported being white, and 15.4 percent reported a white-Hispanic identification. Part of the greater heterogeneity among Hispanics may be due to the fact that Hispanic or Latino is in the census a measure of ethnicity, separate from the usual indicators of race. A sizable number of Hispanics (5.5 percent of the total) identified with some "other" racial grouping in the survey. Among Asians only a small group identified themselves as white in the survey (1.8 percent). A somewhat larger fraction (2.9 percent) said they were some combination of white and Asian. And a non-negligible proportion (4.1 percent) claimed membership in an "other" category. Two main lessons may be drawn from Table B.6. First, there is substantial agreement between how individuals are classified for analysis purposes and how they define themselves in the NSCE survey. We should expect to find this agreement if the analysis is on solid ground. Second, the correlation is not perfect. Within each primary race/ethnicity designation there is much richness in terms of multiple-race affiliations. But the overall picture that emerges is that when there is mixing across different racial groupings, it tends to be between one minority racial group and the dominant white group.

Assigning a Single Race or Ethnicity

For analysis purposes it is desirable to have a single race or ethnicity category assigned to each survey respondent. Table B.7 describes how these assignments were made for each of the 9,085 individuals who completed the NSCE survey. First, each person was assigned to one of the following four alternatives: White, Black, Hispanic, or Asian (WBHA). If an applicant identified with only one race or ethnicity category on her college application form and the corresponding institution reported that information to the NSCE project, that category was accepted as the race or ethnicity for subsequent analysis purposes. More than 90 percent of all survey respondents fell into this category. Second, if a student's race or ethnicity was something other than WBHA or was unknown in the institutional data, we relied on that individual's response to the NSCE race question. If the individual reported only one race or ethnicity and it fell into WBHA, we relied on that response in assigning race. These first two steps permitted a race or ethnicity allocation to all except 214 or 2.4 percent of all survey respondents.

TABLE B.7

Steps in Assigning Single-Race Categories to N = 9,085 NSCE Survey Respondents

Procedure	References	Number of Cases Resolved	Percent of Total
1. Accept institutional single-race designation for individuals labeled White (W), Black (B), Hispanic (H), or Asian (A).		8,209	90.4
2. Use response to NSCE survey race question (s_race). Move people from the institutional "other" or "unknown" category to Asian, Black, White, or Hispanic using these rules: to Asian if s_race is A, P, or AP (N = 125)[a] to Black if s_race is B (N = 37) to White if s_race is W (N = 493) to Hispanic if s_race is H (N = 7)		662	7.3
3. Use individual's race response on the Student Descriptive Questionnaire (SDQ). The SDQ asks students registering for the SAT test to "mark only one" race. Recode as: Asian if SDQ_race is "Asian, Asian American, or Pacific Islander" Black if SDQ_race is "Black or African American" Hispanic if SDQ_race is "Mexican or Mexican American/Puerto Rican/Latin American, South American, Central American, or other Hispanic or Latino" White if SDQ_race is "White"		4	0.04

The remaining steps describe the treatment of the NSCE survey race response (s_race).

4.	If s_race involves two race groups, one of which is I, then recode: WI → W (N = 29) BI → B AI → A, PI → A, API → A (N = 3) HI → H	(Goldstein and Morning, 2000, 2002; Harrison, 2002; CLASS data[b])	32	0.4

5.	Use parents' race from NSCE survey (typically when respondent's race is unknown)
	  a. if one parent's race is specified and the other's is missing, O, or U, use the race that is specified (N = 8)
	  b. if both parents have the same race, use that race for respondent (N = 5)
	  c. if both parents have the same race pairs, one of which is O or U (e.g., WO, WO), ignore O or U and use known race for respondent (N = 5)
			18	0.2

6.	If respondent chooses two race groups from among W, B, H, and A, then: WB → B WH → H WA → W BH → B BA → B	(Qian, 2004a, 2004b; CLASS data) (Qian, 2004a; CLASS data) (Goldstein and Morning, 2000, 2002; Qian, 2004a, 2004b; CLASS data) (CLASS data) (CLASS data)	50	0.6

(Continued)

TABLE B.7 (*Continued*)

Procedure	References	Number of Cases Resolved	Percent of Total
HA→H	(Goldstein and Morning, 2000, 2002; Cole and Barber, 2003; CLASS data)		
or if			
AO→A			
BO→B			
HO→H			
WO→W			
7. American Indian/Native American/Alaska Native		67	0.7

7. American Indian/Native American/Alaska Native
There are N = 67 respondents who marked only "I" on NSCE survey race (s_race). Of these, N = 1 had Asian ancestry in parents' generation and N = 32 had white ancestry among parents. These were recoded "A" and "W", respectively. In addition, N = 27 marked only "I" for self, mother, and father for NSCE race, and N = 7 marked only "I" for self, mother, and father for NSCE race and for self on SDQ_race. These remaining 34 cases were also recoded White.

8.	Manual lookups	43	0.5
	All remaining cases in which there was no information about respondent's or parents' race available on the NSCE survey or from the SDQ data were manually recoded on the basis of name and citizenship status at the time of college application.		
Total		9,085	100.0

Source: National Study of College Experience.

[a]NSCE survey respondents were asked to circle all race/ethnic categories that applied to them. Categories include: I (American Indian/Native American or Alaska Native), A (Asian or Asian American), B (Black or African American), H (Hispanic or Latino), P (Native Hawaiian or Other Pacific Islander), W (White), O (Other Race/Ethnicity), and U (Unspecified Mixed Race).

[b]The Campus Life in America Student Survey (CLASS Project), being conducted at Princeton University, surveyed all freshmen and juniors at Princeton University, Emory University, University of Miami, Michigan State University, Portland State University, and UCLA in the fall of 2004. Among other things, respondents were asked, "What do you consider to be your primary race/ethnicity? (Circle one only)" and then "What else do you consider as describing your race/ethnicity? (Circle one or more)." Possible response categories included American Indian/Native American or Alaska Native; Asian or Asian American; Black or African American; Hispanic or Latino; Native Hawaiian or Other Pacific Islander; White; None; and Other—Specify. Distributions of what students considered to be their primary race when several races were indicated were used to recode multiple-race responses on the NSCE into single-race categories.

Third, students who register to take the SAT test are asked to complete a companion Student Descriptive Questionnaire (SDQ). The SDQ gives students an opportunity to mark one racial or ethnicity category to which they feel they belong. We used these responses to define a race/ethnicity for an additional four survey respondents. Next, if a survey respondent circled two categories in response to the NSCE survey race question, one of which was Native American/Alaska Native and the other one a category in WBHA, we relied on the available literature and data from the CLASS project at Princeton University to designate a category from WBHA as the primary race or ethnicity (Goldstein and Morning, 2000, 2002; Harrison, 2002).[17] These guidelines helped resolve an additional thirty-two cases for individuals whose race or ethnicity was "other" or "unknown" in the institutional data.

Occasionally, a respondent's single race or ethnicity could not be determined from the institutional data, from their own race response in the NSCE survey, or their SDQ response, but respondents told us something in the NSCE survey about their parents' race(s). In eighteen instances, we used information about parents to deduce a race or ethnicity for their son or daughter. Several rules of thumb, listed in Table B.7, were utilized. Most common was the situation of multiple-race individuals in the NSCE survey. If a respondent identified two race/ethnicity categories, a rule of thumb was needed to substitute a primary race or ethnicity. These principles were deduced from the existing literature (Cole and Barber, 2003; Goldstein and Morning, 2000, 2002; Qian, 2004a, 2004b) and tabulations from the CLASS project, and are listed in Table B.7. If white was listed in combination with black, Hispanic, or Asian, black and Hispanic prevailed over white, but white was listed as the primary race when used in combination with Asian. Black prevailed over Hispanic and Asian, and Hispanic was given priority over Asian. If white, black, Hispanic, or Asian was listed together with "other," then the WBHA category prevailed. Fifty cases were resolved using step 6.

There was an insufficient number of individuals responding to the NSCE survey who listed Native American/Alaska Native to constitute a meaningful analysis category. Rather than discard these cases, we assigned them to another category in WBHA (step 7). In half of these 67 cases, there was some information available about parents' race that permitted an allocation. However, in another 34 instances, respondents indicated

[17] The Campus Life in America Student Survey (CLASS project) collected data from more than twelve thousand first- and third-year students at Princeton, Emory, University of Miami, Michigan State, Portland State University (in Portland, Oregon), and UCLA in the fall of 2004. Among other things, students were asked a series of questions about their racial/ethnic identification. More information is available at http://class.princeton.edu/. See also note b in Table B.7.

only Native American or Alaska Native in both their generation and their parents' generation. These individuals were assigned to the white group. Finally, in 43 instances where nothing was known from any available source about respondents' race or their parents' racial identification, it was necessary to make a determination about race or ethnicity by looking up the individual's name and citizenship status. For example, a student who had an Hispanic surname and listed their citizenship as "Mexico" was put into the Hispanic group. Likewise, a respondent with an Asian Indian surname whose citizenship was given as "India" was assigned to the Asian category. Further details are described in Table B.7.[18]

Socioeconomic Status

Recent scholarship has drawn attention to socioeconomic status (SES) or social class as another important lens through which processes of college admission and campus life should be viewed (Bowen, Kurzweil, and Tobin, 2005; Kahlenberg, 2004). An underlying issue is the extent to which academically selective colleges and universities provide opportunities for upward social mobility or, alternatively, reproduce patterns of social inequality from one generation to the next. Our primary measure of socioeconomic status is the answer survey respondents give to the question, "Which one of the following categories best describes your family's social class during your senior year in high school?" Response categories include 1 = lower class, 2 = working class, 3 = middle class, 4 = upper-middle class, 5 = upper class, and 7 = don't recall. More than 97.5 percent of respondents answered in one of the first five categories. Ordinary least squares (OLS) regression was used to impute a response category in the remaining 219 cases where respondents either answered "Don't recall" or left the question blank.

Prediction equations were fit separately to data from each of the three entering cohorts. For example, to impute social class values for the 1997 cohort in the 105 cases where social class is missing, 4,291 known values of social class were regressed on roughly three dozen indicators of social and economic status.[19] The OLS regression provided a good overall fit to

[18] Analyses in this book are conducted using four primary race/ethnic groupings, including white, black, Hispanic, and Asian. Even though the Hispanic category is not usually considered as a "race," and indeed a separate question about Hispanic ethnicity is asked on the U.S. decennial census form, we will frequently employ the shorthand term "race" when we mean a combination of race and ethnicity as these terms are typically understood.

[19] Most of the predictor variables come from NSCE survey data and include, for example, whether the student applied for financial aid or held a campus job, amount of college debt, whether the student took an SAT review course, type of high school the respondent graduated from, how many colleges visited prior to applying, whether respondent is native born,

the data, producing an R^2 of .65. Social class categories were imputed by recoding predicted values (*yhat*) from the OLS regression as follows: lower class if *yhat* is less than 1.5, working class if *yhat* is between 1.5 and 2.5, middle class for *yhat* between 2.5 and 3.5, upper-middle class for *yhat* between 3.5 and 4.5, and upper class if *yhat* exceeds 4.5. As a check on these procedures, predicted values of social class were cross-classified with observed values for all known values of social class in the 1997 cohort. More than two-thirds of the cases (2,891 out of 4,291, or 67.4 percent) were correctly classified with this prediction equation. In only 27 cases did the predicted value differ from the observed value by more than one social class category.[20]

It is also common to base SES measures on other "objective" indicators of social class, including parental education, occupation, and income. Therefore, as a further check on our approach, we conducted a factor analysis of replies to nine questions in the NSCE survey. The twelve variables involved in the factor analysis represent a subset of the predictor variables used in the imputation equations.[21] One principal factor was identified, and nine of the twelve variables loaded on this factor in the expected direction with factor loadings greater than 0.30 in absolute value.[22] In the remaining three cases (household income far above [below] average compared with neighbors, and had own bedroom senior year in high school), the factor loadings had the correct sign but were smaller than 0.30.

Based on these results a factor score corresponding to an underlying dimension of socioeconomic status was computed for each of the 4,396

---

citizenship status, and parental education, occupation, income, and net worth. Respondent's race and state of residence from the application form were also used as predictors. Altogether more than 240 independent variables formed the prediction equations.

[20] We also experimented with an ordered-logit (OL) prediction equation, but it did not perform as well. It yielded a pseudo-R^2 value of .41 in Stata when fit to the 4,291 known social class values. When the OLS and OL prediction equations were used to impute social class values for the 105 missing cases, they resulted in identical imputations in 96 out of 105 cases. OL imputations were developed by assigning the social class category for which the predicted probability is the greatest.

[21] These include parent(s) attended a four-year college; grandparent(s) attended a four-year college; father's occupation is executive, administrative, managerial, or professional; father's highest level of schooling is master's, professional school, or doctorate degree; respondent applied for financial aid to college; total annual household income less than $50,000; total household income greater than $100,000; household income far below average compared with neighbors; household income far above average compared with neighbors; did not have own bedroom senior year in high school; total parental assets less than $10,000; total parental assets greater than $300,000.

[22] The strongest factor loadings (in parentheses) corresponded to father's occupation (.62), father's education (.57), household income less than $50,000 (−.62), and household income above $100,000 (.62).

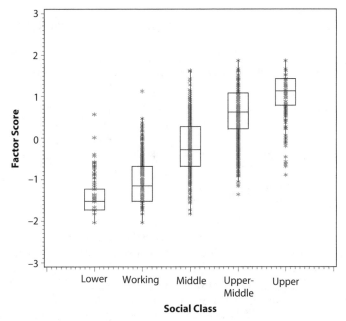

Figure B.1. Box and Whisker Plots of Factor Score for Socioeconomic Status against Reported Social Class, 1997 Entering Cohort (N = 4,396). Note: Social class includes both reported and imputed values. The horizontal lines marking the top, middle, and bottom of each box represent the 75th percentile, median, and 25th percentile, respectively. The length of each whisker denotes the most extreme point within 1.5 times the interquartile range. Source: National Study of College Experience.

respondents in the 1997 cohort. The correspondence between these factor scores and reported values of social class is shown in Figure B.1. In these box and whisker plots, the horizontal line in the middle of each box corresponds to the median factor score, and the bottom and top sides of each box represent the interquartile range, or the 25th and 75th percentiles, respectively. The length of each "whisker" identifies the most extreme point within 1.5 times the size of the interquartile range. In general, as one moves from lower social classes to higher ones, both the median and associated range of factor scores rise, suggesting that reported social class is a good measure of socioeconomic status in one's household of origin.[23]

[23] There also appears to be some compression in both tails of the SES distribution. The "distance" between lower and working classes and between upper-middle and upper classes is not as great as the separation between the three social classes in the middle.

TABLE B.8
Reported and Imputed Values of Social Class in the NSCE Survey

Social Class	Reported		Imputed		Total	
	Number	Percent	Number	Percent	Number	Percent
Upper	335	3.8	9	4.1	344	3.8
Upper-Middle	3,322	37.5	47	21.5	3,369	37.1
Middle	3,391	38.2	142	64.8	3,533	38.9
Working	1,550	17.5	20	9.1	1,570	17.3
Lower	268	3.0	1	0.5	269	3.0
Total	8,866	100.0	219	100.0	9,085	100.0

Source: National Study of College Experience.

Similar procedures were used to analyze data from the 1993 and 1980s entering cohorts.[24] There is a high degree of similarity in results across all three cohorts. OLS regressions provide a good fit to observed social class values, there is a high correlation between reported and predicted social class measures, and the factor analyses are nearly identical.[25] In addition, there is a high degree of agreement among imputed values whether imputations are based on OLS or ordered-logit regressions. Both regression procedures provide identical values in 205 out of the 219 imputed cases, and in the small number of remaining cases there is no evidence that OLS gives either systematically smaller or larger values than ordered-logit regressions. Table B.8 records for all NSCE respondents reported social class categories together with 219 cases where social class was imputed using OLS regression. Imputed values are somewhat more likely than reported social class to be concentrated among middle-class respondents. The final column of Table B.8 displays social class for all NSCE respondents. Three-quarters of sample members (76.0 percent) are about equally divided between middle-class and upper-middle-class families. Relatively few respondents indicated they were either from lower- or upper-class families.

The distribution of social class for each of the principal race and ethnic groups is shown in Table B.9. White and Asian respondents typically describe themselves as having come from higher social class backgrounds than do either black or Hispanic respondents. Slightly more than one-half

[24] The OLS prediction equation for the 1980s included a dummy variable for each cohort year.

[25] R^2 values for the OLS regressions were .72 and .69 in the 1993 and 1980s cohorts, respectively. Reported and predicted social class categories agreed in more than 72 percent of the cases in both cohorts. The magnitude and sign of the factor loadings are nearly identical with those in the 1997 cohort.

TABLE B.9
Distribution of Social Class for Principal Race/Ethnicity Categories

	Race/Ethnic Group							
	White		Black		Hispanic		Asian	
Social Class	Number	Percent	Number	Percent	Number	Percent	Number	Percent
Upper	149	5.8	31	1.0	71	4.5	93	4.7
Upper-Middle	1,316	51.6	640	21.4	484	30.9	929	47.1
Middle	892	35.0	1,352	45.2	576	36.8	713	36.1
Working	177	6.9	834	27.9	355	22.7	204	10.3
Lower	18	0.7	137	4.6	79	5.1	35	1.8
Total	2,552	100.0	2,994	100.0	1,565	100.0	1,974	100.0

Source: National Study of College Experience.
Note: Tabulations based on N = 9,085 NSCE survey respondents.

of whites say their families belonged to the upper-middle class during respondents' senior year in high school in contrast to just over 20 percent of blacks. Nearly 28 percent of blacks described themselves as having working-class backgrounds in contrast to 10 percent of Asians and only 7 percent of whites. For both white and Asian respondents, the two largest social class categories are upper-middle and middle class in that order. The same is true for Hispanics, except that the relative size of these groups is reversed. For blacks, the two largest socioeconomic background groups are middle class followed by working class.[26]

CHAPTER 9: CLOSING THE TEST SCORE GAP

Earlier chapters have documented the substantial differences that exist in a variety of academic performance measures between black and Hispanic students on the one hand and whites and Asians on the other. Some fraction of these differences can be explained by the fact that black and Hispanic families usually have lower socioeconomic status than white and Asian families (Chaplin and Hannaway, 1998). Controlling for these social class differences narrows performance differentials, but racial and ethnic gaps remain. It is these latter differences, after controlling for socioeconomic status, that researchers refer to as the achievement gap or the test-score gap.

[26]When the five social class categories are assigned numerical scores of upper class = 5 through lower class = 1 and weighted averages of social class are calculated for each race/ethnic group, the results are: white (3.5), black (2.9), Hispanic (3.1), and Asian (3.4).

For purposes of analysis in chapter 9, we want to examine what the profile of admitted students would look like if the racial academic achievement gap were closed. In particular, what would be the effect of closing the black-white and the Hispanic-white achievement gap in the presence of affirmative action and, alternatively, if affirmative action were eliminated? This section describes the methods by which new academic performance outcomes are assigned to black and Hispanic students so that achievement gaps no longer exist between them and similarly situated white students.

To motivate the methodology, imagine that we have a sample of black and white applicants to academically selective colleges and universities and all we know about these students are their race, SAT score, and social class. If SAT score is regressed on race, we would expect to find a racial gap in favor of whites. If SAT score is regressed on both race and social class, we would expect the racial gap to narrow but not disappear completely. One mechanical approach to closing the test-score gap involves grouping applicants by social class. Within each social class consider each black student one at a time. For each black applicant, pick at random one white applicant in the same social class and assign that white student's SAT score to the black student. When the new SAT scores for the black applicants and the unaltered ones for white students are regressed on race and social class, we should expect social class to continue to matter and the effect of race to be insignificant.

In practice, we proceeded as follows.[27] Consider first the subset of black and white applicants to the seven NSCE institutions. We estimated a weighted logistic regression equation for the probability that an applicant is black, using as predictor variables an applicant's state of residence, institution to which they applied, social class (in five categories), sex, citizenship, whether a recruited athlete, whether an alumni child, high school type, whether high school is one of seventy-two elite high schools, whether student is a first-generation college student, household size (four or less versus five or more), and number of parents in the household. Based on this regression, applicants were ranked by their predicted probability of being black—from highest to lowest. Starting from the top, applicants were next grouped into bins, making sure there were twenty white applicants in each bin. Then, for every black student i in bin j, a white student from bin j was picked as a "donor" (using independent, random draws with replacement). A (potentially) different white donor was selected for each black student. All of the white donor's academic performance vari-

[27] We thank Bonnie Ghosh-Dastidar from the RAND Corporation for suggesting this methodology. The matching technique relies on propensity scores (see Little, 1988; Rosenbaum, 1995; Dehejia and Wahba, 1999).

ables were assigned to the black applicant, including SAT score, ACT score, number of AP tests taken, number of SAT II Subject (or Achievement) tests taken, mean score on the SAT II tests, high school GPA, high school class rank, and whether the donor is a National Merit Scholar. The same process was followed for each black applicant.

The subset of Hispanic and white NSCE applicants was chosen to perform the imputations for Hispanic students. Procedures identical to those for blacks were followed for Hispanics, including ranking Hispanic and white students by the predicted probability of being Hispanic. Again starting from the top, Hispanic and white applicants were grouped into bins making sure that twenty white applicants were in each bin. In all bins except the three at the top (corresponding to applicants who have the highest predicted probability of being Hispanic), each Hispanic student was paired with a randomly selected white student from the same bin who acted as a donor for academic performance measures.

Different procedures were required for the first three bins, each of which was unusually large owing to the fact that the separate white and Hispanic distributions for the predicted probability of being Hispanic had relatively little overlap at the high end of the distribution. To impute academic performance measures to the remaining Hispanic applicants, we grouped Hispanic students in the top three bins into five social class categories—lower, working, middle, upper-middle, and upper. *All* of the white applicants, regardless of their initial bin assignments, were grouped into the same five social class categories. Then within each social class group, a white student was randomly chosen to serve as the donor for each Hispanic applicant. A separate random draw was made for each Hispanic student.

These matching procedures work very well, as seen in Table B.10. In the left-hand column are eight indicators of academic performance, including the number of standardized tests taken, scores on these tests, high school grades, and whether an applicant is a National Merit or National Achievement Scholar. Each of the academic performance measures was regressed on a fixed set of applicant characteristics, including race, social class, sex, U.S. citizenship status, whether a recruited athlete, legacy status, high school type, whether high school is one of seventy-two elite U.S. high schools, whether first-generation college student, household size, family composition, and dummy variables for state of permanent residence and institution.

The first column of regression coefficients shows the expected effect of race and ethnicity when using the original, unadjusted values of academic performance for black and Hispanic applicants. We find clear evidence for a racial achievement gap. Black and Hispanic students have test scores or other academic performance indicators that are significantly below

TABLE B.10
Race Effects in Academic Performance Measures

Outcome Variables	Race	Before Matching Estimated Coefficient[a]	After Matching Estimated Coefficient[a]
SAT I (Verbal + Math) Score	(White)	—	—
	Black	−133.94***	22.58
	Hispanic	−92.36***	−8.27
	Asian	16.34	23.80
ACT Composite Score	(White)	—	—
	Black	−3.14***	0.55
	Hispanic	−1.79***	0.90
	Asian	0.64	0.53
Number of AP Tests Taken	(White)	—	—
	Black	−0.79***	0.33
	Hispanic	−0.79***	−0.28
	Asian	0.83***	0.90***
Number of SAT II Exams Taken	(White)	—	—
	Black	0.06	0.14
	Hispanic	−0.12	0.08
	Asian	0.40**	0.45***
Average SAT II Exam Score	(White)	—	—
	Black	−53.35***	18.03
	Hispanic	−28.27***	8.06
	Asian	7.77	10.86
High School GPA[b]	(White)	—	—
	Black	−1.27***	0.42
	Hispanic	−0.77***	−0.32
	Asian	−0.18	−0.08
High School Class Rank[c]	(White)	—	—
	Black	−1.46***	0.93**
	Hispanic	−0.89***	−0.34
	Asian	0.03	0.11
National Merit/Achievement Scholar	(White)	—	—
	Black	0.75**	0.36
	Hispanic	0.12	0.35
	Asian	0.37	0.39

Source: National Study of College Experience.

Note: All the models have the same set of independent variables, including race, state of permanent residence (including foreign, other, and unknown states), institutional dummies, social class, gender, U.S. citizenship, whether a recruited athlete, legacy status, high school type, elite 72 high school, first-generation college student, size of household, and whether both parents are present.

[a]Models in the first five rows were estimated with ordinary least squares. Models involving high school GPA and class rank were estimated using ordered-logit models. Whether a student was a National Merit or a National Achievement scholar was estimated with logistic regression. Each model was fit using a different number of observations, mainly as a result of different numbers of valid responses to the dependent variables. The number of cases ranges from 989 for the ACT composite score model to 3,724 cases for the merit scholar model.

[b]High school GPA categories (and codes) are: B + or lower (=1), A− (=2), A (=3), and A+ (=4). The model is also known as the "proportional odds model" (McCullagh, 1980).

[c]High school class rank categories (and codes) are: Bottom 80% (=1), Next 10% (=2), and Top 10% (=3).

*p < .05 **p < .01 ***p < .001

comparable measures for white students in six out of eight instances. In each of these six cases, black applicants perform less well (or certainly no better) than Hispanics do relative to whites. There is no racial achievement gap with respect to the number of SAT II examinations taken, but black applicants are significantly more likely than whites to be designated as a merit scholar. Part of the reason for this latter anomaly has to do with the nature of the merit scholar program. Candidates of all races and ethnicities are eligible to compete in the National Merit Scholarship Program. The National Achievement Scholarship Program, a smaller competition begun in 1964 as a complement to the older National Merit Scholarship Program, is reserved for black applicants.

One can see in the second column of estimated coefficients the effects of matching academic performance indicators of black and Hispanic candidates to those of similarly situated white applicants. We expect that the coefficients for black and Hispanic applicants will be statistically insignificant. This is indeed the case for every performance indicator. The lone exception is the significantly positive coefficient for blacks in the high school class rank regression. These results give us every reason to believe that the propensity-score matching technique we are using has successfully (albeit artificially) closed the black-white and the Hispanic-white test score gap.

Additional confirmatory evidence is provided by the regression coefficients for Asian applicants. Asian test scores, number of standardized examinations taken, high school grades, and whether a merit scholar were not adjusted by our matching methods. The same values for Asian students were used in both sets of regressions. As one should expect, the signs, relative magnitudes, and levels of statistical significance for the Asian coefficients are strikingly similar in both regressions. In seven of the eight cases, the Asian coefficients are positive, suggesting that Asian students perform even better than similarly situated white applicants. In two instances—both centering on the number of standardized tests taken—Asian students take significantly more tests than whites do. Overall, the regressions in Table B.10 suggest that there is an Asian-white academic achievement gap in favor of Asian students.

Appendix C

ADDITIONAL TABLES

The following tables supplement the results in individual chapters.

TABLE C.3.1

Participation in Extracurricular Activities, Use of Other Selective Admission Enhancement Strategies, and Acceptance to Public NSCE Institutions, Fall 1997

	Percent Admitted	
Item	Did Have or Use	Did Not Have or Use
Extracurricular Activities/Awards/Leadership Positions[a]		
Large Number of Total Activities	58.4	54.7
Large Number of Total Awards/Leadership Positions	77.5*[b]	53.0
Large Number of Academic Activities	62.4	54.8
Large Number of Academic Awards/Leadership Positions	89.5***	53.8
Large Number of Performing Arts Activities	50.8	55.7
Large Number of Performing Arts Awards/Leadership Positions	48.2	55.9
Large Number of Athletic Activities	70.3	49.5
Large Number of Athletic Awards/Leadership Positions	72.1	53.8
Large Number of Community Service Activities	68.3	54.2
Large Number of Community Service Awards/ Leadership Positions	80.5	53.7
Large Number of Cultural Diversity Activities	62.9	54.5
Large Number of Cultural Diversity Awards/Leadership Positions	51.3	56.0
Large Number of Career-Oriented Activities	49.7	56.4
Large Number of Career-Oriented Awards/Leadership Positions	54.6	55.2
Held Part-time Job in High School	57.3	52.8
Other Admission Enhancement Strategies[c]		
Attend and graduate from magnet, parochial/religious, or private high school to improve chances of college acceptance	42.2	56.8

(*Continued*)

TABLE C.3.1 (*Continued*)

Item	Percent Admitted	
	Did Have or Use	*Did Not Have or Use*
Attend and graduate from private high school to improve chances of college acceptance	61.8	54.6
Participate in some kind of academic enrichment program(s) during high school years	53.4	56.3
Participate in college-sponsored academic enrichment program(s) during high school years	54.4	55.1
Take an SAT, PSAT, or ACT test preparation course	42.0**	67.1
Use professional consultant or private tutor to select colleges and/or help complete application forms	70.1	52.7
Visit six or more colleges before applying to any schools	61.6	53.4

Source: Educational Testing Service Student Descriptive Questionnaire; National Study of College Experience.

[a]See Note a in Table 3.8 for definitions and sources.

[b]The presence of asterisks indicates a statistically significant difference between the percentages of applicants who had a large number of activities/awards and those who did not, or between the percentages of applicants who used a particular enhancement strategy and those who did not.

[c]Data on the use of other admission enhancement strategies come from the NSCE survey.

*p < .05 **p < .01 ***p < .001

TABLE C.9.1
Effect of Eliminating Affirmative Action at Private Institutions: Simulation Results, Fall 1997

Item	Observed Baseline Applications		Observed Baseline Admitted			No Affirmative Action[a]			Race-Neutral Admission[b]		
	Number	Percent	Number	Percent	Acceptance Rate Percent	Number	Percent	Acceptance Rate Percent	Number	Percent	Acceptance Rate Percent
Total	51,836	100.0	12,233	100.0	23.6	12,233	100.0	23.6	12,233	100.0	23.6
Race											
White	28,894	55.7	7,329	59.9	25.4	7,894	64.5	27.3	6,538	53.4	22.6
Black	3,276	6.3	1,016	8.3	31.0	437	3.6	13.3	345	2.8	10.5
Hispanic	3,615	7.0	964	7.9	26.7	711	5.8	19.7	580	4.7	16.1
Asian	16,052	31.0	2,925	23.9	18.2	3,190	26.1	19.9	4,769	39.0	29.7
Social Class											
Lower	842	1.6	195	1.6	23.2	97	0.8	11.5	46	0.4	5.4
Working	5,528	10.7	1,012	8.3	18.3	765	6.3	13.8	495	4.0	9.0
Middle	19,689	38.0	4,085	33.4	20.7	4,038	33.0	20.5	4,791	39.2	24.3
Upper-Middle	22,271	43.0	6,064	49.6	27.2	6,368	52.1	28.6	6,005	49.1	27.0
Upper	3,506	6.8	878	7.2	25.0	965	7.9	27.5	896	7.3	25.6
Race and Social Class											
Minority, bottom 2 classes	1,831	3.5	548	4.5	29.9	147	1.2	8.0	113	0.9	6.2
Non-minority, bottom 2 classes	4,539	8.8	659	5.4	14.5	715	5.8	15.7	427	3.5	9.4
Minority, top 3 classes	5,059	9.8	1,432	11.7	28.3	1,001	8.2	19.8	812	6.6	16.1
Non-minority, top 3 classes	40,407	78.0	9,594	78.4	23.7	10,370	84.8	25.7	10,880	88.9	26.9
Mean SAT Score	1,340		1,405			1,410			1,415		
High School GPA[c]											
A+	14,012	32.4	4,155	42.1	29.6	4,245	43.1	30.3	4,282	43.6	30.6
A	15,201	35.1	3,745	37.9	24.6	3,712	37.7	24.4	3,798	38.7	25.0
A-	9,783	22.6	1,410	14.3	14.4	1,400	14.2	14.3	1,306	13.3	14.3
B+ or lower	4,271	9.9	569	5.8	13.3	492	5.0	11.5	436	4.4	10.2

No Response	637	—	217	—	34.0	221	—	34.6	267	—	41.9
No SDQ[d]	7,932	—	2,138	—	26.9	2,163	—	27.3	2,145	—	27.0
High School Class Rank[c]											
Top 10%	27,000	67.8	7,610	81.1	28.2	7,752	82.6	28.7	8,036	84.5	29.8
Next 10%	7,856	19.7	1,390	14.8	17.7	1,292	13.8	16.4	1,200	12.6	15.3
Bottom 80%	4,954	12.4	387	4.1	7.8	345	3.7	7.0	274	2.9	5.5
No Response	4,095	—	709	—	17.3	681	—	16.6	578	—	14.1
No SDQ[d]	7,932	—	2,138	—	26.9	2,163	—	27.3	2,145	—	27.0

Source: National Study of College Experience.

[a]This simulation eliminates preferences for black and Hispanic applicants, but keeps the Asian disadvantage.

[b]This simulation removes all consideration of race or ethnicity.

[c]Percentage distribution is calculated on the basis of known outcomes.

[d]These students elected not to complete the voluntary Student Descriptive Questionnaire when they registered to take the SAT examination.

TABLE C.9.2
Effect of Giving More Weight to Low-Income Students at Private Institutions: Simulation Results, Fall 1997

Item	Observed Baseline Admitted			Substitute Black and Hispanic Weights for Lower and Working Classes			Substitute Legacy Weight for Lower Class[a]			Substitute Legacy Weight for Lower and Working Classes[a]		
	Number	Percent	Acceptance Rate Percent	Number	Percent	Acceptance Rate Percent	Number	Percent	Acceptance Rate Percent	Number	Percent	Acceptance Rate Percent
Total	12,233	100.0	23.6	12,233	100.0	23.6	12,233	100.0	23.6	12,233	100.0	23.6
Race												
White	7,329	59.9	25.4	7,035	57.5	24.3	7,283	59.5	25.2	7,002	57.2	24.2
Black	1,016	8.3	31.0	1,143	9.3	34.9	1,035	8.5	31.6	1,160	9.5	35.4
Hispanic	964	7.9	26.7	1,083	8.8	29.9	979	8.0	27.1	1,098	9.0	30.4
Asian	2,925	23.9	18.2	2,973	24.3	18.5	2,936	24.0	18.3	2,972	24.3	18.5
Social Class												
Lower	195	1.6	23.2	631	5.2	75.0	585	4.8	69.5	555	4.5	65.9
Working	1,012	8.3	18.3	1,898	15.5	34.3	979	8.0	17.7	2,075	17.0	37.5
Middle	4,085	33.4	20.7	3,590	29.3	18.2	3,951	32.3	20.1	3,552	29.0	18.0
Upper-Middle	6,064	49.6	27.2	5,354	43.8	24.0	5,872	48.0	26.4	5,300	43.3	23.8
Upper	878	7.2	25.0	760	6.2	21.7	846	6.9	24.1	751	6.1	21.4
Race and Social Class												
Minority, bottom 2 classes	548	4.5	29.9	954	7.8	52.1	624	5.1	34.1	999	8.2	54.6
Non-minority, bottom 2 classes	659	5.4	14.5	1,575	12.9	34.7	940	7.7	20.7	1,630	13.3	35.9
Minority, top 3 classes	1,432	11.7	28.3	1,271	10.4	25.1	1,389	11.4	27.5	1,259	10.3	24.9

Non-minority, top 3 classes	9,594	78.4	23.7	8,432	68.9	20.9	9,280	75.9	23.0	8,344	68.2	20.7
Mean SAT Score	1,405			1,388			1,398			1,386		
High School GPA[b]												
A+	4,155	42.1	29.6	4,050	40.7	28.9	4,055	40.9	28.9	4,073	41.0	29.1
A	3,745	37.9	24.6	3,797	38.1	25.0	3,826	38.5	25.2	3,767	37.9	24.8
A−	1,410	14.3	14.4	1,436	14.4	14.7	1,420	14.3	14.5	1,435	14.4	14.7
B+ or lower	569	5.8	13.3	669	6.7	15.7	624	6.3	14.6	670	6.7	15.7
No Response	217	—	34.0	198	—	31.0	209	—	32.8	197	—	30.9
No SDQ[c]	2,138	—	26.9	2,083	—	26.3	2,100	—	26.5	2,091	—	26.4
High School Class Rank[b]												
Top 10%	7,610	81.1	28.2	7,305	77.4	27.1	7,428	79.1	27.5	7,320	77.6	27.1
Next 10%	1,390	14.8	17.7	1,460	15.5	18.6	1,361	14.5	17.3	1,490	15.8	19.0
Bottom 80%	387	4.1	7.8	668	7.1	13.5	604	6.4	12.2	629	6.7	12.7
No Response	709	—	17.3	717	—	17.5	740	—	18.1	703	—	17.2
No SDQ[c]	2,138	—	26.9	2,083	—	26.3	2,100	—	26.5	2,091	—	26.4

Source: National Study of College Experience.

[a] The legacy weight, equivalent to an odds ratio of 2.858, is based on an estimate for the 1997 cohort in the work by Espenshade, Chung, and Walling (2004, Table 7, p. 1442).

[b] The percentage distribution is calculated on the basis of known outcomes.

[c] These students elected not to complete the voluntary Student Descriptive Questionnaire when they registered to take the SAT examination.

TABLE C.9.3

Effect of Substituting Other Policies for Affirmative Action at Private Institutions: Simulation Results, Fall 1997

Item	Observed Baseline Admitted			No Affirmative Action, More Low-Income Weight[a]			No Affirmative Action, More Low-Income Weight, Less Emphasis on Academic Performance[b]			No Affirmative Action, More Low-Income Weight, No Weight to Academic Performance[c]		
	Number	Percent	Acceptance Rate Percent	Number	Percent	Acceptance Rate Percent	Number	Percent	Acceptance Rate Percent	Number	Percent	Acceptance Rate Percent
Total	12,233	100.0	23.6	12,233	100.0	23.6	12,233	100.0	23.6	12,233	100.0	23.6
Race												
White	7,329	59.9	25.4	7,696	62.9	26.6	7,622	62.3	26.4	7,599	62.1	26.3
Black	1,016	8.3	31.0	495	4.0	15.1	705	5.8	21.5	925	7.6	28.2
Hispanic	964	7.9	26.7	761	6.2	21.1	842	6.9	23.3	892	7.3	24.7
Asian	2,925	23.9	18.2	3,281	26.8	20.4	3,064	25.0	19.1	2,817	23.0	17.5
Social Class												
Lower	195	1.6	23.2	500	4.1	59.4	562	4.6	66.8	610	5.0	72.5
Working	1,012	8.3	18.3	1,567	12.8	28.3	1,831	15.0	33.1	2,038	16.7	36.9
Middle	4,085	33.4	20.7	3,596	29.4	18.3	3,444	28.2	17.5	3,461	28.3	17.6
Upper-Middle	6,064	49.6	27.2	5,716	46.7	25.7	5,491	44.9	24.7	5,162	42.2	23.2
Upper	878	7.2	25.0	854	7.0	24.4	904	7.4	25.8	962	7.9	27.4
Race and Social Class												
Minority, bottom 2 classes	548	4.5	29.9	366	3.0	20.0	503	4.1	27.5	578	4.7	31.6
Non-minority, bottom 2 classes	659	5.4	14.5	1,701	13.9	37.5	1,890	15.5	41.6	2,070	16.9	45.6
Minority, top 3 classes	1,432	11.7	28.3	890	7.3	17.6	1,044	8.5	20.6	1,239	10.1	24.5

Non-minority, top 3 classes	9,594	78.4	23.7	9,276	75.8	23.0	8,796	71.9	21.8	8,346	68.2	20.7
Mean SAT Score	1,405			1,400			1,371			1,329		
High School GPA[d]												
A+	4,155	42.1	29.6	4,175	42.1	29.8	3,255	35.7	23.2	1,701	21.8	12.1
A	3,745	37.9	24.6	3,743	37.8	24.6	3,391	37.2	22.3	2,723	34.9	17.9
A−	1,410	14.3	14.4	1,430	14.4	14.6	1,667	18.3	17.0	2,047	26.3	20.9
B+ or lower	569	5.8	13.3	566	5.7	13.2	807	8.8	18.9	1,322	17.0	31.0
No Response	217	—	34.0	202	—	31.6	191	—	29.9	171	—	26.8
No SDQ[e]	2,138	—	26.9	2,118	—	26.7	2,922	—	36.8	4,269	—	53.8
High School Class Rank[d]												
Top 10%	7,610	81.1	28.2	7,450	79.1	27.6	6,103	72.2	22.6	3,654	54.3	13.5
Next 10%	1,390	14.8	17.7	1,348	14.3	17.2	1,502	17.8	19.1	1,741	25.9	22.2
Bottom 80%	387	4.1	7.8	624	6.6	12.6	846	10.0	17.1	1,329	19.8	26.8
No Response	709	—	17.3	692	—	16.9	860	—	21.0	1,240	—	30.3
No SDQ[e]	2,138	—	26.9	2,118	—	26.7	2,922	—	36.8	4,269	—	53.8

Source: National Study of College Experience.

[a] This simulation eliminates affirmative action for black and Hispanic applicants, but substitutes black and Hispanic weights for lower and working classes, respectively.

[b] This simulation eliminates affirmative action for black and Hispanic applicants, but substitutes black and Hispanic weights for lower and working classes, respectively. The weight given to SAT and ACT scores, high school GPA, and high school class rank is reduced by one-half.

[c] This simulation eliminates affirmative action for black and Hispanic applicants, but substitutes black and Hispanic weights for lower and working classes, respectively. Zero weight is attached to SAT and ACT scores, and to high school GPA and class rank.

[d] Percentage distribution is calculated on the basis of known outcomes.

[e] These students elected not to complete the voluntary Student Descriptive Questionnaire when they registered to take the SAT examination.

TABLE C.9.4

Effect of Top 10 Percent Plans at Private and Public Institutions: Simulation Results, Fall 1997

Item	Observed Baseline Admitted to Private			No Affirmative Action, Admit Top 10% with A+ GPA, Ranked by SAT Score[a]			Observed Baseline Admitted to Public			No Affirmative Action, Admit Top 10% First[b]			No Affirmative Action, Admit In-State, Admit Top 10% First[c]		
	Number	Percent	Acceptance Rate Percent	Number	Percent	Acceptance Rate Percent	Number	Percent	Acceptance Rate Percent	Number	Percent	Acceptance Rate Percent	Number	Percent	Acceptance Rate Percent
Total	12,233	100.0	23.6	12,219	100.0	23.6	14,185	100.0	54.9	14,185	100.0	54.9	14,185	100.0	54.9
Race															
White	7,329	59.9	25.4	7,413	60.7	25.7	12,381	87.3	55.8	12,847	90.6	57.9	12,845	90.6	57.9
Black	1,016	8.3	31.0	217	1.8	6.6	1,110	7.8	58.2	630	4.4	33.1	631	4.4	33.1
Hispanic	964	7.9	26.7	522	4.3	14.4	216	1.5	39.6	222	1.6	40.9	213	1.5	39.3
Asian	2,925	23.9	18.2	4,067	33.3	25.3	479	3.4	39.8	486	3.4	40.3	496	3.5	41.2
Social Class															
Lower	195	1.6	23.2	54	0.4	6.4	70	0.5	57.8	60	0.4	48.9	40	0.3	32.6
Working	1,012	8.3	18.3	1,275	10.4	23.1	864	6.1	51.3	1,097	7.7	65.2	809	5.7	48.1
Middle	4,085	33.4	20.7	5,375	44.0	27.3	5,400	38.1	57.2	4,973	35.1	52.6	5,489	38.7	58.1
Upper-Middle	6,064	49.6	27.2	5,245	42.9	23.6	7,452	52.5	53.4	7,747	54.6	55.5	7,455	52.6	53.4
Upper	878	7.2	25.0	271	2.2	7.7	400	2.8	65.7	309	2.2	50.8	392	2.8	64.5
Race and Social Class															
Minority, bottom 2 classes	548	4.5	29.9	154	1.3	8.4	371	2.6	60.1	205	1.4	33.1	216	1.5	35.0
Non-minority, bottom 2 classes	659	5.4	14.5	1,175	9.6	25.9	563	4.0	47.4	952	6.7	80.2	633	4.5	53.3
Minority, top 3 classes	1,432	11.7	28.3	585	4.8	11.6	954	6.7	52.1	648	4.6	35.4	628	4.4	34.3
Non-minority, top 3 classes	9,594	78.4	23.7	10,306	84.3	25.5	12,297	86.7	55.4	12,381	87.3	55.8	12,708	89.6	57.3
Mean SAT Score	1,405			1,419			1,206			1,233			1,211		
High School GPA[d]															
A+	4,155	42.1	29.6	12,219	100.0	87.2	3,148	26.1	86.1	3,618	27.4	98.9	3,130	25.8	85.6
A	3,745	37.9	24.6	0	0	—	4,549	37.7	69.8	5,479	41.5	84.1	4,819	39.8	74.0

High school class rank / GPA	No.	%	%	No.	%	%	No.	%	%	No.	%	%	No.	%	%
A−	1,410	14.3	14.4	0	—	45.3	1,846	15.3	39.4	2,208	16.7	47.2	1,794	14.8	38.3
B+ or lower	569	5.8	13.3	0	—	—	2,522	20.9	38.3	1,895	14.4	28.8	2,367	19.5	35.9
No Response	217	—	34.0	0	—	—	42	—	8.4	11	—	2.2	32	—	6.6
No SDQ[e]	2,138	—	26.9	0	—	—	2,079	—	53.4	974	—	25.0	2,043	—	52.5
High School Class Rank[d]															
Top 10%	7,610	81.1	28.2	12,219	100.0	45.3	6,112	52.2	63.6	9,610	73.9	100.0	6,430	54.5	66.9
Next 10%	1,390	14.8	17.7	0	0	—	3,550	30.3	65.9	2,612	20.1	48.5	3,467	29.4	64.3
Bottom 80%	387	4.1	7.8	0	0	—	2,047	17.5	39.8	790	6.1	15.4	1,891	16.0	36.8
No Response	709	—	17.3	0	0	—	397	—	22.1	199	—	11.1	355	—	19.7
No SDQ[e]	2,138	—	26.9	0	0	—	2,079	—	53.4	974	—	25.0	2,043	—	52.5

Source: National Study of College Experience.

[a] This simulation admits all applicants in the top 10 percent of their high school class with a GPA of A+ and SAT score of about 1230 or higher.

[b] This simulation admits all applicants to public NSCE institutions who rank in the top 10 percent of their high school class. After eliminating race-based affirmative action for black and Hispanic applicants, the usual criteria were applied to the remaining 32.3 percent of admitted students.

[c] This simulation admits all in-state applicants to public NSCE institutions who rank in the top 10 percent of their high school class. After eliminating race-based affirmative action for black and Hispanic applicants, the usual criteria were applied to the remaining 65.2 percent of admitted students.

[d] Percentage distribution is calculated on the basis of known outcomes.

[e] These students elected not to complete the voluntary Student Descriptive Questionnaire when they registered to take the SAT examination.

Table C.9.5
Effect of Admitting Students by SAT Scores Alone at Private Institutions:
Simulation Results, Fall 1997

Item	Observed Baseline Admitted			Admission by SAT Scores Only[a]		
	Number	Percent	Acceptance Rate Percent	Number	Percent	Acceptance Rate Percent
Total	12,233	100.0	23.6	12,349	100.0	23.8
Race						
White	7,329	59.9	25.4	7,203	58.3	24.9
Black	1,016	8.3	31.0	110	0.9	3.3
Hispanic	964	7.9	26.7	309	2.5	8.6
Asian	2,925	23.9	18.2	4,728	38.3	29.5
Social Class						
Lower	195	1.6	23.2	25	0.2	2.9
Working	1,012	8.3	18.3	276	2.2	5.0
Middle	4,085	33.4	20.7	4,756	38.5	24.2
Upper-Middle	6,064	49.6	27.2	6,263	50.7	28.1
Upper	878	7.2	25.0	1,031	8.3	29.4
Race and Social Class						
Minority, bottom 2 classes	548	4.5	29.9	46	0.4	2.5
Non-minority, bottom 2 classes	659	5.4	14.5	254	2.1	5.6
Minority, top 3 classes	1,432	11.7	28.3	373	3.0	7.4
Non-minority, top 3 classes	9,594	78.4	23.7	11,676	94.6	28.9
Mean SAT Score	1,405			1,512		
High School GPA[b]						
A+	4,155	42.1	29.6	4,933	46.1	35.2
A	3,745	37.9	24.6	4,243	39.7	27.9
A−	1,410	14.3	14.4	1,180	11.0	12.1
B+ or lower	569	5.8	13.3	339	3.2	7.9
No Response	217	—	34.0	80	—	12.6
No SDQ[c]	2,138	—	26.9	1,575	—	19.9
High School Class Rank[b]						
Top 10%	7,610	81.1	28.2	8,761	84.4	32.4
Next 10%	1,390	14.8	17.7	1,455	14.0	18.5
Bottom 80%	387	4.1	7.8	170	1.6	3.4
No Response	709	—	17.3	389	—	9.5
No SDQ[c]	2,138	—	26.9	1,575	—	19.9

Source: National Study of College Experience.

[a]This simulation admits all students with SAT scores of about 1450 and higher.

[b]The percentage distribution is calculated on the basis of known outcomes.

[c]These students elected not to complete the voluntary Student Descriptive Questionnaire when they registered to take the SAT examination.

Table C.9.6

Effect of Eliminating the Racial Achievement Gap and Affirmative Action at Private Institutions: Simulation Results, Fall 1997

Item	Observed Baseline Admitted			Applications with No Achievement Gap		Admitted with No Achievement Gap, but Keeping Affirmative Action[a]			Admitted with No Achievement Gap, No Affirmative Action[b]		
	Number	Percent	Acceptance Rate Percent	Number	Percent	Number	Percent	Acceptance Rate Percent	Number	Percent	Acceptance Rate Percent
Total	12,233	100.0	23.6	51,836	100.0	12,233	100.0	23.6	12,233	100.0	23.6
Race											
White	7,329	59.9	25.4	28,894	55.7	6,702	54.8	23.2	7,363	60.2	25.5
Black	1,016	8.3	31.0	3,276	6.3	1,663	13.6	50.8	983	8.0	30.0
Hispanic	964	7.9	26.7	3,615	7.0	1,233	10.1	34.1	946	7.7	26.2
Asian	2,925	23.9	18.2	16,052	31.0	2,635	21.5	16.4	2,941	24.0	18.3
Social Class											
Lower	195	1.6	23.2	842	1.6	258	2.1	30.6	117	1.0	13.9
Working	1,012	8.3	18.3	5,528	10.7	1,162	9.5	21.0	849	6.9	15.4
Middle	4,085	33.4	20.7	19,689	38.0	4,305	35.2	21.9	4,249	34.7	21.6
Upper-Middle	6,064	49.6	27.2	22,271	43.0	5,700	46.6	25.6	6,113	50.0	27.4
Upper	878	7.2	25.0	3,506	6.8	808	6.6	23.0	905	7.4	25.8
Race and Social Class											
Minority, bottom 2 classes	548	4.5	29.9	1,831	3.5	820	6.7	44.8	303	2.5	16.5
Non-minority, bottom 2 classes	659	5.4	14.5	4,539	8.8	600	4.9	13.2	663	5.4	14.6
Minority, top 3 classes	1,432	11.7	28.3	5,059	9.8	2,075	17.0	41.0	1,626	13.3	32.1
Non-minority, top 3 classes	9,594	78.4	23.7	40,407	78.0	8,737	71.4	21.6	9,642	78.8	23.9
Mean SAT Score	1,405			1,350		1,413			1,418		

(Continued)

TABLE C.9.6 (Continued)

Item	Observed Baseline Admitted			Applications with No Achievement Gap		Admitted with No Achievement Gap, but Keeping Affirmative Action[a]			Admitted with No Achievement Gap, No Affirmative Action[b]		
	Number	Percent	Acceptance Rate Percent	Number	Percent	Number	Percent	Acceptance Rate Percent	Number	Percent	Acceptance Rate Percent
High School GPA[c]											
A+	4,155	42.1	29.6	14,556	34.1	4,526	45.8	31.1	4,544	45.8	31.2
A	3,745	37.9	24.6	14,797	34.7	3,702	37.4	25.0	3,673	37.1	24.8
A−	1,410	14.3	14.4	9,522	22.3	1,274	12.9	13.4	1,301	13.1	13.7
B+ or lower	569	5.8	13.3	3,797	8.9	390	3.9	10.3	395	4.0	10.4
No Response	217	—	34.0	655	—	207	—	31.7	195	—	29.8
No SDQ[d]	2,138	—	26.9	8,509	—	2,133	—	25.1	2,125	—	25.0
High School Class Rank[c]											
Top 10%	7,610	81.1	28.2	27,880	70.4	8,114	85.1	29.1	8,098	85.0	29.0
Next 10%	1,390	14.8	17.7	7,383	18.6	1,102	11.6	14.9	1,124	11.8	15.2
Bottom 80%	387	4.1	7.8	4,354	11.0	314	3.3	7.2	303	3.2	7.0
No Response	709	—	17.3	3,709	—	571	—	15.4	584	—	15.7
No SDQ[d]	2,138	—	26.9	8,509	—	2,133	—	25.1	2,125	—	25.0

Source: National Study of College Experience.

[a]This simulation shows the profile of admitted students assuming the black-white and Hispanic-white achievement gap has been closed. It is further assumed that current admission practices remain in effect, including the positive preferences for black and Hispanic applicants and the Asian disadvantage.

[b]This simulation shows the profile of admitted students assuming the black-white and Hispanic-white achievement gap has been closed. It is further assumed that affirmative action for black and Hispanic applicants has been eliminated, though the Asian disadvantage remains.

[c]Percentage distribution is calculated on the basis of known outcomes.

[d]These students elected not to complete the voluntary Student Descriptive Questionnaire when they registered to take the SAT examination.

TABLE C.9.7
Effect of Eliminating Affirmative Action at Public Institutions: Simulation Results, Fall 1997

Item	Observed Baseline Applications		Observed Baseline Admitted			No Affirmative Action[a]			Race-Neutral Admission[b]		
	Number	Percent	Number	Percent	Acceptance Rate Percent	Number	Percent	Acceptance Rate Percent	Number	Percent	Acceptance Rate Percent
Total	25,826	100.0	14,185	100.0	54.9	14,185	100.0	54.9	14,185	100.0	54.9
Race											
White	22,172	85.9	12,381	87.3	55.8	12,859	90.6	58.0	12,760	90.0	57.6
Black	1,906	7.4	1,110	7.8	58.2	600	4.2	31.5	592	4.2	31.1
Hispanic	544	2.1	216	1.5	39.6	214	1.5	39.4	212	1.5	39.0
Asian	1,204	4.7	479	3.4	39.8	512	3.6	42.5	621	4.4	51.6
Social Class											
Lower	122	0.5	70	0.5	57.8	27	0.2	22.5	27	0.2	22.1
Working	1,683	6.5	864	6.1	51.3	760	5.4	45.1	747	5.3	44.4
Middle	9,447	36.6	5,400	38.1	57.2	5,371	37.9	56.8	5,344	37.7	56.6
Upper-Middle	13,966	54.1	7,452	52.5	53.4	7,632	53.8	54.6	7,673	54.1	54.9
Upper	608	2.4	400	2.8	65.7	396	2.8	65.1	394	2.8	64.8
Race and Social Class											
Minority, bottom 2 classes	617	2.4	371	2.6	60.1	189	1.3	30.7	186	1.3	30.2
Non-minority, bottom 2 classes	1,188	4.6	563	4.0	47.4	598	4.2	50.3	588	4.1	49.5
Minority, top 3 classes	1,832	7.1	954	6.7	52.1	625	4.4	34.1	618	4.4	33.7
Non-minority, top 3 classes	22,189	85.9	12,297	86.7	55.4	12,773	90.0	57.6	12,794	90.2	57.7

(Continued)

TABLE C.9.7 (Continued)

Item	Observed Baseline Applications		Observed Baseline Admitted			No Affirmative Action[a]			Race-Neutral Admission[b]		
	Number	Percent	Number	Percent	Acceptance Rate Percent	Number	Percent	Acceptance Rate Percent	Number	Percent	Acceptance Rate Percent
Mean SAT Score	1,189		1,206			1,210			1,211		
High School GPA[c]											
A+	3,658	17.1	3,148	26.1	86.1	3,146	26.2	86.0	3,164	26.3	86.5
A	6,516	30.4	4,549	37.7	69.8	4,508	37.5	69.2	4,503	37.4	69.1
A−	4,679	21.8	1,846	15.3	39.4	1,807	15.0	38.6	1,844	15.3	39.4
B+ or lower	6,586	30.7	2,522	20.9	38.3	2,549	21.2	38.7	2,516	20.9	38.2
No Response	494	—	42	—	8.4	36	—	7.3	35	—	7.2
No SDQ[d]	3,893	—	2,079	—	53.4	2,140	—	55.0	2,123	—	54.5
High School Class Rank[c]											
Top 10%	9,610	47.7	6,112	52.2	63.6	6,091	52.2	63.4	6,103	52.2	63.5
Next 10%	5,390	26.8	3,550	30.3	65.9	3,538	30.3	65.6	3,568	30.5	66.2
Bottom 80%	5,137	25.5	2,047	17.5	39.8	2,043	17.5	39.8	2,020	17.3	39.3
No Response	1,796	—	397	—	22.1	373	—	20.8	372	—	20.7
No SDQ[d]	3,893	—	2,079	—	53.4	2,140	—	55.0	2,123	—	54.5

Source: National Study of College Experience.

[a]This simulation eliminates preferences for black and Hispanic applicants, but keeps the Asian disadvantage.

[b]This simulation removes all consideration of race or ethnicity.

[c]Percentage distribution is calculated on the basis of known outcomes.

[d]These students elected not to complete the voluntary Student Descriptive Questionnaire when they registered to take the SAT examination.

TABLE C.9.8

Effect of Giving More Weight to Low-Income Students at Public Institutions:
Simulation Results, Fall 1997

Item	Observed Baseline Admitted			Substitute Black and Hispanic Weights for Lower and Working Classes		
	Number	Percent	Acceptance Rate Percent	Number	Percent	Acceptance Rate Percent
Total	14,185	100.0	54.9	14,185	100.0	54.9
Race						
White	12,381	87.3	55.8	12,335	87.0	55.6
Black	1,110	7.8	58.2	1,152	8.1	60.5
Hispanic	216	1.5	39.6	224	1.6	41.2
Asian	479	3.4	39.8	474	3.3	39.4
Social Class						
Lower	70	0.5	57.8	112	0.8	92.2
Working	864	6.1	51.3	937	6.6	55.6
Middle	5,400	38.1	57.2	5,343	37.7	56.6
Upper-Middle	7,452	52.5	53.4	7,395	52.1	52.9
Upper	400	2.8	65.7	399	2.8	65.6
Race and Social Class						
Minority, bottom 2 classes	371	2.6	60.1	433	3.1	70.2
Non-minority, bottom 2 classes	563	4.0	47.4	616	4.3	51.8
Minority, top 3 classes	954	6.7	52.1	943	6.6	51.5
Non-minority, top 3 classes	12,297	86.7	55.4	12,194	86.0	55.0
Mean SAT Score	1,206			1,206		
High School GPA[a]						
A+	3,148	26.1	86.1	3,150	26.1	86.1
A	4,549	37.7	69.8	4,561	37.8	70.0
A−	1,846	15.3	39.4	1,838	15.2	39.3
B+ or lower	2,522	20.9	38.3	2,506	20.8	38.0
No Response	42	—	8.4	74	—	14.9
No SDQ[b]	2,079	—	53.4	2,058	—	52.9
High School Class Rank[a]						
Top 10%	6,112	52.2	63.6	6,114	52.3	63.6
Next 10%	3,550	30.3	65.9	3,547	30.3	65.8
Bottom 80%	2,047	17.5	39.8	2,041	17.4	39.7
No Response	397	—	22.1	425	—	23.7
No SDQ[b]	2,079	—	53.4	2,058	—	52.9

Source: National Study of College Experience.

[a]The percentage distribution is calculated on the basis of known outcomes.

[b]These students elected not to complete the voluntary Student Descriptive Questionnaire when they registered to take the SAT examination.

TABLE C.9.9
Effect of Substituting Other Policies for Affirmative Action at Public Institutions: Simulation Results, Fall 1997

Item	Observed Baseline Admitted			No Affirmative Action, More Low-Income Weight[a]			No Affirmative Action, More Low-Income Weight, Less Emphasis on Academic Performance[b]			No Affirmative Action, More Low-Income Weight, No Weight to Academic Performance[c]		
	Number	Percent	Acceptance Rate Percent	Number	Percent	Acceptance Rate Percent	Number	Percent	Acceptance Rate Percent	Number	Percent	Acceptance Rate Percent
Total	14,185	100.0	54.9	14,185	100.0	54.9	14,185	100.0	54.9	14,185	100.0	54.9
Race												
White	12,381	87.3	55.8	12,805	90.3	57.8	12,726	89.7	57.4	12,796	90.2	57.7
Black	1,110	7.8	58.2	652	4.6	34.2	722	5.1	37.9	755	5.3	39.6
Hispanic	216	1.5	39.6	221	1.6	40.7	236	1.7	43.5	221	1.6	40.6
Asian	479	3.4	39.8	507	3.6	42.1	501	3.5	41.6	413	2.9	34.3
Social Class												
Lower	70	0.5	57.8	81	0.6	66.8	84	0.6	69.1	85	0.6	69.8
Working	864	6.1	51.3	829	5.8	49.2	897	6.3	53.3	797	5.6	47.4
Middle	5,400	38.1	57.2	5,311	37.4	56.2	5,139	36.2	54.4	4,908	34.6	51.9
Upper-Middle	7,452	52.5	53.4	7,570	53.4	54.2	7,681	54.1	55.0	8,032	56.6	57.5
Upper	400	2.8	65.7	395	2.8	64.9	384	2.7	63.2	364	2.6	59.9
Race and Social Class												
Minority, bottom 2 classes	371	2.6	60.1	257	1.8	41.7	283	2.0	45.9	298	2.1	48.3
Non-minority, bottom 2 classes	563	4.0	47.4	653	4.6	55.0	698	4.9	58.8	584	4.1	49.2
Minority, top 3 classes	954	6.7	52.1	616	4.3	33.6	675	4.8	36.8	678	4.8	37.0
Non-minority, top 3 classes	12,297	86.7	55.4	12,659	89.2	57.1	12,529	88.3	56.5	12,626	89.0	56.9
Mean SAT Score	1,206			1,209			1,206			1,184		

High School GPA[d]												
A+	3,148	26.1	86.1	3,162	26.3	86.5	3,165	26.9	86.5	2,376	21.3	65.0
A	4,549	37.7	69.8	4,531	37.7	69.5	4,448	37.8	68.3	3,670	32.9	56.3
A−	1,846	15.3	39.4	1,796	14.9	38.4	1,692	14.4	36.2	1,469	13.2	31.4
B+ or lower	2,522	20.9	38.3	2,542	21.1	38.6	2,466	20.9	37.4	3,634	32.6	55.2
No Response	42	—	8.4	37	—	7.5	75	—	15.1	257	—	52.0
No SDQ[e]	2,079	—	53.4	2,117	—	54.4	2,341	—	60.1	2,779	—	71.4
High School Class Rank[d]												
Top 10%	6,112	52.2	63.6	6,132	52.4	63.8	6,079	53.0	63.3	4,834	44.6	50.3
Next 10%	3,550	30.3	65.9	3,527	30.2	65.4	3,327	29.0	61.7	2,910	26.9	54.0
Bottom 80%	2,047	17.5	39.8	2,036	17.4	39.6	2,059	18.0	40.1	3,090	28.5	60.2
No Response	397	—	22.1	373	—	20.8	380	—	21.1	572	—	31.9
No SDQ[e]	2,079	—	53.4	2,117	—	54.4	2,341	—	60.1	2,779	—	71.4

Source: National Study of College Experience.

[a]This simulation eliminates affirmative action for black and Hispanic applicants, but substitutes black and Hispanic weights for lower and working classes, respectively.

[b]This simulation eliminates affirmative action for black and Hispanic applicants, but substitutes black and Hispanic weights for lower and working classes, respectively. The weight given to SAT and ACT scores, high school GPA, and high school class rank is reduced by one-half.

[c]This simulation eliminates affirmative action for black and Hispanic applicants, but substitutes black and Hispanic weights for lower and working classes, respectively. Zero weight is attached to SAT and ACT scores, and to high school GPA and class rank.

[d]Percentage distribution is calculated on the basis of known outcomes.

[e]These students elected not to complete the voluntary Student Descriptive Questionnaire when they registered to take the SAT examination.

TABLE C.9.10
Effect of Admitting Students by SAT Scores Alone at Public Institutions:
Simulation Results, Fall 1997

Item	Observed Baseline Admitted			Admission by SAT Scores Only[a]		
	Number	Percent	Acceptance Rate Percent	Number	Percent	Acceptance Rate Percent
Total	14,185	100.0	54.9	14,193	100.0	55.0
Race						
White	12,381	87.3	55.8	12,760	89.9	57.5
Black	1,110	7.8	58.2	419	3.0	22.0
Hispanic	216	1.5	39.6	264	1.9	48.5
Asian	479	3.4	39.8	751	5.3	62.3
Social Class						
Lower	70	0.5	57.8	18	0.1	15.0
Working	864	6.1	51.3	788	5.6	46.8
Middle	5,400	38.1	57.2	4,152	29.3	43.9
Upper-Middle	7,452	52.5	53.4	8,834	62.2	63.3
Upper	400	2.8	65.7	402	2.8	66.0
Race and Social Class						
Minority, bottom 2 classes	371	2.6	60.1	133	0.9	21.5
Non-minority, bottom 2 classes	563	4.0	47.4	674	4.7	56.7
Minority, top 3 classes	954	6.7	52.1	550	3.9	30.0
Non-minority, top 3 classes	12,297	86.7	55.4	12,837	90.4	57.9
Mean SAT Score	1,206			1,292		
High School GPA[b]						
A+	3,148	26.1	86.1	2,852	24.0	78.0
A	4,549	37.7	69.8	3,677	30.9	56.4
A−	1,846	15.3	39.4	2,957	24.8	63.2
B+ or lower	2,522	20.9	38.3	2,416	20.3	36.7
No Response	42	—	8.4	431	—	87.2
No SDQ[c]	2,079	—	53.4	1,860	—	47.8
High School Class Rank[b]						
Top 10%	6,112	52.2	63.6	6,494	57.5	67.6
Next 10%	3,550	30.3	65.9	2,551	22.6	47.3
Bottom 80%	2,047	17.5	39.8	2,252	19.9	43.8
No Response	397	—	22.1	1,037	—	57.7
No SDQ[c]	2,079	—	53.4	1,860	—	47.8

Source: National Study of College Experience.

[a]This simulation admits all students with SAT scores of about 1180 and higher.

[b]The percentage distribution is calculated on the basis of known outcomes.

[c]These students elected not to complete the voluntary Student Descriptive Questionnaire when they registered to take the SAT examination.

Table C.9.11

Effect of Eliminating the Racial Achievement Gap and Affirmative Action at Public Institutions: Simulation Results, Fall 1997

Item	Observed Baseline Admitted			Applications with No Achievement Gap		Admitted with No Achievement Gap, but Keeping Affirmative Action[a]			Admitted with No Achievement Gap, No Affirmative Action[b]		
	Number	Percent	Acceptance Rate Percent	Number	Percent	Number	Percent	Acceptance Rate Percent	Number	Percent	Acceptance Rate Percent
Total	14,185	100.0	54.9	25,826	100.0	14,185	100.0	54.9	14,185	100.0	54.9
Race											
White	12,381	87.3	55.8	22,172	85.9	11,777	83.0	53.1	12,143	85.6	54.8
Black	1,110	7.8	58.2	1,906	7.4	1,608	11.3	84.4	1,228	8.7	64.4
Hispanic	216	1.5	39.6	544	2.1	363	2.6	66.7	352	2.5	64.8
Asian	479	3.4	39.8	1,204	4.7	438	3.1	36.4	463	3.3	38.4
Social Class											
Lower	70	0.5	57.8	122	0.5	107	0.8	87.6	92	0.6	75.8
Working	864	6.1	51.3	1,683	6.5	856	6.0	50.8	794	5.6	47.2
Middle	5,400	38.1	57.2	9,447	36.6	5,460	38.5	57.8	5,408	38.1	57.2
Upper-Middle	7,452	52.5	53.4	13,966	54.1	7,357	51.9	52.7	7,497	52.9	53.7
Upper	400	2.8	65.7	608	2.4	406	2.9	66.8	394	2.8	64.8
Race and Social Class											
Minority, bottom 2 classes	371	2.6	60.1	617	2.4	437	3.1	70.9	340	2.4	55.0
Non-minority, bottom 2 classes	563	4.0	47.4	1,188	4.6	525	3.7	44.2	547	3.9	46.1
Minority, top 3 classes	954	6.7	52.1	1,832	7.1	1,533	10.8	83.7	1,241	8.7	67.7
Non-minority, top 3 classes	12,297	86.7	55.4	22,189	85.9	11,690	82.4	52.7	12,058	85.0	54.3
Mean SAT Score	1,206			1,214		1,242			1,237		

(Continued)

Table C.9.11 (Continued)

Item	Observed Baseline Admitted			Applications with No Achievement Gap		Admitted with No Achievement Gap, but Keeping Affirmative Action[a]			Admitted with No Achievement Gap, No Affirmative Action[b]		
	Number	Percent	Acceptance Rate Percent	Number	Percent	Number	Percent	Acceptance Rate Percent	Number	Percent	Acceptance Rate Percent
High School GPA[c]											
A+	3,148	26.1	86.1	4,034	19.1	3,499	29.2	86.8	3,475	28.9	86.2
A	4,549	37.7	69.8	6,589	31.2	4,694	39.2	71.2	4,647	38.7	70.5
A-	1,846	15.3	39.4	4,685	22.2	1,804	15.1	38.5	1,782	14.8	38.0
B+ or lower	2,522	20.9	38.3	5,811	27.5	1,980	16.5	34.1	2,111	17.6	36.3
No Response	42	—	8.4	437	—	30	—	6.9	13	—	3.0
No SDQ[d]	2,079	—	53.4	4,271	—	2,178	—	51.0	2,157	—	50.5
High School Class Rank[c]											
Top 10%	6,112	52.2	63.6	10,282	51.7	6,697	57.7	65.1	6,598	56.6	64.2
Next 10%	3,550	30.3	65.9	5,084	25.5	3,348	28.8	65.9	3,399	29.2	66.9
Bottom 80%	2,047	17.5	39.8	4,536	22.8	1,571	13.5	34.6	1,652	14.2	36.4
No Response	397	—	22.1	1,653	—	392	—	23.7	381	—	23.0
No SDQ[d]	2,079	—	53.4	4,271	—	2,178	—	51.0	2,157	—	50.5

Source: National Study of College Experience.

[a]This simulation shows the profile of admitted students assuming the black-white and Hispanic-white achievement gap has been closed. It is further assumed that current admission practices remain in effect, including the positive preferences for black and Hispanic applicants and the Asian disadvantage.

[b]This simulation shows the profile of admitted students assuming the black-white and Hispanic-white achievement gap has been closed. It is further assumed that affirmative action for black and Hispanic applicants has been eliminated, though the Asian disadvantage remains.

[c]Percentage distribution is calculated on the basis of known outcomes.

[d]These students elected not to complete the voluntary Student Descriptive Questionnaire when they registered to take the SAT examination.

REFERENCES

Advisory Committee on Student Financial Assistance. 2006. *Mortgaging Our Future: How Financial Barriers to College Undercut America's Global Competitiveness.* September. Washington, DC.

Ahmadi, Mohammad, Farhad Raiszadeh, and Marilyn Helms. 1997. "An Examination of the Admission Criteria for the MBA Programs: A Case Study." *Education* 117(4): 540–46.

Ainsworth, James W. 2002. "Why Does It Take a Village? The Mediation of Neighborhood Effects on Educational Achievement." *Social Forces* 81(1): 117–52.

Alexander, Karl L., and Bruce K. Eckland. 1977. "High School Context and College Selectivity: Institutional Constraints in Educational Stratification." *Social Forces* 56(1): 166–88.

Alliance for Excellent Education. 2007. "The High Cost of High School Dropouts: What the Nation Pays for Inadequate High Schools." *Issue Brief*, January. Washington, DC.

Allport, Gordon W. 1979. *The Nature of Prejudice.* Cambridge, MA: Perseus Books.

Alon, Sigal, and Marta Tienda. 2005. "Assessing the 'Mismatch' Hypothesis: Differences in College Graduation Rates by Institutional Selectivity." *Sociology of Education* 78(4): 294–315.

Alves, Julio. 2006. "Class Struggles." *Chronicle of Higher Education*, October 13, 53(8): B5.

American Association for Public Opinion Research. 2000. *Standard Definitions: Final Dispositions of Case Codes and Outcome Rates for Surveys.* Ann Arbor, MI: AAPOR.

———. 2004. *Standard Definitions: Final Dispositions of Case Codes and Outcome Rates for Survey.* 3rd ed. Lenexa, KS: AAPOR.

American College Testing Program. 1997. "ACT Average Composite Scores by State, 1997 ACT-Tested Graduates." http://www.act.org/news/data/97/97states.html (last accessed January 16, 2004).

AmeriCorps. 2006. "AmeriCorps Education Award." http://www.americorps.org/for_individuals/benefits/benefits_ed_award.asp (last accessed June 29, 2006).

Anderson, Joseph M. 1999. "The Wealth of U.S. Families: Analysis of Recent Census Data." No. 233, November 10, *Survey of Income and Program Participation.* Washington, DC: U.S. Census Bureau, U.S. Department of Commerce.

Antonio, Anthony Lising. 2004. "When Does Race Matter in College Friendships? Exploring Men's Diverse and Homogeneous Friendship Groups." *Review of Higher Education* 27(4): 553–75.

Arenson, Karen W. 2002. "Early Admissions Are Rising as Colleges Debate Practice." *New York Times*, December 23, p. A18.

Arenson, Karen W. 2003. "Change on Early Admission Produces Application Shifts." *New York Times*, November 13, p. A27.

———. 2006. "CUNY Reports Fewer Blacks at Top Schools." *New York Times*, August 10, p. B1.

———. 2008a. "Yale Plans Sharp Increase in Student Aid." *New York Times*, January 15, p. A14.

———. 2008b. "Applications to Colleges Are Breaking Records." *New York Times*, January 17, p. A22.

Argetsinger, Amy. 2003. "Legacy Students: A Counterpoint to Affirmative Action." *Washington Post*, March 12, p. A6.

Armor, David J. 2008. "Can NCLB Close Achievement Gaps?" Pp. 323–42 in Alan R. Sadovnik, Jennifer A. O'Day, George W. Bohrnstedt, and Kathryn M. Borman, eds., *No Child Left Behind and the Reduction of the Achievement Gap*. New York: Routledge.

Arnold, Karen D. 2002. "Getting to the Top—What Role Do Elite Colleges Play?" *About Campus* 7(5): 4–12.

Ashenfelter, Orley, and Cecilia Rouse. 1999. "Schooling, Intelligence, and Income in America: Cracks in the Bell Curve." Working Paper 6902, January. Cambridge, MA: National Bureau of Economic Research.

Astin, Alexander W. 1993. *What Matters in College: Four Critical Years Revisited*. San Francisco: Jossey-Bass.

———. 1999. "Student Involvement: A Developmental Theory for Higher Education." *Journal of College Student Development* 40(5): 518–29.

Astin, Alexander W., Leticia Oseguera, Linda J. Sax, and William S. Korn. 2002. *The American Freshman: Thirty-Five Year Trends*. Los Angeles: Higher Education Research Institute, UCLA.

Attewell, Paul. 2001. "The Winner-Take-All High School: Organizational Adaptations to Educational Stratification." *Sociology of Education* 74(4): 267–95.

Attewell, Paul, and David Lavin. 2007. *Passing the Torch: Does Higher Education for the Disadvantaged Pay Off across the Generations?* New York: Russell Sage Foundation.

Avery, Christopher, and Caroline M. Hoxby. 2004. "Do and Should Financial Aid Packages Affect Students' College Choices?" Pp. 239–99 in Caroline M. Hoxby, ed., *College Choices: The Economics of Where to Go, When to Go, and How to Pay for It*. Chicago: University of Chicago Press.

Avery, Christopher, Andrew Fairbanks, and Richard Zeckhauser. 2003. *The Early Admissions Game: Joining the Elite*. Cambridge, MA: Harvard University Press.

Barron's: Profiles of American Colleges. 1998. 23rd ed. Hauppauge, NY: Barron's Educational Series.

Barron's: Profiles of American Colleges. 2000. 24th ed. Hauppauge, NY: Barron's Educational Series.

Basten, Jay, John Cole, Ricardo Maestas, and Katherine Mason. 1997. "Redefining the Virtuous Cycle: Replacing the Criterion of Race with Socioeconomic Status in the Admissions Process in Highly Selective Institutions." Paper presented at the Annual Meetings of the Association for the Study of Higher Education, Albuquerque, NM, November 6–9.

Baum, Sandy, and Jennifer Ma. 2007. *Education Pays: The Benefits of Higher Education for Individuals and Society*. Trends in Higher Education Series. New York: The College Board.

Baum, Sandy, and Marie O'Malley. 2003. "College on Credit: How Borrowers Perceive Their Education Debt: Results of the 2002 National Student Loan Survey, Final Report." Nellie Mae Corporation, February 6, http://www .nelliemae.org/library/nasls_2002.pdf (last accessed September 14, 2006).

Baum, Sandy, and Diane Saunders. 1998. "Life after Debt: Results of the National Student Loan Survey." *National Student Loan Survey: Final Report*, February, Nellie Mae, Braintree, MA.

Baumol, William J., and Alan S. Blinder. 2006. *Economics: Principles and Policy*. 10th ed. Mason, OH: Thomson Business and Professional Publishing.

Becker, Gary S. 1975. *Human Capital: A Theoretical and Empirical Analysis with Special Reference to Education*. 2nd ed. New York: National Bureau of Economic Research.

Becker, Gary S., and Kevin M. Murphy. 2007. "The Upside of Income Inequality." *The American* 4(4): 20–23.

Behrman, Jere R., Mark R. Rosenzweig, and Paul Taubman. 1996. "College Choice and Wages: Estimates Using Data on Female Twins." *Review of Economics and Statistics* 78(4): 672–85.

Beller, Emily, and Michael Hout. 2006. "Intergenerational Social Mobility: The United States in Comparative Perspective." Special Issue on Opportunity in America, *The Future of Children* 16(2): 19–36.

Belluck, Pam. 2002. "Harvard President Backs Raises for Low-Wage Staff; University Works to End Grade Inflation." *New York Times*, February 1, p. A20.

Berger, Joseph B. 2001–2. "Understanding the Organizational Nature of Student Persistence: Empirically-Based Recommendations for Practice." *Journal of College Student Retention: Research, Theory, and Practice* 3(1): 3–21.

Berlak, Harold. 2001. "Race and the Achievement Gap." *Rethinking Schools*, Summer, 15(4), http://rethinkingschools.org/archive/15_04/Race154.shtml (last accessed August 7, 2006).

Bernstein, Elizabeth. 2003. "Want to Go to Harvard Law?" *Wall Street Journal*, September 26, p. W1.

Blinder, Alan S. 2006. "Offshoring: The Next Industrial Revolution?" *Foreign Affairs* 85(2): 113–28.

———. 2007. "Offshoring: Big Deal, or Business as Usual?" Working Paper 149, June, Center for Economic Policy Studies, Princeton University, Princeton, NJ.

Bloomberg News. 2008. "Brown Ends Tuition for Lower-Income Students." *New York Times*, February 25, p. 13.

Blumenstyk, Goldie. 2008. "Endowments Savor Big Gains But Lower Their Sights." *Chronicle of Higher Education*, February 1, 54(21): A1.

Boas, Katherine. 2002. "The Latest Essential for College Applicants: A Summer Already Spent on Campus." *New York Times*, August 21, p. B8.

Bobo, Lawrence D. 2001. "Racial Attitudes and Relations at the Close of the Twentieth Century." Pp. 264–301 in Neil J. Smelser, William Julius Wilson, and Faith Mitchell, eds., *America Becoming: Racial Trends and Their Consequences*. Vol. 1. Washington, DC: National Research Council.

Boggess, Scott, and Camille Ryan. 2002. "Financing the Future—Postsecondary Students, Costs, and Financial Aid: 1996–1997." *Current Population Reports*, P70–83, http://www.census.gov/prod/2002pubs/p70–83.pdf (last accessed November 9, 2007).

Boisjoly, Johanne, Greg J. Duncan, Michael Kremer, Dan M. Levy, and Jacque Eccles. 2006. "Empathy or Antipathy? The Impact of Diversity." *American Economic Review* 96(5): 1890–1905.

Borjas, George J. 1990. *Friends or Strangers: The Impact of Immigrants on the U.S. Economy*. New York: Basic Books.

Bostic, Raphael W., and Brian J. Surette. 2001. "Have the Doors Opened Wider? Trends in Homeownership Rates by Race and Income." *Journal of Real Estate Finance and Economics* 23(3): 411–34.

Bowen, Howard Rothmann. 1997. *Investment in Learning: The Individual and Social Value of American Higher Education*. 2nd ed. Baltimore: Johns Hopkins University Press.

Bowen, William G. 1987. "Admissions and the Relevance of Race." Pp. 422–36 in *Ever the Teacher: William G. Bowen's Writings as President of Princeton*. Princeton: Princeton University Press.

———. 2006. "Extending Opportunity: 'What Is to Be Done?'" Pp. 19–33 in Michael S. McPherson and Morton Owen Schapiro, eds., *College Access: Opportunity or Privilege?* New York: The College Board.

———. 2007. "Getting In . . . and What Comes Later." *Princeton Alumni Weekly* 107(8): 20–23.

Bowen, William G., and Derek Bok. 1998. *The Shape of the River: Long-Term Consequences of Considering Race in College and University Admissions*. Princeton: Princeton University Press.

Bowen, William G., and Sarah A. Levin. 2003. *Reclaiming the Game: College Sports and Educational Values*. Princeton: Princeton University Press.

Bowen, William G., Martin A. Kurzweil, and Eugene M. Tobin. 2005. *Equity and Excellence in American Higher Education*. Charlottesville: University of Virginia Press.

Brainard, Jeffrey. 2006. "U. of Minnesota Expands Scholarships for Low-Income Students." *Chronicle of Higher Education*, February 24, 52(25): A24.

Brand, Jennie E., and Charles N. Halaby. 2006. "Regression and Matching Estimates of the Effects of Elite College Attendance on Educational and Career Achievement." *Social Science Research* 35(3): 749–70.

Brandon, Emily. 2006. "Better Yet, No Tuition; More Programs Offer Students Free Schooling." *U.S. News & World Report*, September 18, 141(10): 74–75.

Brest, Paul, and Miranda Oshige. 1995. "Affirmative Action for Whom?" *Stanford Law Review* 47(5): 855–900.

Brewer, Dominic J., Eric R. Eide, and Ronald G. Ehrenberg. 1999. "Does It Pay to Attend an Elite Private College? Cross-Cohort Evidence on the Effects of College Type on Earnings." *Journal of Human Resources* 34(1): 104–23.

Briggs, Derek C. 2004. "Evaluating SAT Coaching: Gains, Effects and Self-Selection." Pp. 217–33 in Rebecca Zwick, ed., *Rethinking the SAT: The Future of Standardized Testing in University Admissions*. New York: RoutledgeFalmer.

Broh, C. Anthony. 2007. Personal communication. Consortium on Financing Higher Education, Cambridge, MA, April 13.

Bronner, Ethan. 1999. "College Applicants of '99 Are Facing Stiffest Competition." *New York Times*, June 12, p. A1.

Brooks, David. 2002. "Making It." *Weekly Standard* 8(15): 19–26.

Brooks-Gunn, Jeanne, and Lisa B. Markman. 2005. "The Contribution of Parenting to Ethnic and Racial Gaps in School Readiness." *The Future of Children* 15(1): 139–68.

Broughman, Stephen P., and Lenore A. Colaciello. 1999. *Private School Universe Survey, 1997–98*. NCES 1999–319, August. Washington, DC: National Center for Education Statistics, U.S. Department of Education.

Broughman, Stephen P., and Kathleen W. Pugh. 2004. *Characteristics of Private Schools in the United States: Results from the 2001–2002 Private School Universe Survey*. NCES 2005–305, October. Washington, DC: National Center for Education Statistics, U.S. Department of Education.

Brown v. Board of Education, 347 U.S. 483 (1954).

Brown, Betsy E., and Robert L. Clark. 2006. "North Carolina's Commitment to Higher Education: Access and Affordability." Pp. 183–205 in Ronald G. Ehrenberg, ed., *What's Happening to Public Higher Education?* Westport, CT: American Council on Education/Praeger Series on Higher Education.

Brown, Susan K., and Charles Hirschman. 2006. "The End of Affirmative Action in Washington State and Its Impact on the Transition from High School to College." *Sociology of Education* 79(2): 106–30.

Brown, Tamara L. 2000. "Gender Differences in African American Students' Satisfaction with College." *Journal of College Student Development* 41(5): 479–87.

Burd, Stephen. 2003. "Too Much Work? Community Colleges Want Congress to Ease a Penalty That Cuts Aid to Working Students." *Chronicle of Higher Education*, August 8, 49(48): A18.

———. 2006. "Working-Class Students Feel the Pinch: Longstanding Aid Formula Can Make It Seem That Have-nots Have More Money for College Than They Really Do." *Chronicle of Higher Education*, June 9, 52(40): A20.

Butler, Donnell. 2006. Personal communication. Project director, Campus Life in America Student Survey, Office of Population Research, Princeton University, September 21.

Cabrera, Alberto F., Steven M. La Nasa, and Kurt R. Burkum. 2001. *Pathways to a Four-Year Degree: The Higher Education Story of One Generation*. Center for the Study of Higher Education, Pennsylvania State University.

Cage, Mary Crystal. 1995. "For Black Students, an Added Burden." *Chronicle of Higher Education*, April 28, 41(33): A21.

Camarota, Steven A. 2005. "Immigrants at Mid-Decade: A Snapshot of America's Foreign-Born Population in 2005." *Backgrounder*, December. Washington, DC: Center for Immigration Studies.

Cancian, Maria. 1998. "Race-Based versus Class-Based Affirmative Action in College Admissions." *Journal of Policy Analysis and Management* 17(1): 94–105.

Card, David, and Alan B. Krueger. 2004. "Would the Elimination of Affirmative Action Affect Highly Qualified Minority Applicants? Evidence from California and Texas." Working Paper 10366, March. Cambridge, MA: National Bureau of Economic Research.

Cardenas, Diana De. 1998. "Diversity Hit Hard, Fall Admissions Stats Show." *UCLA Today*, http://today.ucla.edu/1998/981109diversity.html (last accessed February 19, 2008).

Carneiro, Pedro, and James J. Heckman. 2003. "Human Capital Policy." Pp. 77–239 in James J. Heckman and Alan B. Krueger, eds., *Inequality in America: What Role for Human Capital Policies?* Cambridge, MA: MIT Press.

Carnevale, Anthony P., and Stephen J. Rose. 2004. "Socioeconomic Status, Race/Ethnicity, and Selective College Admissions." Pp. 101–56 in Richard D. Kahlenberg, ed., *America's Untapped Resource: Low-Income Students in Higher Education*. New York: Century Foundation Press.

Cauchon, Dennis. 2004. "Merit Awards Make College Affordable; Scholarships Help Keep Best Students In-state." *USA Today*, June 28, p. A04.

Chace, William M. 2006. *100 Semesters: My Adventures as Student, Professor, and University President, and What I Learned along the Way*. Princeton: Princeton University Press.

Chaker, Anne Marie. 2005. "Your Money Matters (A Special Report): Family Money; Early Remittance: We All Know about the High Cost of Tuition; But the Bills Can Start Piling Up Well before Your Child Applies." *Wall Street Journal*, November 28, p. R8.

Chan, Jimmy, and Erik Eyster. 2003. "Does Banning Affirmative Action Lower College Student Quality?" *American Economic Review* 93(3): 858–72.

Chang, Mitchell J., Alexander W. Astin, and Dongbin Kim. 2004. "Cross-Racial Interaction among Undergraduates: Some Consequences, Causes, and Patterns." *Research in Higher Education* 45(5): 529–53.

Chaplin, Duncan, and Jane Hannaway. 1998. "Course Taking, Student Activities, School Performance, and SAT Performance." African-American High Scorers Project, Technical Report #3, November. Washington, DC: Urban Institute.

Chapman, Randall G., and Rex Jackson. 1987. *College Choices of Academically Able Students: The Influence of No-Need Financial Aid and Other Factors*. Research Monograph No. 10. New York: College Entrance Examination Board.

Charles, Camille Zubrinsky. 2003. "The Dynamics of Racial Residential Segregation." *Annual Review of Sociology* 29: 167–207.

———. 2006. *Won't You Be My Neighbor? Race, Class, and Residence in Los Angeles*. New York: Russell Sage Foundation.

Chatman, Steve. 2008. "Does Diversity Matter in the Education Process? An Exploration of Student Interactions by Wealth, Religion, Politics, Race, Ethnicity and Immigrant Status at the University of California." *Research and Occasional Paper Series*, CSHE.5.08, March, Center for Studies in Higher Education, University of California, Berkeley.

Cheadle, Jacob E. 2008. "Educational Investment, Family Context, and Children's Math and Reading Growth from Kindergarten through the Third Grade." *Sociology of Education* 81(1): 1–31.

Chinni, Dante. 2006. "Heaven's Gate: Will Gaining Admission to One of the Nation's Elite Colleges Guarantee a Prosperous Future—Or Just a Mountain of Debt?" *Washington Post*, April 2, p. W10.

Chronicle of Higher Education. 2004. "Projections of College Enrollment, Degrees Conferred, and High-School Graduates, 2002 to 2013." *The Chronicle Almanac, 2004–5* 51(1): 18.

———. 2007. "College Enrollment by Age of Students, Fall 2005." *2007–2008 Almanac of Higher Education*. http://chronicle.com/weekly/almanac/2007/Nation/0101502.htm, (last accessed February 21, 2008).

City University of New York. 2006. *Honors College, Admissions, The Application*. http://portal.cuny.edu/portal/site/cuny/index (last accessed August 4, 2006).

Clark, Sanza B., and Sandie L. Crawford. 1992. "An Analysis of African-American First-Year College Student Attitudes and Attrition Rates." *Urban Education* 27(1): 59–79.

Clarke, Marguerite. 2002. "Quantifying Quality: What Can the *U.S. News and World Report* Rankings Tell Us about the Quality of Higher Education?" *Education Policy Analysis Archives*, March 20, 10(16).

Cliatt, Cass. 2008. "Princeton Makes Offers to 9.25 Percent of Applicants in 'Most Selective' Admission Process." http://www.princeton.edu/main/news/archive/S20/71/02Q45/index.xml?section=topstories (last accessed April 12, 2008).

Cohen, Carl, and James P. Sterba. 2003. *Affirmative Action and Racial Preference: A Debate*. New York: Oxford University Press.

Cohen, Katherine. 2002. *The Truth About Getting In: A Top College Advisor Tells You Everything You Need to Know*. New York: Hyperion.

Cohen, Paula Marantz. 2006. "When the Best Is Not Good Enough." *New York Times*, April 24, p. A42.

Colburn, David R., Charles E. Young, and Victor M. Yellen. 2008. "Admissions and Public Higher Education in California, Texas, and Florida: The Post-Affirmative Action Era." *InterActions: UCLA Journal of Education and Information Studies* 4(1), Article 2. http://repositories.cdlib.org/gseis/interactions/vol4/iss1/art2 (last accessed February 12, 2008).

Cole, Michael S., Robert S. Rubin, Hubert S. Feild, and William F. Giles. 2007. "Recruiters' Perceptions and Use of Applicant Résumé Information: Screening the Recent Graduate." *Applied Psychology: An International Review* 56(2): 319–43.

Cole, Stephen, and Elinor Barber. 2003. *Increasing Faculty Diversity: The Occupational Choices of High-Achieving Minority Students*. Cambridge, MA: Harvard University Press.

Coleman, James S. 1968. "The Concept of Equality of Educational Opportunity." *Harvard Educational Review* 38: 7–22.

Coleman, James S., Ernest Q. Campbell, Carol F. Hobson, James M. McPartland, Alexander M. Mood, Frederic D. Weinfeld, and Robert L. York. 1966. *Equality of Educational Opportunity*. Washington, DC: U.S. GPO.

College Board. 1997. "Table 1: Mean SAT® Scores of Entering College Class, 1967–1997." *1997 College Board National Report*, http://www.collegeboard.com/press/senior97/table01.html (last accessed December 15, 2005).

College Board. 1999. *Reaching the Top: A Report of the National Task Force on Minority High Achievement*. New York: The College Board.

———. 2003. *SAT Verbal and Math Scores Up Significantly as a Record-breaking Number of Students Take the Test*. Report N0218, August 26. New York: The College Board.

———. 2005a. "SAT Percentile Ranks." http://www.collegeboard.com/prod_downloads/about/news_info/cbsenior/yr2005/02_v&m_composite_percentile_ranks_0506.pdf (last accessed December 2, 2005).

———. 2005b. "Trends in Student Aid." *Trends in Higher Education Series, Report Number 050341687*, http://www.collegeboard.com/prod_downloads/press/cost05/trends_aid_05.pdf (last accessed May 22, 2006).

———. 2006a. *Advanced Placement Report to the Nation 2006*. New York: The College Board.

———. 2006b. "College Application Requirements: Application Fee." http://www.collegeboard.com/student/apply/the-application/115.html (last accessed June 8, 2006).

———. 2007a. "Trends in College Pricing." *Trends in Higher Education Series, Report Number 070342218*, http://www.collegeboard.com/prod_downloads/about/news_info/trends/trends_pricing_07.pdf (last accessed November 8, 2007).

———. 2007b. *2007 College-Bound Seniors*. Total Group Profile Report, Total Group. 002_0_NP_01 566. New York: The College Board.

Collins, Randall. 1979. *The Credential Society: An Historical Sociology of Education and Stratification*. Orlando, FL: Academic Press.

Collison, Michele N-K. 1993. "Black Students Become More Savvy in Making Their College Choices." *Chronicle of Higher Education*, March 31, 39(30): A28.

Commission on the Future of Higher Education. 2006. *Final Draft Report*. August 9, http://chronicle.com/daily/2006/08/2006081101n.htm (last accessed August 17, 2006).

Committee on Prospering in the Global Economy of the 21st Century: An Agenda for American Science and Technology. 2007. *Rising above the Gathering Storm: Energizing and Employing America for a Brighter Economic Future*. Committee on Science, Engineering, and Public Policy. Washington, DC: National Academies Press.

Committee on Undergraduate Admissions and Relations with Schools (CUARS). 1999. *1998–1999 Report to the Academic Senate at UCLA*. Los Angeles, CA.

Conley, Dalton. 1999. *Being Black, Living in the Red: Race, Wealth, and Social Policy in America*. Berkeley: University of California Press.

Conrad, Cecilia A. 1999. "Affirmative Action and Admission to the University of California." Pp. 171–96 in Paul Ong, ed., *Impacts of Affirmative Action: Policies and Consequences in California*. Walnut Creek, CA: AltaMira Press.

Conrad, Cecilia A., and Rhonda V. Sharpe. 1996. "The Impact of the California Civil Rights Initiative (CCRI) on University and Professional School Admissions and the Implications for the California Economy." *Review of Black Political Economy* 25(1): 13–59.

Cook, Philip J., and Robert H. Frank. 1993. "The Growing Concentration of Top Students at Elite Schools." Pp. 121–44 in Charles T. Clotfelter and

Michael Rothschild, eds., *Studies of Supply and Demand in Higher Education*. Chicago: University of Chicago Press.

Cookson, Peter W. Jr., and Caroline Hodges Persell. 1985. *Preparing for Power: America's Elite Boarding Schools*. New York: Basic Books, Inc.

Cross, Theodore. 1998. "The Thernstrom Fallacy: Why Affirmative Action Is Not Responsible for High Dropout Rates of African-American College Students." *Journal of Blacks in Higher Education* 20: 90–98.

Cruice, Valerie. 2000. "Seeking an Early Edge into Elite Colleges." *New York Times*, May 28, p. 14CN.

Currie, Janet. 2005. "Health Disparities and Gaps in School Readiness." *The Future of Children* 15(1): 117–38.

Curry, Wade, Walt MacDonald, and Rick Morgan. 1999. "The Advanced Placement Program: Access to Excellence." *Journal of Secondary Gifted Education* 11(1): 17–22.

Dale, Stacy Berg, and Alan B. Krueger. 2002. "Estimating the Payoff to Attending a More Selective College: An Application of Selection on Observables and Unobservables." *Quarterly Journal of Economics* 117(4): 1491–1527.

Daniel, Kermit, Dan Black, and Jeffrey Smith. 1997. "College Quality and the Wages of Young Men." Working Paper, June. Philadelphia: University of Pennsylvania, Wharton School of Public Policy and Management.

Davis, James A. 1966. "The Campus as a Frog Pond: An Application of the Theory of Relative Deprivation to Career Decisions of College Men." *American Journal of Sociology* 72(1): 17–31.

Davis, Sampson, George Jenkins, and Rameck Hunt. 2002. *The Pact: Three Young Men Make a Promise and Fulfill a Dream*. New York: Riverhead Books.

Daymont, Thomas N., and Paul J. Andrisani. 1984. "Job Preferences, College Major, and the Gender Gap in Earnings." *Journal of Human Resources* 19(3): 408–28.

Dehejia, Rajeev H., and Sadek Wahba. 1999. "Causal Effects in Nonexperimental Studies: Reevaluating the Evaluation of Training Programs." *Journal of the American Statistical Association* 94(448): 1053–62.

Dickens, William T. 2005. "Genetic Differences and School Readiness." *The Future of Children* 15(1): 55–69.

Dickert-Conlin, Stacy, and Ross Rubenstein, eds. 2006. *Economic Inequality and Higher Education*. New York: Russell Sage Foundation.

Diener, Ed, and Robert Biswas-Diener. 2002. "Will Money Increase Subjective Well-Being?" *Social Indicators Research* 57: 119–69.

DiMaggio, Paul, Eszter Hargittai, Coral Celeste, and Steven Shafer. 2004. "Digital Inequality: From Unequal Access to Differentiated Use." Pp. 355–400 in Kathryn M. Neckerman, ed., *Social Inequality*. New York: Russell Sage Foundation.

Dodson, Lisa, and Jillian Dickert. 2004. "Girl's Family Labor in Low-Income Households: A Decade of Qualitative Research." *Journal of Marriage and Family* 66(2): 318–32.

Donohue, Tambra L., and Eugene H. Wong. 1997. "Achievement Motivation and College Satisfaction in Traditional and Nontraditional Students." *Education* 118(2): 237–43.

Duffy, Elizabeth A., and Idana Goldberg. 1998. *Crafting a Class: College Admissions and Financial Aid, 1955–1994*. Princeton: Princeton University Press.

Dugan, Mary Kay, Nazli Baydar, William R. Grady, and Terry R. Johnson. 1996. "Affirmative Action: Does It Exist in Graduate Business Schools?" *Selections*, Winter, pp. 11–18.

Duncan, Greg J., and Katherine A. Magnuson. 2005. "Can Family Socioeconomic Resources Account for Racial and Ethnic Test Score Gaps?" *The Future of Children* 15(1): 35–54.

Duncan, Greg J., Amy Claessens, Aletha C. Huston, Linda S. Pagani, Mimi Engel, Holly Sexton, Chantelle J. Dowsett, Katherine Magnuson, Pamela Klebanov, Leon Feinstein, Jeanne Brooks-Gunn, Kathryn Duckworth, and Crista Japel. 2007. "School Readiness and Later Achievement." *Developmental Psychology* 43(6): 1428–46.

Easterbrook, Gregg. 2004. "Who Needs Harvard?" *Atlantic Monthly* 294(3): 128–30, 132–33.

Edley, Christopher Jr. 1996. *Not All Black and White: Affirmative Action and American Values*. New York: Farrar, Straus, and Giroux.

Egan, Timothy. 2007. "Little Asia on the Hill." *Education Life, New York Times*, January 7, Section 4A, p. 24.

———. 2008. "The Lords of Higher Learning." *New York Times*, March 18, p. A23.

Ehrenberg, Ronald G. 2002. *Tuition Rising: Why College Costs So Much*. Cambridge, MA: Harvard University Press.

———. 2003. "Method or Madness? Inside the 'USNWR' College Rankings." Cornell Higher Education Research Institute, Cornell University. Paper presented at the Wisconsin Center for the Advancement of Postsecondary Education Forum on the Use and Abuse of College Rankings, Madison, Wisconsin, November 20–21.

Ehrenberg, Ronald G., and Michael J. Rizzo. 2004. "Financial Forces and the Future of American Higher Education." *Academe* 90(4): 28–31.

Ehrmann, Nicholas. 2007. "From the Ghetto to the Ivory Tower: Gendered Effects of Segregation on Elite-College Completion." *Social Science Quarterly* 88(5): 1392–1414.

Eide, Eric, Dominic J. Brewer, and Ronald G. Ehrenberg. 1998. "Does It Pay to Attend an Elite Private College? Evidence on the Effects of Undergraduate College Quality on Graduate School Attendance." *Economics of Education Review* 17(4): 371–76.

Einarson, Marne K., and Michael W. Matier. 2005. "Exploring Race Differences in Correlates of Seniors' Satisfaction with Undergraduate Education." *Research in Higher Education* 46(6): 641–76.

Elliott, Rogers, A. Christopher Strenta, Russell Adair, Michael Matier, and Jannah Scott. 1996. "The Role of Ethnicity in Choosing and Leaving Science in Highly Selective Institutions." *Research in Higher Education* 37(6): 681–709.

Engle, Jennifer, and Colleen O'Brien. 2007. *Demography Is Not Destiny: Increasing the Graduation Rates of Low-Income College Students at Large Public Universities*. Washington, DC: Pell Institute for the Study of Opportunity in Higher Education.

Epple, Dennis, Richard Romano, and Holger Sieg. 2006. "Admission, Tuition, and Financial Aid Policies in the Market for Higher Education." *Econometrica* 74(4): 885–928.

Escueta, Eugenia, and Eileen O'Brien. 1991. "Asian Americans in Higher Education: Trends and Issues." *American Council on Education Research Briefs*, 2(4), http://eric.ed.gov/ERICWebPortal/custom/portlets/recordDetails/detailmini.jsp?_nfpb=true&_&ERICExtSearch_SearchValue_0=ED381103&ERICExtSearch_SearchType_0=eric_accno&accno=ED381103 (last accessed October 2, 2007).

Espenshade, Thomas J., and Chang Y. Chung. 2005. "The Opportunity Cost of Admission Preferences at Elite Universities." *Social Science Quarterly* 86(2): 293–305.

Espenshade, Thomas J., Chang Y. Chung, and Joan L. Walling. 2004. "Admission Preferences for Minority Students, Athletes, and Legacies at Elite Universities." *Social Science Quarterly* 85(5): 1422–46.

Espenshade, Thomas J., Lauren E. Hale, and Chang Y. Chung. 2004. "High School Academic Environment, Class Rank, and Elite College Admission." Unpublished manuscript, September, Office of Population Research, Princeton University.

———. 2005. "The Frog Pond Revisited: High School Academic Context, Class Rank, and Elite College Admission." *Sociology of Education* 78(4): 269–93.

Espiritu, Yen Le. 1992. *Asian American Panethnicity: Bridging Institutions and Identities*. Philadelphia: Temple University Press.

Ewers, Justin. 2003. "The Admissions Maze." *U.S. News & World Report*, September 1, 135(6): 64–70.

———. 2005. "Class Conscious; Low-Income Students Have Long Been a Rare and Invisible Minority at Elite Colleges: That May Be About to Change." *U.S. News & World Report*, May 2, 138(16): 42.

Fain, Paul. 2007. "12 Presidents Sign Anti-Rankings Letter." *Chronicle of Higher Education*, May 18, 53(37): A32.

Farkas, George. 2004. "The Black-White Test Score Gap." *Contexts* 3(2): 12–19.

Farley, Reynolds. 2002. "Racial Identities in 2000: The Response to the Multiple-Race Response Option." Pp. 33–61 in Joel Perlmann and Mary C. Waters, eds., *The New Race Question: How the Census Counts Multiracial Individuals*. New York: Russell Sage Foundation.

Farrell, Elizabeth F. 2006a. "College Searches Gone Wild." *Chronicle of Higher Education*, March 31, 52(30): A39–A40.

———. 2006b. "Following Harvard's Lead, 2 Ivies Make Changes to Help Needy Students." *Chronicle of Higher Education*, September 29, 53(6): A44.

———. 2006c. "U. of Virginia Announces Plans to End Early-Decision Admissions." *Chronicle of Higher Education*, October 6, 53(7): A33.

———. 2006d. "The Power and Peril of Admissions Data." *Chronicle of Higher Education*, October 13, 53(8): A46–A48.

———. 2007a. "Richer Students Receive Much More Merit-Based Aid Than Do Poorer Ones, Study Finds." *Today's News, Chronicle of Higher Education*, Wednesday, January 17, http://chronicle.com/daily/2007/01/2007011705n.htm (last accessed June 8, 2008).

Farrell, Elizabeth F. 2007b. "Consultants Help Families Pay Less for College: A New Breed of Planners Show Parents How to Win More Student Aid." *Chronicle of Higher Education*, October 26, 54(9): A1.

Feld, Scott L., and William C. Carter. 1998. "When Desegregation Reduces Interracial Contact: A Class Size Paradox for Weak Ties." *American Journal of Sociology* 103(5): 1165–86.

Ferguson, Ronald F. 2001. "Test-Score Trends along Racial Lines, 1971 to 1996: Popular Culture and Community Academic Standards." Pp. 348–90 in Neil J. Smelser, William Julius Wilson, and Faith Mitchell, eds., *America Becoming: Racial Trends and Their Consequences*. Vol. 1. Washington, DC: National Research Council.

Fetter, Jean H. 1995. *Questions and Admissions: Reflections on 100,000 Admissions Decisions at Stanford*. Stanford: Stanford University Press.

Ficklen, Ellen, and Jeneva E. Stone. 2002. "Empty Promises: The Myth of College Access in America: A Report of the Advisory Committee on Student Financial Assistance." *Advisory Committee on Student Financial Assistance*, June. Washington, DC.

Field, Kelly. 2008. "Congress's Cost Cure May Have Side Effects." *Chronicle of Higher Education*, February 8, 54(22): A1.

Finder, Alan. 2006a. "Aid Lets Smaller Colleges Ask, Why Pay for Ivy League Retail?" *New York Times*, January 1, p. 1.1.

———. 2006b. "High Schools Avoid Class Ranking, Vexing Colleges." *New York Times*, March 5, p. 1.29.

———. 2006c. "In New Twist on College Search, a First Choice, and 20 Backups." *New York Times*, March 21, p. A11.

———. 2007. "Ivy League Admissions Crunch Brings New Cachet to Next Tier." *New York Times*, May 16, p. A1.

———. 2008a. "Yale Plans to Increase Spending from Its Endowment, with Financial Aid to Benefit." *New York Times*, January 8, p. A12.

———. 2008b. "Elite Colleges Reporting Record Lows in Admission." *New York Times*, April 1, p. A16.

Fischer, Karin. 2006a. "Mass. Merit Aid Fails to Increase Access." *Chronicle of Higher Education*, March 24, 52(29): A29.

———. 2006b. "Elite Colleges Lag in Serving the Needy." *Chronicle of Higher Education*, May 12, 52(36): A1.

Fischer, Mary J. 2007. "Settling into Campus Life: Differences by Race/Ethnicity in College Involvement and Outcomes." *Journal of Higher Education* 78(2): 125–61.

Flanagan, Caitlin. 2001. "Confessions of a Prep School College Counselor." *Atlantic Monthly* 288(2): 53–61.

Fogg, Neeta. 2004. *College Majors Handbook with Real Career Paths and Payoffs: The Actual Jobs, Earnings, and Trends for Graduates of 60 College Majors*. Indianapolis: Jist Publishing.

Foner, Eric. 2004. "The Reconstruction Amendments: Official Documents as Social History." *History Now*, Gilder Lehrman Institute of American History, http://www.historynow.org/12_2004/print/historian.html (last accessed March 6, 2007).

Forster, Greg. 2006. "The Embarrassing Good News on College Access." *Chronicle of Higher Education*, March 10, 52(27): B50.

Frank, Robert H. 2005. "The Intense Competition for Top Students Is Threatening Financial Aid Based on Need." *New York Times*, April 14, p. C2.

Frank, Robert H., and Philip J. Cook. 1995. *The Winner-Take-All Society*. New York: The Free Press.

Freedman, James O. 2003. *Liberal Education and the Public Interest*. Iowa City: University of Iowa Press.

Freeland, Edward P., and Marc Weiner. 2003. *Survey Methodology Report, The National Survey of College Experience*. July 31. Princeton: Survey Research Center, Woodrow Wilson School, Princeton University.

Freeman, Richard B. 2007. *America Works: The Exceptional U.S. Labor Market*. New York: Russell Sage Foundation.

Fryer, Roland G. Jr., and Steven D. Levitt. 2004. "Understanding the Black-White Test Score Gap in the First Two Years of School." *Review of Economics and Statistics* 86(2): 447–64.

———. 2006a. "Testing for Racial Differences in the Mental Ability of Young Children." Working Paper 12066, March. Cambridge, MA: National Bureau of Economic Research.

———. 2006b. "The Black-White Test Score Gap through Third Grade." *American Law and Economics Review* 8(2): 249–81.

Fryer, Roland G., Jr., Glenn C. Loury, and Tolga Yuret. 2007. "An Economic Analysis of Color-Blind Affirmative Action." *Journal of Law, Economics, and Organization*, Advance Access published on December 24, 2007, doi:10.1093/jleo/ewm053.

Geiser, Saul, and Maria Veronica Santelices. 2007. "Validity of High-School Grades in Predicting Student Success beyond the Freshman Year: High-School Record vs. Standardized Tests as Indicators of Four-Year College Outcomes." *Research & Occasional Paper Series: CSHE.6.07*, http://cshe.berkeley.edu/publications/publications.php?id=265 (last accessed October 2, 2007).

Gerald, Danette, and Kati Haycock. 2006. *Engines of Inequality: Diminishing Equity in the Nation's Premier Public Universities*. Washington, DC: Education Trust.

Gertner, Jon. 2006. "Forgive Us Our Student Debts." *New York Times Magazine*, June 11, pp. 60–68.

Gladieux, Lawrence E. 2004. "Low-Income Students and the Affordability of Higher Education." Pp. 17–57 in Richard D. Kahlenberg, ed., *America's Untapped Resource: Low-Income Students in Higher Education*. New York: Century Foundation Press.

Glater, Jonathan D. 2006. "Some Parents Letting Children Choose College, and Pay for It." *New York Times*, April 10, p. A1.

———. 2008a. "Stanford Set to Raise Aid for Students in Middle." *New York Times*, February 21, p. A14.

———. 2008b. "Harvard Law, Hoping Students Will Consider Public Service, Offers Tuition Break." *New York Times*, March 18, p. A14.

Goldberg, Carey. 1997. "Admissions Essay Ordeal: The Young Examined Life." *New York Times*, December 31, pp. A1, B8.

Golden, Daniel. 2006. *The Price of Admission: How America's Ruling Class Buys Its Way into Elite Colleges—and Who Gets Left outside the Gates*. New York: Crown.

Goldstein, Joshua R., and Ann J. Morning. 2000. "The Multiple-Race Population of the United States: Issues and Estimates." *Proceedings of the National Academy of Sciences*, May 23, 97(11): 6230–35.

———. 2002. "Back in the Box: The Dilemma of Using Multiple-Race Data for Single-Race Laws." Pp. 119–36 in Joel Perlmann and Mary C. Waters, eds., *The New Race Question: How the Census Counts Multiracial Individuals*. New York: Russell Sage Foundation.

Gose, Ben. 1998. "Recent Shifts on Aid by Elite Colleges Signal New Push to Help the Middle Class." *Chronicle of Higher Education*, March 6, 44(26): A43–A44.

Goyette, Kimberly A., and Ann L. Mullen. 2006. "Who Studies the Arts and Sciences? Social Background and the Choice and Consequences of Undergraduate Field of Study." *Journal of Higher Education* 77(3): 497–538.

Grace, Stephanie N. 2007. *Dormroom Diversity: Examining the Effects of Racially Heterogeneous College Roommate Pairings*. Senior thesis in the Department of Sociology, Princeton University.

Graham, Hugh Davis. 2001. "Affirmative Action for Immigrants? The Unintended Consequences of Reform." Pp. 53–70 in John David Skrentny, ed. *Color Lines: Affirmative Action, Immigration, and Civil Rights Options for America*. Chicago: University of Chicago Press.

———. 2002. *Collision Course: The Strange Convergence of Affirmative Action and Immigration Policy in America*. New York: Oxford University Press.

Gratz v. Bollinger, 539 U.S. 244 (2003).

Greenhouse, Linda. 2006. "Court to Weigh Race as a Factor in School Rolls." *New York Times*, June 6, p. A1.

———. 2007. "Justices Limit the Use of Race in School Plans for Integration." *New York Times*, June 29, p. A1.

Greenwald, Rob, Larry V. Hedges, and Richard D. Laine. 1996. "The Effect of School Resources on Student Achievement." *Review of Educational Research* 66(3): 361–96.

Gross, Jane. 1999. "Basking in the Hamptons to Coach Students for SATs." *New York Times*, August 9, p. B1.

Grossman, Gene M., and Esteban Rossi-Hansberg. 2006. "The Rise of Offshoring: It's Not Wine for Cloth Anymore." Department of Economics, Princeton University. Paper prepared for the symposium sponsored by the Federal Reserve Bank of Kansas City titled "The New Economic Geography: Effects and Policy Implications," Jackson Hole, WY, August 24–26.

Groves, Robert M., and Lars W. Lyberg. 1988. "An Overview of Nonresponse Issues in Telephone Surveys." Pp. 191–212 in Robert M. Groves, Paul P. Biemer, Lars E. Lyberg, James T. Massey, William L. Nicholls, and Joseph Waksberg, eds., *Telephone Survey Methodology*. New York: John Wiley.

Grusky, David B., ed. 2001. *Social Stratification: Class, Race, and Gender in Sociological Perspective*, 2nd ed. Boulder, CO: Westview Press.

Grutter v. Bollinger, 539 U.S. 306 (2003).

Gryphon, Marie. 2005. "The Affirmative Action Myth." *Policy Analysis*, No. 540, April 6. Washington, DC: CATO Institute.

Guerrero, Andrea. 2002. *Silence at Boalt Hall: The Dismantling of Affirmative Action*. Berkeley: University of California Press.

Gurin, Patricia. 2002. "Expert Report of Patricia Gurin." In *The Compelling Need for Diversity in Higher Education*," for *Gratz et al. v. Bollinger et al.*, No. 97–75321(E.D. Mich.) and *Grutter et al. v. Bollinger et al.*, No. 97–75928 (E.D. Mich.). http://www.umich.edu/~urel/admissions/legal/expert/gurintoc .html, (last accessed on December 8, 2005).

Gurin, Patricia, Eric L. Dey, Sylvia Hurtado, and Gerald Gurin. 2002. "Diversity and Higher Education: Theory and Impact on Educational Outcomes." *Harvard Educational Review* 72(3): 330–66.

Hales, Peter Bacon. 1997. *Atomic Spaces: Living on the Manhattan Project*. Urbana: University of Illinois Press.

Hansen, Fay. 2006. "Employee Referral Programs, Selective Campus Recruitment Could Touch Off Bias Charges." *Workforce Management*, June 26, 85(12): 59–60.

Harris, Angel L. 2006. "I (Don't) Hate School: Revisiting Oppositional Culture Theory of Blacks' Resistance to Schooling." *Social Forces* 85(2): 1–38.

Harrison, Roderick J. 2002. "Inadequacies of Multiple-Response Race Data in the Federal Statistical System." Pp. 137–60 in Joel Perlmann and Mary C. Waters, eds., *The New Race Question: How the Census Counts Multiracial Individuals*. New York: Russell Sage Foundation.

Hart, Betty, and Todd R. Risley. 2003. "The Early Catastrophe: The 30 Million Word Gap by Age 3." *American Educator* 27(1): 4–9.

Harvard College Admissions Office. 2007. "Statistics: Class of 2010." http:// www.admissions.college.harvard.edu/counselors/stats/index.html (last accessed July 14, 2007).

Harvard College. 2006. "Understanding your Financial Aid Award 2006–2007." http://www.fao.fas.harvard.edu/downloads/understanding_your_award.pdf (last accessed June 6, 2006).

Haskins, Ron. 2008. "Education and Economic Mobility." Pp. 91–104 in Julia B. Isaacs, Isabel V. Sawhill, and Ron Haskins, eds., *Getting Ahead or Losing Ground: Economic Mobility in America*. Economic Mobility Project. Washington, DC: Brookings Institution.

Hauser, Robert M. 2004. "Progress in Schooling." Pp. 271–318 in Kathryn M. Neckerman, ed., *Social Inequality*. New York: Russell Sage Foundation.

Haveman, Robert, and Timothy Smeeding. 2006. "The Role of Higher Education in Social Mobility." Special Issue on Opportunity in America, *The Future of Children* 16(2): 125–50.

Hawkins, David A., and Melissa Clinedinst. 2006. *State of College Admission: 2006*. Alexandria, VA: National Association for College Admission Counseling.

Hawkins, David A., and Jessica Lautz. 2005. *State of College Admission, 2004– 05*. March. Alexandria, VA: National Association for College Admission Counseling.

Hebel, Sara. 2007. "The Graduation Gap: Degree Attainment Varies Widely among Colleges that Serve Low-Income Students." *Chronicle of Higher Education*, March 23, 53(29): A20–A24.

Hecker, Daniel E. 1996. "Earnings and Major Field of Study of College Graduates." *Occupational Outlook Quarterly* 40(2): 10–21.

Hedges, Larry V., and Amy Nowell. 1999. "Changes in the Black-White Gap in Achievement Test Scores." *Sociology of Education* 72(2): 111–35.

Heller, Donald E. 2004. "Pell Grant Recipients in Selective Colleges and Universities." Pp. 157–66 in Richard D. Kahlenberg, ed., *America's Untapped Resource: Low-Income Students in Higher Education*. New York: Century Foundation Press.

Herbert, Bob. 2007. "Nightmare before Christmas." Op-Ed contribution, *New York Times*, December 22, p. A25.

Hernández, Michele A. 1997. *A Is for Admission: The Insider's Guide to Getting into the Ivy League and Other Top Colleges*. New York: Warner Books.

Herring, Hubert B. 2005. "Your Child Got into an Ivy: Do You Have to Say Yes?" *New York Times*, April 17, p. 3.8.

Hill, Catharine B., and Gordon C. Winston. 2006a. "A 'Free' Harvard? Now That's Rich." *Los Angeles Times*, April 2, p. M2.

———. 2006b. "How Scarce Are High-Ability, Low-Income Students?" Pp. 75–102 in Michael S. McPherson and Morton Owen Schapiro, eds., *College Access: Opportunity or Privilege?* New York: The College Board.

Ho, Daniel E. 2005. "Why Affirmative Action Does Not Cause Black Students to Fail the Bar." *Yale Law Journal* 114(8): 1997–2016.

Hoffman, Lee McGraw. 1999. *Overview of Public Elementary and Secondary Schools and Districts: School Year 1997–98*. NCES 99–322, May. Washington, DC: National Center for Education Statistics, U.S. Department of Education.

———. 2003. *Overview of Public Elementary and Secondary Schools and Districts: School Year 2001–02*. NCES 2003–411, May. Washington, DC: National Center for Education Statistics, U.S. Department of Education.

Holzer, Harry, and David Neumark. 2000. "Assessing Affirmative Action." *Journal of Economic Literature* 38(3): 483–568.

———. 2006. "Affirmative Action: What Do We Know?" *Journal of Policy Analysis and Management* 25(2): 463–90.

Holzer, Harry J., Diane Whitmore Schanzenbach, Greg J. Duncan, and Jens Ludwig. 2007. *The Economic Costs of Poverty in the United States: Subsequent Effects of Children Growing Up Poor*. January 24. Washington, DC: Center for Economic Progress.

Hong, Peter. 2005. "Students: The Rich Get Smarter; More Scholarships for Wealthy Students Cut Out the Poor Kids." *Los Angeles Times*, October 23, p. M.6.

Hoover, Eric. 2007a. "Hoping to Attract More Middle-Income Students, Amherst College Replaces Loans with Grants." *Today's News*, *Chronicle of Higher Education*, Friday, July 20, http://chronicle.com/daily/2007/07/2007072003n.htm (last accessed June 9, 2008).

———. 2007b. "How Applying to College Shapes Students." *Chronicle of Higher Education*, September 28, 54(5): A1.

Hopwood v. Texas, 78 F.3d 932 (5th Cir. Tex. 1996).

Horn, Catherine L., and Stella M. Flores. 2003. *Percent Plans in College Admissions: A Comparative Analysis of Three States' Experiences*. Cambridge, MA: Civil Rights Project at Harvard University.

Horn, Laura J. 2006. *Placing College Graduation Rates in Context: How 4-Year College Graduation Rates Vary with Selectivity and the Size of Low-Income Enrollment*. NCES 2007–161. Washington, DC: National Center for Education Statistics, U.S. Department of Education.

Horn, Laura J., and Jennifer Berktold. 1998. *Profile of Undergraduates in U.S. Postsecondary Education Institutions: 1995–96*. NCES 98–084. Washington, DC: National Center for Education Statistics, U.S. Department of Education.

Horn, Laura J., Christina Chang Wei, and Ali Berker. 2002. *What Students Pay for College, Changes in Net Price of College Attendance Between 1992–93 and 1999–2000*. NCES 2002–174. Washington, DC: National Center for Education Statistics, U.S. Department of Education.

Hossler, Don, Jack Schmit, and Nick Vesper. 1999. *Going to College: How Social, Economic, and Educational Factors Influence the Decisions Students Make*. Baltimore: Johns Hopkins University Press.

Hout, Michael. 2005. *Berkeley's Comprehensive Review Method for Making Freshman Admissions Decisions: An Assessment*. Report to the Committee on Admissions, Enrollment, and Preparatory Education (AEPE) and the Vice Chancellor for Admissions and Enrollment, May, Department of Sociology, University of California, Berkeley.

Hoxby, Caroline M. 1997. "How the Changing Market Structure of U.S. Higher Education Explains College Tuition." Working Paper 6323, December. Cambridge, MA: National Bureau of Economic Research.

———. 2000. "The Effects of Geographic Integration and Increasing Competition in the Market for College Education." Unpublished manuscript, May, Department of Economics, Harvard University, Cambridge, MA.

———. 2001. "The Return to Attending a More Selective College: 1960 to the Present." Pp. 13–42 in Maureen Devlin and Joel Myerson, eds., *Forum Futures: Exploring the Future of Higher Education, 2000 Papers*, Forum Strategy Series. Vol. 3. San Francisco: Jossey-Bass.

———, ed. 2004. *College Choices: The Economics of Where to Go, When to Go, and How to Pay for It*. Chicago: University of Chicago Press.

Hu, Winnie. 2006. "An Inward Look at Racial Tension at Trinity College." *New York Times*, December 18, p. B1.

Humphreys, Debra. 1998. "The Impact of Diversity on College Students: The Latest Research." *Higher Education, Race & Diversity: Views from the Field*. Washington, DC: Association of American Colleges and Universities. http://www.diversityweb.org/research_and_trends/research_evaluation_impact/benefits_of_diversity/impact_of_diversity.cfm (last accessed May 7, 2008).

Iceland, John, Daniel H. Weinberg, and Erika Steinmetz. 2002. *Racial and Ethnic Residential Segregation in the United States: 1980–2000*. Census 2000 Special Reports, CENSR-3. Washington, DC: U.S. Census Bureau.

Immerwahr, John, and Jean Johnson. 2007. *Squeeze Play: How Parents and the Public Look at Higher Education Today*. Report prepared by Public Agenda for the National Center for Public Policy and Higher Education, San Jose, CA.

International Monetary Fund. 2007. *World Economic Outlook: April 2007, Spillovers and Cycles in the Global Economy.* World Economic and Financial Surveys. Washington, DC: International Monetary Fund.

Isaacs, Julia B. 2007. "Economic Mobility of Families across Generations." *Economic Mobility Project,* an initiative of the Pew Charitable Trusts. Washington, DC: Brookings Institution.

Ishitani, Terry T. 2006. "Studying Attrition and Degree Completion Behavior among First-Generation College Students in the United States." *Journal of Higher Education* 77(5): 861–85.

Ishitani, Terry T., and Stephen L. DesJardins. 2002. "A Longitudinal Investigation of Dropout from College in the United States." *Journal of College Student Retention* 4(2): 173–201.

Jencks, Christopher, and Meredith Phillips. 1998a. "America's Next Achievement Test: Closing the Black-White Test Score Gap." *American Prospect* 40:44–53.

———. 1998b. "The Black-White Test Score Gap: An Introduction." Pp. 1–51 in Christopher Jencks and Meredith Phillips, eds., *The Black-White Test Score Gap.* Washington, DC: Brookings Institution Press.

Johnson, Lyndon B. 1965. "To Fulfill These Rights." President Johnson's Commencement Address at Howard University, June 4, Washington, DC, http://www.lbjlib.utexas.edu/johnson/archives.hom/speeches.hom/650604.asp (last accessed June 9, 2008).

Johnston, David Cay. 2007. "Income Gap Is Widening, Data Shows." *New York Times,* March 29, p. C1.

Jones, Nicholas A., and Amy Symens Smith. 2001. "The Two or More Races Population: 2000." *Census 2000 Brief* #C2KBR/01–6, U.S. Census Bureau, Washington, DC. http://www.census.gov/prod/2001pubs/c2kbr01–6.pdf (last accessed August 17, 2006).

Joyner, Kara, and Grace Kao. 2000. "School Racial Composition and Adolescent Racial Homophily." *Social Science Quarterly* 81(3): 810–25.

June, Audrey Williams, and Peter Schmidt. 2007. "Court Tells Michigan Universities to Comply Immediately with Preference Ban." *Chronicle of Higher Education,* January 12, 53(19): A25.

Kahlenberg, Richard D. 1996. *The Remedy: Class, Race, and Affirmative Action.* New York: Basic Books.

———, ed. 2004. *America's Untapped Resource: Low-Income Students in Higher Education.* New York: Century Foundation Press.

———. 2006. "Cost Remains a Key Obstacle to College Access." *Chronicle of Higher Education,* March 10, 52(27): B51.

Kahneman, Daniel, Alan B. Krueger, David A. Schkade, Norbert Schwarz, and Arthur A. Stone. 2004. "A Survey Method for Characterizing Daily Life Experience: The Day Reconstruction Method." *Science,* December 3, 306: 1776–80.

———. 2006. "Would You Be Happier If You Were Richer? A Focusing Illusion." *Science,* June 30, 312: 1908–10.

Kalil, Ariel, Mary Pattillo, and Monique R. Payne. 2004. "Intergenerational Assets and the Black-White Test Score Gap." Pp. 170–94 in Dalton Conley and

Karen Albright, eds., *After the Bell—Family Background, Public Policy, and Educational Success*. New York: Routledge.

Kane, Thomas J. 1998a. "Misconceptions in the Debate Over Affirmative Action in College Admissions." Pp. 17–32 in Gary Orfield and Edward Miller, eds., *Chilling Admissions: The Affirmative Action Crisis and the Search for Alternatives*. Cambridge, MA: Harvard Education Publishing Group.

———. 1998b. "Racial and Ethnic Preferences in College Admissions." Pp. 431–56 in Christopher Jencks and Meredith Phillips, eds., *The Black-White Test Score Gap*. Washington, DC: Brookings Institution Press.

———. 1999. *The Price of Admission: Rethinking How Americans Pay for College*. Washington, DC: Brookings Institution Press.

———. 2004. "College-Going and Inequality." Pp. 319–53 in Kathryn M. Neckerman, ed., *Social Inequality*. New York: Russell Sage Foundation.

———. 2006. Personal communication. Harvard Graduate School of Education, June 19.

Karabel, Jerome. 2004. "The Legacy of Legacies." *New York Times*, September 13, p. A23.

———. 2005. *The Chosen: The Hidden History of Admission and Exclusion at Harvard, Yale, and Princeton*. New York: Houghton Mifflin.

Karen, David. 1990. "Toward a Political-Organizational Model of Gatekeeping: The Case of Elite Colleges." *Sociology of Education* 63(4): 227–40.

———. 1991a. "The Politics of Class, Race, and Gender: Access to Higher Education in the United States, 1960–1986." *American Journal of Education* 99(2): 208–37.

———. 1991b. "'Achievement' and 'Ascription' in Admission to an Elite College: A Political-Organizational Analysis." *Sociological Forum* 6(2): 349–80.

———. 2002. "Changes in Access to Higher Education in the United States: 1980–1992." *Sociology of Education* 75(3): 191–210.

Katznelson, Ira. 2005. *When Affirmative Action Was White: An Untold History of Racial Inequality in Twentieth-Century America*. New York: W. W. Norton.

Kaufman, Jason, and Jay Gabler. 2004. "Cultural Capital and the Extracurricular Activities of Girls and Boys in the College Attainment Process." *Poetics* 32: 145–68.

Kaufman, Jonathan. 2001. "Campus Currency: At Elite Universities, a Culture of Money Highlights Class Divide—Stock Trades and Cellphones for Some Duke Students—But Not for Ms. Byrd—'I Have 2 Groups of Friends.'" *Wall Street Journal*, June 8, p. A1.

Keister, Lisa A. 2005. *Getting Rich: America's New Rich and How They Got That Way*. New York: Cambridge University Press.

Kennedy, Randall. 2001. "Racial Trends in the Administration of Criminal Justice." Pp. 1–20 in Neil J. Smelser, William Julius Wilson, and Faith Mitchell, eds., *America Becoming: Racial Trends and Their Consequences*. Vol. 2. Washington, DC: National Academy Press.

Kent, Mary Mederios. 2007. "Immigration and America's Black Population." *Population Bulletin* 62(4): 3–16. Washington, DC: Population Reference Bureau.

KewalRamani, Angelina, Lauren Gilbertson, Mary Ann Fox, and Stephen Provasnik. 2007. *Status and Trends in the Education of Racial and Ethnic Minorities*

(NCES 2007–039). Washington, DC: National Center for Education Statistics, Institute of Education Sciences, U.S. Department of Education.

King, C. Judson. 2005. Personal communication. June 9.

King, Jacqueline E. 2005. "Federal Student Loan Debt: 1993 to 2004." *American Council on Education, Center for Policy Analysis Issue Brief*, June, http://www.acenet.edu/AM/Template.cfm?Section=CPA&Template=/CM/ContentDisplay.cfm&ContentID=10777 (last accessed July 1, 2006).

King, Jacqueline E., and Gigi G. Gomez. 2008. *On the Pathway to the Presidency: Characteristics of Higher Education's Senior Leadership*. Washington, DC: American Council on Education.

Kirp, David L. 2003. *Shakespeare, Einstein, and the Bottom Line: The Marketing of Higher Education*. Cambridge, MA: Harvard University Press.

Kirsch, Irwin, Henry Braun, Kentaro Yamamoto, and Andrew Sum. 2007. *America's Perfect Storm: Three Forces Changing Our Nation's Future*. Policy Information Report. Princeton, NJ: Educational Testing Service.

Kirshstein, Rita J., Andrea R. Berger, Elana Benatar, and David Rhodes. 2004. "Workforce Contingent Financial Aid: How States Link Financial Aid to Employment." *The Lumina Foundation*, February, http://www.luminafoundation.org/research/Workforce.pdf (last accessed November 15, 2007).

Klitgaard, Robert E. 1985. *Choosing Elites*. New York: Basic Books.

Knapp, Laura G., Janice E. Kelly-Reid, Roy W. Whitmore, and Elise S. Miller. 2007. *Enrollment in Postsecondary Institutions, Fall 2005; Graduation Rates, 1999 and 2002 Cohorts; and Financial Statistics, Fiscal Year 2005*. NCES 2007–154. Washington, DC: National Center for Education Statistics, U.S. Department of Education.

Kober, Nancy. 2001. *It Takes More Than Testing: Closing the Achievement Gap*. August. Washington, DC: Center on Education Policy. http://www.cep-dc.org/improvingpublicschools/closingachievementgap.pdf (last accessed December 29, 2007).

Kobrin, Jennifer L., Brian F. Patterson, Emily J. Shaw, Krista D. Mattern, and Sandra M. Barbuti. 2008. *Validity of the SAT for Predicting First-Year College Grade Point Average*. Research Report No. 2008–5. New York: The College Board. http://professionals.collegeboard.com/profdownload/Validity_of_the_SAT_for_Predicting_First_Year_College_Grade_Point_Average.pdf (last accessed July 4, 2008).

Konigsberg, Eric. 1996. "Getting In: Everybody Goes to Rusty." *Rolling Stone*, October 17, 745: 103–7.

Kozol, Jonathan. 1991. *Savage Inequalities: Children in America's Schools*. New York: Crown.

Krauthammer, Charles. 2001. "Affirmative Action Fails Again." *Washington Post*, July 13, p. A2.

Krueger, Alan B., and Diane Whitmore. 2001. "Would Smaller Classes Help Close the Achievement Gap?" Department of Economics, Princeton University, http://www.irs.princeton.edu/pubs/pdfs/451.pdf (last accessed May 7, 2008).

Krueger, Alan B., Jesse Rothstein, and Sarah Turner. 2006. "Race, Income, and College in 25 Years: Evaluating Justice O'Connor's Conjecture." *American Law and Economics Review* 8(2): 282–311.

Krugman, Paul. 2007. "Trouble with Trade." Op-Ed contribution. *New York Times*, December 28, p. A23.

Kuh, George D. 2001. "College Students Today: Why We Can't Leave Serendipity to Chance." Pp. 277–303 in Philip G. Altbach, Patricia J. Gumport, and D. Bruce Johnstone, eds., *In Defense of American Higher Education*. Baltimore: Johns Hopkins University Press.

Kuncel, Nathan R., Marcus Credé, and Lisa L. Thomas. 2005. "The Validity of Self-Reported Grade Point Averages, Class Ranks, and Test Scores: A Meta-Analysis and Review of the Literature." *Review of Educational Research* 75(1): 63–82.

LaBrecque, Rodney. 2006. "Unfair Advancement." *New York Times*, September 21, p. A31.

Lang, Kevin. 2007. *Poverty and Discrimination*. Princeton: Princeton University Press.

Lareau, Annette. 2003. *Unequal Childhoods: Class, Race, and Family Life*. Berkeley: University of California Press.

Le, Vi-Nhuan, Sheila Nataraj Kirby, Heather Barney, Claude Messan Setodji, and Daniel Gershwin. 2006. *School Readiness, Full-Day Kindergarten, and Student Achievement: An Empirical Investigation*. Santa Monica, CA: RAND Corporation.

Lee, Jaekyung. 2006. "Tracking Achievement Gaps and Assessing the Impact of NCLB on the Gaps: An In-Depth Look into National and State Reading and Math Outcome Trends." June. Cambridge, MA: Civil Rights Project at Harvard University.

———. 2007. "Can Reducing School Segregation Close the Achievement Gap?" Pp. 74–97 in Erica Frankenberg and Gary Orfield, eds., *Lessons in Integration: Realizing the Promise of Racial Diversity in American Schools*. Charlottesville: University of Virginia Press.

Lee, Sharon M., and Barry Edmonston. 2005. "New Marriages, New Families: U.S. Racial and Hispanic Intermarriage." *Population Bulletin* 60(2): 3–36. Washington, DC: Population Reference Bureau.

Leighley, Jan E., and Arnold Vedlitz. 1999. "Race, Ethnicity, and Political Participation: Competing Models and Contrasting Explanations." *Journal of Politics* 61(4): 1092–1114.

Lemieux, Thomas, W. Bentley MacLeod, and Daniel Parent. 2007. "Performance Pay and Wage Inequality." IZA Discussion Paper 2850, June, http://ftp.iza.org/dp2850.pdf (last accessed June 9, 2008).

Leonhardt, David. 2004. "As Wealthy Fill Top Colleges, Concerns Grow over Fairness." *New York Times*, April 22, p. A1.

Leppel, Karen, Mary L. Williams, and Charles Waldauer. 2001. "The Impact of Parental Occupation and Socioeconomic Status on Choice of College Major." *Journal of Family and Economic Issues* 22(4): 373–94.

Levin, Henry, Clive Belfield, Peter Muennig, and Cecilia Rouse. 2007. *The Costs and Benefits of an Excellent Education for All of America's Children*. January. New York: Teachers College, Columbia University.

Levin, Shana. 2003. "Social Psychological Evidence on Race and Racism." Pp. 97–125 in Mitchell J. Chang, Daria Witt, James Jones, and Kenji Hakuta, eds., *Compelling Interest: Examining the Evidence on Racial Dynamics in Colleges and Universities*. Stanford: Stanford University Press.

Levin, Shana, Colette Van Laar, and Jim Sidanius. 2003. "The Effects of Ingroup and Outgroup Friendships on Ethnic Attitudes in College: A Longitudinal Study." *Group Processes and Intergroup Relations* 6(1): 76–92.

Levine, Arthur, and Jeanette Cureton. 1992. "The Quiet Revolution." *Change* 24(1): 24–30.

Levine, Arthur, and Jana Nidiffer. 1996. *Beating the Odds: How the Poor Get to College*. San Francisco: Jossey-Bass.

Levy, Frank, and Richard J. Murnane. 2006. "How Computerized Work and Globalization Shape Human Skill Demands." Revised May 31. Cambridge, MA: Department of Urban Studies and Planning, Massachusetts Institute of Technology.

Levy, Frank, and Peter Temin. 2007. "Inequality and Institutions in 20th Century America." Working Paper 13106, May. Cambridge, MA: National Bureau of Economic Research.

Lewin, Tamar. 2004. "How I Spent Summer Vacation: Going to Get-Into-College Camp." *New York Times*, April 18, p. 1.1.

———. 2007a. "Colleges Regroup after Voters Ban Race Preferences." *New York Times*, January 26, p. A1.

———. 2007b. "Columbia to Receive Its Largest Gift, $400 Million for Student Aid." *New York Times*, April 11, p. B1.

———. 2008. "2 Colleges End Entrance Exam Requirement." *New York Times*, May 27, p. A19.

Lewis, Valerie A. 2008. "Social Energy and Racial Segregation in the University Context." *Social Science Quarterly* 89(3): 573–93.

Light, Audrey, and Wayne Strayer. 2000. "Determinants of College Completion: School Quality or Student Ability?" *Journal of Human Resources* 35(2): 299–332.

Light, Richard J. 2001. *Making the Most of College: Students Speak Their Minds*. Cambridge, MA: Harvard University Press.

Lillard, Dean, and Jennifer Gerner. 1999. "Getting to the Ivy League: How Family Composition Affects College Choice." *Journal of Higher Education* 70(6): 706–30.

Lindsey, Robert L. 1987. "Colleges Accused of Bias to Stem Asians' Gains." *New York Times*, January 19, p. A10.

Linsenmeier, David M., Harvey S. Rosen, and Cecilia Elena Rouse. 2006. "Financial Aid Packages and College Enrollment Decisions: An Econometric Case Study." *Review of Economics and Statistics* 88(1): 126–45.

Lipka, Sara. 2006. "MIT to Match Federal Pell Grants." *Chronicle of Higher Education*, March 17, 52(28): A49.

———. 2007. "Davidson College, in Move to Increase Access, Will Substitute Grants for Loans for All Students." *Today's News, Chronicle of Higher Education*, Monday, March 19, http://chronicle.com/daily/2007/03/2007031903n.htm (last accessed June 9, 2008).

Lipman Hearne. 2006. "A Report on High-Achieving Seniors and the College Decision: Key Insights." April, http://www.lipmanhearne.com/resources/ (last accessed June 7, 2006).

Lippman, Laura, Lina Guzman, Julie Dombrowski Keith, Akemi Kinukawa, Rebecca Shwalb, and Peter Tice. 2008. *Parent Expectations and Planning for College: Statistical Analysis Report*. NCES 2008–079, April. Washington, DC: National Center for Education Statistics, Institute of Education Sciences, U.S. Department of Education.

Liptak, Adam. 2007. "In Students' Eyes, Look-Alike Lawyers Don't Make the Grade." *New York Times*, October 29, p. A10.

Little, Roderick J. A. 1988. "Missing-Data Adjustments in Large Surveys." *Journal of Business and Economic Statistics* 6(3): 287–96.

Liu, Goodwin. 2007. "Seattle and Louisville." *California Law Review* 95(1): 277–317.

Logan, John R., Brian J. Stults, and Reynolds Farley. 2004. "Segregation of Minorities in the Metropolis: Two Decades of Change." *Demography* 41(1): 1–22.

Lombardi, Kate Stone. 2003. "Ready, or Not." *New York Times*, November 9, p. 4A13.

———. 2004. "Tutoring for the Already Brainy." *New York Times*, May 23, p. 14WC1.

Lomibao, Stephanie, Matt A. Barreto, and Harry P. Pachon. 2004. "The Reality of Race-Neutral Admissions for Minority Students at the University of California: Turning the Tide or Turning Them Away?" Los Angeles: Tomás Rivera Policy Institute, University of Southern California.

Long, Bridget Terry. 2004. "How Have College Decisions Changed Over Time? An Application of the Conditional Logistic Choice Model." *Journal of Econometrics* 121(1–2): 271–96.

Long, Bridget Terry, and Erin Riley. 2007. "Financial Aid: A Broken Bridge to College Access?" *Harvard Educational Review* 77(1): 39–63.

Long, Mark C. 2004a. "College Applications and the Effect of Affirmative Action." *Journal of Econometrics* 121(1–2): 319–42.

———. 2004b. "Race and College Admissions: An Alternative to Affirmative Action?" *Review of Economics and Statistics* 86(4): 1020–33.

———. 2007a. "Affirmative Action and Its Alternatives in Public Universities: What Do We Know?" *Public Administration Review* 67(2): 315–30.

———. 2007b. "College Quality and Early Adult Outcomes." *Economics of Education Review*, doi:10.1016/j.econedurev.2007.04.004.

Loury, Glenn C. 1997. "How to Mend Affirmative Action." *The Public Interest* 127: 33–43.

Loury, Linda Datcher, and David Garman. 1995. "College Selectivity and Earnings." *Journal of Labor Economics* 13(2): 289–308.

Lucas, Samuel R. 1999. *Tracking Inequality: Stratification and Mobility in American High Schools*. New York: Teachers' College Press.

Lucas, Samuel R., and Marcel Paret. 2005. "Law, Race, and Education in the United States." *Annual Review of Law and Social Science* 1: 203–31.

Ludwig, Jens, and Isabel Sawhill. 2007. *Success by Ten: Intervening Early, Often, and Effectively in the Education of Young Children*. Hamilton Project, Discussion Paper 2007–02, February. Washington, DC: Brookings Institution.

Malkiel, Nancy Weiss. 2003. "Truth in Grading: Proposals and Questions." Memo to Members of the Faculty from Nancy Weiss Malkiel, for the Faculty

Committee on Examinations and Standing, February 20, Office of the Dean of the College, Princeton University.

Manski, Charles F., and David A. Wise. 1983. *College Choice in America*. Cambridge, MA: Harvard University Press.

Marcus, David L., and Emily Sohn. 2001. "Didn't Get in? You're Not Alone: Record Applicants and Fewer Openings." *U.S. News & World Report*, April 30, 130(17): 49.

Marks, Marilyn. 2001. "Grants to Replace Loans." *Princeton Weekly Bulletin* 90(15), February 5, p. 1.

Martin, Philip, and Gottfried Zürcher. 2008. "Managing Migration: The Global Challenge." *Population Bulletin* 63(1): 3–20. Washington, DC: Population Reference Bureau.

Martínez Alemán, Ana M. 2000. "Race Talks: Undergraduate Women of Color and Female Friendships." *Review of Higher Education* 23(2): 133–52.

Massey, Douglas S. 2007. *Categorically Unequal: The American Stratification System*. New York: Russell Sage Foundation.

Massey, Douglas S., and Nancy A. Denton. 1993. *American Apartheid: Segregation and the Making of the Underclass*. Cambridge, MA: Harvard University Press.

Massey, Douglas S., and Margarita Mooney. 2007. "The Effects of America's Three Affirmative Action Programs on Academic Performance." *Social Problems* 54(1): 99–117.

Massey, Douglas S., Camille Z. Charles, Garvey F. Lundy, and Mary J. Fischer. 2003. *The Source of the River: The Social Origins of Freshmen at America's Selective Colleges and Universities*. Princeton: Princeton University Press.

Massey, Douglas S., Margarita Mooney, Kimberly C. Torres, and Camille Z. Charles. 2007. "Black Immigrants and Black Natives Attending Selective Colleges and Universities in the United States." *American Journal of Education* 113(2): 243–71.

Mattern, Krista D., Brian F. Patterson, Emily J. Shaw, Jennifer L. Kobrin, and Sandra M. Barbuti. 2008. *Differential Validity and Prediction of the SAT*, Research Report No. 2008–4. New York: The College Board. http://professionals .collegeboard.com/profdownload/Differential_Validity_and_Prediction_of_the _SAT.pdf (last accessed July 4, 2008).

Maxwell, Lesli A. 2007. "The 'Other' Gap." *Education Week*, February 14, 26(23): 26–29.

Mayher, Bill. 1998. *The College Admissions Mystique*. New York: Farrar, Straus and Giroux.

McCormack, Eugene. 2007. "Number of Foreign Students Bounces Back to Near-Record High." *Chronicle of Higher Education*, November 16, 54(12): A1.

McCormick, Marie C., Steven L. Gortmaker, and Arthur M. Sobol. 1990. "Very Low Birth Weight Children: Behavior Problems and School Difficulty in a National Sample." *Journal of Pediatrics* 117(5): 687–93.

McCullagh, Peter. 1980. "Regression Models for Ordinal Data." *Journal of the Royal Statistical Society*, Series B (Methodological), 42(2): 109–42.

McDonald, Judith A., and Robert J. Thornton. 2007. "Do New Male and Female College Graduates Receive Unequal Pay?" *Journal of Human Resources* 42(1): 32–48.

McDonough, Patricia M. 1994. "Buying and Selling Higher Education: The Social Construction of the College Applicant." *Journal of Higher Education* 65(4): 427–46.

———. 1997. *Choosing Colleges: How Social Class and Schools Structure Opportunity*. Albany: State University of New York Press.

———. 2005. "Counseling and College Counseling in America's High Schools." *National Association for College Admission Counseling*, White Paper, January, Alexandria, VA.

McGinn, Daniel. 2005. "Holding Less Sway." *Newsweek*, May 2, 145(18): 12.

McGlynn, Angela Provitera. 2006. "College on Credit Has Kids Dropping Out." *Education Digest* 71(8): 57–60.

McKinney, Arlise P., Kevin D. Carlson, Ross L. Mecham III, Nicholas C. D'Angelo, and Mary L. Connerly. 2003. "Recruiters' Use of GPA in Initial Screening Decisions: Higher GPAs Don't Always Make the Cut." *Personnel Psychology* 56(4): 823–45.

McLanahan, Sara, and Gary Sandefur. 1994. *Growing Up with a Single Parent: What Hurts, What Helps*. Cambridge, MA: Harvard University Press.

McNeil, Michele. 2007. "Rigorous Courses, Fresh Enrollment." *Education Week* 26(36): 28–31.

McPherson, Michael S., and Morton Owen Schapiro. 1991. *Keeping College Affordable: Government and Educational Opportunity*. Washington, DC: Brookings Institution.

———. 1998. *The Student Aid Game: Meeting Need and Rewarding Talent in American Higher Education*. Princeton: Princeton University Press.

———, eds. 2006a. *College Access: Opportunity or Privilege?* New York: The College Board.

———. 2006b. "Introduction." Pp. 3–15 in Michael S. McPherson and Morton Owen Schapiro, eds., *College Access: Opportunity or Privilege?* New York: The College Board.

McPherson, Miller, Lynn Smith-Lovin, and James M. Cook. 2001. "Birds of a Feather: Homophily in Social Networks." *Annual Review of Sociology* 27: 415–44.

Melguizo, Tatiana. 2007. "Latino and African-American Students' Transfer Pathway to Elite Education in California." *Change* 39(6): 52–55.

———. 2008. "Quality Matters: Assessing the Impact of Attending More Selective Institutions on College Completion Rates of Minorities." *Research in Higher Education* 49(3): 214–36.

Menand, Louis. 2003. "The Thin Envelope." *The New Yorker*, April 7, 79(7): 88–92.

Milem, Jeffrey F. 2003. "The Educational Benefits of Diversity: Evidence from Multiple Sectors." Pp. 126–69 in Mitchell J. Chang, Daria Witt, James Jones, and Kenji Hakuta, eds., *Compelling Interest: Examining the Evidence on Racial Dynamics in Colleges and Universities*. Stanford: Stanford University Press.

Millet, Catherine M. 2003. "How Undergraduate Loan Debt Affects Application and Enrollment in Graduate or First Professional School." *Journal of Higher Education* 72(4): 386–427.

Mishel, Lawrence, and Joydeep Roy. 2006. *Rethinking High School Graduation Rates and Trends*. Washington, DC: Economic Policy Institute.

Mishel, Lawrence, Jared Bernstein, and Sylvia Allegretto. 2007. *The State of Working America 2006/2007*. Ithaca, NY: Economic Policy Institute/ILR Press.

Monks, James, and Ronald G. Ehrenberg. 1999. "*U.S. News & World Report* Rankings: Why They Do Matter." *Change* 31 (November/December): 43–51.

Moody, James. 2001. "Race, School Integration, and Friendship Segregation in America." *American Journal of Sociology* 107(3): 679–716.

Mooney, Margarita. 2005. "Does Religion Influence College Satisfaction or Grades Earned? Evidence from the National Longitudinal Survey of Freshmen (NLSF)." Paper presented at the 67th Annual Meetings of the Association for the Sociology of Religion, Philadelphia, August 13–15.

Moore, Calvin C. 2002. *A Report to the Berkeley Faculty on Undergraduate Admission and Comprehensive Review: 1995–2002*. Submitted by the Committee on Admissions, Enrollment, and Preparatory Education (AEPE), May, University of California, Berkeley.

Morales, Pamilla C., and Robbie Steward. 1996. "Biracial Identification, Familial Influence and Levels of Acculturation." Paper presented at the 104th Annual Meetings of the American Psychological Association, Toronto, August 9–13.

Morrison, Peter A. 1979. "The Shifting Regional Balance." *American Demographics* 1(5): 9–15.

Myers, Samuel L., and Chanjin Chung. 1996. "Racial Differences in Home Ownership and Home Equity among Preretirement-Aged Households." *The Gerontologist* 36(3): 350–60.

Myrdal, Gunnar. 1944. *An American Dilemma: The Negro Problem and Modern Democracy*. New York: Harper and Brothers.

National Association for College Admission Counseling. 2003. *Diversity and College Admission in 2003: A Survey Report*. September, Alexandria, VA.

National Center for Education Statistics. 2004. *Digest of Education Statistics, 2003*. Washington, DC: U.S. Department of Education.

———. 2006. "Total Fall Enrollment in Degree-Granting Institutions, by Race/Ethnicity of Student and Type and Control of Institution: Selected Years, 1976 through 2005." *Digest of Education Statistics*, Table 211. http://nces.ed.gov/programs/digest/d06/tables/dt06_211.asp (last accessed March 11, 2008).

———. 2007a. "NAEP Data Explorer." http://nces.ed.gov/nationsreportcard/nde/viewresults.asp (last accessed September 17, 2007).

———. 2007b. *Projections of Education Statistics to 2016*. NCES 2008–060, December. Washington, DC: Institute of Education Sciences, U.S. Department of Education. http://nces.ed.gov/programs/projections/projections2016 (last accessed April 16, 2008).

———. 2007c. "Student Effort and Educational Progress: Transition to College." *The Condition of Education*. Washington, DC: Institute of Education Sciences, U.S. Department of Education. http://nces.ed.gov/programs/coe/2007 (last accessed April 16, 2008).

———. 2007d. *The Integrated Postsecondary Education Data System (IPEDS), Peer Analysis System*. http://nces.ed.gov/ipedspas/ (last accessed October 29, 2007).

National Opinion Research Center. 2000. "A Review of the Methodology for the U.S. News & World Report's Rankings of Undergraduate Colleges and Universities." *Washington Monthly*, http://www.washingtonmonthly.com/features/2000/norc (last accessed August 4, 2006).

National Science Board. 2008. *Science and Engineering Indicators 2008*. 2 vols. Arlington, VA: National Science Foundation.

Neal, Derek A., and William R. Johnson. 1996. "The Role of Premarket Factors in Black-White Wage Differences." *Journal of Political Economy* 104(5): 869–95.

Nellie Mae. 2005. "Undergraduate Students and Credit Cards in 2004: An Analysis of Usage Rates and Trends." May, http://www.nelliemae.com/library/ccstudy_2005.pdf (last accessed June 29, 2006).

New Commission on the Skills of the American Workforce. 2007. *Tough Choices or Tough Times*. National Center on Education and the Economy. San Francisco: Jossey-Bass.

New Strategist Editors. 2006. *Racial and Ethnic Diversity: Asians, Blacks, Hispanics, Native Americans, and Whites*. 5th ed. Ithaca, NY: New Strategist Publications.

Nisbett, Richard E. 2007. "All Brains Are the Same Color." Op-Ed contribution, *New York Times*, December 9, p. 4.11.

Nishimura, Nancy J. 1998. "Assessing the Issues of Multiracial Students on College Campuses." *Journal of College Counseling* 1(1): 45–54.

Nonis, Sarath A., and Gail I. Hudson. 2006. "Academic Performance of College Students: Influence of Time Spent Studying and Working." *Journal of Education for Business* 81(3): 151–59.

O'Regan, Katherine M., and John M. Quigley. 1996. "Teenage Employment and the Spatial Isolation of Minority and Poverty Households." *Journal of Human Resources* 31(3): 692–703.

Office of Analysis and Information Management. 2007. "New Freshmen Admissions by Ethnicity, Fall 1991 to Fall 2007." *UCLA AIM*. http:// www.aim.ucla.edu/Statistics/admisions/NewFreshmenByEthnicityFall2007.pdf (last accessed February 19, 2008).

Ohland, Matthew W., Guili Zhang, Brian Thorndyke, and Timothy J. Anderson. 2004. "Grade-Point Average, Changes of Major, and Majors Selected by Students Leaving Engineering." Paper presented at 34th ASEE/IEEE Frontiers in Education Conference, Savannah, GA, October 20–23.

Oliver, Melvin L., and Thomas M. Shapiro. 1995. *Black Wealth/White Wealth: A New Perspective on Racial Inequality*. New York: Routledge.

Orcutt, Guy H. 1957. "A New Type of Socio-Economic System." *Review of Economics and Statistics* 80: 1081–1100.

Orcutt, Guy H., Martin Greenberger, John Korbel, and Alice M. Rivlin. 1961. *Microanalysis of Socioeconomic Systems: A Simulation Study*. New York: Harper and Row.

Oregon College Savings Plan. 2005. "College Savings Projector." March 15, http://www.oregoncollegesavings.com/pdf/CollegeSavingsProjector.pdf (last accessed May 23, 2006).

———. 2006. "The Future: The Rising Cost of a Four-Year Education." http://www.oregoncollegesavings.com/ (last accessed July 16, 2006).

Orfield, Gary, ed. 2001. *Diversity Challenged: Evidence on the Impact of Affirmative Action*. Civil Rights Project, Harvard University. Cambridge, MA: Harvard Education Publishing Group.

Orfield, Gary, and Chungmei Lee. 2006. *Racial Transformation and the Changing Nature of Segregation*. Cambridge, MA: Civil Rights Project, Harvard University.

Ostrove, Joan M., and Susan M. Long. 2007. "Social Class and Belonging: Implications for College Adjustment." *Review of Higher Education* 30(4): 363–89.

Page, Lindsay C., Richard J. Murnane, and John B. Willett. 2008. "Understanding Trends in the Black-White Achievement Gap: The Importance of Decomposition Methodology." Paper presented at the Annual Meetings of the American Educational Research Association, New York, March 24–28.

Page, Scott E. 2007. *The Difference: How the Power of Diversity Creates Better Groups, Firms, Schools, and Societies*. Princeton: Princeton University Press.

Pager, Devah. 2003. "The Mark of a Criminal Record." *American Journal of Sociology* 108(5): 937–75.

Palmer, Scott R. 2001. "Diversity and Affirmative Action: Evolving Principles and Continuing Legal Battles." Pp. 81–98 in Gary Orfield, ed., *Diversity Challenged: Evidence on the Impact of Affirmative Action*. Civil Rights Project, Harvard University. Cambridge, MA: Harvard Education Publishing Group.

Paneth, Nigel. 1995. "The Problem of Low Birth Weight." *The Future of Children: Low Birth Weight* 5(1): 19–34.

Pascarella, Ernest T., and John C. Smart. 1991. "Impact of Intercollegiate Athletic Participation for African American and Caucasian Men: Some Further Evidence." *Journal of College Student Development* 32: 123–30.

Pascarella, Ernest T., and Patrick Terrenzini. 1991. *How College Affects Students*. San Francisco: Jossey-Bass.

Passel, Jeffrey S., and D'Vera Cohn. 2008. *U.S. Population Projections: 2005–2050*. February 11. Washington, DC: Pew Research Center.

Patterson, Orlando. 2001. "Race by the Numbers." *New York Times*, May 8, p. A27.

Paul, Bill. 1995a. "Getting In: An Inside Look at Admissions and Its Dean, Fred Hargadon." *Princeton Alumni Weekly*, November 22, pp. 11–19.

———. 1995b. *Getting In: Inside the College Admissions Process*. Cambridge, MA: Perseus Publishing.

———. 2000. "Another Roadblock for Equal Access to College: The 'Counselor Advantage.'" *Chronicle of Higher Education*, March 10, 46(27): B9.

Perie, Marianne, Rebecca Moran, and Anthony D. Lutkus. 2005. *NAEP 2004 Trends in Academic Progress: Three Decades of Student Performance in Reading and Mathematics* (NCES 2005–464). Washington, DC: National Center for Education Statistics, Institute of Education Sciences, U.S. Department of Education.

Persell, Caroline Hodges, and Peter W. Cookson Jr. 1985. "Chartering and Bartering: Elite Education and Social Reproduction." *Social Problems* 33(2): 114–29.

Persell, Caroline Hodges, Sophia Catsambis, and Peter W. Cookson Jr. 1992. "Differential Asset Conversion: Class and Gendered Pathways to Selective Colleges." *Sociology of Education* 65(3): 208–25.

Pfeffer, Fabian T. 2007. "Intergenerational Educational Mobility in Comparative Perspective: Persistent Inequality in Educational Attainment and its Institutional Context." Working Paper 2007–09, Center for Demography and Ecology, University of Wisconsin, Madison.

Phillips, Meredith, and Tiffani Chin. 2004. "School Inequality: What Do We Know?" Pp. 467–519 in Kathryn M. Neckerman, ed., *Social Inequality*. New York: Russell Sage Foundation.

Phillips, Meredith, James Crouse, and John Ralph. 1998. "Does the Black-White Test Score Gap Widen after Children Enter School?" Pp. 229–72 in Christopher Jencks and Meredith Phillips, eds., *The Black-White Test Score Gap*. Washington, DC: Brookings Institution Press.

Phillips, Meredith, Jeanne Brooks-Gunn, Greg J. Duncan, Pamela Klebanov, and Jonathan Crane. 1998. "Family Background, Parenting Practices, and the Black-White Test Score Gap." Pp. 103–45 in Christopher Jencks and Meredith Phillips, eds., *The Black-White Test Score Gap*. Washington, DC: Brookings Institution Press.

Pidot, Justin. 2006. "Intuition or Proof: The Social Science Justification for the Diversity Rationale in *Grutter v. Bollinger* and *Gratz v. Bollinger*." *Stanford Law Review* 59(3): 761–808.

Pike, Gary R. 1993. "The Relationship between Perceived Learning and Satisfaction with College: An Alternative View." *Research in Higher Education* 34(1): 23–40.

———. 1994. "The Relationship between Alumni Satisfaction and Work Experiences." *Research in Higher Education* 35(1): 105–23.

Piketty, Thomas, and Emmanuel Saez. 2003. "Income Inequality in the United States, 1913–1998." *Quarterly Journal of Economics* 118(1): 1–39.

Plessy v. Ferguson, 163 U.S. 537 (1896).

Polaski, Sandra. 2007. "U.S. Living Standards in an Era of Globalization." *Policy Brief* No. 53, July. Washington, DC: Carnegie Endowment for International Peace.

Portes, Alejandro, and Rubén G. Rumbaut. 2001. *Legacies: The Story of the Immigrant Second Generation*. Berkeley: University of California Press.

Powers, Donald E. 1993. "Coaching for the SAT: Summary of the Summaries and an Update." *Educational Measurement: Issues and Practice* 12(2): 24–30.

Powers, Donald E., and Donald A. Rock. 1999. "Effects of Coaching on SAT I: Reasoning Test Scores." *Journal of Educational Measurement* 36(2): 93–118.

Princeton Review. 2008. "SAT Tutoring Programs." http://testprep.princeton review.com/coursetutor/search.aspx (last accessed April 29, 2008).

Princeton University. 2007. "Undergraduate Admission and Enrollment." *A Princeton Profile, 2007–08*, http://www.princeton.edu/pr/facts/profile/07/admissions (last accessed January 21, 2008).

Project on Student Debt. 2006. "Quick Facts about Student Debt." April 4, http://projectonstudentdebt.org/pub_home.php (last accessed May 7, 2006).

Pryor, John H. 2007. Personal communication. Cooperative Institutional Research Program, UCLA Higher Education Research Institute, Los Angeles, March 23.

Pryor, John H., Sylvia Hurtado, Jessica Sharkness, and William S. Korn. 2007. *The American Freshman: National Norms for Fall 2007*. Los Angeles: Higher Education Research Institute, UCLA.

Pryor, John H., Sylvia Hurtado, Victor B. Saenz, José Luis Santos, and William S. Korn. 2007. *The American Freshman: Forty-Year Trends, 1966–2006*. April. Los Angeles: Higher Education Research Institute, UCLA.

Qian, Zhenchao. 2004a. "Options: Racial/Ethnic Identification of Children of Intermarried Couples." *Social Science Quarterly* 85(3): 746–66.

———. 2004b. "Race of the Minority Parent and Racial Identity of Children of Intermarried Couples." Paper presented at the Annual Meetings of the Population Association of America, Boston, April 1–3.

Qian, Zhenchao, and Daniel T. Lichter. 2007. "Social Boundaries and Marital Assimilation: Interpreting Trends in Racial and Ethnic Intermarriage." *American Sociological Review* 72(1): 68–94.

Quinn, Jane Bryant. 2006. "New Math for College Costs, We're Seeing More 'Sorting' by Income in American Education: The Average Private College Is Trolling for Students Who Can Pay." *Newsweek*, March 13, 147(11): 43.

Quiñones, Eric. 2005. "Graduates of First 'No Loan' Class Look to Future." *The Princeton Weekly Bulletin*, May 30, 94(28), http://www.princeton.edu/pr/pwb/05/0530/1b.shtml (last accessed June 19, 2006).

Radford, Alexandria Walton. 2008. "Another Shade of White? Indian Immigrants' Identity in the United States." Pp. 86–106 in Charles A. Gallagher, ed., *Racism in Post-Race America: New Theories, New Directions*. Chapel Hill, NC: Social Forces.

Reardon, Sean F. 2008. "Differential Growth in the Black-White Achievement Gap during Elementary School among Initially High- and Low-Scoring Students." Working Paper 2008–03, March, Institute for Research on Education Policy and Practice, Stanford University, Palo Alto, CA.

"Rebuilding the American Dream Machine." 2006. *The Economist*, January 21, pp. 29–30.

Regents of the University of California v. Bakke, 438 U.S. 265 (1978).

Report of the Knight Foundation, Commission on Intercollegiate Athletics. 2001. *A Call to Action: Reconnecting College Sports and Higher Education*. June, John S. and James L. Knight Foundation, Miami, FL.

Rimer, Sara, and Karen W. Arenson. 2004. "Top Colleges Take More Blacks, But Which Ones?" *New York Times*, June 24, p. A1.

Rimer, Sara, and Alan Finder. 2007. "Harvard to Aid Students High in Middle Class." *New York Times*, December 11, p. A1.

Roksa, Josipa. 2005. "Double Disadvantage or Blessing in Disguise? Understanding the Relationship between College Major and Employment Sector." *Sociology of Education* 78(3): 207–32.

Rong, Xue Lan, and Frank Brown. 2001. "The Effects of Immigrant Generation and Ethnicity on Educational Attainment among Young African and Caribbean Blacks in the United States." *Harvard Educational Review* 71(3): 536–65.

Rong, Xue Lan, and Linda Grant. 1992. "Ethnicity, Generation, and School Attainment of Asians, Hispanics, and Non-Hispanic Whites." *Sociological Quarterly* 33(4): 625–36.

Roper Center. 2003. "Time/CNN/Harris Interactive Poll: Terrorism/Iraq/2004 Presidential Election/Affirmative Action." Conducted by Harris Interactive, February 19–20. http://www.ropercenter.uconn.edu/sdaweb/SDA0003.html (last accessed April 4, 2007).

RoperASW. 2002. *Methodology Report, College Student Composition Study*. RoperASW Number: NQMP01. February. Princeton, NJ: RoperASW, NOP World.

Rosenbaum, Paul R. 1995. *Observational Studies*. New York: Springer-Verlag.

Rothman, Stanley, Seymour Martin Lipset, and Neil Nevitte. 2003. "Racial Diversity Reconsidered." *The Public Interest* 151: 25–38.

Rothstein, Jesse M. 2004. "College Performance Predictions and the SAT." *Journal of Econometrics* 121: 297–317.

Rothstein, Jesse M., and Cecilia Elena Rouse. 2007. "Constrained after College: Student Loans and Early Career Occupational Choices." Working Paper 13117, May. Cambridge, MA: National Bureau of Economic Research.

Rothstein, Richard. 2004. *Class and Schools: Using Social, Economic, and Educational Reform to Close the Black-White Achievement Gap*. Washington, DC: Economic Policy Institute.

Rouse, Cecilia, Jeanne Brooks-Gunn, and Sara McLanahan. 2005. "Introducing the Issue." *The Future of Children* 15(1): 5–14.

Rytina, Steve, and David L. Morgan. 1982. "The Arithmetic of Social Relations: The Interplay of Category and Network." *American Journal of Sociology* 88(1): 88–113.

Sabot, Richard, and John Wakeman-Linn. 1991. "Grade Inflation and Course Choice." *Journal of Economic Perspectives* 5(1): 159–70.

Sacks, Peter. 2007a. "How Colleges Perpetuate Inequality." *Chronicle Review*, *Chronicle of Higher Education*, January 12, 53(19): B9.

———. 2007b. *Tearing down the Gates: Confronting the Class Divide in American Education*. Berkeley: University of California Press.

Saks, Raven E., and Stephen H. Shore. 2005. "Risk and Career Choice." *Advances in Economic Analysis & Policy* 5(1): 1–43.

Sander, Richard H. 2004. "A Systemic Analysis of Affirmative Action in American Law Schools." *Stanford Law Review* 57: 367–483.

Sanoff, Alvin P. 1999. "A Parent's Plea: Our High Schools Need Better College Counseling." *Chronicle of Higher Education*, February 12, 45(23): B7.

Sawhill, Isabel V. 2008. "Overview." Pp. 1–13 in Julia B. Isaacs, Isabel V. Sawhill, and Ron Haskins, *Getting Ahead or Losing Ground: Economic Mobility in America*. Economic Mobility Project. Washington, DC: Brookings Institution.

Sax, Linda J. 2007. "College Women Still Face Many Obstacles in Reaching Their Full Potential." *Chronicle of Higher Education*, September 28, 54(5): B46.

Sax, Linda J., Alexander W. Astin, William S. Korn, and Kathryn M. Mahoney. 1997. *The American Freshman: National Norms for Fall 1997*. Los Angeles: Higher Education Research Institute, UCLA.

Sax, Linda J., Alexander W. Astin, Jennifer A. Lindholm, William S. Korn, Victor B. Saenz, and Kathryn M. Mahoney. 2003. *The American Freshman: National Norms for Fall 2003*. Los Angeles: Higher Education Research Institute, UCLA.

Sax, Linda J., Sylvia Hurtado, Jennifer A. Lindholm, Alexander W. Astin, William S. Korn, and Kathryn M. Mahoney. 2004. *The American Freshman: National Norms for Fall 2004*. Los Angeles: Higher Education Research Institute, UCLA.

Schapiro, Morton Owen, Michael P. O'Malley, and Larry H. Litten. 1991. "Progression to Graduate School from the 'Elite' Colleges and Universities." *Economics of Education Review* 10(3): 221–44.

Schmidt, Peter. 2006a. "Educational Testing Service Accused of Suppressing Research on an Alternative to Affirmative Action." *Today's News, Chronicle of Higher Education*, Thursday, November 2, http://chronicle.com/daily/2006/11/2006110201n.htm (last accessed June 10, 2008).

———. 2006b. "Michigan Overwhelmingly Adopts Ban on Affirmative-Action Preferences." *Chronicle of Higher Education*, November 17, 53(13): A23–A24.

———. 2007a. "Legal Battles over a Ban on Preferences Heat Up." *Chronicle of Higher Education*, January 5, 53(18): A1, A24.

———. 2007b. "U. of Wisconsin Discusses Its Plan to Consider Applicants' Race Systemwide and Gets Mixed Reviews." *Today's News, Chronicle of Higher Education*, Tuesday, January 30, http://chronicle.com/daily/2007/01/2007013001n.htm (last accessed June 10, 2008).

———. 2007c. "What Color Is an A?" *Chronicle of Higher Education*, June 1, 53(39): A24.

———. 2007d. "5 More States May Curtail Affirmative Action." *Chronicle of Higher Education*, October 19, 54(8): A1.

———. 2008. "A University Examines Underlying Problems after Racist Incidents." *Chronicle of Higher Education*, March 14, 54(27): A18.

Schwartz, Stephen I., ed. 1998. *Atomic Audit: The Costs and Consequences of U.S. Nuclear Weapons since 1940*. Washington, DC: Brookings Institution Press.

Schwartz, Wendy. 1998. "The Identity Development of Multiracial Youth." *ERIC/CUE Digest*, No. 138.

Schweitzer, Sarah. 2006. "Class Matters: Lower-Income Students Bonding at Elite Schools." *Boston Globe*, May 13, p. B1.

Scott, Janny. 2005. "Life at the Top in America Isn't Just Better, It's Longer." Pp. 27–50 in Correspondents of the New York Times, *Class Matters*. New York: Henry Holt and Company.

Selingo, Jeffrey. 2005. "Michigan: Who Really Won?" *Chronicle of Higher Education*, January 14, 51(19): A21.

———. 2006. "Student-Aid Form Too Long, Scholars Say." *Chronicle of Higher Education*, May 12, 52(36): A34.

Selingo, Jeffrey, and Jeffrey Brainard. 2006. "The Rich-Poor Gap Widens for Colleges and Students." *Special Report, Chronicle of Higher Education*, April 7, 52(31): A1.

Sharpe, Rochelle. 1999. "Education: Beating the Ivy League Odds." *Wall Street Journal*, April 16, p. W1.

Shea, Rachel Hartigan, and David L. Marcus. 2001. "America's Best Colleges: The Competition Is Keener Than Ever; Here's What You Need to Know to Get a Spot at the School You Choose." *U.S. News & World Report*, September 17, 131(10): 88–96.

Shireman, Robert M. 2002. "Enrolling Economic Diversity." *New York Times*, May 4, p. A13.

Shulman, James L., and William G. Bowen. 2001. *The Game of Life: College Sports and Educational Values*. Princeton: Princeton University Press.

Sidanius, Jim, Colette Van Laar, Shana Levin, and Stacey Sinclair. 2004. "Ethnic Enclaves and the Dynamics of Social Identity on the College Campus: The Good, the Bad, and the Ugly." *Journal of Personality and Social Psychology* 87(1): 96–110.

Simmons, Ruth J. 2007. "How Does Life Outside the Classroom Contribute to the Educational Mission of a Residential University?" Princeton University Trustee Retreat, January 19, Princeton University.

Simpson, Jacqueline C. 2001. "Segregated by Subject: Racial Differences in the Factors Influencing Academic Major Between European Americans, Asian Americans, and African, Hispanic and Native Americans." *Journal of Higher Education* 72(1): 63–100.

Singell, Larry D. Jr., and Mark Stater. 2006. "Going, Going, Gone: The Effects of Aid Policies on Graduation at Three Large Public Institutions." *Policy Sciences* 39(4): 379–403.

Singell, Larry D. Jr., Glen R. Waddell, and Bradley R. Curs. 2006. "HOPE for the Pell? Institutional Effects in the Intersection of Merit-Based and Need-Based Aid." *Southern Economic Journal* 73(1): 79–99.

Small, Mario L., and Christopher Winship. 2007. "Black Students' Graduation from Elite Colleges: Institutional Characteristics and Between-Institution Differences." *Social Science Research* 36(3): 1257–75.

Smallwood, Scott. 2006. "People Oppose Government Interference in Academe, Poll Finds, But Some Are Wary of Radical Professors." *Chronicle of Higher Education*, June 16, 52(41): A1.

Smart, John C. 1986. "College Effects on Occupational Status Attainment." *Research in Higher Education* 24(1): 73–95.

Smelser, Neil J., William Julius Wilson, and Faith Mitchell. 2001. "Introduction." Pp. 1–20 in Neil J. Smelser, William Julius Wilson, and Faith Mitchell, eds., *America Becoming: Racial Trends and Their Consequences*. Vol. 1. Washington, DC: National Academy Press.

Smith, Daryl G., Jose Moreno, Alma R. Clayton-Pedersen, Sharon Parker, and Daniel Hiroyuki Teraguchi. 2005. "'Unknown' Students on College Campuses." *Insight*, James Irvine Foundation, December, San Francisco.

Smith, Daryl G., Guy L. Gerbick, Mark A. Figueroa, Gayle Harris Watkins, Thomas Levitan, Leeshawn Cradoc Moore, Pamela A. Merchant, Haim Dov Beliak, and Benjamin Figueroa. 1997. *Diversity Works: The Emerging Picture of How Students Benefit*. Washington, DC: Association of American Colleges and Universities.

Smith, Lauren. 2007a. "Four Decades of Survey Data on American Freshmen Reveal Widening Socioeconomic Gap." *Today's News, Chronicle of Higher Education*, Monday, April 9, http://chronicle.com/daily/2007/04/2007040906n.htm (last accessed June 10, 2008).

Smith, Lauren. 2007b. "Many Public Colleges Have Raised Tuition Despite Increases in State Support." *Chronicle of Higher Education*, October 5, 54(6): A20.

Smith, Sandra S., and Mignon R. Moore. 2000. "Intraracial Diversity and Relations among African-Americans: Closeness among Black Students at a Predominantly White University." *American Journal of Sociology* 106(1): 1–39.

Smith, Tom W. 2003. "A Review of Methods to Estimate the Status of Cases with Unknown Eligibility." September, Version 1.1. Report prepared for the AAPOR Standard Definitions Committee and presented to AAPOR, Phoenix, AZ, May 2004.

Soares, Joseph A. 2007. *The Power of Privilege: Yale and America's Elite Colleges*. Stanford: Stanford University Press.

Southern Regional Educational Board. 2006. "Latest Data Confirm a College Affordability Gap for Students from Middle- and Lower-Income Families." *Fact Book Bulletin*, June, http://www.sreb.org/main/EdData/Bulletin/60E08-June06 .pdf (last accessed June 21, 2006).

Sowell, Thomas. 1972. *Black Education: Myths and Tragedies*. New York: McKay.

———. 1993. *Inside American Education: The Decline, the Deception, the Dogmas*. New York: Free Press.

———. 2004. *Affirmative Action around the World: An Empirical Study*. New Haven: Yale University Press.

Steele, Claude M. 1997. "A Threat in the Air: How Stereotypes Shape Intellectual Identity and Performance." *American Psychologist* 52(6): 613–27.

Steele, Claude M., and Joshua Aronson. 1998. "Stereotype Threat and the Test Performance of Academically Successful African Americans." Pp. 401–30 in Christopher Jencks and Meredith Phillips, eds., *The Black-White Test Score Gap*. Washington, DC: Brookings Institution Press.

Steinberg, Jacques. 2002. *The Gatekeepers: Inside the Admissions Process of a Premier College*. New York: Viking Penguin.

———. 2003. "College-Entrance Preferences for the Well Connected Draw Ire." *New York Times*, February 13, p. A24.

Steinecke, Ann, James Beaudreau, Ruth B. Bletzinger, and Charles Terrell. 2007. "Race-Neutral Admission Approaches: Challenges and Opportunities for Medical Schools." *Academic Medicine* 82(2): 117–26.

Stephan, Walter G., and Cookie White Stephan. 1991. "Intermarriage: Effects on Personality, Adjustment, and Intergroup Relations in Two Samples of Students." *Journal of Marriage and the Family* 53(1): 241–50.

Stern, Robert. 2006. "College Applicants Are Less Willing to Gamble." *Trenton Times*, February 19, p. A1.

Stevens, Mitchell L. 2006. "Organizational Mechanisms of Inequality in Selective College Admissions." Unpublished manuscript, Department of Humanities and Social Sciences, Steinhardt School of Education, New York University.

———. 2007. *Creating a Class: College Admissions and the Education of Elites*. Cambridge, MA: Harvard University Press.

Stinebrickner, Todd R., and Ralph Stinebrickner. 2007. "The Effect of Credit Constraints on the College Drop-Out Decision: A Direct Approach Using a

New Panel Study." Working Paper 13340, August. Cambridge, MA: National Bureau of Economic Research.

Stodghill, Ron. 2007. "Is There Room at the Top for Black Executives?" *New York Times*, November 1, p. C1.

Stohr, Greg. 2004. *A Black and White Case: How Affirmative Action Survived Its Greatest Legal Challenge*. Princeton, NJ: Bloomberg Press.

Straight, Ronald L. 2002. "Wealth: Asset-Accumulation Differences by Race—SCF Data, 1995 and 1998." *American Economic Review* 92(2): 330–34.

Strauss, Linda C., and J. Fredericks Volkwein. 2002. "Comparing Student Performance and Growth in 2- and 4-Year Institutions." *Research in Higher Education* 43(2): 133–61.

Stringer, William L., Alisa F. Cunningham, Colleen T. O'Brien, and Jamie P. Merisotis. 1998. "It's All Relative: The Role of Parents in College Financing and Enrollment." *Institute of Higher Education Policy*, October, http://www.ihep .org/organizations.php3?action=printContentItem&orgid=104&typeID=906& itemID=9257 (last accessed November 9, 2007).

Sum, Andrew, Ishwar Khatiwada, Joseph McLaughlin, and Paulo Tobar. 2007. *The Educational Attainment of the Nation's Young Black Men and Their Recent Labor Market Experiences: What Can Be Done to Improve Their Future Labor Market and Educational Prospects?* February, Center for Labor Market Studies, Northeastern University, Boston.

Suskind, Ron. 1998. *A Hope in the Unseen: An American Odyssey from the Inner City to the Ivy League*. New York: Broadway Books.

Swanson, Christopher B. 2004. *Who Graduates? Who Doesn't? A Statistical Portrait of Public High School Graduation, Class of 2001*. Education Policy Center, Urban Institute, Washington, DC.

Swarthout, Luke. 2006. "Paying Back, Not Giving Back: Student Debt's Negative Impact on Public Service Career Opportunities." *State PIRGs' Higher Education Project*, April, http://pirg.org/highered/highered.asp?id2=23337&id3= highered (last accessed June 21, 2006).

Tatum, Beverly Daniel. 1997. *"Why Are All the Black Kids Sitting Together in the Cafeteria?" And Other Conversations about Race*. New York: Basic Books.

———. 2007. *Can We Talk about Race? And Other Conversations in an Era of School Resegregation*. Boston: Beacon Press.

Taylor, Edward, and Steven G. Olswang. 1997. "Crossing the Color Line: African Americans and Predominantly White Universities." *College Student Journal* 31: 11–18.

Tebbs, Jeffrey, and Sarah Turner. 2006. "The Challenge of Improving the Representation of Low-Income Students at Flagship Universities: AccessUVa and the University of Virginia." Pp. 103–15 in Michael S. McPherson and Morton Owen Schapiro, eds., *College Access: Opportunity or Privilege?* New York: The College Board.

Terrell, Kenneth. 1998. "Are Consultants Worth the Cost?" *U.S. News & World Report*, August 31, 125(8): 80.

Thernstrom, Abigail, and Stephan Thernstrom. 2003. *No Excuses: Closing the Racial Gap in Learning*. New York: Simon and Schuster.

Thernstrom, Stephan, and Abigail Thernstrom. 1997. *America in Black and White: One Nation, Indivisible.* New York: Simon and Schuster.

———. 1999. "Reflections on *The Shape of the River.*" *UCLA Law Review* 46(5): 1583–1631.

Thomas, Clarence. 2003. Dissenting Opinion of J. Thomas. *Grutter v. Bollinger.* 539 U.S. 306, pp. 1–31.

Thomas, Gail E. 1985. "College Major and Career Inequality: Implications for Black Students." *Journal of Negro Education* 54(4): 537–47.

Tienda, Marta, and Sunny Xinchun Niu. 2006. "Capitalizing on Segregation, Pretending Neutrality: College Admissions and the Texas Top 10% Law." *American Law and Economics Review* 8(2): 312–46.

Tilghman, Shirley M. 2007. "Expanding Equal Opportunity: The Princeton Experience with Financial Aid." *Harvard Educational Review* 77(4): 435–41.

Tinto, Vincent. 1993. *Leaving College: Rethinking the Causes and Cures of Student Attrition.* 2nd ed. Chicago: University of Chicago Press.

Tomsho, Robert. 2006. "Saying 'No' to the Ivy League; Families Face Tough Choice as Back-Up Schools Boost Merit Aid for Top Students." *Wall Street Journal*, April 20, p. D1.

Tonn, Jessica L. 2005. "A Leg Up." *Education Week*, August 10, 24(44): 35–38.

Tooley, Jo Ann, and Arnesa Howell. 1995. "A Heavy Loan Burden." *U.S. News & World Report*, September 25, 119(12): 81–82, 84.

Toor, Rachel. 2000. "Pushy Parents and Other Tales of the Admissions Game." *Chronicle of Higher Education*, October 7, 47(6): B18.

———. 2001. *Admissions Confidential: An Insider's Account of the Elite College Selection Process.* New York: St. Martin's Press.

———. 2004. "Confessions of a Recovering Admissions Officer." *Chronicle of Higher Education*, April 30, 50(34): B16.

Tribe, Laurence H. 2003. *Brief of Harvard University, Brown University, the University of Chicago, Dartmouth College, Duke University, the University of Pennsylvania, Princeton University, and Yale University as Amici Curiae Supporting Respondents.* Grutter v. Bollinger, 123 S. Ct. 2325 (2003) (No. 02–241) and Gratz v. Bollinger, 123 S. Ct. 2411 (2003) (No. 02–516).

Turner, Sarah. 2006. "Higher Tuition, Higher Aid, and the Quest to Improve Opportunities for Low-Income Students: The Case of Virginia." Pp. 251–74 in Ronald G. Ehrenberg, ed., *What's Happening to Public Higher Education?* Westport, CT: American Council on Education/Praeger Series on Higher Education.

U.S. Bureau of Labor Statistics. 2008. "Consumer Price Index, All Urban Consumers, All Items." U.S. Department of Labor, http://data.bls.gov/cgi-bin/surveymost (last accessed March 7, 2008).

U.S. Census Bureau. 1974. "Social and Economic Characteristics of Students: October 1972." *Current Population Reports*, Series P-20, No. 260, Table 1. Washington, DC: U.S. GPO.

———. 2000a. "Census 2000 Demographic Profile Highlights." http://factfinder.census.gov/servlet/SAFFFacts?_submenuId=factsheet_1&_sse=on (last accessed April 5, 2006).

U.S. Census Bureau. 2000b. "Projections of the Total Resident Population by 5-Year Age Groups, Race, and Hispanic Origin with Special Age Categories: Middle Series, 1999 to 2100." NP-T4, http://www.census.gov/population/www/projections/natsum-T3.html, (last accessed September 18, 2007).

———. 2003. "No. HS-22. Educational Attainment by Sex: 1910 to 2002." http://www.census.gov/statab/hist/HS-22.pdf (last accessed April 18, 2006).

———. 2004. "Hispanic Heritage Month 2004: September 15–October 15." September 8, http://www.census.gov/Press-Release/www/releases/archives/facts_for_features_special_editions/002270.html (last accessed November 19, 2005).

———. 2005. "Asian/Pacific American Heritage Month, May 2005." April 29, http://www.census.gov/Press-Release/www/releases/archives/facts_for_features_special_editions/004522.html (last accessed November 19, 2005).

———. 2006a. "Homeownership by Race and Hispanic Origin: 2000, Historical Census of Housing Tables." Housing and Household Economic Statistics Division, http://www.census.gov/hhes/www/housing/census/historic/ownershipbyrace.html (last accessed September 15, 2006).

———. 2006b. "Housing Vacancies and Homeownership; Table 15. Housing Inventory Estimates by Age and Family Status." http://www.census.gov/hhes/www/housing/hvs/historic/index.html (last accessed September 9, 2006).

———. 2006c. "Income, Historical Income Tables—Families, Table F-5: Race and Hispanic Origin of Householder—Families by Median and Mean Income: 1947 to 2004." Housing and Household Economic Statistics Division, http://www.census.gov/hhes/www/income/histinc/f05.html, (last accessed September 9, 2006).

———. 2007. "Monthly Population Estimates by Age, Sex, Race and Hispanic Origin for the United States: April 1, 2000 to July 1, 2006." NC-EST2006-ALLDATA-R-File14.dat, http://www.census.gov/popest/national/asrh/2006_nat_res.html (last accessed September 17, 2007).

U.S. Commission on Civil Rights. 1992. *Civil Rights Issues Facing Asian Americans in the 1990s*. February. Washington, DC: GPO.

U.S. Department of Agriculture. 2005. "National School Lunch Program Fact Sheet." Food and Nutrition Service, http://www.fns.usda.gov/cnd/Lunch/AboutLunch/NSLPFactSheet.htm (last accessed November 22, 2005).

U.S. Department of Education. 2003. *The Condition of Education, 2003*. NCES 2003–067. Washington, DC: National Center for Education Statistics.

———. 2006. "Funding Education beyond High School: The Guide to Federal Student Aid, 2006–2007." *Federal Student Aid, Students Channel*, January, http://studentaid.ed.gov/PORTALSWebApp/students/english/publications.jsp (last accessed June 27, 2006).

U.S. News & World Report. 2005. *America's Best Colleges*. 2006 ed. August 29, 139(7). Washington, DC.

United States v. Fordice, 505 U.S. 717 (1992).

University of California, Berkeley. 2006. "Work Study: Students' Frequently Asked Questions." http://workstudy.berkeley.edu/Work-Study%20FAQ.htm (last accessed June 6, 2006).

University of Maryland. 1986. *Understanding and Increasing Students' Satisfaction with College. Maryland Longitudinal Study Research Highlights*.

Executive Summary. College Park: Division of Student Affairs, University of Maryland.

University of Michigan News Service. 2007. "U-M Enrollment Up in 2007–08." November 1, http://www.ns.umich.edu/htdocs/releases/print.php?htdocs/releases/plainstory.php?id=615 (last accessed February 18, 2008).

University of North Carolina at Chapel Hill. 2006. "Carolina Covenant." http://www.unc.edu/carolinacovenant/ (last accessed June 28, 2006).

University of Virginia. 2005. "Student Handbook Federal Work-Study (FWS) Program." Revised August 4. http://www.virginia.edu/financialaid/forms/Documentation/Student%20WS%20Handbook.pdf (last accessed June 6, 2006).

———. 2006. "Learn about Access UVA." http://www.virginia.edu/accessuva/learn.html (last accessed June 7, 2006).

USA Funds Education Access Report. 2004. "African-American-Student Retention Involves Unique Challenges." January 27, http://www.usafunds.org/news/27jan2004/dmp012704a.html (last accessed September 14, 2006).

Usher, Alex. 2006. *Grants for Students: What They Do, Why They Work*. Toronto: Educational Policy Institute, Canadian Education Report Series.

Van der Werf, Martin. 2007. "Endowments Celebrate a Streak." *Chronicle of Higher Education*, January 26, 53(21): 1, 25.

Van Laar, Colette, Shana Levin, Stacey Sinclair, and Jim Sidanius. 2005. "The Effect of University Roommate Contact on Ethnic Attitudes and Behavior." *Journal of Experimental Social Psychology* 41(4): 329–345.

Vars, Frederick E., and William G. Bowen. 1998. "Scholastic Aptitude Test Scores, Race, and Academic Performance in Selective Colleges and Universities." Pp. 457–79 in Christopher Jencks and Meredith Phillips, eds., *The Black-White Test Score Gap*. Washington, DC: Brookings Institution Press.

Verba, Sidney, Kay Lehman Schlozman, and Henry E. Brady. 2004. "Political Equality: What Do We Know about It?" Pp. 635–66 in Kathryn M. Neckerman, ed., *Social Inequality*. New York: Russell Sage Foundation.

Viadero, Debra. 2006a. "Race Report's Influence Felt 40 Years Later." *Education Week*, June 21, 25(41): 1.

———. 2006b. "Rags to Riches in U.S. Largely a Myth, Scholars Write." *Education Week*, October 25, 26(9): 8.

Walster, Elaine, T. Anne Cleary, and Margaret M. Clifford. 1971. "The Effect of Race and Sex on College Admission." *Sociology of Education* 44(2): 237–44.

Washburn, Jennifer. 2004. "The Tuition Crunch." *Atlantic Monthly* 293(1): 140.

Washington Monthly College Guide. 2006. "The RANKINGS: National Universities and Liberal Arts Colleges." *Washington Monthly* 38(9): 30–43.

Wasik, John F. 2006. "Figuring Out College Costs Is a Lesson in Math." *Asbury Park Press*, June 25, p. B7.

Wasley, Paula. 2006. "Stanford U. Increases Aid to Cover Tuition for Low-Income Students." *Chronicle of Higher Education*, March 31, 52(30): A39.

Wei, Christina Chang, and Lutz Berkner. 2008. *Trends in Undergraduate Borrowing II: Federal Student Loans in 1995–96, 1999–2000, and 2003–04*. NCES 2008–179. Washington, DC: National Center for Education Statistics, Institute of Education Sciences, U.S. Department of Education.

Weiss, Kenneth R. 1997. "UC Accused of Bias in Admissions; Education: Civil Rights Groups Allege in Federal Complaint That University Has Retained Graduate School Requirements That Favor Whites and Men." *Los Angeles Times*, March 20, p. 3.

Wertheimer, Linda K. 2002. "New Diversity Law Complicates Texas Graduate Schools' Admissions Policies." *Knight Ridder Tribune Business News*, February 25, p. 1.

West, Cornel. 2001. *Race Matters*. New York: Vintage Books.

Western, Bruce. 2006. *Punishment and Inequality in America*. New York: Russell Sage Foundation.

The White House. 2006. "A Quality Teacher in Every Classroom: Improving Teacher Quality and Enhancing the Profession." http://www.whitehouse.gov/infocus/education/teachers/quality-teachers.pdf (last accessed July 12, 2006).

Wiedeman, Reeves. 2008a. "Ban on Preferences Succeeds in Nebraska; Colorado Measure Remains Undecided." *Today's News, Chronicle of Higher Education*, Wednesday, November 5, http://chronicle.com/daily/2008/11/6652n.htm (last accessed December 5, 2008).

———. 2008b. "Colorado's Singular 'No'." *Chronicle of Higher Education*, November 21, 54(13): A4.

Wightman, Linda F. 1997. "The Threat to Diversity in Legal Education: An Empirical Analysis of the Consequences of Abandoning Race as a Factor in Law School Admission Decisions." *New York University Law Review* 72(1): 1–53.

Wilkins, David B. 2005. "A Systematic Response to Systemic Disadvantage: A Response to Sander." *Stanford Law Review* 57(6): 1915–61.

Winerip, Michael. 2005. "Test Prep Help for Students Who Can't Afford Kaplan." *New York Times*, November 16, p. B9.

Winston, Gordon C., and David J. Zimmerman. 2004. "Peer Effects in Higher Education." Pp. 395–421 in Caroline M. Hoxby, ed., *College Choices: The Economics of Where to Go, When to Go, and How to Pay for It*. Chicago: University of Chicago Press.

Winter, Greg. 2005. "Yale Cuts Expenses for Needy In a Move to Beat Competitors." *New York Times*, March 4, p. B5.

Wise, Timothy J. 2005. *Affirmative Action: Racial Preference in Black and White*. New York: Routledge.

Witt, Daria, Mitchell J. Chang, and Kenji Hakuta. 2003. "Introduction." Pp. 1–21 in Mitchell J. Chang, Daria Witt, James Jones, and Kenji Hakuta, eds., *Compelling Interest: Examining the Evidence on Racial Dynamics in Colleges and Universities*. Stanford: Stanford University Press.

Wolff, Edward N. 2007. "Recent Trends in Household Wealth in the United States: Rising Debt and the Middle-Class Squeeze." Working Paper 502, Levy Economics Institute of Bard College, June, http:// www.levy.org/pubs/wp_502.pdf (last accessed June 10, 2008).

Worth, Robert. 2000. "Ivy League Fever." *New York Times*, September 24, Westchester Weekly Desk, p. 14WC1.

Wray, L. Randall. 2006. "The Burden of Aging: Much Ado about Nothing, or Little to Do about Something?" *Policy News*, No. 5, Levy Economics Institute of Bard College.

Yaqub, Reshma Memon. 2002. "Getting Inside the Ivy Gates." *Worth*, September, pp. 94–104.

Yeung, W. Jean, and Dalton Conley. 2008. "Black-White Achievement Gap and Family Wealth." *Child Development* 79(2): 303–24.

Young, John W. 2004. "Differential Validity and Prediction: Race and Sex Differences in College Admissions Testing." Pp. 289–300 in Rebecca Zwick, ed., *Rethinking the SAT: The Future of Standardized Testing in University Admissions*. New York and London: RoutledgeFalmer.

Zernike, Kate. 2000. "Ease Up, Top Colleges Tell Stressed Applicants." *New York Times*, December 7, p. A1.

Zhang, Liang. 2005a. "Advance to Graduate Education: The Effect of College Quality and Undergraduate Majors." *Review of Higher Education* 28(3): 313–38.

———. 2005b. "Do Measures of College Quality Matter? The Effect of College Quality on Graduates' Earnings." *Review of Higher Education* 28(4): 571–96.

Zimmerman, Marc A., Cleopatra Howard Caldwell, and Debra Hilkene Bernat. 2002. "Discrepancy between Self-Report and School-Record Grade Point Average: Correlates with Psychosocial Outcomes among African American Adolescents." *Journal of Applied Social Psychology* 32(1): 86–109.

Zwick, Rebecca. 2002. *Fair Game? The Use of Standardized Admissions Tests in Higher Education*. New York: RoutledgeFalmer.

INDEX

A Better Chance (ABC), 167n33
academic achievement, inequality in, 394–409
academic mismatch hypothesis, 228, 233, 236, 238, 240, 262
academic underperformance, 12, 238, 248, 252n34, 254, 257
Achieve College Prep Services, 52
ACT test/scores, 92, 93, 114n54; and academic enrichment, 58; and admission preferences, 92; and admission rates, 87, 90, 125n61; and applicants, 39; and application rates and acceptance rates, 69; in Midwest, 162n30, 230n6, 367n33, 370; preparation courses for, 47, 59, 71, 72n10, 75, 118, 120, 122, 126; and school choice, 58
admission, 97, 339; academic bar for, 6; and academic merit, 110–11; and affluence of students, 331; early decision programs for, 77; enhancement strategies for, 54–60, 115–27, 462–63; factors affecting, 11, 62–129; goals of, 74–79; and legacies, 113; and matriculant yield rates, 131; and merit, 78–83; need-blind, 76; and race, 111–12; race-neutral, 376; by SAT scores alone, 472, 480; social class neutrality in, 384; success of enhancement strategies for, 115–27; variety and diversity as goal in, 74
Advanced Placement (AP) courses, 20, 37–38, 61, 75
Advanced Placement (AP) exams, 19, 37, 38, 71, 87, 92, 114n54, 161n28, 239n21, 251, 370
Advisory Committee on Student Financial Assistance, 385
affirmative action, class-based, 12–13, 355–61, 356, 376, 382
affirmative action, economic, 348–55
affirmative action, race-based, 90, 98, 361, 376, 384; and academic self-confidence,
261–62; and acceptance rates, 81; actual beneficiaries of, 298–307; and black descendants, 105; and class rank, 244, 248, 249, 259, 260; controversy over, 4–5, 12, 226–28, 337; definition of, 299–300; developmental, 369; and distributive justice rationale, 305; and educational benefits of diversity, 298; elimination of, 376, 464–65, 473–74, 475–76, 481–82; and graduation rates, 226–27, 258; as helpful to minority futures, 262; increasing restrictions on, 405; lack of need for, 375, 405; and low-income recruiting, 167n33; micro-simulations of elimination of, 341–48; nonremedial justifications for, 302–4; opposition to, 299–301, 337, 339–40; and race-neutral policy, 345–46; and racial achievement gap, 369; remedial justifications for, 304–7; and socioeconomic diversity, 381; substitution of other policies for, 468–69, 478–79; support for, 337; and Ten-percent plans, 362
African/African American Studies, 178, 179, 192, 217, 222
Ahmadi, Mohammad, Farhad Raiszadeh, and Marilyn Helms, 260
Ainsworth, James W., 168
Alexander, Karl L., and Bruce K. Eckland, 16, 259n48
Alliance for Excellent Education, 406, 407, 408
Allport, Gordon W., 181, 313n18, 392
Alon, Sigal, and Marta Tienda, 259n47, 301n2
Alves, Julio, 9
American Civil Rights Coalition, 340n1
American College Testing Program, 70
American Competitiveness and Leadership Project (ACLP), 403–8, 409
American Council on Education, 407n35
American Freshman Survey, 21, 23, 242, 330
Amherst College, 382, 386